Open Learning

Systems and problems
in post-secondary education

A

OPEN LEARNING

Systems and problems in post-secondary education

A report prepared with the support of the Ford Foundation

Norman MacKenzie
Richmond Postgate
John Scupham

Other contributors: Bernard Bartram, Kevin Batt, John R. Beardsley, Bernard Braithwaite, Norman C. Dahl, Kenneth Fawdry, George Grimmett, Stephen Kanocz, Hidetoshi Kato, David C. Kinsey, Peter E. Kinyanjui, Valentin Kuznetsov, W. C. Meierhenry, Fred A. Nelson, Edward A. Pires, Gerald Stone and Charles A. Wedemeyer

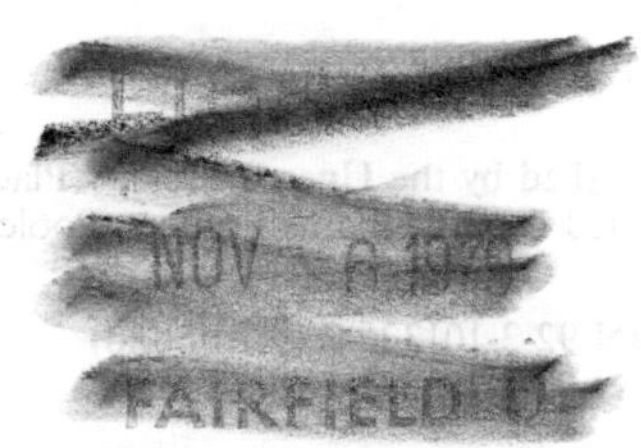

The Unesco Press 1975

Published by the Unesco Press, 7 Place de Fontenoy, 75700 Paris
Printed by Sydenhams Printers, Poole, Dorset

ISBN 92-3-101326-2 (softbound)
ISBN 92-3-101332-7 (hardbound)

This book is dedicated with affection and respect to Sir Peter Venables, Chairman of the Planning Committee of the Open University of the United Kingdom and its first Pro-Chancellor

Acknowledgements

The project team wishes to record its sense of indebtedness and appreciation to all those who made this publication possible: First, to the sponsoring and financing organizations, Unesco and the Ford Foundation, on whose practical support and steadfast encouragement it came to rely; then, to the University of Sussex under whose academic aegis it worked; to the Polytechnic of Central London which afforded it office space, administrative and clerical services and a congenial working atmosphere; and to the staff of the Open University, who helped at many stages, particularly with the arrangements for the rapid publication of this book. Next, to its principal contributors, listed on the title-page, who had to work at great speed and often at some inconvenience to prepare the case studies. Then, to the many organizations consulted for information and opinion. Last, to many individuals who gave advice and help: in particular to Gail Spangenberg, the Assistant Program Officer of the Ford Foundation, and to Herbert Marchl, of the Department of Materials, Methods and Techniques in the Educational Division of Unesco; to John Robinson, Chief Assistant to the Controller of Education, BBC; to Audrey Postgate, who helped pull the text together; and to its tireless Personal Assistant and Secretary, Jackie Williams.

Preface

In 1973, the Centre for Educational Technology at the University of Sussex (United Kingdom) undertook, with the support of Unesco and the Ford Foundation, a project devoted to Open Learning systems at post-secondary level involving the use of modern media. The present work is the outcome of that project. It comprises seventeen case studies dealing with Open Learning in a number of countries—among them Australia, Japan, Kenya, the United Kingdom, the United States and the U.S.S.R.—preceded by a lengthy analytical survey of the subject. This survey attempts to provide a checklist of operational questions which arise when an Open Learning system is set up and to examine current activities throughout the world. It indicates the procedural and organizational problems which may be encountered, together with the opportunities and limitations involved in the transfer of experience.

The original intention was to publish the introductory survey as a handbook and possibly to issue the case studies separately. It was finally decided, however, to combine all the assembled material in one volume so as to facilitate cross-reference and furnish comprehensive documentation. In its present form, the work may be considered virtually unique in its range and detail.

It may therefore fairly be described as an indispensable publication for all educational authorities, planners and advisers concerned with the question and, more especially, for those in the developing countries.

The project team consisted of: Director, Professor Norman MacKenzie, B.Sc.(Econ.), Director, School of Education, University of Sussex, (formerly) Director, Centre for Educational Technology, University of Sussex, member of the Planning Committee and Governing Council of the Open University; Principal Investigator, Richmond Postgate, M.A., (formerly) broadcasting assessor to the Planning Committee of the Open University and member of its Governing Council, former Controller of Educational Broadcasting, British Broadcasting Corporation, and Director-General, Nigerian Broadcasting Corporation; and Principal Educational Consultant, John Scupham, O.B.E., M.A., member of the Planning Committee and Governing Council of the Open University, (formerly) Controller of Educational Broadcasting, British Broadcasting Corporation.

The designations employed and the presentation of the material in this work do not imply the expression of any opinion whatsoever on the part of the Unesco Secretariat concerning the legal status of any country or territory, or of its authorities, or concerning the delimitation of its frontiers. The opinions expressed in the following pages, moreover, are those of the authors and do not necessarily reflect those of Unesco.

Contents

Bibliographical information

***Additionally**, short relevant bibliographies are given at the end of each case study*

Introduction

Over the past ten years there has been a significant growth of interest in Open Learning systems as an alternative to formal, full-time study in post-secondary education. Such systems are designed to offer opportunities for part-time study, for learning at a distance and for innovations in the curriculum. They are intended to allow access to wider sections of the adult population, to enable students to compensate for lost opportunities in the past or to acquire new skills and qualifications for the future. Open Learning systems aim to redress social or educational inequality and to offer opportunities not provided by conventional colleges and universities.

The success of the Open University in the United Kingdom has given a substantial impetus to developments of this kind. That, however, is only one model. Other institutions have experimented with other forms of open admission, devised new methods of reaching part-time or remote students or of satisfying special groups in need of additional training or education.

The pace at which new systems have begun to emerge and the diversity of their purpose and structure have made it difficult to collect and classify information of use to those engaged in their development, and to those planning other similar projects. There has been some exchange of experience, but the lack of substantial reports on many of these innovations remains a handicap. It was felt, therefore, by the Ford Foundation and Unesco that a number of relevant projects might be usefully reviewed in a series of case studies and the main common problems analysed in order to serve as a basis for planners and educational specialists. The project team was commissioned in mid-1973. With the agreement of our sponsors we selected a number of the more advanced projects for study during 1974. Each of the Open Learning systems chosen has been set in its historical, economic and social context and described in such a way as to emphasize the problems involved in planning and launching it.

The method we decided on was to invite contributors with considerable experience in education and communications to undertake a case study under the general direction of the project team. None of the contributors was directly involved in the system studied, but in some cases he had an associate from the country concerned who was unconnected with the enterprise under review. Despite the fact that it proved impossible to make the case studies precisely comparable, because the systems differed so much in origin and character and the data base in so many countries could not be brought into the same framework, yet in all instances the case study was based on a set of similar questions and a concern with common problems.

At first we had intended to restrict the case studies to a small number—between six and ten—but as we went on it became clear that the possible range of systems could not reasonably be covered in such a limited review. As a result the final number of studies was seventeen. Apart from the introductory overview offered in the chapters of Parts One and Two they form the substance of our report.

In Part One we discuss the implications of the term 'Open Learning', and consider its relationship with non-traditional study and continuing education. We consider the educational and social pressures which have induced public and private institutions to move in this direction and draw attention to some important common characteristics. We deal with the relationship between education and communications technology, with special reference to broadcasting, and summarize some of the main problems involved in providing Open Learning facilities.

In Part Two, which is concerned with practical matters, we turn to a series of specific topics of concern to planners and educationists. These are: the students, their situation and needs; research and evaluation; the curriculum and choice of media; the use of broadcasting; making the courses; the use and transfer of experience; effectiveness and costs—the framework; questions for planners; Open Learning—new experiences and new skills; and the impact of Open Learning.

We then turn in Part Three to the case studies themselves, which are listed in the Contents and briefly described on pages 19–20 below.

Each case study normally concludes with three appendixes: Appendix A gives standardized reference data and sources of further information and Appendix B gives a short bibliography. Appendix C is a brief biographical note.

A short general bibliography is given after the case studies, on page 497. A number of the works listed contain bibliographies. This is followed by a short list of directories of international agencies, charitable foundations and the like.

N. M.
R. P.
J. S.

Part One Perspectives

Chapter 1
Open Learning systems

Open Learning is an imprecise phrase to which a range of meanings can be, and is, attached. It eludes definition. But as an inscription to be carried in procession on a banner, gathering adherents and enthusiasms, it has great potential. For its very imprecision enables it to accommodate many different ideas and aims and the two terms of the phrase carry with them emotional overtones that evoked a wide response in the 1950s and 1960s when it came into use, particularly at the later secondary and post-secondary levels with which we are concerned. It was in this period that the concept of learning, as indicating activity by the student and a measure of self-direction, was displacing the idea of the active teacher and the passive taught, the image of the gardener guiding the vigorously growing plant replacing that of the jug and the cup.

The other term, 'open', has many meanings, and the aura of most of them seemed generous and 'charismatic'—open-handed, open-ended, open-hearted, open house, open choice. 'Open' as contrasted with 'closed' carried suggestions of the lessening or removal of restrictions, of exclusions and of privilege; of demolishing or lowering established barriers between subject areas; of enlarging and enriching the areas of activity and experience graded as educational. It symbolized a shift in the relationship between teacher and pupil towards that of student and adviser.

Perhaps the most commonly used sense of 'open' has been the idea of creating opportunities for study for those debarred from it for whatever reasons, be it lack of formal educational attainments or shortage of vacancies, poverty, remoteness, employment or domestic necessities. To seek increased access is, of course, not a recent objective amongst educators. It has a long, honourable history of pioneer effort, over a hundred years or more. London University was created in 1836 as a body to conduct examinations and award degrees and by 1858 admitted matriculated candidates from any part of the world. The work in the United Kingdom of such voluntary agencies as the Workers' Educational Association, the Extension Services and the extramural departments of universities is another expression of the same intention. It has parallels in many other countries, perhaps most notably in the Soviet Union, where today nearly half the students in higher education study on a part-time basis. Openness in that sense is no new phenomenon.

Its use in the title of the currently most conspicuous example—the British Open University—was to some extent an afterthought. When the Labour Party, then in opposition, first put forward the proposal in 1963 the title used was 'University of the Air', and this title was again used when the idea became government policy in 1964. It was changed to 'Open University' by the Planning Committee set up in 1967, largely on account of the adverse publicity that the proposal had received in academic circles, where it was decried as a soft option, an armchair operation that would lower the reputation of university degrees generally.

This change of name was not due to any substantial change in the initial concept, but rather to considerations of prudence and publicity. 'University of the Air' overemphasized the significance of the broadcast media in the learning system planned. Though their contribution was thought essential to attract and secure the adherence of a new student-body at which the university aimed, a more important characteristic was the waiving of formal entry qualifications and, as 'Open' indicated this, the new title was adopted.

In the event, the university is not open in the sense that all applicants are admitted. Various limits are imposed: some because financial constraints restrict the number of places available and some for reasons of policy. A minimum entry age of 21 was decided upon and various occupational and geographical quotas imposed. However, intermittent study is permitted, so that a student once enrolled is entitle to withdraw temporarily and rejoin. But the idea of openness nevertheless exercised its influence. It was expressed eighteen months later in the address of the first Chancellor of the Open University, the late Lord Crowther, when he received the Royal Charter in 1969. He said that the Open University would be open, not only as to entry, but as to place (no campus), as to method (the use of any communication medium that promoted its educational purposes) and as to ideas (in that it would be concerned not only with necessary skills and experience, but with all that human understanding can encompass).

Five years later, the National Association of Educational Broadcasters (the professional association linking all educational broadcasting practitioners in the United States of America) published a report on Open Learning systems. This aimed to look ahead, to see in what direction Open Learning might be expected to go. The NAEB report identified the following essential characteristics:

Essential characteristics of Open Learning systems

The system must guide a student by eliciting, interpreting and analysing goals at the beginning point and throughout the student's contact with the programme of instruction.

The system must formulate learning objectives in such a way that they serve as the basis for making decisions in instructional design, including evaluation, and in such a way that they will be fully known to, accepted by or capable of modification by students.

The system must facilitate the participation of learners without imposing traditional academic entry requirements, without the pursuit of an academic degree or other certification as the exclusive reward.

To provide the flexibility required to satisfy a variety of individual needs, the system should make it operationally possible to employ sound, television, film and print as options for mediating learning experiences.

The system should use testing and evaluation principally to diagnose and analyse the extent to which specified learning objectives have been accomplished. In other words, the system should be competence-based.

The system must be able to accommodate distance between the instructional staff resources and the learner, employing the distance as a positive element in the development of independence in learning.

In the main text the report states: 'We are speaking of a fundamentally new institutional concept of education. It is not simply a variation on traditional academic tunes or relaxed entry requirements. Open education is not a variant form of traditional education but the opposite of it.'[1]

This concept is far removed from that which seems to have been in the minds of the British Planning Committee, a concept which, as those who read the study in this book will see, has many traditional features.[2] The NAEB report drew much of its inspiration from a different source—the thinking and experimentation which, founded and encouraged by large grants from the major charitable foundations, had been exploring 'non-traditional' forms of post-secondary education in the United States since 1960.

The history, structure and traditions of post-secondary education in the United States provided a context different from that based on the European tradition; they have produced a greater and more diversified provision, allowing for the accumulation and transfer of credits between institutions—a flexibility which is another form of openness. Four United States studies are included in this book.[3] The general issues particularly were studied and reported on by the Commission on Non-Traditional Study, set up in 1971 under the chairmanship of Dr Samuel B. Gould, Chancellor Emeritus of the State University of New York. It is of interest that the commission also found some difficulty in defining their subject precisely:

Despite our lack of a completely suitable definition, we always seemed to sense the areas of education around which our interests centered. This community of concern was a mysterious light in the darkness, yet not all mysterious in retrospect. Most of us agreed that non-traditional study is more an attitude than a system and thus can never be defined except tangentially. This attitude puts the students first and the institution second, concentrates more on the former's need than the latter's convenience, encourages diversity of individual opportunity rather than uniform prescription, and de-emphasizes time, space, and even course requirements in favour of competence and, where applicable, performance. It has concern for the learner of any age and circumstance, for the degree aspirant as well as the person who finds sufficient reward in enriching life through constant, periodic or occasional study. This attitude is not new; it is simply more prevalent than it used to be. It can stimulate exciting and high-quality educational progress; it can also, unless great care is taken to protect the freedom it offers, be the unwitting means to a lessening of academic rigour and even to charlatanism.[4]

1. *Open Learning*, Washington, D.C., National Association of Educational Broadcasters, 1974.
2. See 'The Open University of the United Kingdom', page 321 below.
3. See 'The Empire State College, New York', 'The Minnesota Metropolitan State College, Minneapolis/St Paul', 'The Community College of Vermont' and 'UMA/SUN: the Nebraska Approach to a Regional University of Mid-America', on pages 369, 399, 423 and 447 below.
4. Commission on Non-Traditional Study, *University by Design*, p. xv, San Francisco, Calif., Jossey-Bass, 1973.

These ideas also attracted the attention of the international educational community, for whom Unesco acts as a forum of exchange in thinking and practice. *Learning to Be*, published by Unesco in 1972, was the work of a distinguished international team headed by Edgar Faure, former Prime Minister of France and Minister of Education. It surveyed the educational situation globally, with special reference to developing countries, and set out fundamental propositions as to the direction it considered national educational systems should take.

In the course of its survey, it rehearsed all the difficulties and deficiencies of the provision as it then was—the insufficiency of premises and equipment, the lack of teachers, the low level of their education and professional training, the high rates of pupil drop-out and of 'repeaters' (those who fail to pass the terminal examinations of their year and are held back to do the course again), the inappropriateness of curricula to the needs of contemporary life and the disparities between the provision for urban and rural areas.[1] Specific illustrations of this generalized picture are to be seen in three of the studies here: the Institute of Education, Beirut, the Correspondence Course Unit at the University of Nairobi and the Free University, Iran.[2]

The educational, social and economic background of these studies as portrayed in *Learning to Be* was very far from that of the British Open University, the Commission on Non-Traditional Study or the NAEB report. But the suggested long-term responses to both sets of circumstances have many similarities, *Learning to Be* being perhaps the more radical and visionary. It propounded the thesis of lifelong education as the master concept to guide educational development in all countries, developed and less-developed alike.

Learning to Be is not a document in which to seek the hard detail upon which national plans for educational development can be directly based; it is, rather, a work of inspirational significance whose influence will be felt for many years. Its view that Open Learning, even if imprecisely defined, may have relevance at many developmental levels and in many different situations is of special interest.

Though, like Dr Gould, we found ourselves unable to define Open Learning comprehensively and precisely, we also, like his commission, always seemed to sense the areas of education around which our interests centred. In order to establish which institutions and systems should be chosen for study we adopted the working criteria given below, choosing the institutions that met most of them:

Students not adequately catered for at the present time for some reason or other (e.g. remoteness, disadvantage).

Courses outside full-time formal education, but related to some important national purpose and having a substantial following.

Learning systems having some element of 'newness' whether in curriculum, organization, course development and delivery, assessment or support (as group study).

Attainment leading to some recognized qualification.

Efficacy, attempting some form of assessment beyond the gaining of a bachelor degree or certificate.

1. ***Learning to Be: the World of Education Today, and Tomorrow***, Paris, Unesco, 1972.
2. See 'Teachers for Refugees: the UNRWA/Unesco Institute of Education, Beirut', 'Kenya: the Use of Correspondence Education for the Improvement of Teaching' and 'The Free University of Iran' on pages 273, 253 and 183 below.

As a great many institutions and systems could qualify under these headings, in making up the list we also attempted to achieve a geographical spread and a range of developmental levels. Naturally also, the choice was affected by such practical considerations as the size of the team, the availability of suitable collaborators, the money available and the time constraint. All the inquiries were planned to take place in the twelve months between 1 September 1973 and 31 August 1974.

The systems selected

In the event, the systems chosen for study fell into some main groups. First, there were studies of major, well-developed systems:

The Open University of the United Kingdom (page 321). The formation and development of the institution and the first-degree course.

Open Learning in Japan (page 231). The experience, since 1945, of part-time learning by correspondence using radio and television at high school and at university level, and the present plans for a Broadcasting University.

The external degree in Australia (page 95). The experience of the external-degree system since its start in 1909. Also, the reports of the Committee on Open University to the Universities Commission (the Karmel Committee).

Correspondence education at post-secondary level in the Soviet Union (page 313). A study of this immensely important provision was planned, which was to include exemplifications of rural areas, including one in which Russian was not the mother tongue. Unfortunately, for practical reasons this study did not take place. Instead, we present the substance of a lecture given in 1973 by Professor Valentin Kuznetsov, Director, Research Institute of Higher Education, Moscow.

University courses to degree level for part-time adult students in France (page 141). This system, though not large, seemed to involve an important advance in inter-university co-operation.

A second main group is related to the enlargement and improvement of teaching forces:

The UNRWA/Unesco Institute of Education, Beirut (page 273). Since 1963 the institute has provided part-time initial and in-service training to teachers at various levels, and to supervisory and administrative staff, in a growing number of Arab countries in the Middle East.

The Radio College (Rundfunk) in the Federal Republic of Germany (page 163). The system for supplying university-level courses, mainly for teachers, in a number of the constituent states of the republic, using radio, by an unusual collaboration between educational and broadcasting agencies.

The Correspondence Course Unit in the University of Nairobi, Kenya (page 253). The establishment of the unit in 1966 to offer correspondence-cum-radio courses to enlarge and upgrade the teaching force in Kenyan schools, and its subsequent development to undertake new tasks.

External courses for teachers in the remote rural areas of Newfoundland (Canada) by the Memorial University of St John's (page 121). The provision, since 1969, of part-time courses for teachers to raise their educational level and improve their pedagogic skills, through a service relying upon a video-cassette delivery system.

Part-time study to raise the level of general education and of agricultural skills is exemplified in the *Television Agricultural High School of Poland* (page 295), a service provided since January 1973, by collaboration between the Ministry of Agriculture and the Polish Television Service, of facilities enabling full-time farm workers on the many small farms to complete their general and vocational education to secondary level.

A group of studies, prefaced by a short introduction to United States post-secondary education, deals with the 'learning contract' institutions: the *Empire State College, New York* (page 369); the *Minnesota Metropolitan State College* (page 399); and the *Community College of Vermont* (page 423).

It was originally intended that the institutions described should be 'going' concerns, i.e. which had admitted students and discharged at least a first group of them on completion of their courses. But, in the belief that those concerned with educational development are just as interested in the discussions and thinking that preceded the decision to create an Open Learning institution, we later resolved to include three studies of institutions in which only the crucial decision to go ahead had then been taken. These are:

The State University of Nebraska (United States) (page 447), planned to become by 1980 the Regional University of Mid-America (UMA/SUN), a possible prototype of other regional universities of distant learning.

The Everyman's University (Israel) (page 209), aiming, in the first instance, at raising the level of the teaching force with particular attention to the needs of non-European Jews. Due to receive its first students in 1977.

The Free University of Iran (page 183), aiming to introduce a new conception of higher education, and to contribute to the social and economic integration of Iranian society by producing skilled manpower to develop the rural and less urbanized sectors. First intake of students for bachelor degrees in mathematics and science in secondary schools in early 1977. First courses to produce graduates in secondary schools due to enrol early 1977. Special consultancy agreement with the British Open University.

Satellites for education (page 477). In view of the great interest in the possibility of using communication satellites for educational purposes, it was also decided to include a study of this facility for Open Learning and educational development generally.

Chapter 2
The educational issues

Despite disparities in wealth and development and differences in political belief and system, in matters of education much common ground exists between the nations as to its indispensability, its purposes, duration and content. Among the headings of national public expenditure, education occupies either the first or the second place; among developing countries it is usually the first. National spending on education has greatly increased over recent years throughout the world. Between 1960 and 1968 the average increase was 150 per cent, representing an increase in the proportion that educational expenditure bore to both total national public expenditure and to gross national product.

Since 1968 the rates of increase have tended to slacken, but this is attributable more to shortage of resources than to the needs having been satisfied. In less-developed countries, such as Kenya[1] or Iran,[2] expansion is needed at every level. In others, special needs for particular sections of the population exist; for instance, Israel[3] feels particular concern for its population of Oriental Jews and Arabs, and special provision for them is made in the earliest stages of the proposed Everyman's University. But wherever in the educational pyramid expansion occurs, its effect is bound eventually to manifest itself later, at the post-secondary stage. In many developing countries this need has yet to show itself fully; so the real demand for post-secondary facilities is a problem for the future.

Some idea of the size and likely duration of this need may be gained from figures for 1967/68 given in *Learning to Be* of the levels of enrolment in tertiary education expressed as a percentage of the population aged 20 to 24 years. In the world the figure is 10.1, in Africa 1.3, North America 44.5, Latin America 5.0, Asia 4.7, Europe and U.S.S.R. 16.7, and Oceania 15.0 (the figures for Asia and the world omit the People's Republic of China, the People's Democratic Republic of Korea and the Democratic Republic of Viet-Nam). Though these figures were in some cases nearly double those of 1960/61 and will have changed by 1975, the disparities are very evident. If the possession of a first degree remains the conventional aim and hallmark of a completed education, this problem will be with some regions for a great many years.

1. 'See 'Kenya: the Use of Radio and Correspondence Education for the Improvement of Teaching', page 253 below.
2. See 'The Free University of Iran', page 183 below.
3. See 'The Everyman's University, Israel', page 209 below.

Besides being one of the most costly public services, education is also one of the most important on account of the many vital roles it is called upon to play:

It is the main source of the trained manpower needed to realize development plans.

It is a principal and continuing expression of the society that a country or state wishes to create or sustain. More than any other activity, it reflects a society's concept of its identity and way of life. The tenacity with which the states of a federation like Australia assert their right to control their educational system constantly testifies to this feeling.

It has to preserve continuity and tradition, but it is also the agent of change, and thus has to be both stable and adaptable at the same time.

These roles produce many different patterns of specific requirements and sets of priorities; nevertheless the outline of an educational system to which most countries would assent would contain many common items. These would be:

1. Universal basic general education from early childhood to late adolescence, with gradual additions at either end on a less than universal basis until a total span from age 3 to 18 is achieved. For the core of this period, if not for the whole, the provision would be compulsory and free.
2. A wide range of opportunities for general and vocational instruction at the later stages of basic education and for prolonging basic education on a less than universal basis; the provision being kept in rough accord with the needs of the economy and with employment prospects, though deferring to popular demand.
3. Steadily extending opportunities for adults to: (a) requalify themselves for employment as their qualifications become obsolescent or as the need for their skills alters; (b) remedy the deficiencies of their basic education.
4. At all levels, the provision of courses that are appropriate to the geographical, economic and social realities of the particular society, and adjusted to the requirements both of the subject studied and of the needs and situation of the students concerned.
5. Over all, the achievement of an educational service that will assist the society to attain, regain and maintain its political and cultural identity; that will equip individuals to withstand the impact of change and to avoid submersion in the vastness and impersonality of modern life.
6. The economic achievement of all this within the constraints of shortage of finance and of material and human resources imposed by the claims of other areas of public provision.

In many developing countries the distance between such a statement of aim and present reality is daunting and the needs truly comprehensive. The Kenya report summarizes (see page 254) the position facing one country attaining political independence in 1963:

> The situation facing the planners . . . was not unique to Kenya but followed a pattern to be found in many developing countries. This includes a high percentage of illiteracy amongst the adult and working population; an increase in school enrolment as a result of growing public demand for education; increasing numbers of school leavers who cannot be absorbed into the monetary economy; an urgent need to revise and modernize the curricula in schools and colleges; shortage of money; and shortage of qualified and experienced teachers, trainees and administrators.

In such situations it is easier to list the categories of need than to say which is the most important. One main group of categories is numerical; to increase the proportion of the age group, at any level, that is exposed to education. This means more schools, more equipment, more teachers, more trainers of teachers, and less wastage by drop-out and repeaters. *Learning to Be* points out that in half the countries of the world, half the children enrolled at the primary stage fail to complete it; and that in many countries the money spent on children who dropped out before the end of the third year of primary school absorbs between 20 and 40 per cent of the total expenditure on public education. So far, neither advances in communications technology as applied to education nor new thinking about teaching methods have had a deep or very widespread effect in reducing these terrible figures. They still serve to highlight the dominant need revealed by our studies, namely for more and better-trained teachers to teach more appropriate courses.

A notable instance of a successful approach to that problem is the UNRWA/Unesco Institute of Education, Beirut. When it was established in 1963, it was faced with a situation in which 90 per cent of the teachers serving in the UNRWA schools for refugees in Palestine were professionally untrained and uncertificated, and it has now developed a range of courses stretching from basic in-service training courses for elementary school teachers to professional courses for teachers who have completed a minimum of two years of university study. Equally important, the system has been adapted for other Middle Eastern countries.[1]

At the secondary level, besides the aim of increasing the proportion of primary school leavers proceeding to the secondary stage, there is the additional problem of providing greater variety in the curriculum and modernizing such key areas as mathematics, the sciences and languages. In some countries such as Iran, whose economy is undergoing a rapid change from a predominantly rural to a predominantly urban society, the schools have also to adjust long-established habits to prepare for the changed employment situation. It is significant that the bachelor degree courses to be offered by the Free University of Iran are designed to produce teachers of mathematics and science at the secondary level. Decisions along these lines feature in nearly all the studies. Instruction in these subjects has, of course, been the staple of such long-established institutions as the NHK Gakuen Senior High School.[2]

It is at the upper level of the secondary stage—that of the senior high school—that the opportunities for part-time study, in the evening or by correspondence courses with various supporting services, first become significant. The Japan study shows how part-time study can supplement full-time provision over a period of development, and exemplifies the fruitful combination of correspondence education and the broadcast media. The Polish study[3] illustrates a similar combination for agricultural workers in small farms.

Many reports on developing countries stress the priority attaching to three other occupations needed by the State: rural extension workers; community and social workers in rural and urban areas; and assistants and 'paramedicals' in health and family-planning services.

With the tiny proportion of the 20 to 24 age group involved in tertiary

1. See 'Teachers for Refugees: the UNRWA/Unesco Institute of Education, Beirut', page 273 below.
2. See 'Open Learning in Japan', page 231 below.
3. See 'The Television Agricultural High School, Poland', page 295 below.

education in some countries, the bachelor degree or equivalent cannot yet be the normally expected qualification for superior employment; yet, in an objective sense, many of the operations needed in a modern State call for the level of general education with which a bachelor degree is associated. As we can see in the Iran study, the impossibility of reaching this standard has led to the idea of a more functionally oriented qualification. The Free University aims to introduce and establish this conception of higher education. No doubt other countries will explore similar possibilities.

In the developed countries, the basic structures of a full educational system are normally developed and diversified. The tide of post-secondary demand arising from the extension and expansion of the basic system has receded. The new challenges come partly from the wish to raise the general standard of education and teaching (in the first year of the Open University in the United Kingdom a large number of applications were from non-graduate teachers who wished to improve their qualifications by gaining a full degree). Partly the challenges arise from the general and continuing effect of technology upon society as a whole, on its economic, civil and social life, and partly from the demands for new and changed educational services which they generate. Some of the principal categories of these demands are for:

Skills to operate and develop new activities created by technological advance, of which the classic instance is the computer, requiring programmers, operators and managers to exploit its capacities.

Skills called for by the enlarged scale of industrial and civic activity.

Skills to deal with the increasing internationalization and mobility of economic and political life. Examples arise not only from the multinational private and public undertakings, but also from new political groupings such as the European Common Market. The need for awareness of world affairs and competence in handling international relations forces more and more executives and officials to acquire multilingual capacity and understanding.

New skills to replace obsolescent skills and practices previously acquired. As knowledge increases and technology alters equipment and processes the related human qualifications obsolesce also. New specialist skills and new patterns of work involving higher degrees of collaboration between specialists are needed. The education system has to respond with a growing supply of in-service training, retraining, refreshment and reorientation courses. The University of New South Wales, Australia,[1] for instance, operates its external service for graduates on the premise that every graduate needs refreshment at least once every five years. Postgraduate courses of a highly technical nature have been provided; but they are now supplemented by others at lower level, covering communication, statistics, computers, management and engineering.

Opportunities for cultural and personal development. Besides the pressure to expand or redirect their educational systems, both developed and less-developed countries are experiencing varying pressures to transform the educational process itself. Its aims, disciplines, pedagogic practices and the personal relations between student and teacher are all under question, stimulated by new educational and psychological thinking as well as by the new opportunities offered by developments in communications technology.

1. See 'Open Learning—the Australian Contribution', page 95 below.

On the one hand, many of the courses associated with universities, particularly in arts subjects (as for example in the Entente Universitaire de l'Est[1]), though offered primarily to teachers have a wide cultural appeal—in such subjects as English, German, philosophy and history. On the other hand, the desire for cultural development finds a direct response in the 'learning contracts' worked out by students with their advisers ('mentors') in such institutions as the Empire State College, New York.[2]

It is to these changing and complex situations that educational systems have to adjust themselves, and it is to these that the Open Learning initiatives we have studied pay particular attention. Offering part-time study to adults and near-adults with other occupations, they all aim at enlarging access. One important aim of the Open University was to provide a second chance to those for whom university education was not available at the normal age. The Centres de Télé-enseignement Universitaire[1] provide facilities to students of the arts who cannot utilize the normal provision. In the United States, the Empire State College,[2] the Minnesota Metropolitan State College,[3] the Community College of Vermont[4] and the ambitious UMA/SUN Regional University of Mid-America[5] all provide routes to qualification supplementary to and different from the conventional provision. So, too, with the proposed National Broadcasting University of Japan.

But these institutions do not only respond to needs arising from economic and social change. They reflect also the prevalent concern and disillusion about education. It is not only developing countries that need to shed their educational inheritance. In the upper reaches of secondary and in post-secondary education, vocal discontent and alienation among students are commonly encountered, particularly in the western world. Demands for 'relevance', for relaxation of authority, for reform of curricula and of the examination system are all too familiar. Large numbers of adults have closed their minds to any further educational experience. It is to these attitudes that many Open Learning systems pay attention.

But these initiatives are likely to run up against the other main concern of education—preservation and continuity, and the conservative attitudes that they engender. Rejection by the teaching force of educational innovations, especially those involving the use of 'educational technology', is the commonest cause of failure of these schemes at school level.

At the post-secondary level the clash between education as the agent of change and the preserver of cultural inheritance and academic standards is often sharp and explicit. A 1971 report, published by the Organization for Economic Cooperation and Development (OECD), discusses the position of universities in the changing situation of today. It distinguishes between the 'noble' institutions and the 'less noble' having a lower status than that of universities.

The noble institutions, focused on abstract and so-called disinterested study and on disciplines preparing for a small number of traditional professions (e.g.

1. See 'University Distance Learning Centres in France', page 141 below.
2. See 'The Empire State College, New York', page 369 below.
3. See 'The Minnesota Metropolitan State College', page 399 below.
4. See 'The Community College of Vermont', page 423 below.
5. See 'UMA/SUN: the Nebraska Approach to a Regional University of Mid-America', page 447 below.

law and medicine), command much more prestige than the less noble, which emphasize the teaching of knowledge and skills in a wide range of both new and old professions. Noble institutions 'have an almost natural tendency to ignore or neglect innovations introduced by or through the less noble establishments, while the latter, even when innovative at the start, tend ultimately to imitate the prestigeful (in most cases traditional) institutions and thus to discard their initial innovative character'.

Our report on the United Kingdom's Open University[1] emphasizes the conservatism of British universities especially in methods of education, relying upon lecturing without giving any training to their lecturers, and in general 'convinced that any way of providing higher education but their own is necessarily an inferior one'.

The critical attitudes to 'Open Learning' and to 'non-traditional study' in the United States derive to a degree from some of the examples themselves, as the quotation from Dr Gould (page 17) hints. There is no denying that some of the attempts to relax rigidities and restrictions, and to include a range of experiences wider than those traditionally considered to be part of a bachelor degree course, have had dubious results, and have understandably earned contempt from academic opinion.

Educational innovators have also to reckon with institutional inertia and, in some cases, to wrestle with constitutional complexities. The study of the UMA/SUN proposal sets out clearly the particular problems of inserting an innovative institution, one that crosses governmental and educational boundaries, into an established and fully articulated framework of governance.

Over all these activities stand the continuing anxieties about finance. The vast increase in educational expenditure over the last decade and a half itself constitutes a barrier to further expenditure, particularly on untried projects. Current inflation and recession increase the difficulty. Consequently, the anxiety to achieve higher levels of return for educational investment is intensified. Chapter 11 deals with some of these complicated matters.

1. See 'The Open University of the United Kingdom', page 328 below.

Chapter 3

The impact of communications technology

In the past fifty years the field of communications technology has seen a process of invention, application and dissemination as fast, as many-sided and as universal as the developments in education, and equally radical and far-reaching in its long-term effect. Advances in printing, illustration and other forms of reprography; the gramophone; the cinema film; the telephone and telex; the computer; radio, television and record/replay devices—all these developments, the equipment they produce ('hardware') and the associated learning material ('software'), have transformed, and are continuing to transform, the ways by which we communicate with each other.

This tide of technological development is far from being spent: further advances are expected in satellite communications, in the use of coaxial cable and in recording technology, and their effects can only be guessed at. We cannot yet see upon what plateau of communications facilities we shall eventually rest.

Only developed nations have so far had the resources to make substantial use of all these new facilities, but a steady reduction in cost of the most significant items as they come into general use has brought them gradually within the reach of the less-developed countries. It is instructive, too, that these countries show particular interest in some of the most recent and sophisticated developments—for instance, satellite communication—because through them they hope to accelerate the rate at which they can bring the whole of their population within reach of educational communications. (It was for this reason that we included a special study in this book.[1])

As communications technology is concerned with all forms of communication, educators have to accept that the direction and priorities of its development will be determined by the pressures of defence, news and entertainment. These are the big battalions with the money behind them. Education, though always socially and politically important for the reasons discussed in the last chapter, is usually a secondary force and has to accept what it can use as a spin-off from other activities. Equipment is not normally designed, nor systems developed, primarily to serve educational purposes.

Even in the broadcasting field, where public purposes normally play a large part, the exceptions to this are few—the policy decision in India to devote television to developmental purposes, the guarantee of daytime hours to

1. 'The Use of Satellites in Open Learning Systems', page 477 below.

educational programmes in Israel's first television channel, and the long-term commitment to education of the broadcasting agencies in Japan and the United Kingdom.

The relationship between developments in communications technology and education has been continuous, extensive and growing. These developments have been one of the major catalysing influences upon education, but the effect has been patchy and it is hard to discern any consistent pattern of welcome and adoption. Reasons for this hesitancy and ambiguity might include the following:

Widespread chronic poverty of many educational systems overwhelmed by problems of numbers and struggling to provide the most elementary services. The offerings of communications technology are costly to acquire and maintain. While their use may raise the quality of the service, the cost is additional, not substitutional, and must be thoroughly scrutinized.

The new developments have come at such a rate that the implications of the right use of one have not been fully worked out before another with different capacities overtakes it, and diverts attention. Normally, the pedagogic training of teachers is completed by early manhood. Adjustments to thought and practice entailed by the use of broadcasting and other forms of communications technology come as postscripts to their training and must be gained, normally in rather haphazard fashion, from in-service training. In their initial training, when the main lines of their professional skills are laid down, it is still exceptional to find adequate attention given to educational technology.

Some of the products of communications technology take the form of equipment and materials over which teachers have complete control, leaving them free to decide whether to buy the equipment (e.g. a tape recorder), free to choose what material they want, and how and when to use it. But other products, of which broadcasting is by far the most important so far as this study is concerned, invade the area of their control and the privacy of their relationships with their pupils. Broadcasting virtually introduces a second pedagogic party to which they must accommodate themselves. Because of the resources of broadcasting systems, the advantage of high-cost centralized manufacture and low distribution costs, and because of the volume of material transmitted and of the (now normal) printed support material, the use on any substantial scale of broadcasting by a school, college or system alters them to an important degree. It changes, to some extent, the functions, necessary skills and responsibilities of the staff; naturally in such circumstances strong resistances may develop.

The challenges and problems arising from the simultaneous and mutually influential development of communications technology and education gave rise to the study of what is widely called 'educational technology'. It is instructive to note that it was first involved principally with the hardware and how it could be used in an educational context. At that stage it was largely the concern of a minority of enthusiasts. Later, it developed into the applications of scientific method to education itself, thus penetrating from its particular standpoint to the heart of the process. Though the claims of educational technology to recognition as an analyst and a constructive critic of educational practices are widely recognized intellectually, it is not established firmly in most educational systems. It remains on the outside.

So far as broadcasting is concerned, in a few instances, such as the school systems in El Salvador and the Ivory Coast and the Israel Television Centre, it has been made the centre of the whole operation; broadcasting is the main agent not only of teaching but of reform of the curriculum itself, and the educational agency is virtually also the broadcasting agency. In the Open University system, the broadcasting component is an integrated element in the total educational provision supplied by a unique partnership between the university and the BBC.[1] In most other countries educational broadcasting is, for one reason or another, less integrated with the broadcasting systems.

Because of its importance to the Open Learning systems with which we are concerned, Chapter 8 is devoted to the use of broadcasting. At this stage it seems appropriate to make a few general points:

For reasons partly due to history, partly to the wide scope of broadcasting, national broadcasting services are commonly not under educational control. Where they are controlled by government departments, such departments are usually the Department of Information, or Information and Broadcasting. Where broadcasting is controlled by a corporation, the corporation has an overall mandate.

The responsibilities of these bodies normally include a responsibility for educational and cultural broadcasting in a very wide sense, outside the control of a Ministry of Education.

Educational broadcasting systems based on educational institutions such as universities are commonly small in scale and without great resources.

Broadcasting to large audiences commonly results in a capacity to produce high-cost material justified by the large audiences. Recording developments are increasingly reducing the inconveniences of use off-air, though delayed use involves the supply locally of equipment, and expenditure upon its maintenance and supervision.

Educational broadcasting seems likely to remain for many years the cheapest way of transmitting educational material to large audiences, and is therefore likely to be the first solution to be examined by those contemplating the establishment of Open Learning systems in developing countries. But, in other circumstances and as recording technology is further developed, it is important to regard broadcasting as merely one of the many modes, each with its own characteristics, of supplying audio-visual learning material.

All the evidence to date indicates that the full potential of educational broadcasting, when used as part of a deliberate system of learning, is obtained only when the broadcasts are fully integrated into an educational entity.

The best use of this entity may require explanation, mediation and tutorial work at the point of reception, and the supply of staff competent to perform these functions may be a necessary component in the whole learning system.

Training for this purpose is not at the present time a customary element in the pedagogic training of those destined to become class-teachers or lecturers in conventional institutions.

1. See 'The Open University of the United Kingdom', page 349.

Chapter 4
Innovation and planning

There is no inherent reason why the main principles of Open Learning cannot be adopted by existing institutions. Examples of relaxed admission requirements, of remote study, a more flexible curriculum structure or the use of new media as a means of teaching can be found in a number of universities and colleges. In Australia, for instance, the Karmel Committee, after considering the British Open University and many proposals from Australians to create a new institution to broaden access to post-secondary education, decided that it would be wiser and more appropriate to the Australian situation to build an Open Learning programme on the experience and resources of the Australian universities. There are other examples in our case studies—the experiment in Minnesota, for instance—where a significant development has grown out of a conventional college system. In almost all the cases we studied, however, and in other cases where preliminary discussions have been taking place, there has been a distinct and new departure. It has been found necessary to create an Open Learning system, where several components are combined in a systematic attempt to bring new ways of teaching and learning to a new clientele, because the existing post-secondary institutions have been unable or reluctant to take on this role.

We have been primarily concerned with such situations. The case studies review new ventures in which, by comparison with older universities and colleges, objectives have been more clearly defined; in which new agencies have been created as an act of policy; in which special allocations of money and other resources have been required; in which new methods of work have been essential; and in which there has been little previous experience of the academic and other problems involved.

All these ventures have therefore had to develop, implicitly or explicitly, strategies for planning, implementing and monitoring the progress of their work. Though the rapid expansion of post-secondary education in the last twenty years has given both planners and academics much opportunity to deal with the multitude of problems involved in the creation of new institutions, both the novelty of Open Learning systems and the haste with which most of them have been developed have led to a good deal of insufficiently considered improvisation, to frustration, waste of resources and to lost opportunities to set these ventures on a firm foundation. There is much evidence that the staffs and consultants employed have been insufficiently prepared, inadequately qualified by experience or familiarity with research findings, or too pressed for time with limited resources, to produce long-term plans. This has produced, in some instances, redundant activity which could have been avoided if more study of relevant experience had been undertaken. In other cases it has led to enthusiastic but not necessarily sensible attempts to transplant innovations from one national or educational context to another, without consideration of the local needs and constraints. We feel that it should be more widely recognized that the study of the nature of change and the means by which it may be controlled should form part of the training of educational innovators. Where Open Learning developments are concerned, this training should take place if possible before planning begins; otherwise, by means of suitable in-service training.

Those directly concerned with planning need to be familiar with the growing body of research and development work in the field of higher education which has been going on in government and academic organizations, under the aegis of educational foundations, specialist institutes and such international agencies as Unesco, OECD, the Council of Europe and the European Communities. They also need to consider with care the specific experience of comparable projects elsewhere.

There are vital differences, for example, in the character and the setting of Open Learning systems in societies with centrally controlled educational structures and those which have a large degree of devolution and autonomy; between those which are designed for 'captive' audiences (such as training systems in industry or in the armed forces) and those which have to attract their students and to hold their interest; between those where there is access to broadcasting and good postal facilities and those where such resources are inadequate or unavailable. Similar differences can be found between new systems with broad educational aims, operating on a large scale (such as the Open University) and those catering to specialist audiences or populations with special characteristics (as in the rural areas of Poland). There are also important distinctions to be made between new projects sponsored by national governments, those which are the work of broadcasting organizations, those which are regional in scope, and those which may grow from an existing private or public institution. There are, moreover, important contrasts in curriculum patterns, teaching methods, academic awards and relationships to the existing post-secondary institutions.

Finally, in the examples covered by our case studies, there are two main types of innovation: the 'step-by-step' and the 'big leap'. The choice between these types depends upon many factors: the nature and scale of the proposed change, the urgency of the problem with which it proposes to deal, the resources available and the degree to which existing institutions can be modified. The Empire State College, for instance, was an addition to the seventy-one colleges in the State University of New York. It was possible to keep the new college small until, after it had been working along new lines for three years, its promoters felt that the system was sufficiently tested to justify expansion. The Community College of Vermont adopted a policy of combining research and development and has felt its way cautiously. The Centre de Télé-enseignement Universitaire in France, knowing that it was operating in a potentially critical atmosphere, adopted a low-profile tactic of growth almost by stealth, *la politique du fait accompli*. Though this gradualist approach has obvious advantages, it has drawbacks. It takes time. It does not easily attract substantial resources. It may not be big enough to make a demonstrably decisive impact and may easily be regarded as peripheral. It may also miss the opportunity, in a temporarily favourable climate of opinion, to launch a much more ambitious programme.

The larger-scale schemes also have drawbacks. It is harder to get initial support for them, they are much more difficult to plan and to introduce, and much greater risks of failure are involved. Almost all of them have been justified on the ground that they need and can exploit the opportunities offered by using radio and television. Where, as in the case of the Open University, there was an experienced and influential broadcasting system to hand in the form of the BBC, and that system was willing to co-operate fully in the project, it was possible to make a convincing case for a scheme of such magnitude and to count on the BBC experience and facilities to assist in a rapid transition from conception to actual operations. Where this was not the case, as in Nebraska, and where complex administrative and funding problems have had to be tackled by co-operation between many agencies, the initial planning stages can be protracted.

One of the reasons for using a case-study approach in our inquiry was the belief that the needs and circumstances of each example were so different that generalization was not easy, and probably not very helpful. Even the degree of detail that has been possible in each case study cannot cover the precise questions that may be asked by planners seeking to design a new and appropriate system. Used with care, however, case studies may provide some stimulation and guidance at the preliminary planning stage and help in deciding which system should be studied in detail.

The innovation cycle

It is possible, nevertheless, to discern some common features of an innovation cycle in all the examples we have considered.

1 Motives

In each case study we have sought to establish the source of the original initiative. In each there has been a mixture of motives but we have been able to determine the broad and explicit intentions of those sponsoring the innovation. These can be broken down into several relevant categories—educational, social, professional, philosophical, national needs, etc.—and a careful scrutiny of the relevance and influence of each motive is essential as a prelude to planning.

2 Preliminary debate and diagnosis

The nature and the scale of the discussion which preceded a decision to launch an Open Learning system is different in each of the cases studied. In some cases the debate focused upon social and educational problems—the need, for example, to provide new or additional services to deprived or geographically isolated potential students—in other cases, the emphasis was on the opportunity to exploit new methods of teaching and learning, especially the broadcast media;

other cases again raised the question of relative costs, in the hope that the suggested innovations would provide a cheaper means of providing for increasing numbers in post-secondary education. The course (and the location) of the ensuing discussion also depended upon the intended scope of the institution proposed and the degree to which substantial financial support was required. A single institution, such as the Minnesota Metropolitan State College, or the examples studied in Poland and Newfoundland, could move relatively quickly and develop its own policies. Schemes such as the Everyman's University in Israel, the Open University and the Free University of Iran have become matters of national policy decision at a high level. In all cases, however, the essential task of diagnosis—of defining needs, assessing priorities and considering possible resources—has had to be tackled. In this diagnostic phase, when the initial brief for the project has to be drafted, specialist task forces and consultants are particularly valuable.

3 Initial brief

The drafting of an initial brief is crucial to the clarity and effectiveness of the project, whatever its scale. Such a brief is usually necessary before any commitment to fund a project is secured. It is also the basis of the contract between the proposers of an innovation and its political, educational and financial sponsors. Failure to produce it is a common cause of later misunderstanding and confusion. Without such a brief, indeed, any later attempt to compare intention and achievement will be jeopardized. Our case studies contain different examples of this stage. In Iran, for instance, the first brief took the form of a report commissioned by the relevant minister from the person eventually appointed as the first chancellor. In the case of UMA/SUN, a working group set up by the President of the University of Nebraska produced a report proposing the enlargement of an existing educational television service to serve higher education needs throughout the state. The Open University began with the short official report *A University of the Air*, after which, when a Planning Committee had been established, a much more substantial report was prepared, together with a draft charter and statutes for the proposed university, and careful analyses of its expected needs for finance, staff, buildings and broadcasting facilities.

4 Analysis of resources

The initial brief will inevitably be modified as planning proceeds, and in the first instance will usually be modified by the discovery that the broad aims drafted with such enthusiasm cannot be met by the available resources. A careful review of all the resource implications—lacking in several of the projects we have considered—is therefore vital to avoid later truncation and distortion of the new system. The main headings under which such a review should be made are as follows:

People to control and operate the scheme: their experience, training and career prospects.

Political support: the degree to which the innovation commands the required backing from government, other official agencies, and the academic community affected.

Finance: the scale and timing of likely financial underpinning and its adequacy for the intended tasks.

Educational resources: the type and degree of help that can be expected from other parts of the educational system.

Social resources: other facilities on which the success of the project depends, such as broadcasting agencies, libraries, postal services, etc.

External: international aid, foundations, research institutions, consultants, other institutions and agencies.

The case studies contain many examples of this stage. The report on the Open University, for instance, notes:

The Open University teaching system was devised to make full use of most (but not all) modern educational media, and to draw heavily upon all the relevant pre-existing educational and communications facilities. These facilities are essential to its system, and it is heavily dependent on the following external agencies:

(i) Publishers, for guaranteeing the availability of set books.
(ii) Booksellers, for stocking them.
(iii) Universities, for providing summer-school facilities.
(iv) Local education authorities, for providing study-centre and reading facilities, and financial support to students.
(v) Public libraries, for providing background reading facilities.
(vi) The Post Office, for providing postal services, and British Road Transport, for providing home-kit delivery services.
(vii) The BBC for broadcast production and transmission.
(viii) Commercial printers, for printing of course units and handbooks.
(ix) The full-time staff of other institutions of higher education, whose members are employed by the Open University on a part-time basis.

It is instructive to compare this passage with a discussion of the difficulties in the report on Iran (see pages 183–208 below).

5 Review of initial brief

The first draft of the brief can now be revised and converted into a draft plan.

6 Preparations for implementation

If a special agency has been created to direct the project it will at this stage move from preliminary planning to the first operational phase. It should by now have created its own outline organization, secured its first financing and enabled its staff to begin the detailed work necessary to launch the project by the planned date.

7 Building relationships

As the plans are implemented, a complex series of working relationships will be established, with government and with other parts of the educational system, with the potential students and with the whole network of suppliers and services on which the project will depend. The success of projects may vitally depend upon the speed and the effectiveness of the relationships established at this stage.

8 First operations

The first cycle of operations will not only determine the public credibility of the project: it will also reveal new problems, demands for additional resources and greater possibilities. Careful monitoring of the first phase will be needed to provide the corrections for the longer-term plan.

9 Revision of plans and procedures

To some extent, projects of this type will receive continual revision. The organizational structure, however, should from the outset specify the methods whereby the plan is to be revised and procedures modified. Such provision is more necessary in the case of Open Learning systems than in conventional institutions since there is little experience on which to base such projects, and neither time nor opportunity in some cases to undertake pilot schemes.

10 Further development

Few of the cases we studied have passed through the first innovation cycle to the point where they are securely established. The majority are in the planning phase, or merely beginning to operate on a regular basis. Yet it is important, from the outset, to make some preparation for the transition from the experimental state to 'normal' status—the point where a project has demonstrated its viability, secured acceptance and can no longer expect special treatment in terms of financial and political support. Many worthwhile innovations fail at precisely this point because they have not anticipated the problems that arise when they have to be funded and maintained on a comparable basis with conventional systems. Unless a project is designed deliberately for short-term or special needs that will continue to justify preferential treatment, it must be planned in such a way as to hold out a reasonable hope of survival.

In setting out this analysis of an innovation cycle that affects initiatives in the Open Learning field, and in emphasizing the need for those who embark on these developments to equip themselves by study of the research data and experience available, we do not wish to leave the impression that these studies are sufficient in themselves to secure success. They are requirements brought about by the developments in communications technology and the nature of the institutions proposed, and are additional to all the long-established skills recognized as necessary to educational development. The frequent lack of general planning skills, of management skills, of financial forecasting and of elementary care in identifying and co-ordinating major developments in one area with those in another which will be affected—for example education with communications—is more serious still. The two most common causes of failure in new developments are, probably, the two very human weaknesses of impatience and unwillingness to face inconvenient questions. The political necessity for starting the Open University within the lifetime of the Labour Government resulted in a grave underestimate, which might have proved permanently crippling, of the time and energy required to make its courses.

Two other points, about the staff needed for innovatory developments generally, should be made here. The early stages of any new development need people of very high general ability and drive; quality is more important than qualifications: the early stages of innovatory developments make very great demands upon the energy, devotion and leisure of the key staff. The limited commitment revealed in the common practice of holding two jobs is in conflict with the needs of new ventures. Services of high academic quality and deep personal commitment may be hard to attain unless the scheme also provides commensurate career prospects.

Part Two Problems and practice

In the second part of this book we turn our attention from a general consideration of purposes, issues and contexts to a more detailed discussion of practical problems and the solutions adopted to meet them. Since Open Learning is typically student-centred it seemed logical to start with the students, their situations and requirements before moving on to the institutions and systems set up to service them.

This leads us to consider at some length the extent to which Open Learning students need and want personal contact with their teachers, advisers and fellow-students and how this can be provided. Since a number of the studies exemplify distance learning, we give some consideration to the links carrying information, comment and guidance between the centre and the periphery, in both directions.

We then move to the centre itself where the courses are planned and materials made, the tests devised and students' work normally evaluated, where results are registered and recorded, and degrees, diplomas and other qualifications awarded.

As the systems are so various and individual it would not be possible or helpful to give any general description; instead we devote chapters to a number of the main elements. These chapters draw upon and refer to the case studies in Part Three, and refer back to issues treated in Part One; they are also intended to stand on their own.

Chapter 5

The students, their situation and needs

Each case study gives a picture of its student body and, as can be imagined, the pictures differ. Here is one, about the students at which the Correspondence College Unit of the University of Nairobi aims:

A typical male student is between 21 and 40 years old, married, and has more than four dependants, including members of his extended family. His house has no electricity, and he owns very few books. He may have access to a very small library, but it is probably miles away and impossible for him to use regularly. He does not regularly buy a newspaper, but he does own a radio which is his principal source of news and information about the world outside his own small community. . . .

If this were compared with a similar sketch of the typical student of the Minnesota Metropolitan State College, or indeed of any institution in the developed world, the contrast would be extreme. Open Learning, if it is to be of universal significance, must deal with these extremes and all that lies between.

Though there is, obviously, no common picture of the Open Learning student's situation, yet many points of resemblance do recur and are worth calling attention to. The first part of this chapter, therefore, attempts to do this in an impressionistic way. In the second half we deal in greater depth with a single aspect—the student's need for personal contact—and describe attempts to meet that need and what they entail.

Open Learning students vary considerably in age, most being between 20 and 40, though many are older. In countries where the emancipation of women is in process but in which the full-time provision for women is less generous than for men, a high proportion are female.

The majority are in full-time work, a large number of the women working at home. Such students are affected by shifts and irregular working as well as by the strain of full-time work; those who work at home are obliged to harmonize study with the demands and emergencies of family life. For relatively few is study the prime occupation.

As to wealth, it would probably be found that very few of the wealthy are attracted by Open Learning; otherwise the clientele is extremely varied. In many countries, adult part-time students receive some form of financial encouragement. In less developed countries where educational resources are limited, assistance is commonly restricted to study which is judged by the educational authorities to serve the needs of the economy. In the more developed countries, a much wider range of study aimed at cultural and personal development receives assistance.

In contrast to many full-time students (though, of course, by no means all) Open Learning students study where they live—in houses, flats, lodgings, farms. A small proportion, such as members of armed forces, invalids in hospitals and prisoners, live in institutions. But the vast majority are home-students undertaking their studies as and when these can be fitted in with their other work.

In ability, academic attainment and educational background they must be considered very heterogeneous. It is generally true that, among those of the normal age for attending post-secondary institutions, the most capable and well-to-do obtain the full-time vacancies and that part-time evening and correspondence study are the second and third options. Thus, in countries where the full-time provision covers a high proportion of the population capable of post-secondary study, the ability level of part-time students may drop as full-time provision grows. This was the case in Japan. But since few countries are in this position today it is probably not right to think of Open Learning students as normally less able; rather that they are less fortunately placed. The backlog of men and women of ability may be very large. And certainly many of them display above-average qualities of character and perseverance. A high proportion of those who have so far enrolled in the Open University of the United Kingdom had, irrespective of the stage at which they gave up full-time study, already made some attempt to prolong their education.

As to motives, the vocational predominate: to raise, enlarge, update technical or professional qualifications in order to seek advancement, a better job, avoid redundancy, gain some new skill created by a technological advance. The acquisition of skills for public duties and an understanding of public affairs, together with the skills associated with home and family life, are other main areas of adult interest.

Do adult learners differ from other students? Should planners of Open Learning courses take particular pains to meet their needs and deficiencies?

As there is as yet no fully satisfactory theory about the process of learning itself, it cannot be maintained that adult learning differs in any fundamental way from that of, say, 18-year-old undergraduates. But many of those engaged in adult education emphasize a number of points as being frequently neglected:

Adults must be treated as adults, not teenagers. The wrong attitude can emerge in many small ways such as in the wording of letters and forms, the way in which queries and difficulties are handled, as well as in the way the written learning material is arranged and the study-assignments graded and arranged.

As a category adult learners must not be treated as inferior or as less important than another category. As the Australian and Japanese studies show, where internal and external students in a university are taught or looked after by the same lecturers, the external are frequently at a disadvantage. They tend to receive less personal interest from the lecturers, to get inferior attention and to get their work sent back late with perfunctory comments. Where there are separate staff to look after the external students, then their status and work-load compare unfavourably with those of internal staff, and in many other ways the status of the external student is lower and sometimes even the practical value of the qualification he or she gains is less.

Unless they are accustomed to formal learning (as are teachers, for instance) adult students often do not know how to study, and need help in organizing themselves for this purpose in addition to help in the other self-organizing task of creating space and time for study in their working-life.

If their previous experience of education has been authoritarian and mechanical, adults may have great difficulty in adapting to the greater freedom of Open Learning. The 'learning contract' studies (which, of course, ask for self-diagnosis as well as self-teaching) note this as the most frequent cause of student difficulty.

Many adults, too, who 'dropped out' of basic education carry with them a sense of failure. Their reintroduction to education is more a form of therapy than of learning and, in the first stages, self-confidence rather than academic attainment is the main aim. Others display a need for very structured and conventional forms of education, finding too much liberty a source of anxiety.

On the other hand, adults in their mid-20s and above, once they have settled to their studies, tend to show greater perseverance than younger students. Our studies, particularly those concerned with external degrees, confirm this conclusion. In Japan, where the NHK Gakuen Senior High School has a slowly rising retention rate, it is believed that the rising entry age is part of the explanation.

Many adults express the need for some form of personal and social contact in their education, for the stimulus and fellowship of other students, and for a developing relationship with tutors and lecturers and, where possible, with those producing the course material. The satisfaction of these demands presents a major organizational and financial problem to which we now give some attention.

The need for personal contacts

Personal contacts between student and teacher and between student and student are such accepted elements at all levels of education that the need for them in Open Learning systems is liable to go unexamined. Yet, particularly in large-distance learning systems, this necessity must be carefully considered, for to provide such contact is organizationally complicated and costly. The Open University allotted 27 per cent of its total budget in 1973 to student services, which includes the maintenance of 250 local centres grouped under regional offices, and involves 445 full-time staff and over 5,000 part-time tutors. Attendance at local centres is not compulsory and averages less than half of the students. Some make very little use of either the counsellors or tutors. Nor is there yet any established causal relationship between the use made of the centres and success in examinations.

The other two systems conceived on the same scale—UMA/SUN and the Free University of Iran—intend to establish local centres, but are notably cautious about the commitment, realizing that if centres are found to be necessary to a national system they must eventually be universally provided. UMA/SUN regards the learning centres as part of the university's system of delivery, giving effect to its intention to make education more accessible. Centres are to be established on college campuses, in shopping centres and in mobile vans. They will house copies of the course materials for individual and group study. Students will be able to work there, get advice and guidance from staff, use a free telephone to the university centre and meet other students. Four experimental centres out of a planned fifteen are to be established under the supervision of senior members of staff with particular experience in extension work, so that by 1980 the best solution will have been worked out. The Iranian intention is similarly cautious, though for different reasons. The stated purposes of the Iranian centres are: to help students learn how to study on their own; to give general advice, help and encouragement; and to encourage the establishment of self-help groups. In contrast to the British situation, there is no reservoir of qualified people ready to offer part-time tutoring and counselling services.

In Japan, 'schooling', which has long been a feature of correspondence education at high-school level (up to twenty days a year of compulsory attendance for teaching, discussion and guidance), is an accepted and enjoyed feature of correspondence education at the adult level, though it is not compulsory. It is to be an element in the planned National Broadcasting University.

In the external degree systems of Australia, the need for contact is met by vacation schools and by the course lecturers travelling long distances to meet their students. At Macquarie University in Sydney, which teaches external students the physical sciences to full bachelor-degree standard, intensive personal contact is maintained through compulsory vacation courses using laboratories and local study groups, and enrolment is limited to the numbers that the staff can handle in this way.

The Institute of Education at Beirut has, as will be seen in the report, a fully thought-out system of direct and indirect contact.

In the system operated by the Memorial University of Newfoundland, a local tutor watches the (cassetted) television programme with the class, leads the discussion that follows and undertakes to get answers on points of difficulty by the next meeting.

Students of the Polish Television Agricultural High School, which aims to complete the secondary education of young working farmers, are invited to consultative sessions on Sundays in the nearest schools, when the school staff and agronomists are available for advice.

The 'learning contract' institutions are, of course, rooted in personal one-to-one contact of a penetrating and intimate character. The working out, by each student, of his own educational situation and the activity he needs to reach his particular goal is a key element of the educational process; moreover, the plans made to implement the contract frequently involve many other kinds of personal contact.

On the other hand, some systems provide little contact. The French example, derived from the traditions of the national universities, shows that, despite very slight contact, teacher-students seeking to improve their qualifications manage fairly well with only the course material and radio lectures. The Deutsches Institut für Fernstudien was founded to 'research into the possibility of academic studies independent of personal contact' which would make the presence of a teacher unnecessary. The Schramm report on the Everyman's University for Israel advised that the university 'should put its resources into making effective courses for individual study rather than establishing an extensive network of tutorial centres that might grow into formal instructional institutions'. At the same time the report observed that 'it is unrealistic to assume that the motivation and interest of disadvantaged people in Israel or anywhere else will be adequate to sustain them through the long courses of independent home study'. Indeed, it appears to be generally true that those who have the least background of formal education stand most in need of personal help and encouragement.

As experience and conclusions vary, a lot of work has yet to be done. Nevertheless, some general points can be made about the factors to be considered, the kinds of service which can be made available to the student and the implications of providing them.

Four interrelated factors are involved: the personal and the educational characteristics of each student, and his or her native capacity and attitudes. In general, the longer full-time education is prolonged the more positive becomes the attitude towards continuing education and the greater the capacity for it. But much depends also upon the nature of the full-time education received—how authoritarian in tone it may have been, how much centred upon memory and repetition, and upon compliance with instructions; how much opportunity for self-organization, independent study and discretion it afforded; whether it was felt to be useful or irrelevant to the real business of life. The sum of these experiences, together with the original personal endowment of students, conditions their prospects in Open Learning.

In that large sector of part-time study that is vocationally oriented and based on correspondence, certain functional capacities are needed: the skills of purposive reading, of self-expression in writing and of self-organization. Adults who left full-time education early are unlikely to possess these to a high degree, nor is their subsequent work-experience likely to have developed them.

As to personal factors, motivation seems to be the key—motivation stimulated by the hope of financial reward or career advancement in return for taxing study. Maturity, as mentioned earlier, is another factor. There are also temperamental differences between the solitary and the gregarious, and systems have to take account of these. Systems that can satisfy a range of such personality variations have advantages.

The kind of services that satisfy the need for personal contact will be familiar but it may be worth briefly enumerating them:

1. *Offering direct contact:* (a) class teaching, group discussions, tutorials, counselling; (b) the telephone: between individuals; or by one individual on behalf of a group; or 'confra-telephone'.
2. *Offering substitute contact:* the broadcast lecturer or presenter, off-air or in recorded form.
3. *Offering periodical contact:* seminars, weekend meetings, workshops, vacations or summer schools.

In the smaller, one-institution systems, most of these ways of creating contact between the individual student and the management can be contrived somehow, if only by *ad hoc* means. In the larger ones, the student's contact must be with the local representative of the system. Direct contact with the central team is achievable only in occasional summer schools, or in the substitute form of broadcasting.

The decision to build local study centres into the system has to be taken with great care. The implications are best seen by reference in detail to the case-study reports on the Open University of the United Kingdom (page 342), UMA/SUN (page 465), Newfoundland (page 126) and the Free University of Iran (page 197). A study of these will quickly give a clear picture of the problem particularly if some of the key questions are held in mind:

Does the centre provide facilities and activities which are optional or compulsory?
To what extent do the activities of the centre depend upon consumption of broadcasts at the centre on, or near to, the day and time of transmission?
What kinds of qualified staff are needed in the centres and how will the necessary professional relationships with the central providing agency be secured?
Can the centres play a full part in meeting the feedback requirements of distance learning?
When questions such as these have been faced, a number of decisions concerning the external relationship of the Open Learning system to the rest of the educational system will arise. For instance, will the centres use existing buildings, or build new ones? Will they aim at a separate existence, or at becoming generalized local centres of culture? If they are to be developed over a period of years how will the problems of favouring one area over another be resolved?

The links

The material to be conveyed inside an Open Learning system involves either physical transfer—the postal services or substitutes—or the communications media. For the postal service to be satisfactory for Open Learning it must satisfy five criteria:

1. *Universality* It must reach everybody enrolled.
2. *Reliability* It must never fail.
3. *Uniformity* The delivery times must be uniform.
4. *Speed* It must be swift enough to ensure that the student receives back his tutor's comments in time to affect his future work.
5. *Cost* The cost to the student must not cripple him.

Failure at any one of these points can limit the 'reach' of the system, condition the structure and organization of course-planning, and reduce the effectiveness of the work of tutors. Postal concessions to enrolled students are not uncommon. With the general increase in these charges, this could become an important item.

Where postal services are undeveloped or erratic, substitutes involving combinations of rail, road and bicycle transport, sometimes in several stages, can be devised.

The material to be conveyed in the outward direction will be the bulk of the printed course material, sent well in advance. Inwards there will be the student's work, to be sent to the point in the system where it is to be marked and assessed.

Additionally, there may be audio- and audio-visual tapes and cassettes, kits and so forth. It is often found more satisfactory to distribute and collect these valuable items by other than postal means, sometimes by the liaison staff of the system, or through broadcasting or educational personnel.

The telephone, as mentioned earlier, offers a form of personal contact. It can be used effectively to link an individual student to a local tutor or counsellor, or to a representative of the system at the course-providing centre. The UMA/SUN scheme provides free inward contact for students. It can also be effectively used to link a local tutor to the staff at the centre, for the tutor to obtain additional information for his or her group, or to supply feedback inwards. These personal communications are fruitful. Attempts to use the telephone as a conference device have, however, failed and are usually abandoned after a short trial.

In passing it should be said that the operational needs of Open Learning systems for the telephone are very great and ample provision must be made for this in the plans.

As to the communications media, the question of broadcasting, which has been touched on earlier in Chapter 3, is dealt with in detail in Chapter 8.

Chapter 6
Research and evaluation

We use the term 'research' to describe the process of organized acquisition of information which forms the essential basis for making the most reliable forecasts and the best decisions possible in the circumstances. The term 'evaluation' refers to the systems by which the success or failure of policies and their execution are reported and assessed, and also by which the opinions reached by those operating the system, and those experiencing it, may be checked and interpreted. Given these meanings, both terms may involve activities that are simple and straightforward, or complicated and calling for sophisticated statistical and other procedures. They may entail intuitional professional judgements not to be undervalued because they are not susceptible of quantitative verification.

The theme of this chapter is that research and evaluation have greater importance to Open Learning than they have generally been given in conventional education. There are several reasons for this:

1. The circumstances surrounding innovation (discussed in Chapters 2 and 4) make it prudent to buttress innovatory proposals with as much indisputable and relevant data as can be assembled. This is particularly true where the proposals require heavy initial and recurrent expenditure, involve long-term commitments, consume scarce national financial and personnel resources or foreign exchange. In such schemes, the reputations of prominent public figures are likely to be involved.
2. Distance-learning systems involve the advance production and distribution of learning materials which cannot be withdrawn once distributed and must last for a considerable number of years. In the case of printed materials, it is impractical to remedy more than a few errors of fact by errata slips, and quite impracticable to correct major pedagogic misjudgements. Corrections to broadcasts are equally difficult, though the provision of remedial and students' programmes (see page 62) can do something. It is also theoretically possible, where local centres form part of the scheme, to ask the local tutors to make verbal adjustments to the course material; but this involves an extra liaison operation and detracts from the authority of the central provision. In some instances, a conflict of views has developed between those providing material from the centre and the academics interpreting it locally, to the confusion of the students.
3. Open Learning course material is made by highly qualified people necessarily cut off during the process of manufacture from the eventual users,

without continuing easy access to representative students, and in many cases with cultural backgrounds very different from those of the students. The adjustments in style, tone and density which can be carried out intuitively in face-to-face situations can in this kind of teaching only come as a result of the work of a research and evaluation unit.

4. Where open broadcasting is involved and where a favourable effect upon the general public may be considered important, there is always some danger that the dual target may impair the pedagogic effectiveness for the primary student audience, or even turn the secondary audience into the primary audience (which seems to have been the case in Kenya). In such situations research and evaluation can be of value in clarifying the issues, so that any change is the result of a deliberate decision rather than of slide.
5. Just as the educational potential of broadcasting is best realized when it is integrated into an educational entity (see Chapter 3, page 29 and Chapter 7 *passim*), so the potential of research and evaluation is best recognized in a system where it is both the servant and guide of the course-makers and the representative and interpreter of the consumers. The story of the use of 'modern media' over the last thirty years is littered with the disappointments and misunderstandings attributable to this organizational failure. Its inherent need for the services of research and evaluation provides the opportunity for Open Learning to remedy this defect.

Research and evaluation is relevant to every stage of Open Learning operations but its particular contribution is different at different stages. For convenience, we have adopted the classifications of 'Background', 'Formative', 'Summative' and 'Policy' research and we discuss their roles in sequence. After that we discuss the skills which the tasks call for, the scale of resources needed and how they might be secured and organized.

Because, as shown in the 'Innovation Cycle' sketched in Chapter 4 above (page 32), research is needed when a project is still only a tentative proposal, it seemed logical to place this chapter dealing with research before those dealing with curriculum intentions and their realization.

Background research

Background research is concerned with the information needed to establish the case for the proposed institution or service and to describe it sufficiently for plans to be made that will carry conviction. In some instances, such as the plans to increase and upgrade the teaching force (Kenya, Lebanon), the needs given by governments are specific, and the attention focuses on how Open Learning systems can meet them; this involves considerable study of the organization of the educational system and of the situation of the students. In other cases the starting-point may be a generalized wish; for instance, to increase access to higher education by means of an institution of a new type (UMA/SUN, the Open University). Here it is necessary to validate and quantify the needs and the interests of the potential students as well as to examine the appropriateness and viability of the scheme proposed and, in the case of UMA/SUN, its acceptability to a range of authorities.

At this stage, much of the information is already available in published reports and through existing agencies. It may, however, be considered necessary to conduct some form of poll of the potential students.

In some instances, the proposal may derive from a high-level request to use a particular facility, often an existing television service, so as to meet an educational need. Here a first concern must be to get behind the proposed solution to the need itself and explore it thoroughly, because of the possibility that some other solution might meet it more effectively and economically.

Relevant passages of our reports are to be found in: UMA/SUN (page 450 ff.); the Open University of the United Kingdom (page 321), the UNRWA/Unesco Institute of Education, Beirut (page 273) and the Free University of Iran (page 189).

Formative research

Formative and summative research are complementary. In the simplest terms, the first is undertaken, in conjunction with the course creators, to help produce a product that will 'work', and the second to see whether it did work, and if not, why not. The stage of formative research is where the academic staff and the media staff (where these are separate) first form a professional working relationship with those who, through their knowledge and contact with the target audience, can help guide the creative process. According to the size of the system, this relationship may involve academics, course designers, writers, broadcasters, producers and directors of all kinds of audio and audio-visual material, graphic designers and editors. It is an area of considerable sensitivity and delicacy, where the work normally proceeds under high pressure. Considerable skill is needed to secure and maintain the kind of personal relationships that are productive. Much depends on the tact and skill of the research and evaluation staff.

Summative research

Since this stage is primarily concerned with the results, objectivity and detachment are at a premium. It is common to enlist external research at this stage, and it has provided, for instance in Kenya (see page 256), a good occasion for seeking external aid. Yet there is also much to be said for using the organization's own research staff, particularly where the problems relate to the spanning of a cultural gap between the course-providers and the target clientele (as, for example, the non-European Jews in Israel, or the rural populations in India for whom the SITE satellite television programmes are designed), and many crucial points concern the detail of content, approach, density of information and presentation.

Policy research

The need for on-going research on the functioning of an Open Learning system—what is often called 'institutional' research—cannot be stressed too strongly. Such a system, which may be highly innovative at the outset, will undoubtedly need continuous monitoring to ensure that it is carrying out its proposed work effectively, to make the inevitable adjustments in structure and methods of operation and to indicate the lines of development for future policy. Such monitoring, which will extend to administrative as well as academic activities, may well be the responsibility of a special section or department, though all sub-units of the system should be expected to review their work regularly and to make suggestions for future policy. There should be, for example, a systematic scrutiny of the teaching system itself and of its effectiveness, of the responses, behaviour and characteristics of its students, of the relative costs incurred by each part of the system, and of the means for policy control within the whole organization.

The scale of such policy research and the means whereby it is conducted will of course vary from one Open Learning system to another. A relatively small-scale enterprise, with limited objectives, will not need to create a substantial organization specifically for this purpose. It may, moreover, be able to enlist outside specialist help for specific and restricted purposes. For instance, a university department of sociology or psychology might well be able to undertake surveys of students; a government agency might contribute to studies of organization and management; an independent consultant could assist with technical communications problems; or a broadcasting organization could give advice on possible developments in the use of radio and television.

In the case of the British Open University, a decision was taken at the outset to establish its own Institute of Educational Technology with a specialist staff able to help the academic faculties in designing and developing courses, devising methods of assessment and studying student performance. This institute, with a staff of more than thirty, still performs only part of the necessary work of policy research, which is also conducted by the academic faculty units, the regional organization and units of the central administration. Our report on the British Open University, however, summarizes (see page 332) the main purposes of this institute and indicates the range of activities thought appropriate to it:

> . . . the university soon came to the conclusion that it needed a counterbalance to its preoccupation with academic distinction. Its teaching must be systematic and must make the fullest use of the techniques available in the light of the best recent work on educational technology and on the psychology of learning. It could not be left to the intuitive methods of gifted teachers, inspiring though those can be in a face-to-face situation. It therefore set up an Institute of Educational Technology (IET) staffed by people who had studied, and whose business it would be to study further, the basic problems of course design, construction, and evaluation. The academic staff proper is primarily concerned with course content. The staff of the IET is concerned with the formulation of objectives, with performance tests, with the developmental testing of course material through its use with sample groups, with assessment and examination, with the conceptual difficulty, grading and continuity of courses, with student feedback, and with the necessary modification of courses. It undertakes studies of groups within the student population and of their learning styles, of the services given by tutors and counsellors, and of the functions of the various components of the university's teaching.

It is difficult to suggest a target figure for the budgetary allocation to institutional or policy research. A figure sometimes used is an approximate 2 per cent of the operating budget. In the case of the British Open University the proportion of the budget allotted to the IET was originally just over 2 per cent, but with the large-scale expansion of the last three years this has now fallen to 1.5 per cent, though the absolute amount has increased. In addition to this budgetary item, however, resources are also devoted to institutional research through other departments, such as regional tutorial services, the project control and examination offices; a significant proportion of uncosted faculty time is also taken up with review and policy-planning activities.

The experience of institutional research, like the emergence of educational technology, is still too recent to offer more than general proposals for organizing the work needed or to suggest the best place for it within the organizational structure. There are arguments for assigning responsibility for its general direction close to the top—under the immediate control of the central administration; there are equally strong arguments for giving such a unit (or units) a measure of independence—especially in the field of research, thus allowing it to operate without the staff as a whole seeing it as an agency of the central administration. In practice, a compromise between these two positions will usually be found, though the structure, responsibilities and modes of work of such a unit should be kept under review as the system develops. At this stage in the development of the British Open University, for instance, serious consideration is being given to a reorganization of institutional research in general and of the terms of reference of the IET in particular.

The role of educational technologists

It is already clear that there are problems involved in the establishment of a separate unit, just as there are other problems if no part of the organization has a direct and continuing responsibility for guiding academic colleagues, for monitoring the scheme's operation, for feeding in the results of its own research and for serving as a line of contact to comparable work going on elsewhere. Where, as in the case of the Open University, a distinct institute has been established, it is likely that the academic staff will come to question its usefulness as they become increasingly informed and experienced in design and presentation. The educational technologists, for instance, undertook many tasks in the early stages of the Open University, when their academic colleagues lacked knowledge of relevant techniques of course design or correspondence education, of new methods of evaluation and assessment, production scheduling and statistical control. That initial contribution was vital; to the degree that it was effective, the relevant skills and activities were disseminated throughout the whole of the Open University. The ensuing question is whether the IET should continue to play a similar role in the future or whether it should take on other types of activity. There are some who feel that the contribution of research and educational technology staff should henceforth be restricted largely to routine tasks—such as assisting the practical work of course teams—and to acting as a service centre for projects requested by the academic staff. There is some resistance to the idea that any quasi-independent unit should undertake long-term or 'state of the art' research, or have any significant say in shaping the future strategy of the university, or even play an investigative role by examining the developing structure and effectiveness of the institution as a whole.

Such difficulties, which arise increasingly as an Open Learning system becomes successfully established, cannot easily be resolved: they derive, in part, from the desire of academic faculty to retain as much control as possible over the system. They may be less acute where the system is restricted to a small range of activities, or where there has been strong central control of the operation from the outset.

Even so, the issue is essentially one of organization, not of function. The kind of research needs summarized earlier remain, wherever the work is located and however it is conducted. Irrespective of the political or management decisions taken in a particular case, it is clear that there will be a requirement for staff with certain kinds of skill for the performance of defined tasks.

The institutional research function, which deals with such matters as student characteristics and performance, the deployment and use of facilities and the relative costs of different parts of the operation, requires staff with statistical, psychological and sociological training, of a type commonly needed in market or survey research.

The course design function, which includes evaluation and assessment, needs the services of staff broadly classified as educational technologists. Since training facilities for such staff are a very recent development, most of the personnel will have been recruited from academic subject specialists, or from staff trained in educational theory and organization.

In both cases, however, the initial training of the staff involved will prove to be less significant than their subsequent experience. Work in institutional research and educational technology demands a range of skills, including the handling of complex interpersonal relations, which can only be developed 'on the job'—and which may depend as much upon personality as on formal qualification. It is also important to realize that the aim of any Open Learning system must be to promote the emergence of such skills throughout its entire staff, who are engaged in a co-operative venture in which there cannot be hard-and-fast working divisions. A polarization between academics, administrators, researchers, educational technologists and broadcast producers is undesirable and counterproductive.

For this reason a special responsibility falls upon research and educational technology staffs to engage in in-service training, both for themselves and for their colleagues in the institution as a whole, and one of the best forms of such training is collaborative participation in specified projects. While researchers and educational technologists will inevitably spend more time on consultant, advisory and research activities than do the 'content' specialists, it must be accepted as an aim of policy that the institution as a whole has a concern for such functions. Effective feedback and dissemination of vital information are almost impossible unless this is the case.

More difficult problems arise when long-term strategy, rather than the day-to-day operation of the system, is at issue. At this point the existence of a separate cluster of specialists, concerned with the skills needed for the development as well as the maintenance of the system, may be invaluable. It can provide the resources for investigating fundamental problems as well as for assessing the implications of the system's performance to date. It does, nevertheless, face the difficulty that confronts any body of presumed 'experts' who operate to some extent outside the normal structure: it can be seen as 'non-responsible' (for instance, to the academic staff) and possibly as 'impracticable', being thought too remote from the practical problems encountered by the mass of the staff.

There are no simple or standard solutions to this problem. Its existence is one reason why it usually proves difficult to secure funds for a separate research and development unit, or to find a role for such a unit once a new institution begins to move from its initial phases into regular and routine operations. Another reason for this resistance is that, in the initial stages, the contribution of research and educational technology is substantial, since it is based upon accumulated experience and knowledge. It is not possible, without a considerable investment of time and resources, to begin to produce a comparable effort at the second level. Institutional research and educational technology have developed too recently, and the systems with which they are dealing are too novel, for 'new' research results and 'new' techniques to emerge easily and quickly. Most of the work undertaken so far is drawing upon the level of knowledge at the end of the 1960s. The analysis and application of the systems created in the last ten years is likely to take several years: it may well be 1980 before significantly new work is available in a form which can affect practice.

This means that all new learning systems have a general responsibility to contribute to that research: without providing some resources for this purpose, even if immediate results are not obtainable, they will be failing to undertake their share of this investment in research and development work. How they do this, and on what scale, may well be vital, to their own future operations as well as to the 'state of the art' generally. To require that research and consultancy be limited to what is urgently demanded by a system is not merely short-sighted, it also lacks hindsight. Such an attitude fails to recognize that the emergence of Open Learning systems in the first instance—the overall objectives, their organization and their methods of work—was to a considerable extent the outcome of research and of the repertoire of concepts and procedures loosely described as educational technology. Planning for the future must provide for such work to be continued, extended and improved.

Chapter 7
The curriculum and choice of media

The curriculum of an Open Learning system may be old or new. It may consist of the established curriculum (or some part of it) of a sponsoring university or other educational institution, or may be that required for the attainment of some recognized educational qualification. It may be an adaptation of such a curriculum, or it may be devised to meet a special need. It may be aimed at a single specific audience, for example teachers of science, or it may offer a varied provision for a more general public to choose from. (This description does not, of course, apply to those institutions which base their work upon separate curricula for each student.)

The design of any curriculum will be determined and shaped by a number of factors; primarily by the need which it exists to serve, but also by the capacities and circumstances of the students, the strengths and limitations of the educational media available, the judgements of the academic staff engaged in planning the operation and the financial constraints peculiar to distance learning and to the particular project.

The needs which Open Learning systems try to meet were considered in Chapter 2. One overwhelming priority emerged: the need for teachers, for enlargement of the teaching force, improved professional standards, and modernization of teaching methods, particularly in mathematics and science. In all instances, the requirement was for part-time courses, mainly for the in-service training of existing teachers.

Open Learning systems of distance teaching more commonly offer arts subjects than science subjects. In Japan, the Ministry of Education was for a number of years opposed to the teaching of science by correspondence. In France the organization known as Télécnam, an offshoot of the Conservatoire Nationale des Arts et des Métiers, caters for students of technology but the university systems cater only for the arts. In Australia, the large and firmly established external service provided by the University of New England covers some 160 courses, but their range is limited to arts and education; in science, only elementary biology is offered (page 105). The institutions that include science in their curriculum have used special resources. Télécnam uses television as a substitute for laboratory demonstration. The Macquarie University in Sydney, Australia (as mentioned earlier) teaches science to bachelor-degree level by an intensive system including compulsory vacation courses, local laboratories, study-groups, audio-tapes and home kits for experiments. The

Open University, which has a growing range of specialized science courses developing from a broadly based introductory course, discourages the enrolment of applicants without access to television, which forms a vital component of the course. It furnishes enrolled students with kits which may include expensive items such as microscopes and colorimeters; and it insists for each course on a week of attendance at which there is intensive laboratory practice under personal guidance. For these reasons the cost of science courses is much higher than that of arts courses (as is the case in conventional universities).

Newly established Open Learning institutions are likely to have a positive attitude towards innovatory schemes, towards interdisciplinary study, towards the new needs of society (for instance the new scientific approach to industrial management) or indeed, towards intellectual adventure of one kind or another. These institutions will introduce new and different content into courses. The steady democratization of post-secondary education and the increasing emphasis on lifelong education brings in new and different people as students. The two combine to challenge educators to present the material in new ways appropriate to students who have never acquired, or have forgotten, the background knowledge which can be taken for granted among those recently qualified.

The design of Open Learning curricula for mature students must take account of their life experience and their personal situation. The courses must be suitable for part-time students and, preferably, for intermittent students. For such students the credit type of progression familiar in American universities has advantages of flexibility over the tightly consecutive, unvariable and lengthy work-programme which in Europe leads to a single final examination. Distance-teaching systems that aim to offer a range of options approaching those of conventional universities need to provide a large number of interlocking courses. (Paradoxically, this web of options can develop into a structure that becomes more inflexible as it grows in sophistication. The additions being made to the Open University courses, for example, make it impossible to reconsider the main course structure itself, and the four-year life of each course slows the rate of possible change.)

The modular nature of the credits approach also facilitates movement from one mode of education to another as, for example, when a student commences on a part-time basis and is able later to move to full-time study. But flexibilities of this type must not so diminish the structure of a bachelor degree that it becomes unacceptable to other universities or to employers.

The bachelor-degree structure of the Open University (see page 333 ff.) has six main lines of study (arts, science, mathematics, technology, the social sciences and educational studies) and four levels. The regulations are designed to require both a certain width of study and an amount of higher-level study, together with as wide a range of choice as possible.

The problem facing university management in constructing a full bachelor-degree system is to reconcile the need for economical working with the aspirations of students and of academic staff, which can at times conflict with this need. The cost of course development is very high; the cost per student will be low for the basic foundation courses with a large enrolment, but rises rapidly as this number is fragmented into smaller and smaller groups of advanced students. Many students, and especially those with vocational advancement in view, will wish to concentrate on particular lines of study and towards specialisms. Many academics support this aim as enhancing the prestige and standing of the university. The university has to recognize the difficulty of attracting and retaining staff of high calibre unless it can provide opportunities for advanced work that offers both intellectual stimulus and the prospect of advancement in other universities.

This major dilemma facing many Open Learning institutions can present itself in the following way. First, is it better in any given circumstances to aim at a comprehensive provision and an effort spread over a large field, or to concentrate on doing those things which can be done best and most economically? Secondly, how many courses should be provided, bearing in mind both the need for economy and the need to present the student with an adequate but not excessive or bewildering range of choice? Thirdly, can the system afford to devote resources of the same kind and on the same scale to advanced courses with small enrolments as it does to more basic courses?

There remains a difficulty which every institution with a radically innovative curriculum, either in content or structure, is likely to encounter: that is, the difficulty of having the degrees or other awards which it grants recognized as of equal worth with those of more conventional institutions. If there is not a national validating machinery, this may call for the establishment of some form of academic advisory body or specially created agency drawn from the ranks of higher education; even given the approval of such a body, negotiations may be needed with professional associations that set standards for their own membership and may not at first be willing to accept the validity of a new curriculum. It may indeed prove necessary for the new institution to be especially severe in the application of its own standards of examination during its early and formative years. (The Council for National Academic Awards performs this function in the United Kingdom.)

Selection of educational media

The selection of media logically succeeds the framing of the curriculum, but in practice the two processes are indivisible. Nowadays there are available, at least in theory, a very wide range of media. It may be appropriate to recall them. Broadly classified they fall into the following groupings:

Printed material. Correspondence texts. Specially written textbooks. Set books already published. Packets of pictures. Directed reading using the resources of libraries (including newspapers and periodicals). Assignments of work for tutorial comment, or for computer assessment. Self-assessment problems, exercises and questions. Material ancillary to the other modes of teaching used, e.g. notes on broadcast programmes; instruction for the use of scientific 'kits'.

Audio-visual material other than print. Slides, filmstrips, film loops and film. Audio tapes. Audio tapes synchronized with filmstrips. National or local radio or television broadcasts, to be used 'live' or to be recorded locally for later or repeated use. Locally made video-tape.

Practical activities. The use of home science 'kits'. Directed work in local laboratories. The undertaking of research activities (e.g. social surveys) or field-work (e.g. collecting of geological specimens) in the student's locality.

Face-to-face teaching and other interpersonal activities. Counselling (on choice of courses, methods of study, etc.). Study by correspondence, including communication by telephone. Lectures and seminars. Self-help groups. Supervised professional activities (e.g. teaching, and the preparation of teaching material). Attendance at summer schools or other short residential courses. Attachments for short periods to schools, colleges or community centres. Internships. Directed travel.

All these are 'media'. The Lebanon study makes a useful distinction between 'direct' and 'indirect' forms of training, the former being those that involve direct contact between the student and the teacher. We shall use these terms. In conversation, the 'media' is often loosely used to mean radio and television. To avoid confusion we shall call them the 'broadcast' media, or 'broadcast-based' media, the latter covering cassetted material prepared as for broadcast transmissions.

Each medium has its own strong and weak points. There is no standard or ideal combination. Some systems make no use of radio and a larger number make no use of television. Some dispense with face-to-face teaching. What must be stressed as emerging from our case studies is that success depends very largely on the close and effective knitting together of such resources as are used. As our report on the UNRWA/Unesco Institute of Education in Beirut puts it (page 283):

It must be said that the several media involved in the institute's multi-media approach have little that is innovative about them if they are considered individually and separately. All of them have been used, at one time or another, and in different combinations, in the training of teachers, pre-service or in-service. The uniqueness of the institute's experiment lies in the integrated manner in which these different media are being used. The key concept in the institute's multi-media approach is integration—a fusion of these media into one organic whole in which there are clearly observable interrelationships. . . . For example, seminars are not conducted without reference to specific study assignments, and guidance in classroom teaching is considered to be most effective when it is provided with reference to what has been learnt by the trainees from the assignments, and in the seminars.

The report on the British Open University makes the same point (page 338):

The unique character of the teaching obviously resides not in the use of any or all of these teaching media, but in the degree of integration achieved and in the organic relationship between the planning of course content and the planning of teaching methods for each course.

A great deal of research effort has been devoted to exploring the capacity of the broadcast media for different teaching tasks or different subjects, but very little so far to precise comparative studies of the effectiveness of the various educational media in specific contexts. Professor Wilbur Schramm sums up the present state of the evidence as follows:

. . . given a reasonably favourable situation, a pupil will learn from any medium—television, radio, programmed instruction, films, filmstrips or others. This has been demonstrated by hundreds of experiments. In general, the same things that control the amount of learning from a teacher face-to-face also control the amount of learning from educational media; among others, the relevance and clarity of the content, individual abilities, motivation to learn, attention, interest in the subject, respect and affection for the teacher, emphasis and replication of the central points to be learnt, and rehearsal by the learner.[1]

Thus, in the present stage of verified information and judgement no special pedagogic magic can be attributed to any one of the available educational media. The distinguishing advantage of the broadcast media lies in their reach. But considered as a means of dissemination their availability varies sharply from country to country, and within each country they vary markedly in cost. Since, over a wide field of subject matter, the various educational media can apparently teach with broadly equivalent success (with science as the most obvious exception), considerations of cost and availability, both to the providing organization and to the individual student, must inevitably play a major part in determining which media should be used, and in what proportions. Thus, the planners of Israel's Everyman's University believe that the use of television will be greatly limited by two practical constraints, limited air time and cost of production and transmission, and should be used only when essential pedagogically; while Japan, with its prosperous economy and intensively developed use of television, is planning a Broadcasting University which will provide eighteen hours of television a day. The British Open University, operating in a small country with good communications, can insist that its students should attend summer schools. This would be plainly impracticable for the Memorial University of Newfoundland, serving remote rural communities, some as far as 800 miles away from the centre.

Working within the limits of the practicable and the economically possible, each teaching organization is, however, obliged to allocate particular media to particular purposes. In the absence of clear research findings it must make commonsense judgements, building as best it can on its own experience and that of others. Every teaching system must minister to three phases of the learning process. First, there must be exposition, written, spoken and in some subjects visual; second, the student must make the facts and concepts presented to him his own by using them, and must undertake regular work, some of which may involve self-correction, but some of which calls for outside assessment. Finally, there must be attention to his individual problems and difficulties. The whole process must, moreover, be so designed as to provide the student with an effective stimulus, and to reinforce his urge to go on learning. We now consider some of the characteristics of the most important teaching media.

Printed material as an expository medium is familiar to the student. It allows him to go at his own pace and pause over his difficulties. It leaves him with a permanent record for revision. It can set out problems and exercises, including multiple-choice questionnaires for computer-marking for the student to undertake in his own time. It can readily incorporate the techniques of programmed learning. Printed material can provide the nucleus round which an integrated sequence of broadcast programmes, of directed activities, of discussion groups and face-to-face teaching can, as resources allow, be built up.

As an element in correspondence education, printed material is the basic and only method of personal instruction capable (wherever postal services

1. W. Schramm, *What the Research Says*, in: W. Schramm (ed.), *Quality in Instructional Television*, p. 44–79, Honolulu, The University Press of Hawaii, 1972.

exist) of indefinite expansion to new subjects and new audiences. Correspondence study has also the practical advantage that, unless it is geared to broadcasting (which has fixed dates), entry to the course, suspension and renewal can be adjusted to the student's convenience, within the limits of the system's administrative tolerance. The use of recorded, cassetted material does not affect this flexibility, nor need it reduce the pacing effect of periodic issues of the printed learning material.

For all these reasons the 'package' of printed material dispatched to the student at regular intervals is an indispensable component of all the systems that we have studied. The stimulus to learning which it offers depends primarily on the teaching skills which it incorporates, and on the sense of progressive mastery of the subject which the student derives from it; but it may be worth adding that attractive format and typography together with well-produced illustrations also have a part to play in assuring him that he is in good hands, that the teaching organization considers him important, and that learning can be a pleasure.

Broadcasting: radio and television

The use of broadcasting in either of its two modes depends more than the use of any other teaching medium on extrinsic rather than pedagogic considerations. The availability of air time, the range of resources and professional skills which can be devoted to educational purposes, the degree of integration which can be achieved between the academic planning of courses and the provision of a broadcasting component of the teaching operation—all these factors are so intimately bound up with the organization and practice of broadcasting in each country that they are the subject of special consideration in the next chapter. Here it is only necessary to touch on them incidentally, and in relation to the major pedagogic decision to be made.

One of the the oldest forms of teaching at post-secondary level is the lecture to a large group of students. It is used throughout the world as the principal instrument for the first and basic expository phase of teaching, carrying the main burden so far as verbal communication is concerned. It is the simplest and cheapest way of giving the student a broad and up-to-date conspectus of a field of knowledge. It is also the most economical of the time of lecturers. The tradition of professor and lecture has a time-honoured prestige and acceptance, although it is also bitterly criticized.

Lectures can be transmitted by broadcasting in the form in which they were prepared, or with slight modifications, and there is evidence that results at least as good can be obtained in this way. It is the practice in two of the systems studied (the Australian and the French) and lecturing is established as the normal broadcasting form in Japan.

Before considering further the contributions that radio and television can make and what role they may be given in Open Learning distance systems, the cardinal fact must be stressed that broadcasting cannot by itself carry the main teaching burden of even a carefully restricted national operation without the use of air time at those peak hours when students are at home and able to listen and view. This is rarely possible, especially in television, and the Broadcasting University of Japan is unique in so far as its planners are thinking in terms of courses taught 'by radio and television, supported by special textbooks and other printed material' (see page 242).

The suitability of the lecture-form in Open Learning systems using broadcasting needs further consideration. The French report has some relevant passages (see page 150):

> The great majority of broadcasts are ordinary university lectures modified to fit the 30 minutes transmission times. In these programmes the standard of delivery is high, but no use is made of the more sophisticated properties of radio. . . . Some broadcast lectures too, are heavy with factual material which might be more appropriately provided in written documentation.

Discussing the attitudes of the responsible planning staff (page 158):

> Some of the university lectures, they feel, now hang like millstones around their necks . . . because they are inappropriate to the needs of the distant learner, and because their existence tends to act as a brake on innovatory thinking about educational communication.

These comments can be seen from two angles: from one they illustrate the disadvantages likely to arise when material made for one set of circumstances is used to serve a second and different set. From another they show the significant differences in style between material designed to impart information and material designed to promote reflective and imaginative responses in the student.

These quotations emphasize again the need to integrate the broadcasting component into the total teaching system by a form of organization that will enable the system to make the most of the media selected. The British Open University has recently included in its evidence to the Committee on the Future of Broadcasting in the United Kingdom (under the chairmanship of Lord Annan) a detailed paper analysing the first four years of the university's course production, and the contributions which it has been found that radio and television can make. The substance of this paper is reproduced below (see pages 60–62). It is of some interest that, among twenty-three specific functions listed for television and nine for radio, only one, and that in radio, refers to the lecture-form. It should also be said that the relevance of this analysis, though it relates to experience in using broadcasting, is not confined to that form of dissemination. It would be applicable also to material created for distribution in cassette or tape form; in other words it is concerned with the role of audio and audio-visual material as a form of 'indirect' education.

But however freely broadcasting is used, the vital need for material permanently available, such as print, remains. Indeed it is necessary not merely to the development, consolidation and revision of what has been presented by broadcasting, but as a preparation for the broadcasts themselves. The more heterogeneous the audience, the more important it is that they should be given beforehand an apparatus of concepts and a vocabulary which will make the broadcast an effective act of communication.

According to the nature of the course and the capacities of the students (for instance, the case of science referred to earlier and the discussion on the role of local centres), it may also be essential to arrange for tutorial contact if the full value of the broadcast material is to be obtained.

Two other advantages to the students may result from the inclusion of broadcasting in a system. First, it can be a strong pacing agent, keeping the student up to the mark, imposing a rhythm on his work and home routines and reinforcing the requirements of the correspondence course where the two are used. Drop-out may be reduced in this way. Secondly, the use of broadcasting as a limited form of face-to-face communication between the course-providers and the students (see items 6 and 21 (television) and item 1 (radio) of 'The Pedagogic Value of Broadcasting' below) can help students to feel that they are members of a corporate body, and in touch with its teaching staff who are in turn responsive and attentive to their reaction to the course material.

These advantages accrue only when broadcasts are directly linked to the progress of the course. They are lost where there is little or no connexion in time between the broadcast and other components, as in many correspondence study systems which permit entry at any date.

Finally, open-circuit broadcasting may influence the general public. The programmes, particularly those of the introductory foundation courses, can allow men and women to sample the broadcast components of a course and to measure their own capacity as potential students. In this way some who might otherwise think themselves incapable of this level of study may be encouraged to try.

The programmes may also have a cultural value for a much larger body of viewers and listeners, an important consideration in the use of an expensive medium like television. The appreciation of this wider audience may help to promote a generally favourable attitude towards the venture.

The pedagogic value of broadcasting

We reproduce below, by kind permission of the Open University and with acknowledgments to Professor Ralph C. Smith (Pro-Vice-Chancellor, Planning) and Dr A. W. Bates of the Institute of Educational Technology, the following analysis of the uses of television and radio found to be appropriate to British Open University programmes.

Television

1 To demonstrate experiments or experimental situations, particularly:
  (a) where equipment or phenomena to be observed are large, expensive, inaccessible or difficult to observe without special equipment.
  (b) where the experimental design is complex.
  (c) where the measurement of experimental behaviour is not easily reduced to a single scale or dimension (e.g. human behaviour).
  (d) where the experimental behaviour may be influenced by uncontrollable but observable variables.

2 To bring to students primary resource material, i.e. film or video-recordings of actual situations which, through editing and selection, can demonstrate principles covered in the units. This material may be used for a number of purposes, for example:
  (a) film of naturally occurring events (e.g. teaching situations, mental disorders, medical cases) to enable recognition of categories, symptoms, etc.
  (b) film of naturally occurring events to enable students to analyse a situation, using principles or criteria established elsewhere in unit.

(c) to provide students with a selection of sources of evidence to analyse. Besides contemporary material, it may also include archive film or historical material.

3 To record specially events, experiments, species, places, people, buildings, etc., which are crucial to the content of units, but may be likely to disappear, die or be destroyed in the near future.

4 To bring to students the views or knowledge of eminent people, who are often prepared to be televised or filmed but not to write material specially for the institution.

5 To change student attitudes:
(a) by presenting material in a novel manner, or from an unfamiliar viewpoint.
(b) by presenting material in a dramatized form, enabling students to identify with the emotions and viewpoints of the main participants.
(c) by allowing the students to identify closely with someone in the programme who overcomes problems or himself changes his attitudes as a result of evidence presented in the programme or televised exercise.

6 To explain or demonstrate activities that the students are to carry out (e.g. home experiments, survey interviewing).

7 To feed back to students 'mass' or total results of activities or surveys carried out by the students themselves, where the 'turn-round' time is too short for printed feedback.

8 To illustrate principles involving dynamic change or movement.

9 To illustrate abstract principles through the use of specially constructed physical models.

10 To illustrate principles involving two-, three-, or *n*-dimensional space.

11 To use animated, slow-motion, or speeded-up film or video-tape to demonstrate changes over time (including computer animation).

12 Through performance, to demonstrate methods or techniques of dramatic production, or different interpretations of dramatic works.

13 To demonstrate decision-making processes:
(a) by filming or observing the decision-making process as it occurs.
(b) by dramatization.
(c) by simulation or role-playing.

14 To condense or synthesize into a coherent whole a wide range of information which in print would take up considerable space and would not provide the richness of background material necessary for students to appreciate fully the situation.

15 To demonstrate how basic principles have been applied in the real world, where visualization of the application in its total environment is necessary to understand the way the principle has been applied, and the difficulties encountered.

16 To test students' ability, by requiring them to apply concepts or principles learned elsewhere in the course; by explaining or analysing 'real-life' situations presented through television.

17 To demonstrate the use of tools or equipment, or the effects of tools or equipment.

18 To demonstrate methods of playing instruments, and the relationship between music, musicians and their instruments.

19 To increase students' sense of belonging; identification of and with course designers; to make the teaching less impersonal.

20 To reduce the time required by students to master content.

21 To pace students; to keep them working regularly; to break the inertia in beginning evening study.

22 To recruit or attract new students (either to the university or to specific courses); to interest general viewers in subject matter.

23 To establish academic credibility of the course to 'outside' world.

Radio

1 To provide remedial tutorials, or some other form of tutorial, based on feedback.
2 To provide corrections, alterations or updating of material, where print remake budgets are limited, or where print cannot reach students quickly enough.
3 To bring to students primary resource material, i.e. recordings which, through careful editing and selection, can demonstrate principles covered in the units. This material may be used in a number of ways, for example:
   (a) recordings of naturally occurring events, e.g. political speeches, children talking, concerts or performances, talks previously recorded for other than Open University purposes (e.g. Reith lectures), eyewitness interviews at historical events.
   (b) to provide students with a selection of sources of evidence to analyse.
4 To bring to students the views or knowledge of eminent people who can condense in a full or edited form, so as to provide the essential points, what in written form may be more complex or lengthy.
5 To record specially the voices of people who have not been recorded before, but whose contribution to the course would provide a unique experience (e.g. famous poets reading their own work, civil servants talking—perhaps anonymously—about their role in decision-making).
6 To change student attitudes:
   (a) by presenting material in a novel manner, or from an unfamiliar viewpoint.
   (b) by presenting material in dramatized form, enabling students to identify with the emotions and viewpoints of the main participants.
7 To demonstrate methods or techniques of drama or music, through performance.
8 To provide the student with a condensed argument, in lecture form, which may:
   (a) reinforce points made elsewhere in the course.
   (b) introduce new concepts not covered elsewhere in the course.
   (c) provide an alternative view to that presented in the correspondence text and/or television programmes.
   (d) analyse material contained elsewhere in the course, more particularly in specially written broadcast notes or television programmes.
   (e) summarize the main points of the block or course as far as it has gone, providing integration and orientation.
   (f) draw on quotation, recorded information, interviews, etc., as evidence in support of (or against) the argument.
9 To enable students to perceive that different points of view exist, and to observe ideas being challenged, through discussions and interviews.

Chapter 8

The use of broadcasting

There are two main reasons for considering the use of broadcasting in Open Learning systems: its reach and its pedagogic versatility. Broadcasting, which uses installations already supplied for other national purposes, can reach very large audiences which already have receiving apparatus (the transistor radio set), or can be supplied with community television receivers at not too great a cost until home television receivers become normal household possessions. Until that stage arrives, the community receiver provides a ready-made opportunity for providing group-work and tutorial reinforcement of the educational message.

By virtue of centralized production, broadcasting can afford to spend considerable sums on making programmes which will be received by so many that the cost per user is very low, even when the cost of the support material is allowed for. Using the best authorities and the best expositors, it can serve as an incomparably rapid means for the diffusion of the newest knowledge and ideas. The versatility of the two media is very high, as the experience of the British Open University (outlined on pages 60–62) indicates. The 'best teacher' argument, so frequently put forward at the school level, inadequately represents the true capacity of the broadcast media to extend and enrich educational experience.

The capacity of broadcasting to reach very large audiences applies to distance-teaching on many scales—local, regional and national—though it is most marked where the potential audience is largest, provided, of course, that the same programmes can satisfy the whole audience. In multilingual societies where transmission in several languages is essential, either additional air time is needed or multi-voice simultaneous transmissions, potentially available at present only from satellite distribution systems.

Recent developments in recording technology have removed or lessened a number of the disabilities of off-air transmission, though at some additional cost. Local recording avoids the necessity of using a programme when transmitted, and makes it available to more students for single or repeated use. If the expense of blank tape, of storage facilities, of technical maintenance and of the administrative implications of an audio-visual library can be met—and such expenses are considerable—broadcasting can become a source of semi-permanent new material instead of a momentary experience. In this way the problems of insufficient and unsuitable air time can be side-stepped. No system has yet taken the logical further step of organized automatic night-time recording, but this is due to economic rather than technical considerations; also to continuing scepticism about the achieved, as distinct from the potential, benefits of educational broadcasting.

The audio disc and audio cassette are now coming within the financial reach of many systems and are widely used as an ancillary means of disseminating material to be used over a period of time; but for the primary dissemination to large audiences, broadcasting remains, and is likely to remain for many years, the cheapest available method of making and distributing audio and audio-visual material; for developing countries it is virtually the only method.

If it is accepted that there is a strong pedagogic case for using broadcasting in a particular Open Learning project, then the next step is to consider how these services may be obtained on terms that will ensure that broadcasting fulfils the role the project wishes it to play. This is a much more complex and sometimes intractable problem, and attempts to resolve it vary greatly from country to country, both in outline and detail, since it involves the establishment and maintenance of satisfactory relationships between two national systems—education and broadcasting—which are sovereign, powerful and already well-established in forms which themselves will shape the pattern of the new relationship.

It is therefore of first importance that the situation of the country concerned be studied realistically and in depth at a very early stage.

Broadcasting pre-dates educational broadcasting, though the intention to use broadcasting services to serve educational ends has normally been one of the stated reasons for establishing a service. It pre-dates by a great many years the concept, central to this study, of the necessity, so far as distance-learning systems are concerned, to integrate broadcasting into a total teaching/learning system. (This concept is applicable to all levels of education; but so far it has been realized completely at school level only in a handful of recent and still tentative experiments—in Samoa, El Salvador and Ivory Coast among others—all of which have involved the restructuring of the entire educational system. The reference to school-level systems is important since in most cases the relationship between education and broadcasting was first worked out at school level, and success or failure in that context affects the confidence of the parties in applying it to the post-secondary level.)

Designers of Open Learning systems wishing to use broadcasting have, therefore, to regard the broadcasting system as a datum to which they must accommodate themselves, as they do to the other relevant social services, for instance the postal services.

Broadcasting systems are normally large, with heavy capital investment and big recurrent incomes, politically powerful and very close to the sources of power in government. Their constitution and structure is settled; their responsibilities, degree of independence, attentiveness to popular opinion, sense of identity and purpose are developed and strongly held.

The systems fall into three main types, each with its own characteristics, and distinctive attitudes towards education. First are the public-service systems which are usually national in scope, funded by grants-in-aid or licence income. These are run as government departments, usually by a Ministry of Information, or by an independent or semi-independent corporation. Such bodies normally have a major educational role of a generalized nature for which they are not answerable to the Ministry of Education. They also commonly provide instructional broadcasting services at school level according to the requirements of the educational authorities under agreements which vary from the provision of transmission facilities only up to the supply, on an agency basis with a high degree of executive discretion, of a full service of programmes, literature and evaluation, as well as participation in the initial and in-service training of classroom teachers in the use of broadcasting. These services are mostly transmitted nationally, but there may also be sub-national services, notably in countries with a federal political structure, or where major cultural and linguistic minorities exist.

Second, there is the commercial tradition in which the income and life-blood is drawn from advertising revenue. These systems are commonly required by the authorizing government agency to supply educational services as a condition of their franchise. This requirement produces a weaker commitment to education than in the public-service systems, and in countries where this situation prevails it is common to find educational systems run by educational institutions such as the education department of a member state in a federation, or by universities. These systems are in many cases smaller and have fewer resources than the national systems, though in some circumstances, for example in Canada, the position is reversed.

Third, there are the hybrid systems in which both the public service and the commercial principles obtain; sometimes, as in Italy, within one organization, sometimes in two parallel agencies as in the United Kingdom or Japan. Many other patterns exist.

The range of possible relationships between broadcasting and education is conditioned also by the nature of the educational systems themselves, and their attitude towards the use of broadcasting for educational purposes. The educational system may be highly centralized with a single obligatory curriculum and detailed syllabuses, prescribed textbooks and teaching procedures, and even a universal timetable. Or it may give a high degree of choice and discretion in the selection of examinations and textbooks, in teaching methods, internal organization and staff/student relationships. Or, in a federal situation (where responsibility for education is almost always incumbent on a state) several traditions may be found within the coverage area of the national broadcasting system. In very large countries, such as Nigeria, Australia, Canada and India, big problems of coverage have to be faced which may further involve the complications of different time zones, as in Canada. Since television is often not available to country-dwellers, the effectiveness of broadcasting may be restricted to the unfashionable medium of radio, unless and until the country invests in satellite transmissions and can also provide electricity in rural areas. In Australia, the Karmel Committee was faced with this situation; the non-existence of a nationwide television coverage was one practical factor which precluded the adoption of a British-type Open University solution.

In consequence, agreements in respect of educational broadcasting made between educational and broadcasting agencies differ widely. Frequently, one agreement applies to the school level and another to the post-school level. Agreements have also tended to change as the estimate of the value of broadcasting to education changes. At the present time, a prolonged debate is in process in the Scandinavian countries (in which the development of and the attainment in school broadcasting have been outstanding) as to whether the balance of direction and control should not be shifted from the broadcasting to the educational partner. Broadly speaking, the more educational opinion values educational broadcasting, the more it seeks control and a share in its operation. The British Open University partnership (described in detail on page 350) and the Japanese decision that the new university should have its own broadcasting system (page 242) are cases in point.

Returning now from this excursus to the questions which the proposer of an Open Learning system on a national scale might face, the situation might be as described below. It is assumed that there is general educational approval for the idea that an Open Learning system might help solve some post-secondary problems and that this idea has been sufficiently explored to point to the use of broadcasting. Broadcasting in the area may be controlled by a government department with only a secondary concern for education and possibly in an ambiguous and fluctuating relationship with the Ministry of Education; or it may be operated by a powerful corporation with a cherished independence of action. A choice would then have to be made between three possible courses:

1. To commission specific services: transmission, access to studios and technical facilities, with the use of technical and, sometimes, programme presentation and direction staff. In such a case, the educational agency provides the programmes and literature, undertakes publicity and is wholly responsible for the educational aspects. The broadcasting agency has a minimal involvement. The points likely to cause discussion are: the volume, timing and stability of the transmission hours; the broadcasting agency's concern for the technical quality of the material supplied for transmission, and its legal responsibilities as a publisher. Because of its non-involvement, the broadcasting agency may be less sympathetic than in the other relationships to the inevitable problems that arise at the start of any new venture, and to requests to use broadcasting as a promotional or student-recruiting agency.

At the school level, the Israeli Government laid down which daytime hours on the first television channel were to be made over to the educational broadcasting agency but has made no such decree at the post-school level. It is always easier to negotiate weekday daytime hours than evening and weekend hours; the latter may prove very difficult not only because of the claims of entertainment but also because of the need to accommodate the broadcasting agency's own educational programmes.

2. To enter into some form of partnership with the broadcasting agency, utilizing the programme-making expertise of the agency's staff, their organization and contacts and their access to programme material in their own libraries and all over the world. Many patterns of association fall under this head, and deserve detailed study by both parties before a decision is made. The negotiation should take place at the highest level since fundamental questions of principle and responsibility are involved for each organization. They will determine the number and quality of the staff required by each partner, and call for the working-out in great detail of operational, day-to-day routines between the professional staffs concerned.

In a partnership the public reputation of both bodies is involved, and both share in the credit or discredit of the new venture.

Since this kind of relationship seems likely to be one frequently selected we give it more attention in the next chapter.

3. To commission the broadcasting agency to provide the programme services and all that goes with them in accordance with some general brief agreed to from time to time. This alternative, which gives the greatest degree of discretion to the broadcasting agency, is commonly the result of an initiative on its part, arising from its general sense of responsibility towards education. Such a scheme is more frequently concerned to provide particular services thought desirable than to create an institution. A number of the courses may not be directed primarily at a recognizable qualification though the scheme may provide for the taking of an examination as an option. Examples of study areas include adult literacy, the study of the native language and its literature, courses for migrant workers, spoken foreign languages, etc. Some of these projects may serve a short-term requirement, though all may need the supporting organization which an Open Learning institution sets up on a permanent basis. As and when the idea of continuing education takes hold, it may well be found desirable to create some co-ordinating organization to bring order to a patchwork of unsystematic activities. Among the questions that will then arise is whether such an organization should be rooted in an existing institution, or whether a new one should be created.

Any proposal for partnership between an Open Learning system and a broadcasting organization involves an assessment of the latter's capacity as a partner in an educational venture, and this involves consideration of the broadcasting agency's internal organization for making educational programmes. Relevant questions on this matter would include the following:

1. Is the educational activity under the direction of an educationally qualified chief officer, and what position does he occupy in the management structure?
2. Does the organization use general production staff, or educationally qualified staff?
3. Are the payments to contributors to educational programmes at the same or a lower level than those paid to contributors to comparable general programmes?
4. Are decisions about the allocation of resources to educational programmes on a par or at a lower level than in respect of other programmes?
5. What criteria govern the allocation of air time between educational and other programmes?
6. To what extent and in what categories of programmes are programme decisions guided by representatives of outside educational interests?
7. What degree of detailed control over content and choice of contributors is accorded them?
8. Are the programme staff assigned to educational programme familiar with and sympathetic to the concept of research and evaluation outlined in Chapter Six?

Chapter 9

Making the courses

Open Learning systems depend upon the assembling or making (or both) of the materials which form the course itself. In the individualized learning contract systems operating in highly developed areas such as the State of New York, the design of an individual's programme of work is to a considerable extent a matter of selection and compilation from the wealth of educational materials and opportunities already on offer; though the Empire State College, for example, has made and keeps available a large number of 'Organized Programmes' which are complete multi-media study programmes in a wide range of subjects (see page 383 ff.).

Among the systems not dependent upon individual programmes of work, a broad distinction can be made between those which use material created by academic staff for their internal students and then made available with minimal alterations and additions to external students, and systems in which the material is planned from the start with the needs of external students as the prime concern.

The first category is exemplified in our studies by the Australian universities and post-secondary institutions offering external degrees (page 95) and by the Centres de Télé-enseignement Universitaire in France (page 141). The lectures given to the internal students are printed or broadcast almost as first delivered, and the same texts are studied. The additional material supplied is intended to compensate the external student for the lack of frequent personal contact with the staff.

Most of our studies fall into the second group, where the course material is specially designed for the home student, and must carry as much as possible of the information and experiences from which he is to learn. The various attempted solutions can be seen in the case studies themselves; here we wish to draw attention to some of their main characteristics, differences and implications.

The complexity of the task before the Open Learning planner can best be appreciated by studying the most complicated system—that of the Open University. The scale of this undertaking has made it possible to identify the component skills and functions required by the system, and to appoint separate specialists to apply or carry them out. This analysis has been carried further in the Open University than in any other system and the Open University consequently relies heavily upon interpersonal collaboration, a quality essential to successful Open Learning operations, but which, like creativity, is difficult to recognize, measure or predict.

The central thesis of the Open University teaching method is that 'the academic content of courses and the ways in which they will be taught must be thought of as a single operation by a single group of people', approaching 'their task as a democracy of equals, each with specialist knowledge and functions, but all concerned with every aspect of the course'. This group, named the Course Team, has total responsibility for realizing a course approved by the Senate and the University's Planning Board (page 338 ff.):

> Its task is to consider the needs of the student body that it envisages, to map out in detail the ground to be covered, and to decide how the various teaching methods at its disposal can best be used to attain its objectives. It has as its chairman a senior member of the academic staff nominated by the dean of the faculty concerned. Its members include those of his staff whose special province is involved, together with experts from outside the university if required. It also includes representatives of those departments of the university primarily concerned with learning strategies, teaching methods and media production, and the BBC radio and television producers who will be responsible for the broadcast components of the course. They are present not as narrow experts in a particular mode of educational communication, but as full course-team members, and are able to make their contribution to the team's thinking about course objectives and content, just as the academic staff may contribute to thinking about presentation. An editor in each team is responsible for the co-ordination of the work.

The course team adopts a systems approach with the learner as the key figure. That is to say, it specifies educational objectives; breaks down the students' task into successive stages; identifies the learning processes involved; considers the appropriateness of the teaching methods available at each stage; combines the methods to make an integrated whole; and provides for feedback, evaluation and assessment. Several points should be made at this juncture:

First, that the members of the course teams are drawn predominantly from permanent staff. The university staff have tenure, and the BBC staff, after a probationary period, have, as do all BBC staff, the right to apply for posts elsewhere in the corporation, whose total staff is nearly 25,000. Specialists are engaged on a shorter term to work on a particular course team for the duration of its existence, which may be two or three years, but there is always a considerable core who will have had the advantage of working together.

Second, that the broadcasting staff assigned usually have academic qualifications in the subject matter of the course as well as experience of educational broadcasting.

Third, that the role of the staff of the Institute of Educational Technology must be stressed. This was discussed earlier in Chapter 6. The relevant passage in the case-study report is on page 332.

Fourth, that the work entailed in making the courses was originally very much underestimated. On the most recent calculation of academic productivity, after making due allowance for research work not related to production (which is a contractual right of the academic staff), the number of units of a 32-unit credit course which can be made per man per year is 2.5 for arts courses, 2.3 for social sciences, 1.6 for educational studies and mathematics and 1.4 for science and technology. In other words, while an arts course requires the work of a team of six for just over two years, a science course calls for twice that number. And this figure relates only to the academic staff, not to the BBC staff, nor, of course, to the substantial administrative support.

Fifth, that because the component courses of the fully developed bachelor-degree programme are so many—there are to be sixty-five 36-week courses (or their equivalent) in 1976—the university is now in one sense a great factory of educational material, with an operational need for clearly defined targets, a strict adherence to schedules and a disciplined co-ordination of all its activities.

The methods of production of UMA/SUN are influenced by its objectives, its administrative structure, the delivery systems to be used and by the national traditions of broadcasting. In sharp contrast with the single elaborated course structure of the Open University, the objectives of UMA/SUN are pluralist and diffused. Certainly the new university has to stand comparison with the other universities of the region of Mid-America, but its statement of objectives, as formulated in 1971, expresses a concern for 'drop-in' and 'drop-out' students and envisages them qualifying for a variety of certificates, for associate degrees as well as the traditional bachelor degree.

Consumer demand is to be a continuing factor in determining what the university offers; the first two course subjects (psychology and accounting) were selected on the results of a market-research-type inquiry. When the target for 1980 (fifty-five courses) is reached, the courses will represent an agglomeration, not the components of a single intellectual scheme.

There is to be no single delivery system, each state being legally responsible within its own borders, and a variety of teaching media will be employed, including television (in broadcast or recorded form), audio-tapes, course books, newspaper articles; but no correspondence-course teaching, which is the core of the Open University's system.

Patterns of production are similarly varied, including both courses designed, made and listed by the university, and existing courses acquired and used with much or little adaptation. The most expensive courses will have a heavy television ingredient and take a minimum of twelve months to prepare.

The production teams are to be assembled *ad hoc*. A specimen team for the introductory accounting course is led by an executive producer drawn from commercial television and two professors as resident consultants. The team includes an instructional designer, a professional writer, a research associate and media production specialists. A clear influence is the successful team-work of the Children's Television Workshop that produced *Sesame Street* and *The Electric Company*.

The system of the UNRWA/Unesco Institute of Education, which offers a carefully planned combination of direct and indirect training varied according to the educational task, is described in the Lebanon case study in Part Three. There are perhaps four aspects which are of particular interest in this pioneering and highly successful service:

First, the great care taken by the central international staff of the institute in preparing written documents of guidance, both for the students (mainly the Guided Assignments which form a key component of their programmes of work) and for the field tutors, all nationals of the host country (principally in the guide 'The Conduct of Seminars', a comprehensive manual of principle and practice).

Second, despite the fact that national radio and television services are not available to the institute, there is a considerable audio-visual element in the courses, obtained by closed-circuit television and other audio-visual teaching media.

Third, great attention has been given to securing a good mixture of theory and practice in what is required of the students, who for the most part are practising class teachers.

Fourth, the way in which delays of several months in returning students' work on the Guided Assignments were overcome.

We noted earlier the care taken to explore fully the situation of every new country to which it was proposed to extend the system.

The Newfoundland system also depends heavily upon televised instruction, distributed by cassette and used in local centres where the students see the programme with a local tutor. The course material consists of a manual outlining the course structure and giving a synopsis of each video-tape and its main teaching points, and selected readings and diagrams related to the visuals on the tape. These are supported by other printed materials, either existing or specially made. The programmes are largely illustrated lectures. The course is created by collaboration between an academic selected from the appropriate faculty of the university under contract, and a producer/director from the university's educational television unit, with other specialists as needed. There is no organized pre-testing of the programme, but a fairly constant flow of feedback from the local tutors who, being themselves qualified in the subject matter, are professionally capable of amplifying the written and recorded course material.

The Polish Television Agricultural High School proceeds informally. The general framework of the courses and the examinations are settled by consultants engaged by the Department of Education in the Ministry of Agriculture. The course materials comprise television programmes, student guide-workbooks, the standard textbook used in the normal high schools, and articles in the weekly journal of the Union of Socialist Village Youth.

The television and print material are produced by the Agricultural Department of Polish Television, which engages its own consultants in collaboration with the relevant government departments.

The three responsible agencies—the Education Departments of the Ministry of Agriculture and of Polish Television, and the Union of Socialist Village Youth—by a series of consultative conferences, and by using the comments of students channelled through the consultative sessions in high schools, provide feedback about the televised and printed material, including the standard textbooks. An important feature of the system is the harmonious and easy relationship between the various departments of the government and of Polish Television, which has been built up by previous successful collaborations in the past.

Some general problems are emerging in systems committed to the preparation of new course materials. The first is the question of cost. In conventional teaching systems the academic staff are engaged in curriculum design and teaching; during the initial stages of new courses there is an investment in course design, but the faculty will normally rely upon material—textbooks, general literature and audio-visual materials—already available in the market. The faculty's main continuing effort is in face-to-face teaching. In Open Learning systems using substantial amounts of new and specially designed materials for teaching and learning, the greater part of the faculty effort is devoted to the writing and designing of those materials. To this cost must be added a much higher cost of production, through printing, broadcasting and other media. This means that there must be a substantial enrolment of students for such courses if the unit-cost per student is to be reasonable and lower than in conventional institutions. The only circumstances in which unusual costs will be justified is where, on such policy grounds as national need or lack of viable alternative provision, an Open Learning system is introduced in full awareness of the special financial burden involved.

The expected level of student enrolment is thus an important constraint on the investment of time and effort in designing, producing and disseminating course materials. Careful investigation may show that economies can be achieved, where the enrolment is lower, by the selection and use of pre-existing materials (textbooks, films, television and radio programmes) and their planned incorporation in the learning system. Moreover, some of the systems studied, including even the large-scale Open University, use elements of face-to-face teaching (tutorials, discussion groups, residential schools and study centres) which supplement the distance-teaching system, and, where they are feasible, these may be cheaper.

Variations of this kind may be needed for other than cost reasons. Certain elements in the learning system may require the students to interact with each other or to use special facilities, such as laboratories. Variation may also be needed to provide greater flexibility, both in dealing with the learning problems of individual students and in making adjustments to the system as it develops. One of the main disadvantages of a sophisticated and expensive pattern of course development, involving the production of new materials, is that the initial cost is so high that there is a strong temptation to amortize it, not merely by a large enrolment in any one year, but by re-using the materials over a period of years. While the Open University recognized the need to improve courses and to prevent their ossification by revising them regularly (say, after three or four years), the effort and expense involved can be very great—with rising price-levels, a major revision could begin to approach the initial investment. If an Open Learning system is to remain adaptive and responsive to the learning behaviour and experience of its students, in budgeting for its course design and materials development care must be taken that the initial commitment is not too large relative to expected resources. Otherwise, what begins as an innovation may prove to be a costly barrier to further growth and improvement.

A further problem, which we discuss elsewhere, arises when the provision of learning materials involves an integral relationship between print and broadcasting. The need to invest in television and radio programmes, on which some of the systems we studied depend, not only adds considerably to the costs of the operation and to the expense of revision; it adds an additional element of inflexibility. Broadcasting schedules have to be planned some way ahead, and programmes have to be prepared long in advance of transmission. While print and correspondence materials can be fairly quickly and easily revised, the same is not true of a sequence of broadcasts. Serious thought must therefore be given to the degree to which one set of materials is integrated with those in a different medium.

An important field for further research, on which only a beginning has so far been made, is the relative effectiveness (and relative ease and cost) of providing students with course materials in different media. Experience has already shown that the quality of design and presentation substantially affects student performance, but far too little is currently known about the impact of learning materials presented, for instance, in print as compared with television and radio. Nor is much known about, or much attention given to, the non-measurable, non-intellectual effect of such materials.

It is important that all Open Learning systems should study and report their experience in these respects for their mutual advantage.

Chapter 10
The use and transfer of experience

All development needs to take advantage of existing experience to avoid the repetition of mistakes. In the relatively uncharted sector of development in education and educational communications to which Open Learning belongs, it is especially important to feed into new schemes the experience of those already established. This applies as much to developed countries, offering a non-standard alternative to an existing system, as to developing countries which seek to provide a non-standard extension to a system which may itself be undergoing radical reform.

At first sight it might seem that information about Open Learning must be easy to come by, that from the flood of literature, the plethora of conferences, seminars and gatherings, good advice and real help should not be difficult to secure; but this is in fact not the case. Though the printed matter is voluminous, there is little signposting of the most important documents. The material goes out of date rapidly, much of it is discursive and unpointed, or marred by a flavour of public relations. So, too, the conferences, though necessary for a continuing collective exchange of ideas, consume an amount of time out of all proportion to the benefit obtained. The jaundiced comment that their greatest value consists in what happens between the sessions is often not far from the truth.

To secure and receive advice, to transfer 'know-how' and skills, is not a simple process nor one which is quickly concluded. The best sources of advice, the points upon which advice can most profitably be sought, the machinery for obtaining it, the means by which skills can be transferred and the preparation of those who are to acquire them—all need more care and attention than they sometimes receive, particularly when national, cultural and linguistic barriers have to be crossed. No transnational contacts are without some political or politico-cultural overtones, and much advice is coloured, openly or covertly, by commercial motives, or by the zeal to promote some educational or communications doctrine. Awareness of these factors can induce reservations in the minds of the recipients, who then impose restrictions making it difficult for the advisers to be as useful as they might be. In an attempt to cut costs, the periods of contact may be so reduced that the experience cannot be transferred. Some countries, trying to avoid over-influence by one source, will seek advice from several, so running the risk of confusion between different but possibly equally satisfactory traditions.

The whole process can be a delicate one. The agencies through which advice, experience and financial assistance can be obtained are legion, and the range of help on offer, both general and specialized, is very wide. Choice between agencies is of key importance, together, of course, with that of financial aid. For aid, whether charitable, political or international, always involves conditions. Among the sources, there is the group of organizations stemming from the United Nations, co-ordinated by the Resident Representative of the United Nations Development Programme in each recipient country. Of the specialized agencies connected with UNDP, it is mainly Unesco and Unicef which cover the ground of Open Learning. The International Bureau of Education (Geneva) is a major source of information.

Then there are the international specialist organizations connected with broadcasting, such as the International Telecommunications Union (Geneva) and the regional associations of the broadcasting agencies in the various continents.

The Commonwealth Education Secretariat (London) is another important source. The two ex-colonial powers, France and the United Kingdom, maintain, in AUDECAM and the British Council, agencies offering advice and training facilities, in the case of France to the French-speaking countries of Africa and to Madagascar; in the case of the British Council to the ex-imperial countries, but also to developed countries.

Advice and aid can also be sought from many developed countries, which offer them as part of their international and bilateral aid programmes, and channel them in some instances through agencies specializing in educational assistance.

Assistance from the charitable foundations has also been of great significance to educational innovation generally, and particularly to Open Learning.

Consultancy on a commercial contract basis is available from a wide range of agencies. The first educational institution to offer consultancy services specifically connected with Open Learning is the British Open University; its first contract was made recently, with the Free University of Iran.

As there are so many agencies in each of these categories, we thought it better not to detail what they offer; instead, a list of a few useful directories is given after the general bibliography at the end of this volume (page 498).

The usefulness of external experience is not confined to the first stages: the preparation of the plan and its initial operation. It may be vitally necessary to the initial and subsequent training of the staff, until they themselves become a cadre of fully competent people able to operate the system, refine and improve it, and train new intake.

Personnel development must be regarded as a concomitant of general development. New schemes often fail to provide adequately for the various aspects of training—scholarships, working attachments, formal courses—which must be extended over several years.

It was suggested above that the Institute of Educational Technology has an important role in improving the British Open University practice. This function is closely allied to that of training, as both contribute to the same objective, that of making the whole system better.

It may be worth mentioning some points to which special attention might be paid, and some common pitfalls:

In a totally new scheme, it is of cardinal importance that the chief executive, and the key group around him, inform themselves in a general way about the possibilities of Open Learning as well as, in depth, about those systems most akin to their particular scheme. This demands a good deal of arduous personal preparation for the round of visits to selected institutions that is likely to follow. Much more will be got from these visits by those who have prepared themselves adequately and know what they are looking for. As an example of a rounded, though costly scheme, the programme of familiarization given to the first staff of the Israeli Everyman's University (described on page 219) may be of interest.

If the scheme depends on the use of a new technology, it is essential that nationals of the country should be sufficiently trained in its essentials to participate fully in plan-making. This point is emphasized in the essay on using satellites for education (page 484). Over the past thirty years, when radio and television were new technologies, many of the failures or part-successes of brave schemes can be partially attributed to the imposition of systems that came from outside and were never fully assimilated and therefore collapsed when external help was withdrawn.

External experience can be particularly useful at a number of stages of planning (see Chapter 4, especially page 33), in particular: (a) in identifying the problems to be solved, leading directly to the brief; (b) in ensuring that the main operational plan is truly comprehensive; (c) in the design of evaluation systems; (d) in the conduct of assessments, particularly if the occasion is also used as a training opportunity for the staff who will later be responsible for this work; an example is the series of assessments carried out by an external foundation in the case of Kenya (page 259).

As to pitfalls, there are, of course, many and much depends upon the choice of advisers, their experience and personality. But some frequently occurring points might be made:

Faced with a strange language and a strange culture a foreign consultant may find it difficult to give advice which will be at once professional and acceptable. To understand the country and its traditions he may need longer than his contract allows and in consequence, he may give advice that is either too narrowly restricted to his particular skill and takes insufficient account of national circumstances, or which is too tentative and guarded to be worth while.

A large number of short-term consultants from a variety of cultural traditions—a feature of some international teams—may produce confusion.

The provision of national counterparts, an excellent policy in itself, can be rendered ineffective if the counterpart is not relieved of enough of his normal work while the consultant is in the country.

Foreign consultants must be very clear as to their role and should not be asked or agree to go outside it, unless the matter has been very carefully considered by both parties.

Transfer of experience can take the form of transferring the product itself—the syllabus, the course material (printed, audio and audio-visual)—either in its original form or modified to some extent to make it more suitable to the second customer. Since the start of radio and television, this possibility has been frequently studied and experimented with, for it seems hard to accept prima facie that all the work and skill which goes into the preparation and production of broadcast material should not have a second exposure; and this would be one way in which the greater resources and skill of the big organizations in developed countries could be used to the benefit of others less well-placed.

Yet, over the years, this well-meaning idea has not had much success at any level of education. To be effective, educational communications have to be tailored closely to the needs of the student and his situation, to his cultural and linguistic background, to the style of the education of his country. The approximations inevitable in the use of foreign material make its use difficult, even if the reluctance to use other people's material does not prove a barrier. Even when the same basic language is used, as it is throughout the English-speaking countries, there may be local differences of pronunciation which make radio and television programmes much less acceptable than in the country of origin. Again, students of history, literature and the social sciences are more at ease if instances and illustrations are drawn from their own national heritage and background. These difficulties are least troublesome in relation to the sciences and to mathematics where the task of translation is straightforward, and the subject matter independent of national culture, but even in arts subjects the barriers have sometimes been surmounted.

One of the early acts of the planners of the UMA/SUN project was to examine all the existing English-language material available and catalogue it for possible use; and one of the intentions of the university is to use this material with a greater or lesser degree of adaptation (pages 448, 464). Three American universities—Maryland, Houston and the State University of New Jersey (Rutgers) have used on an experimental basis three of the Foundation courses of the Open University. At Houston, the humanities and science courses were offered to full-time 'traditional' students on campus. At the other two, the courses were offered to part-time students, local study-centres being set up for the purpose, manned by part-time tutors recruited from the existing full-time staff.

In the fifties and sixties, attempts were made by the education divisions of broadcasting organizations, notably by the members of the European Broadcasting Union, to organize co-operation and programme exchanges on a multilateral or bilateral basis, but in general these schemes were not particularly successful except where the participants had very strong cultural links, as in the Scandinavian countries, and they have declined in recent years.

Chapter 11

Effectiveness and costs—the framework

The two questions most frequently asked about Open Learning are:
How effective is it in a pedagogic sense?
Does it cost less than conventional forms of education?
The case-study reports show how hard it is to give confident and precise answers to either question. Yet these questions have to be asked, for whether or not the answers given are reliable, decisions of great weight in policy and administrative consequence have to be taken and these two questions inevitably enter into the decisions. This chapter discusses the issues involved.

Pedagogic effectiveness

Pedagogic effectiveness interpreted in its narrowest sense can be held to be represented by the ratio between the number enrolling for a course leading to a qualification within a planned period of time and the number who follow the course and receive the qualification. This is an arithmetically measurable yardstick, easily quoted. But this ratio, regarded as a major factor in evaluating an institution or in the decision to create another on similar lines, is inadequate for a large number of reasons, particularly when a comparison is made with conventional, full-time institutions leading to the same qualification level. For example, part-time study to bachelor-degree level is normally expected to take at least a quarter longer than full-time study, and over the five or six years involved, the student is exposed to domestic and employment pressures that are totally unrelated to the pedagogic quality of the course. This yardstick also rates as failures those who get some way in the course and gain some credits (if the course is organized as a series of credit-gaining units). It ignores the intermittent student. It ignores also the important minority of students who pursue the course to its end but choose, for one reason or another, not to submit themselves to the examination. Again, there are those who fail by inability to fulfil some compulsory residential component, such as attendance at a summer school (as specified for all Foundation-course students at the Open University) or as residential students for some part of the course (as in some university-level courses in Japan and in the Television Agricultural High School in Poland). For a complete evaluation the ratio is not a fair or efficient basis; nevertheless it remains an important one, as a pointer to a matter of concern.

In Chapter 2 figures were quoted showing that up to 40 per cent of educational expenditure in some countries went on providing primary education to children who dropped out before the education could have any substantial or lasting effect. Though in the field of Open Learning at post-secondary level there are as yet no established norms for this ratio, some must eventually be looked for.

In reaching a decision whether or not to establish an Open Learning system other factors have to be considered: for example, the effect of such an institution upon the national educational system as a whole. A successful innovatory institution may exercise a major influence upon the attitudes and practice of the teaching profession and demonstrate and disseminate new ideas in curricula, syllabuses and methods. This is particularly true of systems using broadcasting. Such systems can also influence the general public. These long-term effects are neither predictable nor measurable but may, as mentioned in the Iran report, be a major motive for establishing the new university. These uncovenanted benefits are the 'bloom on the grape'.

Returning to arithmetical ratios, there are several others which can be usefully measured if the system is set up to produce the data. There is the ratio between applicants and admitted students, which over the years may establish a trend of demand, though the trend may say more about the development of society as a whole than about the acceptability of the institution. There are ratios between the enrolled students and those who gave up after one, two or more months. It is a universal experience that drop-out is heavier at the start than later. Then there are the ratios between the initially or firmly enrolled (if the system recognizes these two stages) and those who complete the course, those who present themselves for the examination, those who pass it, and those who enrol for the next stage; and the interrelationship of these several ratios.

Figures for all these can be taken out for each stage of each course; the total picture gives a much more realistic indication in arithmetical terms of the institution's characteristics and its points of strength and weakness.

A major factor influencing all such figures relates to the composition of the student body. The institution will be set up to provide for a need which will have been as closely delineated as possible when the proposal was put forward. It is likely that some groups with high motivation will form a considerable proportion of the intake in the first years. In the case of the British Open University, though entry was open to all, a large proportion of the early students were teachers with pedagogic qualifications, but not degrees; they had therefore a high motivation, since the gaining of a degree would raise their salaries. They were also accustomed to academic work and private study. As students, they were 'good bets'. As this backlog of entrants is worked off, the composition of the student body will change and the later groups may not possess the same high motivation. The experience of the NHK Gakuen Senior High School over twenty years shows that the extension of the full-time system of high school education influenced the volume and quality of the school's intake. In so far as Open Learning systems are ancillary to a changing full-time system of post-secondary education they are not likely to achieve the steady state that will allow factors of pedagogic effectiveness to be completely disentangled from developmental factors.

Consequently, figures produced in this area need to be handled with caution and interpreted by those with intimate knowledge of the institution concerned.

Their suitability for making comparisons with conventional institutions or institutions abroad is very limited.

No doubt this was one reason why the figures kept by some of the institutions studied were surprisingly fragmentary. We wish to suggest that, subject to available resources, figures as full as possible should be collected and analysed, particularly in large-scale distance systems, for they can be used very constructively to indicate points at which the design and operation of the systems could be improved. Some instances follow:

At entry, particularly where no qualifications are required, some students are bound to find themselves unable to cope with what is expected of them. Analysis of these cases may reveal the inadequacy of publicity or counselling arrangements, or the need to establish better systems for preparatory courses or supervised study.

Quality of the course material. The key importance of this element has been frequently stressed. Analysis of drop-outs may indicate points of weakness.

Radio and television. It is commonly said that the quality of good programmes helps students to stay the course; also that their regular use paces the student, and encourages regular habits of study. The high cost of television, the shortage of air time and further development of recording technology could mean in some instances that this second function will lessen (see pages 60, 63).

The study of 'drop-out' figures may indicate the points at which personal contact is most needed by the students and what form it should take (see page 41).

Similarly, such study may suggest students' satisfaction or discontent with the way they are handled by tutors and administrators.

Cost and cost-effectiveness

The case studies contain a certain amount of information as to the cost of specific learning systems, but they do not, taken as a whole, provide the basis for any fundamental comparative study. The only reasonably full analytic account is that relating to the British Open University. The reason for this state of affairs and the considerations which should be borne in mind in assessing the costs and cost-effectiveness of any proposed operation are discussed below.

Some systems preclude separate costing. Institutions like the Chicago Junior College and the distance-teaching centres of the universities of Eastern France aim primarily at the extension to an extramural audience in a largely unmodified form of courses already prepared for their internal students. In such instances it is not customary, and would be largely arbitrary, to apportion part of the cost of course development and maintenance to the external operation.

Institutions like the Australian universities, which exist primarily to serve their internal students but which offer external degrees and devote some of the energies of their staffs to the preparation of correspondence courses, also find it impracticable to arrive at a realistic division of costs between the two overlapping activities.

Again, if there is a partnership with a broadcasting organization for either the production or the transmission of educational programmes, it is unusual for that organization to separate off the relevant costs; and still more unusual for it to take any share of capital expenditure into the reckoning. That this was done in the case of the Open University was due to the insistence of the BBC that no part of the cost of its contribution to the university should fall upon its licence revenue.

Even in dealing with a wholly or largely self-contained operation there are problems in arriving at reliable and meaningful statements of cost; particularly those dealing with such figures as cost per enrolled student and cost per qualification gained, or those making comparisons with conventional institutions and institutions in other countries. These problems derive to a large extent from the nature of Open Learning institutions and the way their costs arise.

In such an institution the relationship between 'fixed overhead costs' and the direct student costs, that vary in exact proportion to the number of students, is different from that in conventional institutions. In the Open Learning institution the principal headings in the first category are academic staff salaries (which account for most of the cost of course development), charges for the production and transmission of radio and television broadcasts, and the cost of development and initial production of printed material. In the Open University these may be as high as £250,000 for a single one-year course (i.e. one-sixth of a bachelor-degree course). All courses intended to have a life of at least four years, but particularly those in science, need regular updating and a periodical radical remaking. The period of years for which a course is valid varies with the subject, and the pace of change in the body of knowledge which it represents.

These fixed costs also include charges, such as expenditure on administration, on computerized records, and on local premises, that rise with increases in student numbers, though not in direct proportion. The principal items of 'direct student costs' are the salaries of any full-time or part-time tutors and counsellors, the additional cost of printed material for each additional student, science kits and the cost of residential courses or summer schools.

The consequence of this pattern of expenditure, which reverses the pattern of conventional universities, is that the marginal cost of each additional student is much less than the existing average costs, and that cost-effectiveness can be considerably increased by raising the number of students. The long-term cost-effectiveness of a venture therefore depends upon the size which is practicable (in terms of the number of potential students, the resources available, and other factors) and which it is allowed to reach. The total social cost of the operation will include not only the costs borne by the providing organization but also the costs borne by the individual student in fees, if they are charged, in the purchase of broadcast-receiving apparatus and books, in travel to centres for face-to-face instruction, and in residential expenditure where this is required. Any or all of such costs may or may not be reimbursed, either by the providing authority or (as in the instance of the Open University) by local education authorities. Furthermore, there are necessary provisions made by the educational system (e.g. of buildings for tutorial and laboratory work, etc.), which may or may not be costed in.

Given an assessment of total expenditure for a given number of students there still remains the problem of determining what end-product shall be set against it. In relation to the enrolled student body three possible criteria may be used. The total cost may be set against the gross number of students on the roll. It may be set against the number of 'credits' gained in a modular system; or these may be ignored as having no intrinsic value, and the cost analysis may be based only on the number of degrees or other final qualifications attained.

Whichever of these criteria is adopted, the average time taken by a student to obtain a credit, or a degree, will be a factor of importance, because in those instances in which the costs of the institutions are regulated by setting a ceiling to the student population, the intake capacity will be regulated by the number of exits.

The cost-evaluation of individual courses provides further complications. The first courses launched by a system which intends to provide more advanced courses as part of its curriculum will in the nature of things have more students than will these later courses. Their cost per student will be comparatively low, while the cost of advanced courses after 'drop-out' has taken its toll, will be high, especially if a wide latitude of choice is allowed. It may be argued that it is reasonable to consider the average cost of courses, treating the more expensive courses as a necessary part of the provision which is set off by the less expensive. This in turn raises the question of how much choice of advanced courses it is possible to offer.

All these considerations must be weighed; and for all of these reasons it is hazardous to compare the cost of Open Learning systems with those of conventional institutions. For example, a study of the Open University made in 1973 by a research group based on the London School of Economics (taking two years as an Open University student to be broadly equivalent to one year as a student in a campus university in terms of hours spent on study and of progress towards graduation) concluded that the cost per full-term equivalent student was very substantially less at the Open University than elsewhere. However, since this study was based on the early courses presented in 1971 and 1972, it is subject to all the reservations expressed above.

Summary

In sum, it is not possible to answer either of the two questions posed at the start of this chapter without many reservations. Some of the reasons for this will diminish as the experience of Open Learning systems accumulates, but many will not. It will be wiser to base the decision to launch an Open Learning system on the conviction that it will achieve nationally important purposes that would not otherwise be achieved, and that it will do so at a cost that the country can afford, rather than on any fallacious monetary calculation. It should always be borne in mind that the students involved are normally in full employment throughout, contributing to the gross national product, and are not withdrawn like conventional students from the effective labour force.

Chapter 12
Questions for planners

Not infrequently the first move in the direction of a new institution may come from a political quarter, perhaps in some colloquial form like the following: 'This Open University seems to be getting a reputation. Oughtn't we to consider it for ourselves? Please let me have your view on a couple of pages by Monday, as I expect to have a chance of talking to. . . .'

As will be seen the request relates to the solution not to the problem. This familiar reversal has been the starting-point of many disappointments. For a solution successful in one set of circumstances can be a formula for failure in another. The person—official or minister—to whom such a request is made has somehow to invert the sequence, to identify and analyse the problem first, and then to estimate whether the solution suggested, or something quite different, will meet it. Chapter 4 was concerned with this.

But such a request once made has to be answered. Because of its frequency we thought that it might be helpful to gather together, from the case studies and our own experience, a checklist of items which cover the main points and which can be used as a framework for designing a full study. We have been helped by two authors in particular, Professor Charles A. Wedemeyer who undertook the study of UMA/SUN and John R. Beardsley, who has written about the Free University of Iran. It has been assumed that the request concerns the possibility of an 'Open University'; but the points might be relevant to other requests also.

Long-range purposes

What kind of university is aimed at? A university pursuing scholarship as well as the education of the young; a teaching/learning and an examining university; an examining-only university; a consortium of existing universities providing co-operatively fresh teaching/learning facilities; an institution to be called a university but in fact providing other than university-level studies?

Justification of the proposal

What national and economic needs will it serve? To what subject areas, to what qualifications is priority attached—in importance and time-sequence? Who are the target students—number, age, sex, occupations, location, prior educational level, capacity—for the type of study proposed? Has their prior experience prepared them for the Open Learning modes of study?

Nature of the institution/system proposed

In what particulars does the proposed institution differ from existing institutions, and why? Do the proposed differences have a permanent validity?

If the request assumes that the institution is to resemble the British Open University, or say, the University Without Walls, is the nature of each fully understood (e.g. the British example, which is a correspondence-based system using, in closely integrated form, a combination of 'direct', e.g. face-to-face, teaching, and 'indirect', e.g. radio and television, media, and awarding its own degrees of a standard acceptable to conventional British universities)?

What alternative systems exist within the country or could be created to fulfil the accepted aims?

Awards

How will awards (credits, degrees/certificates) be awarded, and how validated? Will the institution's awards be accepted by other academic institutions and by employers? Will the new institution accept the awards of other institutions? By what steps is it proposed to reach reciprocal arrangements? What assurances can be given to student applicants in the first years about the practical value of the qualification in the eyes of employers?

Resources involved

Academic and pedagogic

What resources are needed to establish the curriculum, syllabuses and sequence of development? Are appropriately qualified persons obtainable within the country? If an 'Open University' (as described) is aimed at, are its requirements—the basic organization, installations and operational experience of each component of the system—already in existence or do they have to be created, enlarged or secured by negotiation? Similarly, do the means for dissemination exist, or have they to be created, enlarged, or access to them secured? If the system involves local centres, what is their precise role in the proposed system, and what relationship will they have to existing local publicly provided facilities?

Evaluation

How will arrangements for evaluating the degree of success or failure of the institutions be established, particularly so that comparisons can be made with comparable existing institutions?

Assistance

At what points, if any, is external advice or assistance expected to be necessary? Is this assistance political or fiscal? Can the difficulties of securing it be foreseen?

Training

Staffs of the institution: What initial/remedial/conversion training will be required to make staff capable of working in the institution? *Students:* What preparatory training/experience/orientation will be required to ensure success in the course?

Prevalent attitudes to the proposal

What are the attitudes of relevant groups, and what steps will be needed to assist the proposal: (a) in governmental circles; (b) among professional educators; (c) among professional communicators; (d) among the target students; (e) among the general public?

Management and control

What structure of control and direction will be appropriate? Where will policy decisions be taken, both long- and short-term, as to: (a) objectives; (b) student admissions; (c) tuition and other fees; (d) curriculum and course content; (e) development; (f) dissemination; (g) evaluation of course material; (h) evaluation of student performance; (j) aids to students?

If the institution has a commitment in principle to such elements of 'openness' as the participation by students in collective and individual programme design, how will this participation be achieved at the formative stage?

Scale and development

What size (number of students—total and per course) is intended: (a) initially; (b) after five years; (c) eventually? (The total and per head costing forecasts require these estimates.)

What development strategies are advised, e.g. step-by-step or major initial commitment?

Cost and return on investment

What initial and recurrent costs are seen to be involved in: (a) new expenditure by the institutions; (b) additional costs to other institutions involved; (c) estimated unit costs—per enrolled student, per qualification gained?

From what source(s) are these costs to be met? What level of public funding is required, and over what period?

Success of the institution

At what stages of its existence will results emerge that can influence opinions of the value of the institution on the part of: (a) the sponsors; (b) the critics; (c) the general public?

Chapter 13

Open Learning—new experiences and new skills

We have seen the variety in design, scale and complexity of Open Learning systems. How far are the experiences of students in them different from what they would be in conventional systems? What would be the difference between one Open Learning system and another? Further, what different pedagogic skills, if any, are called for from those in direct contact with the students?

As to the first question, concerning the experience of the student, the answer depends to some extent upon the purposes of the system. Of those we have studied, most have vocational aims or provide alternative ways of gaining established qualifications—a degree or some professionally recognized award. The content of such courses cannot depart greatly from the normal; the differences in experience therefore arise more from the presentation of the course material, or from the situation of the student, e.g. his isolation and the steps taken to reduce it. In effect, they arise more from the system than from its purposes, and the action needed relates more to the third question, concerning the different pedagogic skills called for, to which we return later in this chapter.

But some Open Learning systems have distinctly and explicitly different objectives. Examples are the three learning-contract institutions.[1] We must briefly recall their common features.

The basic belief underlying them is that the true end of education is to create the 'lifelong, self-directing learner committed to excellence in his learning', to quote the Minnesota phrase. The holder of a degree is expected by this college to be a whole person (not merely a knowledgeable person), capable of further learning and displaying social awareness, civic, recreational and vocational competence, to be active in his society, and alive and responsive to the changes taking place around him.

These beliefs lead to others, concerned with the responsibility of the student towards his own education, with the range of material that can properly form the content of a course leading to an externally recognized qualification, and with the ways in which attainment of the components of a programme of work should be tested. They also influence the nature of the professional services which the students need.

1. Empire State College, New York (page 369), Minnesota Metropolitan State College (page 399), Vermont Community College (page 423).

The conviction is that all students should have responsibility for, and authority over, their own education individually. They should be responsible for developing their own programmes of work, setting out the components of the plan, and proposing how and by whom their achievements should be assessed. In doing this, they are assisted by the staff of the institution. The latter help students to assess themselves, their previous educational experiences and present attainments. The staff also advise students as to the facilities upon which they can draw to make their plans, and on the adequacy of the assessment procedures they propose. When the plan has been agreed between the parties and the work has taken place, the institution awards the qualification.

These institutions encourage the inclusion, whether in courses or as attainments justifying exemptions from a work programme, of a wide range of items not usually recognized for academic courses. The list at Empire State College includes: works published, pictures painted, patents obtained, machines designed, scientific exhibits; languages spoken, musical instruments played; internships (working attachments) in government and social agencies, work and study with theatre and dance-groups, museums, television and radio organizations, libraries, laboratories and centres; co-operative membership of groups undertaking urban, ecological and cultural studies of problems of a particular area in their own or other countries. The problem of assessing experiences of this kind against traditional academic attainment raises difficult questions of testing and of basic and relative evaluation. The institutions are well aware that the problem has not been solved to general satisfaction, and it is to this point that academic quarters direct most of their criticisms of Open Learning. If, in the democratization of post-secondary education, we are to arrive at an agreed new concept of what possession of a 'degree' should mean, then a great deal of discussion has yet to take place. It is of interest that one of the planned Open Universities states aims that are not too far away from that of the Learning Contract institutions. The aim of the Japanese Broadcasting University is to cultivate in students a 'capacity for understanding problems, the intelligence to solve them and a creative policy to plan for the future in a changing world' (page 242).

A further consequence of this approach is the greatly enhanced importance attached to the process of self-diagnosis and evaluation that precedes the formulation by the student of his particular plan. In many instances, this is considered to be the most educative part of the course, and it is to this activity that the institutions apply their best and most experienced talent. As a corollary, some institutions use teachers who are not basically teachers, but people who have regular jobs in the community practising the skill they teach, and who are brought in on a part-time basis to help students acquire that skill. In the Community College of Vermont these helpers are paid nominal sums and they look to professional 'teacher-supporters' to assist them. At Minnesota, there is a large number of part-time staff drawn from the community (called 'adjunct faculty') who are available to students who need their particular skills. They are drawn from many occupations: accountants, lawyers, architects, local government officers and so forth. Thus the range of people considered capable of contributing to increased access to adult education is, conceptually at least, very much enlarged. This is a point which might be considered very seriously in developing countries where the supply of qualified adults is limited; it indicates that, although the learning-contract institutions developed inside a country of great wealth and high educational development, their ideas might be applied at other developmental levels. The fundamental beliefs are both radical and of universal relevance.

The pedagogic implications of Open Learning systems for those in direct contact with the students are different in distance learning systems and in the Learning Contract institutions. In the former, those who meet the students are not those who present the material, nor will they have participated in its preparation. They are intermediaries, whose role is to interpret, explain, supplement and generally assist. Their assistance may be needed with the materials, or with the students' own situations or problems. The first role is broadly 'tutorial' and the second 'counselling', but they will frequently overlap or be indistinguishable from each other. The students' need may be for assistance from one personality only.

The tutor clearly needs appropriate academic qualifications. He also needs access to channels of communication to and from the source of the material. If he does not understand the material or the intention of its makers, he may confuse the students or substitute a rival view, so some form of briefing may be necessary. This could be achieved by the issue of special notes to tutors only and by periodic communication or meetings. In the other direction, the tutor may need to seek further clarification of difficulties experienced by the group which he cannot explain himself. Furthermore, the central agency may need feedback from him about the students' reaction.

Systems meet these problems in a variety of ways, corresponding to their circumstances. The cases of Newfoundland, Poland, and the British Open University may be instanced. In the early days of the Newfoundland system, the student groups were serviced by a technician who was there primarily to see to the video-tape equipment, but was asked also to undertake administrative duties (registering attendance, distributing course literature and assignments and collecting work done). Later a tutor was appointed who, in addition to the duties mentioned, watched the programme with the students, led the subsequent discussion, and telephoned the course-producers about unresolved difficulties.

In Poland, the students are entitled to attend consultation meetings at high schools on Sundays and use local primary schools and rural agricultural laboratories; it is part of the work of the staffs of these institutions to help them. (In this instance school teachers are in a tutorial relationship to adults. This is not always found to be a fruitful relationship, particularly with adult illiterates. The class-teacher frequently does not make a good adult tutor, without special training.)

In the Open University the requirements and duties of the 5,000 local counsellors and tutors are being examined in a fundamental fashion and the findings when issued should be of general interest.

In the learning-contract institutions, the heavy reliance upon one-to-one counselling produces its own problems. Can this load, which has resulted in heavy overwork for the pioneer staff, be sustained on a regular basis? Or can group- or peer-counselling reduce it? Can the idea of self-help of adult students be fostered, and what are its limits? Are we witnessing the emergence of a new form of adult educator? If so, where in the pedagogic hierarchy is he to be placed? Questions such as these have no answer yet.

Chapter 14
The impact of Open Learning

Since this inquiry was launched, the concept of Open Learning has attracted increasing interest and support. In addition to the ventures described in this volume several other schemes are now being planned or developed; at the same time, hitherto conventional institutions are beginning to introduce elements of Open Learning into their programmes.

Such diversity makes it difficult to define Open Learning precisely. It is, in part, a social change, permitting access to post-secondary education for groups outside the scope of formal full-time teaching. It is, too, a change in the methods of teaching, using modern methods of communication to overcome the problems of distance, or to satisfy the need for part-time study. And it is also a change in educational assumptions, depending upon new styles of curriculum development, student learning and assessment. The combination of these three factors leads us to believe that it is a substantial and soundly based innovation which will have enduring and far-reaching effects on systems of higher education.

The experience of the experimental schemes so far launched has shown the difficulties as well as the potential of Open Learning: much of the value of this pioneering work, indeed, lies in the fact that it throws new light upon old problems as well as in the fact that it raises a series of new challenges. Traditional assumptions about campus-based education, for instance, have to be revised—assumptions about the length of course as well as about its content and teaching techniques, about the nature of student learning, about formal examination procedures controlling entry to higher education or the award of qualifications. Open Learning, moreover, may prove to be more flexible, able to adapt to new needs in the working population and to the personal requirements and capabilities of students, encouraging greater self-dependence and more independent learning.

For all these reasons we consider that Open Learning may properly be considered as a new movement in educational ideas. It is true that the initial Open Learning schemes emerged as expedients designed to meet exceptional situations—to reach students who, for one reason or another, were excluded from full-time institutions—but it is already clear that these schemes reflected a much more profound change in attitude. The developing concern with continuing education, variously expressed as *éducation permanente* or 'lifelong learning', is another expression of the same trend towards the enlargement and diversification of opportunity.

All the ventures described in the following case studies are part of that movement towards a new educational frontier. They are first attempts to cross into new territory and to draw tentative maps of teaching and learning to help explore it. It was, therefore, sensible to summarize their experience so far. It seems to us, however, that in the next stage of development it would be profitable to focus attention less upon specific institutions and more upon problems and processes. Because each venture operates in a specific context, and for a fairly specific purpose, its organizational structure has only limited relevance outside that context: it is not systems which are capable of transfer so much as assumptions and methods.

We therefore suggest that any studies, conferences or working relationships that may arise from this report will achieve more if their emphasis is shifted away from reporting on complete systems and on to the analysis of concepts and techniques. Open Learning has begun to make a successful impact as a principle; it has been demonstrated that it is needed and that institutions based upon this principle can operate effectively. What those involved in its further development now need is information, research, training and interchange at the operational level. The next task is to devise the appropriate ways in which this can be achieved.

Part Three **The case studies**

Open Learning: the **Australian** contribution

Bernard Braithwaite
and Kevin Batt

Contents

I The national context

1. Australia is a vast continent of nearly 3 million square miles with a population density of well under five to the square mile, yet with over 8 million (61 per cent) of its population of 13 million concentrated in the capital cities of its six states and two territories. Thus, in spite of its size, it has a highly urbanized population with the remainder scattered thinly over wide expanses of land.

2. It developed through the nineteenth century as an offshoot of the British Isles and, therefore, until after the Second World War was essentially a British community with British traditions and institutions based on those of the United Kingdom. However, the nature and resources of the Australian environment, its problems of distance, of interior aridity and internal communications have been accepted and overcome to produce institutions which are essentially Australian. The result today is a country with one of the highest standards of living in the world (GNP per head is over U.S.$3000), self-sufficient for food and developing fast economically.

3. The provision and maintenance of schools in the public sector is the responsibility of the states, which jealously guard their independence of action. Non-government schools enrol some 20 per cent of school-age pupils, about 80 per cent of whom attend Roman Catholic schools. Education in the public sector is free and attendance is compulsory from age 6 to 15 (16 in Tasmania). Because of lack of transport or because of distance, some children may be excused from compulsory attendance if they live too far from a school to attend daily, and Australia has, in consequence, pioneered developments in the teaching of school children by radio and correspondence. In the process it has made a small but valuable contribution to the education of isolated individuals.

4. In tertiary education, provision of universities and colleges has been a state function supported by grants from the federal government. There are no private universities or universities founded by churches. They all, including the Australian National University set up by the federal government, operate under, and are limited by, an act of one of the parliaments, which lays down the conditions to which the university must conform. All charges for teaching in tertiary education have been abolished since January 1974, the whole cost having become a charge on the federal government. In addition, all full-time, non-bonded Australian students admitted to any tertiary education institution can obtain a maintenance allowance, assessed after a means test, up to a

maximum of $(A)850 annually if living at home and $(A)1,400 if living away from home. External and part-time students benefit by having to pay no fees. The social impact of this change has not yet had time to become manifest.

5. Tertiary education, up to 1973, was provided by (a) universities, (b) colleges of advanced education, (c) teacher-training colleges, (d) technical colleges, (e) organizations and bodies conducting adult or continuing education of a non-vocational, and often informal, nature. There are 18 universities, several of which have been founded in the past decade, and expansion continues. About 80 per cent of the undergraduate enrolments are for pass degrees only. Total student enrolment in 1973 was 132,733, including over 5,000 students taking higher-degree courses. Of this total, 47,027 or 35 per cent were part-time or external students. The proportion of the 17 to 22 age group enrolled is about 9 per cent. The development of universities has mainly been in the great capital cities, leaving the hinterland almost devoid of such provision.

6. In recent years there has been a trend towards incorporating or converting other institutions, particularly the teacher-training colleges, into colleges of advanced education. These last-named numbered 79 in 1973 and enrolled 94,882 students, of whom 36,294 or 38 per cent were part-time or external students. Some 36 of the 79 colleges were formerly teacher-training colleges and the others were technical or arts institutions of varying types offering continuation courses, mainly vocational in nature. The colleges are distributed over a wider range of population centres than are the universities. They are oriented towards the needs of industry, commerce and government, emphasizing the practical application of knowledge at levels below senior degree work.

7. While there is thus a variety of provision for tertiary education, much more remains to be done, particularly in external work. The Committee on Open University in its 1974 report states this specifically, indicating that only two Australians in a hundred are tertiary students and pointing out that the facilities for enrolment as an external student vary greatly from state to state. The evidence presented to this committee (see section VII) overwhelmingly indicated unfulfilled demand.

8. The organization of broadcasting, unlike the tertiary education system, is highly pluralistic in control, with private commercial interests strongly represented. In every part of the country, except the most remote areas, it is possible to receive one channel of public services television, in competition with one, two or three channels of commercial television. The public-service television and radio are provided by the Australian Broadcasting Commission; the commercial stations are for the most part owned by newspaper and airline interests. Both population coverage and distribution of receivers are high, and quality of reception in the urban areas is generally good.

9. In addition to being pluralistic, control of broadcasting is to a high degree decentralized. The Australian Broadcasting Commission is a national organization, but gives a substantial measure of autonomy to its state divisions, with only a light national control. The commercial companies are essentially state-based or area-based, though in many cases they form part of national chains of commercial interest. In both the public and commercial services, a strong sense of state and local loyalty is cultivated and national programming is kept within strict limits.

10. The Australian Broadcasting Commission provides an extensive service of broadcasts for schools, which has operated in radio since 1932 and in tele-

vision since 1963 (following pilot programmes from 1958). This service is directed and co-ordinated at national level, but largely provided at state level, in close co-operation with the state education departments. The relationship with state curricula and examinations is an important factor; but strong efforts are made to provide series that are appropriate to many states and such series often achieve national coverage. Because of the competitive system, described in paragraph 8, it is inevitable that the pressure on evening and weekend programming should be towards seeking consistently large audiences and that no time can be found for more specialized interests such as systematic adult education. At present, therefore, the only adult education broadcasts in Australia are from the small number of university stations that provide a useful but limited coverage in their immediate area (see paragraphs 52–58).

11. A recent reconsideration of allocations in the A.M. band showed that by the adoption of revised planning standards many more allocations would become available. The Report of the Independent Inquiry into F.M. Broadcasting issued in March 1974 recommended that full advantage should be taken of these frequencies. The report further recommended that F.M. radio broadcasting should be introduced as soon as possible; that the number of A.M. radio stations should be substantially increased; that a network of F.M. stations should be developed for national broadcasting purposes; and that non-profit-making community stations and public-access stations should be developed for radio broadcasting. If these recommendations are implemented, there should be significant new opportunities for adult education by radio. In the present situation, as the Committee of Enquiry into Open University observed in its draft report, there is little chance of any radio broadcasting time being available for systematic tertiary education purposes.

12. As to television for these purposes, the prospective frequency situation is such that any substantial national or state-by-state coverage for adult education is unlikely unless public pressure were to become a great deal stronger than it is at present. There is little scope for the wider use of the V.H.F. band in the big cities, although some further stations in country areas may be possible in this band. So far, however, the U.H.F. band, which is widely used elsewhere, has not been employed for television in Australia. The report recommends that this band should be so used. At present, television receivers in Australia have no U.H.F. tuners. The report recommends that as soon as possible receivers should be adapted for these bands.

II The historical background

13. The Australian pattern of settlement and cultural development began on the coast at isolated points with good harbours and thence spread outwards into the fertile coastal areas. Beyond these areas, the terrain, water shortage and vast distances limited population growth, so that it was largely confined to the principal settlements. This has continued throughout Australian history. It has resulted in powerful urban nuclei controlling large, relatively empty surrounding areas, with a few large units of government, the states, as highly centralized semi-autonomous authorities. The states guard their rights carefully and among the social services have retained control of education. Though the federal government has increased its authority in the last three decades, the

original structure has been durable enough to survive and to determine the shape of institutional life. Because there were no other institutions outside the main centres of population, the states have tended to initiate development. The result is a state-centralized system, highly unified within each separate state.

14. This structure has been used in social life and education to further the Australian creed of a basic minimum for everyone. There is a firm belief in a basic wage and a standard of living below which none should fall, and a basic education to which all should have access. This latter presented problems of implementation in the nineteenth century, both numerically and geographically. It seemed more important to ensure basic schooling of a reasonable and similar standard than to provide advanced quality education for a minority, as had occurred in older civilizations in Europe. This has resulted in schools which provide a roughly equivalent but not outstandingly high standard of teaching for everyone up to the age of 15 and at university level, a general (80 per cent) rather than an honours (20 per cent) degree.

15. The concern to provide fair and equal access to education irrespective of geographical location has resulted in special emphasis on the needs of the isolated student. Schooling by correspondence and radio tuition has already been mentioned (paragraph 3), and in tertiary education the part-time and external degree, associate or diploma qualification has been developed which forms the special Australian contribution at this level. The desire for fair access to educational opportunity produced a problem as education expanded with growing population and longer school life, namely a need for more and better-qualified teachers. The cheapest and quickest way of raising quality is by in-service training, which avoids teachers having to be withdrawn from the schools to get full-time training. In Australia, the impetus for external studies, via the state-controlled universities, derives from the need for better teachers in the state schools. The provision of upgrading external courses (and the use made of them) varies from state to state, with some making relatively little such provision.

16. It is thus important to realize that the special contribution made by external studies in Australia has grown out of the country's own peculiar needs and history. It was an Australian solution to an Australian need in the Australian ethos and the Australian setting. It did not specifically set out to produce new media, new curricula, new techniques or new ideas, and such of these as have developed have arisen, *sui generis*, from the need to perform a specific task.

III External studies: the universities

17. Legislative provision for external students dates from the Act of 1909 which established the University of Queensland in Brisbane. This act required that: 'Provision shall be made in the Statutes for the granting after examination of degrees and the diploma of education to persons engaged in the profession of teaching or other persons in cases where such teachers or other persons are unable to attend lectures at or in connection with the University.' From this origin, external work in Australia has grown, changed its pattern, been incorporated deliberately as a major function of three universities and accepted in the tertiary colleges. It has thus had over sixty years to develop and its contribution must be judged in the light of (a) the use made of this opportunity,

and (b) the extent to which other nations have drawn on it for their own purposes.

The special claim for external studies is that they permit the individual student to work at his or her own pace at a place and time of his or her own choosing. This is particularly valued by mature students, who can organize themselves more effectively than 18-year-olds and have more commitments than have younger persons. It applies particularly when a student already has a job and is unable, for reasons of distance or inconvenience, to attend lectures on a campus as a part-time student. It thus enables tertiary studies to be undertaken by persons who could not or would not otherwise obtain them.

18. In spite of its early start, the growth of external studies in Australia has been slow, almost reluctant. It has had to face shortage of resources and much opposition from academic staff, ranging from neglect to active hostility. The established universities in four of the six states (Victoria, South Australia, Western Australia and Tasmania) have almost no provision for external studies. Where full-time internal study has proved impossible, orthodox academic opinion has preferred part-time study at the campus to external study. Thus part-time university studies have grown and make a considerable contribution, namely 29 per cent of the total enrolments for 1973. By contrast, the proportion of external students has remained low at 6.4 per cent. In fact, the proportion of both part-time and external students has fallen since 1961 from 36.5 per cent and 10 per cent respectively, due to the more rapid enrolment of full-time students in existing and new universities. The provision for external degrees is concentrated in three institutions, which in 1973 provided between them 7,394 out of the total of 8,517 external students. These are the universities of Queensland, where external students make up 19.1 per cent of the total enrolment, New England 54.0 per cent and Macquarie 8.1 per cent (details are given in section V). The new Murdoch University at Perth, due to take its first students in 1975, has a built-in commitment to external students and is planning that they should account for 10 per cent of its enrolment.

Certain characteristics of external studies are given below to indicate the special features of Australian provision, such as the degree structure, the composition of the student body, the techniques used and the success rates.

Degree structure

19. All Australian universities insist that the external degree shall, so far as is possible, be identical with the internal degree. There are no special courses for external candidates and courses, curricula and examinations are identical for all. This is to ensure that both types of degree are equal in status and to avoid the suspicion that the external degree is an inferior product. The only concession is that external students take fewer courses at a time and consequently are allowed longer to gain their degrees. Most external students have to pass the standard matriculation requirement to enter, but relaxations have recently been permitted for mature students. Prescribed textbooks are the same for all students. External provision simply enables students to pass the standard examination where regular attendance on the campus is impossible.

Student body (1972)

20. By far the majority of external students are teachers (University of Queensland 66 per cent, University of New England 72 per cent and Macquarie University 80 per cent of total enrolments). Even in the large college of advanced education, the Western Australia Institute of Technology (WAIT), teachers form the biggest occupational group among external students, namely 40 per cent. The evidence indicates that the main incentive in providing external studies has been to upgrade the quality of the teaching profession. This is certainly made clear in the original University of Queensland Act of 1909 (paragraph 17). External students are older than internal students. In the University of New England they have averaged 29 years for almost a decade.

Techniques

21. Because Australian universities have been emphatic that all degrees shall, so far as is possible, be identical, most universities use the same staff to teach both internal and external students. The exception is the University of Queensland where some forty-two staff members are engaged by the department of external studies primarily for external teaching.

As external students cannot attend lectures on campus, various means have been adopted to convey the content of the lectures to them. These were initiated at the University of Queensland when some students began taking notes which were subsequently typed and circulated to external students. Then stenographers were used to get more accurate results. From these crude beginnings have evolved methods whereby lecturers prepare notes in advance for external students and, in addition, issue either their own exact lectures in print, or specially modified ones including supplementary notes and cross-references. Some internal lecturers use a microphone to record their lectures and these are then circulated on audio-tape to external students. Others record some of their lectures, specially bearing in mind the needs of their external students, and the tapes are distributed, one copy to each external student taking the course. In addition special course books have been developed. These contain a synopsis of the course and give references to source books, summaries of lectures and various diagrams, statistics and illustrations to help the external students. The supply of textbooks to students is of course essential, and some universities provide special libraries for use by external students only, so as to ensure a fair opportunity for such students and to avoid their being at a disadvantage compared with internal students. Supplementary aids such as slides, loops, records and films are available for certain courses—tapes and records being essential for language study.

22. The institutions specifically examined (section V) have all set up special departments to assist external students. In New England, Macquarie and WAIT, there are 'servicing' departments which distribute lecture notes, course books and supplementary aids, handle assignments and organize vacation schools. They have no authority to intervene in curricula or the teaching methods adopted by the teaching staff, although some have produced notes or aids on teaching techniques. Only in Queensland does the department also employ academic teaching staff directly.

23. The main instrument of teaching is by correspondence, with lecture notes and course books mailed regularly, and students returning to the teacher assignments which are marked and assessed. In addition, study groups and vocation schools are organized by the external department so that students can have access to facilities on the campus and benefit from face-to-face contact with the lecturer, which is considered of great importance for both parties. The vacation courses are indispensable in science courses.

24. Vacation courses and study groups are supplemented by visits of academic staff to groups of students or even to individuals. These involve the lecturer in frequent travelling if the contacts are at all systematic. When groups of four or more students studying the same topic can meet regularly in one spot, the University of Queensland provides a tutor, usually an appropriately qualified graduate living locally, to provide the 'give and take' so important in tertiary education. Attendance at these centres is optional, but if attendance falls the tutor is withdrawn. Attendance at summer schools may be compulsory (e.g. New England and Macquarie) or optional (e.g. Queensland). Radio and television broadcasts play no part in external first-degree work, though they are used in special fields (paragraph 52). No textbooks are specifically written for external students and the course books are limited and unimaginative by comparison with those available in the British Open University.

Higher degrees

25. While many students working for bachelor's degrees may already possess a degree, Australia provides opportunities for students to take higher degrees by external study. Such degrees are permitted by universities other than the three which make substantial provision for external first degrees. Thus the Universities of New South Wales and Adelaide had 69 and 78 higher-degree external students enrolled in 1971, though their undergraduate external students in each case were fewer than 150 out of a total of 14,000 and 7,300 respectively. Altogether, such degrees, for masters, doctorates and higher doctorates, totalled 216, though this represented a drop from 357 in 1962. No special facilities or techniques have been adopted for higher-degree students, other than the part-time courses outlined in paragraphs 52–58.

Extra-state developments

26. External students are, as a rule, only admitted to a university in the state of their domicile. An exception is the University of Queensland, which assumed responsibility for external studies in the Northern Territory, Papua-New Guinea, Fiji and students in certain countries in the Colombo Plan. While responsibility for Fiji has now been taken over by New Zealand, and universities have been established in Papua-New Guinea and the South Pacific, external students in the areas still study with the University of Queensland. These are mostly Australians living in the territories and no specific provision is made by the University of Queensland for the indigenous inhabitants of the areas served.

Success rates

27. Since external students may be allowed unlimited time to take their degree, it is not easy to assess the proportion who succeed. What can be stated in the light of studies in particular universities is that the withdrawal rate is high in the first year and then flattens off. In the University of New England, where records have been kept since 1955, this in the first year is now about 24 per cent but in later years is around 12 per cent. Of those who survived and sat their final examinations in the Faculty of Arts, the pass rate of 87 per cent in 1971 was 1 per cent higher than for internal students and has been an average of 1 per cent higher since 1955. In Macquarie University and at WAIT there is similar evidence of good examination results from those who persist in their courses, though first-year withdrawal is high (about 30 per cent) in both institutions. The comparable figures at Macquarie for full-time students show a drop-out rate of some 10 per cent in the first year with an overall drop-out of 25 to 30 per cent while total external drop-outs are some 50 to 55 per cent.

IV External studies: the colleges of advanced education

28. The colleges of advanced education (paragraph 6) at present number 79, though the total will change as various tertiary institutions are added or reorganized. Though there are facilities for some external study in all states other than Tasmania, only four such institutions (the Royal Melbourne Institute of Technology, the Mitchell College of Advanced Education, the Torrens College of Advanced Education and the Western Australian Institute of Technology (WAIT)) had more than 500 external students in 1973 and between them accounted for 2,594 of the 5,324 enrolments. WAIT is included in detail in this study (see paragraphs 45–51). Enrolments in external studies represent 5.6 per cent of total enrolments in colleges of advanced education (11.5 per cent in WAIT), with commercial and business studies forming some 49 per cent of subjects studied. Students study either for associateship, degree or diploma courses, but in some subject areas only part of the course may be undertaken externally, the remainder having to be by internal study. Accrediting of the courses studied is by a state body, such as the Western Australia Tertiary Education Commission and at national level by the Australian Council on Awards in Advanced Education. The curriculum and examinations are the same as for internal students. There is an overlap between working full- and part-time and considerable flexibility exists to enable students to take advantage of whichever way is more convenient to them. Course books are used, rather more written work is expected of external students, and weekend and vacational schools operate as in the universities. Teaching is undertaken by the same staff as for internal students. WAIT has one full-time external study centre as the first of a planned series of outposts to meet the needs of its external students. No special techniques have been devised to help external students other than the provision of course books and substantial use of audio-tapes. The course books at WAIT are not very imaginative and few of them have been made with special consideration for the needs of external students. Technical subjects

cannot be taught well to external students so the range of studies available is largely limited to non-scientific subjects or to theory in scientific and technical areas.

V Patterns of external studies

The University of Queensland, Brisbane

29. This university pioneered teaching and examinations for external degrees in Australia (paragraph 17) and for over forty years from its inauguration provided most of the external work undertaken in this regard. Thus it remains one of the two universities having the largest external student provision, with some 3,302 enrolments in 1973. The methods and organization adopted for external studies have not been followed by other Australian universities entering this field.

30. In Queensland a department of external studies handles all matters relating to the enrolment of students and provides the academic staff which supplies 78 per cent of the external teaching. Present policies will extend this until virtually all such teaching is done by the department's staff. Nevertheless the curriculum and subject range is effectively controlled by internal staff to ensure that external students receive degrees identical to internal students. Throughout its development the external department has had a considerable measure of responsibility for the care of its students, for tutorial and other help, and for teaching aids and methods. In the 1950s over one-third of the university's students were external, but the recent national provision for more full-time students had reduced the proportion to 19.1 per cent by 1973.

31. The staff of the department now numbers 42 with 29 administrative support personnel. There is a special library for external students of 66,000 volumes, half of which are issued annually. Course books for external students are compiled as a supplement to lecture notes. The first course specifically designed in the external department and taught only to external students has now been issued. It relates to a period of Napoleonic history in which the external staff considered their students were interested. Audio-tapes are used, but no television or radio teaching is provided, even in metropolitan Brisbane, despite the fact that the university has its own television station there, which is used for technical instruction in engineering but not for wider educational purposes. Vacation schools are organized on the campus but are not compulsory. Tutorial groups for four or more students are organized weekly or bi-weekly and a tutor is paid to teach and help them in the same way as for a seminar in internal university teaching.

32. The external studies department claims that its students receive a better service when taught by staff specially selected for, and working full-time in, external work. They argue that the staff know the students' needs, visit them regularly and handle their problems more effectively than could internal staff, whose main loyalty is to their internal students.

The department and its staff compile outlines and course aids which give such help to the external students that, it is claimed, they are sometimes better served than the normal internal student. This is borne out by the fact that there is a 'black market' in external lecture notes, which are officially only available to external students, but are purchased from them by internal students! Additionally, the university has had to verify carefully the actual domicile of students, because metropolitan residents were found to be using country addresses in order to enrol as external students. When metropolitan residents who were already graduates were allowed to enrol for a second first degree as external students, the university had an embarrassing flood of applicants. Fifteen per cent of external students now live in Brisbane, an indication of the preference for external methods of study. The department prepares an annual report on the performance of all external students. This is greatly appreciated as a morale booster. It is also claimed that external work has a special appeal so that staff who are personally attracted by work in the external field, and hence of especially good quality, are being recruited.

33. There are several weaknesses in the Queensland situation. The external department is less well endowed with senior posts. University promotion tends to require research achievements and because of the nature of their work and the travelling involved, external staff are unable to do much work of this kind. Advanced courses have therefore to be given by internal staff because they are better qualified. Hence, opinion in the university is that external work is denigrated and regarded as inferior. Promotion is more difficult for external staff who tend to be 'condemned' to this activity unless they get out quickly. This has, in the past, produced high staff turnover. There is no teaching for honours work externally, for the reason just given, and similarly postgraduate work has been precluded. The student/staff ratio is much higher for external teachers, the submission to the Karmel Committee stating that in 1973 the 41 staff members taught 36 subjects with an enrolment of 3,800 students.

34. In spite of the disadvantages, the trend in Queensland would seem to be towards a steady increase in external enrolments, as these have doubled in twenty years. With bigger numbers, more staff and better support services, the department feels it can now stand on its own feet and improve its contribution. As numbers expand the advantages of specifically appointed external teaching staff increase and if such growth occurs, the university feels well adapted to handle it.

The University of New England, Armidale

35. As part of its grant of independent status, this university was committed to providing external studies from its inception in 1955. As it is situated well away from centres of population in a small town of about 15,000, it would barely be viable without its external students who made up 54 per cent of its 1973 enrolment of 6,502. The arrangement for handling external studies differs from that of Queensland in that all staff appointed to the university may be called on to teach both internal and external students. The external studies department employs no academic teaching staff, but is a purely administrative and service department. It organizes and co-ordinates but takes no responsibility in academic matters affecting curricula, content or method. This approach minimizes differences between internal and external teaching and the university claims that it has gone to the limit to achieve this integration.

36. The basic features of external study are, again, the lecture notes, supplemented by course outlines, assignments marked by the lecturers undertaking

the teaching, face-to-face contact between teachers and students in weekend study groups and compulsory vacation schools. Tutors are appointed for groups undertaking the same course. Costs are impossible to assess accurately, because the same staff teach both internally and externally. The general consensus is that there is not much difference in cost per graduate whichever method of study is adopted. The range of studies is limited to arts and education, but covers some 160 courses. Only elementary biological studies are undertaken in science. Some postgraduate courses (e.g. educational administration) are offered to persons living outside New South Wales.

37. Special developments in matriculation practice are of interest. Initially, applicants for external studies were required to have the same qualifications as internal students, but the university has since relaxed this requirement for maturer applicants so that students over 21 years can be granted provisional matriculation on a minimal academic record. Provided that they pass at least one course per year they may continue their studies. Some 25 per cent of students enter external studies in this way and their performance compares satisfactorily with those admitted on the basis of formal standards. It must be remembered, however, that 72 per cent of students are teachers who can therefore be assumed to have maintained contact with education even if they had not previously attained formal university matriculation. This easing of entry has been extended for 1974 to 39 entrants who have no educational qualifications at all, so a beginning has been made for genuinely 'open' admissions.

38. The New England model has been widely publicized all over the world and what would otherwise be a little-known university in a remote part of New South Wales has become famous because of its external study programme. Visitors from many countries have examined its achievements, and copies and variations of its techniques have been used widely. Nevertheless, the system is not without its drawbacks. To gain real benefit, an external student must be fortunate enough to be allocated to a teacher who will make more than the minimum effort demanded for internal teaching. It is found that many staff do not do this, as they are often busy people and therefore tend to give priority to their internal students who are present on the campus. Moreover, when completed, the planning, curriculum and course outline must be delivered to the external department by fixed times for duplication and distribution. Similarly assignments must be planned, set and marked on fixed schedules. All this involves requirements which a staff member not specifically appointed to undertake external teaching may find difficulty in meeting. Because the external department is administrative only, it cannot do more than request, persuade and possibly cajole in order to get a fair deal for the external student. Supplementary aids are a matter for the lecturer alone to decide. Some go to the trouble of providing these; many do not. Team-work in course construction does not exist and the efficiency or otherwise of the teaching depends heavily on the inclination and adaptability of the individual lecturer, who is not chosen for his capacity to teach external students. No training in external teaching techniques is given, though the external studies department can make suggestions.

The New England model has now been running for some twenty years and it has made a tremendous contribution both to its own external students and to the whole world of external studies. But its very success has put it in danger of becoming too set in its ways because of its insistence on integration. This insistence has inhibited developments which could have occurred to the benefit of the external student and therefore means that application elsewhere is limited in scope. Change in the pattern does not appear likely at present.

Macquarie University, Sydney

39. This is a new university, situated in the northern suburbs of Sydney, which opened in 1967. Its special contribution to external studies lies in the realm of science, where, in conjunction with its Department of Part-Time Studies, it has developed special courses which, in respect of New South Wales, complement the external provision in the humanities and education at the University of New England. The 1973 enrolment was 584, being 8.1 per cent of the university's total of 7,190 students. By decision of the New South Wales Government, subjects taught at New England may not be taught at Macquarie. Between 70 per cent and 80 per cent of the annual intake are teachers of science.

40. Teaching follows the New England pattern, being undertaken by the same staff for internal and external students. Special features are (a) the Department of Part-Time Studies, which is responsible for service, welfare and liaison for all part-time students including external students, and (b) the fact that admission means entry to the university and not just to a particular category of student. Thus, within certain limits, students once admitted can change courses. The university is particularly flexible in its enrolment policy, which allows for relaxed matriculation for mature students and has already proved its value. Lectures are circulated in print or by audio-tape, supplemented by course notes and study guides. Unlike the practice in other universities, some of these are also circulated to internal students.

41. Numbers in the external courses are small, there being at present a limit of 650 places. This means that personal contacts between staff and students are facilitated and they are effected through compulsory vacation courses on the campus, using the laboratories and local study groups. The university has made a special effort to teach the physical sciences to full degree standard, subjects which had not been previously taught off campus in Australia. This has not been done by diluting the course. The period of study and its concentration of laboratory work for chemistry may differ for an external student, but the number of hours involved is the same as for an internal student. The drive to undertake external science teaching was the need to upgrade teachers of science in schools and to equip them for advanced work, normally entrusted only to science graduates. The university feels that the intensive techniques used at Macquarie, while doing the job they set out to do, are expensive, and not every member of staff is willing to undertake such work. They are not, therefore, applicable to mass instruction and there is a limit to the amount of such external physical science teaching that the university could and would undertake. This is because the target has been specific and limited, namely, as stated, to upgrade science teachers to degree standard so that they can do more advanced work. The enrolments are overwhelmingly from serving teachers (paragraph 39). The teachers are strongly motivated and gain a specific salary increase when they graduate.

42. Among the support services, special mention must be made of audio-tapes. The use made of these ranges from the taping of lectures as they are being delivered to the making of special tapes for external students by the lecturers to

illuminate particular topics. Indeed, it is claimed that courses are sometimes devised specifically for external or part-time students and then used for internal students. In addition, home kits for certain aspects of science have been added, though initially these were not used because they might interfere with the students' contact with the staff. The Macquarie staff claim that their intensive personal contacts with their external students in vacation school laboratory work provide valuable help in shaping their general university teaching to all students. There appears little doubt that the general aim of producing a quality product in a difficult curriculum area is being achieved.

43. Although the first generation of external students is only just graduating after the normal five to six years of study, interesting data are being accumulated by the head of the Department of Part-Time Studies about the performance of mature part-time students who lack the normal entry matriculation qualifications. In simplified terms these appear to show that: (a) the biggest drop-out is among young part-time students, i.e. those under 20 years of age; (b) for mature students over 24 who have to pass in two matriculation subjects in the year prior to entering university, their scores in these subjects are as good a prognosis as are five such subjects taken at age 18 by the normal entrant; (c) the perseverance rate for students over 24 years of age is better than for those under that age, regardless of the method of gaining entry.

These findings are preliminary only and relate to part-time rather than to external students. Nevertheless, if corroborated, they are important to the general field of external studies where the students are almost all of mature age.

44. External studies at Macquarie are too recent to enable a satisfactory general critique to be applied, but they have proved that the physical sciences can be taught externally using intensive laboratory sessions with staff who, though not specifically trained for the job, are enthusiastic, have keen students and a strong support department to assist them. Critics point out that numbers are small and such techniques do not have extensive application. This is true and is admitted by the university.

The Western Australia Institute of Technology (WAIT), Perth

45. Though the title differs, and the institution is a very large one, this institute can be classed as one of the new colleges of advanced education. It opened in 1967 and it has a substantial external service providing for 729 students, 13 per cent of its total enrolment in 1973. Most students in the institute work for associateships in social science and commercial subjects. External students also predominate in these areas, only 13 per cent studying engineering, applied science and architecture. This to some extent is explained by the occupations of the external students, 40 per cent being teachers and 38 per cent accountants and administrative officers. The explanation of the small amount of scientific subject matter being taught externally is stated to be lack of demand and the practical difficulty of such studies for external students. These have to undertake some on-campus study in any case, even if they do part of their scientific work as external students. An interesting difference from the usual university pattern of external studies is that residents in metropolitan Perth are freely allowed to take external courses, for example, if they can demonstrate that

it is difficult or inconvenient to attend daily at the campus. As a result some 35 per cent of the external students live in metropolitan Perth.

46. The external studies department also provides repeat courses for internal students who fail in a particular subject. This use of external studies as an alternative to the provision of special internal courses is claimed to be a major resource saver and about 8 per cent of the internal students are at present doing such courses. For external studies as a whole the institute considers that costs are high, mainly because numbers in the many courses are relatively small.

47. The pattern of external teaching follows that of New England, being undertaken by the same staff as teach internally, but some external part-time tutors are also hired. This is for the same reason as obtains in most Australian universities, namely, to ensure parity of status for the qualification. Curricula and examinations for external and internal students are identical. There are no residential facilities and this represents a constraint on vacation schools. Consequently tutor/student contact is less than in New England or Queensland, being limited more to weekend study groups. The main media of instruction are the usual course books, study guides and lecture notes, with written assignments marked by lecturers. There is a special library for external student borrowing. Considerable use is made of audio-tapes. These, like the other aids to study, are produced in a special educational services department which serves all the institute, including external studies. While tapes are made directly, during lectures, recent developments have been towards making special tapes for external students, and, as in Queensland, it has been found that these are also much appreciated by internal students. Elaborate tape-copying machines have been installed to duplicate tapes at speed so they can be dispatched quickly to students taking the relevant course. Cassettes have almost replaced reel-to-reel tapes. Students buy their own playing equipment. The servicing department also controls a bookshop which issues books C.O.D. to external students, thus eliminating difficulty and delays.

48. The WAIT practice reflects the same difficulties and limitations on external study development as are found elsewhere in Australia. The service could expand as there is evidence of unsatisfied demand but, apart from financial limitations, it appears that, as internal enrolments rise, lecturers tend to neglect their external students. As some lecturers display no interest in external students, the trend is for the latter to be allocated to the relatively small number of staff members who are happy to teach them. This may lead to the recruiting of staff specially for external teaching, resulting in the Queensland situation. If, therefore, there is to be a substantial expansion of external studies, this may become the pattern.

49. Difficulties arise, as elsewhere, when lecturers fail to prepare material adequately for their external students. The external department has no mandate to require such preparation, and, since many WAIT staff have no pedagogical training, the quality of teaching varies considerably. This is a particular problem in an institute which specializes in teaching commercial and business studies, because many of the staff are recruited from business rather than from the teaching profession.

50. Western Australia has even greater problems of distance than the rest of Australia. It is therefore particularly difficult to get staff to travel out from Perth to visit and help external students. This is particularly unfortunate because a number of industries are developing in the north of the state and firms are

finding that both subject knowledge and staff morale in remote areas is improved where extension-study facilities exist. Some such firms go so far as to provide study centres to encourage external work. In this situation, and pending the development of local institutions, there seems to be considerable potential for growth in external studies. Such studies would be needed in technical and administrative areas and would combine theoretical knowledge, provided as at present through external study, with practical work undertaken in the workshops and/or laboratories of interested firms. To this could then be added sandwich courses of intensive study at WAIT during vacations when the existing laboratory and workshop capacity is available. Development along these lines would meet a need in the growing area of the northern coast and could make a valuable contribution to the special problems of this vast state, but it is not yet clear if it will take place.

51. A small but interesting recent development in adult education has been made possible by a special grant supplemented by one from the Farmers' Society. One research worker has been specially seconded to provide non-vocational courses of interest to some twenty or so adults, widely scattered over an area of up to 200 miles from Perth. Special visits and advice on courses of study are being arranged at the request of the individuals concerned, staff members sometimes travelling by light aeroplane. These visits are said to contribute considerably to the morale of persons compelled to work in isolation, many of them women. It is of particular interest that a farming organization deems such a development worth supporting, even though the courses bear little relation to the industry. Though strictly adult-education courses and not external studies are involved, the innovation may add impetus to, and widen the extension of, external education in Western Australia.

Radio and Television Universities, Sydney and Adelaide

52. Two universities, New South Wales and Adelaide, broadcast courses of study by radio and television. Particularly in New South Wales, these make a specific, though limited, contribution to university extension work in specialist postgraduate updating studies.

53. In 1961 the University of New South Wales installed and operated the first Australian radio station to be used exclusively for education. Until the University of Adelaide followed suit in 1972, this was the only such station. In 1966, a television station was added, again solely for education. An audio-tape service for those living beyond the range of the broadcasting stations is also available.

54. The initial thinking behind the establishment of these transmissions was that every graduate in a profession needs a refresher course at least once every five years. The courses are therefore of a highly technical nature with specific target audiences in the professions. To the postgraduate studies have now been added others at lower levels. For postgraduate studies in 1972, there was an enrolment of 1,956 to which must be added 1,302 enrolled for tape correspondence courses, a total of 3,258. Courses were in subjects such as communication, statistics, computers, management and engineering. The institute of administration organizes similar courses for 525 students, and for postgraduate medical courses there were another 1,111 enrolments. Other courses enrolled

619, and there were 351 students for whom bridging courses between school and university were organized in science. This gives a grand total of 5,864 enrolments in specific radio and television courses.

55. Students pay fees for almost all the courses, ranging from $(A)7 upwards, for which sum details of the programmes, times of broadcasts and lecture notes are provided. The latter are essential to understand the broadcasts. Some courses are supplemented by tutorials at various centres and some of the administrative courses have residential requirements for which the fees rise to $(A)750. Certain courses involve laboratory work at the university. Some of the courses count for credit towards higher degrees such as Master of Engineering and others qualify for the graduate Diploma in Human Communication.

56. Whilst the co-ordinator of postgraduate extension studies (who heads the station) and the producers are on the establishment of the university, which therefore pays their salaries, the lecturers' fees and all other expenditure including transmission, publications and tapes, are covered by student fees. The cost per student hour of broadcasting is stated to be $(A)1 an hour. There has been no development for first-degree work. The university has limited its broadcast teaching to the specific areas mentioned.

57. The University of Adelaide has operated a small radio station since 1972 and broadcasts a variety of programmes within its limited means and with a tiny staff. The programmes are more in the realm of adult education as they are mainly enrichment or background broadcasts, ranging from school-age to postgraduate topics. No credit courses are given. About 2,000 fee-paying listeners are enrolled; lecture notes are issued for roughly half the courses. The service is still in its infancy and, like the stations of the University of New South Wales, has to cover operating costs from student fees.

58. Though the broadcasts of the University of New South Wales have, as stated, been in operation for thirteen years and clearly make a contribution to those in its specific target areas, they do not appear to have developed a great deal since their inception. Cassettes and tapes have been added to extend the scope of the original radio lectures, and television has been further added to extend visual scope, but the range of audiences remains limited. No attempt seems to have been made to integrate the work of the broadcasting stations or lecturers' knowledge and techniques into external courses within the university. This may well be because the university only offers external courses in health administration and enrols only 1 per cent of its student body externally. It is unfortunate for the development of external studies in Australia that neither of these university broadcasting stations exists in universities which have substantial extension programmes. (Adelaide has only 2 per cent of its students enrolled externally.) No attempt has been made to integrate external studies by using the established Australian techniques (correspondence, course books, lecture notes, study groups, vacation schools and audio-tapes), combined with these university broadcasting facilities. The stations therefore represent, particularly in New South Wales, a successful attempt to do a specific job in upgrading professional persons in a limited range of professional subjects, which is what they were designed for. These broadcasting efforts show no interest in developing ideas or methods of mass communication and they do not try to appeal to a wider audience or to enlarge the range of undergraduate studies. Their contribution to the wider field is therefore limited.

VI Appraisal of the Australian contribution

59. The Australian contributions to tertiary education at a distance are considerable and should be recognized. They have not only met a definite need in Australia, but have provided information and stimulus for development elsewhere. They have been built up slowly, with only one institution contributing for forty years, though subsequent developments have been quicker.

60. The motivation for extended tertiary educational growth has been the states' need for improved quality of teachers and public servants. Such students today number some 60 per cent of external enrolments. There has been little extension beyond this to the public at large. The feed-in has therefore mainly comprised professional personnel, who already possess some qualification and who gain professional advancement and financial reward from successful further study.

61. The general pattern having been established, developments have only been marginal. Though all the known uses and forms of the broadcasting media are to be found in Australia, there has been no real co-ordination to maximize their impact. Development has been sporadic, often in the face of academic opposition. The educational contribution has been supplementary rather than radical, both in conception and delivery.

62. There have, however, been real innovations. These include postgraduate specialist instruction, direct instruction at advanced level by radio and television, substantial development in the use of audio-tapes and initiative in the teaching of science to first-degree standard. Regretfully, these (and the main work of external studies) have been limited through concentration on providing recipients with a qualifying 'ticket' rather than on increasing further education as such.

63. The targets which have been achieved are important. They are also relevant to other countries, particularly the less developed. Unfortunately the Australian model, by its insistence on standard matriculation and the use of full-time university staff both to write the curriculum and teach it, severely limits the potential for transfer to less developed countries, where there is a lower standard of literacy, greater communication problems and fewer qualified staff.

64. In spite of these criticisms there has undoubtedly been substantial impact on developments elsewhere. Thus, virtually all the technical ideas found in the highly innovative United Kingdom Open University delivery system already existed in Australia, although they were never brought together in the same place at one time. Australia's individual institutions may have paid the penalty of being pioneers and of resting content with their efforts to the neglect of continuous innovation. Nevertheless, the merits and disadvantages of what has been achieved are well worth summarizing.

65. The advantages of the system are as follows:

The external degree course allows the student to study at home, in his own time, at his own convenience, allows him to continue in his job, to live with his family and to save money on his maintenance. It has special appeal for the mature student.

The external degree has equal status with all other degrees; this achievement is not in question.

The external student in most cases is taught by the same staff as the internal student, has the same lectures and takes the same examinations. He can therefore feel he has access to the same educational opportunity as the full-time internal student.

Valuable experience has been gained in helping external students and this has been of benefit for internal students.

There is growing recognition that mature students of low formal academic attainment can overcome this disadvantage and do well.

The Australian university and college pattern allows substantial flexibility in structure between full-time, part-time and external studies in order to get a degree. This is of substantial benefit to students in the states where the service is offered.

Postgraduate work has been effectively carried out by external studies.

Audio-tapes have been utilized as a valuable medium of instruction.

Some development towards 'open' admissions is being made.

Australian experience has been of help to representatives of developing countries who have visited Australian institutions and who have then introduced correspondence education in their own areas.

66. The main disadvantages of the system are as follows:

No special courses have been developed to meet the needs of external students. Such students can study only for certain of the existing degree courses in universities or colleges. The system is therefore unduly rigid.

The general requirement of the same matriculation as for internal students greatly limits the student body and inhibits development.

The external service has not met the demand. All 200 submissions to the special Committee on Open University for Australia stress the need for expansion.

Australian universities tend to restrict the credit they give to each other's students. External students who move from their state may lose the fruit of much of their efforts.

The use of identical academic staff to teach both internal and external students in general works to the detriment of the latter, because the staff tend to give preference to their internal students.

There is a high drop-out and wastage of external students, particularly in the first year.

There has been a disappointing lack of development in technical subjects in non-degree areas.

The student body is overwhelmingly in public service. There is little general appeal in the external studies offered.

Many of the universities with prestige make little or no provision for external studies and the existing coverage is consequently uneven.

There are severe limitations on external enrolment for students living in metropolitan areas in spite of the evidence of demand.

Costs in external education are not demonstrably lower than for internal courses.

To less developed countries the Australian model has limited appeal since both internal and external studies make similar demands on scarce resources and there is little cost-advantage to be obtained from the external system.

The pattern of development selected in recent years (i.e. using the same staff for both types of students) has resulted in external departments which are purely service-oriented and administrative. This has inhibited development or modification of curricula.

The existing machinery and pattern shows little sign of producing radical change in the development of external studies.

VII Future developments—the Karmel Report

67. The contributions of Australian universities and colleges to students who cannot study on a full-time basis are considerable and have formed the basis for much that has been done elsewhere. Nevertheless, there exists a considerable demand for further facilities. This, coinciding with the advent and success of the Open University in the United Kingdom, resulted in the establishment in March 1973 of a committee under the chairmanship of Professor P. H. Karmel, Chairman of the Australian Universities Commission 'to enquire into the desirability and means of expanding opportunities in Australia for extra-mural degree courses at university standard and to make recommendations'. In so doing, the committee was to have regard to the aims and methods of the Open University. The committee was allowed to widen its scope to include the work done in colleges of advanced education and to look at efforts other than those of the United Kingdom model.

68. It is natural that such an inquiry should produce a range of reactions. In Australia, with its long-established pattern of external-degree work, it was to be expected that very strong views would be put forward, and this indeed occurred. But on one major issue there has been complete consensus of opinion. More extramural work is needed and all submissions to the committee appear to have stressed this. The issues arose as to ways and means, and since proposals were drafted for further discussion final decisions still remain to be taken at the time of writing. The main argument inevitably turns on whether the existing pattern will suffice for the further development needed or whether a new institution or institutions must be established for the task.

69. At the same time, the Australian trend is towards more 'openness' of admission and greater flexibility of options, courses and methods. Additionally, a number of minority groups such as social and welfare workers and handicapped persons have made their views and needs more public, and if there is to be quantitative expansion the traditionally rigid matriculation requirements will have to adjust to more open admissions. It has also been made clear that Australian tertiary institutions have been slow to adopt modern educational media compared with schools. The unusual geography of Australia has also to be considered as well as the technological limitations of the media services available.

70. Australia does not, therefore, present a situation where innovation and development can start *de novo*. Patterns of development are inevitably affected by recent history and in Australia this weakens any argument for inaugurating novel institutions. It is natural to build upon what already exists and the situation in the United Kingdom differs considerably from that in Australia. A major reason for the success of the Open University was that it was operating, as a public body, in virgin territory. No United Kingdom university taught for external degrees; only one, London, even examined. All British universities had high, competitive entrance requirements and all require attendance on campus for instruction. None of these situations prevails in Australia, and the creation of a new institution charged with special responsibility for open education in external degree work would inevitably have discouraged existing institutions in their present functions and deterred others from starting external work.

71. In the light of this, and numerous detailed arguments, it is not surprising that the Committee on Open University should have opted for the expansion of existing services, based on existing institutions but with more open admissions,

better technology in communication and more participating institutions. A new national institute of open tertiary education is proposed, to act as a stimulant to initiate collaboration and development with universities and colleges, to make awards on the basis of credits earned in more than one tertiary institution, to survey needs, to provide information and to encourage new programmes of study and ways of teaching. To do this, a network of courses would be developed from a selected number of existing and new institutions, and one new university, to be founded, would have special responsibility for providing open education. The main base would, however, continue to be those institutions which exist at present and no institution would be pressurized into undertaking external work if it did not wish to.

The situation in Australia therefore presents a challenge to the structure which has served it so well hitherto. Educational institutions are notoriously slow to change and new ideas often have to battle against vested interests and traditions. The pattern of external services which has proved so helpful to other countries will now itself have to undergo a change if it is to meet the new needs for more, and more open, extramural education in Australia.

VIII Postscript: final report of the Karmel Committee

72. The report of the case study was completed in late 1974, at which time the interim report of this committee had been recently published. The final report of the committee, *Open Tertiary Education in Australia*, was issued in December 1974. This postscript brings the position up to date.

73. The committee noted that several universities and colleges of advanced education were already offering off-campus courses and that there were many opportunities for part-time study. It concluded, however, that 'significant barriers to access to tertiary education still exist'. These constraints affected such matters as entry qualifications, the range of courses, modes of learning, transferability between institutions and student finance. Though these bore on groups deprived socially and economically at earlier stages of their education, the committee felt that a number of measures could be adopted which would lead to an expansion of tertiary studies by adults.

74. The main proposal was to establish a National Institute of Open Tertiary Education to encourage and facilitate wider access. Rejecting the United Kingdom model of a single institution with its own courses and teaching facilities as inappropriate to Australia, the committee felt that the new agency could work through existing institutions. It would promote the admission of students without the normal qualifications for entry; stimulate new courses to meet the needs of off-campus students; encourage the transfer of credits; and assist the introduction of new methods of teaching and learning. It did not consider the extensive use of broadcasting media desirable on educational grounds or feasible in practical terms in the Australian setting.

75. The main strategy proposed is the development of a network of off-campus opportunities. The committee nevertheless felt that one new university, at Albury–Wodonga, should be allocated resources to carry out 'a commitment to open education in the widest sense'. It also suggested that local study centres and special library facilities should be provided to meet the needs of off-campus students; and that existing universities and colleges of advanced education should be expected to extend their provision for students of this kind.

Appendix A Standardized reference data

Country, state or province *Australia*

Area and climate	2,967,909 square miles. Tropical through mediterranean to alpine.
Population	
Total (latest year)	13,131,600 (1973).
Estimated population aged 18	220,202 (1970).
Estimated percentage under 15	29.53.
Current annual growth rate (percentage)	1.9 (1965–72).
Government	
Main organizational structure	Delegation of major administrative responsibilities through federal system.
Political type	Parliamentary democracy: constitutional monarchy in British Commonwealth.
Economy	
Political type	Predominantly extensive agriculture. Some state control via legislation.
Gross national product	
Total (latest year)	$(A)40,984 million (1972–73) ($(A)1=U.S.$1.19).
Per head	$(A)3,121 (1972–73).
Average annual increase (percentage)	3.1.
Communications	
Ground/air	All-round efficient communication services, particularly through countrywide system of roads and air transport.
Mail/telephone	Good mail service; 34 telephones per 100 inhabitants (1972).

Broadcasting	
Main system(s) operating/ Principal authorities responsible	Australian Broadcasting Commission, independent but a public body responsible to parliament. Commercial services operate under licence from Ministry of Media.
Radio	
Transmission coverage of main programme services in percentage of population reached	100.
Receiving capability for main programme services (percentage)	85 (1973) (based on number of licences and average number of 4 persons per household).
Television	
Transmission coverage as defined for radio (percentage)	97.
Receiving capability for main programme services (percentage)	97 (1973) (based on number of licences and average number of 4 persons per household).
Monochrome or colour	Both; colour since 1 March 1975.
Education	
Type of system(s)	Predominantly publicly controlled and financed at state level.
Main authorities responsible and powers	
At school level	Federal government controls education in national and capital territories, and gives some financial aid to other states; 20 per cent of pupils in non-government schools, 80 per cent of these in Roman Catholic institutions.
At post-secondary level	State control plus very few grants from federal government, private or church institutions.
End of full-time school attendance	
Legal	Education is compulsory and free between 6 and 15 (16 in Tasmania).
De facto	10,000 children through disability or distance from regular schools learn by correspondence education.
Proportion of 18-year-old age group involved in education (percentage)	
Full-time	9 (17–22 age group) (1970).
Part-time	8.8 (17–22 age group) (1970).
Major developments in provision	
Over last five years	Emphasis on quantity not quality. Since 1973, trend towards incorporating other institutions, particularly teacher-training colleges, into colleges of advanced education.

Over next five years	The Committee on Open University (1974) proposal recognized universal demands for expansion of tertiary education, particularly for external students.

Institution/system under study

Brief for study and reason for inclusion	External distance studies at post-secondary level. Early development of external studies by correspondence at all levels contrasting with demands for expansion and change, backed by Australian belief in a basic minimum for everyone.
Description of subject studied	
Origins	1909 Act of Parliament which established provision for external study in charter of University of Queensland.
Educational authority(ies) and roles/Communications authority(ies) and roles	External study concentrated in four universities and one proposed institution: University of Queensland and Brisbane (UQ); University of New England at Armidale (UNE); Macquarie University at Sydney (MU); Western Australia Institute of Technology at Perth (WAIT). Two other universities broadcast courses by radio and television. Broadcasting authorities have no particular involvement with educational institutions or extension programmes.
Services provided	Upgrading of standard of teachers in state schools by in-service methods and over large areas to graduate level. Also upgrading of public servants.
Eligibility to study	
(a) categories	Adults, usually of mature age.
(b) qualifications	Relaxed entrance requirements for those over 21: 1974 experiment of small entry with no qualifications. Science teachers: MU 80 per cent. Teachers: UQ, 66 per cent; UNE, 72 per cent; WAIT, 40 per cent. Administrators and accountants: WAIT, 38 per cent.
Terminal qualifications	First degree B.A., B.Sc.; except WAIT—commercial diplomas.
Instructional means used	Mainly correspondence backed up by typed and taped lectures. Science kits, special notebooks, library facilities and audio-visual material—slides, loops, etc. Study groups attend vacation courses, optional at UQ and compulsory at MU and UNE.

Pedagogical effectiveness	High first-year drop-out rate at UNE (24 per cent first year), 12 per cent other years, older students stay better. Pass rate at WAIT 85–93 per cent (1969–72): 1 per cent higher than for internal students. At MU and WAIT 30–40 per cent first year drop-out.

Numbers involved

Students	
Enrolment	1973: UQ 3,302; UNE 3,508; MU 584; WAIT 729.
Academic staff	
Full-time/Part-time	As role of external and internal staff not separable, figures not available. At UNE and MU academic staff same as for internal students. At UQ members of external studies department do 78 per cent of external teaching. At WAIT 12 staff in department of external studies.
Other professional staff	
Number	At UQ 29 administrative personnel, 9 library personnel. External studies department at UNE purely administration and service personnel.

Finance

Recurrent expenditure	
By providing authorities (latest year)	Costs—much as for internal students—at MU extension studies not funded separately. UQ Department of External Studies: $(A)602,820 (1973).
Average annual outlay by student	At UQ no tuition fees. At MU no tuition fees.

Sources of further information

Education	Department of Adult Education, Australian Government Publications Service 1973, Canberra. Commonwealth Bureau of Census and Statistics, Canberra.
Broadcasting	Australian Broadcasting Commission, 145–149 Elizabeth Street, Sydney 2000. G.P.O. Box 487–2001.

Appendix B Short bibliography

COMMITTEE ON OPEN UNIVERSITY. *Open tertiary education*. Canberra, A.C.T., 1974. Report by the committee to the Australian Universities Commission.

DEPARTMENT OF EDUCATION. *Education in Australia*. Canberra, A.C.T., Australian Government Publishing Service, 1973.

PARTRIDGE, P. H. *Society, schools and progress in Australia*. Oxford, Pergamon Press, 1973.

SHEATH, H. *Report on external studies*. Armidale, N.S.W., University of New England, 1973. Available on request.

WATTS, F. *A.B.C's education department and its work*. Sydney, Australian Broadcasting Commission, 1974. (Mimeo.)

WHITELOCK, D. (ed.). *Adult education in Australia*. Oxford, Pergamon Press, 1970.

Appendix C Biographical note

Bernard Braithwaite was Chief Education Officer for East Sussex before becoming Director of Education in the Bahamas and later General Educational Specialist for the World Bank. He has been consultant to the World Bank, Economic Development Institute, Rothschild Foundation from 1971.

Dr Kevin Batt is on a two-year secondment to the Australian National University from the federal Department of Education. He is working as Research Fellow with Professor Donald Anderson on a study of regional colleges of advanced education.

Improving the skills of remote teachers—a project of the Memorial University of Newfoundland, **Canada**

George Grimmett

Contents

I The general background

1. The Province of Newfoundland, whilst claiming to be the oldest settled part of the New World, is the most recent to join the Canadian Federation (1949). Its economy has mainly developed round the fishing industry, hence the relatively small population (roughly half a million) is mostly settled in small seaports and 'outport' communities along the tortuous 6,000-mile coastline. Mountainous country makes internal communications difficult, and many of the outports are not served by any recognizable road at all. Indeed a tourist brochure currently boasts 'that this country . . . offers some of the world's most rugged, exciting terrain, over 140,000 square miles of essentially virgin territory, covered with thousands of lakes and streams and evergreen forests . . . accessible only by float plane . . .' etc.

2. The Avalon Peninsula juts out into the Atlantic from the eastern coast of the island of Newfoundland. The capital of St John's, at the north-east tip of this peninsula, has grown up around fishing and seafaring activities over a period of at least 600 years. Remains of Viking settlements in the neighbourhood date from over 1,000 years ago.

3. This pattern of settlement and development is very different from that of the rest of Canada and North America and has given the Newfoundlanders their own character and identity. Accents, for example, echo the soft brogues of southern Ireland and the west of England, as indeed do many of the place names.

4. Inland, forestry and logging settlements, and more recently paper and pulp mills, help to boost the economy, whilst significant iron ore and hydro-electric plants in Labrador have been and are being developed.

5. But in spite of this economic activity the *per capita* income is less than two-thirds of the Canadian average. Thus Newfoundland needs to derive roughly 60 per cent of its income from the federal government to enable it to maintain some kind of parity with national development.

6. The trans-Canada highway has given Newfoundland alone some 540 miles of good motorway from St John's in the east through to the ferry on the west that links with the mainland. A railway line follows this road and offers a limited passenger service. Air transport is probably the most significant communications development, and eight licensed airports permit a network of local services (backed by self-drive car hire). Two networks of radio and television retransmission stations aim to cover the settled areas. However the nature of the country is such that in many distant communities no television signals, or signals

of only fringe quality, can be received. Telephone services reach most of the significant communities through the activities of three commercial companies, and result in a distribution of approximately one telephone to every four people.

II The educational background

7. Education is the responsibility of the provincial government, although the federal government undertakes the retraining of adults and offers financial support (up to 50 per cent) for post-secondary education, and gives grants-in-aid for research personnel and university equipment.

8. The Newfoundland educational system, established in 1874, was denominational until 1966. At this date the main Protestant denomimations amalgamated, forming twenty-one local school boards. Other denominations (mainly the Roman Catholics) still continue to form their own school boards (twelve) to manage their own schools. The provincial Department of Education (a political minister has a professional educationist as his deputy) provides an inspection service; offers central specialist services ranging from audio-visual aids and broadcasting to curriculum development and a consultation service for all subject areas; pays teachers' salaries and arranges transportation (the school bus service) and is responsible for the overall planning and development of education, including vocational and adult education.

9. Schooling is compulsory between the ages of 6/7 and 15/16, with the more recently built schools making provision for kindergarten education from the age of 5. Thus two patterns of schooling tend to be emerging. In the first an elementary school (kindergarten and grades 1 to 6) caters for ages of 5 to 11 years, and is followed by a central high school (grades 7 to 11) covering ages from 12 to 16 years. In the second, an elementary school caters for ages of roughly 5 to 13 years (kindergarten and grades 1 to 8) with a regional high school continuing education up to the age of roughly 16 (grades 9 to 11). There are also some junior high schools and a number of all-grade schools.

10. Vocational training is not offered in secondary schools, but there are 14 district vocational schools in the province offering 46 separate subjects ranging from aircraft maintenance and beauty culture to weaving, welding and wood-scaling.

11. At the tertiary level, the Memorial University of Newfoundland, at St John's, provides bachelor-degree courses in arts, science, commercial and business administration, education and applied sciences. Certificate courses are offered in public administration and banking.

12. At other institutions, non-university courses are offered in trade and technology subjects such as fishing, navigation, marine engineering, electronic engineering and hospital services.

13. However, probably the most significant recent educational activity has been in developments in the secondary sector. These have included the gradual disappearance of the 'one-class school' (over a period of seven years no less than 372 of these school houses, against a current total of 755 schools of all grades, have been closed down and replaced by 1,639 classrooms in other schools). This has been accompanied by a professional upgrading of the teaching force. The more highly qualified teachers are certificated (in grades 1 to 7 according to academic qualification). Others are licensed if they have no academic qualifica-

tion. Between 1966 and 1973, the ratio of certificated to licensed teachers has increased from 3.3 per cent to 58 per cent. Teachers with four or more years of academic training thus now constitute about 50 per cent of the teaching force (compared with 70 per cent as a Canadian national average and 10 per cent in Newfoundland a decade ago). This has been accompanied by a lowering of the proportion of teachers with less than one year's training to under 3 per cent (compared with a 1 per cent Canadian national average and 40 per cent a decade ago).

The total teaching force currently numbers just under 7,000 for about 162,000 pupils of all grades. This, incidentally, compares with a total teaching force of approximately 6,000 five years ago for a similar number of pupils. The upgrading of qualifications is accompanied, of course, by an increase in salary and it is relevant to note that over the last ten years the average annual salary of Newfoundland teachers has more than doubled, from a median of $3,000 p.a. in 1962 to over $8,000 p.a. in 1972.

14. This rationalization of educational method has not, however, been achieved without overcoming many and varied problems. For example, considerable extra provision has had to be made to transport children to and from schools, and the 1972/73 annual report from the Department of Education shows that 839 buses transported 63,792 students 21,450 total miles daily at an annual cost exceeding $6 million.

The use of educational media

15. Throughout the province emphasis has been placed on the wider use of educational media and technology to overcome the shortage of basic library facilities in many schools. Films, filmstrips, projectors, tape recorders and audio-tapes have been made available through the assistant director of instructional materials in the Department of Education. Broadcast radio and television programmes from the national network, but with some inputs of locally produced programmes, are the basic responsibility of the Canadian Broadcasting Corporation (CBC). Local television production facilities are not, however, available to the Department of Education. The department has its own radio studio capable of broadcast-quality production, on a limited scale, which can be fed into the CBC network. Every effort is being made to increase the effectiveness of the radio programming by producing supporting visuals such as slides, filmstrips and overhead projector transparencies to accompany the school broadcasts.

16. Audio-visual services, generally, have expanded steadily over the years and plans are now evolving, in conjunction with local school boards, for more effective distribution systems and for establishing resource centres for districts. The single central film-library/resources facility which has, so far, served the educational system can no longer cope with the volume of demands made upon it by schools. It is reported that regular use is now being made of the department's audio-visual services by over 500 schools.

17. Short 'media usage' workshops for practising teachers have been held in co-operation with the Centre for Audio-Visual Education at the Memorial University of Newfoundland.

18. Newfoundland is developing libraries as community centres providing information and resources as well as reference materials. Film collections, with

audio cassettes and records, are increasingly appearing in many of these libraries (*per capita* expenditure on public library services is approximately $2.25 p.a.). Two 'bookmobiles' are in operation as an experiment for areas lacking established library services. The library development plan envisages the division of the province into five regions with one bookmobile for each region.

III The Memorial University of Newfoundland, Department of Summer Sessions and Extra-Mural Studies

19. The Memorial University was created to serve the needs of all the peoples of Newfoundland and Labrador. However, its geographical location, combined with transportation/communication difficulties, have tended to restrict its part-time (extramural or 'off-campus') activities to people living in the proximity of its campus.

20. The Department of Summer Sessions and Extra-Mural Studies is responsible for: (a) off-campus credit courses; (b) summer sessions; (c) on-campus evening credit courses.

21. This report is concerned with the first of these activities by which, in 26 centres scattered throughout the province, the opportunity of full university credit courses is offered to the vast majority of people. Even then, there are certain areas where, because of scattered populations, it is not feasible to establish centres (the Labrador Coast, the South Coast and certain areas of the Northern Peninsula). For these people, the university is now considering placing courses on audio-tape and offering sophisticated correspondence courses. Its optimism and confidence are based on experience gained with 'mediated' off-campus credit courses developed since 1969, and it is the result of this experience which is condensed in the following paragraphs.

IV Development of 'off-campus' courses

22. In 1969, the university, through its Department of Summer Sessions and Extra-Mural Studies, decided to offer full university credit courses to remote students through a special programme of activities. This called for collaboration from many departments as well as the creation of a new infrastructure of administrative support. Careful initial planning, together with constant on-going refinement of techniques and methods, has led to the evolution of a system based on the concept of a centrally prepared multi-media package to support a tutorial role played by an inexperienced and possibly underqualified 'volunteer' at a remote outport. The printed word, personal interaction and educational television all play mutually supporting roles.

23. The main need for this type of assistance was in the teaching profession, where a very large number of teachers, in the remote schools particularly, were underqualified by Canadian standards. Practising teachers and many other individuals can now, through part-time study, acquire university credits equivalent to those obtained by the full-time students attending the university.

24. Essentially, the administrative design and overall responsibility rests with the Department of Summer Sessions and Extra-Mural Studies within the university; the academic content comes from faculty members in the various

specialized departments of the university and the supporting educational-television component is produced by the ETV Centre of the university. Each of these can only treat the off-campus involvement as a part, although a significant one, of its total responsibility within the university. Their respective roles are described more fully later in this study.

The first four years of operation

25. During 1969/70, the first year of the operation of the new service, university courses were offered at 12 centres with a total enrolment of approximately 600 students for a total of 963 courses. Of these, some 200 took the psychology course offered through educational television, with the remainder registered in 31 other courses, which were taught by locally recruited instructors.

26. The choice of 'The Psychology of Learning' for this first experiment was determined by the following considerations:

(a) It was known that most off-campus students would be teachers; thus a course particularly useful to teachers would ensure maximum enrolment and maximum benefit.

(b) Many off-campus courses in remote centres had run into difficulties through deficiencies in library requirements or in laboratory facilities. The psychology course, although a third-year course, was relatively self-contained and not bound by prerequisites that could not be obtained off the parent campus.

(c) The instructor (i.e. the university faculty member responsible for the academic content of the course) had already had experience with television in psychology courses on campus, and thus did not enter the project untried.

(d) The necessary texts for the course were few and well conceived. The main text was partially programmed with the techniques the course itself promoted, and the minimum library requirements were compiled into a book of readings.

(e) Granted that this project was an experiment, it was considered that most of the experience gained through the application of this particular course would be valid on expansion of the project.

27. In the next academic year (1970/71) the number of off-campus centres was increased to 19 and 3,180 students were registered for the 27 available courses, 4 of which were offered via educational television with the rest being taught by local instructors.

28. In 1971 the number of centres was increased to 20 with 3 courses offered by educational television and 14 by local instructors. Later in the 1971/72 academic year an additional 7 centres were added, bringing the total to 27 with 8 courses offered by educational television and 39 by local instructors. By this time the total student course enrolment was 4,651.

29. In the 1972/73 academic year the location of some of the centres was changed as it was felt that this would be beneficial to the users, and one extra centre was added. This, it was felt, gave an adequate network to cover the present requirements of the province and it is not envisaged that this will be increased significantly in the foreseeable future. Fifty-six live courses and 6 educational-television courses satisfied a student course enrolment of 4,829.

In retrospect

30. Looking back over this four-year period of development it is interesting to note that whilst the number of 'live' courses offered (139) is greater than the number of educational-television courses (19), the number of students benefiting from educational television (total 6,581) is comparable with, and indeed has in some years exceeded, the number benefiting from live courses (total 7,042). This, of course, arises from the fact that each 'live' course can be given only in one centre whilst the educational-television courses have been offered in roughly half the centres in operation at any particular time.

31. At this stage two expressions need to be clarified: (a) 'Educational television', in the context of the Memorial University Off-Campus Course, refers to an important component of the media package which has been prepared by the ETV Centre staff using the academic advice of the faculty member responsible for the course. This may frequently be no more than a recording on video-tape of a carefully presented academic lecture, which the student may play back at the study centre. In fact the full range of skills of the production centre staff combines to yield a very effective communication of the academic message. (b) 'Local instructor' is a term used to describe the academic who delivers a course in a remote study centre. He is completely responsible for the entire study experiences of his students. He may or may not use material which has been centrally prepared. However, when a student elects to take one of the ETV courses he will not have a local instructor, but a tutor. The difference between their two roles may seem slight but it is nevertheless significant. Whilst every effort is made to find a tutor with high academic qualifications in the particular field, it is recognized that this is not quite so demanding as in the case of a 'local instructor'.

User profile

32. The types of people taking off-campus courses have changed as the scheme has developed. At first almost all the students were teachers seeking to upgrade their qualifications. The salary scale applicable to the teaching profession encourages teachers to acquire better academic qualifications, by generous salary increments. Also, more qualified graduates were applying for teaching posts and the security and promotion prospects of unqualified teachers were diminishing. However, in a recent and typical enrolment the occupations of welfare officer, businessman, Royal Canadian Mounted Police officer, tradesman, sales clerk, bank teller and clergyman accounted for about 86 per cent of the students. Some of the students register for courses after they have completed their high-school education, and whilst they are trying to decide whether they are suited for university.

The evolution of the educational-television component

33. There is a deep-rooted feeling in the faculty of the Memorial University that personal contact is necessary between students and staff. During the planning of the new off-campus courses it was realized that Memorial University had a great potential asset in the largest and most sophisticated university

educational-television centre east of Montreal. Fully equipped to broadcast standards, the ETV Centre had been producing programmes for broadcast and closed-circuit use since 1967.

34. Such media developments within a university were unusual at that time. However an active extension service had pioneered the way at least five years before the ETV Centre was established and it was this experience that gave the initial impetus to the development.

35. These origins ensured that the technical and production staff of the university ETV Centre had a background of experience in broadcast television (this, moreover, has created its own problems over the years since university salaries, generally, have not kept pace with broadcasting organization salaries and skilled staff are liable to be poached from the university). The director, who ranks as a departmental head within the university hierarchy, has a background of experience in commercial broadcasting and university television. He has also other qualities relevant to his present role: he is a musician, an artist and an experienced photographer. These are important in enabling him to lead the team and earn the respect of academic colleagues.

The use of video-tapes

36. To broadcast educational-television lectures to distant students imposed immediate unacceptable limitations as the broadcasting services did not cover the entire population, particularly in the more remote areas. Added to this the signals were often of only fringe quality. These considerations, coupled with the obvious advantages of group viewing, particularly with a tutor present, led to the decision to use video-tapes. Six centres were chosen for the experiment, all in remote areas and separated by enormous geographic distances, but with suitable physical facilities and personnel able to operate a 1-inch video-tape recorder.

37. These 'operators' played an important part in the project. Their functions were stated to be to operate and maintain the video-tape equipment, to check attendances, to distribute materials and reference books for the course, and to collect assignments and forward them to the university. The operators, and later the tutors, were recruited by the local co-ordinators and liaison officers (see 'Administrative Structure' below) and were given short training courses by the staff of the university. Experience led to the operators being replaced by tutors, who basically undertook the same function, but in addition were academically qualified and had a direct responsibility for the groups' tuition. It is considered that this has been a major factor in upgrading the quality of the educational-television courses. It is also, possibly, relevant to record the strong impression that the spirit of service to the community, amongst all working in this project, and particularly amongst the part-time staff, is exceptionally high (and appears to be a far more important motivating factor than the honoraria paid for services).

38. Each of the chosen centres served a population large enough to make the experiment valid and economic. The first course chosen for educational-television treatment was educational psychology. Within the university, a faculty member designed a course which included a series of lectures which he gave in a television studio and which were recorded on video-tape. There were 33 separate presentations, each lasting approximately half an hour and followed by a

number of questions which the viewers had to answer. Separate copies of each video-tape were produced and distributed to each of the six centres. Print material was also produced (described below under 'Course Materials').

39. The subsequent growth in the number of centres to 27 and the increase in the number of educational-television courses has necessitated the development of a video replication facility in the university and the investment of approximately $240,000 in video-tape.

Experiments with conference telephones

40. Each centre was equipped with a conference telephone and on alternate weeks the remote groups would be connected to the faculty member in the university in St John's responsible for the course. The telephone element of this experiment was a failure. It failed in a technical sense since although each centre was equipped with conference telephones and loudspeakers (rented through commercial telephone companies) the telephone companies were unable to make the system function to specification. For example, while in most attempts each class could hear the control instructor it was never possible to ensure that the centres could hear each other. This led to failure from an educational point of view since the tensions caused by these uncertainties inhibited the students in the use of the equipment, well beyond the level which could normally be expected because of shyness. Although the initial experiment called for six centres to be connected to the university simultaneously only three were actually involved in the experiment at a time. But even with three centres competing simultaneously for attention, it proved impossible to have useful discussions over thousands of miles of telephone line.

41. The objective of this experiment was to see if discussion could be generated between the instructors and students in different centres. In practice the telephone calls degenerated to questions for the instructor to clarify as 'the authority' and this, it was felt, could be more effectively and economically handled by other techniques.

Experiments with two-way flow of audio cassettes

42. The following year the telephone conference technique was discontinued. In its place audio cassette recorders were issued to each centre. After each educational-television lecture, question tapes were prepared by the students and sent by post back to the university. The course instructors then tape-recorded answers and mailed them back to the centres. However, a careful evaluation of this technique showed that it was not producing the desired result, particularly since the time lapse between the question being asked and recorded and the answer being received, after the tape had travelled by road and air to the university and back to the centre, was regarded as unacceptable by the vast majority of students.

The evolution of the local 'tutor'

43. The latest development is to recruit a 'tutor' who watches each educational-television programme with the class. He leads the discussion afterwards and is responsible for noting any points of difficulty and obtaining

an explanation from the course instructor in the Memorial University in time for the students' next meeting. This he may do by a normal telephone call.

44. The tutor acts as a quasi-teacher performing normal classroom duties. His main function may be described as a 'stand-in' for the educational-television instructor who has composed the course back at the university. The tutor must have a basic degree with some depth of knowledge in the subject area of the course. Where possible the university tries to obtain an individual with a master's degree in the subject area, although there are a number of occasions when an individual with a bachelor's degree, including courses in the subject area, has proved acceptable. The availability of such a person living in reasonable proximity to any study centre is a critical factor in deciding whether or not that centre can offer a specific educational-television course. An individual with the required academic background, and willingness to serve, is identified by the local co-ordinator and appointed by the university liaison officer, who also arranges such in-service training as is appropriate in technical and administrative procedures.

Administrative structure

Headquarters staff

45. In the Department of Summer Sessions and Extra-Mural Studies, the following staff are involved in the off-campus courses as well as their other duties: the director, who is responsible to the vice-president of the university for the overall success of the operation; an assistant director; a secretary; a stenographer and two clerks. In the ETV Centre the director is aided by the assistant director who is a producer and has also carried out a major research survey concerning attitudes towards the off-campus courses. Three other producers assist in turning out a total of about 200 hours of educational-television programmes per year for all faculties of the university, including the off-campus courses. There are also 7 technicians, 4 photographers and 3 graphic artists. A dozen students work on studio-crew duties on a part-time basis. The educational-television unit organizes workshop sessions for interested faculty members and trains each local co-ordinator in the operation and maintenance of his video-tape recorder.

University liaison officers

46. In the academic year 1971/72 the services of 4 permanent employees called University Liaison Officers were obtained. These were stationed in strategic outposts and were responsible for a number of centres in which they organized and administered courses, distributed all materials such as course books, reference books, video- and audio-tapes and kept stand-by video-tape recorders, in case of breakdowns. They also compile payrolls, recruit tutors and off-campus instructors, and survey their area to ascertain the demand for courses and act as student advisers. They are responsible for providing information about university matters to schools within their areas, and generally act as the university's agent.

Part-time co-ordinators

47. In each centre there is a part-time co-ordinator responsible for direct administration. Where centres have 100 or more students there is also an assistant co-ordinator. The co-ordinator needs a forceful, dynamic personality with a strong interest in educational matters and above all the respect of the local people. He registers students, makes up class timetables, arranges a system of lending reference books, etc.

The local tutor

48. One of the important elements in the success of the system is the selection of a local tutor, who assumes responsibility with a group of students in a particular centre for a particular course. Indeed, before a particular course is offered in any centre it is essential that such a tutor can be identified and the availability of tutors of this calibre has often dictated the type of course which a centre is able to offer. In the identification of such a suitable local personality the co-ordinator plays a leading role.

Working method

49. The initiative for the production of educational-television courses originates with the Division of Extra-Mural Studies and may follow one of several procedures. There may, for example, be a demand for a particular course from educationists in the field (district superintendents, supervisors, principals, as well as teachers, may often focus the need for a course).

50. A provincial Department of Education sometimes needs to help teachers with particular difficulties (for example, the education of exceptional children) and the Extra-Mural Division has responded to this approach. The changing pattern of educational practice requires teachers to be brought up to date with certain conceptual skills and a specific course is being developed to meet the need.

51. Finally, there is the broad band of elective courses that students can take at all levels to satisfy their own interests and to contribute towards the credits they require for a degree.

52. Once this type of decision is made relating to the subject area, the next step is to contact the head of the academic department concerned to obtain his agreement as to the necessity for such a course, and his help in choosing a suitable faculty member who has the time, ability and inclination to write and produce an educational-television course.

53. When this individual has been identified and has consented to produce a particular course, he meets with the director of the Educational Television Unit and the director of the Extra-Mural Studies Department to discuss responsibilities and working relationships. It is particularly important that the faculty member should understand the immense amount of work involved in undertaking this project—not just in writing scripts and preparing the course manual but in preparing and recording the lectures on video-tape and in the administration and support of the course once it is going out. The remuneration for this type of work is generous as a matter of policy, since it is felt that this is

more likely to encourage the most able people to come forward and offer their services. University tutors are allowed release time from their faculty duties for one semester to prepare a course; or, alternatively, $1,000. A fee of $400 is paid to a tutor who undertakes the production of course materials including the educational-television component. For subsequent supervision of the students' work an additional fee is payable which ranges from $500 (up to 100 students) to $1,200 (where there are over 401 students). Should it be necessary at a subsequent date to update a tape, a further fee of $50 is payable for each tape. In addition 'residuals' are payable for the third and fourth semester ($400 per semester) and for the fifth and sixth semester ($200 per semester). When agreement has been reached all round, the ETV Centre allocates a producer-director to work with the instructor and work begins on the development of course scripts and the production of video-tapes. Other specialists are employed as required.

Course materials

54. The course manual generally outlines the course structure and then gives a synopsis of each of the video-tapes and the main teaching points contained in each tape. For each video-taped lecture a selected reading list is given together with diagrams relating to the visual presentations in the educational-television lectures. Series of practical exercises are included for the student to work on at home. In courses requiring laboratory work the manual includes an additional laboratory section.

55. In addition to the manual there may be a book of readings including articles from well-known journals in the subject area. This may involve additional expenses in hiring a research graduate and in obtaining permission to use copyright articles. The book of readings is then published by the university with a foreword by the instructor and offered for sale to students as an extra textbook. It is interesting to note that there is a brisk sale of these books among the students taking 'on-campus' lecture courses as well. The instructor may prefer to prescribe a textbook as background material for his course of lectures. These are purchased in bulk and shipped together with the other materials out to each centre and sold by the co-ordinator to the students at the same price as would be paid to the university.

56. The course designers are concerned by the scarcity of reference material available at the centres. It is clearly impossible to duplicate the university library's holdings in each of the centres, but a compromise has been effected by the production of a library box of relevant reference material which can be shipped out to the co-ordinator at each centre. The off-campus students also have the same right as their on-campus counterparts to borrow materials from the main university libraries, although they must, of course, plan well ahead.

57. About a year is required to produce, assemble and prepare all the elements of an off-campus course. Whilst no budgetary restrictions are imposed upon any particular programme series, the unit has developed a series of effective audio and visual communications at low cost.

58. Thus the 'talking head' is often used, but in conjunction with relevant models, specimens, diagrams and charts or photographs, and very occasionally cine film. The emphasis is always to ensure that the student hears clearly and

sees clearly whatever is relevant to the instructor's teaching point at that particular time. The enthusiasm and professional ability of the university instructors come across well, with the result that interesting programmes are made which, as far as could be judged (the investigator spent considerable time viewing samples of programmes chosen at random and visited study centres to meet and observe students), were regarded by the students as interesting and valuable contributions to their studies.

Utilization

59. In the early days, a student from each class of the off-campus credit courses was paid a nominal fee to operate the television equipment. However, it was felt necessary to have someone in charge of the class to organize discussion groups and to be able to answer questions arising from the television lectures (the local tutor). Where possible an attempt is made to obtain an individual with a master's degree in the subject area although there have been occasions when an individual with a bachelor's degree has been successful. It is assumed that students will attend the centre two nights a week for a period of 75 minutes, during which the educational-television tape will be played for about 30 minutes; the remainder of the time will be devoted to answering questions, conducting classroom discussions, conducting laboratory sessions if required and noting any particular points of difficulty which the students have experienced. The tutor is able to phone the educational television instructor on the main university campus with problems or questions which must have an immediate answer. Thus the tutor not only provides an invaluable service for the students, but is also a means of feeding back information from the study groups to the university.

60. Administrative machinery ensures that supplies of all necessary materials are delivered to the centres in time by road and air, through the offices of the university liaison officers and the centre co-ordinators, and that an adequate staff exists to see that all logistical requirements are met. The educational-television service technicians visit each centre during the summer period and service all the educational-television equipment. This preventive maintenance has paid off well and in four years of operation very few problems have arisen which can be attributed to technical breakdowns. Nevertheless, stand-by equipment is located at strategic points and, should a fault occur, replacement equipment can be installed with very little interruption to the learning process whilst the defective equipment is taken away for repair. It has been found adequate simply to issue one stand-by video-tape recorder to each liaison officer.

Evaluation

61. Apart from the routine feedback obtained from the tutors working with each study group and the usual type of 'evaluation' through the examination system, two separate evaluative exercises have been conducted on aspects of two of the educational-television courses. The first looked in particular at the academic results and attitude ratings of the off-campus television course in

psychology offered in 1969/70: 177 students in six separate locations off-campus compared with 124 students in daytime courses on-campus and 78 students at night-time courses on-campus. It became clear from this that the degree of motivation was higher in the part-time students than in the full-time students, and that the former were, by and large, older and more mature. In all cases the drop-out rate was extremely low (5 per cent or less) and in the final marks there appeared to be no significant difference between the performance of the various groups. Attitudes to various components of the course were examined carefully. The report finished with the following conclusion: 'It is felt that on grounds of both academic results and attitude ratings the "Off-Campus" television course was amply justified . . . and there is every reason for supporting and predicting an increasing offering of "Off-Campus" ETV courses in subsequent years.'

62. The second survey, conducted in 1973, surveyed attitudes towards a geography course taken by off-campus students. This is a careful and detailed piece of research which examines various components of the course in depth.

V Adaptability

63. This is a delivery system for academic courses which is particularly well suited to the requirements of tertiary education. The production techniques can meet a wide range of educational and instructional situations. These two aspects are, clearly, capable of adaptation to meet the needs of other parts of the Commonwealth where problems arising through isolated distant communities and educational need have to be met with limited resources. However, the strength of the Memorial University system appears to lie in the way in which each course package has been specifically designed to meet identified local needs, particularly in terms of the relevance of the academic content. Growing support from extramural students shows the value of this careful preparation.

VI Economic considerations

64. An outline has been given of the manpower requirements. It is impossible to quantify these meaningfully in cash terms but it is important to emphasize the high degree of professionalism manifest in all aspects of this operation. Again, an attempt to quantify capital costs is unlikely to be useful. The electronic system was installed many years ago and anyone designing such a system nowadays would undoubtedly use newer and possibly smaller and cheaper equipment.

65. This system is effective, economical and provides an important social service to people who could easily feel isolated and neglected.

66. The immediate benefit is enjoyed at 28 remote centres where about 3,000 adults (out of a total population of just over 500,000) are, each year, able to enjoy the opportunities that further university study offers. Again, this cannot be quantified in cash terms, yet few would doubt that Newfoundland and her people will derive great benefit from this activity.

67. Costs will need to be examined carefully in any attempt to reproduce elements of this system elsewhere, particularly if there is a possibility of distributing the signals satisfactorily by means other than the physical distribution of

video-tapes. Newfoundland, with 28 centres, has possibly reached the optimum level of development of the present system. In a larger operation, economies might be effected by micro-wave or even satellite distribution; even then the small video-tape recorder at the classroom end will remain critically important.

VII Future plans

68. There will be a growing requirement for the in-service training of teachers on a continuing basis, perhaps to introduce a new approach to the teaching of a particular subject, perhaps to produce specialized materials for groups of teachers in workshop sessions and short seminars in remote parts of the province, perhaps to offer second-degree courses. The pioneering work of the Memorial University in Newfoundland has shown that educational television has a tremendous potential to assist in solving these problems effectively and efficiently.

Appendix A Standardized reference data

Country, state or province	*Canada (the Province of Newfoundland)*
Area and climate	Newfoundland: 41,164 square miles. Labrador: 101,881 square miles. Total: 143,045 square miles.
Population	
Total (latest year)	522,104 (1972).
Estimated population aged 18	13,000 (1972).
Estimated percentage under 15	34.8 (1972).
Current annual growth rate (percentage)	1.5 (Canada).
Government	
Main organizational structure	Autonomous province under control of Federation of Canada; elected state legislative.
Political type	Democratic state organization.
Economy	
Political type	Predominantly agricultural: mainly fishing, hunting, forestry. No federal or provincial controls.
Gross national product	
Total (latest year)	\$(C)1,523 million (1972) (\$(C)1 = U.S.\$ 1.004).
Per head	\$(C)1,523 (current costs); \$(C)1,079 (at 1961 constant costs).
Average annual increase (percentage)	3.2 (Canada).
Communications	
Ground/air	All-round efficient communications services, particularly through air transport.
Mail/telephone	Mail regular and reliable except to remote outposts in adverse weather. Telephone: 27.5 per 100 population (1 in 4).

Broadcasting	
Main system(s) operating	A.M., F.M.; television.
Principal authorities responsible	Canadian Broadcasting Corporation (CBC), a public body operating on a national scale. Canadian Television Network (CTV), a private body, the counterpart of CBC.
Radio	
Transmission coverage of main programme services with percentage of population reached	In Canada as a whole 300 private radio and television stations; 97.3 per cent (1972).
Receiving capability for main programme services (percentage)	100 (1972).
Television	
Transmission coverage as defined for radio (percentage)	93.4 (1972). Poor in remote mountainous areas.
Monochrome or colour	Colour but local educational-television production through university in monochrome.
Education	
Type of system(s)	Predominantly publicly controlled and financed, althoughr eligious schools are independent of both federal and provincial control.
Main authorities responsible and powers	
At school level	Provincial government, Department of Education.
At post-secondary level	As at school level but federal government undertakes retraining of adults and gives support (50 per cent of costs) for post-secondary education and informal education.
End of full-time school attendance	
Legal	Education is compulsory between the ages of 6/7 and 15/16.
De facto	As above.
Proportion of 18-year-old age group involved in education (percentage)	
Full-time Part-time	} 10 (approx.).
Major developments in provision	
Over last five years Over next five years	{ Teacher upgrading and provision of more resources. Reduction in number of 'One-class' schools.

Institution/system under study	*Memorial University, St John's, Newfoundland*
Brief for study and reason for inclusion	Off-campus university credit courses; evening credit courses. 1. Upgrading of teaching forces. 2. Spread of ideas concerning new technology. 3. Off-campus function for an on-campus educational-television system. 4. Low drop-out rate. 5. Apparently high transference capacity. The provision of full university degrees.
Description of subject studied	
Origins/Educational authority(ies) and roles	Natural development of extramural studies programme through initiative of individuals within the Memorial University.
Communications authority(ies) and roles	Some courses broadcast on national networks, others in remote areas are relayed by video-tape.
Services provided	Satisfying personal aspirations of practising unqualified teachers in line with government policy for increasing quality of education.
Eligibility to study	
(a) categories	All adults.
(b) qualifications	High School Diploma (Grade 11 Completion) waived for mature students.
Terminal qualifications	First degree (ordinary) 40 courses; (honours) 45 courses; B.Ed. 12 courses additional to first degree.
Instructional means used	Multi-media course notes, extra reading material and video-taped lectures/demonstrations. Tutor in study centre.
Personal input from student	Two nights per week for 45 minutes at study centre for 25 weeks per credit course and home study.
Normal duration of study	Up to four years for full degree, but at present, main requirement is for additional courses to upgrade qualifications.
Pedagogic effectiveness	High; drop-out 5 per cent or less.
Numbers involved	
Students	
Intake (latest year)	4,829 (1972–73).
Graduating (percentage)	75.
Academic staff	
Full-time/Part-time	Course tutor for each course unit, plus tutor or instructor for each group of students at study centre, plus co-ordinator for each of 27 study centres.

Other professional staff	
Number	Five administrators; four liaison officers, local part-time co-ordinators. Educational-television production unit.
Finance	
Recurrent expenditure	
By providing authorities (latest year)	Extramural studies and summer schools: $(C)360,000 p.a. (not a true indication as educational-television and academic staff have other duties).
Average annual outlay by student	$(C)50 per course.
Non-recurrent expenditure	
Gross, over first five years of new institution	Meaningless to quantify since high degree of experimentation with technological equipment, some of which was initially purchased for other purposes.
Special assistance received	
Non-financial	Enthusiasm of population in isolated communities.

Sources of further information

Educational	Director of Summer Sessions and Extra-Mural Studies, Memorial University of Newfoundland, St John's, Newfoundland, Canada.
Broadcasting	Director of Educational Television, Educational Television Centre, Memorial University of Newfoundland, St John's, Newfoundland. Education, Information and Research Department, The British Council, Tavistock House, London WC1 H94.

Appendix B **Short bibliography**

DEPARTMENT OF EDUCATION, GOVERNMENT OF NEWFOUNDLAND AND LABRADOR. *Annual report*. (For current year.)

DEPARTMENT OF SUMMER SESSIONS AND EXTRA-MURAL STUDIES, UNIVERSITY OF ST JOHN'S. (Director's) *Report*. (For current year.)

MCNAMARA, W. CRAIG. *A study of off-campus TV courses in geography and attitudes towards this course*. Newfoundland, Memorial University of St John's.

MOORE, D. L. *Psychology 341—off campus ETV project*. Newfoundland, Memorial University of St John's, 1969.
STARCHER, DUANE B. *Educational television in remote locations—what to do outside the wired city*. Newfoundland, Memorial University of St John's.

Appendix C Biographical note

George Grimmett was Deputy Director of Education, Information and Research for the Centre for Educational Development Overseas before the centre became part of the British Council. He is now involved in educational technology work for the Education, Information and Research Department for the British Council.

University distance learning centres in eastern **France**

Kenneth Fawdry

Contents

I Distance learning at post-secondary level in France

1. The distance learning centres to which this study relates are spread over a wide area of eastern France: they are located at the universities of Dijon, Nancy II,[1] Strasbourg II,[1] Besançon and Reims. Associated with them, in that they enlist students without originating courses, are the new University of Metz and the University Centre of Mulhouse. These seven institutions are grouped together for the purposes of distance learning in an association (l'Entente Universitaire de l'Est) which involves a sharing-out of tasks and an agreement on the validation of diplomas, but which has as yet no statutory framework. One of the centre's directors acts as general secretary to the Entente as a whole.

2. There are in France some fifteen other centres providing distance learning at post-secondary level. Most of these are associated with conventional universities: several of them can show examples of inter-university co-operation in catering for distance learning students, but only those in the Entente de l'Est can claim a solid record of joint activity, extending over several years, for this purpose. An important exception to the university-based norm is the organization known as Télécnam, an offshoot of the Conservatoire National des Arts et Métiers, which caters for students of technology and (unlike most of the others) provides its broadcast instruction on television and on a national as opposed to a local basis.

3. The activities of all these centres are kept under review and are funded by a department[2] of the national Ministry of Education. In particular this department has to approve arrangements with RTF,[3] the national broadcasting organization, for the broadcasting facilities which the centres require, and to meet the bills for these services.

4. Otherwise, each centre remains part and parcel of its parent university.

1. In 1968 universities containing substantially more than 10,000 students were split up. This applied to the universities of Nancy and Strasbourg.
2. This department is known as DISUP 8 de la Direction chargée des Universités et des Établissements d'Enseignement Supérieur et de Recherche.
3. The ORTF (Office de Radiodiffusion-Télévision Française) ceased to exist as such on 1 January 75, its functions being split between six separate associations. Since, however, the State's monopoly of broadcasting services remains unimpaired and the precise relationship between these six associations is not fully worked out, the term RTF (Radiodiffusion et Télévision Françaises) will for convenience be used in this report to signify French national broadcasting as a whole, or any part of it.

Main purposes

5. The primary purpose of the distance learning centres (Centres de Télé-enseignement Universitaire—CTUs) is to extend opportunities for study at university level and for acquiring university diplomas and bachelor degrees to those unable to attend as full-time students. They will be for the most part people already in paid employment, but will include also housewives and those incapacitated by illness.

6. An important secondary purpose is to contribute to *éducation permanente* by providing courses which will help people in their chosen careers without involving them in university examinations, or which will simply enhance their general culture.

II Courses provided by the university distance learning centres (CTUs) of eastern France

Courses leading to university awards

7. All the courses provided by the centres of the Entente de l'Est lie within the field of the humanities (*lettres*). Each of the five providing centres specializes in a particular discipline: Dijon in *lettres modernes* (but this includes an element of Latin!); Nancy in English; Strasbourg in German; Besançon in history; and Reims in philosophy. These allocations were agreed between the members of the Entente as fields in which each was felt to have a distinctive strength.

8. An aspiring CTU student is required first to enrol as a member of his local university. Thereafter, however, the CTU providing the discipline of his choice undertakes entire responsibility for him. Thus, should he live in or near Besançon but wish to study for a diploma or bachelor degree (*licence*) in English, he will enrol as a member of Besançon University, then apply to CTU Nancy for registration as a distance learning student; and his work will be supervized by CTU Nancy. If he is successful in his examinations he will be awarded the relevant diploma or degree of Besançon University; this qualification will be indistinguishable from that obtainable by a normal full-time student there who has followed a conventional course.

9. All five centres offer courses leading, after a minimum of two years, to the DEUG (*diplôme d'études universitaires générales*)[1] and after a minimum of three years to the *licence* (bachelor degree). In addition, the Dijon and Reims CTUs prepare students for the *maîtrise* (master's degree) in *lettres modernes* and philosophy respectively.

10. Each course provided by the CTUs gives scope for a certain number of options, though not quite as many as are available to conventional university students.

1. This is a rather more broadly based diploma than the DUEL (*diplôme universitaire d'études littéraires*), which it is in process of replacing.

Courses serving other purposes

11. Besides preparing students for university diplomas and degrees, individual centres have enlarged the range of their activities in various ways. This is particularly true of Nancy and Strasbourg, which are both concerned with modern-language teaching and therefore offer a product which has a direct and manifest usefulness to a wide range of students.

12. Thus, for the benefit of students wishing to further their '*formation permanente*' in English rather than simply to achieve a university qualification, Nancy has developed a technology of learning and a whole range of new materials designed to assist the autodidact, with the emphasis on improving comprehension of the written and spoken langage. In addition, it includes in its broadcast provision a series of weekly programmes of special usefulness to teachers, being designed to update their English and to enhance their professional expertise.

13. Strasbourg, for its part, runs correspondence courses, supported by tapes, in eight different modern languages in addition to German; and also a course for aspiring teachers of German, designed to prepare them for the CAPES (*certificat d'aptitude professionelle à l'enseignement secondaire*).

14. Dijon offers courses in musicology of interest to a wide public outside university students, and has recently initiated, in association with Strasbourg, a new course in *sciences religieuses*, thus enlarging the range of options open to students and introducing a new cross-disciplinary element.

III Student numbers and characteristics

15. The number of students enrolled in the CTUs of the Entente de l'Est in 1972/73 with the object of preparing for university diplomas or degrees was 1,450. Figures for the latest year (1973/74) show a further intake of 700 students.

16. If we look at a particular CTU—Nancy—in 1972/73, we find that of the 1,450 Entente students, 402 had elected to follow the English courses there. They were enrolled in the universities of the Entente in very unequal numbers: nearly half of them at the University of Nancy and nearly a quarter at Dijon, with the remaining enrolments spread over the other five universities of the Entente. It is no doubt natural that each CTU should attract a substantial proportion of its students from among people in its own locality. Some 10 per cent of the students at CTU Nancy lived outside eastern France, the majority of these being resident abroad.

17. In the same year, CTU Nancy enrolled a further 70 students who were not aiming at university qualifications but whose intentions were sufficiently serious to require the complete range of services the CTU provides (i.e. excluding more casual followers of the radio broadcasts only). When all such students at the Entente's five CTUs are counted in, the total number of distance learning students within their orbit probably now exceeds 2,000.

18. The great majority of students (82 per cent) in the Entente's CTUs are teachers or *surveillants* (monitors) aspiring to full teacher status. The prevalence of practising teachers among CTU clients is such that on Wednesdays, when French schools are not in session, CTU radio programmes are transmitted throughout the day instead of in the early evening only.

IV History of the CTUs

19. The history of the CTUs now forming the Entente de l'Est is one of continuous development over fourteen years.

20. Dijon was first in the field, in 1960. It offered one-year correspondence courses for students wishing to prepare for the examination known as the *propédeutique*, or 'preliminary examination' (later replaced by the two-year DUEL) and unable to attend the university full-time. The operation was on a very small scale, and at this stage no broadcasting was involved. It was essentially an enterprise stemming from within the university itself.

21. The first initiatives at ministerial level came in 1963, when all French universities were sounded as to their interest in setting up distance learning centres which would use radio as well as correspondence. According to M. Guy Lecomte, who directed the centre at Dijon until 1973, these first steps owed much to the encouragement of M. Pompidou, then Prime Minister of France, who saw major troubles ahead for the universities (they erupted in 1968) owing to overcrowding, understaffing and antiquated organization and methods, and was favourably disposed to changes that would improve their image.

22. A more specific reason for providing new opportunities for people in employment to work for university degrees was the need to increase the teaching force in secondary schools, as it was planned to raise the age of compulsory schooling to 16 in the near future. Secondary school teachers in France are required to possess a university degree (*licence*), and distance learning facilities opened the way for primary school teachers (normally without degrees) to work for them. These teachers were for the most part better equipped in arts than in science subjects, so would naturally specialize in an arts field in preparing their *licence*. Thus the lack of science and maths courses in the services offered by the CTUs was no impediment to their development, though of course it meant that they could do nothing to redress the imbalance in the additional teaching force available for secondary schools.

23. The CTUs of Dijon, Nancy and Strasbourg were set up in 1963. Their policy was then, and has been since, to proceed by stealth and to justify themselves by results. No elaborate research or consultation preceded their inauguration, and no trumpet-blowing accompanied it. The department of the Ministry which oversaw their activities and secured broadcasting time and facilities for them imposed no guidelines and issued no directives. The CTUs had indeed no statutes at this stage: these were not formulated until 1972. It was essentially a grass-roots operation.

24. There were informal discussions between the directors of the three CTUs (soon to be joined by a fourth, Besançon), so the germ of the Entente was already present by 1964. At this stage 12 hours of broadcasting time were available weekly: later this number was increased to 16, where it remained until 1974.

25. In the early years, each CTU undertook courses in several disciplines, using the broadcast transmitters in its own locality. After two years' operation, however, it became clear that this was a wasteful and inefficient procedure, and the CTUs agreed among themselves to rationalize their work so that each concentrated on a particular discipline. This was a major step forward, entailing not simply an agreement among the CTU directors, but a substantial declaration of mutual confidence between the universities themselves, and particularly

between the deans of their humanities faculties. For university A to agree to some of its enrolled students having their courses of study both organized and examined by university B, and to accept the successful examinee as qualified for a diploma or degree of university A, was quite a new development. It was facilitated by the prior existence, unconnected with the CTUs, of the Association Inter-Universitaire de l'Est, through which the deans of faculties of the several universities met informally. The necessary administrative steps towards the formation of the Entente could not have been achieved without their active collaboration.

26. The Entente thus became a working reality, with M. Lecomte elected in 1968 as its co-ordinating secretary; and the way was open for each CTU, in response to the now manifest expectations of its students, to enlarge the range of courses offered within its discipline. Thus by 1968 Dijon, for instance, was catering for both years of the two-year diploma; in 1970 it also accepted students preparing the *licence* and in 1972 a certain number of master's degree students also. Meanwhile Reims, and later Metz and Mulhouse, had joined the Entente, and increasing attention was being paid to the claims of *éducation permanente* outside the area of university qualifications.

27. All the steps in this progression have been achieved by what Guy Lecomte describes as '*la politique du fait accompli*'. 'If we had waited for advice', he says, 'or tried to secure the full co-operation of all our university colleagues before advancing to the next stage, we should never have got where we are.' By the same token, although the CTUs have had to face during this decade of progress considerable indifference and some hostility among some university colleagues, they clearly owe much to the willing collaboration of others, particularly within the faculties (or the UERs—*unités d'enseignement et de recherches*—to use the terminology current since the reforms of 1968), whose work parallels their own. These 1968 reforms did not contribute directly to the progress of the CTUs: indeed, by their emphasis on the autonomy of French universities they might appear to have made more difficult the kind of development represented by the Entente de l'Est. Yet it is likely that their indirect effects have been favourable to CTU growth, by bringing about general improvements in university staffing and by fostering a climate in which new departures have been made more acceptable, individual initiatives encouraged and the ideal of democratizing opportunities for higher education proclaimed.

V Organization and control

28. The statutes of each CTU derive from a decision of its parent university, requiring a two-thirds majority. They allow for federation by agreement with other CTUs, but the Entente de l'Est as a whole has no collective statue.

29. The statutes for CTU Nancy, to take an example, provide for a controlling council of twelve members having a three-year (renewable) term of office. Membership consists of:

(a) The president of the university or his nominee, as chairman.

(b) Three teaching staff and three students of the university, elected by their peers on the University Council. These should normally be chosen from among teachers and students participating in the work of the CTU.

(c) Three members (one teacher, one administrative and one technical staff) chosen by and from among CTU staff.
(d) Two members from outside the university, elected by the other members of the CTU Council.

30. The director of the CTU attends the CTU Council meetings in a consultative capacity. Meetings take place at least twicc a year, and more often, if requested by one-third of the membership. Minutes are published within the university.

31. The main duties of the CTU Council are to approve the outlines and oversee the execution of the CTU's operational programme, and to endorse its annual budgetary request (which is then submitted to the University Council for approval) and its annual report. The operational programme must reflect the general objectives of the CTU, including not only the preparation of students for university examinations and the CTU's role in *éducation permanente*, but also research in the technology of audio-visual education.

32. The director of the CTU is nominated by the University Council, on the recommendation of its president, for a three-year term of office (renewable). He or she is selected from among the teaching staff attached to or collaborating with the CTU and has complete executive charge of the CTU's operations and personnel: requests for CTU staff, as for money, are initiated by the director and forwarded to the Ministry of Education by the university. The CTU statutes also provide for the *ad hoc* engagement under contract of other university staff to collaborate in the work of the CTU.

33. Basically, the funds of the CTU derive from the relevant department of the Ministry of Education, which earmarks a certain sum specifically for the use of the CTU. The university, however, has discretion to augment this from its general financial resources should it choose to do so.

34. The statutes also allow for student contributions to the financing of the CTU: these must figure in its budget. (The normal student's fee is the very small one of 100 francs—about U.S.$21—annually.)

35. The broadcast facilities to be provided each year are negotiated between the university and RTF, but the prior approval of the Ministry of Education (which subsequently meets RTF's bills) is essential.

36. This is the formal picture of organization and control; but it must also be borne in mind that the CTUs are quite small bodies (at Nancy the permanent staff—teaching, technical and administrative together—number no more than 8). Their impetus is very much self-generated. The CTU councils are in practice not very influential: a good deal of their business is formal, and their role mainly a watchdog's rather than a dynamic or initiatory one. There are certain matters, however, which they consider in some detail: for instance, the ways in which the conventional examinations need to be modified to meet the situation of CTU students (such modifications are kept to a minimum, to avoid the charge that the CTUs are a soft option, but some are almost always necessary).

37. On the larger issues, however, almost everything depends on the energy, drive and diplomacy of the director, who will naturally be in continuous informal consultation with his small teaching staff. How far he can develop his service will depend on his persuasive powers vis-à-vis his colleagues in the relevant faculty (on whose collaboration much of his work depends), the president of his university, and the head of the responsible department at the Ministry. These powers will naturally be enhanced if he can point to growing

numbers of students applying for CTU enrolment and a good level of examination successes among them; if he can give evidence of providing services which are valued by ordinary students in the university as well as by CTU students (for instance, radio programmes or audio-visual materials which usefully supplement university lectures); if he can advance the reputation of the university through the CTU among the discerning public at large; and if he can acquire, vis-à-vis the Ministry, the reputation of bidding for only a little more than he can reasonably hope to get.

VI Staffing of CTUs

38. The permanent staffs of the CTUs consist in the main, as one might expect, of young people, the teaching members being in the earlier rather than the later stages of their university careers. This is likely to be true of the directors as well as their subordinates.

39. There is indeed a certain ambivalence in the situation of the director. In so far as his job carries opportunities for innovation and involves considerable independence and responsibility, it naturally has its attractions: on the other hand, since its incumbent carries a substantial administrative load and is preoccupied with developing the specialized techniques that multi-media approaches to learning require, he lacks the time to pursue his scholarly interests. And while running one's own show brings with it a certain prestige, this is a waning asset if it involves stepping aside from the ladder which conventionally leads to university promotion. For the CTU, while largely autonomous, is too small to give its director the standing within the university which naturally attaches to, say, a reader (*maître de conférences*), let alone a professor.

40. This is a problem which the CTUs and their parent universities have not yet satisfactorily resolved. It applies, in a measure, to the other teaching members of the permanent CTU staff also; though less severely since they are likely to be younger—in their twenties perhaps rather than their thirties—and have not necessarily set their sights firmly on a university career. It is perhaps pertinent to record that M. Lecomte was invited to take charge of CTU Dijon after experience as an inspector of primary schools in the Department of the Creuse, and that he resigned the CTU directorship after ten successful years in order to have time to complete his dissertation.

41. The permanent teaching staff of the CTUs—including the director—are expected to take their share in all the activities of the CTU: not only planning courses, lecturing, correcting the work of students and maintaining contact with them in other ways, but also preparing supplementary materials of all kinds, in print, as sound cassettes and for radio broadcasts. Now that, experimentally, some television programmes are beginning to feature in the output, a certain amount of specialization (for instance in radio or television) is starting to become necessary within the small team.

42. The status and career prospects of technical and administrative staff attached to CTUs also give rise to some concern. For the former, job satisfaction is naturally much enhanced where the work of the CTU gives opportunities for a really creative contribution on the technical side (for instance at Dijon, where the CTU produces its own programmes; and at Nancy, where the production of sound cassettes is very extensive).

VII Qualifications for entry to CTUs and examinations

43. As CTU students aiming at university examinations have first to enrol at their local university, the qualification they require is the same as for conventional university students: the *baccalauréat*[1] (roughly equivalent to 'matriculation'), which automatically carries the right of admission to any university. No qualification is required for those wishing to enrol as *auditeurs libres* (i.e. not preparing a university examination).

44. The form of the examinations varies with different universities. Most use a system of credits (*unités de valeur capitalisables*); or if they do not, they allow students to spread what is normally a single year's work, examinable at the end of the year, over two years, with the relevant examination similarly split into parts, which gives a comparable flexibility. Some universities, too, use examination systems which include continuous assessment, others do not. At Besançon, for instance, a student can elect, instead of the end-of-year written examination, to be assessed on his performance in two exercises done during the year under controlled conditions, and the best of two others done at home.

45. As in conventional university examinations, the oral examination is important. Students normally have to take this at the CTU whose course they are following: written examinations, on the other hand, can be taken at the student's local university.

VIII The elements of the CTU courses

The broadcast element

Radio: extent, timings and transmission

46. The programmes are broadcast on V.H.F. (F.M.) on the network of France-Inter, the most popular of the French radio services, from fourteen transmitters in the east of France. Geographically, the coverage of eastern France by these transmitters is virtually complete. Students are strongly advised to record programmes (or get a friend to record for them) so that they are available for detailed study instead of for a single hearing only. The small proportion of students living outside the area of coverage (mainly abroad) may arrange to have broadcasts sent to them in recorded form.

47. For several years up to 1974, the five CTUs providing courses were broadcasting 32 programmes in all of 30 minutes each for 24 or 25 weeks of the year (November to May). Transmission times were between approximately 5 p.m. and 8 p.m. from Monday to Friday inclusive, with an additional morning period (9 a.m. to 12 a.m.) on Wednesdays.

48. For 1974/75, however (and no doubt subsequent years also), RTF have reduced the hours available to the Entente de l'Est from 16 to 11 hours weekly. This substantial cut, officially made known only two months before the start of

1. The concept of the *baccalauréat* as a passport giving automatic right to university entry is likely to be modified shortly. As student options in secondary education become wider, university aspirants will be expected to have achieved higher than 'pass' marks in special subjects of their own choice.

the university year, was not altogether unexpected. Inevitably, what the CTUs claim for their students and what RTF conceives as its obligation to its wider public do not coincide and short of a degree of governmental compulsion that is almost inconceivable, the last word lies with RTF. The problem has been that, after dark, medium-wave reception is less reliable than VHF; and darkness falls long before 8 p.m. during most of the period when the CTUs are on the air. Consequently, RTF has considered it no longer reasonable to reserve its VHF frequencies for the tiny CTU audience after 7 p.m. RTF has never been willing to release weekend times, which presumably would suit CTU students better still.

Nature of radio programmes

49. The great majority of broadcasts are ordinary university lectures modified to fit the 30 minutes transmission time. In these programmes the standard of delivery is high, but no use is made of the more sophisticated properties of radio. Thus, the single voice predominates even where radio practitioners would normally without question use more than one (for instance where quotations from a literary text are used in the course of a lecture). Some broadcast lectures, too, are heavy with factual material which might be more appropriately provided in written documentation, with radio reserved for comment and discussion. The programmes do, however, regularly have written material in support.

50. Efforts are continually being made, moreover, to widen the scope of the radio broadcasts and to seize opportunities for deploying the special strengths of radio as a medium. Thus, CTU Dijon has produced programmes which include radio dramatizations of parts of set books, and round-table discussions of elements in the courses are becoming a more frequent feature of their programmes. Participants in these discussion programmes may include, besides a range of academics bringing a variety of expertise to bear on the subject, people from other walks of life with especially valuable contributions to make.

51. CTU Nancy, for its part, draws substantially on recordings of BBC programmes (panel games and light entertainment as well as more serious material) for its broadcasts designed to foster aural comprehension of English, while radio is much used in conjunction with written material, for instance for illumination and discussion of extracts from newspapers which are included in the associated documentation. Radio may also be used to provide correct versions of exercises previously set to students.

Participants in radio programmes

52. Besides the members of CTU teaching staffs, university lecturers of the faculty concerned regularly contribute to the output of the CTUs: as many as a dozen in any one university will probably take part in the course of a year. These contributions are arranged on a contract basis, being additional to the normal work of the lecturers concerned: no member of the university staff is required so to contribute. There is a scale of payment which takes account both of the status of the contributor in the university hierarchy, and of what has been involved for him or her in making the contribution (at the lowest level, this could simply be a normal lecture recorded in the lecture hall or at the lecturer's residence; at the highest, a specially prepared contribution requiring many

hours of additional work and substantial rehearsal). Copyright in the recorded contribution will normally remain with the university, though there are complications which are the subject of current study.

Production of radio programmes

53. In most cases this is undertaken by RTF in its regional studios. However, the services it offers for production are minimal; and where the programme in question is not a straightforward lecture, many of the elements within it will have been prepared by CTU staff. Nancy, for instance, regularly undertakes the preparation and editing of tape material for insert; only the final assembly and recording are done in the RTF studio.

54. CTU Dijon is an exception to this general practice. It has a fully equipped radio studio, and produces and records its own programmes in their entirety: RTF handles only their transmission.

Why radio?

55. The simple answer is: because it was available; because it is a suitable vehicle for carrying much of the information and comment appropriate to arts courses; and because it provides a feeling of personal link between teacher and taught which is absent from courses relying on correspondence. In language teaching, it can readily offer a variety of native voices and the direct experience of different styles of communication.

Experimental television programmes

56. Over the last two years a few television programmes have been produced experimentally in Paris for the CTUs of eastern France and transmitted on RTF's second television channel (Chaîne 2). This is a colour channel of 625 lines, with coverage extending over upwards of 75 per cent of the country.

57. These programmes (of 30 minutes' length, like the radio programmes), have been mainly or entirely on film. In the case of Dijon, much of this has been specially shot: Nancy has been assiduous in seeking material available at low cost from RTF's film library.

58. It is already evident that repeated programmes are likely, in view of the substantial costs, to figure importantly in any growth of the use of television in the CTUs: Nancy, for instance, has been allotted funds for only four new programmes in 1974/75, with a recommendation to rebroadcast those made last year. This observation is not, of course, to be read critically. Quite the contrary, for a substantial proportion of repeats each year should be a feature of this type of enterprise; and it is to be expected that as professional expertise in programme-making develops, more radio broadcasts too will be re-used than is apparently the case in some of the CTUs today.

The Centre Audio-Visuel de Saint-Cloud

59. The Saint-Cloud centre is associated with the École Normale Supérieure de Saint-Cloud (the highest teacher-training establishment in France). It has staff trained in the preparation and production of audio-visual materials of all

kinds, including radio and television; it also runs a wide range of training courses and undertakes much research into the methodology and the impact of audio-visual techniques in education. It has close relationships with the department of the Ministry (DISUP 8) which oversees the work of the CTUs, acting as a '*bureau d'études*' or study centre (something wider than a research bureau) on its behalf.

60. The centre is ready to co-operate in the production of television programmes for CTUs on request. CTU Dijon has availed itself of this co-operation, as have several other CTUs outside the Entente de l'Est. The average budget for such productions is 40,000 francs (about U.S.$8,000).

61. The centre also conducted research into the impact of seven television programmes transmitted within the Entente de l'Est during the period February to April 1973, by means of a detailed questionnaire to students, supplemented by interviews. The proportion of questionnaires returned was not, however, high. Moreover, while students' opinions of the value of television in this context were by and large very favourable (as one would surely expect), this can hardly be said in itself to provide any very clear pointers for the future. Replies to the questionnaire also revealed that a not insignificant number of students did not have access to a television set (and of course, virtually none would have facilities for recording and replaying television programmes).

The correspondence element

Nature of the correspondence element

62. The correspondence element is central to all courses, whether designed to prepare for university awards or for *éducation permanente*. In either case it consists of a variety of written material and of recorded sound. The former includes: support literature for broadcasts; original texts; bibliographies; exercises; fair copies; corrections to students' work; general instructions and advice. 'Original texts' has a wide connotation: at Nancy, for instance, newspaper articles are drawn on a great deal, as are press advertisements—both copy and illustrations (especially in the courses designed for *éducation permanente*). None of this material is printed: its preparation is carried out within the CTU, which is equipped for reprography.

63. The material sent to students on sound cassettes complements the material distributed over the air. It includes, naturally, all oral material which is not suited to radio transmission, either by its nature or because it does not extend to half-an-hour in length or necessarily exceeds this; and in a linguistic course it will tend to include whatever material it is most important for the student to have available for repeated hearing, without the possible hazards of recording off-air. A small charge (reimbursable) is made to students for the cassettes lent to them.

Extent of the correspondence element

64. Packages are sent to students every two to three weeks during the academic year. A typical package for a student enrolled for *éducation permanente* at CTU Nancy would consist of four cassettes, with mimeographed

accompanying documents: one analysing and commenting on documents designed for comprehension of the written word; two containing material for aural comprehension; and one consisting of 'actuality' material culled from newspapers, radio programmes, etc. In all, the package would provide material for 4 hours' listening, or a minimum of 8 hours' work.

65. The example of CTU Nancy will also serve to give an idea of what a year's operation involves for the correspondence service. During the year 1972/73 it prepared and distributed to students a total of over 3,000 sets of documents ('*fascicules*'—each of some 50 to 100 foolscap sheets loosely bound together); over 100,000 duplicated sheets; and about 10,000 sound cassettes.

Responsibility for preparation of material

66. Responsibility for preparing written material designed to accompany broadcasts rests with the lecturer concerned, whether a CTU staff member or a university lecturer under contract; and the same applies to the correction of written work. Where sound cassettes are associated with the courses of contract lecturers, their preparation involves a co-operative effort by the lecturer and one of the CTU staff. However, to take the example of Nancy again, a great deal of new material is constantly being generated, especially in the service of the growing body of students pursuing *éducation permanente*; and from this a substantial library of sound cassettes is being built up (representing, by 1973, a total of 200 hours' listening material, and since then much increased). This is in addition to its stock of recorded broadcasts, and is a development that is very much dependent on the energies and resourcefulness of the small permanent CTU staff.

The tutorial element: contact with students

67. Three times a year every CTU student has the opportunity to come to the CTU headquarters for a day (or sometimes two days) of tutorial sessions (*stages*). Students are of course encouraged to attend, but they are not obliged to do so; and only a relatively small minority do. This is not altogether surprising when research suggests that over 60 per cent of students, in 1973, were living more than 50 kilometres from their nearest university. For most, the journey to their CTU would be much further.

68. The prime purpose of the *stages* is to enable students to meet their teachers—and each other—face to face. An important secondary purpose is to give them the opportunity of doing some work under controlled examination conditions. For foreign-language students, these days can also provide a welcome opportunity to put the language they are studying to social use: Nancy assembles British and American students, of whom there are always at least a handful, to meet them socially at the university.

69. Apart from this, students who live close to their CTU can make informal contact at other times, and use its library of sound recordings. They may also borrow from this library as may other students at the university—but this facility is not publicized to the latter, as it is felt that the demand would exceed the library's capacity to meet it.

70. The CTUs are also willing to help in arranging meetings of students, where there are sufficient numbers of them and sufficient evidence of demand, at convenient points away from the CTU; but very little has as yet been achieved in this respect.

71. There is no organized counselling or tutorial service on anything like an individual basis—much less anything in the nature of summer schools. To anyone used to thinking of university work as characterized by the tutorial group, or familiar with the very extensive services to students provided by, for instance, the Open University in the United Kingdom, this must seem a major weakness of the Entente de l'Est and its constituent CTUs; and it is certainly one of the aims of the CTUs themselves to achieve an improvement here, for a sense of isolation is recognized as the commonest reason for student drop-out where this occurs. One must remember, however, that in France there has never been a strong tradition of individual tuition or pastoral care for university students; and even the reforms of 1968 have not in the event brought this much nearer.[1] So it would be wrong to suppose that CTU students have great expectations in this direction which are disappointed in the event. Indeed, in the opinion of M. Lecomte, distance learning students feel as much in contact with their teachers as do conventional ones—perhaps more so, since the radio voice speaks more intimately than that of the lecturer in the large hall, where numbers may even today be large enough for some students to prefer to to purchase the lecture in the form of an impersonal '*polycopié*'.

72. The distance learner, too, remains for his teacher an individual free from the danger of submersion among a mass of other students; and the necessity for frequent correspondence can underline the individuality of his or her circumstances in a way which chance encounters in the lecture hall or even the seminar rarely permit.

73. By the same token, however, there is no forum for the expression of collective CTU student opinion (if one excepts the occasional opportunity to complete a questionnaire, and the presence of student representatives on the CTU Council, neither of which would be likely to exercise a marked influence on the orientation of the CTU's work). But CTU students do not expect to develop any strong corporate outlook. What they want is effective professional help in working on their own towards the objectives they have set themselves; and this they are getting, it would appear, generally to their satisfaction.

IX Teachers, students and work load

74. We need to look finally at the CTU course as a whole, as distinct from its separate elements, to become aware of certain important features. The first is that the majority of the teaching, and all that goes with it, is done by ordinary university staff under contract to the CTU rather than by the small number of specialist CTU staff. They will bring to their job varying experience, though not of the special problems. The opportunities open to them will likewise vary: not all, for instance, will have the chance to use radio even if they wish to.

1. This kind of tutor–student relationship is the prerogative of those who enter the 'Grandes Écoles', which annually cream off, through highly competitive examinations, the ablest students of university age.

Audio cassettes will be a new medium to many: they will probably find it time-consuming to learn to use them effectively. Initial enthusiasm may well be tempered by the discovery of what is involved.

75. The work load will vary not only with the nature of the preparation required, but with the numbers of students following the particular course. For there is work to be corrected as well as work to be set: a single broadcast can reach 100 or more students, but the work coming back is still 100 separate units of work, to be corrected and annotated. A job which was attractive and comparatively well paid when student numbers were small can become progressively less so as they increase. For there is no back-up force (much less any system of marking by computer) to take the load of handling students' work off the teacher.

76. In these circumstances, while thought is given—within the limitations of what is possible—to the choice of medium for putting information or experience across, there is little time to consider in depth how far (if at all) problems of organizing the learner's experience so that it best meets his solitary situation differ from those of teaching in a conventional university context.

Student progress

77. Despite the foregoing reservations, CTU candidates achieve if anything slightly better results in their examinations than do conventional students. Success rates during the years 1971–73 in the CTUs of the Entente de l'Est have averaged 57 per cent for first-year students, 58 per cent for second-year students and 69 per cent for third-year students.

78. The proportion of drop-outs, on the other hand, is a little higher in the case of CTU students (hardly surprising in view of the arduous undertaking on which they have embarked—and at an early age, the vast majority being under 30 and substantially more of these in their earlier than their later twenties).

X Summary of present situation and prospects

The scope of the Entente de l'Est in perspective

79. In terms of the number of students served through the CTUs, the Entente de l'Est is not large. The universities of the region have a total population of about 84,000 students, some 26,000 of whom are in the humanities faculties. The CTUs of the Entente, including the registered '*auditeurs libres*', have a little over 2,000 students. They have thus increased the number of those enjoying university education of any kind in this part of France by about 2.5 per cent and of those studying humanities at university level by some 8 per cent.

80. In terms of the satisfaction of national needs, an increase in the number of students obtaining arts degrees or diplomas is not of major significance. The national university population has vastly expanded in the last two decades, and now amounts to some 800,000 students. A *licence* (bachelor degree), in France as in many other developed countries, is no longer in itself a passport for entry into many vocations: it may, or may not, be a useful step towards this

(it does, as we have seen, open up the field of secondary teaching to teachers previously confined to work in primary schools).

The significance of its work

81. The importance of the CTUs (apart of course from the personal satisfaction they provide for successful students) lies rather in their recognition of the need for study, research and experimentation in the techniques and methods appropriate to distant learning. Some see this need essentially in terms of course-building—in the programming of experience to achieve maximum impact on the distant learner. Others emphasize rather the change in scale—from cottage industry to mass production—which modern media make possible for the dissemination of knowledge, and the ready market which distance learning provides for this. On neither count have the CTUs as yet done much more than skim the surface of the problems and the opportunities; but their experience has at least brought them—and through them, the university world to which they belong—face to face with these opportunities and their associated problems.

82. Equally significant, however, are the questions which the relative success of the CTUs raise about the appropriate forms that post-secondary study might take for a wider range of students, including some straight from school. CTUs were established expressly for, and limited to, students who were unable to attend university full-time in the normal way: now they are asking why the option should not be open to any aspiring student to study for a bachelor degree through a CTU should they so prefer—in combination perhaps with a full- or a part-time job. A lot of students abandon conventional university studies without attaining a degree; and there is some concern over the numbers from school who drift into universities without much motivation, perhaps without the temperament for three or four years' full-time study, and often without secure career prospects at the end of it. CTU courses are already flexible: they could no doubt be made even more so if it seemed advisable for more students to spread their studies over a longer period.

83. The Entente as such has also performed the important job of showing that universities are capable of collaborating on practical tasks. One must not make too much of this: collaboration between the universities of the Entente has mainly been limited to the agreement to share out tasks between the CTUs. Once this agreement was made, each CTU was free to plan the courses in its particular discipline without reference to the others. Two examples only of inter-university co-operation at the teaching level have been recorded (between Dijon and Strasbourg for a course in *sciences religieuses,* and between Dijon and Reims for a psychology course). Yet the achievement, however limited, has been both real and significant; and to have attempted to go faster might well have had the effect of frightening off altogether the CTUs' parent universities, with their strong traditions of independence. Moreover, detailed co-planning, while it should lead eventually to rationalization and greater cost-effectiveness, is initially demanding—to some extent of money, but particularly of time.

84. The moment has now come for further initiatives. The 'grass-roots' tradition in the CTUs is still strong, and will not be abandoned (even if they admire the United Kingdom's Open University, they are not averse to describing

the concept as 'Napoleonic'); but local loyalties will increasingly have to give way to the need to organize at least certain services on a regional or a national basis.

XI Some problems

Relations with RTF

85. The relationship between the CTUs and RTF is essentially one of business and policy. At the operational level, while RTF personnel have, of course, a professional attitude to their work, there is no real sense of involvement in the CTU programmes. It would therefore be stretching words to speak of a 'partnership' of academics and broadcasting people in this context; and recent events do not suggest any strong commitment to the enterprise on RTF's part in the face of counter-pressures.

86. The CTUs' response to RTF's cuts in radio transmission hours must, surely, lie in an extension of their cassette distribution to students. The diminished contact of the CTUs with the discriminating public at large which the loss of radio broadcasts entails is, of course, regrettable; but the change need not be to the student's disadvantage (possibly the contrary), nor necessarily damaging to the economics of the operation, since RTF costs accounted, before the recent cuts, for as much as 30 per cent of the total expenditure on the CTUs.

87. Television does not, at present, have the same problems of air time; but then its scale is as yet extremely small. As it develops, it can hardly escape one day meeting the same problems as radio if the distribution of programmes is dependent on the existing national networks.

Prospects for television

88. It was inevitable that the CTUs should have ambitions to enter the television field, for without it the range of what they can offer is necessarily limited. Yet apart from possible difficulties in the longer term over transmission time, any substantial increase in its scale will have serious budgetary repercussions. The cost-effectiveness of the Entente's operations, in so far as one can fairly separate these from other university costs, compares very favourably with that of conventional universities; but even over the whole Entente the student clientele for any given broadcast is very small, and the addition of, say, 50 television programmes per annum would add significantly to the cost per student. Larger regional groupings, and arrangements for the regular exchange of programmes across those groupings, would seem to be a necessity if television's contribution is to be both substantial and reasonably cost-effective.

University substitute or specialized distance learning institution?

89. Some members of CTU staffs feel that in the longer run there is a basic conflict between these two functions, or at least that the CTU cannot fulfil both

satisfactorily. Originally, this argument runs, their purpose was clear: to be a university substitute for limited categories of people. The broadcast university lecture then lay at the centre of what they provided. But the exploration of the problems of distance learning, particularly in the context of *éducation permanente*, has tended to draw them away from this function—and towards a more interesting and significant one. Some of the university lectures, they feel, now hang like millstones around their necks—not because they lack distinction in themselves, but because they are inappropriate to the needs of the distant learner, and because their existence tends to act as a brake on innovatory thinking about educational communication.

90. It is difficult to see the outcome of this dilemma—particularly as it is likely to be felt with differing intensity in the various disciplines represented in the Entente (and perhaps not at all in some). An institution concerned primarily with language teaching, for instance, might be quite happy to develop on lines which would have the flavour of polytechnic rather than university education. A school of philosophy could hardly feel the same way. But whatever the outcome of the dilemma (if such it is), the raising of the question is somehow symptomatic of the arrival at maturity of an association of organic institutions which has hitherto been able to grow naturally, almost casually, and without fuss, but now finds itself confronted with the problems of adulthood.

Appendix A Standardized reference data

Country, state or province	*France*
Area and climate	213,000 square miles. Temperate.
Population	
Total (latest year)	51,700,000 (1972).
Estimated population aged 18	830,000 (1972–73).
Estimated percentage under 15	24.6 (1972).
Current annual growth rate (percentage)	0.9 (since 1968).
Government	
Main organizational structure	Unitary, with highly centralized administrative functions through centralized ministries to regional departments.
Political type	Parliamentary democracy; republic.
Economy	
Political type	Mixed: largely small-scale farming and also industrialized; state interest in developing regions.
Gross national product	
Total (latest year)	U.S.$163,000 million (1971).
Per head	U.S.$3,180 (1971).
Average annual increase (percentage)	4.7 (1966–71).
Communications	
Ground/air	Quick and easy countrywide system of roads, motorways, bus, rail and air transport services.
Mail/telephone	Adequate postal services. Growing telephone services now (1971) 19.9 per 100 population.

Broadcasting	
Main system(s) operating	A.M., F.M.; television.
Principal authorities responsible	Office de Radiodiffusion-Télévision Française (ORTF), a government controlled body. Now Radiodiffusion et Télévision Françaises (RTF).
Radio	
Transmission coverage of main programme services with percentage of population reached	90 per cent reached by all channels and F.M.
Receiving capability for main programme services (percentage)	90.
Television	
Transmission coverage as defined for radio (percentage)	Chaîne I: 98. Chaîne II: 75. Chaîne III: 25.
Monochrome or colour	Chaîne II and Chaîne III transmit in colour.
Education	
Type of system(s)	Predominantly publicly controlled and financed. Less than 10 per cent attend private institutions. Highly centralized control of standardized curricula.
End of full-time school attendance	
Legal	Compulsory and free 6 to 16 years.
De facto	Increasing numbers stay voluntarily until 18.
Proportion of 18-year-old age group involved in education (percentage)	
Full-time	20.
Part-time	Not known.
Major developments in provision	
Over last five years	University reforms aimed at: (a) giving greater independence; (b) modernizing curricula and methods: (c) breaking the power of the individual faculties; (d) promoting concept of *éducation permanente*; (e) development of technological institutions at university level; (f) liberalization of secondary-school curricula.
Over next five years	Drive to provide pre-school education for all five-year-olds and most four-year-olds by 1976.

Institution/system under study

Brief for study and reason for inclusion	To study the Centres de Télé-enseignement Universitaire of the Entente Universitaire de l'Est as an example of multi-media distance teaching.

Description of subject studied

Origins	The institution and its first degree system. Largely self-generated but with ministerial encouragement in the early 1960s.
Educational authority(ies) and roles	Financed by Ministry of Education Distance Learning Centres set up in five universities.
Communications authority(ies) and roles	RTF for transmitting broadcast element.
Services provided	Wider opportunities of university education for adults, both for vocational and non-vocational purposes, through face-to-face and multi-media methods of tuition.
Eligibility to study	
(a) categories	Those prevented by occupation or physical disability from full-time university study.
(b) qualifications	For those requiring university qualification, the *baccalauréat* (matriculation).
Terminal qualifications	*Diplôme d'études*: *général*, two years; *licence*, three years; *maîtrise*, four years.
Instructional means used	Correspondence, sound tapes and cassettes. Study guides. Radio. Television limited and very experimental.
Personal input from student	Ten to twelve hours weekly.
Normal duration of study	Two to three years.
Pedagogical effectiveness	Compares satisfactorily with systems of conventional students.

Numbers involved

Students	
Intake (latest year)	700 (1973/74).
On roll	1,700.
Academic staff	
Full-time	25 approximately.
Part-time	50.
Other professional staff	
Number	Administrative and technical 20.

Finance

Recurrent expenditure	
Average annual outlay by student	100 francs. Plus returnable deposit on expensive items of equipment.
Non-recurrent expenditure	
Gross, over first five years of new institution	Impossible to estimate, as distance learning centres grew up over a number of years.

Special assistance received

Financial	None.
Non-financial	Advice of director, Audio-Visual Centre of Saint-Cloud.

Sources of further information

Educational/Broadcasting

Relations with broadcasting authorities: M. André Deprad, Chef de Bureau au Secrétariat d'État aux Universités, Ministère de L'Education Nationale, Bureau Disup 8, 110 Rue de Grenelle, 75357 Paris.
Distance learning at university level in France and western Europe: M. Robert Lefranc, Directeur, Centre Audio-Visuel, Ecole Normale Supérieure de Saint-Cloud, Ofratème, 29 Rue d'Ulm, 75230 Paris.
The Entente de L'Est in particular: M. Clement Bouillon, Directeur, Centre de Télé-enseignement, BP 3397, 54015 Nancy, France.

Appendix B **Short bibliography**

COUNCIL FOR CULTURAL COOPERATION. *The combined use of radio and television and correspondence courses in higher education.* Strasbourg, Council of Europe, 1974. 150 p., bibliog. This authoritative work, in French and English, surveys the field over the whole of western Europe, and contains many references to the Entente de l'Est and its constituent distance learning centres.

INSTITUT NATIONAL DE RECHERCHE ET DE DOCUMENTATION PÉDAGOGIQUES. *L'organisation de l'enseignement en France.* Paris, the institute, 29 Rue d'Ulm, 75230 Paris, 1973. Index, bibliog. (In French.) A useful book for reference to the French educational system.

Appendix C **Biographical note**

Kenneth Fawdry is a graduate in classics and modern languages of Cambridge University, United Kingdom. After teaching in secondary schools and at London University he joined the BBC and in 1950 became Senior Education Officer to the School Broadcasting Council, which guides the BBC in its school broadcast provision. From 1959 to 1972 he was Head of BBC School Television. He is a former Vice-Chairman of the European Broadcasting Union's Study Group for School and Educational Television.

Part-time higher education using radio—an example from the **Federal Republic of Germany**

Stephen Kanocz

Contents

I Introduction

1. The Radio College (Funkkolleg) in the Federal Republic of Germany has been chosen for this study because of some unique features which distinguish it from other Open Learning systems of the world. It is probably the only educational institution of university level that has neither premises nor full-time staff of its own. In the pursuance of its aims it has achieved a very close working relationship between state authorities, autonomous public service broadcasting organizations, universities, a government-funded school for distance studies, a private computer firm and several adult-education organizations.

2. It can look back on eight years of successful activity, during which more than 150,000 persons have enrolled as students and (of the 108,670 who enrolled before the current year) over 37,000 have obtained its certificate.

3. It is held in high esteem in the German-speaking countries of Europe—and only recently German-speaking Switzerland decided to join it.

4. It compares very favourably with other German educational establishments, and with Open Learning systems in other countries, as regards expenditure per student, partly because it uses only the cheaper of the two broadcasting media: radio.

5. Funkkolleg also seems to be the first establishment of higher education relying entirely on a computerized evaluation of examinations.

6. Funkkolleg offers a different curriculum every year and each new course is guided by a different group of academic experts.

II Background

7. The Federal Republic of Germany is one of the two German States that came into existence in 1949, four years after the end of the Second World War and the disappearance of the united Germany founded in 1871. Although the Allied powers were originally committed to the restoration of German unity, west and east Germany were completely divided both economically and politically by 1948. The two states set up in 1949 have since been recognized as fully sovereign by all powers, including each other, and have acquired separate membership of the United Nations.

8. The Federal Republic has, as its name suggests, a strongly federalist constitution with wide powers reserved to its ten member states, including the

realms of education and broadcasting. Although the majority of the member states are artificial post-war creations, federalism itself is deeply rooted in Germany history.

9. The Federal Republic has evolved into a firm and stable democratic State. The number of political parties has dwindled, by a process of natural elimination, to three, which by now consistently poll well over 90 per cent of the votes cast in all elections, in a proportion of roughly 4 : 4 : 1. The two larger parties are Christian-conservative and Social-democratic respectively in inspiration, the smaller one is Liberal. They govern at all levels of the federal structure, usually in coalitions of two parties in varying combinations.

10. The area of the Federal Republic is 100,000 square miles and its population is just under 62 million. After 1948 the country made a rapid recovery from the ravages of war, enjoying a remarkable rate of economic growth leading to a high level of prosperity. The first stage of this development has become known as the German economic miracle ('Wirtschaftswunder'). In the last year of the post-war firm exchange-rate system, in 1971, the Federal Republic had the largest gross national product after the United States and Japan, the highest *per capita* income after the United States, Sweden, Canada, Kuwait and Switzerland, and was in fourth place in providing development aid after the United States, Japan and France. International economic developments since 1973 have brought the growth of the economy, at least temporarily, to a halt. On the other hand, there has been no decline in the country's prosperity and the Deutsche Mark has remained one of the strongest of the world's currencies.

III Education

11. Education in Germany has been traditionally the concern of state governments. Although free compulsory education was introduced in the German Reich in the nineteenth century, only primary and the lowest level of secondary education remained free and non-selective until after the Second World War.

12. Compulsory schooling (6 to 15, part-time until 18) starts at the *Volkschule*, lasting four years, after which there is a choice of three levels of secondary education:

(a) Lowest level (five years), which is the continuation of the *Volkschule* until 15.
(b) Middle level (*Realschule*), which lasts six years.
(c) Highest level (*Gymnasium*), which lasts nine years and ends with an examination known as the *Abitur*—once the only means of university admission.

University courses in Germany changed little in form before the late 1960s and the main vehicle of teaching remained the lecture rather than individual or group tutorials.

13. The swift rise in living standards after 1948 created new social ambitions, one of which was for children to enjoy higher levels of education than their parents had done. Many who would have acquired jobs after gaining the *Abitur* went instead to university, and many whose parents would previously have accepted a *Realschule* education, went instead to a *Gymnasium*.

14. The result of this was that by 1960, although the population of the Federal Republic was only 10 per cent below that of pre-war Germany in 1937,

with 26 universities compared to 33, the number of students was 190,000 as against 60,000. Between 1960 and 1971, the number of university students doubled again while the number of pupils in the *Gymnasien* doubled between 1950 and 1971. Although more universities were founded in the 1960s, they could hardly cope with the increase in the number of students.

15. Social inequalities in the recruitment of university students resulted partly from the need to undergo thirteen years of schooling before admission. To correct these, two reforms were made after the creation of the Federal Republic in 1949:

(a) Evening grammar schools (*Zweiter Bildungsweg*—second-chance education) were introduced. In 1965, however, there were only 2,000 pupils at these evening grammar schools, compared with nearly 1 million at the ordinary *Gymnasien.*

(b) The second attempt at reform (1957) was the institution of special entry examinations for the highly gifted (*Begabtensonderprüfung*), who had to prove that despite their lack of traditional schooling and *Abitur*, they could benefit from university studies. The condition of entry to this examination was the provision of testimonials from two university professors to the effect that the candidate had an aptitude for university studies. These testimonials were usually granted after the student attended lectures as a guest student for a half-year term and passed a small examination known as the *Kolloquium*. Although no exact figures are available, there is no doubt that few people entered university through this special examination, and only a handful have graduated since its introduction.

IV Broadcasting

16. German radio was divided into regional organizations by the Allied Powers in 1945. Under the constitution of 1949 control of broadcasting became a matter for state governments. The main source of income of broadcasting organizations is the licence revenue collected from owners of television and radio sets. Advertising is allowed only in blocks clearly separated from programmes.

17. Funkkolleg was started by Hessischer Rundfunk (HR) in 1966, and in 1969 this Hessen broadcasting organization joined three other stations—Saarländischer Rundfunk (SR), operating in Saarland (headquarters in Saarbrücken), Süddeutscher Rundfunk (SDR), operating in the northern half of Baden-Württemberg (headquarters in Stuttgart), and Südwestfunk (SWF), operating in Rheinland-Pfalz and the south of Baden-Württemberg (headquarters in Baden-Baden)—to form the so-called Quadriga and thus effect economies in television and radio production. The Quadriga also took over the broadcasting sponsorship of Funkkolleg, which in this extended version became part of a multi-media teaching system. The sponsoring organizations were joined by Radio Bremen (operating in the city-state of Bremen) in 1971, when the name Quadriga was officially dropped.

V The development of Funkkolleg

First plans (before 1966)

18. The plan for a radio college grew from requests from the educational radio department of Hessischer Rundfunk for an increase in the output of adult education on radio. The head of the department was (and is) Professor Gerd Kadelbach, who is also part-time professor of mass media studies at Frankfurt University. The management of HR agreed on two conditions. The first condition was that the impact of new series should meet national or regional needs, and to fulfil this condition a college was envisaged with formal enrolment and a system of examinations and certificates which would encourage students to persevere with their studies, but with no enrolment fees and no admission requirements. To meet the second condition the radio college was expected: (a) to ease the pressure on the universities by providing courses for existing university students; (b) to correct the social injustices inherent in university selection by providing an alternative method of preparation for the special examination for the highly gifted (see paragraph 15(b) above); (c) to pioneer the use of modern telecommunication techniques in university education; and (d) to support the educational policies of the government of Hessen by training teachers of social studies and by upgrading secondary school teachers from the lowest to the middle stratum (see paragraph 12). This was linked to a long-term policy aim of making the middle-level *Realschule* available to all children in Hessen, thus prolonging their education to 16.

19. The basic aims of Funkkolleg were outlined by Professor Kadelbach as follows:

To open the universities to all those capable of study and not just a privileged minority. In practice this meant an alternative means of admission to the *Abitur*, the evening grammar schools and the system of testimonials.

To provide a way of updating their qualifications for those following a professional career.

To ease the strains caused by overcrowding and antiquated teaching methods in the universities by introducing new teaching methods and using telecommunications, enabling lectures to be delivered over the air.

To encourage a more critical approach towards professors as a result of their confrontation with each other over the air.

The first Funkkolleg (1966–69)

20. The development of university-level courses and the upgrading of secondary school teachers required more teachers possessing higher university-level educational standards. In an attempt to achieve these aims, Hessischer Rundfunk in 1966 introduced a three-year course of university-type lectures on 'The Understanding of Modern Society'. The course was given with the co-operation of Frankfurt University and was divided into one term of general introduction and five terms of more specialized study.

21. A professor was in charge of each term course but was not necessarily the only speaker. Reading lists and other printed material were distributed on a small scale but texts of broadcasts were not made available to students.

22. Only those students who produced two or three items of homework per term were admitted to the written and oral examination at the end of the terms. There were two terms each year and certificates were awarded to students passing a term examination. Two of these certificates were to be the equivalent of the two testimonials from professors (see paragraph 15(b) above), and to lead to the special examination (*Begabtensonderprüfung*).

23. Special alternatives were arranged to regulate the use of Funkkolleg certificates so that teachers could gain additional qualifications. The subject of this course, 'The Understanding of Modern Society', was chosen primarily for the benefit of teachers who would have to teach social-science courses.

Results of the course of 1966–69

24. The number of active participants in this course varied between 550 and 850. Approximately one-third of these were admitted to the examinations after completing the required homework. Of those admitted, 85 per cent attended the examinations, from which a total of 79 university students and 341 teachers obtained certificates. Sixty-three participants obtained the two passes needed for admission to the *Begabtensonderprüfung* examination.

25. Results were rather disappointing with regard to pioneering new teaching methods for universities, as the series failed to make use of the full potentialities of radio and consisted mainly of traditional lectures rather than of documentary recordings and/or dramatizations.

The impact of the first Funkkolleg (1966–69)

26. A sociological survey commissioned by Funkkolleg showed that the new course had done little to correct the social injustices of the educational system, even in Hessen itself. Seventy per cent of the Funkkolleg students were white-collar workers, particularly civil servants, which in the Federal Republic includes teachers; 20 per cent were university students or grammar-school pupils; and only 5 per cent manual workers. Almost all participants were found to be 'habitual' further-education students.

Further opportunities for tutoring

27. Although the first Funkkolleg did not provide personal tutoring, a number of optional evening classes (*Studienbegleitzirkel*) were set up by the adult-education institutes (*Volkshochschulen*) of Hessen, and others were formed by private initiative. Those who attended the evening classes did significantly better at the examinations than the other participants.

VI The progression of Funkkolleg into a multi-media teaching system

28. In 1969 Hessischer Rundfunk joined with three broadcasting agencies, SDR, SR and SWF (see paragraph 17) in sponsoring Funkkolleg, which also

became a multi-media teaching system operating over four states. (It was joined in 1971 by Bremen.) The radio stations now take it in turns to produce the courses for each year. Programmes are broadcast twice by each station, usually at different times. A predominant part in the new system is played by the German Institute for Distance Studies (Deutsches Institut für Fernstudien, abbreviated DIFF; see paragraph 34).

29. Partnership in Funkkolleg was also extended to the educational departments of the governments of the four states (five when Bremen joined), which helped to pay for the examinations and subsidize the evening classes, and the state administrations of adult-education institutes. In order to give Funkkolleg full university status, the bodies representing the universities in each participating state were also invited to take part in planning its work.

30. Responsibility for the teaching syllabus of each year is no longer incumbent on individual professors, but on teams appointed by the 'acting' broadcasting organization (i.e. the one whose turn it is to produce the programmes) with the help of DIFF. The teams are made up of groups of professors and lecturers of one or several universities.

31. Each course is divided into one-hour programmes comprising two half-hour lectures delivered either by members of the team or others commissioned by the radio station and DIFF.

32. Funkkolleg has no full-time staff, premises or money of its own. Apart from a small administrative office in Frankfurt, it operates through committees, working parties and teams.

33. The cost of preparatory consultation and payments of authors and speakers is met by the 'acting' broadcasting organization, supported by DIFF, and partially refunded later by the other organizations roughly in proportion to their overall income, which depends on the number of licence-holders in their area.

The role of the Deutsches Institut für Fernstudien (DIFF) in Funkkolleg

34. DIFF was founded in 1967 by the Volkswagen Foundation for the purpose of carrying out research into the possibility 'of academic studies through media independent of personal contact, to create and test such possibilities which make the (physical) presence of a teacher unnecessary and may lead to the realization of multi-media teaching at university level'. (Initially, DIFF was part of Tübingen University.) Particular attention was to be paid to the in-service training of teachers, and the institute is bound by its statute to co-operate with universities and 'other bodies'. It comprised a staff of dedicated educationists, some of whom were later to co-operate with the academic teams of Funkkolleg.

35. Before joining Funkkolleg as a partner, DIFF had acquired some experience in teaching English to non-graduate teachers through a combination of teaching pamphlets and tape recordings and had started developing other courses of distance study.

36. In 1972, DIFF, together with its staff of 100 academic and 50 non-academic employees, was taken over by the state governments of the Federal Republic. By that time it had become involved in developing and testing a total

of 23 distance teaching courses as well as participating in the work of Funkkolleg. Most of the DIFF courses outside Funkkolleg are designed for teachers or for teacher training (see paragraph 34) and some courses are linked to broadcast programmes.

37. DIFF not only pays for the drafting of the basic syllabus, including the fees and expenses of the academic teams of Funkkolleg (although not their broadcasting fees), but also provides approximately half the production cost of the printed brochures which accompany the courses and which are distributed to students. The brochures (known as *Studienbegleitbriefe*) are compiled by DIFF in co-operation with the academic team and distributed on its behalf by a private publisher, the Julius Beltz Verlag. Some of the costs of these publications, which amount to some 30 per cent of the total budget of Funkkolleg, are recovered from the students through registration fees.

The role of adult-education institutes

38. Evening classes (*Studienbegleitzirkel*) were set up by the adult-education institutes (*Volkshochschulen*) of Hessen and by private initiative to provide optional personal tutoring for anyone so desiring. In order to ensure that the evening classes would be able to function as an effective part of the radio college, Funkkolleg would have had to arrange for special notes to be published for tutors. Since this presented a problem because of the tight schedules of the other broadcast work, special optional meetings and seminars were arranged for the tutors instead, but these have been largely unattended for personal or professional reasons. (These meetings account for 1 per cent of the Funkkolleg budget.)

39. Although universities in the Funkkolleg states take part in planning its work, they do not contribute to its costs. They may, however, arrange seminars working with the material provided by Funkkolleg and they may accept the Funkkolleg certificate instead of the normal seminar certificate required from students.

VII How Funkkolleg functions

40. During each one-year course there are about 30 radio programmes, each lasting one hour, which are divided more or less evenly into the two terms or semesters that make up a course (known as a *Modell*). In later years they have totalled 33, with additional feedback programmes.

41. Before the first term there are four introductory programmes of 30 minutes each, the texts of which are made available to the students.

42. For the other programmes, about twelve brochures are distributed to the students—approximately one for every three programmes. An additional brochure is sent out each term which contains a set piece of homework to be completed and returned by the student during the term.

43. At the end of the term students are required to sit for a written examination held in special centres. Both homework and examinations are drafted by the Funkkolleg team with the help of the broadcast authors and DIFF experts.

44. The homework and examinations provide questions with five alternative answers of which at least two, and not more than four, are wrong. Another set of multiple-choice tests is made for reserve examinations which take place each term for those students who, for medical or other reasons, failed to attend the terminal examinations. (Reports of Funkkolleg programmes are said to be hindered by the limited number of possible multiple-choice questions applicable to the course material.)

45. Marking is done by computer and a student is given a full account of his or her results as well as explanations as to why certain answers are wrong.

Subjects taught

46. The choice of subjects to be taught is the prerogative of the Planning Commission of Funkkolleg, which acts in a general supervisory capacity. Since 1969 this has been composed of representatives of the four (from 1971, five) state governments, the university federations and adult-education institutes of the states, the four (from 1971, five) broadcasting stations, DIFF, and a representative of the academic team of the previous year.

47. Since Modell I, subjects have lasted for one year or two terms (semesters) and have changed every year:

1969/70	Education (course known as Modell II).
1970/71	Mathematics (Modell III).
1971	Political economy (Modell IV) half a year only; in fact a repeat of a term of Modell I.
1971/72	Linguistics (Modell V).
1972/73	Educational psychology (Modell VI).
1973/74	Biology (Modell VII).

The study year of Funkkolleg is linked to that of the schools and adapted to school holidays.

48. The choice of education as the subject of Modell II virtually imposed itself in the major crisis of the educational system in 1968. The subject of mathematics was chosen particularly for older teachers unacquainted with new teaching methods; the linguistics course aimed to update the knowledge of German and foreign-language teachers. The educational psychology course chosen for 1972/73 had the highest enrolment figures so far, which reflects the continuing interest in educational problems in the Federal Republic.

Development of team and radio co-operation

49. It was not until the linguistics course began in 1971 that a first attempt was made to exploit the full potentialities of radio by presenting the 'living language' in scenes, dialogues etc. This new departure was abandoned, however, during the course. Another and more vigorous attempt to establish radio expertise inside the Funkkolleg team was made by Saarländischer Rundfunk (SR), when, in 1973, a scientist was appointed as radio editor of the biology course and given two assistants qualified to speak on the subject. The academic nucleus of the team at this time happened to be particularly responsive to suggestions by DIFF educationists and the SR broadcasting experts.

50. DIFF has a special influence in Funkkolleg, being the largest contributor to the budget and the only factor of continuity amidst changing teams. Its integration in the process of producing radio studies was established very early and its influence has grown ever since.

Content of the texts and brochures

51. While the 'acting' broadcasting organization is responsible for the programmes, it is the team which distributes air time between its members and other scholars, agrees on the final text of the course with its author, and supervises the writing of the course brochures together with a member of DIFF and the author of the course, and, where possible, the radio editor. During the biology course the radio editor and his two assistants also take an active part in discussions about the printed material.

Publications

52. Both team and printers have to cope with very tight time schedules for printing the course material. In the case of the political-economy course in 1971, which was a repeat of a term in Modell I (see paragraph 47), more time could be allotted to the elaboration of printed material since lectures were ready before the broadcasts even started.

53. The cost of publicity is borne by the broadcasting organizations. Publicity consists of advertisements in the press, radio commercials and billboards as well as the free dispatch of the text of the introductory programmes of the latest model and a pamphlet describing the course, which includes a printed enrolment card to be sent in by each student.

54. The brochures and publicity handouts are printed by a private publisher, the Julius Beltz Verlag, which also bills students for the fees payable. Another publisher, the Fischer Bücherei, prints the texts of the broadcast lectures, but well after the examinations for the Modell.

Fees

55. Fees for each course cover enrolment, the marking of homework and examinations, and the cost of brochures and postage. Inflation has caused a steady rise in fees from DM.12 per term in 1969 to DM.32 in 1974. An additional fee of DM.20–30 is sometimes charged for evening classes (see paragraph 38).

Examinations

56. Two commissions were set up to supervise the computerized multiple-choice tests (see paragraph 44): the Certificates Commission (*Zertifikatskommission*) and the Examinations Commission (*Prüfungskommission*).

The Certificates Commission

This commission comprises one representative from each of the five states in which Funkkolleg broadcasts, representatives of the academic team (see paragraph 30) and DIFF. Its yearly meetings are arranged by the 'acting' broadcasting organization. The commission makes fundamental decisions about examination procedure as well as recommendations with regard to the merit of certificates obtained. The merit of the certificates in relation to the special admission procedure to universities (see paragraph 15(b)) and the advantages the certificate may offer practising teachers is decided by the state government; but the extent to which a certificate may be recognized as a substitute for university seminars for existing university students is decided by the individual universities.

The Examinations Commission

A larger Examinations Commission carries out the practical work connected with the computerized examinations and includes representatives of the Educational Centre of IBM Deutschland, the firm processing the examinations.

Advantages of the computerized evaluations of examinations

57. During a testing process, computer experts test questions on students of a university which is outside the operational area of Funkkolleg, in order to eliminate badly phrased and misleading questions and those with low or negative discerning value. Questions which the majority of candidates can answer correctly are deemed to have a low or fractional discerning value, while questions answered incorrectly by the better candidates (because, for example, they suspected a trap where there is none) and correctly by candidates with poorer overall results are considered to have a negative discerning value.

58. Multiple-choice questions can test theoretical understanding and factual knowledge. However, they cannot reveal anything about the candidate's ability to use his or her knowledge in a creative way.

59. Funkkolleg has no means of introducing additional examinations and, even if it had, there would be some opposition to their introduction on the grounds that candidates with a good educational background would have an unfair advantage and results would no longer be assessed with absolute objectivity.

60. It might be expected that some candidates would be confused by computer feed-in forms. However, at the examination after the 1969/70 education course, only 0.2 per cent of candidates made incorrect markings that required the entries to be copied before they were fed into the computer. Surprisingly, there was not a single case in which the intentions of the candidates had not been clear and it can be assumed that the familiarity of candidates with computerized multiple-choice examinations has since improved.

61. Depending on the number of students and other conditions, computerized tests can be considerably cheaper than other examinations. In January 1974 the cost per student of the Funkkolleg examination was only

DM.1.60 (U.S.$0.70 or £0.28p). However, in the case of Funkkolleg there would have to be about 3,000 students to make this more economical than other forms.

62. In principle, basic computer programmes used for the Funkkolleg multiple-choice examinations are of universal application.

VIII Students

63. Students of the Funkkolleg are officially described as 'participants' (*Teilnehmer*) and range from candidates seeking special university admission, to university students and pupils of the last two years of grammar school, as well as teachers and others. Participants do not have to be of German nationality or live in the area served by Funkkolleg; they do not have to have any educational qualifications and there is no age limit. Selection or aptitude tests are conducted according to the principle of first come, first served. Inhabitants of Austria and Switzerland have been encouraged to join, and in 1974 1,026 Swiss university students enrolled.

Candidates seeking admission to university

64. For candidates without the necessary *Abitur* who want to enter university the certificate gained after one year at Funkkolleg replaces one of the two testimonials from a university professor required under the special admission procedure (see paragraph 15(b)). In Bremen one certificate replaces both testimonials, and students can thus qualify for the examination with one Funkkolleg certificate. With this exception, two years of study are generally required to qualify for the second stage of the special entry examinations.

University students

65. In the case of university students the certificate may serve as a substitute for a university seminar, though one year's study at Funkkolleg will be considered at most as the equivalent of one (half-year) term of a university seminar, unless Funkkolleg offers a subject for which there is no provision in the university's own curriculum. Where they cannot provide a course themselves, some universities are glad to make use of the Funkkolleg provision. For instance, in 1973/74, universities without a biology course in their medical curriculum used Funkkolleg Modell VII. Other universities, however, see the Funkkolleg as a source of interference.

Grammar school pupils

66. The role of Funkkolleg in secondary school education is unclear. In the case of grammar schools offering laboratory workshops for science courses in the higher forms, the Funkkolleg course in biology may have provided inspiration or served as a substitute for that work.

Teachers

67. Although upgrading or promotion prospects are held out to teachers with Funkkolleg certificates, these prospects have on the whole lessened in importance since 1969.

Other students

68. With regard to other students, the value of Funkkolleg certificates is unclear. It is, for instance, suggested in prospectuses that successful candidates 'may ask their employers to put their FK certificates on their personal files.'

IX Practical effects of Funkkolleg

69. Until 1966 Funkkolleg operated in one state only and the number of Funkkolleg students was under 1,000. But the number had increased to 17,000 by 1971/72 and to 41,000 in 1972/74 when educational psychology was offered as a subject. For the biology course in 1973/74 the number dropped to 20,000.

70. Teachers have outnumbered other types of students because the choice of subjects was nearly always influenced by provincial governments wishing to update the qualifications of certain categories of teachers and train others for new tasks. Teachers are classified as part of the group of civil servants making up 50 per cent of the student population. Only half of 1 per cent of all participants are workers. A slightly larger percentage are described as apprentices and trainees, and at least some of these are bound to be children of working-class families or young people in blue-collar jobs. The larger part of the findings of a special DIFF unit on the social composition of the student body has so far remained unpublished, but is available in typescript form on request.

71. The number of university students enrolling increased from 12 per cent in 1970 to 26 per cent in 1973, which may indicate a growing recognition by the universities of Funkkolleg, or an increased desire by students to supplement their studies.

72. The percentage of participants wanting to gain a certificate to enter university without the *Abitur* has decreased from 10 per cent in 1971 to 4 per cent of the total number of students in 1973. Because of the increase in the total number of the student population, however, the strength of this group has in fact increased in absolute figures.

73. The proportion of female students increased from 18 per cent in Modell I (1966–69) to 47 per cent in 1972. The latter figure is only slightly lower than the proportion of women in the adult population of the Federal Republic of Germany (55 per cent). The course of educational psychology of 1972/73 may have been particularly attractive to women and was officially advertised as useful to mothers, but the same cannot be said of the course on linguistics in 1971/72 in which the proportion of women was 42 per cent, i.e. only slightly lower. The increase in the number and proportion of women can in fact be regarded as part of an even wider and more significant trend in the development of Funkkolleg and its student population. Since 1970 at least there has been a

steady increase in the number of students enrolling without such motives as the hope for promotion or social betterment, or the intention to start full-time studies at university. By now the majority of students enrol because of an interest in the subject offered, or higher learning in general. These students have but vague, if any, ideas about the practical use they can make of their acquired knowledge.

74. An increasing number of 'participants' have taken the final examination —29 per cent in 1969 rising to 36 per cent in 1973. (The number dropped during the mathematics year of 1970/71 to 24 per cent.) This may be partly due to the increasing number of participants who re-enrol—in 1973 the proportion was 25 per cent. The success rate of examinations was over 90 per cent.

75. The high rate of success may also be due to the increase in the percentage of university students used to formal examinations, and the fact that about one-third of students now tape-record the broadcasts, which makes preparation for examinations much easier. A drop-out rate would be hard to define since the intention to obtain a certificate is not a prerequisite of enrolment. Some participants, for instance, are only interested in obtaining the cheap student brochures.

76. Fees for the course have remained low—the 1973 biology course amounted to DM.64 per year (£10 or U.S.$25)—and there are no additional expenses such as the buying of books, since the brochures provide all that is needed. Extras amount simply to paying for the postage of returned homework and fares to the nearest site where the examinations are held. To attend evening classes many students may have to pay an extra DM.20 to DM.30, but maximum expenditure during 1973/74 did not amount to more than DM.100 (or approximately the equivalent of one year's combined radio and television licence fee). Present inflation and rising costs may mean a substantial increase in fees, however. Total or partial exemption from payment of fees is very seldom accorded. There is no reduction in fees if several members of the same family enrol and could share the price of the brochures.

77. The payment of fees is the only condition of admission (see paragraph 63).

X Finance

78. Half of Funkkolleg's revenue is contributed by DIFF, which itself is financed by the state governments, including those in whose areas Funkkolleg does not broadcast. The governments of the five states in which Funkkolleg operates altogether contribute one-third, partly through their further education administrations, and the rest is provided by the five radio organizations.

79. Expenditure figures for Funkkolleg compare favourably with other Open Learning systems. Estimates for 1974/75 foresaw costs amounting to DM.180 (£30 or U.S.$75) per student, making a total expenditure of DM.3.6 million (about £0.6 million, U.S.$1.5 million) for 20,000 students. Since about one-quarter of this will be recovered from enrolment fees, public expenditure per student is of the order of DM.100 to DM.150 (about £17 to £25, or U.S.$40 to U.S.$60)—a figure which compares favourably with the 1970 figure for full-time university education in the Federal Republic of Germany. In that year DM.7,000 million was spent on the higher education of fewer than 400,000

students (roughly DM.20,000 per student). Even after taking into account differences between full-time and part-time education and the fact that a large part of university budgets is spent on research while Funkkolleg spends nothing in this field (except on sociological surveys of its own students), the proportion of 1 to 200 in Funkkolleg's favour (and that at a later stage of inflation) must be regarded as most impressive.

XI Extent of Funkkolleg success

80. During its eight years of existence, a total of 150,000 students have enrolled in the courses up to and including 1974/75. As there are no records available it is not known how many Funkkolleg students entered university after obtaining a certificate, but the number is believed to be very low. A total of nearly 40,000 certificates have been issued to participants, excluding figures for 1974. Though many students may have obtained more than one certificate, it is estimated that 0.2 per cent of the total population of the area covered by Funkkolleg has completed one or more courses with full success, while over 1 per cent of the adult population in the Funkkolleg area has enrolled for at least one of the university-level multi-media courses.

Funkkolleg radio lectures and publications have gained much prestige for the college and radio lectures and printed teaching material have been successfully combined, although imaginative use of radio potentialities is still limited. Computerized evaluation of examinations and homework has been a striking innovation, but remains of limited value in assessing creative use of knowledge.

By achieving free, flexible and enthusiastic co-operation with many institutions, Funkkolleg has proved that an extensive multi-media learning system can function without becoming an established institution.

XII Conclusion

81. Though Funkkolleg appears to have had little influence on the established academic methods of the educational system in the Federal Republic, it has shown that a large proportion of the population is interested in and capable of assimilating university-level studies. It has proved that modern technology can be used in co-operation with decentralized institutions to provide university-type teaching at a low cost to an unlimited audience.

Appendix A **Standardized reference data**

Country, state or province	*Federal Republic of Germany*
Area and climate	100,000 square miles. Maritime to continental.
Population	
Total (latest year)	61,700,000 (1971).
Estimated population aged 18	500,000 (1970).
Estimated percentage under 15	Approximately 12 per cent (1970).
Current annual growth rate (percentage)	0.6 (1965–72).
Government	
Main organizational structure	Delegation of major administrative responsibilities through federal system's 10 states.
Political type	Parliamentary democracy; republic.
Economy	
Political type	Predominantly industrialized, agriculture and forestry developed. Little state control.
Gross national product	
Total (latest year)	U.S.$235,000 million (1971) (1 Deutsche Mark=U.S.$0.238).
Per head	U.S.$3,800 (1971).
Average annual increase (percentage)	4 (1970–71); 3 (1971–72).
Communications	
Ground/air	Quick and easy countrywide system of roads, motorways, bus, rail and air transport services.
Mail/telephone	Adequate postal services. Growing telephone services, 26 per 100 inhabitants (1972).

Broadcasting	
Main system(s) operating/Principal authorities responsible	ARD (Arbeitsgemeinschaft der Öffentlich-rechtlichen Rundfunkanstalten Deutschlands): a public body responsible for the planning and transmission of radio and television services in 9 regional organizations. ZDF (Deutsches Fernsehen) second channel. Both non-profit-making.
Radio	
Transmission coverage of main programme services in percentage of population reached	Virtually 100.
Receiving capability for main programme services (percentage)	Virtually 100.
Television	
Transmission coverage as defined for radio (percentage)	Approaching 100.
Receiving capability for main programme services (percentage)	Approaching 100.
Monochrome or colour	All channels in colour (PAL) with compatible monochrome.
Education	
Type of system(s)	Public controlled (insignificant private sector), under strict state supervision, some religious schools forming part of public sector.
Main authorities responsible and powers	
At school level	Land (autonomous state) governments maintain schools subject to financial and administrative influence of federal government.
At post-secondary level	Land governments.
End of full-time school attendance	
Legal	Compulsory and free between 6 and 15.
De facto	Thirty per cent stay voluntarily till at least 16, about 20 per cent till 19.
Proportion of 18-year-old age group involved in education (percentage)	
Full-time	20.
Major developments in provision	
Over last five years	Introduction of *numerus clausus* at most universities.
Over next five years	Lowering of school entry age from 6 to 5 years.

Institution/system under study	*Funkkolleg*
Brief for study and reason for inclusion	State of Hesse. The Funkkolleg is not an institution but a functional co-operative effort by broadcasting stations, Land governments and DIFF (German Institute for Distance Studies). Included as an example of multi-media distance teaching.
Description of subject studied	The institution and its certificate.
Origins	Founded in Land of Hessen (1966).
Educational authority(ies) and roles	Land governments finance via DIFF basic syllabus and study material. Also administration and examinations.
Communications authority(ies) and roles	ARD and ZDF provide air time and pay for lectures on the air.
Services provided	Wider opportunities of university education to adults both for vocational and non-vocational purposes, through face-to-face and multi-media methods of tutoring.
Eligibility to study	
(a) categories	Adults.
(b) qualifications	None.
Terminal qualifications	Zertifikat (Certificate).
Instructional means used	Multi-media, i.e. radio, printed study letters and (optional) seminars.
Personal input from student	4 to 10 hours per week.
Normal duration of study	One year, but up to 25 per cent enrol again for the next course in the following year.
Pedagogical effectiveness	Pass rate now 40 per cent and constantly increasing.
Numbers involved	
Students	
Intake (latest year)	40,000 (1972/73), 20,000 (1973/74).
On roll	40,000 (1972/73), 20,000 (1973/74).
Graduating	Over 14,000 (1973).
Academic staff	
Full time/Part-time	No full- or part-time staff but a few DIFF staff allocated to Funkkolleg full-time, others part-time.
Other professional staff	
Number	3 clerical staff.
Finance	
Recurrent expenditure	
By providing authorities (latest year)	DM.3.6 million (1974/75). Of this about DM.1 million to be recovered from students.
Average annual outlay by students	Under DM.100.
Non-recurrent expenditure	
Gross, over first five years of new institution	No capital expenditure.

Special assistance received	
Financial	None beyond public funds and a contribution of one-sixth by broadcasting associations.
Non-financial	Funkkolleg dependent upon existing educational and communications infrastructure and co-operation with ARD educational services.

Sources of further information

Educational	Zentralbüro des Funkkollegs, 6 Frankfurt am Main 90, Robert-Mayer-Strasse 20 (Federal Republic of Germany).

Appendix B **Short bibliography**

FUNKKOLLEG. *Forschungsreport, Modell I, Modell II.* Weinheim u. Basel, Beltz Verlag, 1972. (Tübinger Beiträge zum Fernstudium, V.)

——. *Forschungsreport, Modell V, Modell VI.* Weinheim u. Basel, Beltz Verlag, 1975. (Tübinger Beiträge zum Fernstudium, VIII.)

HOFFBAUER, H. The Quadriga-Funkkolleg. In: *Pedagogy*, p. 82–104. Munich, Internationales Institut für das Jugend und Bildungsfernsehen, 1971.

KADELBACH, G.; KLAFKI, W.; REBEL, K. *et al.* Das Quadriga-Funkkolleg 'Erziehungswissenschaft'. *IBM Nachrichten* (Sindelfingen), vol. 202, August 1970.

——. Modell der multimedialen Erwachsenenbildung. *IBM Nachrichten* (Sindelfingen), vol. 205, February 1971.

REBEL, K. The Quadriga Funkkolleg. In: *Multimedia systems in adult education*, p. 73–81. Munich, Internationales Institut für das Jugend und Bildungsfernsehen, 1971.

INFRATEST/DIFF. Research reports by Infratest/DIFF can be consulted at the five radio stations co-operating in Funkkolleg (Hessischer Rundfunk, etc.), in the offices of DIFF at the University of Tübingen and in the Central Office of Funkkolleg in Frankfurt.

Appendix C **Biographical note**

Stephen Kanocz holds the Licence des Lettres Allemandes of the University of Louvain and the Licence en Philologie Germanique of the University of Brussels. He became the producer of German School Programmes for the BBC in 1963 and between then and 1971 wrote, produced and published the audio-visual audio-lingual German course as well as several other programmes about the Federal Republic of Germany today.

The Free University of **Iran**

John R. Beardsley

Contents

I Introduction

1. The Free University of Iran is an attempt to introduce and institutionalize in Iran an entirely new concept of university education. Its basic aim is to contribute to the national policy of social and economic integration of Iranian society by providing skilled manpower for the development of the country's rural and less urbanized sectors. If successful, the Free University will develop as a viable alternative to the present structure of higher education, with different premises as to who is to be taught, what is to be taught and how teaching is to be carried out.

2. The university will receive its first intake, approximately 6,000 students, early in 1977. Employing a variety of instructional materials and methods, the Free University will develop a system to teach its students at a distance. Since integration of the rural areas is a basic aim, it will attempt to bring learning resources as close as possible to its students' places of residence and work.

3. This paper is intended to provide a survey of the Free University's aims, objectives and proposed teaching system.

II The national context

4. Iran lies in south-west Asia, stretching from the Persian Gulf and the Gulf of Oman in the south to the Caspian Sea in the north. On the east it is bounded by Afghanistan and Pakistan: on the west by Turkey and Iraq. In addition to its coastline on the Caspian in the north, Iran has an extensive common border with the U.S.S.R. (1,200 miles).

5. The total area of Iran is 636,000 square miles, greater than the combined areas of Belgium, Denmark, France, the Federal Republic of Germany, Italy and the United Kingdom. One-third of the country consists of a mountainous plateau some 4,000 feet above sea level, one-third of vast desert expanses and one-third of a mixture of wooded slopes and arable plains.

6. Persian, an Aryan language of the Indo-European group written in Arabic characters, is the official and dominant language. Other important languages include Turkish, spoken by over 20 per cent of the population, Caspian dialects, Kurdi, Baluchi, Arabic and Armenian. Approximately 35 per cent of Iran's population speak a language other than Persian as their mother tongue.

7. In 1966, the year of the last census, Iran's population stood at 25.8 million. In 1972–73 the population was estimated by the National Plan Organization to be 31.2 million. In 1966 approximately 38 per cent of the total population were living in urban areas (towns of less than 5,000 population being designated as rural). In 1972–73 the estimated urban population was 43 per cent. The percentage of the urban population should rise to approximately 47.2 per cent by 1978.

8. Iran is a constitutional monarchy with a bicameral legislative body. The nation is ruled by the Shahinshah Mohammed Reza Pahlavi. The present constitution, instituted in 1906, provides for: a senate with sixty members, half of whom are appointed by the Shah, with fifteen elected from the capital city, Tehran, and fifteen from the provinces; the Majlis (Parliament) with 198 popularly elected members; a cabinet of ministers headed by the Prime Minister, appointed by the Shah; and local governors and governors-general for the provinces, appointed by the government.

9. Iran's modern era can be said to have begun in the 1920s when Reza Khan staged a *coup d'état*, forcing the last of the Qajar Shahs to leave the country. In 1925 he made himself Shah and founded the Pahlavi dynasty. In the middle sixties, after having launched 'a revolution from the throne' which called for electoral reform, land redistribution and the end of serfdom, and which provided the impetus for rapid industrialization, the present Shah began to assert successfully the power of his monarchy. Today Iran is relatively stable. Her vast oil revenues fuel the development of the economy, technological modernization and many social and educational reforms.

10. Although oil provides about one-quarter of the gross domestic product, Iran's economy is still predominantly agricultural. But it is becoming less so. Of the country's labour force, 49 per cent were employed in agriculture in 1967, while by 1972 the comparable figure was only 40.1 per cent. The oil industry is not labour-intensive, but, as might be expected, both in general industry and in services the proportion employed has risen appreciably.

11. If, instead of the labour force, finance is taken as a yardstick, the change shows even more sharply. Examination of the gross national product shows that in 1959 agriculture's share was almost three times that of industry, and more than three times that of oil. Since then a radical change has taken place. By 1972, agriculture's share had halved, industry's had increased by about one and a half times and oil had doubled its share, giving a breakdown of 19 per cent for agriculture, 23 per cent for industry and 19 per cent for oil. Yet though Iran has experienced a dramatic growth of modern industrial products over recent years, three-quarters of the country's exports are still traditional and agricultural goods.

12. Such deep and swift social and economic changes as the foregoing demand changes in the educational patterns of the country. In Iran, a thoroughgoing effort is being made to bring about the process by planning and reform. The new system should be completely implemented throughout the country by the end of the Fifth Plan, that is, by March 1978. In the new system, students complete a five-year full elementary stage and later a three-year guidance cycle which is free and has been made compulsory. This guidance cycle represents an attempt to rationalize secondary education and to eliminate unsuitable entrants from this stage, regarded as preparatory to university education. At the end of the cycle, all students are required to take a national examination which is a

basis for establishing eligibility to enter either the academic or the vocational/technical branches of the upper secondary level. The academic branch lasts four years, with the final year offering specialization in one of the following four areas: (a) literature and arts; (b) natural sciences; (c) physics and mathematics; (d) social science and economics.

13. In 1971, the proportion of pupils enrolled for the primary and secondary levels was approximately 77 per cent and 32 per cent respectively of the appropriate age group. According to the Plan Organization, these figures should rise to 88 per cent and 44 per cent by the end of the Fifth Plan, with 80 per cent of rural children being accommodated in primary schools. The number of students at universities and institutions of higher education was 108,000 in 1972/73; approximately 154,000 students are to be enrolled in 1977/78.

14. The total financial allocation for education was 134,000 million rials in the Fourth Plan. Before the increase in oil prices, 405,000 million rials were allocated for the Fifth Plan. Government investment in education is expected to rise from 3.4 per cent of gross national income at the end of the Fourth Plan to some 6 per cent by 1978.

15. Centralized control of primary and secondary education is exercised by the Ministry of Education. Each province has its own director of education directly responsible to the ministry. Higher education is much less centralized. The Ministry of Science and Higher Education, established in 1968, exercises no executive control over the universities and can set institutions of higher education only vague requirements and standards, which they can easily adapt to meet their particular circumstances.

16. The educational system in Iran, including the post-secondary level, is beset with problems common to most developing nations: the pressure of numbers; an inadequate supply of trained and competent teachers; lack of resources; and the emphasis on memorization of facts as a primary teaching objective, if not in terms of what is desired at least in terms of what is actually achieved. It is in this context that the Free University was designed and will attempt to develop its unique teaching system.

III The establishment of the Free University

17. In January 1971, influenced considerably by information about the British Open University, the Ministry of Science and Higher Education in Iran (MSHE) began to consider the possible implications of long-distance teaching as a means of solving some of its own problems.

18. Enrolments in universities and institutions of higher education in Iran had increased fourfold since 1963; the existing educational structure was stretched to the breaking point. It was clear, moreover, that the demand for post-secondary qualifications was not going to abate during the period of the fifth National Development Plan (March 1973 to March 1978). It was equally clear that the system of higher education, while it would enrol approximately 154,000 students in 1978 (as opposed to 97,000 in 1971/72), would absorb a lower percentage of the secondary school leavers.

19. It was the British Open University's claim that it could cut the cost of university education per pupil eightfold, together with the fact that the system required little capital investment, no large teaching facilities and could

reach thousands of scattered students, which attracted the Iranian planners.

20. The idea to study the Open University took form in the MSHE and in the Institute for Research and Planning in Science and Education (IRPSE). IRPSE is an independent governmental body concerned with all aspects and elements of the educational system in Iran. It has, however, no executive responsibility or authority. While the institute is ostensibly concerned with the entire system of education, it seems to have a much closer working relationship with the Ministry of Science than with the Ministry of Education. It was created as part of the MSHE and separated later; the Minister of Science is, *ex officio*, chairman of its board of trustees.

21. In June 1971 the Minister of Science instructed Dr A. Ahmadi, then deputy-director of the institute, to request a visit to the British Open University in order to study its methods and operations. In addition to the Open University, Dr Ahmadi visited Telekolleg in Munich and KTRU (Committee for Television and Radio in Education) in Stockholm.

22. In November 1971, Ahmadi submitted his initial report to the Prime Minister. The report included: an enumeration and discussion of crucial (and obvious) problems besetting the system of higher education in Iran; a description of the Open University's teaching system; a summary of benefits which might be derived from introducing such a system into Iran and the obstacles likely to be encountered; and an estimate of development costs involved.

23. The report did not suggest a commitment to create an 'Open University' in Iran or offer a basis for any specific designs. It recommended the establishment of a Planning Council which would be comprised of prominent academics, broadcasters, and government planners. The council would undertake studies 'to determine the appropriateness, feasibility, and likely design of a correspondence-based educational system at the post-secondary level'. It was suggested that the council be chaired by the Prime Minister.

24. The winter of 1972 was occupied in devising the overall planning strategy for creating the university. The objective at this stage was to commit the government as well as the officers of the university to certain courses of action (e.g. a deadline for the first intake of students, a philosophical orientation, a certain educational approach, etc.) which were felt to be appropriate to the conception of the university and which would, once the decision to go ahead had been taken, be feasible. The planning was to be completed in ten months.

25. The main essentials at this stage were, therefore, to identify the decisions to be made, the activities to be carried out and the personnel required. For this a timetable had to be drawn up to co-ordinate the various planning activities. First, eleven elements of the final document were identified. These elements constituted the framework of the planning stage. Second, the planners listed the constraints which they felt to be operative at the time. Third, they enumerated basic questions which they believed would have to be answered within each of the elements—questions considered 'strategic' in nature. Having set up a planning structure and decided upon a timetable, they identified manpower requirements at different points, including the need for consultants.

26. The elements of the plan and some of the questions which were posed are set out below. The following questions do not constitute a comprehensive list, either in terms of what was asked or what should be asked, but they do serve to illustrate the range and complexity of issues which have to be faced by governments or institutions which aim to embark upon a similar study.

The long-range goals of the proposed university—are they justified?

Who are the students in need? What are their characteristics in terms of age, sex, occupation, academic background and geographical location?

What are the national and economic needs of the country in terms of manpower?

What general education would it be appropriate for the proposed university to presume?

Is the correspondence-based multi-media system of the proposed university the most appropriate to satisfy the needs, or are there better alternatives either within the country or elsewhere?

What are the educational priorities?

What skills and what subject areas can be defined at this stage, bearing in mind the production strains of the initial years?

Admission policy and degree structure

To what extent should these, or can these, differ from those of the conventional university?

The instructional system

Given the basic pattern of the British Open University, to what extent should Iran make adaptation in, e.g., the degree of decentralization in the planning and use of some course material, the role of television, the emphasis to be placed on face-to-face tuition and the mix of the media?

The support system

What support systems (e.g. publishing, printing and distribution) must be set up and how can they be incorporated into the university?

Course-material creation

Given limited manpower in Iran, is the course team of the British Open University a feasible proposition? What are the alternatives?

Size and scope of the university

What should be the target for student numbers in the first two years? How many of Iran's thirteen regions should be covered?

Government and management structure

What should be the authority and responsibilities of the university's supreme governing body, both externally vis-à-vis the MSHE and internally vis-à-vis its staff and students? How should the various policy-making, administrative and operational functions be structured within the university?

Financing

What division should there be between capital and recurrent expenditure? What is a realistic estimate of costs over the first five years?

Initial commitments

What initial commitments have to be made to give a reasonable chance of success? A foreign advisory service, a long-term staff training scheme and an initial foundation of a size and scope to give university status seem essential. Are there others?

Institutional relationships
What formal external relationships should the university foster and what form should they take (e.g. with National Iranian Radio and Television)?

27. The strategic planning stage was organized at three levels. There was a Planning Council, chaired by the Prime Minister, and made up of very high-level academic administrators. Its membership included the Minister of Science and Higher Education, the Director of the Plan Organization, the Director of National Iranian Radio and Television (NIRT), the Vice-Chancellor of Tehran University, the Minister of Education, and the director and deputy-director of IRPSE. The council assumed overall responsibility for the planning of the university but, as it met very infrequently, its primary, if not its only, role, though an extremely important one, was to lend political authority to decisions generated further down the line.

28. At the end of the line, a planning unit was organized within IRPSE. It consisted of Dr Ahmadi, the director of educational planning, and four staff members of IRPSE. This unit was made responsible for deliberating upon and carrying out studies related to the issues listed above. It drew upon the resources of an Iranian consulting firm, the Industrial Management Institute (IMI), for much of the detailed work related to the organization of the university, and dealt at both the staff and policy levels with NIRT. Between the planning unit, within IRPSE, and the Planning Council, a third body was created. It was called the Executive Committee of the Planning Council and consisted of six of the council's members.

29. The Executive Committee was very much a working body and met at least three times a month during the autumn of 1972 and the winter of 1973. The strategic plan, submitted by the council to the Shah in June 1973, should be considered, therefore, as the result of a joint effort.

30. The initial plan underwent a number of slight revisions during the summer of 1973. During this same period, Dr Ahmadi was also requested to submit a more detailed development strategy which would ensure the availability of the skills required to design and operate the systems proposed.

31. In December 1973 the Free University was established by imperial decree. Dr Ahmadi was chosen to be its first chancellor.

IV Aims and objectives

Problems and needs

32. The Free University has been designed to respond to three very basic needs: the need to satisfy the ever-increasing demand for higher education while holding costs to society within acceptable bounds; the need to accommodate a demand no longer limited to specific socio-economic and age groupings; and the need to provide highly skilled manpower in areas critical to national integration and development.

The pressure of demand

33. In Iran, as elsewhere, rapid population growth, the expansion of primary and secondary school systems, changes in popular expectations and rapid technological changes have all contributed to an enormous increase in the demand for higher education during the past two decades. Starting from a very low base, Iran rapidly expanded its system of higher education during the 1960s. In 1962/63, a total of 24,456 students were enrolled at seven universities and four institutes of higher education. By 1972/73, the total enrolment figure exceeded 115,000; one university and over 100 institutes had been created. The universities' share of the total fell from 88 per cent in 1962/63 to 41 per cent in 1972/73. The current role of private institutions in absorbing much of the demand is clearly important; while these institutions were not included in 1963/64, they accounted for 21 per cent of total enrolment in 1972/73.

34. To fuel this growth, the government increased higher education's percentage of the total education budget from under 10 per cent in 1964 to practically 20 per cent by 1968; by 1972 it had dropped to 14 per cent. Of the three main levels of education (elementary, general secondary, and higher) higher education had the highest rate of total growth during the period 1964–72.

35. But by the end of the Fourth Plan (March 1973) it was abundantly clear that the demand for higher education was far from its peak. It was also apparent that the ability of the existing system to respond to the demand was extremely limited, especially if serious efforts were to be launched to upgrade the quality of instruction.

36. There has been a considerable rate of expansion at secondary level over the past decade. Despite efforts to hold down this expansion during the Fourth Plan, enrolments soared from 781,507 in 1968 to practically 1.2 million in 1972/73. The planned rate was considerably more modest. According to the fourth National Development Plan, the target for the school year 1972/73 was approximately 950,000. In 1968, 31,049 were graduated from the upper secondary level; in 1973, the figure was 66,000, practically all of whom sat for the university entrance examination. For those who failed to gain admittance it was not a question of entering the job market, but rather of waiting to attempt a second, third or even fourth time. It cannot be expected that attempts by the Ministry of Education to diversify and rationalize secondary education will have much effect upon demand for the studies which lead directly to post-secondary qualifications, especially university qualifications. In most educational systems where only a small percentage reach the upper secondary level, the demand is the same and one should not expect Iran to be any different.

37. Finally, the fact that the net annual population growth rate of over 3 per cent is not likely to abate in the near future, taken together with the government's public commitment to the democratization of the first eight years of schooling, presents additional evidence that Iran's system of higher education has just begun to feel the pressure of numbers.

38. But the issue of numbers, of course, is not simply one of aggregate figures. In 1969/70, approximately 8 per cent of third-level students came from working-class or farming families; most of these were enrolled in technical or agricultural institutes. Slightly more than one-third of the entire student body

was born in the Central Province, which in 1966 contained only 18 per cent of Iran's population. Moreover, nearly half had received their secondary education in the capital city. Though no distribution breakdown is available for 1972/73, it would not be surprising to find a reduction in the regional distribution of students in the higher education system. Of the additional 14,000 students in the private system, practically all would have come from Tehran or its environs. If it were not for the addition in 1971 of two-year teacher-training colleges to the list of post-secondary institutions, the distribution would be even more skewed.

39. None of the above, however, is surprising in a situation where only 4 per cent of the 18 to 22 age group are enrolled in post-secondary institutions. It is equally obvious, moreover, that the system of higher education is going to be pressed to accommodate a larger and more heterogeneous and geographically dispersed student body, as the secondary level expands and extends its scope.

40. The burden of responding to the demand for higher education, moreover, is most accurately measured in terms of the costs to the quality of education. Few would disagree that the rapid expansion of the system during the last decade has been achieved at considerable expense of quality. Human and material resources have been stretched to breaking point. Half the teaching staff at Tehran University, for example, work part-time; the provincial universities, with one exception, rely heavily upon teachers whose sole interest is to avoid military conscription. It is universally felt that the quality of instruction will be further diluted unless the present system has the opportunity to launch serious attempts at self-improvement. And yet, according to a report of IRPSE, the system will have to expand at a greater rate over the next ten years than it has in the last ten, just in order to maintain the ratio of acceptances to graduates.

41. A final aspect of the nature of the ever-increasing demand for higher education is reflected by the 'youth-centredness' of the Iranian higher educational system. Higher education in Iran, as in most societies, is clearly based upon the assumptions that knowledge and skills obtained in youth are sufficient for life and that they are most effectively and efficiently transferred in a 'lockstep' fashion. However, in any society which is in transition from an agricultural to an industrial economy, from a static and traditional society to a more socially dynamic and economically fluid one, and in whose development continued training and education are called for, entirely youth-centred educational systems are anomalies.

42. But the educational problems of the adult are very different, of course, from those of young people. The adult needs to integrate his studies freely with his everyday working and social activities; he needs a very flexible means of gathering new knowledge and skills; one which allows him to study at a time and place of his own choosing.

43. It was felt by the end of 1971 that expansion could only be achieved through a capital-intensive approach (as opposed to a labour-intensive one—which, is, in fact, exemplified by most educational institutes) if costs to society were to be held to a minimum. It was also felt that, if the adult with his particular needs was to be accommodated, a system would have to be developed which brought learning resources to the student rather than requiring him to travel to reach them.

Manpower requirements

44. The existence of demand, however important in both social and political terms, does not, of course justify the development of the means to satisfy it. Very few societies can afford the 'social demand' approach to educational planning. For Iran, the solution to the demand problem does not lie in merely expanding the existing system; to do so might well result in creating unemployed graduates instead of unemployed school leavers. Expansion, it is argued, should be achieved in a way which is as congruent as possible with the developing requirements of the economy as a whole, and with the manpower requirements of different sectors in particular.

45. Because of the above considerations, it was agreed in the early planning stages that the Free University would not aim to produce scholars or students with a subject-discipline orientation. It was decided that the initial focus of the university (for at least the first decade of its existence) would be upon the pre-service and in-service training and education of professionals. It was further decided to launch two programmes during the first year; one in teacher education and the second in health services education.

Teacher education

46. Reports received from a number of sources, including the planning staff of the university, reached very similar conclusions about the primary obstacle to the qualitative improvement of the Iranian educational system: namely, the shortage of teaching personnel and the widening gap between the numbers of students and the numbers of teachers.

47. The shortage has been most severe in the case of secondary education in rural areas where the rate of increase of teachers has been nearly half that of students. A considerable number of elementary school teachers were upgraded in an attempt to fill the gap; but the student–teacher ratios continued to deteriorate. Moreover, the transfer had a deleterious effect upon the quality of primary education, since those with the highest qualifications were transferred.

48. Within the secondary level, the severest shortage in terms of type of teacher appeared to be in science and mathematics. Moreover, out of a total number of 29,569 secondary teachers in 1971/72, less than half had a bachelor's degree. The remainder lacked university education; many had only a ninth-grade certificate.

49. Teachers of science and mathematics at secondary level do not represent the only need. There is also a need for more and better trained and educated teachers throughout the entire educational system of Iran. For example, one finds: (a) untrained high school teachers training prospective elementary school teachers; (b) few and inadequate training programmes for guidance-cycle counsellors, although they are a crucial factor in the success of the new system of education; and (c) elementary school teachers (whose importance to the effectiveness of the educational system in general goes without saying) with only an elementary education. Consequently, while one of the first two professional programmes of the Free University will aim to create new secondary school teachers from high-school graduates, the programmes will be designed in

module form so that elements taken alone or in combination with one another are also appropriate for existing teachers at a number of other levels.

Health services education

50. A second priority identified by the university planners is in the area of health services. Numerous studies over the past three years have examined the inadequacies of the existing health-care system in Iran. Their conclusions, reached more or less independently, are very similar; they call for a radical restructuring of the entire health-care delivery system. They note that, despite a considerable improvement in the health standard of the country as a whole and the eradication of such epidemic diseases as malaria, the deficiencies of the present system are such as to deny three-fourths of Iran's population adequate medical services—for this portion of the population, the doctor–population ratio is 1 to 16,000. More important, the reports underscore the immediate need to develop a cadre of para-professionals to substitute for medical doctors.

51. But the concept of a graded system of medical practitioners is a new one in Iran. There does not yet exist a clear idea of what different levels (in terms of skills, functions, education and training) should and could exist. Consequently, while the Free University has committed itself to the development of an educational programme within the area of health services, it cannot say at this point what the product or nature of that programme will be. Following the principle of the systems approach to programme development (to be discussed below), the university intends to work closely with the appropriate agencies to define the skills and knowledge required by the different medical practitioners who are to implement the new network of health-care services.

Development of rural skills

52. It was clear from evidence supplied by the Hirsch Commission that a key to the promotion of co-operatives, both rural and urban, as an institutional framework for development, was the availability of trained personnel, especially managers of co-operatives. The report noted the existing education and training programmes at a number of universities and underlined the concern of the authorities that existing programmes were insufficient to cope with the current situation, let alone the massive developments planned in co-operatives and the extension of their activities.

53. Co-operative management was just one skill which the Hirsch Commission identified. The university launched a study in the spring of 1975 to determine what other specialist services should be produced to support the development of the rural areas over the next five to eight years.

The conceptual framework for programme selection

54. While the educational programmes of the Free University are to be derived from concrete manpower needs of society, the university has chosen to limit its initial priorities to those skills and knowledge required for 'the

reconstruction of rural society' and the minimization of the socio-economic disparities and imbalances which have developed over the past fifteen years.

55. The focus on rural society might at first appear incongruous, given Iran's exceptionally impressive economic development over the part ten years. The success of Iran's development policies during this period in terms of the total production of goods and services alone is apparent to the casual observer and the economic analyst alike. As pointed out by at least one economic study, ambitious public and private investment programmes and considerable diversification and expansion of the industrial sector have contributed to uninterrupted growth and development. Moreover, the modern sector, initially concentrated in Tehran, has spread to most of the major cities, which are increasingly becoming growth points for their surrounding regions and centres of the evident dynamism of the Iranian economy.

56. The same observers point out, however, the absence of a built-in catalytic agent that ensures a sustained development. They point to serious imbalances which have occurred over the past decade; imbalances which threaten the ability of the economy to absorb accelerated investment. They point to the classic symptoms of dualism in the economy: stagnating agricultural output, large regional disparities, high rates of rural underemployment, very rapid urbanization and a consequent unintegrated economy. At the heart of this is the widening gap between the rich and the poor; between, in effect, the urban and rural populations.

57. It is the size and direction of this gap which is considered to be the most serious threat to the continued growth and development of the Iranian economy. Development, it is argued, is much more than a matter of encouraging economic growth within a given social structure. It is rather the modernization of that structure, a process of social, economic and political change, that requires the remaking of society in its most intimate as well as its most public attributes. In more prosaic terms, as stated by the International Labour Office, 'More equitable distribution of income is a prerequisite for the expansion of domestic markets on which industrial expansion will largely depend.'[1] It is, moreover, within the rural sector that the income level must rise. The implication, as suggested by many students of development, is not the introduction of the 'modern sector' into the rural sector (i.e. capital-intensive mechanization), but rather the formation of and commitment to a policy for attacking the problem by direct means in order to energize the rural population through providing capital, an infrastructure, jobs and services.

58. The Free University, as a producer of highly skilled manpower is, of course, only one such element; indeed a very weak one when considered separately from a general policy aimed at the reconstruction of rural society and the integration of Iran's two economies and societies. But, though a policy framework is still lacking, a public commitment to attack the income gap has been made, and the Free University considers itself part of that commitment.

V The teaching system of the Free University

59. The proposed teaching system of the Free University has been arrived at

1. *Employment and Income Policies for Iran*, Appendix I (Educational and Vocational Training) p. 26, Geneva, ILO, 1972.

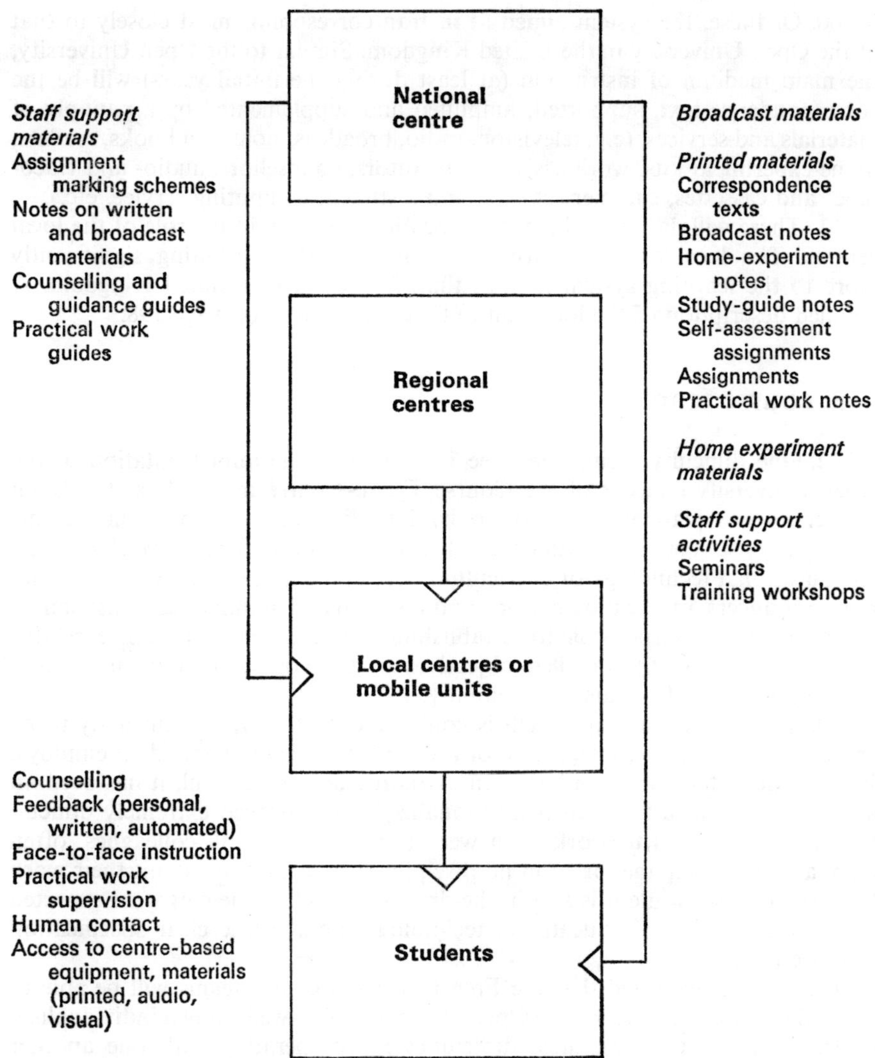

FIG. 1. The teaching system of the Free University

after studying a number of distance teaching methods being developed at varying educational levels in other countries, including the Open University in the United Kingdom, public service broadcasting in collaboration with the Ministry of Education in Japan, the Telekolleg in Munich, teacher-training provision administered by UNRWA-Unesco in Algeria, correspondence courses for students in higher education in the Soviet Union, and a multi-media teaching system for engineering studies to a first-degree level in Poland.

60. Of these, the system aimed at in Iran corresponds most closely to that of the Open University in the United Kingdom. Similar to the Open University, the main medium of instruction (at least during the initial years) will be the correspondence text, supported, amplified and supplemented by a panoply of materials and services, (e.g. television, radio, broadcast notes, set books, readers, home-experiment kits, work assignments, tutors, counsellors, audio- and video-tapes and cassettes, summer schools, and a student computing service, etc.).

61. There will, however, be one major difference, i.e. in the role of the local centres. The local centre network is envisaged as contributing significantly more to the learning system in Iran than it does in the United Kingdom. A detailed description of the local centre function is given on page 198.

The course team

62. One difficulty facing the Free University is the implementation of the Open University concept of the Course Team. Course materials at the Open University are planned and written by interdisciplinary teams. Such teams usually consist of subject-matter specialists (ten to twelve for a 32-week course), an educational technology or curriculum development specialist, television and radio producers, publication editors, and research and administrative assistants. Course teams are responsible for establishing the broad aims of their respective courses, specifying the detailed objectives of the course (unit by unit), and selecting the various media to be employed.

63. The course-team approach is considered by the Open University to be crucial for the effective integration of the various teaching methods it employs. But, although the approach has been extraordinarily successful, it has been an arduous and difficult one to institutionalize. It has proved extremely difficult for many academics to work on a week-to-week basis with colleagues, often from another discipline, or from no discipline *per se*, and to submit their work to open criticism while it is still in the draft stage. All academics were expected to learn something of educational technology, notably the clear specification of objectives.

64. It is not expected that the Free University course teams will be able to avoid the problems faced by the Open University. The well-known individualism of Iranians and their manifest difficulties in co-operating with one another might make it impossible to implement fully the course-team approach. But, because of the apparently positive correlation between the quality and 'integratedness' of course materials and the course-team approach, the Free University will attempt to adapt this experience.

The selection of media and methods

65. At the beginning of the strategic planning phase, it was hoped—a rather naive expectation in retrospect—to find a set of practical procedures, based upon sound psychological and pedagogical foundations, which would allow the planners to define overall objectives for different media used by the university, and which would serve as guidelines for the selection of media between and within individual programmes and courses. In the event, there was

considerable high-level discussion of abstractions, and no significant criteria were elucidated. A series of difficult analyses were often found to end in some commonsense decisions.

66. In the last resort, the selection of media in the Free University was guided by several non-pedagogical factors: ignorance, logistics and external politics. Print, for example, was chosen as the main medium of instruction for a combination of such reasons. First, it allows the student independence and freedom to decide where and when he will study and provides him with a permanent and easily accessible record of his courses; difficult objectives to achieve with television or radio. Second, the printed medium would seem to be more familiar to and easily managed by academics. Third, the correspondence texts in the Open University appear to have been very effective. Finally, written texts do not have to be maintained; power failures and breakdowns would not threaten the system.

67. In addition to the frequently enunciated objectives for the use of television, namely to motivate students, to pace students, to expand the boundaries of the institution and to convey instruction, twenty-five functions have been identified for television. These were arrived at by applying two criteria: that they would be difficult or impossible to achieve by any other means or that they would be more economically achieved in terms of student time and cost to the institution.

68. On-going research in this area might result in a set of practical guidelines for the university's course teams. But the decision of the university regarding television was to limit its use in the initial years and to provide video-cassette recording equipment in local centres. Educational broadcasting is a recent phenomenon in Iran and has yet to reach a very high standard. Though it would have been impossible to disregard broadcasting completely, for political reasons, the university very wisely decided to concentrate its efforts and those of NIRT on the production of a limited number of programmes to a reasonable standard.

69. That radio has become a much neglected medium of instruction is a fact. But despite the considerable amount of experience with radio, few concrete suggestions were found for its use. Since the production time for radio is much shorter than that for television, it is hoped to employ it as a means for providing feedback and remedial advice. In addition, because radio production facilities exist at the regional level in Iran, it is also hoped to see it used as a means to 'decentralize' certain elements of the teaching system and to involve the regional staff directly in the system itself.

The regional and local centre network

70. It was mentioned earlier that the learning systems of the Free University will be based more on local centres than are other centralized distance learning systems. The extent to which, and the means by which, face-to-face contact is provided in a distance learning system vary considerably. It can be: continuous on a week-to-week basis; voluntary or mandatory; limited to summer residential courses, to practical work experiences or to preparatory periods for examinations. The tutorial services of the British Open University, for example, are voluntary and provided continuously throughout the academic year. The Telekolleg requires attendance at what it calls '*Telegruppen*' twice a month.

71. There is, on the one hand, no hard evidence to show that tutorial services are crucial to the effectiveness of a correspondence-based system. Attendance at the Open University study centres averages below 50 per cent over the year. Seventy-five per cent of those students formally enrolled in 1971 received credit for courses taken. There is considerable evidence, on the other hand, that the provision of such services on a large scale is very expensive; approximately 27 per cent of the recurrent budget of the Open University in 1973 was allocated to the tutorial services. It was the lack of hard evidence and the experience of the Open University which prompted the planners for the Everyman's University in Israel to argue that money for tutorial services is better spent on course-material development.

72. The Free University's decision to allocate a significant role to its regional and local centre network was based on a number of considerations. First, it was obvious that none of its prospective students would have had any experience in self-directed study. Second, as many of them will be recent high-school graduates, moreover, they are bound to lack the motivation of the more adult Open University students. Third, their geographical location is bound to compound the problem of isolation and depersonalization experienced in all distance learning systems.

73. Fourth, individual access to television (and even radio) cannot be assumed: it is obvious that community resources such as those existing in the United Kingdom are simply not available. Fifth, the programmes of the Free University will require practical work experience and those experiences will require organization, guidance and supervision. Sixth, the university aims to play a role in the development of the communities where centres are located.

74. Lastly, it is believed that much of the success of the university will depend upon the extent to which three basic needs of the students are met: (a) the need to learn how to study effectively and efficiently on one's own; (b) the need for general advice, help and encouragement; (c) the need for assistance to set up and to run self-help groups.

75. It was for all these reasons that the university decided to construct local centres, to make full provision for equipping and staffing them, and to give active encouragement to student attendance for the many activities they undertake. It was also decided to develop mobile units to bring the resources of the centres to students who are unable to attend them.

76. A detailed description of the premises, staff and daily activities of the centres is not yet possible. While it is clear that the Free University intends to develop a 'centre-based' system, many of the operational decisions have yet to be made, and the thinking within the university is bound to change over the next few months as implications are discussed and hard decisions made. It should be noted, moreover, that the university does not intend to restrict itself to one mode of operation during the early years. There is considerable room for experimentation; as many alternatives as possible will be explored in the search for the most cost-effective ones.

77. The equipment and facilities which the centres will provide in one form or another, however, are fairly straightforward and have been identified in general terms. In all probability, these will include: laboratory space and equipment; video-cassette and audio-tape recording equipment; reference material on microfiche or film; lecture and large-group viewing facilities; space for individual study and small-group learning; facilities for micro-teaching and

practical work under clinical conditions; and space and facilities for social gatherings and informal discussions.

78. It is a stated aim of the university to lessen the dependence of its students upon the centres, particularly its human resources, as they progress through the system. A concerted effort will be made to develop a cadre of counsellors whose primary responsibility will be to guide students towards self-directed or self-disciplined learning and in the use of their fellow students as a major source of academic assistance.

79. As full-time staff, centre counsellors will also be responsible for much of the didactic work for the foundation and, possibly, for second-level courses as well.

80. Efforts are now being made to identify suitable third- and fourth-year students at provincial universities. In 1975 and 1976, these students will be put through an intensive summer internship programme as well as additional training sessions of varying lengths. It is hoped from this to develop an adequate pool of people from which centre counsellors will be drawn in January 1977, when the first students start. Another source in the future should be the university's own students.

81. Tuition in the subject matter of the upper-level courses and the supervision of practical work will undoubtedly have to be carried out by part-time staff, either on a peripatetic basis, from the regions, or recruited locally. The possibility of hiring some of this staff on a full-time basis does exist, but the number will probably be very small.

82. In concluding this section on the Free University's teaching system, it must be said that many fundamental decisions which will have to be made in the run-up period about the university's operational system will only be confirmed after some experience has been gained. Those related to the regional and local centre network are likely to remain particularly fluid, at least in the minds of the university's officers, until experience shows a 'hunch' to have been either right or wrong or somewhere in between.

VI A principle of programme planning and course development

83. One of the university's primary objectives will be the application of systems design principles to the planning and development of its programmes and courses. In theory, the application of systems design principles to education implies that each element of an educational programme and the programme itself fulfil three purposes. First, there must be a specified and measurable result. Second, evidence concerning its effectiveness at attaining this result must be continuously available. Third, the programme or element should be easily adapted or corrected in the light of that evidence. This is the case whether the element in question is a segment of instruction within a programme (e.g. a 50-page booklet, or a single television programme), or the entire student evaluation system, or the programme itself.

84. The Free University's commitment to the systems approach exists for several reasons. First, to incite programme planners and designers to focus on the effectiveness of their programmes and to avoid the tendency simply to transpose and translate material which exists elsewhere. Second, to provoke the

programme designers and planners to examine the context within which the graduates of their programmes will function. It is inevitable that paramedical workers and teachers in Iran, faced with a very different set of economic, social and cultural realities from those of their counterparts in the United States or Europe, will require many different skills, attitudes and behaviours. The differences of background are rarely, if ever, reflected in transplanted material. Third, to provoke planners to be explicit about what they intend to produce and how: to force programme and course designers to question continually their assumptions regarding the relationships between ends and means. Finally, to force the university to recognize the importance of programme evaluation in addition to student evaluation.

85. As the first step towards implementing its commitment to systems design principles, the Free University will design a programme in teacher-education according to competency- or performance-based standards.

86. Briefly stated, the aim of the planning project is to establish objectives for the first teacher-education programme which define the expected roles and behaviours of secondary school teachers of mathematics and science. The objectives, when clustered and sequenced over a three-year period, will constitute the syllabus of the teacher-education programme. In addition, there are two major secondary aims of the project: first, that the objectives or expected teacher behaviours be derived from explicit assumptions regarding the context within which Iranian teachers work; second, that individuals who are intimately familiar with the educational process in Iran be used as sources for aims and objectives for the programme.

VII Course structure and curriculum

87. The course and degree structures of the Free University have yet to be worked out in detail. Consequently, it is only possible to note very general points about them. At other universities in Iran, 140 credit-hours constitute the normal basic requirement for a bachelor of arts degree. At the Free University, credits will be based on its courses, not on the credit-hours system; and students will not be required to write theses.

88. Operating on a 32-week academic year, the university will produce courses of 8, 16, 24 and 32 weeks in length. The courses will be designed on the assumption that, on the average, they will not require more than 12 hours work per week. In all probability, the requirements for the first degree will be either twelve or thirteen 16-week courses. The total work load of Free University students should be slightly higher than that of conventional universities.

89. At least 32 units (or one full-year course) will required in fields of study outside a student's professional specialization. The university is at present engaged in designing four 16-week foundation-level courses in science, mathematics, English language, and social sciences and humanities. These courses will be ready for the university's first academic year. The first set of specifically professional courses will not be offered until the second year, that is, in 1978.

90. Each course, regardless of length, will include a final examination. It is not clear yet whether the university will also institute a set of comprehensive examinations to be taken upon completion of required individual courses. The

continuing assessment and evaluation policy leading up to the examinations also remains to be formulated.

VIII Government and organization

91. Iranian universities and institutions of higher education are classified according to their sources of finance and employment regulations as State or private institutions. The Free University is a State institution. Such institutions are established by legislation or by special charter and are almost entirely financed by the government. They have administrative and financial autonomy under their respective boards of trustees. The non-academic employees of these universities and institutions of higher education are usually considered as civil servants and, therefore, come under the ordinary regulations of government employees. The academic staff are employed under special employment regulations approved by the boards of trustees. In the case of the Free University, because of the extraordinary need for high-level and expensive 'non-academic' skills, special employment regulations for technical staff have been drafted and approved by the board of trustees.

92. The board of trustees of State universities acts as a legislative body, ratifying regulations concerning the employment of academic staff, finance and the universities' budget. All funds from public agencies and private revenue received by the universities are, in the final analysis, allocated by the board of trustees to the various parts of the institution. The chancellors of universities are nominated by the board of trustees and are presented to the Shah through the Ministry of Science and Higher Education. The Shah makes the final appointment.

93. The organization of the Free University provides for two internal policy-making bodies: the University Council and the Academic and Research Council. According to the charter of the Free University, the University Council is the supreme decision-making authority in such matters as resource allocation. It consists of the chancellor (as chairman), the vice-chancellors, the deans of faculties, the director of the Institute of Educational Technology, the heads of centres (e.g. physical planning and technical services), and the regional directors.

94. The Academic and Research Council is the supreme academic authority, although decisions which have resource implications (e.g. the number of courses to be offered in the teacher-education programme) must be approved by the University Council. The Academic and Research Council will consist of the chancellor or his designate (as chairman), the vice-chancellor for academic and research affairs, the deans of faculties, the director of the Institute of Educational Technology, directors of programmes and three members of the university to be selected by the chancellor.

95. The university has established three faculties: science and technology; natural sciences; and humanities and social sciences. Academic staff will hold appointments in one of these faculties and in some cases there will be joint appointments, to a faculty and to the Institute of Educational Technology. The teaching (i.e. course-preparation) of the university, however, will for the most part not be carried out within the faculty structure. As the university will be developing professional programmes, the educational needs of which cut across

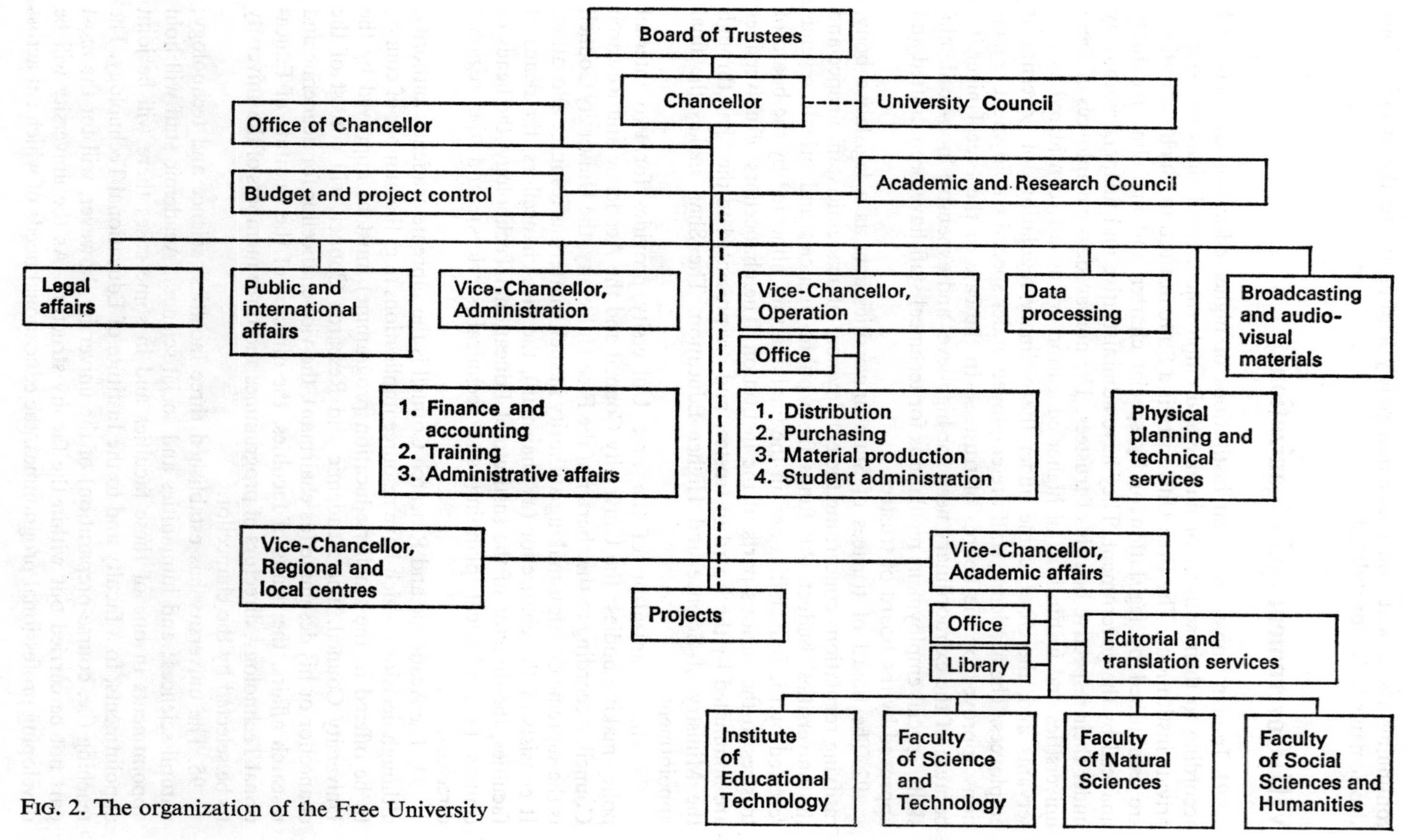

FIG. 2. The organization of the Free University

the three faculties, academics will work in course teams under the authority of a programme director or committee.

96. In a sense, the university will attempt to institutionalize the project management principle of organizational design with functional groups representing a secondary-authority network superimposed on the primary-authority network of the formal organizational structure. The university decided to develop a matrix organization in order to ensure that the focus of the academics' course-preparation activities remained on the needs and demands of the programme and not on those of the academic discipline. The project director (or committee) and the chairman of each course team will be selected by the Academic and Research Council. Course-team members will be assigned by the council, though, naturally, after consultation with the individuals concerned.

IX Reflections on criteria of feasibility

97. There are four different but interrelated sets of criteria which must be considered when discussing the feasibility of the Free University. Two concern the development of the operational and administrative systems of the university. A third concerns the university's programme planning and design. The fourth concerns the final product, i.e. whether a sufficient number of graduates work in the jobs for which they have received training.

98. For present purposes, the scope of the discussion has been limited to the first set of criteria; to those which must be satisfied if the university is to develop its systems to a minimally acceptable standard. For example, is the structure going to be capable of distributing and retrieving course materials on time? Are production staff going to be capable of producing programmes on schedule, and will the programmes be universally accepted as 'better' than they have been in the past?

99. The problems causing concern are numerous; for some, they are too numerous for the project to be accepted as feasible. Writing in 1971, a staff member of IRPSE asserted that the idea of establishing an Open University in developing countries is 'naive and most likely to be the imaginative effort of some people involved in the field of education'.

100. The absence of sufficient skilled personnel is evident in all aspects of the university's work. Experience elsewhere shows that the planning and preparation of course materials (including television and radio broadcasts in a correspondence course) is neither an individual nor single-discipline effort. In successful cases such materials are developed by teams, consisting of subject specialists, curriculum development specialists, television and radio producers, tests and measurement specialists, and editors. The planning and design skills of the curriculum development specialist are extremely rare in most countries but their existence is necessary to a successful team. In June 1973 and again in April 1974, advertisements for such persons in Iran produced no result.

101. Outside Iran's seven largest cities, there are no universities or institutes of higher education, nor are there many persons with more than a high-school diploma. The background, supporting, conventional educational system is practically non-existent. Moreover, the Free University's need to establish co-operative links with other institutions and with ministries might well prove difficult in Iran where co-operation of this kind is extraordinarily rare.

102. Home study, especially for those with domestic and work responsibilities, is an extremely demanding way to obtain a degree and one that requires not only self-discipline but also the existence of an environment conducive to study, namely, a private, quiet and well-lit room. Conventional universities provide such an environment. But it is unlikely to be true of the home of the average Free University student.

103. Correspondence courses require efficient distribution and communications. Television programmes must be received without distortion; delays in distribution of correspondence texts and other home-study materials will disrupt students' study patterns. The time factor is especially important when it concerns student–tutor communication. Obviously, the shorter the lapse of time between the exchange of communications, the better. If students have to wait up to two or three weeks before receiving responses to questions and reactions to work submitted, the effectiveness of the system can be jeopardized. Will the existing communications structure in Iran have the capacity to meet these demands?

104. The list of minimum criteria within each of the areas discussed above is formidable enough. Yet, the significance of these pales in comparison with the absence of management and administrative skills. Backward personnel policies, the lack of any effective reward system, dilatory procedures, the lack of co-operation and co-ordination, inadequate accounting and financial control systems, lack of initiative, the centralization of authority (if not control) are all characteristics of Iranian bureaucracies. But, in a university whose very existence will depend heavily upon close, effective co-operation between its different parts, upon decisions being taken and acted upon swiftly and upon establishing a 'production-line' attitude of mind, such attributes might be not merely deleterious; they could be fatal.

105. In order to mitigate some of the problems, the university has decided to limit its initial size and scope. As a matter of policy, it has been decided that only four 16-week courses should be produced for the first year; that 6,000 students should be enrolled (as opposed to the entering cohort of 25,000 at the Open University); and that only five regions (out of a possible thirteen) should initially be covered. Moreover, the courses for paramedical students should be limited to in-service education, if a pre-service programme appears to be beyond the university's capabilities. In addition, the university recognized the fact that it would have to go outside Iran in order to find many of the skills in short supply—persons who will be able to contribute directly to the development of the university's systems and to the training of its staff.

106. No member of the Free University is under any illusion regarding the obstacles which must be overcome if even a minimally acceptable standard is to be achieved. But the very challenge posed by such obstacles, the opportunity to participate in the creation of an innovatory educational system, and the anticipation of what success will mean in terms of personal satisfaction and goals, have served at least in part to attract a core of highly capable and committed individuals. If the present degree of commitment can be maintained as the university grows in size, and assuming that certain skills can be obtained over the next two years, there should be no reason to expect that future problems will prove to be insurmountable.

Appendix A Standardized reference data

Country, state or province	*Iran*
Area and climate	636,000 square miles. Temperate continental.
Population	
Total (latest year)	27.8 million (1966), 31.2 million (1972–73).
Estimated population aged 18	15–19: 2,520,000 (1966).
Estimated percentage under 15	46.3 (1968).
Current annual growth rate (percentage)	3.2.
Government	
Main organizational structure	Unitary with delegated responsibilities. Inequalities in urban and rural development and provisions. Fourteen administrative provinces.
Political type	Shah has strong control; parliamentary democracy; constitutional monarchy.
Economy	
Political type	Predominantly subsistence agriculture in a desert country. Domestic industry only, but oil important.
Gross national product	
Total (latest year)	1,149,000 million rials (1972/73) (1 rial= U.S.$0.132).
Per head	U.S.$490.
Average annual increase (percentage)	7.2 (1965/72)
Communications	
Ground/air	Adequate road (many roads unpaved), rail and air-transport services, but poorly developed in many areas.

Mail/telephone	Increasing (telephone): 1.5 per 100 people (1972).
Broadcasting	
Main system(s) operating	34 radio stations. 15 television stations.
Principal authorities responsible	Under aegis of director-general of National Iranian Radio and Television.
Radio	
Transmission coverage of main programme services with percentage of population reached	75 (area of country).
Receiving capability for main programme services (percentage)	78.
Television	
Transmission coverage as defined for radio (percentage)	50.
Receiving capability for main programme services (percentage)	24.
Monochrome or colour	Monochrome.
Education	
Type of system(s)	Predominantly public provision but numerous and important private institutions.
Main authorities responsible and powers	
At school level	Publicly controlled at school level by Ministry of Education with local education authorities directly responsible to ministry.
At post-secondary level	Less centralization at post-secondary level. Ministry of Science and Higher Education has no executive control and sets general standards which are pragmatically adopted. Institute for Research and Planning in Science and Education. State institutions centrally funded. Twenty-one per cent of enrolment in 1972/73 in private institutions.
End of full-time school attendance	
Legal	Eight compulsory and free years, ages 6 to 15 (five primary, three secondary).
De facto	54 per cent of eligible age group attend school.
Proportion of 18-year-old age group involved in education	
Full-time/part-time	Four per cent of age group 18 to 22 in post-secondary education.
Major developments in provision	
Over last five years	Fourfold increase in enrolment in institutions of higher education since 1963.

Over next five years	Fifth plan, to be completed by 1978, provides for 5-year elementary school, plus 3-year secondary-level course. Raising of proportion attending school to 66 per cent, plus increase in financial provision.

Institution/system under study — *Free University of Iran (FUI)*

Brief for study and reason for inclusion	Based on British Open University and other institutions around the world, but adapted to specific needs and objectives of Iranian society, particularly the rapid increase in demand for post-secondary education of high quality for an increasingly heterogeneous and geographically dispersed student body.
Description of subject studied	
Origins	Attraction of Open University in United Kingdom.
Educational authorities	FUI established 1973 after research by Ministry of Science and Higher Education and Institute for Research and Planning in Science and Education.
Communications authority	National Iranian Radio and Television. Limited use of television in early years.
Services provided	In first decade, to concentrate on providing skilled manpower, particularly for development of rural areas (e.g. teacher training, health services); and to give preference to rural areas as element in overall policy of developing country through reform of educational system.
Eligibility to study	Expected to be high-school graduates, i.e. 18-plus.
Terminal qualifications	First degree.
Instructional means used	Multi-media, but mainly written word, i.e. correspondence supplemented by other materials and services (television, radio, set books, tutors, summer schools and especially local learning centres).
Personal input from student	Twelve hours per week per course.
Normal duration of study	Twelve or thirteen 16-week courses.
Numbers involved	
Students	6,000 to be enrolled in first year, 1977.
Academic staff	Central university body. Work in course teams. Many part-time local-centre tutors; a few full-time planned.
Other professional staff	Institute of Educational Technology.
Finance	
Recurrent expenditure	Financed by government.

Sources of further information

Educational	Free University of Iran, Shah Reza Avenue, Tehran (Iran).
Broadcasting	National Iranian Radio and Television, P.O. Box 33–200, Tehran (Iran).

Appendix B Short bibliography

HOUSTON, ROBERT W. Designing competency-based instructional systems. *Journal of teacher education*, vol. XXIV, no. 3, 1973, p. 201.

INSTITUTE FOR RESEARCH AND PLANNING IN SCIENCE AND EDUCATION. *The system of higher education in Iran*. Tehran, IRPSE, 1972.

——. *The financing of higher education in Iran. An analytical study*. Tehran, IRPSE, 1973.

JACOBS, N. *The sociology of development: Iran as an Asian case study*. New York, N.Y., Praeger, 1966.

MACDONALD-ROSS, M. *Behavioural objectives—a critical review*. Bletchley, England, The Open University, 1973. (Mimeo.)

MANZOOR, C. University reform in Iran: problems and prospects. Unpublished doctoral dissertation.

SCHALOCK, H. D.; HALE, J. R. *A competency-based field-centered systems approach to elementary teacher education. Final report*. Vol. 1. Washington, D.C., United States Government Printing Office, 1969.

UPTON, J. M. *The history of modern Iran: an interpretation*. Cambridge, Mass., Harvard University Press, 1960.

ZONIS, M. *The political elite of Iran*. Princeton, N.J., Princeton University Press, 1971.

Appendix C Biographical note

John R. Beardsley graduated from Princeton University in 1964. Until 1967 he was a teacher in the Peace Corps in Tunisia and in Saudi Arabia. He returned to the United States to resume his studies and received his master of arts degree in Islamic studies from the University of California at Los Angeles in 1969. In the autumn of 1969 he entered the doctoral programme in educational planning at Harvard University. He went to Iran in 1971 to complete work on his dissertation. He was involved in the initial planning of the Free University and at present serves as a consultant to its chancellor.

The Everyman's University, **Israel**

Fred A. Nelson

Contents

I Introduction

1. On 2 October 1973 Israel's Council for Higher Education unanimously authorized the establishment of 'Everyman's University (Pilot Project) in Israel', and the institution was legally incorporated under this name on 14 April 1974. The conception, birth and early infancy of this Open Learning system are probably unique among similar programmes around the world.

Everyman's University (EU) represents a new kind of university, established with private support and no public funds, but with the clear understanding at the outset that if, after three years, the venture looks promising, it will be gradually adopted by new public parents with increasing tax support. This private-to-public process of establishing a nation-wide Open Learning system may serve as a useful example to other countries and to other institutions.

2. Despite the obvious newness of the EU itself, it has already demonstrated some qualities which may offer helpful lessons to others. In both the planning and early operational stages, Israel's leaders and the EU staff have systematically drawn upon, and are still drawing upon, the experience of several other countries with Open Learning systems. The idea has not been simply to replicate or transplant *in toto* what has been done elsewhere, but rather to profit from other successes (and failures) and to adapt and adopt ideas and programmes to the particular needs, experiences and capabilities of Israel.

II The Israeli context

3. Israel is a nation with an extremely complex history marked by a series of violent conflicts. The events since its creation as an independent State have reinforced its sense of nationhood. A very high proportion of the gross national product, which in 1973 amounted to U.S.$6,250 million, or U.S.$1,890 per head, is devoted to defence.

Geography and demography

4. To many visitors the small size of Israel comes as something of a surprise. In pre-1967 figures, the total area is only 20,500 square kilometres or 8,023 square miles. From north to south the nation is just 320 miles long and from

east to west only 120 miles wide at the maximum. In United States terms, Israel is just under the size of the State of Massachusetts. (Israel at present occupies four times this area and now includes no less than 1 million Arabs.) Three million three hundred thousand people live in Israel, which is a very small population base when one considers the level of government spending on defence and education. The great majority of Israel's people live in the coastal plain, and over 80 per cent of the population live in towns or urban areas. Over 1 million people live in the greater Tel Aviv area alone, and another 220,000 in Haifa, the country's principal port. Historic Jerusalem, which is also the nation's capital, has a population of about 200,000. The well-known social experiments, the *kibbutzim*, house only 3 per cent of the total population, or about 85,000 people in all.

5. The population of Israel, like the geography and the climate, is surprisingly diverse. In 1973 there were 2,810,400 Jews in Israel, 375,000 Moslems, 76,000 Christians and 46,000 Druses. The Jewish population itself is composed of a large number of varying communities. Even though an increasing percentage of Israelis are native-born, the diversity of backgrounds leads to greatly differing expectations and educational standards. Hence the great concern about the educational gap between the so-called European Jews, on the one hand, and the Oriental Jews and Arabs on the other. One source estimates that about 43 per cent of the population are 'European' Jews, while 10 per cent are Arabs. European Jews, whose values dominate the nation, are actually in the minority, and are over-represented in the educational system at all levels.

Economic resources

6. Unlike those of her oil-rich neighbours, the oil fields of Israel are able to produce only 5 per cent of local consumption. As a result, the chief national resource is the rich soil of the coastal plain which, when combined with intensive irrigation and the use of fertilizers, gives Israel a very advanced agricultural industry. Despite the lack of raw materials, Israel has a considerable industrial development, largely based on imported materials. Given the isolation of Israel and the great distance to its markets, it is possible to feel concerned about the immediate and long-range economic future of the nation. The lack of great natural wealth is generally recognized, and the future of the country will therefore depend on the ingenuity and technical skills of its people. All of this gives even greater importance to the role of education in Israel's future.

Existing higher education

7. In 1973, there were 918,702 students at all levels of education, which is no less than 28 per cent of the entire population. About 50,000 of these students were in higher education. It seems to be believed that higher education in Israel, in general, is more fully developed than either primary or secondary education. Indeed, about 40 per cent of the government's education budget is spent on these 50,000 students. Here again we see the influence of the European Jewish tradition which places a high value on traditional academic higher education and pure research.

8. Seven universities currently exist in Israel, including the Weizmann Institute of Science. About one-fifth of all university students are graduates, and the current policy in these universities is to increase the number of graduate students while keeping undergraduate enrolment at the present size. The existing universities can meet the demand, with the exception of that in some fields like medicine and psychology.

9. In addition to the seven universities providing higher education for 50,000 students, there are about 7,000 students in twenty teacher-training colleges who take a three-year course introduced in 1971 to replace the previous two-year training course. The majority of teachers in secondary schools, as contrasted with the primary and intermediate schools, come from the existing universities, which offer a special course for teachers corresponding to the postgraduate certificate course at British universities.

10. Given the small geographic area of Israel, the relatively small population base, the existence of a number of large universities and other institutions of post-secondary education, the large current expenditure on higher education, and the limited economic resources available for further expansion, one might well ask: why have another university in Israel?

III Conceptions of the project

The Instructional Television Centre (ITC)

11. Any new venture owes its existence, not to any single person or institution, but to a confluence of forces, events, interests and people. As early as 1963, the Rothschild Foundation (or 'Hanadiv') set up and funded Israel's Instructional Television Centre (ITC), originally named the Instructional Television Trust. Like many developing countries, Israel hoped to modernize her curriculum and teaching methods through the use of television. By January 1966, ITC had moved into its new building, located next to the Tel Aviv University, and in March of 1966 it was ready for its first transmission. The Rothschild Foundation assumed responsibility for funding ITC and for its operation, and Max Rowe of the Rothschild Foundation served as the initial director of ITC. At the same time, the Ministry of Education and Culture assumed responsibility for educational priorities, programme content, and liaison with schools. This privately funded project was judged to be a success, and in 1969 ITC was turned over to the Ministry of Education and Culture for a two-year trial period. The trial period came to an end in 1971, and Israel's Parliament (the Knesset) voted to maintain the ITC as a separate entity from the Broadcasting Authority and as an integral part of the Ministry of Education and Culture. The Knesset at the same time amended the Broadcasting Law to assure ITC access to the one national television network during the daytime hours, which now run from 7.30 a.m. until 5.30 p.m.

12. Here we have the important precedent of a privately funded experimental project, after its trial period, being handed over to, and supported almost entirely by, the government. Here too we have an early and major national commitment to the use of television for educational purposes in both schools and individual homes.

The Centre for Educational Technology (CET)

13. During 1970 the Rothschild Foundation established the Centre for Educational Technology to help improve the quality of learning and increase the efficiency of teaching within Israel's education system by investigating, developing and evaluating applications of educational technology. After completing the trial period with instructional television, the foundation wanted to test the applicability of a wider spectrum of media to planned instruction. For this purpose it created the Centre for Educational Technology, which is still under Rothschild sponsorship, and is conducting a number of important projects, particularly at the elementary, secondary and technical levels. The centre at present has a full-time staff of more than forty people.

Committee on Post-Secondary Education

14. Late in 1969, the same year that the ITC became a permanent part of the Ministry of Education and Culture and the same year that Britain's Open University was created, Yigal Allon became both Deputy Prime Minister and Minister of Education and Culture. Mr Allon was a friend of the United Kingdom's Harold Wilson, whose political speech in 1963 gave rise to the scheme for a 'University of the Air', which evolved into the now famous Open University, and Allon was both interested in and impressed by this development.

15. The Ministry of Education and Culture and the Council for Higher Education appointed a Committee on Post-Secondary Education on 5 May 1970. The committee was chaired by Professor Shneior Lifson, the head of the Department of Chemical Physics at the Weizmann Institute of Science. Its broad mandate was to review all facets of post-secondary education in Israel, excluding university education. Included in the brief to the committee was the request by the council for the committee to discuss the possibility of making use of television, radio and postal services.

16. In March 1971, nine months before it issued its final report, the Lifson Committee proposed to examine ways of establishing an 'Open University' (based on the model of the United Kingdom's Open University) which, with the co-operation of the network of colleges proposed earlier by the committee, would provide higher education at the bachelor-of-arts level to students in all parts of the country. The Lifson Committee in its final report[1] formally recommended (a) the gradual development of a national network of colleges as the main way of expanding and deepening post-secondary education, (b) that a national centre for post-secondary education (colleges and post-secondary institutions) should be established by the Council for Higher Education, and (c) that an experimental programme for establishing an Open University should be commenced. The committee suggested that, despite the name 'Open University', the programme suggested should be limited to college education, leading wholly or partly to a first academic degree. The committee believed that the Open University's methods would be particularly important for the training of teachers in the sciences and in mathematics for junior and senior high schools.

1. Committee on Post-Secondary Education, *Report to the Council for Higher Education*, Appendix 11a, p. I, Jerusalem, December 1971.

The Lifson Committee had two objectives in mind: 'Firstly, this proposal would offer an appropriate solution to an urgent and important problem. Secondly, it would be a pioneer experiment, whose purpose would be to develop new methods of learning technology and apply them particularly to those regions and populations where a suitable alternative is not available.'

The Rothschild proposal for an Everyman's University

17. Independently of the work of the Committee on Post-Secondary Education, and indeed without knowing of its existence, Hanadiv, the Rothschild Foundation, was pursuing its own inquiries about the creation of an Open Learning system at university level.

18. Early in 1971, Max Rowe, Secretary-General of the Rothschild Foundation, visited Professor Wilbur Schramm, then at Stanford University in California. The possibility of an Everyman's University was then considered. On his return to Geneva, Mr Rowe submitted a memorandum, dated 17 March 1971, to Lord Rothschild. This memorandum analysed the needs for an alternative system of higher education outside the conventional universities. It was not, however, to be a replica of the Open University of the United Kingdom; it was not to rely so heavily on television but rather to use simpler and less expensive technology.

19. The memorandum concluded with the recommendation that Hanadiv should invite a small group of experts to examine the problem and submit recommendations. It further suggested that, subject to experts' views, Hanadiv should, in due course, create an 'Everyman's University' and carry out some pilot experiments before handing it on to a public authority.

20. Hanadiv adopted these recommendations, provided that the Minister of Education (at that time Yigal Allon) was also in agreement.

The Schramm Commission

21. The minister agreed and in October 1971, Hanadiv set up a study commission on what was by then called an Everyman's University for Israel. The commission was appointed with Professor Wilbur Schramm as chairman, and with Professor David Hawkridge and Harold Howe II as members. Professor Schramm was then Director of the Institute for Communications Research at Stanford University, and now occupies a similar post at the East–West Centre at the University of Hawaii; Professor Hawkridge is the Director of the Institute of Educational Technology at the Open University of the United Kingdom; and Mr Howe is Vice-President for Education and Research of the Ford Foundation and a former United States Commissioner of Education. The Schramm Commission visited Israel twice during 1972, and issued its final report on 15 September 1972: *An Everyman's University for Israel.*

Problems and solutions

22. This three-man commission was asked by Hanadiv to inquire into 'the

feasibility, practicability, and economics' of an Everyman's University (EU) in Israel.

23. Given this broad mandate it went ahead and identified major problem areas to which the EU might address itself. The most demanding problems, in the view of the commission, were those related to the needs of the less advantaged portion of the population made up largely of Oriental Jews and Arabs. In its report the commission emphasizes that 'this problem is much broader than education, and even the related educational needs are greater than could be met by any single new institution'. The commission identified two related problems to which the new EU might make a significant contribution. The first was the upgrading of the elementary and secondary teacher corps. The second problem area was to provide a 'second chance' to students who, for one reason or another, had fallen just short of completing secondary school or of possessing the Bagrut (matriculation) examination. In addition, the commission identified a third special need to be fulfilled by the EU: 'the continuing education of Israeli people able to profit from learning opportunities at the post-secondary and higher level'. Max Rowe has expressed the view that adult education—for professional upgrading and enriching leisure time—may ultimately become the most significant task of EU.

Role of existing institutions

24. The commission concluded that 'despite the impressive amount of effort already under way within the educational system, greatly expanding existing institutions and services would not be an efficient way to accomplish the ends in view. Greater flexibility seems to be required than traditional institutions provide . . .'.

25. Israel has about 50,000 in a single age cohort going through elementary school. Of these, about 40 per cent, or 20,000, complete grade 12 and go on to some form of post-secondary education. Approximately 10,000 students, or 20 per cent of the cohort, pass the matriculation examination and go to a university to seek the first degree. The commission believed that Israel's seven universities were coming close to meeting the educational needs of all students able to pass the matriculation examination. On the other hand, there were large and serious needs which the universities, by natural tradition, are less well equipped to meet. For these and other reasons, the Schramm Report recommended that Israel, rather than depending entirely on its present institutions, should consider what new educational institutions and new patterns of instructional technology might help to meet the urgent needs already discussed.

26. The earlier Lifson Committee had proposed the gradual development of a national network of colleges as the main way of expanding and deepening post-secondary education. The Schramm Commission not only expressed great concern about the cost of developing such a network of colleges, but it also pointed out that 'the experience of other countries has been that regional and community colleges have an almost irrepressible tendency to want to grow into full-fledged universities'.

27. For these and other reasons, the Schramm Commission recommended in some detail the establishment of the Everyman's University as an institution:

... committed to delivering learning opportunities to people where they are and when they are motivated to learn, and opportunities of the kind best fitted to their needs and capabilities. We envisage it as committed to finding solutions for Israel's most urgent problems not being met by the present system, particularly for education beyond its secondary level and for repairing upper-secondary deficiencies in order to qualify students for matriculation.

IV The birth of Everyman's University

To be or not to be a university

28. A central dilemma confronting any new Open Learning system is the level of students it is to serve and the level of curriculum it should provide. Some educational leaders in Israel felt that the EU should be a true academic university even though it might have to achieve university status in stages, and might also have to offer preparatory courses. But the Schramm Commission came down on the side of other national priorities, namely, the need to raise the standards of teachers already in the profession and to mitigate the social inequality of the disadvantaged in Israeli society.

29. A major question surrounding the establishment of the EU was whether to start at the 'top' (as a 'true academic university') and 'work down', or to start at the 'bottom' (at the pre- or sub-academic level) and work up. When recently asked about this choice, Elal Pelled, the Director-General of Israel's Ministry of Education and Culture, and a member of the new Council of the EU, said 'I would start in the middle!' By this he meant a degree completion programme for existing teachers. Mr Pelled suggests this approach in order 'to have immediate success' rather than having an excessively drawn-out waiting period for the first EU graduates.

30. Max Rowe, the President of the new EU, has said, 'Obtaining university status (as conferred on the EU by the Council for Higher Education) was essential in order to give Everyman's University the academic prestige without which we might not be able to attract staff of the highest calibre and also because we would be authorized to award the first academic degree.'[1]

31. But the Schramm Commission admittedly used the term 'university' in a 'somewhat different sense than the name is typically used in Israel'. Indeed the commission expected some questions to be raised about calling the proposed institution a 'university', although it hoped that Israel would consider the matter carefully before deciding not to call it by the honourable and esteemed title of university. The commission preferred to think of a 'university', like Alfred North Whitehead, as 'a place where the adventure of action meets the adventure of thought'.

Further developments

32. Considerable discussion and debate both preceded and followed the publication of the final Schramm Commission report on 15 September 1972.

1. Speech by Max Rowe, *Everyman's University*, p. 6, Report to the Open Learning Conference, Lincoln, Nebraska, January 1974.

A first draft of the commission's report was submitted to leading educators in Israel earlier that year, and many of these individuals provided comments on the draft report, either in writing, or in meeting personally with the commission in July 1972. Some of these comments were incorporated into the final report.

33. After the Schramm Commission issued its final report, the Rothschild Foundation sought the advice of yet another consultant, B. S. Braithwaite, formerly an educational adviser to the World Bank, as a 'referee'. Mr Braithwaite endorsed the proposal that there should be an Everyman's University, although he urged that it should be a true university and one which would allow more face-to-face contact than envisaged by the Schramm Commission.

Formal authorization

34. Following the Schramm Commission's report and the subsequent advice of Mr Braithwaite, discussions took place between the Rothschild Foundation and the Ministry of Education and Culture. Finally, on 19 August 1973, almost a year after the Schramm Commission completed its work, Israel's Cabinet unanimously approved the establishment of the Everyman's University. Then, on 2 October 1973, the Council for Higher Education also unanimously authorized the establishment of the university.

35. The Schramm Commission estimated that it would be unlikely that the EU would cost more than U.S.$8 million in the first seven years of the project. The Rothschild Foundation, as it had already done with the ITC and CET, agreed to meet the total expenses of the project for its first three years, but made it clear that, thereafter, steadily increasing government support would be required if the project looked promising. For this basic reason, agreements between the Rothschild Foundation and the Israeli Government (the Ministry of Education and the Cabinet) had, exceptionally, to be obtained before approval by the Council for Higher Education could be sought. Without this assurance of exemption from taxation and of government support at a future time, the project could not be started at all.

36. This unique agreement between government and a private philanthropic organization formed the basis of a letter from Yigal Allon, Minister of Education, to Dorothy de Rothschild, dated 11 November 1973. The principles set out in that letter form the operational charter for Everyman's University (Pilot Project).

37. The Rothschild Foundation has committed U.S.$5 million to the project for a trial period of seven years, including all of the cost for the first three years of the project; the government has agreed to provide, as from the fourth year, the balance of the funds required for operating EU during the trial period.

Incorporation of the university

38. The university became legally incorporated as a non-profit-making corporation and charitable trust on 14 April 1974. The memorandum of association for 'Everyman's University (Pilot Project) in Israel' lists twenty-one objects for which the university corporation is established. Most of these 'objects' read much like the legal wording of any incorporating document for any conven-

tional university: to confer degrees (including honorary degrees); to carry out research; to provide or secure a staff of tutors; to demand and receive fees; to acquire facilities; to co-operate with the Ministry of Education, etc. There appears to be no legal limitation as to the trend and level of the degrees, diplomas, certificates and other academic distinctions' to be granted by the university.

39. The first object (a) of the memorandum of association is worth quoting *in toto*:

To set up, establish and operate an Everyman's University for the advancement of learning and knowledge by research and teaching, by a diversity of means such as broadcasting and technological devices appropriate to higher education, by correspondence tuition, residential courses and seminars and other relevant ways, to provide education of university and professional standards for its students and to promote the educational well-being of the community generally.

Early reactions

40. Hence the initial steps, which began as early as 1968 with the setting up of the Instructional TV Trust, and were followed in 1970 by the creation of the Centre for Educational Technology, steadily gained momentum in 1971 through the advice of Wilbur Schramm and in 1972 through the work of the Schramm Commission. These steps led to the eventual establishment of the Everyman's University in late 1973, and to its incorporation in April 1974.

41. As with any new programme or institution whose purposes are not clearly defined or understood, reporters and others in Israel could define for themselves what they either wanted, or feared, the new Everyman's University to be. Despite some criticism, negative reactions and outright scepticism, the project came into being with a great deal of support, particularly at various governmental levels, and in university circles.

V Staff selection and training

Initial senior staff

42. The charter of Everyman's University states that 'the Chief Executive of the University shall be nominated by Hanadiv after consultation with the Ministry of Education and Culture'. This was done, and Max Rowe, the director of the Rothschild Foundation, was named as president of the new university.

43. The role of president is unique by either British or United States standards. The president is the administrative and academic head of the fledgeling university, even though he also serves as the director of the Rothschild Foundation, so that only a part of his time can be devoted to the EU. His role lies somewhere between that of a chancellor and of a vice-chancellor in British terms; and in United States terms between a chancellor and a president. Professor Schneior Lifson was named rector of the university, a post familiar in European universities; and an official of the British Council has been seconded to serve as Secretary of the EU.

Present organization

44. The university is governed by a seven-man council which acts as a board of trustees.

45. There are plans to add another major administrative position as vice-president, but that position has not been filled.

Recruitment of new academic staff

46. One of the first, and most difficult, tasks confronting any new institution is the recruitment and selection of academic staff. A general advertisement was placed in the Israeli press, and in addition a number of letters were written to existing universities to seek nominations and applications.

47. In all, between 400 and 500 applications were received. The selection boards consisted of well-known academics. In what may or may not have been appropriate for such an innovative institution, candidates not holding the doctorate were eliminated. Finally, about 100 candidates were invited for interviews. Of the 100 candidates personally interviewed, 22 were invited to participate in a five-week 'training programme' held in Tel Aviv during July and August of 1974, under the direction of Professor Edward Stasheff of Michigan University and Professor Maxim Bruckheimer, then of the Open University of the United Kingdom.

Training programme for new academic staff

48. One of the training programme's major problems, which could easily be corrected in similar future efforts, arose from the term 'training programme'. Many of the 22 candidates selected for this five-week training programme thought that they would almost certainly be engaged by the university even before the programme began. As it turned out, only 7 of the 22 were engaged at the programme's conclusion. This problem could be overcome by making the possibility clearer to the participants at the outset. All of the 22 candidates were paid adequately for the time involved in the programme, whether they were hired or not, so that none could say that they volunteered their time fruitlessly.

49. Perhaps the greatest lesson of the training programme was that it provided a mutual inspection tour both for the candidates and for the university itself. The primary objective of the training course was to introduce these young academics to Open Learning systems in general and to the specific tasks they would have to perform if they were to join the EU academic staff. Many of these tasks, as the United Kingdom Open University has learned, are quite different from the typical working experience of a traditional academic.

50. The 22 candidates were divided into small groups or mini-course teams, and in the fourth week of the programme each group had to submit a self-study package and related materials. This task included the writing of explicit learning or behavioural objectives, itself a unique experience for many of the participants. In short, these groups had to attempt to do in a brief time and on very small scale the kinds of things they would have to do later in working in an EU course team.

51. In addition each candidate in one week of the programme had to study one complete unit for an Open University course in a subject area other than his or her own field. In other words, each candidate had to become an Open University student for a week. They read the materials, watched the film, heard the tape, and submitted computer-marked assignments. In another week of the programme, each candidate conducted a five-minute television production which was video-taped. Some part of the time could be spent in straightforward lecturing, but some had to be spent using primitive visual aids. Each candidate also recorded a five-minute 'radio' broadcast, so that all had the opportunity to hear and see themselves as EU students might eventually see them, which can be a most humbling experience.

52. As another activity in the programme, each candidate had to choose a specific target audience and write and compile an appropriate learning package for that audience. These tasks, when combined, demonstrated to the prospective new staff the problems of putting together self-study courses and the problems of using media in an Open Learning system.

53. Even though the course lasted five weeks, it was essentially a late afternoon and evening activity. Almost all of the candidates were employed elsewhere, which prevented daytime participation. Besides these tasks and activities, in the evenings the candidates heard a number of speakers and saw other presentations.

54. All of the (now) eight new academic staff at the EU who have been engaged are in their thirties, with the exception of one man who is 40 years of age and one 'old-timer' of 50. Hence the initial academic staff are all quite young. Their academic fields include: computer science, engineering, mathematics, biological sciences, earth sciences, Jewish studies and chemistry. In addition, six more academics have since been engaged on a part-time basis. None of the staff has tenure during the trial period of EU. In fact, the agreement with the ministry was that a special allowance should be paid to staff in lieu of tenure. Their initial contracts are for two years, and can be terminated after one year by either side. Several of these provisions tend to emphasize the provisional nature of the EU; and many of these new staff members, like the small number of senior staff, may retain appointments elsewhere. It seems to be a custom, if not now an economic necessity, for Israeli academics to maintain two or more jobs. But this situation had led one friend of the university to say: 'I do not see anybody committed to it—no full-time commitment.' By contrast, the initial small staff at the United Kingdom Open University had placed their own careers at risk to ensure that the OU was a permanent success.

Future staff training

55. All through the initial planning of Everyman's University there has been a consistent effort to draw on the experience of other experts and other Open Learning systems, and not just the Open University of the United Kingdom. In accordance with this philosophy, President Rowe in October 1974 took all of the new academic staff personally to visit Munich, Federal Republic of Germany, to see the Telekolleg and Lehrerkolleg and to Tübingen to visit DIFF, the Deutsches Institut für Fernstudien (Institute for Distance Studies). Following their experiences in the Federal Republic of Germany, the staff spent some time at the Open University in the United Kingdom before going to the United

States. In the latter, they did not visit Open Learning systems but instead listened to a number of experts, such as Dr Samuel B. Gould, chairman of the Council for the Progress of Non-Traditional Study, and Professor Cyril Houle, author of the recent book, *The External Degree.*

56. Certainly this Open Learning 'grand tour' is one way, and a relatively expensive one, to introduce staff first-hand to what others in the field are doing. Since educational technology is so foreign to most academics, a variety of efforts and training programmes are useful, if not necessary, adequately to introduce faculty to the issues, problems and techniques involved. Furthermore, the personal contacts established may help the staff cope with the many unforeseen, as well as the foreseen, problems which lie ahead.

VI The future dimly seen

Future difficulties

57. In a speech in June 1974 President Rowe raised some of the difficult and as yet unanswered questions:

How shall we prevent distance between teacher and learner leading to a depersonalization of the learning process and an alienation between the two?
Shall we avoid an over-emphasis of media over content?
Who will do the job?
Shall we find the right people in sufficient numbers within a short period of time?
Will the EU attract a sufficient number of students to make the operation worth while?
Shall we succeed in producing material of such quality as to upgrade the learner, sustain his motivation and reduce the drop-out rate to acceptable proportions?
Shall we resist the temptation of copying conventional institutions?
Shall we win over the educators to the new synthesis of direct and indirect learning?
Will the country bear with us, or will the people be impatient for results before we can deliver them?
Can we keep the cost within reasonable limits?

Students to be served

58. The evolution of the planning of the EU demonstrates the increasing emphasis on the in-service academic education of school teachers which will, in fact, receive the highest priority. The hope persists that EU may be successful in helping these teachers to find, in the words of the Schramm Commission, 'ways to be more successful than they are now with Orientals and Arabs'.

59. Teachers without academic degrees therefore receive the highest priority for the EU's programmes. But the first students to experience the EU first-hand have been immigrants of widely varying educational backgrounds. In the early part of 1975, EU joined the Centre for Instructional TV in the distribution of a televised course in Hebrew-language instruction designed for individuals with no more than a 500-word vocabulary in Hebrew. This programme was made possible by a special grant from the Rothschild Foundation and was of three months' duration and clearly 'pre-academic' or 'sub-academic'. Some critics of the EU would say that a 'university' should not be involved with this kind of instruction in the first place.

Curriculum

60. Besides the three-month non-academic course in Hebrew offered early in 1975, the EU hopes to offer another preparatory or sub-academic course in English, for both its own students and others interested, and another in electronics (in association with the Centre for Educational Technology).

61. The EU has agreed with the Ministry of Education that its first academic courses, those for teacher training, should include mathematics, science, technology, and Jewish studies, which includes Hebrew language, Jewish history and Jewish thought. In fact, the new, young, academic staff are now beginning to plan these courses, which they hope will be ready for students by October 1976. The EU expects to develop 'modular courses', each of about 12 weeks in length. Nine such courses would be necessary for a B.A. for a practising teacher, with perhaps as many as 18 or 20 such modular courses necessary for a B.A. for all other students.

62. Even with a clearly defined 'target' student population, many questions remain to be answered. Should the 'target' be attacked with a rifle or a shotgun? That is, should a course be so specific that it would only be of interest to teachers or should it be made broader to appeal to a more general adult student population? The possibility exists that as a course becomes more general it may also, at the same time, become less relevant to its target population.

63. The EU will, whenever appropriate, buy course materials from others, such as the Open University or the UMA/SUN Project.

Entry qualifications

64. The qualification of students to be served is inextricably related to the basic purposes of the institution and to the students who actually will be served. The Schramm Commission believed that the openness of the system should be guaranteed as far as possible. The commission went on to emphasize this point: 'Above all, it [the EU] should not develop restrictive academic entry requirements.' They also recognized the obvious: that an open admissions policy for the EU would raise questions of standards.

65. The dilemma, of course, is how to be 'open' and 'maintain standards'? Can one have a semi-open or sort-of-open university? The British Open University is open to anyone over 21, but though participation in these Olympics is available to all comers, the height of the first hurdle is fixed and the same for everyone. The EU rector would like to have a 'self-test', which might consist of a unit or two of a course, to be offered before a course starts. From this experience, a student should be able to estimate more accurately his or her prospect of success in the course and reduce the risk of 'dropping-out' and taking up a place another might have filled. The trials should also help to keep the courses adjusted to the students' capacity. The educational concern here, according to the rector, is to ensure that the courses are 'not above the heads of our students. We want to hit them.'

66. President Rowe believes that if the EU is true to its purposes as an Open Learning system, it must have an open admission, without requiring any entrance examinations. He believes that 'standards are not set by the students who enter without entrance qualifications but by the university itself'.

67. So a question that bedevils most Open Learning systems remains unanswered at the EU. Future plans may resolve the dilemma of how to be egalitarian and elitist at the same time, of how to mitigate social inequality without changing the rules that establish 'inequality' and of how to serve appropriately the educational needs of individuals and of the larger society.

The role of television

68. Even though the Schramm Commission strongly urged that new patterns of instructional technology should be devised, its recommendations regarding the use of television by the EU were surprisingly cautious. 'We think that the general rule for Everyman's University should be that television should be used only where absolutely necessary.' Elsewhere the commission asserted that

> . . . more television, more radio, more films, more instructional talk of any kind have never solved basic educational problems anywhere in the world. Solutions lie not in the media, but in the instruction for which they are used and the instructional systems of which they are a part.

69. Television will no doubt play some important role in EU's future. The government has assured the new university that it will 'use its best offices to provide the university with broadcasting time on the national television network, when the same will be found necessary for the operation of the university'. While this is a supportive statement, it is hardly like the firm commitment and legal contract between the United Kingdom's Open University and the BBC. There is only one television channel in Israel, but because of the country's small size there is virtually 100 per cent coverage. Instructional Television, which has the use of that one channel from 7.30 a.m. until 5.30 p.m., is under the direct control of the Minister of Education, but the use of the one channel after 5.30 p.m. is under a public broadcasting authority.

70. There is no absolute assurance that broadcasting time will be forthcoming, but the EU has a 'good neighbour' relationship with Israel's ITV 'with some potential for a marriage at a future date'. The director of the Centre for Educational Technology feels that the EU use of broadcast television will be greatly limited by two practical constraints: limited air time and cost of production and transmission.

71. The Centre for Educational Technology, supported by the Rothschild Foundation, and already operational and successful, will provide a number of services related to both television and the other media. These services could include publishing, producing audio-visual materials, duplicating audio cassettes, providing computer services, and acting as an agent for television production, both in definition of programme content and budget matters.

72. The president foresees the day when, if the EU is successful, the CET, ITC and the EU could be combined under one umbrella in a single public agency. He hopes that such a combination would not be under the Ministry of Education, but rather a more autonomous and new public body. Initially, the EU expects to occupy the third floor of the large new building being erected for the CET, which is adjacent to the building in which the ITC is housed. The Everyman's University is temporarily located in a remodelled villa very near to

the new building of the CET, the existing ITC facility and the large campus of the University of Tel Aviv.

Role of study centres and tutors

73. If television is not to be extensively utilized in the future at the EU, by what means will instruction be provided in this Open Learning system? The Schramm Commission saw the EU as a learning resource for all of Israel. At the same time it suggested that the EU try to put its resources into making effective courses for individualized study rather than into establishing an extensive network of tutorial centres that might grow into formal instructional institutions.

74. The rector hopes that the EU will be able to do much of its work without establishing study centres on its own. Such centres, he feels, might antagonize other institutions, would be expensive and perhaps even unnecessary. At the same time, Professor Lifson has strong feelings about the importance and efficacy of group activity by students. The Schramm Commission also expressed the view that it was unrealistic to assume that the motivation and interest of disadvantaged people in Israel or anywhere else would be adequate to sustain them through the long courses of independent home study.

75. Unanswered questions remain about how the EU can or will provide 'group activity' and/or face-to-face contact. Professor Lifson hopes to obtain the co-operation of local or regional colleges and various adult educational programmes by establishing a kind of 'structural association' with existing institutions. Lifson believes that one idea might be to co-opt EU graduates of the previous year to work with the new EU students in group activities, such as working through open-ended questions or other group tasks.

76. Obviously many critical questions must be answered before the EU can become operational. The questions of what 'delivery systems' are to be used and in what ratio for what courses have yet to be resolved. Whether and how to provide face-to-face human contact has yet to be determined.

Costs

77. There really is not much that can be said concerning the cost of the EU. The Schramm Commission (in 1972) estimated possible staff requirements and capital and operating expenses, and came up with a figure of about U.S.$8 million for the seven-year trial period of the project. Some observers believe that this estimate is now far too conservative, but nobody has been able to produce a more accurate figure.

78. As mentioned earlier in this report, the Rothschild Foundation has committed U.S.$5 million to the project over the first seven years, including all support for the first three years. The government has committed itself to provide the funds needed in the last four years of the 'trial period'.

79. Mr Rowe has said that since the EU has 'no solid predictions about enrolments, there can be no estimate of what costs per student might be'.

80. The other, and too often neglected, side of the costs coin is cost *to* the student rather than the institutional cost *per* student. What does the student

get for what he or she pays? At the Open University, as at other British universities, student fees provide only 12 to 13 per cent of its operating budget, because the fees charged to students are so very low. At the Open University a student pays only a U.S.$20 registration fee and about $91 for each foundation course, and up to $143 for each upper-level course. There are, of course, other expenses such as books, deposit on science kits, and a modest summer-school fee. By contrast, students at Israel's University paid 1,500 Israeli pounds tuition fees per semester, or about U.S.$750 dollars per academic year, during 1973/74, and the fees were to go up by a further amount during 1974/75.

81. The pressure of the market-place exists only when the customer has a choice. Does the student have a choice between Sussex and the Open University, or between Hebrew University and Everyman's University? If the student has a choice, what does he or she get for what he or she pays for at the various alternatives? If the student does not have a choice, then is the single option worth the expense? The chief expense for Open University students is the sacrifice of their spare time. Will this be the case for the EU students? Will the charges made to students be another barrier? It is obviously too early to say, since the entire subject of student fees and financial barriers to higher education, both in actual costs and in earnings forfeited by the prospective students has yet to be considered or experienced.

VII Summary

82. The new Everyman's University, like other Open Learning systems around the world, hopes to serve certain national needs. In the case of the EU, these are to provide: (a) teacher training for in-service teachers without academic degrees; (b) a 'second chance' for people unsuccessful in their first encounter with education at the secondary or post-secondary level; and (c) adult education to upgrade skills and to enrich leisure time. These goals are clearly part of the now world-wide trend of expanding educational opportunity to more and more people.

83. Departures from tradition can include risks; and the EU presents an excellent case study of how private funds through 'creative philanthropy' can undertake risks which governments may be unable or unwilling to do. The Everyman's University has come into being and will be supported for its first three years entirely by the Rothschild Foundation (Hanadiv). Then, if the project looks promising, it will be gradually and increasingly supported with public funds for the remainder of the trial seven-year period, to be ultimately supported entirely with public funds. The Rothschild Foundation has similarly created (in 1963) Israel's Instructional Television Centre and (in 1969) the Centre for Educational Technology. There is the hope that, eventually, these obviously related efforts (including the EU) can be amalgamated under some single public body or agency creatively serving Israel's educational needs.

84. Besides this unique 'conception and birth', the EU also provides an excellent example of how high-level advice and expertise can be obtained from other countries to help in both the planning and the implementation of an Open Learning system. The EU's staff-selection and distinctive staff-training programmes can also be useful models to other nations and other Open Learning systems.

85. Because of its very early stage of development, it is far too early to judge the EU either a success or failure; but it certainly has a good start in its hope 'to serve in the building of a better society in Israel'.

Appendix A Standardized reference data

Country, state or province	Israel
Area and climate	8,023 square miles (pre-1967). The 'territories': 26,476 square miles. Mediterranean to desert.
Population	
Total (latest year)	(1973) Jews 2,810,400, non-Jews 497,100, total 3,307,500.
Estimated population aged 18	Approximately 50,000.
Estimated percentage under 15	Under 18: 34 per cent (1973).
Current annual growth rate (percentage)	Jews: 3.2 (1973), non-Jews 4.3 (1973).
Government	
Main organizational structure	Unitary; single-chamber parliament.
Political type	Republic.
Economy	
Political type	Mixed public and private.
Gross national product	
Total (latest year)	£(I)37,500 million (U.S.$6,250 million) (1973).
Per head	£(I)11,340 (U.S.$1,890) (1973).
Average annual increase (percentage)	24.2 (1970–74).
Communications	
Ground/air	Adequate system of highways. Some intra-national air service, excellent international services.
Mail/telephone	Adequate postal services. Automatic dialling.

Broadcasting

Main systems operating	One national television channel. Serving general and instructional television.
Principal authority(ies) responsible	1. Ministry of Education (Instructional Television). 2. Broadcasting Authority (semi-autonomous). 3. General Television (autonomous public body represented politically by Ministry of Education).
Radio	
Transmission coverage of main programme services with percentage of population reached	100.
Receiving capability for main programme services (percentage)	85.7 (based on radio licences, 1973).
Television	
Transmission coverage as defined for radio (percentage)	Almost 100.
Receiving capability for main programme services (percentage)	78.5 (based on television licences, 1973).
Monochrome or colour	Monochrome.

Education

Type of system(s)	Religious and Jewish State schools.
Main authorities responsible and powers	
Elementary schools	Ministry of Education. Unified public control.
Secondary school level	Municipal and private but Ministry of Education sets unified examinations and gives scholarships liberally to cover school fees.
Teacher colleges	Ministry of Education.
Post-secondary	Council for Higher Education.
End of full-time school attendance	
Legal	14 years of age.
De facto	14 years of age.
Proportion of 18-year-old age group involved in education	
Full-time	45 per cent (25,028 in 1973).
Major developments in provision	
Over last five years	Reform of 1968–70 to provide 'Mixed system' of junior high and senior high schools until 1977.
Over next five years	New emphasis on under-privileged (Ministry of Education). Individualized instruction at elementary schools (CET) and at post-secondary level (EU). New impetus to adult education (EU).

Institution/system under study	*Everyman's University, Israel*
Brief for study and reason for inclusion	A recently established Open Learning institution. Unique private-to-public funding.
Description of subject studied	
Origins	Joint decision by Rothschild Foundation and Ministry of Education in 1971.
Educational authority(ies) and roles	Educational priorities subject to the approval of Minister of Education and Culture.
Communications authority(ies) and roles	Government will 'ensure' that the Instructional TV Trust shall 'co-operate with the University'. Because of high cost of television, EU will only make limited use of it.
Services provided	1. In-service teacher training. 2. 'Second-chance' secondary school completion and higher education. 3. Adult education.
Eligibility to study (a) categories	1. Teachers without academic degrees. 2. 'Disadvantaged' Oriental Jews and Arabs. 3. Other adults.
(b) qualifications	None; 'open entry'.
Terminal qualifications	B.A., B.Ed., or diploma.
Instructional means used	Yet to be determined, but probably multi-media, modular, 12-week courses, plus guided work groups and seminars.
Personal input from student	Yet to be determined. Norm: 10 hours per week.
Normal duration of study	18 courses required for bachelor degree. Teachers will be given credits for existing qualifications.
Pedagogical effectiveness	Evaluations will be carried out continuously. Until EU has its own evaluation, the Education School of Hebrew University will carry out the evaluations.
Numbers involved	
Student intake (latest year)	Between 1,500 and 2,500 in first year, 1976.
Academic staff	
Full-time	10 (March 1975).
Part-time	8 (March 1975).
Other professional staff	Secretary of the University Financial Controller.
Finance	
Recurrent expenditure (by providing authorities, latest year)	U.S.$1.1 million (1975).
Non-recurrent expenditure	U.S.$1.5 million (1973–76).

Special assistance received

Financial	The Rothschild Foundation has committed U.S.$5 million to the project, which will cost U.S.$8 million (at least) during first seven years. Actual costs likely to be much higher.
Non-financial	Extensive contact with other countries; Schramm Commission study and report.

Sources of further information

Max Rowe, The Rothschild Foundation, 14, Chemin Riev, 1208 Geneva (Switzerland).

The Secretary, Everyman's University, 35 Rechov Mishmeret, Afeka, Tel Aviv (Israel).

Appendix B **Short bibliography**

HAWKRIDGE, D. *Everyman's University—the Israeli OU.* Milton Keynes, The Open University Information Services, Milton Keynes, MK7 6HA, United Kingdom.

ISRAEL. INSTRUCTIONAL TELEVISION CENTRE. *Instructional television in Israel. Some facts and figures.* Ramat Aviv, Israel, ITC, 14 Klausner Street, Ramat Aviv, 1971.

ROWE, M. *Open Learning—Everyman's University, Israel.* Speech delivered at the United States Cultural Centre, Tel Aviv, 3 June 1974. (Available from: The Rothschild Foundation, 14 Chemin Riev, 1208 Geneva, Switzerland.)

SCHRAMM, W. *An 'Everyman's University' for Israel.* Tel Aviv, 1972. Report submitted to Hanadiv by the Enquiry Commission (Wilbur Schramm, chairman, David Hawkridge, Harold Howe II), 15 September 1972. (Available from: Everyman's University, 35 Rechov Mishmeret, Afeka, Tel Aviv, Israel.)

UNITED KINGDOM. THE OPEN UNIVERSITY. *Open line*, no. 2, May 1974. (The OU/BBC Overseas Newsletter, available from: The Open University Information Services, Milton Keynes, MK7 6HA, United Kingdom).

Appendix C **Biographical note**

Dr Fred Nelson is Vice-President for Administrative Affairs at Nova University in Florida and a visiting fellow at the Open University, where he served two years as co-director of the Office of New Degree Programmes, a joint activity of the College Entrance Examination Board and the Educational Testing Service.

Open Learning in **Japan**

Hidetoshi Kato
and Richmond Postgate

Contents

I Introduction

1. This study describes the experience of Japan in providing opportunities for adults and young adults to gain qualifications by part-time study; sets this experience in the context of the country's history and circumstances; and considers the prospect for continuing change.

2. It focuses particularly upon provision involving the combined use of correspondence education and broadcasting at senior high school, university and college levels, and upon the current discussions about the proposal for a broadcasting university. It comments, finally, on the possible relevance of Japanese experience and practice to other countries facing problems of educational development.

3. Grateful acknowledgement is made by the authors to the Japanese Broadcasting Corporation (Nippon Hoso Kyokai—NHK) and to the Japanese Ministry of Education, and to many individuals for help, information and advice.

II The background

4. Japan consists of four main islands and innumerable islets off the east coast of the Asian mainland. Eighty per cent of its land area is mountainous and its population of 108 million (1973) lives mainly in the densely populated urban areas. It has a parliamentary form of government, very good facilities for travel and communication, and ample public broadcasting services. The national corporation, NHK, has two television and three radio networks with national coverage, and these are supplemented by 52 commercial radio and 86 television companies. A notably high proportion of NHK resources is devoted to educational programmes in the broad sense (18 per cent of the programme budget in 1973). Two complete channels are devoted to education, one in television and one in radio, besides a large volume of quasi-educational material in other programme services.

5. In recent times growth and development in all directions have dominated Japan. The population has tripled in the last 100 years. In the past fifteen years economic development has taken place at unprecedented rates (GNP registering an average annual real growth of 10 to 12 per cent during the period). In 1973 Japan was the richest country in the Far East.

6. Japan is one of the most educationally conscious and competitive countries in the world. Over 11 per cent of public expenditure is spent on education and large amounts are contributed by industry, charitable foundations and informal groups. The private institutions are very numerous and important, particularly at the post-secondary level.

7. Attendance at school is free and compulsory for nine years until age 15 (six years primary and three years junior secondary). Above this level tuition fees are charged. In 1973, 90 per cent of those who completed the junior secondary course went on to voluntary attendance at the senior high schools (16 to 18). A third of high-school leavers enter universities and junior colleges, and the proportion is growing annually; it is expected that it will rise to 35 per cent by 1985 and to 40 per cent in 1990. With the full support of parents, Japan is fast becoming a graduate society (*kogakureki shakai*). This situation has in fact developed despite the fact that there are virtually no educational grants to high school and university students in Japan. A small number of students receive modest loans; but the common practice is for families to save for this purpose and for students to help by working their way through college.

8. The roots of the situation lie far in the past. In mediaeval times the influence of Chinese culture led to a high respect for the educated literati, for literacy and a capacity for elegant poetic composition. Between 1615 and 1865 the Tokugawa Government kept Japan at peace internally and isolated from the outside world. This long period helped to incubate the people's educational aspirations. It also fostered the growth of cultural homogeneity and the intuitional understanding between the Japanese which seems to underlie the talent for team-work which so many inside and outside Japan have remarked upon.

9. It is estimated that by the middle of the nineteenth century, 40 per cent of the population were literate, an unusually high figure for a country not yet industrialized.

10. The two major historical convulsions since then—the Meiji Restoration of 1868, which opened Japan to the world, and the reconstitution of society that followed the Pacific War in 1945—both stimulated and encouraged the young and vigorous to realize their capacities through success at school and university. The spirit of Samuel Smiles' *Self Help*, one of the earliest foreign books to be translated into Japanese during this period, set an attitude which is still dominant today. Their capacity for hard work and the high level of their education are characteristics of which Japanese are most proud.

11. Entry into the post-secondary stages of education was (and is) by competitive examination set by the individual institutions, a system which can be traced back to the early years of the Meiji period. The examination at 18 dominates and, in some eyes, deforms Japanese education today, for its influence reaches backwards into the primary level imparting a competitiveness that negates the comprehensive philosophy upon which the compulsory system rests. On account of the traditions of lifelong employment in a single concern, and of the rigid, though unwritten, ranking of universities, this examination assumes critical importance in a young man's career and its results place him permanently in an occupation and define his social status and expectations. For these reasons some 200,000 candidates may be held up for as much as five years while attempting repeatedly to gain entry to the institution of their choice. The description of this experience as *shiken jigoku* ('examination hell') is not surprising.

Higher education in Japan, 1973

Universities/ Junior colleges	*Type of institution*	*Number of institutions*	*Number of students*
Universities	National	76	333,273
	Local public	33	49,623
	Private	295	1,214,386
	Total	404	1,597,282
Junior colleges	National	24	11,296
	Local public	45	16,873
	Private	430	281,655
	Total	499	309,824

12. The institutions of higher education relevant to this study are universities and junior colleges. Universities offer a first degree course of four years. They fall into three categories: national institutions, generally the oldest and most esteemed, which supply recruits to the public services and the big private corporations; the local-authority (prefectural) universities, which followed later; and the private universities, founded by groups or individuals and established as charities. Some of the latter enjoy high esteem, but the majority do not. Private universities tend to serve the business world. Four-fifths of university students are male.

13. The junior colleges, developed after the war, again fall into the same categories: national, local public and private. They offer two- and three-year courses to diploma level, predominantly in the humanities, and are attended mainly by girls.

14. The accompanying table, giving figures for higher education, shows the very great dependence in Japan on the private sector. National institutions are favoured in a number of ways. For example, the average staff/student ratio in national universities is 1 : 7, compared with 1 : 30 in private institutions. The expenditure per student is similarly disproportionate. The level of fees in national universities is lower than that in private institutions.

15. In private institutions, fees account for two-thirds of the income; public resources constitute 15 per cent; the remainder comes from industry, business and private sources. These institutions are frequently in financial difficulties and, in consequence, though with some outstanding exceptions such as Keio, Waseda, etc., their educational standards and standing are lower. It is commonly said that the institution a young man attends is, in terms of his future employment, more important than his performance in his final examination.[1]

16. Mention should also be made of two particularly Japanese features of the national education system: social education and what are called 'miscel-

1. This survey omits the files of technical education headed by the five-year technical colleges, since part-time education is not available in this sector.

laneous schools'. Both are extensive and reinforce the very high level of commitment to education in all sections of Japanese society.

17. Social education is part of the national system and consists of organized educational activities, mainly for youths and adults, in schools or higher education institutions. These are carried on by official and non-official bodies in community centres, 'youth houses', museums and public libraries. More than 90 per cent of municipal bodies maintain such centres.

18. 'Miscellaneous schools' (*kakushu gakko*) or 'non-school schools' form another, and specifically Japanese, category of unofficial private institutions and groups outside the purview of the ministries. They organize activities and training that do not usually lead to any formal qualification. These may be vocational courses for boiler-men or bankers, classes in flower arrangement which meet in the instructor's home, or foreign-language schools with an enrolment of thousands. It is estimated that in Tokyo alone 750,000 may be engaged in these activities.

19. The tone of Japanese education stresses learning by rote. Such practices as collective chanting and the reproduction of factual information in examinations play a large part in the educational experience. Discovery methods of learning and individualized study by project are not common. This tradition must be borne in mind when the developments and innovations now proposed are considered.

III Part-time education

20. Part-time study to gain recognized qualifications by students above the legal school-leaving age has existed in Japan for many years. It has taken the two usual forms: evening study on several nights a week and correspondence education based on postal communications between student and tutor. Both forms are available at senior high school, university and junior college levels. At senior high school level, part-time study is offered at about eighty schools, involving 425,000 students, of whom 158,000 are studying by correspondence.

21. At university level, part-time study is available (1973) at 16 universities involving 234,000 students. Of these part-time students, 99,000 are studying by correspondence.

22. At junior college level, a quarter of these colleges offer part-time studies involving 83,000 students, of whom 43,000 are studying by correspondence.

23. It is with these correspondence students, totalling 300,000 in all, that this study is concerned. The Japanese postal system is very efficient, and the turnround rate between the moment the student dispatches his work and its return marked by his tutor is normally seven days.

24. For all of these students, radio and television support is available, as well as some form of tutor/student contact. Apart from this common characteristic the systems have significant differences at the different levels; so they will be looked at in turn.

25. The first beginnings of correspondence education in Japan date back to the 1880s. In 1883 Madoka Maeda started a correspondence course in reading the Chinese classics, sending material to students twice a month. After the invention of Japanese shorthand in 1884, correspondence courses in this subject were developed, notably at Waseda University.

26. The real development occurred at the end of the Pacific War in 1945 when the educational system was radically reformed along democratic lines. At that time, with the destruction of school buildings and the poverty which prevented many parents from keeping their children at school, education by correspondence could provide an important extension of high school study. It was needed too, for adults, both for those whose education has been interrupted by the war, and for those who wished by gaining educational qualifications to fit themselves to take part in the new society and realize its cultural aims (*bunka kokka*).

27. One main principle of the new educational policy was that opportunities for higher education should be universally available as a civic right, irrespective of birth, wealth, status or location. Correspondence education was seen as a way to secure this, and its development is attributable more to this factor than to the relative costs to the State of correspondence and full-time education.

IV Correspondence education at high school level

28. Although this report is primarily concerned with higher education, the earliest and most comprehensive attempt to use combined resources for teaching students not in full-time attendance at an educational institution was at the high school level. Since experience gained in this field has strongly influenced Japanese thinking about the teaching of adults, and since many of the pupils of the correspondence high schools are in fact adults, that experience is dealt with at some length below.

29. Considering the high percentage of students leaving full-time education at the age of 15 in the post-war years, it was natural that correspondence education should begin at the high school level. After consultation on ways and means with the Education Institute of the United States Armed Forces, correspondence education was introduced into the Japanese system in 1948. Article 45 of the School Education Law (Gakko Kyoiku Ho) authorized the local-education authorities (prefectures) to set up high schools to teach students in their areas by correspondence.

30. The learning system then established (and still operating) enables a student to gain in four years the same qualification that an internal student should gain in three. The correspondence student is required to study specified textbooks, chosen from the range approved by the Ministry of Education, alongside special manuals of guidance, and to submit written work once a month on subjects prescribed by the school. Students must also attend at the school or some other centre for face-to-face sessions on twenty days each year. These sessions consist of direct teaching, discussions, guidance and testing and are known as 'schooling'. Students sit subject examinations three times a year, and a general promotion examination annually. The school year starts in April.

31. The courses consist of compulsory subjects, such as Japanese, English and mathematics, and a wide range of optional subjects. The courses offered have varied according to demand and to the extent to which the subjects were catered for in the expanding full-time provision. Between 1962 and 1972 vocational courses were much in demand, but diminished as more and more young people stayed on at high school and then sought entry to universities. There is now a swing towards the provision of social and cultural courses.

32. It is instructive to note how the extent, following and role of correspondence education has changed over the past twenty years, as can be approximately indicated by the destinations of junior high school leavers. In 1953, 44 per cent became full-time students at senior high schools. Ten years later this figure was over 60 per cent and in 1972 nearly 90 per cent. The percentage discontinuing education dropped from 31 to a mere 7 over the period. The remainder, those continuing their education part-time, fell from 209,000 at the start to 102,000 by the end; but the proportion studying by correspondence rose from under 10 per cent to nearly 50 per cent. In other words, some 50,000 leavers from junior high schools were taking their senior high school education by correspondence.

33. It is also of interest that, particularly in the last ten years, the age of entrants to correspondence senior high schools has been edging upwards. In 1963 students under 21 accounted for two-thirds of the entry; now they form about half. The average entry age is nearly 25, with more women than men. For a special adult-education-type course started in 1973, the average age of entrants was over 32.

34. These figures seem to suggest not only that correspondence education is suitable for adults and adolescents alike, but also that the greater freedom to choose their own working pattern makes adults prefer this form of part-time study. The educational administrator may see how flexible and adaptable is this correspondence mode and reflect on the saving of capital expenditure on expensive fixed installations.

Use of broadcasting

35. After a local trial, NHK began offering broadcast contributions to senior high school correspondence students on its educational networks, first by radio in 1953, and then by television as well in 1960. By 1963 a majority of the subjects of the curriculum were covered, the same subjects being frequently offered in both media.

36. Students following the courses were excused some of the 'schooling' sessions, three-tenths in the case of radio, five-tenths in the case of television and six-tenths if they followed both. Since the inability to meet the 'schooling' requirements has proved one cause of drop-out, these concessions were valuable. That the student is following the broadcast courses is known because of the reports he has to send on each broadcast. It should also be said that 'schooling', although it is compulsory, is not resented; on the contrary, it is regarded by most students as a source of great pleasure.

37. In 1963, when less than two-thirds of junior high school leavers were continuing their education at senior high schools as full-time students, NHK set up its now internationally famous broadcasting correspondence high school, the NHK Gakuen Correspondence High School. The motives were twofold: to serve as a testing ground and as a demonstration of the potentialities of linking correspondence education with broadcasting; and to offer services on a nationwide scale. NHK Gakuen was established as a private institution under the management of a corporation independent of NHK, financed by tuition fees and a grant from NHK. Today its annual enrolment for high-school qualifications averages 2,700; its student population is around 12,000. It has a staff of

150, and premises in the suburbs of Tokyo which can offer residential accommodation for 100 students. The NHK course is comparable to the courses of other correspondence high schools, though not identical with them. The course materials, both printed and broadcast, are prepared in close and constant consultation between the school staff and the NHK broadcasting staff. The broadcasts 'teach' the course, and are regarded as central and essential to it. They duplicate and explain the written material and are prepared by a prolonged collaborative process in which the lecturer/broadcaster, the academic staff of the school, the NHK producers and experienced teachers from other schools all play a part. The broadcast producer's role is, in television, to 'audio-visualize' the material provided by the educational side. The results, regarded as broadcasting, tend to be unexciting and prosaically didactic; but the programmes are inexpensive and chime in with the expectations of students, who place a high value upon the sense of personal contact with the broadcaster that the lecture format gives.

38. Each subject normally receives one television and one radio programme a week. The transmission times are, for television, 9 to 11 p.m. on weekdays and 3 hours spread over Sunday morning and afternoon; for radio 8 to 11 p.m. daily, with an extra hour on Sunday. 'Schooling' sessions are provided during the week and at weekends at the NHK school and at 69 other centres in the country, mainly other correspondence high schools. These sessions are the main source of feedback from the students to the course-providers.

39. NHK Gakuen students have thus the stimulus and pacing of both schooling and broadcasts. Students at other correspondence high schools may, of course, use the broadcasts, and many do.

40. It may in fact be useful at this point to give a general impression of how most correspondence students work, when taking the high school courses. First of all the students will be working in parallel in about eight subjects. For each of these subjects they will try to follow one or two broadcasts each week and will then get down to their reading and written work. This they will do mainly in the evenings, often working late into the night. With a five-and-a-half-day working week, it is not surprising that Japanese workers enjoy their one day of leisure; and the parks and gardens of Japanese cities are thronged with people on any fine Sunday. But, every two weeks for most of the year, students must give up their precious free Sunday and travel anything up to one hundred miles to attend their day of 'schooling'. Here they will go to a succession of classes, conducted formally by the school's teaching staff, and including probably some more private study, in which they can ask questions of the teachers. They will probably also have a chance during the day to take part in games and other physical activities, such as gymnastics and country dancing. Then back to another week of work and evening study. This pattern of work will probably continue for four or five years before students complete their high school qualifications and become eligible for any higher education.

41. The main and endemic drawback of correspondence education—drop-out—remains a cause of anxiety. The reader is referred to a study made in 1969 by a team of Japanese experts under the chairmanship of Professor Wilbur Schramm. The essential facts are these: of the enrolment in senior high schools of all correspondence students, only 17 per cent graduate after four years; but of the enrolment in NHK only, the figure is 19½ per cent. The Schramm report studied the annual drop-out rates of cohorts of entrants over the four

years of the NHK course over a number of years and shows that the drop-out rates were steadily falling. For the last three years to 1974 the proportions remaining in this system were, successively, 16.7, 18.8 and 23.8 per cent. Those responsible believe that this reflects the rising entry-age and the greater persistance displayed by mature students.

42. It is worth recording that over ten years 14,402 NHK Gakuen students have graduated.

43. An attempt to give some idea of the comparative cost-effectiveness of full-time and correspondence high school education was made; but as the complete data needed to make this very complicated comparison were not available, it was felt better not to make any statement, particularly since, as noted earlier, correspondence education in Japan is provided at least in part for reasons of social justice.

V Correspondence education at university and college levels

44. Correspondence education at higher educational levels also began in the late forties, authorized by article 54 of the Education Law, but has been provided only by a handful of private institutions. Today 16 universities and 8 junior colleges offer correspondence courses. Most of them offer courses in only one or two subjects. It is a story of independent initiatives on the part of separate institutions and individuals within them, leading to what today can only be described as a miscellaneous patchwork, working to no overall national plan. Where several institutions offer the same subject, there are no agreed textbooks and no standardization of the content of the courses between the institutions. The aggregate of courses offered thus forms only a partial university extension service.

45. Initially, the principal function of the service was to familiarize adults with the new post-war society and to bring in previously underprivileged groups such as women at home and residents of rural areas. In the 1950s, when a national campaign to improve the quality of the teaching force was launched, and a large number of non-graduate teachers needed to obtain degrees to teach in high schools, a new phase opened. During the 1960s, the years of the great economic development, vocational, professional and technical courses flourished, as well as updating courses for those whose initial qualifications were becoming obsolete. Towards the end of that decade and in the 1970s a new clientele emerged, comprising people who look to home study as a means of obtaining a liberal adult education.

46. The pattern of study, both at university and college level, is similar to that at high school level. A degree course consists of 124 units for credit spread over five years. A student receives textbooks and assignments of work to be sent to his tutor, who comments on them and returns them with advice. The material and the staff are the same for correspondence as for internal students. Staff are paid extra for this external work.

47. A quarter of the credits (a minimum of thirty) must be earned in residence. Many working students find this impossible, unless they are among the small number, e.g. civil servants studying law, who are granted exemption for this purpose. The requirement is a major cause of drop-out.

48. Applicants must be high school graduates or hold equivalent qualifications. There are no institutional entry examinations, though entrants may be

given academic tests after acceptance. Applications are treated on a first come, first served basis. Applicants without the High School Diploma may follow the course, but not for credit. Substantial numbers do this—about one-third at university level and one-half at college level. Today there are in all 150,000 students, of whom over 40 per cent are women.

49. 'Schooling' in the high school sense does not exist; instead there are forms of unofficial contact and two-week or three-week summer schools, in addition to the credit units for which residence is compulsory.

50. As the courses derive from the private sector, students share in the disadvantages of less favourable staff/student ratios and lower expenditure per student. Moreover, the fees that can be charged for correspondence courses are to some extent affected by the amount of the subsidized fee chargeable to full-time students at national universities. But though no direct financial aid is given to these institutions, the government has made some concessions in such matters as reduced postal rates for correspondence material, subsidized travel for students attending summer school and income tax concessions for students enrolled for credits. In the fiscal year 1974 a grant was made for the first time to the Association of Private Correspondence Universities to be spent on the revision and production of course textbooks.

51. It is not surprising that as a result of these conditions, the work load on the staff concerned is extremely heavy, the return of assignments sometimes delayed and the comments perfunctory. Furthermore, correspondence students rarely enjoy any cultural or social life connected with the institutions. Though the qualifications theoretically have equal status with those gained internally, it does not follow that they are held in the same esteem. Indeed, there is a good deal of evidence that correspondence qualifications are less highly regarded. One way and another, correspondence students tend to be underprivileged.

Use of broadcasting

52. Broadcast courses for university correspondence students were first offered in the 1960s. NHK now broadcasts programmes approved as part of college courses on radio and television for six days a week in the early morning; these are repeated in the late evening, with an additional afternoon repeat for radio at 5 p.m. The programmes are prepared through a form of collaboration similar to that at high school level, but the situation is complicated by the fact that there is no single national syllabus to which the broadcasters can relate the broadcasts. Broadcasts are supported by printed textbooks written by the broadcaster/lecturers and distributed by the college. In some cases, groups of students meet at the local NHK station for contact and mutual help.

53. Broadcast offerings at university level present special difficulties because the courses tend to reflect the individual attitudes of the academic staff who plan them; these attitudes sometimes come into conflict with the views of the broadcasters whom NHK may, after consultation, invite to prepare the programmes. All these factors create circumstances that are unfavourable for developing the close harmony that prevails at the senior high school level. The educational agencies are autonomous and act independently of each other and of NHK. NHK has its own independent and very extensive educational broadcasting activities unconnected with courses.

54. Since 1947 some 50,000 students at university and college level have obtained the qualifications they were seeking through university correspondence courses. The fact that these represent about 6 per cent of the total enrolments over that period should be seen not so much as indicating that 94 per cent have failed, or failed to gain the complete qualification, but rather that nearly 900,000 persons, half of them women, were sufficiently keen to attempt courses (some of which involved following broadcasts at inconvenient times). The fact that a substantial proportion of the students did not possess the basic entry qualifications suggests that they were as much interested in the experience as in the reward at the end. These are points which are relevant in considering the Broadcasting University proposal.

VI The Broadcasting University proposal

55. The Broadcasting University project is not an isolated proposal designed to exploit the educational potentialities of the broadcasting media. It is one of a number of measures designed to reform, reshape and develop higher education in Japan, and it is necessary to see it in that context.

56. In common with most other countries, Japan has found it necessary to rethink its policies and practice in this field. The immensely rapid developments of the last twenty years have resulted in strains and stresses which might have been avoided at a lower growth rate and which give particular urgency to this review.

57. In 1970, after five years of deliberation and, towards the end of that period, against a background of worrying student unrest, the Central Council for Education, which is the major body tendering policy advice to the Ministry for Education, issued a Master Plan for the Reform of Education. The plan made comprehensive and radical proposals: to enlarge and diversify the system to meet the numbers which it was anticipated would want higher education by 1985; to provide improved facilities for graduate research and research study; to improve the quality of teaching in formal and informal education by more widespread use of audio-visual teaching methods; and to eliminate a number of unacceptable features in the existing system. In putting forward the plan, official thinking recognized that higher education must aim at multiple and sometimes apparently contradictory objectives which must be met and reconciled. The increase in the proportion of adults wanting higher education meant that the plan must provide for an increasing range of demands from an enlarged body of students of a wider range of ability than hitherto. At the same time, the system would have to provide for the fullest development of fundamental and applied research, and for the training of more research workers for this purpose.

58. University curricula had to be revised and modified to produce graduates with all-round ability and a basic stock of information and skills, together with a capacity for reacting positively to a complex and rapidly developing society.

59. Some of the features of the plan which have a bearing on the present study are noted below.

60. The Central Council saw as obstacles to the wider diffusion of higher education the gruelling examination at the age of 18, the general difficulties of access to educational opportunities at the higher level, the isolation and inward-

looking posture of some universities and academics, and the rigidities and inflexibilities in the content and administration of higher education generally. In particular, it wished to encourage the replanning of undergraduate courses so as to avoid requiring students to spend two years on general education before they could begin on work more relevant to their own aims and their eventual employment, though this recommendation of the council met a considerable amount of opposition. Finally, it wished to see a readjustment in the relative functions of teaching and research in universities which would place a great emphasis on teaching, especially for the correspondence student.

61. The strategy of reform had four prongs: first, to make administrative changes in ways which would encourage existing institutions to undertake reforms of their own accord; second, to create a university of a new type which would give concrete expression to new educational thinking and serve as a testing-ground and model for future developments; third, to establish a five-year programme of initial and in-service training for school teachers, backed by a generous school equipment policy; and, fourth, to create a new national institution for part-time study to degree level, leaning heavily on radio and television.

62. The discussion stimulated by the plan has been intense and prolonged and will no doubt continue, for it involves many conflicting political and educational interests and views. To those connected with the educational use of radio and television it is of interest that it was felt necessary at this stage to mount a massive training campaign amongst teachers about audio-visual education; and this fact is a reminder of how difficult it is to change established teaching practice. To restate the point from the angle of the educational technologist: a solution to the problem of utilization of programmes must be reached before even the most extensive broadcast services can realize their full potential.

63. The Broadcasting University (Hoso Daigaku) has been under discussion for nearly ten years and two different exploratory official committees have made a number of proposals. The second of these bodies, the Research Conference for the Establishment of a Broadcasting University, released its latest plan in March 1974.

64. Under this plan, the aim of the Broadcasting University is to 'cultivate a capacity for understanding problems, the intelligence to solve them and a creative policy to plan for the future in a changing world'. If the plan goes ahead, this will be achieved through degree courses lasting for a minimum of four years, composed of three terms of 15 weeks, with broadcast programmes on seven days a week for the first two years.

65. The courses will be interdisciplinary in character, departing from traditional faculty divisions, and will consist of compulsory and elective subjects giving students a wide choice. The material will fall into four broad areas: 'nature and humanities'; 'social and international relations'; 'science and engineering'; and 'science of living'.

66. The course will be presented by radio and television, supported by special textbooks and other printed material, and by face-to-face 'schooling' contacts of between 10 and 20 days a year at centres giving individual guidance and practical work.

67. For this purpose the university will require a broadcasting licence and frequencies for radio and television giving national coverage over 18 hours a

day, and will make its own programmes. The university will be financed by a grant from the Ministry of Education and either directly or indirectly by students' fees.

68. The basic unit of production will be a course team comprising a chairman, who will be a senior member of the academic staff, a broadcasting lecturer, an educational technologist and a broadcast producer. Each team will be directly answerable to the president of the university, and will be responsible for all the learning material (broadcast and printed), for securing tutor/student contacts in regional centres and for continuing evaluation of student progress based on computerized feedback.

69. The university is expected to make substantial use of part-time and short-time contracts. Any adult graduate of a high school will be eligible for entry without further testing. Applications will be accepted in 1975 for a start in 1976. The fees to be charged are not decided yet, but will not be more than those of regular national universities (60,000 yen: U.S.$220 a year).

70. Initially the university will operate only in the densely populated Kanto area (in which Tokyo is situated) and one rural area. An initial entry of 8,000 is contemplated, building up to a student population of 40,000 in four years. Expansion into other areas will depend upon the experience of the first year.

71. It will be seen from the above that the university's proposed use of the broadcast media is central to its teaching and a major part of its provision, and that the broadcasts are not to be provided by the national broadcasting agency, NHK. This decision is of great interest in view of the long and deep commitment by NHK to education, and its extensive provision of educational broadcasting, both on its own initiative and in association with educational agencies at all levels. The Broadcasting University has been the subject of public discussion for at least five years and during this period pilot schemes for providing broadcasts for the university both in radio and television have been mounted, in which NHK and certain commercial companies have participated. However, it has not proved possible up to the present to reach agreement between NHK and the ministry for any continuing partnership. Consequently, as noted above, the university will need its own production and transmission services to provide the broadcast services.

72. The establishment of the university is unlikely to affect the general educational provision of NHK, though it might attenuate the volume of the present university-linked courses.

VII Some reflections

73. This section endeavours to relate the Japanese experience to the general objectives of the project described in the Introduction to the present book.

74. Five points have been singled out:

(a) The relationship between correspondence education and educational development and change.

(b) The influence of national attitudes to learning upon educational provision and styles of teaching and learning.

(c) Modes of combining correspondence education with other forms of learning.

(d) The relationship, in respect of educational broadcasting, between the national broadcasting organization and the educational system.
(e) The significance of educational institutions employing full-time staff for their Open Learning systems.

These points are now considered in detail.

The relationship between correspondence education and educational development and change

75. The present report suggests a number of roles for correspondence education:

(a) As a temporary auxiliary supplying substitute facilities for full-time education until the full-time provision catches up with the demand.
(b) As a continuing component of the total provision supplying alternative services to a sizable minority for whom full-time study is impossible, difficult or distasteful.
(c) As a means of discharging an accepted political responsibility to provide access to further education to all as a civic right.
(d) As a means of providing flexibly and without heavy capital expenditure for new needs and subject areas as they occur.

The influence of national attitudes to learning upon educational provision and styles of teaching and learning

76. It has been observed: (a) that the present high level of education rests not only upon the two periods of high development starting in 1868 and 1945, but upon the rate of literacy achieved before 1868; and (b) that the high respect for scholarship and the master–pupil relationship inherited from mediaeval times is a major factor in the present-day attitudes of students to hard work, to the dominance of factual learning and to acceptance of the lecture as the principal mode of learning, attitudes which find expression in didactic and austere presentation in broadcasting.

Modes of combining correspondence education with other forms of learning

77. The following points should be noted:

(a) The fact that 'schooling' in some form or other is a feature of all the systems studied, while it is a reflection of the high respect for scholarship observed above, is a reminder that effective adult education normally requires a social element to supply contact and support between student and student, and student and tutor.
(b) Broadcasting can supply elements useful to and valued by the student which are not otherwise available, such as penetration into the home, pacing students' study, and personal contact between student and lecturer.
(c) These possibilities are more likely to be realized when there is a high degree of co-operation at management and professional levels between the providing agencies, as this will result in a close relationship between the broadcast and printed learning materials.

The relationship, in respect of educational broadcasting, between the national broadcasting organization and the educational system

78. It will have been noted: (a) that a national broadcasting organization, independent of government, with a high commitment to education and culture and with adequate resources, can make outstanding contributions to education at all levels, and constantly take initiatives in response to new situations; but (b) that these initiatives require close and continuous contact between education and broadcasting, and positive steps by the appropriate authorities to secure adequate initial and in-service training of teachers; and (c) that where, as in the Broadcasting University proposal, the main burden of teaching is to be carried by the broadcasts, separate and additional segregated transmission facilities are required, and that the educational agency is less willing to surrender its editorial control in order to secure the skills of the broadcasting agency.

The significance of educational institutions employing full-time staff for their Open Learning systems

79. The example of NHK Gakuen shows that the success rates of such an institution made possible by a partnership between a national broadcasting agency and an independent 'private' institution are higher than the comparable existing patterns of association.

It would appear that the needs of correspondence students are better served when they are the prime concern of an institution than when they form a clientele additional to a full-time student body whose needs come first.

80. Perhaps, as a final comment, it should be added that, though some studies have been made of the causes of, and remedies for, drop-out among correspondence students, there does not as yet appear to have emerged a coherent body of tested experience and practice which can easily be studied by interested outsiders.

Appendix A Standardized reference data

Country, state or province	*Japan*
Area and climate	142,812 square miles in 4,000 islands. Temperate maritime to semi-tropical maritime.
Population	
Total (latest year)	108,580,000 (1973).
Estimated population aged 18	1,880,700 (1970).
Current annual growth rate (percentage)	Population tripled in last 100 years. In recent years, annual increase 1.24 per cent.
Government	
Main organizational structure	Unitary state with delegation of administrative responsibilities to State ministries.
Political type	Parliamentary democracy: *de facto* power does not lie with emperor.
Economy	
Political type	Mixed economy.
Gross national product	
Total (latest year)	95,564 million yen (1972) (U.S.$1=270.8 yen approx.).
Per head	711,030 yen (1972).
Average annual increase (percentage)	12.
Communications	
Ground/air	Quick and easy countrywide system of railways and unpaved roads. Air transport on rapid increase.
Mail/telephone	Good mail and telephone services.
Broadcasting	
Main system(s) operating	Public service and commercial systems of radio and television.

Principal authorities responsible	NHK (Japanese Broadcasting Corporation), a public service providing two radio networks, one F.M. radio and two television networks, financed by user's fees; commercial companies, radio and television.
Radio	
Transmission coverage of main programme services with percentage of population reached	Virtually universal.
Receiving capability for main programme services (percentage)	100.
Television	
Transmission coverage as defined for radio (percentage)	NHK coverage 100 per cent.
Receiving capability for main programme services (percentage)	87 per cent of households can receive NHK television.
Monochrome or colour	Monochrome and colour.
Education	
Type of system(s)	Public and private coexist.
Main authorities responsible and powers	
At school level	Predominantly public institutions, controlled and financed by central local authorities. Proportions provided by private bodies: small at primary level, one-quarter at senior high school level.
At post-secondary level	Junior colleges: 499, of which 430 private. Universities: 404, of which 295 private. 70 per cent of university students attend private universities. Prestige of private, with few exceptions, lower than that of public.
End of full-time school attendance	
Legal	Free compulsory education between ages of 6 and 15.
De facto	89.4 per cent enter senior high schools (16 to 19) voluntarily (1970).
Proportion of 18-year-old age group involved in education	
Full-time	27.7 per cent (1970) of age group enter some form of further education.
Part-time	Over 20 per cent involved in junior colleges and university evening education.
Major developments in provision	
Over last five years	All-round expansion.
Over next five years	Expected proportion of secondary school leavers to enter universities: 35 per cent (1985); 40 per cent (1990).

Institution/system under study

Brief for study and reason for inclusion

1. Japan is a pioneer of part-time study, at ages between 16 and 23, for qualification by correspondence assisted by broadcasting.

2. Discussion of establishment of national university based on distance teaching relying heavily on broadcasting.

Description of subject studied

Origins

1. Major development of correspondence education after end of Pacific War as component of education for new democratic society, complementing full-time provision and ensuring universal access. Initially aimed to benefit underprivileged (such as women and rural dwellers) and to upgrade qualifications and teachers. Later, general updating of vocational qualifications; today, increased emphasis is on general adult education.

2. University proposed as component of wide-ranging reform of higher education, introducing new concepts of higher education and enlarging access.

Educational authority(ies) and roles

1. Education authorities responsible for content and methods of courses leading to examinations approved by the ministry. Private institutions, established as juridical persons, alone provide correspondence facilities at junior college and university level.

2. The ministry will establish university, which will acquire and operate its own broadcasting production and transmission facilities.

Communications authority(ies) and roles

1. In consultation with educational authorities, NHK supplies radio and television courses: comprehensive at senior high school level and selective at junior college and university level. NHK established, and supports financially, an independent, linked senior correspondence high school, NHK Gakuen, to which it supplies broadcast element. This institution now expanding into adult education.

2. NHK not involved in proposed broadcast university as supplier of broadcasts (1974).

Students engaged on part-time study[1]

Level	*Institutions*	*Total part-time*	*Total correspondence*
Senior high school	80	425,358	158,502
Junior college	120	82,780	43,253
University	16	233,599	98,588
Total	216	741,737	300,343

Changes in the destination of leavers from junior school since 1953 (000s)

Year	*Leaving junior high school*	*Entering senior high schools*		
		Full-time	*Part-time evening*	*Part-time correspondence*
1953	1,558	697	191	17
1963	2,440	1,527	162	36
1972	1,523	1,317	70	45

NHK Gakuen (Senior High School): composition of entrants (1963–73)

Year	*Age of students at entry*					
	18 and under	*19 to 21*	*22 to 30*	*30 to 40*	*Over 40*	*Average*
1963	6,095	2,109	2,299	1,054	164	21.2
1969	8,102	2,793	5,720	1,788	233	22.5
1971	5,600	3,168	4,209	3,426	991	24.2
1973	4,447	2,556	3,290	3,236	727	24.8

Composition by sex of entrants

In 1973, 54.4 per cent of the entry was female; the proportion is steadily rising.

1. The information of particular interest in this study is presented in a different form at this point, so as to bring out: (a) the role of correspondence education in part-time education; (b) the changes in the educational destination of students leaving junior schools from 1953 onwards; (c) the changes in the age composition of students in NHK Gakuen; (d) the pedagogical effectiveness of broadcast-assisted correspondence study.

Retention of students: percentage of enrolled students remaining at the start of each year of study

Year	Year of study			
	First	*Second*	*Third*	*Fourth*
1966	44.8	25.3	13.5	16.4
1969	41.9	25.0	19.6	13.5
1970	37.7	26.3	19.4	16.6
1971	39.2	25.4	19.8	15.6
1972	35.3	28.0	20.0	16.7
1973	27.9	28.3	25.0	18.8
1974	28.6	22.8	24.8	23.8

The proportion of students graduating after four years (the minimum permissible) is 19.5 per cent for NHK Gakuen and 17.2 per cent for all senior high school students studying by correspondence.

Special course for adults: numbers of entrants

Year	*Total*	*Male*	*Female*
1973	3,487	1,463	2,024
1974	6,190	2,476	3,714

Age of entrants, 1973 and 1974

18 and under	*10 to 21*	*22 to 30*	*30 to 40*	*40 to 50*	*Over 50*	*Average*
890	631	2,032	2,506	2,177	1,441	32.4

Sources of further information

Education

Ministry of Education (MOMBU-SHO), Higher Education and Science Bureau, 3–2–2 Kasumigaseki, Chiyoda-Ku, Tokyo 100 (Japan).

Broadcasting

Mr Tadashi Yoshida, Special Assistant to the President, NHK, Uchisaiwai-Cho, Chiyoda-Ku, Tokyo (Japan).

Mr Storu Takatsuka, Principal, NHK Gakuen, Nippon Hoso Kyokai, Jinnan, Shibuya-Ku, Tokyo (Japan).

Appendix B — Short bibliography

JAPAN. MINISTRY OF EDUCATION. *Education and broadcasting in Japan.* Tokyo, 1969.

——. *Hoso daigaku no setsuritsu ni tsuite* [On the establishment of Broadcasting University]. Tokyo, 1970.

——. *Hoso daigaku ni kansuru junbi chosa no keii* [Summary of preparatory research on broadcasting university]. Tokyo, 1972.

——. *Hoso daigaku no kihon koso* [Fundamental outlines of Broadcasting University]. Tokyo, 1974.

SCHRAMM, W. *et al. The broadcast correspondence high school.* Munich, Internationales Institut für Jugend- und Bildungsfernsehen, 1971.

Appendix C — Biographical note

Hidetoshi Kato is a graduate of Hitotsubashi University, Tokyo, and of its postgraduate school. He has taught at Kyoto University, Iowa State University and the University of Hawaii. Currently he is a professor of sociology at Gakushuin University, Tokyo, and is working for the East–West Communication Institute, Honolulu, on a part-time basis.

Richmond Postgate, M.A. Camb., is a senior research fellow at the University of Sussex; broadcasting assessor to the Planning Committee of the Open University, he was formerly member of its governing council. Sometime Director-General of the Nigerian Broadcasting Corporation and former Controller of Educational Broadcasting, BBC.

Kenya: the use of radio and correspondence education for the improvement of teaching

Peter E. Kinyanjui

Contents

I Background

Geographical, economic and political background

1. Kenya is a large country (225,000 square miles or 582,647 square kilometres) with a current population of around 12 million, most of whom (95 per cent) live in rural areas and derive their livelihood either directly or indirectly from farming. The government is the largest employer in the monetary sector of the economy, though private enterprise in small commercial and manufacturing industries is encouraged.

The gross national product in 1971 was estimated at £(K)520 million so that *per capita* income was an estimated £(K)47 per annum. The average annual increase was reckoned to be 8 per cent.

Kenya attained political independence in December 1963 when a democratic republic was set up within the Commonwealth. Since then she has embarked on a series of four-year development plans to guide the social, economic and educational development of the country.

Educational background

2. One of the most vital needs facing the new republic was the development of facilities for primary and secondary education, which in its turn presupposed the need for a corresponding increase in facilities for the training or upgrading of teachers.

3. The situation facing the planners during the early years of independence was not unique to Kenya but followed a pattern to be found in many developing countries. This includes a high percentage of illiteracy amongst the adult and working population; an increase in school enrolment as a result of growing public demand for education; increasing numbers of school leavers who cannot be absorbed into the monetary economy; an urgent need to revise and modernize the curricula in schools and colleges; shortage of money; and shortage of qualified and experienced teachers, trainees and administrators.

4. In order to meet immediate needs, the Ministry of Education had to employ considerable numbers of underqualified or even unqualified teachers. It also increased enrolments in the primary teacher training colleges to the extent that total enrolment in colleges rose from 4,579 in 1963 to 6,732 in 1970. At the

same time the colleges themselves were reduced in number from 32 to 24 in an attempt to consolidate the facilities and resources then available.

5. In spite of these developments in teacher education, the total output of the training colleges could not match the rising demand for qualified teachers or even replace the existing unqualified staff in the schools. Hence the Ministry of Education mounted in-service teacher-training and upgrading programmes as the only way of providing more qualified teachers.

6. These programmes were quickly accepted by teachers because they permitted them to obtain academic and professional qualifications while continuing to be employed.

7. Correspondence education, another possible source of training, was not highly regarded in Kenya at that time, mainly because of the unsatisfactory record of the numerous commercial colleges which were operating throughout the East African region. These colleges were based in the United Kingdom and the United States and the courses they offered were irrelevant and out of date, while the fees charged were usually very high. The drop-out rate of students enrolled was reckoned to be in the region of 70 per cent. None the less, many adult students enrolled with these commercial colleges since, as most of them admitted, there were no other possibilities for self-improvement for those who did not gain admission to formal institutions and who lived too far away from the main towns to attend evening classes.

8. It was against this background and the urge to increase the speed of Kenya's educational development that the Ominde Commission was set up.

II The Ominde Commission and the setting up of the Correspondence Course Unit (CCU)

9. The Kenya Education Commission, under the chairmanship of Professor Simeon Ominde, was set up to look into the whole of Kenya's educational system and to make recommendations to the Minister of Education.

10. The report of this commission, which was published in two parts in 1964 and 1965, has influenced and guided national policy for education in Kenya since independence. It was the Ominde Commission (as it became popularly known) which first proposed that the Ministry of Education should establish radio/correspondence education in Kenya. The commission urged consideration of a 'combination of lessons by radio with an approved correspondence course'. Furthermore, the commission suggested that if the required facilities could not be provided by the established commercial correspondence colleges, it might be necessary for the ministry itself to enter the field of education by correspondence.

11. Following this recommendation, the Government of Kenya sought technical assistance from the United States Agency for International Development (USAID) for the establishment of the Correspondence Course Unit (CCU) in the Institute of Adult Studies, University College, Nairobi (now the University of Nairobi). USAID contracted the University of Wisconsin Extension to provide three specialists to assist in the setting up of the project and to train Kenyans for the first three years beginning April 1967. External aid also covered the cost of some printing and recording equipment. The Government of Kenya provided the physical facilities, printing and postage, office equipment and supplies and free air time for radio broadcasts on the national broadcasting

system: the Voice of Kenya. In spite of the inevitable complications of dealing with four different organizations, namely, USAID, the University of Wisconsin Extension, the Ministry of Education and the University of Nairobi, the CCU succeeded in establishing its place within the Kenya educational system chiefly because of the careful initial planning of its programmes, the training of local staff and the efficiency of its operations.

12. The decision to set up the CCU within the University of Nairobi was organizationally sound in that the unit had easy access to the facilities and expertise of the University of Nairobi, while at the same time operating as a service agency for the Ministry of Education as well as other government departments and voluntary organizations. As an integral part of the Institute of Adult Studies, the CCU was able to utilize the facilities of the institute's Extra-Mural Department while arranging for face-to-face contact with students in different parts of the country, and to utilize the Adult Studies Centre for the occasional tutorial in residence during vacation. The unit has also been in a position to co-operate with international organizations, particularly in the field of evaluation. As a result of this co-operation, the unit has been able to conduct continuous evaluation and on-going research, which have contributed a great deal to the improvement and modification of its programmes and methods of instruction.

13. The CCU was inaugurated in 1966 with the main object of helping primary school teachers by a combination of radio lessons, correspondence courses and face-to-face teaching. It began effective action in 1968 and had a twofold task: (a) to increase speedily the overall numbers of qualified teachers to cope with increasing demand; and (b) to provide unqualified teachers with a chance to qualify while remaining in their posts as teachers.

14. The size of the problem is indicated by the *Annual Report* of the Kenya Ministry of Education which states that in 1968 there were 37,923 teachers employed in Kenya's primary schools.

15. Of these, over one-quarter (10,438) had no professional teaching qualifications at all. Of the remainder, three-fifths (16,992) had qualifications only for the lowest grade (P3). Such teachers had had only seven or eight years of primary education, and two years of teacher training. To become eligible for promotion to the next grade (P2) they had to pass a national examination: the Kenya Junior Secondary Examination (KJSE). Prior to 1968 a candidate for this examination was required to pass five subjects together in a single year.

III The organization and management of the CCU

The courses offered and their objectives

16. In 1968, at the recommendation of the CCU staff, it was agreed by the Ministry of Education that P3 teachers should be allowed to sit their KJSE two or more subjects at a time, and carry forward credits from one year to the next, until they had accumulated the necessary five credits. The first CCU courses in 1968 were therefore aimed at preparing these teachers, and other adults who had completed primary education, for the KJSE.

17. Following this, in 1969 the CCU undertook a second programme to run concurrently with the KJSE Preparatory Courses. At the request of the Ministry

of Education, the CCU agreed to co-operate with the Kenya Institute of Education (KIE) in its in-service training course for unqualified teachers (UQT). The UQT upgrading course is intended to improve the teaching effectiveness of previously untrained teachers. The programme is conducted in two phases. The first is professional training in methods of teaching, organized by the KIE and consisting of a year's study divided into three short residential courses during school holidays. Between the residential sessions, the courses are supplemented by radio lectures. Candidates who successfully complete the first phase of the programme are then admitted to the second year's academic course conducted by the CCU. The unqualified teachers, however, study only three subjects (English, mathematics and either history or geography) at the first-year secondary level. Those who successfully complete the correspondence course and pass the final examination are upgraded to P3 status.

The learning package and the organization behind it

18. To date, the CCU has offered the following subjects at both first- and second-year levels of the secondary course: English, Kiswahili, history, geography, mathematics ('modern'), biology and physical science. These courses are not merely 'cram' courses for the KJSE, but are designed to cover the academic work normally done in two full years of study in secondary school. Moreover, the *modus operandi* of the CCU involves planned and systematic selection, preparation and presentation of teaching materials, as well as recording and assessing what the student has learned. Hence, the instructional programme provided by the CCU comprises a synthesis of the following: (a) correspondence-study guides, textbooks and other teaching materials such as maps, mathematical instrument sets, science-experiment kits etc.; (b) supplementary radio broadcasts covering the material in one or more lessons of the study guide; (c) marking of students' lessons by qualified secondary and university teachers; (d) occasional face-to-face teaching during residential courses.

19. The instructional process operates through machinery for establishing and maintaining contact between the student, the teacher and the unit, and through the systems for recruitment, enrolment, distribution of study materials, the handling of lessons and end-of-course examinations.

20. The unit is equipped with its own printing, duplicating and binding facilities; with registration, mailing, records and accounts sections; with a self-contained radio recording and production studio; and with a small science laboratory. The Adult Studies Centre adjacent to the CCU provides all facilities for residential courses for up to 60 students. The CCU staffing complement comprises 11 members of academic staff, all appointed under the university's terms of service. The academic staff consists of the head of the unit who is also an assistant director of the Institute of Adult Studies, seven correspondence tutors, a course-development tutor, a radio/television specialist and a course editor. The ancillary staff includes an administrative assistant, an accountant and a team of typists, printers, stores, mailing and records clerks. In addition the CCU draws upon the services of about fifty practising teachers in and around Nairobi as part-time course markers.

21. All lessons in the study guide contain selective (rather than exhaustive) self-test exercises with which the student checks his understanding of the study

material. Alternate lessons also require written assignments to be submitted to the CCU for marking.

22. Enrolment is open throughout the year, and students can work as fast as they are able to, depending on the amount of time they can devote to their studies and on their knowledge of the subject. Some students have been able to cover the two-year KJSE programme in one year. Others have taken longer than two years.

23. A survey conducted in 1968 revealed that a large proportion (90 per cent) of CCU students are teachers. The remaining 10 per cent include clerks, farmers, housewives and members of the armed forces, the police and staff of the co-operatives. A typical male student is between 21 and 40 years old, married, and has more than four dependants, including members of his extended family. His house has no electricity, and he owns very few books. He may have access to a very small library, but it is probably miles away and impossible for him to use regularly. He does not regularly buy a newspaper, but he does own a radio which is his principal source of news and information about the world outside his own small community. It is mainly for this reason that radio programmes prepared by the CCU and broadcast over the Voice of Kenya are used to supplement the correspondence instruction. Although the written materials which the students receive from the CCU are self-contained and give all instruction necessary, radio broadcasts have been used regularly to supplement instruction in each subject in the same way that a classroom teacher would offer extra help to the slower students to encourage them, sustain their interest, answer their questions and help them solve their problems. The radio programmes have proved to be particularly useful for speech-work in the two language courses as well as for maintaining good *rapport* between the student and the teacher. It has been established that a large proportion of the enrolled students make a point of listening to the radio programmes regularly, although many of them may be working through their lessons either well ahead or behind the radio schedules.

24. The CCU has realized that, apart from the enrolled students, there are other people using its study materials in less formal ways. It is difficult to estimate the number of teachers and other adults not registered with the CCU who are using the study guides and textbooks for their private study. Nevertheless, it seems reasonable to assume that this 'overflow' is quite substantial and that it has some broad social benefit. Similarly, the radio broadcasts have attracted very many casual listeners besides the students enrolled with the CCU. A survey conducted in 1969 by the Voice of Kenya revealed that there are a minimum of 318,000 and a maximum of 817,000 adult listeners who have their radios on when the CCU broadcasts are on the air (i.e. between 5 and 6 p.m.). Consequently, the CCU has been modifying the radio programmes into a more flexible format to cater for those listeners who are not studying for examinations but find the programmes interesting and informative. This is another by-product of the CCU project.

IV Evaluation of the CCU Kenya Junior Secondary Examination programme

25. After five years of operation, the Correspondence Course Unit was

anxious to evaluate its work. This was made possible through the generosity of the Friedrich Ebert Foundation of the Federal Republic of Germany in seconding a research fellow to carry out the evaluation. The final report of the evaluation produced some interesting assessments of the unit from the students' viewpoint, as well as many useful recommendations for improvement based on students' comments, criticisms and suggestions.

26. The survey was carried out through a questionnaire sent to students enrolled in the KJSE programme. It was thought best to concentrate the survey on KJSE students since the inclusion of students from the unqualified teachers' programme, with its careful selection and high student motivation, and the structured approach of the programme, would have biased the results of the survey. It was based on a large sample of 2,200 KJSE students, random except that it was modified to secure a representative picture of all the provinces involved.

27. The questionnaire was first tested on a number of students and adjusted in the light of the responses received.

28. Out of the 920 questionnaires sent to students (a sample quota of roughly 40 per cent), 270 questionnaires came back filled in correctly, i.e. a response of 29.3 per cent. Compared with previous surveys the response was satisfactory. Looking at the rural/urban distribution, we find that 25 per cent of the response came from urban areas (defining Nairobi, Mombasa, Kisumu and Nakuru as urban), and 75 per cent from rural areas.

29. One section of the questionnaire dealt with some of the major difficulties students found themselves confronted with during their study process. Roughly 60 per cent of the obstacles to study were found to be environmental difficulties, particularly lack of sufficient time to study, personal and family problems and unfavourable conditions. The actual pedagogic difficulties that faced students were found to constitute only about 10 per cent of the total.

Drop-out rate

30. From some of the answers to the questionnaire, we can derive some information about the drop-out rate of the CCU students, although we can argue only indirectly. It was not possible to ask directly: 'Do you think you are a drop-out?' This would have been a pejorative suggestion. But taking into account the fact that about 56 per cent of CCU students had registered for the KJSE, one could say that such students could not be considered as drop-outs. Others indicated that they were not yet prepared to sit for the examination while a few referred to personal and 'other' difficulties. The CCU enrolment also includes quite a number of students who do not study in order to sit for the KJSE, while another group consists of those who, having passed the examination, feel they still need to complete the course in which they initially enrolled and for which they had paid.

31. Another factor which makes it difficult to quantify the drop-out rate of the CCU students is that no time limit is imposed on students once enrolled. They are at liberty to study at their own pace depending on their personal circumstances and their previous knowledge of the subject. The radio programmes which supplement the printed materials are repeated every four months during the year and students can therefore benefit from the radio at any time.

Nevertheless, the research fellow estimated the drop-out rate of the CCU students as somewhere between 15 and 25 per cent.

32. There is no doubt that since the majority of CCU students are teachers they are very highly motivated by the immediate benefits in terms of the promotion and the increased salaries they receive on passing their examinations. Many of them have also become aware of the urgent need to upgrade themselves in their professions as the lower grades are gradually being phased out and as there is more competition for jobs. It is not surprising then that the completion rates are high.

Examination results

33. Since 1968 the CCU has carried out various analyses of students' performance in the KJSE. The results reveal that candidates who have studied with the CCU have performed better than other candidates sitting the same examination.

34. The average pass rates for CCU candidates were 42 per cent in 1968, 46 per cent in 1969 and 51 per cent in 1970, as compared with school candidates who achieved 16 to 30 per cent in the various provinces, while private candidates achieved 8 to 15 per cent pass rates. In 1970 when the government-aided schools averaged 47 per cent, the unaided schools 20 per cent and the private candidates 13 per cent, the CCU candidates achieved 51 per cent pass rates. In the various subjects offered by the CCU, the average pass rates have gone as high as 76 per cent in Kiswahili, 57 per cent in English and 55 per cent in history. In looking at these figures, it is perhaps unfair to compare the performance of private candidates with that of teachers, because, while the former must pass in at least five subjects at one sitting, the latter are allowed to take examinations in individual subjects until they accumulate passes in five subjects.

35. In analysing the reasons for their failure in the examinations the CCU students tended to be self-critical in their replies. Roughly 50 per cent said that they did not work hard enough on their study materials, 17 per cent indicated that they did not submit enough written assignments, and 11 per cent quoted insufficient radio listening. The general tendency with all teachers was to register for the examination almost every year and in more subjects than they could objectively pass, with the hope that they might collect the required number of passes in the shortest time possible. This does therefore cause some statistical inaccuracies in the official reports.

36. It is too early yet to conclude that the above results indicate success. It has yet to be demonstrated that a P3 teacher, for example, improved his or her performance in the classroom after being upgraded to the P2 grade. Nevertheless, for most CCU students, this was the first time they had ever been engaged in an organized and systematic form of study since they left formal institutions, and the first time that they had received individual and personal tutoring through the post and through the radio from teachers they probably had never met.

37. Many letters from successful students confirm that they felt they had benefited from these courses.

V Evaluation of the unqualified teachers' programme, 1969–72

38. As stated earlier, the Kenya Institute of Education (KIE), which is the body responsible for teacher education and upgrading, selects the teachers for the unqualified teachers' (UQT) programme and handles the professional aspects of the upgrading course, while the CCU deals with the academic content.

39. The UQT in-service training programme is the only means by which unqualified teachers can be upgraded to P3 status. After serving further in the profession, they may attempt higher examinations to attain even higher status. The candidates are carefully selected from among those who have been teaching for over three years and have given evidence of ability and motivation. The programme is controlled by the KIE through its field officers, and the course proceeds in defined stages. The residential sessions held during school vacations are compulsory, and the final examination is conducted at the end of the year. It is thus a rigidly controlled, single-purpose and 'closed' in-service programme, and it has proved to be highly successful in terms of completion rates of assignments and pass rates in the final examination.

40. Since 1969 the UQT programme has produced very encouraging results. About 82 per cent of those who enrolled in the programmes from 1968 to 1970 completed their courses successfully and were awarded P3 teachers' certificates. In 1969, the percentage of passes in the final examination in academic subjects was: English, 95 per cent; geography, 96 per cent; mathematics, 90 per cent; and history, 86 per cent. But one must look beyond figures such as these when evaluating the project as a whole. A more important consideration is whether the teachers upgraded by this method improve their performance in their jobs. It is worth noting that, according to the assessment of the KIE, the unqualified teachers who successfully completed the course and were issued with teaching certificates compared very well academically and professionally with those qualifying from the teachers' colleges. This, however, needed to be verified, and the CCU staff accordingly conducted the follow-up study described below.

41. During 1969–73 over 10,000 unqualified teachers successfully completed their upgrading courses through radio, correspondence and residential study and were awarded P3 teachers' certificates. The follow-up study was carried out with a sample of these teachers. It consisted of questionnaires and face-to-face interviews at two different levels.

42. At the first level, the study was concentrated on the teachers themselves. According to their replies, the in-service course had been useful to them professionally. About 99 per cent of them felt that their performance in the classroom had improved as a result of the course. Many of them indicated that they felt greater confidence in their teaching, and that they commanded greater respect from their fellow teachers than before. A number of these teachers also indicated that the course in 'modern mathematics', which they had taken as one of the compulsory subjects in their own examination, had proved to be very useful in their classroom teaching, given recent changes in the primary schools mathematics syllabus based on the 'modern mathematics' approach.

43. It was also evident that the upgraded teachers were more secure in their jobs and stood a better chance of further promotion after three or four years of service than the unqualified teachers.

44. In fact, the unqualified teacher in Kenya is constantly under threat of being phased out of the teaching service as more qualified teachers join the

profession. This, in effect, has provided one of the strongest motivating factors for the in-service training course. The other factor is the substantial salary increase that a teacher enjoys after being upgraded.

45. More significant, perhaps, than these subjective assessments of the value of their course, is the fact that about 48 per cent of the respondents had pursued further courses of study after achieving their initial qualification. Most of these teachers had sat for the KJSE in additional subjects over and above the three compulsory subjects needed for the upgrading. About 20 per cent of them had even gone on to study for the East African Certificate of Education (equivalent to the British GCE 'O' level). This means that, given proper directions for study, a teacher might, in time, attain the higher primary teaching grades of P2 or P1 through in-service training. Another significant point to note is that none of the successful students who were interviewed had changed careers after being upgraded, and they did not know of any colleagues who had done so.

46. Among the suggestions put forward by the respondents was a request for an increase in the number of academic subjects offered in the UQT upgrading programme. Many teachers felt that an option only between history and geography was insufficient and that the authorities should consider including other subjects relevant to classroom teaching as well as to examination purposes.

47. The one-year professional training was also considered to be inadequate by many teachers who suggested extending it into the second year of academic study. It should be possible through the combined efforts of KIE and the CCU to incorporate most of these suggestions in future plans for in-service teacher-training programmes.

48. At the second level, the follow-up study was directed towards the educational authorities, and in particular the headmasters, education officers and supervisors of those schools where the teachers who had replied were employed. It was important not only to get a recorded opinion from these authorities on the quality of teachers upgraded, but also to obtain their reactions towards the whole idea of training teachers by unorthodox methods.

49. The authorities interviewed felt that about 95 per cent of the teachers under their supervision had improved their performance in the classroom after the upgrading course. This was evident particularly in the three subjects they had studied, namely English, mathematics and either history or geography. More important was the observation that there had been visible improvement in the classroom performance and the examination results of the pupils taught by these teachers. The effectiveness of a teacher is still measured in most cases, unfortunately, by the performance of his pupils in the national examinations. Of the cases examined, 90 per cent reported some improvement in the pupil's performance.

50. The educational authorities interviewed were, on the whole, favourably impressed by the quality of the teachers upgraded. They often commented on the apparent determination of these teachers to improve themselves further by attempting higher examinations. None of the teachers had changed their careers. One or two headmasters reported cases where there was not enough checking of pupils' work because the teachers were busy at night studying for further qualifications. But on the whole there was general agreement among the authorities that the more diligent teachers striving to improve themselves were more committed to their jobs, while the lazy teachers tended to neglect their studies as well as their pupils. All the authorities encouraged the teachers to

continue to improve themselves in their profession. A few criticized the UQT programme, particularly in respect of the inadequacy of the professional training. The period spent on this part of the programme was considered too short and many authorities recommended its extension into the second year. The academic part of the programme was better handled, but it was suggested that the number of subjects should be increased in order to provide more options for the teachers.

51. All the authorities agreed that the in-service training courses offered the best opportunity for most teachers to improve their knowledge and skills, and that the traditional teacher-training colleges were not able to cope with the increasing demands for qualified teachers in Kenya. They agreed also that in-service training courses gave the teachers a good opportunity to apply their knowledge and skills in the classrooms, and to test their suitability or otherwise in actual teaching situations. One schools' supervisor went further and suggested that an extension of radio and correspondence methods should be used to disseminate the latest information about curricular changes, teaching methods, and educational policies amongst teachers, administrators and parents throughout Kenya.

52. The follow-up study revealed many good qualities in the in-service training programme which should be maintained and improved. It also revealed some weaknesses. Many constructive suggestions for improvements were offered by teachers and educational authorities. Effective action on these suggestions calls for a joint effort not only on the part of the KIE and the CCU but also of the Ministry of Education and the Teachers' Service Commission.

53. One of the greatest supporters of the teachers' upgrading programmes has been the Kenya National Union of Teachers which has been urging its members to enrol so that they could enhance their bargaining powers with their employers. Teachers who have improved themselves through radio and correspondence studies have been an important source of encouragement for those who have not yet enrolled.

VI Future plans, 1974–78

Changes in teacher education programmes, 1974

54. On the tenth anniversary of Kenya's independence, a presidential decree introduced free primary education in standards I to IV with effect from 1 January 1974. This measure resulted immediately in enrolments in primary schools rising to 2¾ million (2,765,615), which was ½ million more than the number estimated by the Development Plan figure for that year. To deal with this number it was estimated that a primary teacher force of over 72,000 was required. Hence, although considerable progress had been made since 1968 in providing a larger and better qualified core of teachers, the problem was growing faster than the provision. Whereas the total number of unqualified teachers in primary schools was reckoned at only 12,000 by the end of 1973, the sudden jump in numbers required for 1976 meant that at least 25,000 of the newly appointed teachers would inevitably be unqualified.

55. To meet this situation the Development Plan for 1974–78 scaled down

the previous long-term policy of developing more P2 and P1 teachers and introduced further interim measures to meet the immediate emergency.

It recommended an increased output of P3 teachers by combining a revised training-college and in-service course. The normal two-year residential college course was to be reduced to one year. After that the student would become a teacher and in-service training would be conducted over a two-year period through a series of radio, correspondence and vacation courses. During the in-service course training period teachers would progress towards certification on a credit system. This whole scheme has come to be known as the '1 plus 2 teacher-training programme'. It is estimated that over a period of three years, this programme should double the number of trained teachers entering the profession, that is, from 4,000 to 8,000 per year. Side by side with this emergency programme it is intended that the upgrading of unqualified teachers will continue as before, though the annual intake will be increased to take into account the extra numbers of teachers who have, of necessity, been employed without professional qualifications. The two programmes will run simultaneously, but it has been accepted that people from other institutions beside the KIE and the CCU will have to share in the responsibility for these expanded in-service teacher-training courses. These will include primary school inspectors, district education officers, teacher-training-college tutors and the curriculum development teams. The KIE will continue to select the teachers due for training, to organize the residential sessions and to conduct the examinations and final assessments.

The CCU will handle all the operations of correspondence teaching, written assignments and student records as well as the accompanying radio programmes. The CCU staff will also train correspondence-course writers and markers from other institutions for any additional course to be included in the expanded programme. College tutors, for instance, will be selected to write correspondence courses after they have attended training workshops, and will be released from other duties in order to work in course development teams. It is hoped that such institutional co-operation will make better use of the qualified personnel available to produce more educationally viable courses than before. It has been recognized that the present syllabus being followed in the KJSE and other teacher-upgrading programmes is inadequate, and although the CCU in its teaching has tried to enlarge and liberalize what is a course crammed with facts it is still too much geared to secondary school pupils and is often unsuitable for adult teachers. By bringing together a group of educationists, practising teachers and school inspectors, it is hoped that a better in-service teacher-training programme will be developed.

56. The Ministry of Education indeed recognizes that, in the long run, a continuing process of teacher education will be the best way to deal with current and future problems. It is also committed to the use of new methods and techniques, changes in curricula and the use of mass media in the process.

The Mass Media Centre: rural education

57. The 1974–78 Development Plan has stressed that 'correspondence courses and radio programmes must remain the main vehicles of out-of-school education'. It has therefore recommended an expansion of the CCU facilities

at Kikuyu into a Mass Media Centre. One of the strong arguments in support of this expansion is that there already exists within the CCU considerable expertise and experience on which to build. Another argument is that, properly utilized, mass media provide a means whereby the best teachers available can make the maximum impact on the quality of education through the country as a whole.

58. Apart from the enrolled students there are many thousands of casual listeners to the CCU radio programmes. Several institutions, including the Ministry of Education, the Ministry of Information and Broadcasting (Voice of Kenya), the Institute of Adult Studies and the CCU have agreed to co-operate in a pilot project to capture this audience. An experiment is to be made with the integrated use of three media, namely film, radio and newspapers. These will be used in conjunction with organized discussion groups in various rural areas, and if successful they will be developed and multiplied on a national scale. Key figures will be the local leader in the community, whose co-operation will be needed to prepare the ground, and the tutor who travels with a mobile unit to show the films and evaluate the effect of the project.

Vocational and technical courses

59. Proposals have been put forward by the Institute of Adult Studies (and accepted in principle) for the CCU techniques of correspondence courses combined with radio and face-to-face tuition, which have proved successful with teacher training, to be extended to business and technical courses for adults. First priority would be given to adults already employed in business and industry so that they, like teachers, would have an opportunity to upgrade themselves and improve their efficiency.

Degree courses

60. The University of Nairobi has accepted in principle the introduction of external degree courses in 1975. The CCU will be responsible for the general administration of these courses, while the teaching and conduct of examinations will be the responsibility of the university faculty conferring the degree.

VII Factors in the case of Kenya of more general application

61. The Kenya case study has demonstrated amongst other things the need for a definite commitment from the government in an educational venture such as the one described here. Its success has, to a large extent, been due to close consultation and co-operation between many different bodies: the Ministry of Education, the Ministry of Information and Broadcasting, and the Institute of Adult Studies of the University of Nairobi. The fact that the CCU was set up within the university enabled it to attract and recruit staff of high calibre and also gave it access to a wide range of expertise.

62. In the beginning the major emphasis put by the assistance of USAID

and the expertise provided by the external specialist staff seconded from the University of Wisconsin was in the training of local staff.

63. The flexibility of the CCU's structure and its willingness to adapt to Kenya's changing needs has been crucial. Over the first five years of its existence, the CCU has developed into a viable 'service unit' which can provide specialized administrative machinery combining correspondence courses, radio and face-to-face tutorial teaching for students at varying levels of teacher training. Now it is preparing for a widening of its activities to include, at the one extreme, mass rural adult education and, at the other, external-degree courses for the University of Nairobi.

64. The changing use made of the radio component in the learning package also illustrates the need for a flexible approach. In 1964 the report of the Ominde Commission urged a 'combination of lessons by radio with an approved correspondence course'. In the event when the CCU operation was set up a change of emphasis had already taken place by which the correspondence course had become the core of the teaching package and the radio broadcasts were an integral but supplemental part of the students' work. By 1969 when it was found that a large 'eavesdropping' audience was listening to the programmes, the CCU took the decision to modify the radio component into a more flexible format and so try to capture the listeners who, though not studying for examinations, obviously found the programmes interesting and informative. It might be argued that in so doing the specific needs of the students were in danger of being submerged by the general needs of the community. But the subsequent development of mass-media rural education for the general adult audience should relieve any clash between the two, provided sufficient time and resources are available. At present the CCU has been allocated five hours per week free air time for radio broadcasts on the Voice of Kenya.

65. However, in the face of increasing demands for educational broadcasting the Voice of Kenya has embarked on a fresh audience survey.

66. This survey will attempt, among other things, to provide a breakdown of the types of programmes people like, whether in the category of entertainment, information or education. It is hoped that the survey will further strengthen the case for a separate educational radio channel for which there is provision in the Development Plan. The current educational-radio air time is used by CCU, Schools Broadcasting and other government departments. The rest of the prime time is taken up by commercial programmes, since Voice of Kenya has to raise about one-third of its running costs through advertising. The argument for a separate educational channel is that with it there would be less competition between educational and other programmes. The argument against is the possible loss of the large casual audience for educational programmes if these were transmitted through a strictly educational channel. It might mean that, if an educational channel is provided, a more exact distinction would have to be made between formal and non-formal educational programmes, with provision for the occasional exchange of selected programmes between the two. The results of the survey will assist the authorities in reaching a fair decision. However, one thing is clear, namely, that the potential of the transistor radio is gradually being realized in many developing countries such as Kenya where a large majority of the people live in the rural areas, and that it now remains to utilize it to its full capacity.

67. On the cost side, a project such as the CCU is an attractive economic

proposition to a government with limited resources trying to expand secondary education.

68. For example, recurrent expenditure in Kenya on secondary education during 1970/71 was about £(K)4.7 million in about 310 government-aided schools with an enrolment of some 75,000 students. In addition there were nearly 500 unaided secondary schools in Kenya with approximately 53,000 students. In comparison, of the CCU annual budget of about £(K)75,000, £(K)45,000 was met from government funds with the balance from students' fees. As enrolment increases with more courses offered, the unit cost of the CCU will be progressively lower.

69. The experience of the CCU has been put to profitable use by other institutions in Africa and elsewhere which are embarking on similar educational projects. The unit has offered advice on techniques of correspondence instruction, administration and course development to all those interested. National institutions which have been assisted in this way by the CCU include the Co-operatives College of Kenya, and correspondence institutes in the United Republic of Tanzania, Ethiopia and Thailand. The CCU was also a founder member of the African Association for Correspondence Education, which will play a leading role in developing correspondence education in Africa.

70. Perhaps the most successful experiment which the unit has conducted has been in the application of different media used in combination: in particular, the use of correspondence materials supplemented by radio broadcasts and occasional face-to-face instruction to reach a widely scattered adult population throughout the country.

71. The flexibility of the unit's structure and operation have made it possible to cope with the changing educational needs of the country and to cater for different groups of students at different levels. The efficiency of the central service agency which handles the practical day-to-day operations in correspondence instruction has been crucial for the success of the CCU. The occasional breakdown of these operations in the past only serves to underline the importance of efficient machinery to handle communication between the unit, the student and the teacher.

72. Economies of scale have gradually been realized as student enrolments have continued to rise. There has been no increase in the fees charged to the students since the CCU started offering its courses, and the government's annual contribution to the recurrent budget of the unit has been maintained at about the same level as in 1968 although the student numbers have more than doubled since that time. The recent changes in teacher-education programmes in Kenya will mean even higher student enrolments and consequently a much lower recurrent cost per student than at present. It will be of interest to see whether the CCU will be able to keep up the standards of its operations as it undertakes more programmes and as the student enrolments continue to rise. The challenge facing the CCU and other co-operating agencies is the maintenance and improvement of the quality of the programmes and the efficiency of the operations in current and future undertakings.

73. However, each country has its own priorities and ways of organizing its development programmes. The Kenya case study described above must be viewed as only one of the ways of solving particular problems at a particular time in the development of a particular country. It is also important to stress that the CCU is only one of the many government and non-government agencies

which are involved in the various aspects of the social and economic development of Kenya. But the need for co-operation and consultation at every stage cannot be overemphasized.

Appendix A **Standardized reference data**

Country, state or province — *Kenya*

Area and climate	225,000 square miles. Tropical.
Population	
Total (latest year)	10,942,705 (1969).
Estimated population under 15 (percentage)	48.4.
Current annual growth rate (percentage)	3.3.
Government	
Main organizational structure	Unitary; delegated administrative responsibilities to provinces, with local administrative councils.
Political type	Democratic republic; Commonwealth nation.
Economy	
Political type	Predominantly agricultural subsistence economy.
Gross national product	
Total (latest year)	£(K)520 million (1971).
Per head	£(K)47 (U.S.$170).
Average annual increase (percentage)	4.1.
Communications	
Ground/air	Road communication network good. Major towns served by East African Airways.
Mail/telephone	Adequate postal services. Telephone services in major towns only; 0.8 per 100 persons (1972).

Broadcasting

Main system(s) operating	A.M. Television. Voice of Kenya. Two national services and three regional ones. Television in Nairobi region under Ministry of Information and Broadcasting.
Principal authorities responsible	Ministry of Information and Broadcasting.
Radio	
Transmission coverage of main programme services with percentage of population reached	90 per cent of population reached.
Receiving capability for main programme services	41 receivers per 1,000 people (1972).
Television	
Transmission coverage as defined for radio (percentage)	40.
Receiving capability for main programme services	3 receivers per 1,000 people (1972).
Monochrome or colour	Monochrome. No immediate plans for colour.

Education

Type of system(s)	Predominantly publicly controlled and financed. A few private schools.
Main authorities responsible and powers	
At school level	Primary and nursery schools are responsibility of district education boards, subject to financial influence of central government. Self-help (*harambee*) and mission schools subject to central government.
At post-secondary level	Central government.
End of full-time school attendance	Attendance not enforced. No figures available. Free for first four years.
Proportion of 18-year-old age group involved in education	
Full-time	6.8 per cent.
Part-time	2.5 per cent.
Major developments in provision	
Over last five years	Rapid increase in number of secondary schools.
Over next five years	Emphasis on technical and vocational schools. Growth of colleges of technology.

Institution/system under study

Brief for study and reason for inclusion	University of Nairobi.
Description of subject studied	
Origins	Kenya Education Commission, 1964.

Educational authority and role	University of Nairobi in response to Ministry of Education request.
Communications authority and role	Voice of Kenya provides free air time.
Services provided	Wider opportunities for secondary-level education for adults for both vocational and non-vocational purposes through face-to-face and multi-media methods of tuition. Home-based students remaining in employment.
Eligibility to study (a) categories	Adults over 16 who are out of full-time educational institutions.
(b) qualifications	Completed primary education.
Terminal qualifications	Junior Secondary Certificate; East African Certificate of Education; National Teachers' Certificate.
Instructional means used	Multi-media, i.e. correspondence work, radio, face-to-face teaching.
Personal input from student	Average 12 hours/week, 36 weeks/year.
Normal duration of study	Two years for unqualified teachers. No limit for others.
Pedagogical effectiveness	As good as orthodox methods. Better results than school candidates.

Numbers involved

Students	
Intake	475.
Academic staff	
Full-time	12.
Part-time	45.
Other professional staff	None.

Sources of further information

Education	Head, Correspondence Course Unit, P.O. Box 30688, Nairobi (Kenya). Director of Education, Ministry of Education, P.O. Box 30040, Nairobi (Kenya).
Broadcasting	Director of Broadcasting, Voice of Kenya, P.O. Box 30456, Nairobi (Kenya). Radio Specialist CCU, P.O. Box 30688, Nairobi (Kenya).

Appendix B Short bibliography

GOVERNMENT OF KENYA. *Development plan, 1970–74*. Nairobi, Government Printer.

——. *Development plan, 1974–78*. Nairobi, Government Printer.

——. MINISTRY OF EDUCATION. *Annual report*. Nairobi, Government Printer, 1968 to date.

——. MINISTRY OF INFORMATION AND BROADCASTING. *An audience survey report in Kenya*. Nairobi, Government Printer, 1969, 1974.

KENYA EDUCATION COMMISSION. *Report*. Pt I. Nairobi, Government Printer, 1964.

KRIVAL, A. S. *Radio/correspondence education project*. Washington, D.C., USAID, 1970. (Report 615–11–650–129, USAID/UWEX.)

RAJU, B. M. *Education in Kenya: problem and perspectives in educational planning and administration*. Nairobi, Heinemann, 1973.

TREYDTE, K. P. *Evaluation of the Radio/Correspondence Preparatory Course for K.J.S.E. of the Correspondence Course Unit*. Nairobi, Institute of Adult Studies, 1972.

Appendix C Biographical note

Peter Kinyanjui is head of the Correspondence Course Unit of the University of Nairobi. He is currently on a two-year secondment as a Director of the International Extension College in Cambridge. Mr Kinyanjui is also chairman of the African Association for Correspondence Education and a vice-president of the International Council on Correspondence Education.

Teachers for refugees: the UNRWA/Unesco Institute of Education, Beirut, Lebanon[1]

Edward A. Pires
with Bernard Bartram

Contents

1. The views expressed in this paper are those of its authors and do not commit anyone, either at the UNRWA/Unesco Institute of Education or the UNRWA/Unesco Department of Education.

I Establishment of the institute

1. The Institute of Education was established in December 1963 to meet an urgent need of the United Nations Relief and Works Agency (UNRWA)/ Unesco school system for Palestinian refugees who were then living in the Gaza Strip, Jordan, the Syrian Arab Republic and Lebanon. The need arose from the fact that over 90 per cent of the teachers serving in the UNRWA schools were professionally untrained and uncertificated, which naturally affected the quality of education imparted to the children enrolled in these schools. The high incidence of untrained teachers in the UNRWA schools stemmed from the fact that when provision was made on an emergency basis in the early years of the agency for the education of Palestinian refugee children, the emphasis was naturally on opening as many classrooms as were required from year to year and on finding teachers for these classes regardless of whether those opting for the job had or did not have the necessary professional qualification and, in many cases, even the minimum academic qualification of a general secondary school certificate.

Since fully qualified persons were in short supply, the majority of those available were selected to fill administrative and supervisory posts. Moreover, quite a few qualified teachers left to take jobs in other Arab countries where, too, there was an acute shortage of trained personnel.

2. To withdraw these untrained teachers from their schools, even in instalments, in order to train them through a full-time programme at a pre-service training institution would have meant heavy additional expenditure for UNRWA on two counts: first, paying for substitute teachers who would be needed to fill their places, and second, meeting the higher cost of full-time pre-service training as compared with the cost of an in-service type of training. The agency was not in a position to meet this additional expenditure. The solution lay in using methods of learning and teaching suited to a form of 'on-the-job training' that did not involve the withdrawal of teachers from their normal school duties.

3. Preparatory to the establishment of the institute, an expert was appointed by Unesco in early 1963 to study the situation and propose a practicable solution to the problem of providing the UNRWA schools with qualified teachers. The draft plan submitted by the expert proposed the establishment of an Institute of Education to operate an in-service teacher-training programme. This plan was studied by the UNRWA authorities who decided 'in principle' to organize

such an institute, after which negotiations were begun to finance it. Unesco agreed to second experts to fill the key posts in the institute.

4. Recruitment was then undertaken to fill the Unesco international posts as well as the local posts, including those of field representatives who would be serving as local tutors to the teacher trainees enrolled in the institute. The latter were appointed in the spring of 1974 and given three months training to prepare them for their responsibilities in the special system of teacher training that the institute would be embarking upon.

5. As the UNRWA/Unesco schools were operating in four host countries, it was found necessary to make an analytical study of the educational systems and requirements of these countries to ensure that the programme of training that would be drawn up would get the approval of their governments. An inquiry was also made into the professional qualifications of the UNRWA teaching staff with a view to establishing needs and priorities for training.

6. The first group of 862 trainees was recruited in the autumn of 1964 for a two-year programme of professional training for teachers who had obtained a State general secondary education certificate or an equivalent secondary diploma. In the following year, provision was also made for a three-year programme for teachers who had not completed their secondary education. This latter programme had a dual objective: to improve the educational background of the teachers as well as to provide them with professional training.

7. To meet the operational costs of the institute, a draft plan was prepared and submitted to UNRWA, Unesco and to the Swiss Government, which expressed an interest in the enterprise. These negotiations resulted, in May 1965, in a tripartite agreement between the two United Nations agencies and the Swiss Government's Service for Technical Co-operation under which the latter provided financial support for the institute, over a two-year period in the first instance.

II Development of the institute during the last ten years

Development of programmes for Palestinian teachers and other educational personnel

8. Since the establishment of the institute in 1964, its work has expanded considerably, particularly in respect of the kinds of training programmes it has been able to offer. It is convenient to divide this development into four or five phases, even though there is an overlapping of these phases.

9. In the *first phase* (from 1964/65 to 1973/74) the main preoccupation of the institute was to provide basic in-service training for elementary school teachers. Two types of courses were organized for this purpose: a two-year course for qualifying elementary school teachers with a full secondary education and a three-year course for upgrading elementary school teachers with qualifications below the secondary level. A total of 3,983 teachers, representing about 80 per cent of the elementary teacher population in 1973/74, has benefited by these courses. The comparable percentage when the institute started its operations was about 10 per cent.

10. In the *second phase*, which began in 1967/68, training programmes were provided for the upgrading of teachers teaching at the preparatory, inter-

mediate or lower secondary level, covering grades 7 to 9. Three types of courses have been organized for such teachers:

(a) Specialized two-year courses in various subjects taught at the preparatory school level, namely, Arabic, social studies, mathematics, science, English, home economics, physical education, handicrafts, and art education (introduced in 1974/75). An essential requirement for these courses is the completion of a basic course of in-service or pre-service training.

(b) A one-year professional course for teachers who have completed a minimum of two years of university study, majoring in a subject area related to the preparatory school curriculum.

(c) A three-year course for holders of a general secondary school certificate appointed to teach at the preparatory level.

The total number of beneficiaries from these courses up to the school year 1973/74 is 1,812, which represents about 85 per cent of the teacher population in that category compared with less than 10 per cent in 1964/65.

11. The *third phase* was introduced in the school year 1969/70, when courses for the training of key educational personnel were started. In that year a course was organized for head teachers, which was followed in 1970/71 by a course for school supervisors and in 1971/72 by a course for teacher-training instructors teaching in the four UNRWA pre-service teacher-training institutes. Since the introduction of this phase of training, 495 head teachers, 54 school supervisors and 71 teacher-training instructors have benefited by these courses.

12. The *fourth phase* or type of training was also introduced in 1969/70 when the first of a series of special or *ad hoc* courses was started. This was the 'Global Method of Teaching Arabic' course. In 1970/71, a course in art education was offered for the first time. Since then, a number of such special courses has been offered to meet the needs of schools in the different host countries where the institute operates. The list of such courses includes the 'Source Method in the Teaching of the Social Studies'; 'Physical Education'; 'Multigrade Teaching'; 'Tests and Measurements'; 'Home Economics'; 'Educational Research'; 'Contemporary Mathematics' (for lower elementary classes); 'Teaching of Religion at the Preparatory Level'; 'Course for Teacher Librarians'; and a course in 'Audio-visual Media for Teachers of the Social Studies at the Preparatory Level'.

Another development in the same direction was the introduction of re-orientation or refresher courses, the first of which was introduced in 1971/72 when a 'Reorientation Course for Grade One Teachers' was organized. Since then the following refresher courses have been organized: 'General Refresher Course for Lower Elementary School Teachers'; 'General Refresher Course for Upper Elementary School Teachers'; 'Mathematics for Preparatory School Teachers'; and 'Contemporary Science for Preparatory School Teachers'. These are all one-year refresher courses, except for the mathematics course, which has been organized as a series of seminars spread over a five-year period. Since the introduction of this phase in 1969/70 and up to the end of 1973/74, a total of 1,540 educators have benefited by pursuing these *ad hoc* and refresher courses.

13. The anticipated enrolment in 1974/75 in these four general categories of training programmes gives some idea of the emphasis:

Basic courses for training elementary school teachers	250
Courses for training preparatory-level teachers	196
Courses for training key educational personnel	57
Refresher and special *ad hoc* courses	766
	1,269

As these figures indicate, the main stress now is on special refresher courses organized to meet the needs of the schools in the different fields of the institute's operations. The continuation of basic training courses for elementary school teachers after ten years of the institute's operation is explained by the fact that in some fields the output of the pre-service training institutes is inadequate to meet the needs of expansion; thus untrained teachers who have to be trained on the job must be employed. Courses for the training of preparatory-level teachers also have to be maintained because of the increasing enrolment in the preparatory grades, requiring the employment of more teachers or the promotion of teachers from the elementary to the preparatory cycle.

Development of the institute into a regional institution

14. A significant and major development of the institute was its involvement in the in-service training of teachers and other educational personnel in the Arab States. This began in May 1969 when the Government of Jordan expressed an interest in developing a programme of in-service training for the large number of untrained elementary and preparatory school teachers serving in its government schools. After a careful study of the institute's approach and programmes, the government decided in 1971 to set up an institute for the certification and in-service training of teachers, with the financial support of Unicef (the United Nations Children's Fund) and the professional and technical guidance of the UNRWA/Unesco Institute. The Jordan Institute for In-service Training began to function in the school year 1971/72 after the staff recruited for its work had undergone a month's intensive programme of training at the UNRWA/Unesco Institute. Further training for its subject specialists was organized in Beirut later in the same scholastic year.

15. Immediately after the establishment of the Jordan Institute, other Arab States began to show interest in developing similar programmes of in-service training. The earliest of these were the Syrian Arab Republic, Iraq and the Sudan. To cope with the work involved, Unesco established the post of Extension Services Officer, which was financed by Unicef. The latter agency also provided funds for meeting the costs of materials that would have to be provided to the Jordan Institute and other in-service training projects, as well as for covering the costs of running the newly created Extension Services Section of the UNRWA/Unesco Institute, including travel to interested countries.

16. After the initiation of the Jordan programme, orientation programmes for key ministry officials from the Syrian Arab Republic, Iraq and the Sudan were organized at the institute between November 1971 and April 1972. This was followed, in the summer of 1972, by training programmes for the staffs of the in-service training projects in the school year 1972/73 in the Syrian Arab Republic and the Sudan.

17. After the establishment in 1972 of a Continuous Training Section in the

Syrian Ministry of Education and an In-Service Educational Training Institute in the Sudan for the in-service training of elementary school teachers, the attention of the Extension Services Section of the UNRWA/Unesco Institute was focused on assisting these three projects (including the one in Jordan) to develop their training programmes along effective lines while, at the same time, assisting other Arab States in organizing new in-service training programmes. Iraq, like the Syrian Arab Republic, was interested in developing a reorientation or refresher course for several thousands of its qualified elementary school teachers; Bahrain wanted to set up a programme like that of Jordan and the Sudan for 1,000 of its elementary school teachers who were professionally unqualified. Each of these five countries had its own peculiar problems arising out of the conditions prevailing therein, and so the training programmes had to be adapted and geared to meet these special conditions and circumstances. In all the projects developed in these five countries, the multi-media approach followed by the UNRWA/Unesco Institute (see section III below) was adopted, with some modifications necessitated by local needs or circumstances. The Bahrain project was under way in the year 1973/74 but commencement of the Iraqi project was delayed until 1974/75. Because of the greatly increased activities of the Extension Services Section, an assistant Extension Services Officer was appointed in 1972, and the Unicef budget for the section for 1974 allowed for two more posts: a second assistant Extension Services Officer and a professional assistant to the three Extension Officers.

18. Besides the five countries that have adopted the multi-media approach to in-service training, a number of other Arab countries have sought the assistance of the Extension Services Section in organizing programmes of training for teachers and school supervisors that are not based on the multi-media approach *in toto* but embody some of its features. These include the Sultanate of Oman, the Yemen Arab Republic and the People's Democratic Republic of Yemen. Head teachers and school supervisors from these countries have come to Beirut to attend courses at the institute that have been specially planned to meet their needs and purposes, and institute staff members have visited these countries to offer advice and on-the-spot guidance in the effective organization and conduct of the training programmes.

19. In 1974, the Extension Services Section of the institute organized a conference of directors of in-service teacher-training projects, which was attended by representatives not only of the five projects in Jordan, the Syrian Arab Republic, the Sudan, Bahrain and Iraq (which are following the institute's multi-media approach) but also of the three other Arab States where in-service training of educational personnel is being conducted with financial assistance from Unicef and technical guidance from the institute. In addition, there were representatives from Lebanon, which was to organize a multi-media project in 1974/75, and from Saudi Arabia and the Libyan Arab Republic which have recently expressed an interest in the institute's approach. The conference had the following specific objectives:

(a) Exchanging experiences gained by the participants in the organization and implementation of the in-service teacher-education programmes of their respective projects.

(b) Sharing of new ideas related to the organization, implementation and evaluation of in-service teacher education programmes adopting the multi-media approach.

(c) Exploring ways and means of more effective collaboration among the various projects, on the one hand, and between the projects and the UNRWA/Unesco Institute of Education and its Extension Services Section on the other. Among the several things that were highlighted during the conference was the need felt by the directors of the projects for more guidance from the institute on the effective implementation of the multi-media approach, not so much through the provision of more documentation on the various aspects of the approach (although this was also requested) but more through on-the-spot training and guidance provided to the staffs of the projects by the various specialists from the institute.

III The multi-media approach to in-service training

20. As has already been stated, the institute had to adopt an approach or a methodology that would not only enable teachers in service to be trained without withdrawing them from their schools in order to send them to pre-service training institutions but would also ensure a high quality of training. The traditional method of training such teachers without pulling them out of their schools was to provide a series of short, intensive courses, especially during vacations. This procedure has limitations: the training tends to be almost entirely theoretical since it is undertaken with little or no relation to actual classroom practice except, perhaps, for the organization of a limited number of demonstration lessons. In other words, this traditional method makes it extremely difficult, if not impossible, to link theory and practice sufficiently closely for the teacher educator to obtain adequate and immediate feedback on the extent to which, and the success with which, the teacher trainee has been able to apply the ideas communicated in the theory classes.

21. The approach devised by those responsible for the establishment of the institute and its operation in the early years of its existence is what has now come to be called the multi-media approach, because it combines indirect and direct forms of training. There have, naturally, been some developments and modifications in the various techniques used by the institute as constituent elements in this approach since its establishment in 1964, and these changes will be indicated in the following paragraphs, which outline the different forms of indirect and direct training.

22. The first category of indirect methods consists of: (a) guided study assignments, including some programmed materials which have been used on a very limited basis; (b) the use of reference books in the field libraries; (c) a quarterly journal published by the institute; (d) closed-circuit television; (e) other audio-visual media. Because the institute's programme is confined to personnel in the UNRWA/Unesco education system, it has not been able to make use of the facilities provided by national radio and television establishments, which are two other media of indirect training that should be utilized in national programmes of in-service teacher education.

23. The direct forms of training include: (a) periodic seminars (fortnightly, weekly or more often, depending upon the nature of the course and its duration); (b) supervised practice in the trainees' own institutions and other forms of practical training on the job (such as micro-teaching, preparation of teaching units, teaching materials and visual aids, training in the conduct of co-curricular

activities, etc.); (c) action research and experimentation (including the organization and implementation of school improvement projects); (d) summer sessions in which the stress is on activities and experiences that cannot be easily provided for in the regular periodic seminars.

24. The study assignments that are prepared by the institute, either by its own technical staff or by outside specialists, are generally accompanied by guidelines indicating what written or practical work is expected of the trainees in connexion with each assignment and suggesting teaching-learning procedures that may be usefully employed by the seminar leader concerned with conducting the weekly seminar based on the assignment. The guidelines also provide an indication of post-seminar activities or follow-up work expected of the trainees. More recently, the practice has been adopted of incorporating such guidelines in the study assignment itself.

25. It may be pointed out here that from 1964 to 1969 trainees were required to submit their written work related to the study assignments to their respective field tutors who, in time, forwarded these exercises to the institute headquarters for assessment and comments. There were several difficulties with this practice. For one thing, it was extremely difficult for a tutor to receive the written work of all his students on a given assignment on time and it then took several weeks for the institute headquarters to have the assignments corrected by external assessors; as a result, sometimes as many as three or four months elapsed before a trainee got his work back. Because such work was assessed, the trainees were tempted to cheat in doing their exercises and this did not promote true learning.

26. In 1970, therefore, this practice was abandoned and the trainees are now required to work on their 'pre-seminar activities' (as these are now called because they may involve other exercises than the usual form of written work, such as seeking the opinions of their colleagues, recall of personal experiences, preparing group reports, etc.) in preparation for their participation in the related seminar. As the quality of such participation is now assessed, the trainees are motivated to work more regularly on their pre-seminar activities, the execution of which can also be checked by the field tutor. Moreover, a system of short periodic tests (four to six in a year) was introduced in the same year as another substitute for the assessment of weekly written work.

27. An institute document entitled *The Conduct of Seminars* offers general suggestions to the institute's field tutors and to outside resource persons invited to lead periodical seminars. The document enunciates principles that need to be borne in mind in the effective conduct of seminars and enumerates pitfalls to be avoided in order to ensure spontaneous but relevant discussion. It also makes a reference to the variety of procedures (such as symposia, workshops, panel discussions, short lectures by the participants, demonstrations, practical activities, reports on experiments, etc.) that may be adopted in a seminar session for the most satisfactory achievement of the objectives of the study assignments.

28. Each study assignment—and its related seminar—is expected to achieve certain specific objectives in terms of learning outcomes related to the general objectives of the training programme. If these objectives have not been spelt out in the assignment itself, then they should appear in the guidelines or working paper for the conduct of the related seminar which is prepared by the course tutor. The number of trainees that constitutes a seminar group does not normally

exceed twenty-five. As a general rule, the tutors themselves are expected to conduct the seminars for the groups they are tutoring, except when they feel that they are not competent to do so, in which case they may obtain the services of an available outside specialist. This is becoming increasingly necessary as the basic courses for elementary school teachers are being gradually phased out and more *ad hoc* special courses are being organized. When field tutors feel the need for calling in specialists to conduct seminars, they have the following groups of educators to choose from: (a) professional staff members from the UNRWA field offices, including the school supervisors; (b) teacher-training instructors in the four UNRWA/Unesco pre-service teacher-training institutes; (c) resource persons from colleges, universities and ministries of education in the host countries; (d) the institute's staff at headquarters; and (e) specialists in the UNRWA/Unesco Department of Education.

29. Wherever it is deemed necessary, the institute's study assignments contain illustrations intended to help the trainees understand their contents. From time to time, the institute also provides its field tutors with materials and audio-visual media such as transparencies, charts, slides, audio- and video-tapes that can be used in the conduct of specific seminars. The field tutors are expected, in addition, to prepare their own seminar media. Since the institute is not in a position to use the facilities of national radio and television stations in its in-service training programmes, it has organized a closed-circuit television studio that prepares video-tapes of demonstration teaching, micro-teaching, panel discussions, experiments in science and psychology, etc.; copies of these are sent to the field for use in the seminar sessions and summer courses. As the institute's experience with the use of closed-circuit television is recent and therefore limited, video-tapes are not yet being used on the scale one would expect in a programme based on the multi-media approach.

30. The five field offices of the institute have been provided with audio-visual equipment and with libraries of reference books, textbooks, courses of study, samples of tests, pamphlets, periodicals and other reading materials. A limited use has been made by the institute of programmed instructional materials in its study assignments. If more funds were available, the field libraries could be considerably improved; at the moment, there are 600 to 1,000 volumes, covering 200 to 500 titles in each field library. Funds are not the only obstacle to providing books suitable for teachers; another major impediment is the paucity of available books in Arabic that could supplement or reinforce most of the modern concepts and practices which are presented to the trainees in the institute's study assignments. Reference has been made to the periodical *Journal* which is published by the institute. This is distributed among all its trainees and copies of it are also sent to the schools in the UNRWA/Unesco system. The *Journal* seeks to present useful and stimulating materials, both professional and academic, to complement study assignments.

31. The annual summer courses provide further opportunities for trainees to profit directly from the expertise of specialists. The summer courses are intended to supplement, consolidate and integrate learning acquired through self-study and seminar participation. Most of the activities and experiences provided in these courses are of a practical nature and such that they could not easily be provided in the two-hour weekly seminars. Illustrations of such activities are: (a) translating curricular objectives into teaching/learning experiences and practices; (b) practical training in the construction of tests and examinations;

(c) laboratory work in science and improvisation of science equipment; (d) training in practical geography; (e) critical study of textbooks; (f) performance and discussion of some experiments in learning; (g) lesson planning with emphasis on the definition of specific aims and their expression in behavioural terms; (h) preparation of self-rating scales for teachers; (i) developing creativity through opportunities for various forms of self-expression; and (j) review of selected research studies submitted by the trainees.

32. The discussions and activities in the summer courses are based on working papers prepared by the institute headquarters staff and on other supplementary documents and materials that are considered relevant and necessary, depending upon the nature of each activity. The working papers indicate the teaching-learning techniques considered most appropriate for the different activities and the special materials and audio-visual media (films, slides, audio- and video-tapes, etc.) that could profitably be used.

33. Supervised teaching and professional guidance on the job constitute another important means of direct training employed by the institute. This is primarily the responsibility of the field tutors, who are placed in charge of specific groups of trainees and who visit their charges in their own schools to follow up the training imparted in the seminars and to report to the institute headquarters on the progress of the trainees. The institute headquarters staff also participate, to the maximum extent possible, in this aspect of training. Such visits to trainees in their schools are normally followed by individual or group discussions, sometimes in the presence of the head teacher.

34. Other practices used in providing on-the-job guidance are: demonstration lessons; micro-teaching sessions with or without the use of audio- and video-tapes; small-group conferences to discuss such matters as pupil activity in the classroom, the preparation and use of teaching aids, effective home assignments, improved home-school relations and co-curricular activities; and guidance in the conduct of action research studies and school improvement projects.

35. An important element of training that has been incorporated since 1969 in all the institute's courses, both for teachers and for key educational personnel such as head teachers, school supervisors and pre-service teacher-training instructors, is action research. Trainees at all these levels are required to select a problem with which they are personally confronted in their day-to-day work and to conduct as methodical a study as they possibly can to resolve their problem. To assist them in this task, seminars on action research are organized and these are followed up by individual and group guidance. In the courses for key educational personnel, another expectation or requirement is involvement in selected school-improvement projects. Both these requirements are aimed at achieving the basic function of the institute—improvement in the quality of education imparted in the UNRWA/Unesco schools.

36. In the system of evaluation used by the institute, the trainees' progress in their theoretical studies is assessed not only through a series of periodic tests (four to six in each school year) and end-of-year written examinations but also on the basis of their active and effective participation in the weekly seminars and summer courses; special recording forms have been devised to evaluate this participation. Development of teaching efficiency is evaluated through supervisory visits by field tutors to the trainees in their classrooms during the course of their training, supplemented by special visits by evaluation panels at the end of each year. Some weightage in the total assessment is also given to the quality

of the action-research studies required of the trainees. In the case of head teachers, the emphasis is on the nature and extent of improvement affected by them in their respective schools as a result of their training, and this is supplemented by a comprehensive written examination which aims at evaluating not so much the factual knowledge gained by the trainees as their ability to use this knowledge in concrete situations and to apply it to the solution of specific educational problems. Trainees in all courses are encouraged to evaluate their own progress through the use of specially constructed self-evaluation forms and rating scales. Until recently such self-evaluation by trainees was general in nature, but now the staff of the Extension Services Section has developed more specific self-evaluation forms for such aspects of a teacher's work as 'Questioning in the classroom', 'Classroom written examinations', 'Effective use of textbooks' and 'Assignment of effective homework for pupils'.

37. It must be said that the several media involved in the institute's multi-media approach have little that is innovative about them if they are considered individually and separately. All of them have been used at one time or another, and in different combinations, in the training of teachers, pre-service or in-service. The uniqueness of the institute's experiment lies in the integrated manner in which these different media are being used. The key concept in the institute's multi-media approach is integration—a fusion of these media into one organic whole in which there are clearly observable interrelationships. Neither the earlier description of the approach, namely, the combined-method approach, nor the current one, namely, the multi-media approach, highlights its essential feature of integration. For example, seminars are not conducted without reference to specific study assignments, and guidance in classroom teaching is considered to be most effective when it is provided with reference to what has been learnt by the trainees from the assignments and in the seminars. Similarly, the summer courses are organized to supplement and enrich the provisions in the training programme found in the study assignments, seminars and classroom practice. Action research, again, seeks to relate to the specific and real problems encountered by the teachers in their own day-to-day work—problems that are within the capacity of each teacher to solve on his own, guided of course by his tutors or by other available advisers—the necessary background for such research being provided at appropriate times through study assignments, seminars and tutorial sessions.

IV An assessment of the approach

38. The significance of the multi-media approach is threefold. First, it makes it possible for governments and other agencies (such as UNRWA and private-school bodies) concerned with teacher training to provide in-service training to their teachers without having to withdraw them from their schools and find substitutes. Second, as the training courses can be spread out over some time—one, two or, if necessary, three years—it allows sufficient time for the trainees not only to develop and enrich the concepts and ideas acquired in the course of their training but also to experiment with some of these ideas in their day-to-day work and, through such experimentation, to improve the quality of their teaching. This is something that is extremely difficult, if not impossible, to provide for in the traditional crash or emergency programmes of short, intensive

training. Third, it facilitates the organization of carefully planned follow-up or supervisory measures intended to provide on-the-job guidance and assistance to individual teachers in their respective schools and during the training programme itself. All these advantages make this approach particularly valuable in the in-service training of unqualified teachers and the reorientation or updating of qualified teachers.

39. The institute has demonstrated that its approach can be both effectively and economically applied to the in-service training of unqualified teachers and to the upgrading and updating of qualified educational personnel. Between 1964 and 1973, the proportion of trained teachers in the teaching force has been transformed. In 1964, 90 per cent of 4,500 teachers were untrained; in 1973, over 80 per cent of a total force of 7,400 were either trained or undergoing in-service training. Moreover, the cost of in-service training at the institute per student-year has been found to be considerably less than half of what it is for the pre-service training courses offered by the UNRWA/Unesco teacher-training institutes.

40. Although no systematic or objective assessment of a comparative nature has been made of the products of the institute and those of the pre-service training institutes, there have been no complaints from school supervisors or school administrators about inferiority in the institute's graduates. Nor have the governments of the host countries in which the institute's programmes have been operating raised doubts about the effectiveness of the institute's approach. On the contrary, the approach has been adopted and is being implemented in Jordan, the Syrian Arab Republic and Lebanon (all host countries) either for the training of unqualified teachers or for the upgrading and updating of qualified teachers.

41. It may be mentioned here that for the purpose of internal evaluation of the various aspects of the multi-media approach, a set of criteria have been developed. These criteria, which are entitled 'Evaluative criteria for in-service teacher-training projects', have also been supplied to the Unicef-supported in-service teacher-training projects in the region and been used by some of them in conducting their own evaluation of their operations.

Factors contributing to the success of the institute's programmes

42. In speaking of the success of the institute's programmes, the term is used in a relative sense. For one thing, not all the institute's training programmes have been equally successful; we must pinpoint the reasons for this variability. Also, when we talk about the success of a programme, we need a clear idea of what we mean. Do we measure the success of a course in terms of the percentage of trainees who received passing grade, or do we judge it by the kind and extent of impact the training makes on the quality of education that is being provided in the UNRWA/Unesco school system?

43. Neither UNRWA nor Unesco[1] has made any scientific assessment of

1. In 1966 the International Institute for Education Planning sent a team to make a case study of the institute's methods and activities. This case study was part of a world-wide research survey of more than twenty educational projects using new educational media.

the institute's impact on the quality of education in the UNRWA/Unesco schools. Therefore, the judgements here are based on the author's impressions acquired through contact with the institute and the UNRWA/Unesco system over the last five years.

44. One impression that is quickly gained by anyone working at the institute is that those trainees who are highly motivated get more out of the institute's courses than those who are not; such motivation can be either intrinsic or extrinsic or both. Teachers who join courses half-heartedly or because they are compelled to join them, generally end up as drop-outs or failures, unless an external incentive such as an increment in salary helps to sustain the minimum interest needed for passing the course. However, it has been found that in some courses, such as the course for head teachers, no extrinsic incentive was needed to motivate the participants to do their best. Perhaps the fact that they were regarded by the administration as being more responsible than teachers and that they could aspire to higher positions in the educational hierarchy made them take their training seriously.

45. The variations between one area of study and another in the success of training (as judged by the successful completion of the course) may be attributed largely to the higher level of motivation displayed by the students in those areas of employment in which there are few or no alternatives to teaching. Another possible explanation for such variations both between and within the different fields is the comparative enthusiasm and efficiency of the institute's field tutors.

46. To the extent that the institute has succeeded in fulfilling its role of upgrading the quality of teachers in the UNRWA/Unesco schools, its success can be attributed to the following factors: (a) the quality of its staff, both international and local, especially in the early years of its operations; (b) its organizational and administrative structure, which has facilitated and smoothed out its operations; (c) the care with which its training programmes have been formulated and presented; and (d) what has already been sufficiently stressed, the integrated approach that has been followed in the implementation of these programmes.

47. It must be admitted that the institute was fortunate in the first five or six years of its existence to get the services of competent and dedicated educators who had a good vision of what was expected of it and who worked wholeheartedly to realize these expectations. After this period, however, the institute began gradually to lose its experienced staff members, both international and local, and it became increasingly difficult to fill the local positions with equally competent and dedicated persons. One reason was a stagnation in the salary scales, which were no longer sufficiently attractive to draw educators of a high calibre. Another reason was the prevailing circumstances which make it difficult to recruit local staff from areas other than Lebanon. This has resulted in a steady decline in the efficiency of the professional staff at a time when the institute has embarked on an extensive programme of special *ad hoc* courses as well as a variety of refresher or reorientation courses to meet the needs of the schools in the various fields of its operations.

48. The second factor responsible for the success of the institute's operations was its organizational and administrative structure, which has several distinctive features. First, the institute is a division of the UNRWA/Unesco Department of Education which has a number of Unesco specialists and associate specialists attached to it whose assistance and guidance can be sought by the institute staff

whenever they feel the need for it. In the case of some of the Unesco specialists in the department—for whom there are local counterpart assistant specialists at the institute—very close collaboration between them is a matter of policy. Second—and this is very important—the institute has its representatives in the host countries or fields where it operates who are primarily responsible for the direct instructional media which constitute the institute's multi-media approach. These media are the periodical seminars, generally held once a week, on-the-spot supervision and guidance in classroom work in the schools where the trainees teach, guidance in the trainees' action-research studies provided on an individual or group basis according to the needs of a tutorial group, and the annual summer courses. Not all field tutors are equally competent or enthusiastic and so the institute headquarters staff have to use a variety of methods to keep them from lagging or stagnating. Such methods include the organization of periodic seminars and workshops for their benefit, frequent visits to the field by the headquarters staff to collaborate with the field tutors, and a carefully devised system of regular feedback to the headquarters on the conduct of seminars, on supervisory visits to teachers, on the progress of trainees in their action-research studies and on the conduct of summer course activities. For administrative purposes, the field tutors are under the Field Education Officer, who is a member of the UNRWA office in a specific field or host country and is responsible for the provision and development of educational facilities in that field or host country. This arrangement obviates the need for the institute to have its own additional administrative personnel in the field to take care of a number of administrative matters such as transportation, supply of materials, disbursement of stipends, etc., which are all taken care of by the UNRWA field offices.

49. With administrative matters in the field left almost entirely in the hands of the field offices, the institute has been able to concentrate on its professional responsibilities. This has enabled it to bestow the maximum possible care on the preparation of curricula, training programmes, working papers and guidelines to field tutors and other part-time educators (such as assignment writers, seminar leaders, assessors of periodic tests, action-research studies and final examinations, both theoretical and practical, etc.), self-evaluation forms, recording and reporting forms for obtaining feedback, and the writing of a proportion of the needed assignments, depending upon the time available for this purpose and upon the expertise of its staff. As a result of long experience, a pattern for the development of training programmes based on the multi-media approach has been gradually developed which normally includes the following components: (a) the objectives of the course stated in terms of training outcomes; (b) the course contents or syllabus divided into units comprising related topics; (c) the learning experience and activities designed to help the trainees achieve the designated results through specific media or channels of training; (d) the methods of evaluation and feedback appropriate to the course; (e) the organization of the course (i) during a training year (in terms of a schedule of self-study assignments, related seminars, various practical training activities, action research, periodic tests, etc.) and (ii) during the summer vacation (in terms of summer course activities and the end-of-year written examination). The care with which the course programmes have been prepared, embodying the features enumerated above, and the extent to which the several professional responsibilities listed in the opening part of this paragraph have been adequately

performed in respect of each of the institute's numerous courses, have resulted in the comparative success of these courses.

V Adoption of the approach by other countries

50. Perhaps the best indicator of the value and practicability of the multi-media approach is the fact that within a period of only three years six Arab countries, including the institute's host countries, Jordan, the Syrian Arab Republic and Lebanon, have either adopted the approach or are on the point of doing so. The five countries that have already implemented teacher-training programmes based on this approach are Jordan, the Syrian Arab Republic, the Sudan, Bahrain and Iraq, while Lebanon has made preparations to do so in the school year 1974/75. In addition, selected aspects of the approach are being applied in the Sultanate of Oman, the Yemen Arab Republic and the People's Democratic Republic of Yemen. Two other Arab countries, the Libyan Arab Republic and Saudi Arabia, and one Asian country, Afghanistan, have expressed an interest in this approach; the Ministry of Education in Afghanistan has sent two groups of teacher educators to the institute for one month's orientation to the approach.

51. It goes without saying that each of the countries which have adopted the multi-media approach has made certain adaptations, not only in the training curriculum but also in the use of the various media involved in the training programme, to fit the conditions prevalent in their countries and to meet the special or unique needs of their teachers. Bahrain requires its trainees, who are all elementary school teachers, to specialize in one of several subject areas such as: language and social studies; mathematics and science; English; physical education; lower elementary teaching; and school administration (for head teachers). This has been done because of the current practice in the majority of elementary schools, especially in the upper-elementary grades, to rely on specialized teaching. The result is that the curriculum has become heavier in Bahrain than in the other countries training elementary school teachers, necessitating two seminars per week instead of one as in the other programmes. In Jordan, the Institute for In-service Training has adopted the credit system in organizing its courses—which no other project has done. Moreover, the training programme covers grades one to nine (the compulsory cycle of education in that country). Jordan also offers courses in specialization, because these teachers may be required to teach in any one of the first nine grades of schooling. An organizational arrangement that will be adopted in Iraq from 1975/76 uses regular school supervisors as field tutors following a special course in school supervision training, with emphasis on the effective use of the multi-media approach to in-service training. The supervisors selected in each district to serve as field tutors will be given a relatively lighter load of regular school supervision. The project in Iraq, as in the Syrian Arab Republic, is for the reorientation of qualified teachers, and the training programme for this purpose will be moved from one set of districts to another until all the qualified elementary school teachers in the country have been refreshed and updated in the newer concepts and practices in elementary education. This process may take anything from five to seven years, depending upon how big an intake will be feasible each year after the first pilot phase of experimentation.

52. These national programmes of teacher education, unlike the UNRWA/Unesco programme, are in a position to make use of their national systems of television and radio broadcasting if they wish to do so. Very little has been done yet in this direction, although in two or three of the projects some initial experiments have been conducted. All of the projects, however, are using audio cassettes and video-tapes in their seminars and summer course programmes, albeit in varying degrees and with varying success, to supplement the usual audio-visual media.

53. Some of the projects have achieved better results than others, and there are two factors that are mainly responsible for this divergence in achievement. One factor is the calibre of the headquarters and field staffs that have been provided to the projects by their respective governments. Another is the adequacy or inadequacy of the administrative and organizational infrastructure facilitating or impeding such aspects of the training programmes as: the quality of printed study assignments; their timely delivery to trainees; easy accessibility of the seminar centres; employment of effective feedback tools and procedures; transportation facilities for headquarters and field staffs for such purposes as visiting trainees in their schools, contacting assignment writers and seminar leaders to brief them about their responsibilities and tasks and carrying supplementary reading materials and audio-visual equipment, if and when necessary, to the seminar centres; the smooth and efficient conduct of examinations; the timely correction of papers and publication of results; and the organization of periodic meetings and conferences of staff members both for discussions of problems faced by them and for their professional growth and development.

Projects in which these and other organizational and administrative requirements have been given careful and serious consideration by the administrators concerned have made better headway than those in which they have been overlooked or neglected. It has been the experience of the institute that these various 'transplants' of projects need continuing nurture by the institute for an appreciable period of time. This can be affected by advisory missions undertaken by institute specialists, through a careful study of as much feedback as can be provided by the projects in respect of the implementation of each aspect of the multi-media approach, and through the continuous supply of useful curricula and other materials. The effective use of the multi-media approach is not something that can be acquired through a month's period of orientation, however intensive that might be, and neophytes to the approach need a great deal of guidance and counselling to be successful. This is especially true in respect of innovative techniques, processes or media such as systems analysis, action research, etc., that the project staffs might be enthusiastic about introducing.

VI General observations on transferability of the approach

54. As can be gathered from what has been said about the development of the institute from an institution for the in-service training of educational personnel in the UNRWA/Unesco school system into a regional centre for in-service training and about the rapid expansion of in-service training projects in the Arab region, there can be few doubts concerning the basic transferability

of the institute's multi-media approach to other countries faced with the problem of unqualified staff.

55. There are three important principles, however, that need to be observed to make such transfer smooth and fruitful. First, the people selected by a government to introduce such an approach in its school system need to be persons of at least average ability. They then need to be properly trained both in the philosophy of the approach and in the techniques related to the use of the different media that constitute the approach. Such training cannot be a one-time affair: it has to be continuous and protracted.

56. Second, a project of in-service training using the multi-media approach must be provided with an adequate administrative set-up. An essential prerequisite is a detailed curriculum and programme of training, prepared sufficiently in advance to ensure the smooth operation of the training course, and indicating as clearly as possible the links and interrelationships among the various media that are to be used. Providing trainees with a regular flow of study materials is an essential feature of the approach. Giving them timely advice and guidance not only in improving their teaching techniques but also in such matters as how to study, how to observe other teachers, how to write reports, how to participate in group discussions, how to evaluate themselves, etc., is another important consideration. What is needed here is a planned programme of training and guidance in the above, which is incorporated in the curriculum. Obtaining regular and adequate feedback on the trainees' progress and development is another *sine qua non* of the approach, and this too has to be carefully planned and programmed. Feedback entails the preparation and use of a diversity of recording and reporting forms and the establishment of practicable procedures which are understood and accepted by everyone in the system. Preparation of an exhaustive list of part-time educators who can be called upon to co-operate in the writing of study assignments, in the conduct of seminars and summer-course activities, in the assessment of periodic tests and end-of-year examinations—and the proper briefing of such educators both through direct contacts and through a supply of literature on the various aspects of the multi-media approach—are vital.

57. Third, it is obvious that each in-service training project will need to adapt the institute's approach to its own needs, conditions and circumstances. Carbon copies of the institute's programmes and arrangements cannot be expected to work; thus, flexibility in the application of the approach becomes an important principle.

Appendix A Standardized reference data

Country, state or province	***Lebanon***
Area	**Covers Lebanon and also the Syrian Arab Republic, Jordan and the Gaza strip.**
Explanatory note	**The UNRWA/Unesco Institute of Education is a division of the UNRWA/Unesco Department of Education, which is a department of UNRWA, the United Nations Relief and Works Agency for Palestine Refugees in the Near East. UNRWA is a subsidiary organ of the United Nations General Assembly, created under General Assembly resolution 302 (IV) of 8 December 1949. It commenced operations in May 1950.**
Population	**1,583,646 Palestine Arab refugees, registered with UNRWA as at 30 June 1974.**
Services	**Relief services (rations, shelters, welfare); health services; education.** **UNRWA's headquarters are in Beirut. It has field offices in Lebanon, the Syrian Arab Republic, Jordan (Amman and Jerusalem) and the Gaza strip; there are also liaison offices in New York, Geneva and Cairo.**
Departments of UNRWA	**Four departments comprise: relief operations; health; education; administration (finance, legal, personnel, public information and contributions, supply, technical).**

Budget	UNRWA's budget in 1974 was U.S.$88.7 million and the income for this budget was from contributions of Member States of the United Nations and of non-governmental organizations and other international organizations.
Education	
Type of system	Education services are provided through the UNRWA/Unesco Department of Education. By an agreement with Unesco dating from August 1950, UNRWA undertakes the administrative responsibility and Unesco the technical responsibility for the education services to the refugees. Under its responsibility, Unesco provides the director of education and nineteen other internationally recruited senior educators and subject specialists to guide and supervise the education programme.
Organization of the education services	Headquarters unit in Beirut comprises four divisions: school education; higher education (responsible for pre-service teacher training and university scholarships); vocational and technical education; in-service training of teachers (by UNRWA/Unesco Institute of Education). Five field education offices, one in each field area; these offices, headed by a Field Education Officer, are mainly responsible for the day-to-day operations.
Statistical information on UNRWA/Unesco education services as at 30 June 1974[1]	
(a) number of schools	562 elementary (primary) and preparatory (lower secondary).
(b) number of pupils	Elementary: 209,201. Preparatory: 59,123. Total: 268,324.
(c) number of teachers	7,662.
(d) number of supervisory staff	70.
(e) number of training centres	Eight, of which three are combined teacher- and vocational-training centres, four are vocational-training centres and one is a teacher-training centre.
(f) number of trainees in vocational and technical courses	3,072.
(g) number of trainees in pre-service teacher-training courses	1,240.

1. UNRWA does not operate schools at the upper secondary level; refugee pupils may enrol in government and private secondary schools, for which allowances for tuition fees and/or books may be paid by UNRWA.

Education budget for 1974	U.S.$38.7 million or 43.8 per cent of the total UNRWA budget of U.S.$88.7 million.
Educational curriculum	Follows that of each host country where refugee schools are located.

Institution/system under study

Brief for study	The UNRWA/Unesco Institute of Education was a pioneer institution in the design and use of a multi-media approach to in-service teacher training.
Reason for inclusion	An example of a multi-media system of adult learning at a distance.
Description of subject studied	
Origins	In 1962 the then Director of the UNRWA/Unesco Department of Education drew attention to the discrepancy between the quantitative expansion of UNRWA's general education system and the qualifications of its teaching staff. Based on the recommendations of the twenty-fifth International Conference on Public Education (on the further training of teachers in service), it was suggested that traditional methods would not solve the problem. A Unesco consultant, in 1963, reported on the problem and recommended a system combining indirect and direct methods of instruction to enable many teachers to be trained in a short period of time. Negotiations between UNRWA/Unesco and the Swiss Government resulted in the signing of a Tripartite Agreement in May 1965 covering the plan of operations, staffing and financing of the institute. Training operations actually commenced in school year 1964/65.
Types of courses offered, entry conditions and terminal target qualifications	
(a) basic two-year course for training unqualified teachers (primary level)	Requirement of full secondary certificate, plus appointment as UNRWA teacher with some teaching experience; leading to an institute teaching certificate.
(b) basic three-year course for training unqualified teachers (primary level)	Completion of preparatory (lower-secondary) schooling plus some years of experience as UNRWA teacher; leading to an institute teaching certificate, provided secondary education is gained in meantime.

(c) specialized two-year course for subject teaching (lower-secondary level)	Completion of basic in-service or pre-service teacher-training course plus appointment or potential appointment as subject teacher in lower secondary school; leading to institute certificate for subject teaching in lower secondary.
(d) professional one-year course for subject teaching (lower-secondary level)	Completion of at least two years of university course with major in subject area of school curriculum, plus appointment as subject teacher in lower secondary school; leading to institute certificate for subject teaching at lower-secondary level.
(e) three-year course of professional training and subject content for teaching (lower-secondary level)	Full secondary certificate plus appointment as subject teacher at lower-secondary school; leading to institute certificate.
(f) one-year course in school administration for head teachers (school principals)	Possession of basic pre-service or in-service teacher-training certificate plus appointment as head teacher; leading to institute certificate.
(g) one-year course in school administration and supervision for school supervisors	Possession of basic pre-service or in-service teacher-training certificate plus appointment as supervisor; leading to institute certificate.
(h) Up to one year *ad hoc* course to meet special needs	Requiring teaching in the particular target subject area; leading to institute certificate.
(i) one-year refresher course for qualified teachers	Requiring completion of basic in-service or pre-service teacher-training courses; leading to institute certificate.
(j) one-year professional refresher course for teacher-training instructors	No entry conditions; leading to institute certificate.
Instructional means used	Multi-media, i.e. correspondence lesson assignments, weekly or fortnightly seminars for teachers in training, video-tapes, filmstrips, tape recordings, reference books, overhead transparencies used in seminars, compulsory summer-school attendance, classroom visits made to teachers for guidance and assessment of classroom practice and techniques, action research.

Numbers involved

Enrolment in 1973–74	Of UNRWA/Unesco teaching staff total of 1,048: 257 teachers followed basic courses for unqualified teachers teaching at elementary (primary) level. 123 preparatory (lower-secondary) teachers followed specialized courses. 134 followed courses for head teachers, supervisors, teacher-training instructors. 534 qualified teachers followed *ad hoc* and refresher courses.

Academic staff		
	(a) Full-time	At institute headquarters: 26; in the field: 20.
	(b) Part-time	Lesson-writers, correctors, translators, lecturers (no data available).
Finance		
	Institute income for 1974	Approximate figures (U.S.$): Unesco, $71,188; UNDP, $329,416; Unicef, $88,626; Swiss Government, $87,963; UNRWA, $23,252. (Institute trainees do not pay any tuition fees).
	Estimated budget for 1974	Recurrent: $477,997. Non-recurrent: $13,798. Extension services: $114,650. Total: U.S.$606,445.

Appendix B — Short bibliography

UNRWA/UNESCO INSTITUTE OF EDUCATION. *Better teachers: an experiment with in-service teacher training*. Paris, Unesco, 1970.

——. The in-service training programme for UNRWA-Unesco teachers. In: W. Schramm (ed.), *New educational media in action: case studies for planners*, vol. 2. Paris, Unesco/IIEP, 1967.

Appendix C — Biographical note

Dr Pires was the second director of the UNRWA/Unesco Institute of Education, Beirut, and director of the Unesco Centre for Regional Training in Manila. As an Extension Service Officer of Unesco, he is concerned with imparting the techniques of the institute to other countries.

Bernard Bartram, who was working with Unesco in Nigeria, the Libyan Arab Republic, the Middle East and the South Pacific, is now director of the Audio-Visual Department of the institute.

The Television Agricultural High School (Telewizyjne Technikum Rolnicze), **Poland**

Gerald Stone

Contents

I The national context

Population

1. The Polish People's Republic has the seventh largest population in Europe. The number of inhabitants on 8 December 1970 was 32,642,000, and in 1972 it was estimated at 33,068,000. The total area is 120,664 square miles and the population density (274 per square mile) is above the European average.

2. A little more than half the population lives in towns (52.3 per cent). On 8 December 1970, 17,064,000 were living in towns and 15,578,000 in the countryside.

3. The population of Poland is comparatively young. In 1972 there were 8,952,300 people aged between 15 and 29, i.e. about 27 per cent. It is estimated that in 1975 the age group 15 to 24 contained 6,811,300 people, i.e. 20 per cent.

4. Poland is divided administratively into seventeen voivodeships with their centres in: Białystok, Bydgoszcz, Gdańsk, Katowice, Kielce, Koszalin, Kraków (Cracow), Lublin, Łódź, Olsztyn, Opole, Poznań, Rzeszów, Szczecin, Warsaw, Wrocław, Zielona Góra.

Economy

5. Poland is a Socialist country and a member of the Council for Mutual Economic Assistance. It is still a largely agricultural country and until 1955 more than half the population made a living in agriculture. The proportion of Poles working on the land has steadily declined, however, and it is now about 30 per cent.

6. The gross national product (1972) is £19,623 million (941,900 million zlotys). (The conversion here, as elsewhere in this report, has been calculated at the basic exchange rate of £1=48 zlotys.) The monetary income per head for the total population is £598 (28,700 zlotys) (1972 figures). Total State expenditure in 1972 was £9,026 million (433.25 million zlotys).

Communications

7. Poland has a highly developed and efficient communications system. The

number of passengers conveyed by socialized means of transport in 1972 was 2,795,845,000. 1,080,858,000 passengers were carried by rail.

8. On 31 December 1972 there were 1,200,329 telephone subscribers in Poland, i.e. 36.2 telephones per 1,000 inhabitants. At the same time there were 7,768 post and telegraph offices, i.e. 23.4 per 1,000 inhabitants.

Broadcasting

9. All broadcasting is under State control. The responsible body is the Committee for Radio and Television Affairs (Komitet do Spraw Radia i Telewizji), which has a constitutional position similar to that of a ministry. There are 28 television transmitting stations and 52 transmitters. Television centres are situated in Warsaw, Cracow, Poznań, Szczecin, Gdańsk, Łódź, Wrocław and Katowice. There is a radio centre in the main town of each of the 17 voivodeships.

10. There are 5,200,000 registered television sets and 5,795,000 radio licence holders. This means that there are 157 television sets and 175 radios per thousand inhabitants. About 60 per cent of all families have television sets. There are two television channels: Channel I covers virtually the whole country; Channel II covers most of it.

Educational broadcasting

11. Educational broadcasting is well developed. Apart from the Television Agricultural High School, whose programmes are transmitted 12 hours a week, Polish Television broadcasts the following educational programmes (hours weekly): (a) language courses, 6; (b) schools broadcasts, 4 to 7; (c) Television Polytechnic (Politechnika Telewizyjna) (preparation for entry to higher technical education), 3; (d) popular scientific programmes, 2 to 2½; (e) agricultural broadcasts (apart from the Television High School), 1; (f) Teachers' Radio and Television University, 1½ (the number of hours shown includes repeat broadcasts).

12. The most recent innovation is the Teachers' Radio and Television University (Nauczycielski Uniwersytet Radiowo-Telewizyjny—known from its initials as NURT, which also means 'current'). It came into operation in January 1974, following an agreement between the Ministry of Education and Upbringing and the Committee for Radio and Television Affairs. Like the Television Agricultural High School it provides vocational training. The majority of students are teachers, who gain help in their external studies for the master's degree (the usual first degree).

Educational system

13. Poland's educational system is controlled and financed by the State. Education is provided free of charge at all levels, and roughly 25 per cent of the entire population (about 8 million people) are receiving full or part-time education of one kind or another.

14. Primary education (*szkoła podstawowa*) is compulsory, and lasts for eight years. In addition, before starting school, one year's attendance at a kindergarten (*przedszkole*) is obligatory. Children start school on 1 September in the calendar year in which they reach the age of 7 years (e.g. those born in 1960 started school on 1 September 1967). Following primary education there are three possibilities at the secondary school level (*szkoła średnia*), namely:

(a) Basic vocational school (*zasadnicza szkoła zawodowa*), which lasts for two years. The most common type of basic vocational school in country districts is the basic agricultural school (*zasadnicza szkoła rolnicza*).

(b) High school (*technikum*), which lasts five years. This type is also vocational and includes agricultural high schools (*technikum rolnicze*). High schools have evening and external departments.

(c) General education secondary school (*liceum ogólnokształcące*), which lasts four years and has evening and correspondence departments.

15. High schools and general-education secondary schools, entry to either of which depends on passing an entrance examination, provide a full secondary education. Basic vocational schools (which have no entrance examination) provide only a partial secondary education, but pupils who have successfully completed the course at such schools and have been given the Vocational School Certificate (*zaświadczenie ukończenia szkoły zawodowej*) are entitled to continue their education at a high school of the same type.

16. Both high schools and general-education secondary schools lead to the Secondary School Certificate (*matura*), which is the first step in obtaining entry to an institution of higher education (*uczelnia wyższa*). The latter may be a university, a polytechnic, or one of a number of such institutions, all of which have equal status and award first and higher degrees. Alternatively, on finishing high school a certificate may be awarded simply confirming that the pupil has successfully completed the course (*świadectwo ukończenia technikum*).

17. Most examinations are oral—important exceptions are the mathematics and Polish-language examinations in the Secondary School Certificate—and are conducted either by the teachers who have taught the subject or by a committee.

18. Total State expenditure on education in 1972 was approximately £823 million (39,503 million zlotys), i.e. about 9 per cent of total State expenditure or approximately 4.20 per cent of the gross national product. Expenditure on education is divided up as follows: kindergartens, primary schools and general-education secondary schools, £460.94 million (22,125 million zlotys); vocational schools, £187.60 million (9,000 million zlotys); higher education, £174.54 million (8,378 million zlotys).

19. Approximately 88 per cent of all pupils continue their education in one way or another on completion of the obligatory eight-year primary school. In 1972/73 75 per cent of all children in the age group 15 to 18 were attending school. In the same year the numbers attending various types of educational institutions were as follows: (a) primary schools, 4,978,400; (b) general-education secondary schools, 609,400; (c) vocational schools, 1,829,700; (d) institutions of higher education, 364,300. Of those in higher education only 229,000 were day students. The evening and external systems are highly developed.

Library facilities

20. In 1972 there were nearly 54,000 libraries in Poland, of which over 31,000 were open to the general public.

Teaching qualifications

21. The number of unqualified teachers in Poland has been rapidly falling and has now reached insignificant proportions. Most teachers are two-year trained, having completed their training (*studium nauczycielskie*) at the end of their secondary education, i.e. after high school or general-education secondary school. Such training is not considered part of higher education, even though it begins at the age of 19 or later. A fair number of teachers have higher education. Recent figures are apparently not available, but in 1966–67 15.6 per cent of all school teachers had higher educational qualifications. At that time 10.7 per cent of the total teaching force was not properly qualified, but this figure has probably dropped considerably in the last eight years.

22. Among proposals at present under discussion are measures to raise the status and skills of teachers. New incentives to attract graduates to teaching are foreseen in order to increase the proportion of teachers with higher education.

Future developments

23. A draft programme for important reforms in the educational system has been prepared by the Ministry of Education and Upbringing and is now under discussion. It foresees the introduction of universal obligatory secondary education within the next eight or ten years. It is also proposed that all children be obliged to attend school from the age of 6 and to attend a kindergarten for one year beforehand.

24. It is expected that the new system will involve the expansion of co-operation with other institutions, including the press, radio and television. The importance of special provision for young people in rural areas is emphasized, in order to modernize both attitudes and agricultural processes. It is envisaged that in 1975 about 70,000 school leavers will be accepted for higher studies, and about 220,000 in the year 2000.

25. Various plans are under discussion for changing the system of admission to higher education. One possibility is that all holders of the Secondary School Certificate (*matura*) will be automatically allowed entry. Since October 1973, as an experiment at the Jagiellonian University in Cracow and at the University of Wrocław, anyone holding this certificate has been permitted to enrol for certain subjects. It seems likely that the real selection will take place in the examinations at the end of the first year.

II Purpose and scope

26. The Polish Television Agricultural High School is a multi-media system of teaching both agriculture and general subjects above the basic vocational

school level. It enables people working full-time on the land (or in other occupations) to complete their secondary education with vocational training in agriculture.

27. The system is based on the principle of 'guided self-education' (*samokształcenie kierowane*). Pupils receive instruction through the medium of television, but they are also external pupils of conventional agricultural high schools, where they obtain guidance in their studies and take examinations.

III The origins and history of the project

28. The idea of the Television Agricultural High School grew up in the 1960s among young people working on the land, especially those active in the Union of Socialist Village Youth (Związek Socjalistycznej Młodzieży Wiejskiej). This is a political youth organization which has as one of its permanent main objectives the furtherance of education among young agricultural workers. The union works to overcome the prejudice that agricultural skills are best learned in practice, being handed down usually by parents to their children. It tries to show that agricultural work can be attractive and that the study of agriculture is a worthwhile pursuit. It aims thereby to raise the number of agricultural workers with a full secondary education (including vocational education in agriculture) and so to increase agricultural efficiency.

29. It was known that there were many young people working on the land who would have liked to complete the secondary stage of their education without interrupting their work, but who, for practical reasons, were unable to do so. There was always the possibility of enrolling in either the evening or external department of an agricultural high school, but many were deterred by the problem of distance.

30. The conventional external system entails travelling to the high school three times a semester for a week's residence on each visit, and many farm workers complain that they live too far from their nearest high school to undertake regular visits for such long periods, especially as this entails interruption of many of the continuous processes and occupations characteristic of agriculture. Would-be students frequently find themselves unable to leave their animals and crops unattended. It was therefore thought that instead of pupils being required to travel long distances to receive concentrated doses of instruction, the lessons could be brought to them in their homes in less concentrated form through the medium of television.

It was through the Union of Socialist Village Youth (following a resolution of its fourth congress in 1970) that suggestions were addressed simultaneously to both the Ministry of Agriculture and to the Polish Radio and Television Service for the establishment of a new way of providing agricultural secondary education, making use of television. The Department of Education in the Ministry of Agriculture was already looking for means of increasing the efficiency of the external departments of agricultural high schools, for their pass rate (usually no more than 25.3 per cent of pupils complete the course successfully) is exceptionally low.

31. The Union of Socialist Village Youth was, however, not only the original motive force behind the discussions leading to the establishment of the Television Agricultural High School. It has been much more than this, for it

continues to play an important part in the school's operation and pursues a policy of encouraging young people to enrol and of helping them with their studies.

32. In view of the fact that educational broadcasting in general was already highly developed (including agricultural educational broadcasting) and that the regional centres (in the form of the 77 existing agricultural high schools with external departments) were already built, fully staffed and operational, it was felt unnecessary to carry out preliminary research. At the same time the entire project was regarded from the outset as experimental, and therefore to be adjusted in the light of experience, especially of the reactions of pupils.

33. Overall responsibility was assumed by the Department of Education in the Ministry of Agriculture. In 1971 the department called meetings with representatives of the Union of Socialist Village Youth and of Polish Television, and by 1972 programmes were already in the making. The last date for registration for the first semester was 15 January 1973, and the first television transmissions began in February that year.

IV Courses and curriculum

34. The curriculum has the same content as that for full-time and conventional external students, but it is arranged somewhat differently. It consists of seven semesters, i.e. 3½ years, but only four semesters (the first four) are covered by television instruction. During the final three semesters the pupil is subject to the normal conditions of the external system and has to put in the usual number of attendances for a week at a time at the school where he or she is enrolled.

35. During the four television semesters the following eleven subjects are studied: Polish language, history, mathematics, physics, chemistry, zoology, botany, plant cultivation, plant preservation, animal husbandry, and agricultural mechanization.

36. New subjects, introduced in the final three semesters—the sessional semesters (*semestry zjazdowe*)—are as follows: Russian language, introduction to sociology, evolutionism, horticulture, safety and hygiene of work, economy and organization of agricultural work, and agricultural counselling.

37. Only four of the subjects studied in the television semesters are continued in the sessional semesters, namely: Polish language, history, mathematics, and agricultural mechanization.

38. Seven subjects are completely covered in the television semesters. They are: physics, chemistry, zoology, botany, plant cultivation, plant preservation, and animal husbandry.

V Teaching methods and examinations

39. The four main teaching media are: television lessons; guide-workbooks; textbooks (which are the same as those in use in conventional high schools); and consultations with teachers at the pupil's high school.

40. A minor additional aid is provided by the special pages (usually three or four) in the weekly journal of the Union of Socialist Village Youth, *Mlody Rolnik* (The Young Farmer), which appears in an edition of about 100,000 copies.

Under the heading 'Wiedza Twoja Szansa' (Knowledge—Your Opportunity), it discusses and complements the television programmes, and enables pupils to air their opinions. It also announces the times and subjects of broadcasts. (These are, of course, already known to registered pupils.)

41. Advice to pupils on how to organize their studies is given in special television lectures (which constitute an integral part of the overall syllabus). There are three such lectures in each of the first three semesters and two in the fourth.

42. The dates and subjects of television lectures for the forthcoming term are known to pupils from a general information pamphlet supplied free of charge to anyone interested. Registered pupils also receive free of charge a guide-workbook for each subject to be studied in the forthcoming semester, telling them how to prepare for each television lecture. The guide-workbook also explains how to make the best use of the appropriate textbook for each subject, which the pupils are expected to acquire for themselves, and tells them how to consolidate what they have learned by testing themselves after the lesson. The guide-workbook contains questions for self-assessment tasks to be carried out and exercises which the pupils complete and send in to their schools within a specified time.

43. In June 1974 the television lectures were transmitted at the following times: 1.45 p.m. and 2.30 p.m. on Tuesday, Thursday and Saturday (Semester I); 12.45 p.m. and 1.25 p.m. on Monday, Wednesday and Friday (Semester III).

44. Lectures last 30 minutes, and each pupil is expected to follow three hours of television time (six half-hour lectures) a week. All programmes are repeated the following morning at 6.30 a.m. and 7.00 a.m. which means a total daily transmission time (first broadcasts and repeats) of 2 hours, except on Sunday (repeat only: 1 hour) and Monday (first broadcast only: 1 hour).

45. When the Television Agricultural High School first started the repeats were broadcast at 10 p.m., but this was changed when it was discovered that this was an unpopular time with pupils who start their working day early.

46. Consultation sessions with teachers take place at the local high schools every Sunday. Pupils are under no obligation to attend them, but it is generally expected that they will attend them at least occasionally. In practice they attend them frequently, and there is nothing to prevent a pupil attending every week, if he or she feels it necessary. Pupils take their guide-workbooks and completed work with them to their consultation sessions or send them in advance by post. These help the teacher to assess progress.

47. Attendance at one session each semester for the purpose of examinations is obligatory, however, and these naturally take place at the end of the semester. Pupils are required to bring their guide-workbooks with them to examinations to give the examiner a general idea of the term's work, but they do not count towards the result.

48. Semestral examinations, which are basically all oral, are conducted by the teachers who give consultations at the Sunday sessions. The examiners, at their own discretion, may give written tests. The examination system is essentially the same as for other secondary-school pupils. Those who complete the seven semesters successfully receive the certificate confirming this fact (*świadectwo ukończenia technikum*). They are then entitled to take the Secondary School Certificate (*matura*).

49. Pupils of the Television Agricultural High School are also entitled (and

encouraged) to make use of the local educational facilities in their own villages. They may turn to their local primary schools or to local agronomists and agricultural stations for guidance and the use of laboratories. The Union of Socialist Village Youth takes steps to systematize the use of local facilities. It forms television pupils into groups and arranges for the groups to have the use of television sets at the times of transmissions. It engages local teachers or agronomists as instructors to these groups, and arranges for the use of the premises of village clubs as consultation centres. It even ensures priority for the repair of television sets used by pupils of the Television Agricultural High School.

VI Enrolment

50. There is no entrance examination for pupils of the Television Agricultural High School, but applicants must submit the following documents to any agricultural high school with an external department: application to join; *curriculum vitae*; school record; testimonial from place of work or from the Village People's Council; copy of identity card; two photographs; doctor's certificate of state of health.

51. The general information pamphlet issued before the beginning of each academic year (which for television and other external pupils coincides with the calendar year) gives the addresses of all agricultural high schools with external departments. This document also contains details of the curriculum, dates of television lectures and enrolment instructions.

52. Apart from those who have successfully completed the course at a basic agricultural school (the usual entrance requirement), applicants with certain other qualifications are accepted, provided that they undergo a preparatory course of one semester in general-education subjects.

53. Most applicants for the Television Agricultural High School choose to register at the school nearest to their home. This may have distinct practical advantages, especially as it is possible to change from the television system to the sessional system at the end of any semester (or vice versa). In the final three semesters all pupils follow the sessional system.

VII Organization, control and staffing

54. Since the experimental stage is not yet over, the organization and administration of the Television Agricultural High School have been kept as informal as possible. It has no constitution or book of rules. The entire project depends on the good-will and co-operation of the three responsible bodies, namely, the Ministry of Agriculture, Polish Television and the Union of Socialist Village Youth. The possibility of having a board of governors at some time in the future has been discussed but not everyone favours the idea.

55. The degree of informality is not as surprising as it might otherwise be, if one bears in mind the fact that the Television Agricultural High School is not really an institution at all in its own right, but rather an arrangement between existing institutions.

56. Academic consultants on methodological problems are appointed by an inspector of the Department of Education in the Ministry of Agriculture. These

consultants (who hold other, full-time appointments) arrange the general framework of the course, including examinations, and write some of the teaching materials. They are paid by the Ministry of Agriculture.

57. According to present arrangements a general conference of high-school teachers dealing with television pupils is held once a year in the summer to discuss problems, to exchange opinions with representatives of the ministry and to make recommendations. About twice a year conferences of the academic consultants and representatives of the three responsible bodies are held. In addition, further small meetings of staff are held as and when considered necessary by the head teachers of the high schools involved.

58. The pupils are able to make their views felt by (a) turning to their teachers in the high schools with suggestions (which the teacher is required to communicate to the Ministry), or (b) writing to the Agricultural Education Department of Polish Television. There is, however, no live contact between the television lecturers and pupils.

59. Pupils' views are also sought by the Centre of Public Opinion and Broadcasting Research of Polish Television, and by an inspector of the Department of Education in the Ministry of Agriculture who travels round the country, inspecting arrangements in agricultural external departments and meeting pupils.

60. The television lectures are, of course, the responsibility of the Agricultural Education Department of Polish Television, but they are planned in consultation with the other two responsible bodies. The television editor of a given programme or series of programmes engages the services of an academic consultant or consultants. Wide use is made of outside broadcasts. Visits are made to students' farms. Actors are employed in dramatized episodes in the Polish-language programmes. Lecturers are chosen jointly at the conferences held twice yearly. Responsibility for the various subjects is distributed regionally to television centres as follows: Gdańsk, physics and chemistry; Poznań, animal husbandry and agricultural mechanization; Szczecin, plant cultivation, zoology, and botany; Warsaw, plant preservation and the Polish language; Łódź, history; and Wrocław, mathematics.

61. Programmes are transmitted to the whole country simultaneously on Channel I.

The academic year runs as follows: Semester I, February to June; vacation: July to August; Semester II, September to December. The first year began in February 1973.

62. During the vacation there are weekly half-hour television programmes to enable pupils to maintain contact with their studies. In September to December 1974 Semester IV was transmitted and Semester II rebroadcast.

VIII Finance

63. Little information is available on the finances of the Television Agricultural High School, owing to the fact that it is not a separate institution with its own budget, but an arrangement between existing institutions. The main financial burdens fall on Polish Television and the external departments of agricultural high schools, under various larger headings in whose budgets the costs of the Television Agricultural High School are hidden. All its funds,

however, have their origin under various headings of the State budget. Hardly anyone is employed full-time in the school and it is not possible to assess what proportion of the work of those involved is applied to this particular aspect of the external system or what proportion of their salary relates to this work.

64. Although the Ministry of Agriculture has overall organizational control, it does not have financial control. The cost of television programmes is met from the budget of Polish Radio and Television, and each agricultural high school is financed from its own voivodeship. Capital outlay was minimal as all the buildings and equipment were already in existence. The overall annual cost to public funds, however, is estimated by the Ministry of Agriculture at 600 to 700 zlotys (£12.50 to £14.50) per student.

65. From the pupil's point of view, costs are low; as in the case of full-time and external education of all kinds, there is no registration fee and tuition is free. The guide-workbooks are provided free of charge at the beginning of each semester. When they attend Sunday consultations or examinations, pupils are accommodated free of charge on the school premises. The cost of textbooks, travel and meals during consultations is borne by the pupils themselves.

66. In each high school, certain staff members are selected to be teachers of television pupils. No separate appointments are made for this purpose. So far as possible a teacher's time with television pupils will be arranged to constitute part of his normal 22 contact-hours a week. But if this load is exceeded he is paid overtime (like any other teacher). It is not possible to say how much overtime is incurred due to the demands of the Television Agricultural High School.

IX Audience research

67. Opinion research among the pupils was initiated almost simultaneously with the beginning of the television lectures. Since March 1973 the Centre of Public Opinion and Broadcasting Research (Ośrodek Badania Opinii Publicznej i Studiów Programowych) has been carrying out research of two kinds: (a) to find out about the pupils themselves, their attitudes and motivation; (b) to assess the efficiency of the teaching system.

68. It has been established that the overwhelming majority of pupils (83 per cent) are working in agriculture or occupations linked with agriculture. Individual farmers constitute 70 per cent of the whole. The majority of pupils are young: 81 per cent are under 30, and only 1 per cent is over 50. Those who left school no more than five years ago constitute 63 per cent whereas only 12 per cent left school more than ten years ago. The proportion of men to women is almost even: 52 per cent men and 48 per cent women.

69. One question which the researchers set out to answer was whether pupils regarded their studies as a way of leaving the land by gaining a secondary education, or as a way of continuing (or entering) employment in agriculture. The results of the research show that, in the main, study in the Television Agricultural High School is regarded as a road to employment in agriculture.

70. The researchers also looked into the question of why pupils chose the television system, and discovered that the most widespread reason was the ability to study at home.

71. An experiment was carried out to discover the pupils' reactions to two different television chemistry lectures, representative of two different pedagogical

approaches. The first (1) attempted to stimulate the pupil's curiosity and then to satisfy it by explanation. The second (2) presented information in a ready-made form.

72. The research showed that the increase in knowledge (assessed by tests conducted immediately before and after the lectures) was considerably greater after type (1) than after type (2). Research also showed a marked preference among the pupils for type (1). In other words, type (1) was shown to be not only more popular but also, objectively, more efficient.

73. Research has also been carried out into such matters as suitability of the level of instruction to the pupils' level of preparation.

74. Whereas the individual farmer to a large extent can arrange his own day and hence arrange his studies accordingly, the employed farm worker is in a more difficult situation. Approximately half the employed pupils have stated that their employing organization looked favourably or very favourably on their decision to study in the Television Agricultural High School. The others encountered either indifference or lack of approval. Of those interviewed 39 per cent stated they had no one to turn to in case of difficulty with their studies; 83 per cent were taking part in Sunday consultations, generally (according to their statements) less often than once a month. The evidence is that some pupils feel that a consultation once a month is not enough for the most difficult subjects.

75. Opinions on the textbooks show that most were generally regarded as 'good'. Only three had a bad reception: the category 'bad' was applied by 31 per cent to the mathematics textbook; by 13 per cent to the chemistry textbook; by 6 per cent to the agricultural mechanization textbook. Opinions of the guide-workbooks were similarly distributed: almost 20 per cent applied the category 'bad' to the mathematics guide-workbook; 7 per cent to the chemistry guide-workbook. It is thought that these assessments may to some extent be determined by the nature of the subject and by the unfamiliarity of the aids: 20 per cent said that the guide-workbooks became more useful towards the end of the semester.

76. Research has included the straight evaluation of certain courses by pupils in terms of 'interesting/boring', 'too short/too long', 'useful/of no use to farmers', etc. The results were discussed at a conference after the first semester, and this resulted in a number of changes, notably in the times of repeat broadcasts and the methods of teaching mathematics.

77. Audience research shows that of the pupils registered in the first semester, 46 per cent were continuing their studies in the second semester (September to December 1973). Since the average overall drop-out rate among external students is about 75 per cent and the majority of drop-outs occur in the first year, the figure of 53 per cent (1 per cent transferred to the sessional system) is considered small. In February 1973, 10,500 pupils began their studies in the first semester of the Television Agricultural High School. At the beginning of the second year there were only 5,000 left. The number registered to begin the first semester in the second year (February 1974) was 6,000.

X Conclusions

78. Despite the opportunities offered by the conventional external departments of agricultural high schools, external pupils working full-time on the land

have great difficulty in completing their secondary education, owing both to the nature of their work and to the inaccessibility of rural areas. The Television Agricultural High School is an extension of the conventional external system, which attempts to reduce this difficulty by (a) the use of television, and (b) the organization through the Union of Socialist Village Youth of local study groups and teaching facilities.

79. It is hoped that the Television Agricultural High School will increase the pass rate among external students, and it seems that it may produce something in the neighbourhood of 2,000 to 3,000 farm workers with secondary vocational qualifications out of every annual intake. (The entry of 10,500 in the first year was probably exceptional and is likely to settle down to something like half that number in the future.)

80. The television system attracts pupils who would not otherwise have been able to pursue their secondary education and therefore (whatever its efficiency expressed as a pass-rate percentage) it will undoubtedly increase the total number of farm workers gaining secondary vocation qualifications.

81. While it is impossible to arrive at any figures, the use of existing buildings and staff clearly makes the cost very low, even if measured only in terms of the rather small proportion of pupils who are likely to graduate.

Appendix A Standardized reference data

Country, state or province	*Poland*
Area and climate	120,664 square miles. Maritime to continental.
Population	
Total (latest year)	33,068,000 (1972).
Estimated population aged 18	685,958 (1970).
Estimated percentage under 15	33.13 (1962).
Current annual growth rate (percentage)	0.8 (1965–72).
Government	
Main organizational structure	Unitary, with delegated administrative responsibilities to seventeen voivodeships and five provincial cities.
Political type	Socialist parliamentary government; people's republic.
Economy	
Political type	Mixed farming and developing industry. Key industries nationalized, but farms and small businesses can be privately owned.
Gross national product	
Total (latest year)	941,900 million zlotys (1972) (1 zloty= U.S.$0.05).
Per head	U.S.$1,425.
Average annual increase (percentage)	4.0 (1965–72).
Communications	
Ground/air	Quick and easy countryside system of roads, bus, rail and some air transport.
Mail/telephone	Adequate postal services; 3.6 telephones per 100 of population (1972).

Broadcasting

Main system(s) operating/ Principal authorities responsible	Komitet do Spraw Radia i Televizji (KSRT): a State-controlled body responsible for the planning and transmission of all radio and television services.
Radio	
Transmission coverage of main programme services with percentage of population reached	17 per cent. Proposed additional network with 100 per cent coverage.
Receiving capability for main programme services (percentage)	Virtually 100.
Television	
Transmission coverage as defined for radio	Chain 1: virtually 100 per cent. Chain 2: eight conurbations plus fifteen environs.
Receiving capability for main programme services (percentage)	56 (1973).
Monochrome or colour	Some colour. SECAM system.

Education

Type of system(s)	Entirely publicly controlled and financed.
Main authorities responsible and powers	
At school level	Ministry of Education and Upbringing.
At post-secondary level	Ministry of Science, Higher Education and Technology.
End of full-time school attendance	
Legal	Compulsory and free between 6 and 15.
De facto	75 per cent voluntarily stay until 18 (1972).
Proportion of 18-year-old age group involved in education	Total 45.7 per cent (1970).

Institution/system under study

Brief for study and reason for inclusion	Polish Television Agricultural High School. An example of multi-media teaching at a distance through co-operation between existing institutions.
Description of subject studied	The institution and its vocational secondary education for farm workers.
Origins	Resolution of the Union of Socialist Village Youth (fourth congress 1970).
Educational authority(ies) and roles	Department of Education in the Ministry of Agriculture has overall responsibility.
Communications authority(ies) and roles	Polish Television Authority, Agricultural Education Department.
Services provided	Wider opportunities of secondary education to adults both for vocational and non-vocational purposes. Should redress the imbalance in educational standards between town and country.

Eligibility to study	
(a) categories	Aged 17 and over.
(b) qualifications	Farm workers with Vocational School Certificate.
Terminal qualifications	Agricultural High School Certificate. Same academic content as conventional studies.
Instructional means used	Multi-media, i.e. set books, correspondence work, television, face-to-face schooling in high schools.
Personal input from students	Voluntary attendance at course centres for advice and tuition. Compulsory attendance at one session each semester for examinations.
Normal duration of study	Seven semesters in 3½ years; first four semesters through television, last three usual external studying.
Pedagogic effectiveness	54 per cent drop-out after first semester (usual external studies drop-out 75 per cent).

Numbers involved

Students	
Intake (latest year)	6,000 (February 1974).
Academic staff	
Full-time	No separate appointments; but there are academic consultants holding other full-time appointments who arrange general framework including examinations.
Part-time	Teachers in established agricultural high schools.
Other professional staff	
Number	Staff of Agricultural Education Department of Polish Television.

Finance

Recurrent expenditure	
By providing authorities (latest year)	600 to 700 zlotys per student.
Average annual outlay by student	No registration or tuition fees; purchases own textbooks and pays for incidental expenses.
Non-recurrent expenditure	
Gross, over first five years of new institution	Minimal capital outlay as all buildings and equipment already in existence.

Special assistance received

Financial	None beyond public funds (KSRT) and Agricultural High School funds.
Non-financial	University dependent upon existing educational communications infrastructure and co-operation with KSRT educational services.

Sources of further information

Educational

Dr Wanda Barcikowski, Education Specialist, Department of Education in Polish Ministry of Agriculture.

Broadcasting

Mr Maciej Znainecki, Chief Editor, Polish Television, Agricultural Education Department.
Dr Janina Frentzel-Zagorska, Senior Research Worker, Centre for Public Opinion, Research and Programme Studies, Polish Television.

Appendix B **Short bibliography**

The following four titles are especially useful:

Concise statistical yearbook on Poland 1973. Warsaw, 1973.
FRENTZEL-ZAGORSKA, J.; WYKA, A. *Research on effects of adult education*. Warsaw, 1973. (Paper given at GEAR conference, Hilversum, June 1973.)
Poland. A handbook. Warsaw, Interpress Publishers, 1974.
Resolution of the Seym of the Polish People's Republic, 12 April 1973. Unofficial translation released by Polish Interpress Agency.

See also:

Draft programme of universal secondary education. 1973. Unofficial translation released by Polish Interpress Agency.
Report on the state of education. 1973. Polish Interpress Agency (release). (Discussion.)
MAKOWIECKI, M. The growing role of agriculture. *Polish perspectives*, no. 2, 1974, p. 9–16.

Appendix C **Biographical note**

Gerald Stone is a graduate in Russian language and literature of London University and a Ph.D. After teaching languages at Bexhill Grammar School he became a lecturer at the University of Nottingham and later at Cambridge University. Since 1972 he has been a university lecturer in Slavonic languages at Oxford and a Fellow of Hertford College. He is the author of books and articles on Slavonic languages and peoples.

Correspondence education in the **Soviet Union**

Valentin Kuznetsov

The scale and range of part-time study at the post-secondary level in the Soviet Union is so great that any general review which failed to cover the experience of the U.S.S.R. would be seriously inadequate. Such a study was proposed and planned in some detail, the report to be the joint work of a member of the project team and of Professor Valentin Kuznetsov, now deputy director of a recently established specialist research bureau within the Ministry of Higher Education. The report would have been particularly timely since reforms of the present system to raise its efficiency and make greater use of the broadcast teaching media are under active consideration. Unfortunately, practical difficulties made it impossible to carry this plan into effect; instead, by the kindness of Professor Kuznetsov, we reproduce the gist of a lecture given by him in 1973. This gives a general idea of the situation at that date.

1. Higher education by correspondence has been in existence in the U.S.S.R. for more than fifty years, turning out highly trained persons in various branches of science ('specialists'[1]), technology and culture. The social significance of this system is difficult to overestimate: it offers a huge number of working people, regardless of age, an opportunity to receive a free higher education without having to leave their jobs.

2. All things considered, it is safe to assert that the system of higher education by correspondence has proved its worth and viability. It has an important role to play in the training of 'specialists' for the national economy.

3. Despite still current views to the contrary, correspondence education provides a high standard of training. Many alumni of higher correspondence education institutions have made outstanding achievements in their professional fields—they include Lenin and State prizewinners, top-ranking managerial workers and prominent scientists. Among them are Obolensky, Deputy Minister of Power Engineering of the U.S.S.R.; Dolgi, Director of the Podolsk Boiler Works; Glushkov, Doctor of Physics and Mathematics, Vice-President of the Academy of Sciences of the Ukrainian S.S.R.; and Predtechensky, Vice-Rector of the Moscow Civil Engineering Institute.

4. The backbone of the system consists of fourteen specialized institutions established as centres for research into the methodology of correspondence education, each concerned with a specific branch of the national economy. Twelve institutions of this kind, known as all-union (national) correspondence institutes and referred to here as Moscow correspondence institutes, are situated in Moscow, one is in Leningrad, and another in Kharkov. The names of a few of these institutes will suggest the fields of study covered; finance and economics, agriculture, mechanical engineering, civil engineering and electrical engineering. There are three polytechnical correspondence education institutes—in Moscow, Leningrad and Kharkov—whose purpose is to train engineers in many fields.

5. Apart from specialized institutes, many normal institutions of higher learning, which offer primarily full-time courses, have correspondence departments.

1. The Russian *spetsialist*, often translated into English as 'specialist', simply means a person who has trained for a particular profession (or even trade). It does not, as in English usage, imply knowledge of a high level in a restricted field.

6. While noting the importance of correspondence education in enabling people employed in the national economy to acquire higher job qualifications, and its beneficial effect on the all-round development of the individual, it must be accepted that to combine work and study at the same time is extremely difficult. With this consideration in mind, those who conceived the correspondence education system in the U.S.S.R. and developed its methods and practice based their work on a realistic view of man's capacity to combine these two activities, but they did so without lowering the standard of attainment.

7. This brings us to the conditions that should enable this goal to be realized. In my view, the conditions are these:

(a) Correspondence education should be designed to ensure that students are able to cover the whole course within the time prescribed.

(b) Persons who decide to enrol for a course without leaving their jobs should be provided with every facility to allow them to combine productive work in industry with the successful pursuit of studies.

8. In the case of the Soviet Union the following arrangements have been made in an attempt to meet the above conditions.

9. In the first place, a number of concessions has been given to persons engaged in correspondence studies. By government decree, correspondence students who make satisfactory progress are entitled to additional paid leave at their places of permanent employment: in the first and second years of study, 30 calendar days each year for laboratory practice, tests and examinations; in the third and subsequent year, 40 calendar days each year for laboratory practice, tests and examinations; additionally, 30 calendar days to take the State final examinations, and four months to prepare and present a diploma thesis.

10. The right to such additional paid leave is confined to students who make satisfactory progress (i.e. those whose work for the previous semester is not in arrears and those who have completed satisfactorily all oral and written tests by the start of the examinations).

11. Correspondence students are entitled to one day off from work every week for ten months prior to the presentation of their thesis or their final examination, the remuneration being half of the fares paid by a student in travelling to and from his place of study.

12. Correspondence students also enjoy some other privileges, including exemption from overtime and night shifts,

13. All this indicates that work-places which have an interest in their workers improving their knowledge take every step to ensure that productive work and study can be satisfactorily combined.

14. Now we turn to the other aspect of making highly trained 'specialists': the principles on which the system of correspondence education is based. We deal first with the study areas and areas of special study offered by correspondence education institutions. Naturally this list is not identical with that normally available in institutions offering full-time instruction.

15. Indeed, as the individual branches of science and technology make further progress, study becomes increasingly complicated. However much normal educational establishments may try, in some subject areas it is not practicable to organize correspondence courses. This limitation applies particularly to study involving a large amount of laboratory work and practical training. It is for this reason that physicians and anthropologists, for example,

and experts in some areas of physics, chemistry and radio electronics are not trained by correspondence in the U.S.S.R. (to mention only a few professional areas).

16. It must also be borne in mind that, as well as making certain fields of study more sophisticated, scientific and technological progress also produces new technical aids and new teaching techniques which facilitate the clear and convincing exposition of new scientific laws and the elucidation of complex processes. Consequently there is periodic revision of the list of subject areas thought suitable for correspondence education.

17. The correspondence education system in the U.S.S.R. is basically an efficient way of improving the qualifications of those at work. Because of this, the existing regulations governing enrolment give preference to persons choosing fields of study in line with the jobs they hold, and having a service record of at least six months in the professional areas concerned.

18. The educational establishments regularly send their staff out to the various relevant institutions which require their skills to recruit as many gifted young people for training as possible. Most of the higher-educational establishments run 8- to 10-month preparatory courses which make it possible for prospective applicants to cover the entrance examination syllabus for a reasonable fee. Free preparatory courses are launched a month before the entrance examination is due to begin. Those qualifying to take the competitive entry examinations are entitled to an additional 15 days leave without pay.

19. Owing to the arrangements outlined above, a high proportion of students at higher-educational establishments are studying subjects in line with their employment. Nearly all students at the Moscow Railway Engineering Correspondence Institute, the Moscow Textile and Light Industry Correspondence Institute and the Moscow Civil Engineering Correspondence Institute work and study in the same professional areas.

20. In whatever way the courses are arranged, the training of specialists in the correspondence system falls into two parts: theoretical teaching and practical work. The disadvantage of having a limited number of lectures and infrequent contact with a tutor is overcome by the provision of comprehensive study materials, by the student's own close contact with the conditions of production and by the opportunities he has to put his knowledge to immediate practical use. The two elements are closely linked. It can fairly be claimed that the correspondence education system ensures a full and close connexion between study and productive work.

21. New curricula are under consideration at the present time, which would lay down programmes under which correspondence students would be moved around work-places in accordance with a training plan.

22. In his first or second year, a student taking a correspondence course, let us say, at a civil engineering institute, might work as a fitter or concrete worker. In his third or fourth year he is in a position to discharge the duties of a middle-level technician, and in his final year, those of an engineer.

23. An important role has been played by the wide network of off-campus study and consultation centres set up in the U.S.S.R. under the aegis of the appropriate correspondence institute. This step has brought educational establishments closer to the students' homes, thus assisting them towards more regular habits of study.

24. Let us take the example of Podolsk—some forty kilometres from

Moscow. Before a study centre of the Moscow Polytechnical Correspondence Institute was set up there, students residing in and around the town had to go to Moscow for practical training, laboratory practice, lectures, tests and examinations. Today this town has a study centre of its own, and the students can do all their academic work in their home town. They now have more time to devote to their studies.

25. Special advisory committees have been established at many correspondence institutes. Composed of representatives of both teaching staff and the industrial enterprises concerned, all of whom serve in a voluntary capacity, these committees not only systematically supervise the students' progress but also give them all possible assistance, among other things seeing that they are promoted to higher posts in accordance with their academic achievements as they complete each successive year of study. Such committees are working well at the Stavropol Agricultural Institute and the Moscow Railway Engineering Correspondence Institute, to name only two educational establishments.

26. One of the most vital tasks confronting the Soviet higher-education system is to organize teaching and learning on a scientifically sound basis. With this aim in view, long-term plans are now being drawn up for the development of correspondence education in the next fifteen to twenty years, in terms of scope and educational standard. Eminent Soviet scientists and scholars are helping higher-education authorities to tackle this question.

27. A solution to the problem of putting education on a scientifically sound basis can hardly be possible unless new teaching techniques and modern teaching aids are employed in the correspondence-education system. We are making every effort to ensure that each study centre is provided with tape-recorded lectures by experts on fundamental problems covered by the courses, and also with films, filmstrips and slides. The study centres must have television and radio links with industrial enterprises and institutions where large groups of their students work.

28. I should like to emphasize that television is one of the most efficient vehicles for improving the content of instruction, in particular for correspondence education. There is every reason to believe that the incursion of scientific and technological progress into the domain of education is a fact which is independent of whether or not teachers are prepared to incorporate the products of educational technology into systems of teaching.

29. Though educationists are as yet far from unanimous as to the advantages and disadvantages of television as a means of instruction, it has already displayed wide-ranging teaching potential which has been proved in practice. We do not propose to present here a thorough analysis of the special qualities of television, and its consequent teaching potential—a description of this kind would take too much space. Instead, we should like to examine one specific aspect of the problem—that of using television as a means of keeping the content of instruction up to date and introducing new teaching techniques.

30. I do not think that many educationists would claim that university and college courses react promptly to every manifestation of scientific and technological progress. Let us consider chemistry—a science which is advancing rapidly. The amount of material published on problems of chemistry and chemical technology is growing fast, since nearly 40 per cent of the research, experimentation and design in the world is carried out in this particular field. At the present rate the amount published in this field should double every ten

years. Yet the content of chemistry courses is slow to change—despite the fact that chemistry is one of the fundamental sciences that lie at the basis of all mankind's achievements. As to specialized, applied disciplines, their content becomes obsolete very fast as the scientific and technological revolution proceeds.

31. A teacher thus has an essential obligation to revise his course constantly so that it is always up to date in its content and, incidentally, in methods of presentation. As the scientific and technological revolution accelerates one should be constantly ready to renew the study matter. Every new development in science and technology should be reflected in instruction.

32. Television seems to be indispensable in this respect. 'Today's scientific discovery or practical advance is part of tomorrow's university course'—this motto, which until recently could only be regarded as fantasy, is becoming routine practice with teachers who, both theoretically and practically, appreciate the educational potential of television, including its ability to help them keep up with the times; they realize that they will not fulfil their educational mission if they cling to the old ways.

33. A printed lecture, a book, a slide or even a film becomes in fact obsolete the moment it is produced. Science and its applications are developing at such a rate that much of what has just been discovered may become antiquated even before it finds its way into textbooks and lecture courses. This is where television comes in: it makes possible the delivery of updated information to the student—a circumstance of first importance at a time of technological revolution.

34. Televised programmes for correspondence students have been broadcast regularly in the U.S.S.R. since the 1964/65 academic year. Lecture courses of social sciences and general science and technical subjects, as laid down by the correspondence education curriculum, are televised in twenty-three cities of the Soviet Union, including the capitals of nine constituent republics.

35. Lecturers of high academic standing are invited to read the lectures, which are accompanied by demonstrations of experiments, working models, animated cartoon filmstrips, etc.

36. Television is used on a large scale by the Moscow and North-Western Polytechnical Correspondence Institutes, the Tyumen Industrial Institute, the Urals Polytechnical Institute, and a number of higher schools in the Ukrainian S.S.R., Uzbekistan, and the Byelorussian S.S.R. An analysis of the academic achievements of correspondence students who systematically view instructional programmes on television makes it clear that such students keep up with the curriculum with less effort, do test work better and more punctually, and reveal a more profound knowledge in examinations.

37. We feel, however, that despite the immense contribution made by the wide use of television and other technical aids, the decisive factor is still sufficiently highly qualified teaching staff. Contact between correspondence students, scientists and scholars not only helps with the assimilation of knowledge but provides intellectual stimulation.

38. Now a few words about university education by correspondence. I should like to make it clear that university education is regarded in the U.S.S.R. only as one specific form of higher education—along with the higher education provided by institutes, academies and higher technical schools. This means that the diplomas awarded by all institutions of higher learning in the U.S.S.R. have the same validity and testify to the same level of education. A specific feature of

our university system is that it develops on a uniform socialist economic basis, and follows uniform principles in organization, academic activity and the instruction and education of students. Specialists are trained on the basis of uniform curricula, syllabuses, textbooks and study materials. All this opens up broad possibilities for the co-ordination of university education, the exchange of experience, mutual assistance and mutual influence.

39. All universities in our country—of which there are sixty-one—offer education by correspondence. There are many universities at which much emphasis is laid on specialist training by correspondence. We would single out the Rostov-on-Don State University, which offers eleven correspondence courses: in Russian language and literature, mathematics, mechanics, history, philosophy, political economy, geography, jurisprudence, biology, geology, and journalism.

40. New functions of correspondence education have become increasingly pronounced in recent years, especially in the area of university education. Correspondence education offers:

(a) Higher education with a view to: (i) providing a theoretical foundation for a job already being performed (for example, journalists without professional qualifications in journalism, a thousand of whom are currently taking the journalism course at the Moscow University alone; or working teachers without diplomas, especially those teaching in senior forms in village schools); (ii) satisfying the growing intellectual and cultural needs of people in our society.

(b) A second higher education with a view to: (i) change of career; (ii) advanced training (for example, for graduate engineers wishing to improve their knowledge of mathematics, or for physicians of psychology).

41. As all the spheres of endeavour in society become amply supplied with graduate staff and the standard of living of the working people continues to rise, the emphasis will shift increasingly to the last function mentioned above.

The Open University of the **United Kingdom**

John Scupham

Contents

I Introduction

1. This study of the British Open University aims to tell the story of its invention, creation and development and to bring out the circumstances and influences that affected it.

2. The study is confined to the first-degree courses. It does not deal with other aspects—postgraduate study, post-experience courses—or with its consultancy services.

3. The conclusions (section XIII) call attention to certain characteristics considered to be of interest to those in other countries concerned with the provision of adult learning opportunities of a non-traditional type, and make suggestions about the possible relevance of the Open University experience.

II The national context

4. The United Kingdom is a compact, highly industrialized and predominantly urban country with a parliamentary government. Its population at the last (1971) census was 55,347,000. It has easy communications, good postal services and a well-established public-service broadcasting system (supplemented by commercial services) with two television channels and four radio channels at its disposal, all of them with virtually complete national coverage.

5. In 1972 the gross national product stood at £53,940 million, and the current expenditure of public authorities on goods and services at £11,702 million, with education accounting for nearly £3,000 million, i.e. about one-quarter of the total. In the same year the total income of the forty-four United Kingdom universities from all sources was about £300 million, of which some 80 per cent came from government grants for teaching and research.

6. The educational system of the country is at all levels predominantly publicly controlled and publicly financed. The persistence of private schools is statistically of little importance; 95 per cent of children attend State schools. There are at present no universities or institutions of higher education outside the orbit of the State-financed system.

7. The ultimate responsibility for the national complex of educational institutions lies with the Department of Education and Science of the central government. The immediate control and conduct of educational establishments

of all kinds within the public sector (with the exception of universities) is, however, in the hands of local government authorities in their capacity as local education authorities, and forms a major part of their responsibilities. The universities, in spite of being State-supported, enjoy a very high degree of academic and administrative independence. The scale of their operations and the direction of their capital expenditure are nevertheless subject to government decisions enforced by financial sanctions. Government money is channelled to them through a government advisory body known as the University Grants Committee, the members of which are drawn from the universities themselves. Its allocations of money to them, for broadly specified purposes in accordance with current government policy, are made on a quinquennial basis.

8. Since the Second World War, the United Kingdom has been engaged in remedying the deficiencies of its educational system and has embarked on a massive programme of educational expansion. Since 1950, the annual growth of educational expenditure, running at an average rate of nearly 5 per cent, has greatly exceeded the percentage growth of the gross national product. The school-leaving age was raised from 14 to 15 years in 1946, and again to 16 years as recently as 1973. Concurrently there has been a steady shift from a highly selective bipartite school set-up, which provided places in secondary schools with an academic bias (known as grammar schools) for about 20 per cent of the population, and assumed that the rest was incapable of much academic progress, towards a system of 'comprehensive' all-ability schools.

9. Under the older system, only the grammar schools offered extended secondary education beyond the age of compulsory school attendance and prepared pupils for the academic school-leaving examination taken at the age of 18 years, the Advanced Level of the General Certificate of Education ('A' level) which serves as the normal entrance requirement of United Kingdom universities. Boys and girls who failed at the age of 11 years to secure entrance to a grammar school, or who left the grammar school at the age of 16 years, were thus debarred from proceeding to a university education, except in so far as there were limited opportunities for transfer from non-academic ('secondary modern') schools to grammar schools at 16, and for study after that age in colleges of further education.

10. Concurrently with the change in the system, there has been a large and continuing increase in the number of secondary-school pupils staying voluntarily at school to take this examination, and a constant percentage of those attaining university entrance standards (i.e. 'A'-level passes in at least two subjects) has actually sought university admission. The country has conseqently become involved in a large expansion of its conventional university provision. In 1939, there were only 50,000 full-time students at the twenty-four then existing United Kingdom universities. By 1972, ten new universities had been founded, ten colleges of advanced technology had been upgraded to university status and the total number of students was 246,000. A landmark in this development was the report of a government Committee on Higher Education (the Robbins Report) in 1963 which enunciated the principle, accepted by all subsequent governments, that 'courses of higher education should be available to all who are qualified by ability and attainment to pursue them, and who wish to do so'. The report called for the provision of enough new places by 1980 to raise from 8 to 17 per cent the proportion of the age group entering full-time higher education.

11. The consequent expansion has not only transformed the universities proper, but has also led to the designation of thirty technical colleges as centres of advanced study. These thirty, called polytechnics, offer full-time, part-time and 'sandwich' courses (i.e. courses interspersed with work experience) leading to technical qualifications, and particularly to the Higher National Certificate[1] which is the approved professional qualification in a number of technological fields. They also provide courses leading to degrees, mainly in scientific subjects, which are validated by a new body, the Council for National Academic Awards, set up for this purpose in 1964, and courses leading to the external degrees of the University of London. The University of London is the only United Kingdom university which admits to its degree examinations external students (who must have satisfied its ordinary matriculation requirements). It offers them no teaching (except on a very limited scale in the field of commerce). This is provided for those who want it either by the technical colleges and polytechnics, or by commercial correspondence colleges catering for the home-based student. In 1970, 14,493 students at the colleges and polytechnics were studying for a London University first degree, 1,474 for a university higher degree and 21,597 for degrees of the Council for National Academic Awards. A million and a half students attend day-release or evening classes in colleges of further education or technical colleges maintained by local education authorities. Most of them are aiming for lower-level technical and vocational qualifications. A further million and a half are enrolled in classes, mainly of a cultural or recreational kind, at evening institutes of the same authorities.

12. To complete the picture, it should be added that nearly all the United Kingdom universities have extramural departments which provide courses and organize classes of a non-vocational nature. They work in partnership with local education authorities, and with various voluntary bodies which are grant-aided for the purpose by the central government, in particular the Workers' Educational Association. In 1971, more than a quarter of a million students were enrolled in such classes, but mostly for short courses, and only a very small minority could be reckoned as serious students working at university level on sustained courses.

13. One other background factor has had a very direct bearing on the development of the Open University. Teachers in the grammar schools and 'public'[2] schools, and specialist teachers in the new comprehensive schools have been, and are, drawn from the ranks of university graduates. In the past only a minority of them had undertaken a further professional training as teachers, though this has now become almost universal. Teachers in primary schools and in other types of secondary school were, and still are, mainly drawn from training colleges for teachers with lower academic admission standards than universities. At these colleges of education (as they are now called) the student undertakes a concurrent study of selected academic subjects and of pedagogy, leading to a qualification known as the Certificate in Education. Until 1959, those entering the colleges enrolled for a course of only two years duration. It then became a three-year course, and from 1970 onwards a small number of students of high academic ability have been allowed to undertake a

1. Designated the Higher National Diploma when achieved by full-time study.
2. The most expensive and exclusive private schools of the United Kingdom are traditionally designated 'public' schools.

fourth year of more specialized studies leading to the new degree of B.Ed. (Bachelor of Education) awarded by the local university with which the college of education is affiliated. In 1970/71 there were 112,177 students in these colleges. The long-term national policy is to establish a wholly graduate teaching force; but there will be a continuing output of non-graduates from the colleges of education for many years. In the meanwhile, graduates are on higher salary scales than non-graduates.

14. As far as the Open University is concerned, the following conclusions emerge from the foregoing survey:

(a) Since it has proved possible thus to increase the proportion of the population going on to university studies without any lowering of examination standards or increase in the failure rate, there must be large reserves of potential academic ability that has never been fully developed in the adult population. Even as late as 1966, the acceptance rate of qualified applicants for university places was no more than 66 per cent, and some 30,000 boys and girls failed to satisfy their academic ambitions. Looking further back, the Planning Committee of the Open University estimated that there must be at least 1 million people born too early to reap the benefits of increasing educational opportunity who would have been eligible for university entrance if the targets set by the Robbins Report had been reached thirty years ago. While it could not be supposed that a majority of them would be able and willing to undertake advanced study after a gap of years, it was clear that there were among them large numbers of men and women who had pursued some form of vocational or cultural study since leaving school, and who might well wish to go further.

(b) In particular, that group includes a large number of certificated non-graduate teachers (some 250,000 in a total teaching force of some 400,000) who did not have the opportunity to take the B.Ed. degree or otherwise to attain graduate status.

(c) There will probably be a continuing shortage of places for qualified school leavers in the established universities and polytechnics now that the school-leaving age has been raised to 16 years, though the latest figures show a marked decline in demand, and some 80 per cent of applicants are now securing places.

(d) There is a massive demand among the adult population for educational facilities, and especially for vocationally oriented educational facilities. At the lower levels, this demand is satisfactorily met by the local education authorities.

(e) Until the advent of the Open University, the mature man or woman in full employment had only very limited opportunities of proceeding to a degree. Those who left school early and who wished to take an external London degree had to face the preliminary hurdle of matriculation, involving them in lengthy studies outside the range of their adult interests. Those who possessed the necessary qualifications for enrolment as degree students had teaching available to them only if they lived within range of an institution offering instruction at the right level in their chosen subjects, or if they enrolled as paying students of a correspondence college using limited traditional methods.

15. It may be added that whereas all students accepted for full-time courses in higher education receive through the local education authority a mandatory

grant sufficient to cover their tuition and living expenses (subject to a parental means test on a sliding scale), part-time students receive such grants only as an act of grace at the discretion of the authority. Some authorities are much more generous than others.

III The origins and history of the project

16. The idea of a national institution which would remedy these deficiencies and contribute to a fuller use of the national pool of ability derives from a number of scattered sources, but owes its embodiment to the British politician Harold Wilson. New British universities of the conventional pattern have owed their origin to local action, though the actual establishment by charter is an act of State. The initiative in establishing the Open University came from the Labour Government of 1964–70, and their role in the creation of this novel and politically controversial institution was decisive.

17. On 8 September 1963 Mr Wilson, the leader of the Labour Party, then in opposition, announced that his party was working on plans for a 'University of the Air'. The new institution, as he saw it, would provide through television and radio programmes, reinforced by correspondence tuition, tutorial classes and short residential courses, a new way of obtaining formal qualifications of university standard. It would also offer professional and technical refresher courses. In the spring of that year, he had visited Chicago to examine the city's Television College. He has since spoken of successive visits to the Soviet Union in the course of which he was greatly impressed by the organization of its university correspondence courses.

18. Mr Wilson's party took office in the autumn of 1964 and, early in the next year, he transferred Miss Jennie Lee (now Baroness Lee), to the Department of Education and Science as a Minister of State with special responsibility for the arts and for the development of his new educational project. That summer, she established a small Advisory Committee to explore the possibilities, taking the chair herself and making it clear from the start that a policy decision which she fully endorsed had already been taken. The university thus had its origins in the realm of personal conviction, and not in any systematic survey of the educational needs of the adult population. It found a place in the Labour Party's plan for education without public debate, and its claim on public resources was never publicly weighed against other educational claims to limited resources.

19. Miss Lee came of a mining family, had found her way to a Scottish university and was familiar with the pursuit of knowledge under difficulties both through her own personal experience and through that of her late husband, Aneurin Bevan, a miner's son and a leading left-wing politician of his generation. It was her determination that everyone, no matter what his formal schooling might have been, should in mature life have access to the highest levels of educational opportunity, and her pertinacity which ensured the survival of Mr Wilson's scheme. It was her insistance that nothing less than the creation of a new university primarily concerned with degree courses would meet the needs of the students whom she had in mind which determined the form which that scheme took.

20. The deliberations of the Advisory Committee resulted in an official

White Paper which met with a hostile, or at best tepid, reception. The decision of the government to go ahead was in no sense a response to pressures from outside, or to public demand; it was a political act of faith, calling for determination. The scheme was consonant with the basic philosophy of the party as the champion of the educationally underprivileged, and with its emphasis at the time on its role in making the fullest use of the latest technologies for the modernization of the United Kingdom. Even so, there were sceptics in the Labour cabinet, which accounted for some delay. It is not surprising that a dubious plan put forward as part of a party political programme encountered direct opposition from the rival party. Furthermore, the White Paper was published at a time of financial stringency and cuts in government expenditure on education. Both the local education authorities and the universities were anxious that public money should not be diverted to an untried venture at the expense of their own plans for educational expansion. It seemed likely that the project would have few friends and would be in danger of abandonment if there should be a change of government. An institution in being might, however, have a better chance of survival than a paper scheme. There was therefore a sense of urgency about the next stages of the planning process.

21. The Advisory Committee was succeeded in September 1967 by a government-appointed Planning Committee. Its formal brief was to work out a comprehensive plan for an Open University as outlined in the White Paper, and to prepare a draft charter and statutes. (A United Kingdom university can be established and can operate only under the authority of a royal charter, issued in the name of the sovereign by the Privy Council. This is a non-political organ of government consisting of men eminent in many fields, appointed for life by successive governments. Draft university charters must not only undergo the scrutiny of its staff and members. They must be open before issue to inspection, comment and objection by any interested body, and notably by the established universities.)

22. Since it was already clear that the Open University would need the practical co-operation of the existing agencies in the field of higher education, it was important that they should all be represented on the Planning Committee. Since also the prestige of the new university and its degrees would in its early years depend largely on acceptance by the existing universities, it was essential that the Planning Committee should include a strong contingent of men and women of distinction drawn from the university world who themselves had faith in the venture, and whose authority would give it credence with their unconvinced colleagues. In view of the prevailing scepticism and hostility in university circles, such men and women were not easy to find. The government fortunately found the ideal chairman in Sir Peter Venables, the vice-chancellor of the University of Aston in Birmingham, who had been responsible for the transformation of that institution from a college of advanced technology into a modern technological university, and who was acutely aware of the resistances to be encountered. Four other vice-chancellors and ex-vice-chancellors also agreed to serve on the committee, together with representatives of the local education authorities, of the university extramural departments and of the voluntary bodies concerned with adult education.

23. The business of the Planning Committee was to produce a workable outline plan which enabled a start to be made without predetermining too many of the questions which would be the concern of the permanent staff. In addition

to its formal duties, it had to undertake a major task of public relations, involving detailed consultation with many interests. It had furthermore to secure the interest and enlist the expertise in educational broadcasting of the British Broadcasting Corporation (BBC), and negotiate an agreement with the BBC for the production and transmission of the radio and television required, to appoint a vice-chancellor and assist him in the recruitment of senior staff and to select a site for the headquarters of the university. The committee held its first meeting on 23 October 1967, and altogether held ten full meetings. At these, it discussed reports and papers from the three working groups that it established, namely, ways and means, students and curriculum, and constitution and organization. These groups held in all forty-one meetings, which included discussions with representatives of a wide range of public bodies and institutions, and the consideration of evidence submitted by such bodies and individuals.

24. The report of the Planning Committee was completed by the end of 1968 and published early in 1969. Since it was necessarily the work of busy men sparing what time they could for its deliberations, the task could not have been accomplished in less than fifteen months. The committee remained in being to continue the recruitment of staff until July, when it handed over its powers to the council and senate as constituted by the university charter. Twelve of its members were appointed to the council, providing a valuable element of continuity.

IV Planning and university status

25. It must be emphasized that the pedagogic approach, the teaching methods and the pattern of operation described later could prove equally effective and appropriate whatever the academic level of the course and whatever the governing bodies of the institution might be. In these latter respects the decisions of the Planning Committee were determined by the intention to create a university which would come to enjoy parity of esteem with other universities. For that purpose, acceptance by the existing universities was judged to be essential. The committee, constituted as it was, was concerned to pay full regard to their views, susceptibilities and interests, and the attitudes then prevailing within them could not be ignored. From a formal point of view they would have the right to comment on the draft charter, and would wish to ensure that it conformed to their accepted standards. Beyond that, the acceptance of the university as academically respectable was of vital importance for the recruitment of staff of the right calibre, and for the public recognition of Open University degrees as having parity with others.

26. The university world is, however, deeply conservative in habits of thought, especially in so far as methods of teaching are concerned. British universities have in the past given hardly any systematic attention to that aspect of their work (as was shown by a government report published in 1964, the Hale Report on University Methods of Teaching). They have relied on lecturing without giving any training to their lecturers; and they have attached an importance to personal contacts and face-to-face teaching in very small groups which can find only a very imperfect reflection in the swollen and cost-conscious modern university. They have been very slow to use closed-circuit television and other new teaching techniques for their own purpose, and have

hardly begun to explore the possibility of recorded courses shared among universities. They have undervalued the possibilities of broadcasting as an educational agency, associating it with 'show-business' and the exploitation of personality. The idea of teaching at a distance was therefore wholly alien to them, and the phrase with which Mr Wilson had launched his idea, 'A University of the Air', was a handicap which soon had to be discarded, since it merely suggested to the university world a meretricious attempt to provide a highroad to learning without effort. 'Degrees while you dust' as one popular newspaper put it. Indeed, the universities were, and remain, convinced that any way of providing higher education but their own is necessarily an inferior way; a substitute for those who have unfortunately missed, or are excluded by circumstances from, the real thing. But the teaching function of the university is nevertheless still undervalued in relation to its function in the advancement of knowledge, and appointment and promotion depend very much more on research and publications than on teaching skills.

27. In these circumstances the Planning Committee tended to work on the unspoken assumption that bold educational innovation would be more readily accepted in the United Kingdom if it were tempered by conservatism, and that the Open University should not diverge unnecessarily or too far from the practice of other universities in its general ethos, its modes of government or its academic curriculum.

28. The decisions that sprang from those assumptions were not inevitable in the United Kingdom, and might not be at all appropriate elsewhere. Those relating to the age of admission and to lower-level courses may prove to have been tactical decisions with no long-term validity. They were, however, all taken advisedly after careful consideration, and have had a continuing and in some ways self-perpetuating influence on the development of the new institution. Their implications are dealt with in the separate sections below, and are only summarily dealt with in the next two paragraphs.

29. In the first place, it was decided that the university must aim at providing a wide and comprehensive range of courses, including advanced courses. It must not operate initially at any lower level than first-degree courses, since other universities did so only through specialized extramural departments whose work lay outside the main stream of university activity, and even to offer lower-level courses would be to lose caste and be reckoned a second-rate institution. It must recruit a highly qualified academic staff, using the same criteria for appointment as used by other universities. It must initiate and provide facilities for research. Finally, it must not trespass on the preserves of existing institutions, or give any colour to the belief that it could offer a satisfactory and cheap way of extending facilities for higher education to students of school-leaving age which would obviate the need to create conventional university places for all qualified applicants. In the view of the Planning Committee it was always preferable for those aged 16 to 21 years in employment to be released from that employment for sandwich courses at technological universities and polytechnics, and only those whose circumstances made that impossible should be enrolled in courses of the Open University.

30. As a legacy of this tenderness towards existing institutions and conformity to their norms, there are some strains in the university between its more radically and its more traditionally minded members of staff. They find expression over comparatively trivial issues, like university ceremonial and the

adoption of academic dress for graduates of the university, and over larger issues like the desirability of examinations. These strains are in all probability no greater than those in long-established institutions.

V The government and organization of the university

31. The charter of the Open University states that its objects are the advancement and dissemination of learning through teaching and research by a diversity of means such as broadcasting and technological devices appropriate to higher education, by correspondence tuition, residential courses and seminars, and in other relevant ways. The university is also required to provide education of university and professional standards for its students, and to promote the educational well-being of the community generally.

32. Otherwise it follows fairly closely the pattern of other university charters issued since the last war. The university is governed by a council which includes among its membership representatives of the academic staff, of the part-time counselling and tutorial staff, of students and of a number of external organizations such as the Privy Council, the Committee of University Vice-Chancellors and Principals, the BBC, the Royal Society (the leading British scientific body) and the local education authorities. Subject to the academic powers of the senate, the council exercises general control over the university's affairs but is particularly concerned with its finances and property, and with staff matters.

33. Some governing bodies are ciphers. The council of the Open University is not of merely formal importance. It holds nine meetings a year, including a two-day residential meeting, to decide major matters of policy referred to it by its own committees and by appropriate university bodies. As an innovating and rapidly expanding institution with nation-wide ramifications and external relationships, the university has needed the guidance of lay members' experience in business and in local government as well as in higher education. It is chaired by the pro-chancellor (until mid-1974 the former chairman of the Planning Committee), who needs to have political acumen as well as wide educational knowledge and administrative ability, and has as an *ex officio* member a treasurer chosen for his skill and experience in large-scale finance.

34. The senate is the academic authority of the university. It comprises over 450 members at present, and includes all the central and regional academic staff and other senior central staff, with elected representatives of the part-time tutorial and counselling staff, course assistants and research assistants, the twelve senior BBC producers and six further BBC producers elected by the BBC staff. It is chaired by the vice-chancellor and meets four times a year.

35. The senate controls the university's teaching and research, regulates its examinations and is concerned with the institution of courses of study and degrees.

36. With an average attendance of 150 members, the Senate is obviously too large for effective discussion and decision-making, but the staff concerned attach so much importance to the conception of the university as a complete democracy that they are unwilling to transform the senate into a smaller representative body. In this respect, they afford a cautionary example and warning against constitution-making which falls too unguardedly into line with current modes of thinking.

37. The charter also makes democratic provision in accordance with the temper of the times for a general assembly consisting of representatives of the senate, of part-time counselling and tutorial staff, and of students elected on a regional basis, which meets once a year and is empowered to comment to the senate on any matter affecting the university. It also elects staff and student members of itself to the council.

38. A final statutory body is the Academic Advisory Committee, which consists of distinguished academic staff from other universities. It is charged with the task of ensuring that the university's academic standards, particularly in the field of examination and assessment, and the university's procedures for appointing academic staff conform with those of other institutions. The committee must present an annual certificate to the university stating its satisfaction with the conduct of these matters. (At an appropriate time, this committee may be dissolved by the Privy Council at the request of the council of the university.)

39. The experience of the university suggests that the existence of three distinct, though overlapping, bodies with the functions stated above is vital to the conduct of any similar enterprise quite apart from the organ of government through which financial resources are channelled. There must be a lay governing body more familiar with the constraints imposed by financing with public money, more sensitive to public opinion and more closely in touch with a wide range of outside institutions and interests than the self-contained university community can hope to be. There must be academic autonomy exercised through a democratic structure; and there must be an outside tribunal of unimpeachable academic authority to validate the university's procedures and degrees until it is firmly established.

40. As for the necessary substructure, it consists, so far as the council is concerned, of two parts. A number of committees of its own members, who must be committed fully to the enterprise and have some time to give to the work, report to it on specific matters including finance, public relations, and terms and conditions of service. The council is also responsible for all appointment, promotion and salary review procedures through appropriate committees including the Staff Salaries and Grading Committee, although the actual appointment of academic staff is a senate responsibility.

41. The council has also established an advisory and liaison committee structure with the general aim of promoting the interest and support of a wide range of outside individuals and organizations. The function of the committees varies widely. The Advisory Committee on Adult and Higher Education is a large forum for wide-ranging discussion. The Advisory Committee on Computing is a small group of experts willing to guide the university on all computer applications. The Advisory Committee on Services Education is a partner in a common enterprise, the provision of Open University courses for members of the armed forces overseas. Other committees are concerned with help to the disabled, with the publishing problems of the university, with the education of teachers and with the problems arising from co-operation with local authorities over library services, over accommodation and facilities for study centres, and over discretionary grants for students.

42. Internally, the university conducts its business through university boards, each of which has a number of committees reporting to it. The Staff Board is responsible to the council; the Academic Board and the Student Examination and Awards Board are responsible to the senate; the Planning Board is respon-

sible to both council and senate. Membership is drawn from the council, the senate, the faculties and the regions. They meet, on an average, four to six times a year. A General Purposes Committee which includes the chairman of the council and is presided over by the vice-chancellor meets frequently to deal with urgent business and questions of co-ordination between the boards. The work of the boards must be undertaken within the financial and resources restraints established by the Planning Board, which allocates resources to spending units. Their members must be acutely aware of the constraints imposed by the fact that the university is in one of its aspects a great factory of educational material, with an operational need for clearly defined targets, a strict adherence to scheduled dates and a disciplined co-ordination of all its activities.

43. It will be noted that council members are closely involved together with members of the staff of the university in all of the major decision-making bodies. This intimacy of contact has done much to foster the sense of a common enterprise and to dispel any idea of the council as a remote controlling body unaware of the practical problems involved. There have in fact been no serious disagreements between senate and council. It will also be noted that membership of committees makes enormous demands on staff time.

VI Academic staffing

44. The recruitment of the academic central and regional staff, now some 400 strong, has, then, been based on the belief that the prestige of the university would be dependent on the calibre of the staff as specialists in their own subjects. The emphasis has been mainly on scholarship, not teaching; and not at all on experience or skill in teaching through the audio-visual media. The bias towards conservative academic attitudes which that policy might have introduced has, however, been tempered by the fact that the novelty of the venture has appealed to the more adventurous and open-minded of the academic community. Nevertheless, the university soon came to the conclusion that it needed a counterbalance to its preoccupation with academic distinction. Its teaching must be systematic and must make the fullest use of the techniques available in the light of the best recent work on educational technology and on the psychology of learning. It could not be left to the intuitive methods of gifted teachers, inspiring though those can be in a face-to-face situation. It therefore set up an Institute of Educational Technology (IET), staffed by people who had studied, and whose business it would be to study further, the basic problems of course design, construction and evaluation. The academic staff proper is primarily concerned with course content. The staff of the IET is concerned with the formulation of objectives, with performance tests, with the developmental testing of course material through its use with sample groups, with assessment and examination, with the conceptual difficulty, grading and continuity of courses, with student feedback and with the necessary modification of courses. It undertakes studies of groups within the student population and of their learning styles, of the services given by tutors and counsellors and of the functions of the various components of the university's teaching.

45. The existence of the IET, and the establishment of a close working relationship between its staff, the staff of the academic faculties and the BBC staff concerned with broadcast production have been vital in the development

of effective teaching methods. The right relationship has been achieved largely through the course teams (see section VIII below).

46. A further reinforcement of the university as a teaching institution and contribution to the realism of its approach is made by the existence of a strong body of full-time but regionally based staff tutors working within the framework of the regional organization (described in paragraph 85 below). The role of the staff tutors is a dual one, linked both to a region and to the central campus. They are recruited as subject specialists with wide teaching experience. On the one hand, they are concerned with the tutorial arrangements for students in the region. On the other, they are concerned with advising the course teams on the basis of their direct experience with students on the effectiveness of the courses and the various teaching methods.

47. The academic staff could not have been recruited without the assurance that the university would offer time and facilities for their own researches and writings as generously as other universities. This has entailed a level of staffing which allows for study leave as a right (and for longer periods of sabbatical leave as a privilege), and the provision of certain basic academic requirements. These include a university library which cannot hope to rival the greater collections, but which already has a strong bibliographical section, and the essential works of reference and periodicals in many fields. The science and technology staff, at present in temporary accommodation, are shortly to be provided with more adequate laboratory facilities. It must be added that the intense pressure of work involved in the building up of a new institution has not yet allowed time and scope for research on the scale which the university hopes ultimately to make possible.

VII Course structure and curriculum

48. It was apparent from the start that it would be impracticable and uneconomic for the university to offer a wide range of courses leading to specialized honours degrees of the same type as the external degrees of the University of London, i.e. each programme of courses tightly planned on a three- or four-year cycle, without cross-reference to the others, and each appealing to a small number of potential students. It would be impossible in terms of air time as well as expense to support such courses with radio and television programmes, since that would involve the concurrent broadcasting of programmes at each grade level for every course to meet the needs of students starting in different years. Nor would such courses be best suited to the needs of the adult student in employment who would be faced with an inflexible and lengthy work-programme culminating in a single cumulative examination.

49. The university therefore operates on a 'credits' system modelled originally on the general degree courses of the Scottish universities, and akin to that of the United States. It utilizes the 32- or 34-week one-year course as its basic full-credit unit, but achieves a wider range of choice for the student through half-credit courses at the more advanced levels, spread over the full length of the academic year. The aim has been to encourage breadth of study, and at the least to ensure that such specialization as proved practicable should rest on broad foundations. This aim is in line with recent tendencies at the conventional universities, which are increasingly offering interdisciplinary degree courses.

50. The one-year courses are grouped in six main lines of study: arts, educational studies, mathematics, science, the social sciences, and technology. They are of four academic levels. For each line of study (except educational studies), there is a 'foundation course', designed as a general introduction to a whole field of discourse. No student is allowed to proceed to any course of the second or any later level until he or she has successfully completed and acquired a credit in one foundation course. Thereafter students may choose to specialize (as most do) but they have considerable freedom if they wish to draw on courses from other faculties, and unless they have credit exemptions they must at some time during their undergraduate studies take one more foundation course. The B.A. degree is awarded to a student who obtains six credits, two in foundation courses and four at second or subsequent levels. The B.A. (honours) degree calls for an additional two credits, and of the total eight, two must be at third or fourth levels. In neither instance need courses be taken in successive years, and no more than two credit courses can be taken in the same year. To meet changes of personal circumstances, students can 'bank' their credits for a term of years and resume their studies when they are able to do so.

51. The system allows for a very large measure of individual choice. Entry to some of the more advanced courses inevitably assumes that the student has reached the 'credit' standard of some specified earlier course, especially in mathematics and the sciences, but even in these cases the university only advises the student.

52. For example, a student entering the university this year and taking the foundation course in science might move on next year to the foundation course in technology or in the social sciences, or, for that matter, arts. In that second year, he or she might feel able to add a half-credit in, say, quantum theory and atomic structure, or in the history of science and belief from Copernicus to Darwin, or even both. With the aid of the university prospectus, the students will, when the full range of courses is developed, be able to map out their total journey for the years ahead, and take their own time over it, though once embarked on any one of the courses they must follow a rigorous timetable of assignments.

53. In terms of equivalence of the degrees of the university with those of other universities, the full credit course is reckoned as 360 hours of student work, and the student is advised that he must have a minimum of ten hours a week to devote to it. In practice, for the average student, this is an underestimate. The hours worked tend to range from ten to fifteen hours a week for a single full-credit course, with the average probably nearer the upper figure. The university drives its students hard—perhaps too hard in some subjects—because it must not risk the imputation that it offers an easy option or that it covers the subject superficially. At the same time, the enthusiasm and sense of commitment of the students leads them to spend much longer on their studies than the courses' creators intended. It is significant that the proportion of applicants who wish to take two full credits in their first year dropped from 45 per cent to 18 per cent as the demands made by the work became known.

54. The university believes in the maximum possible transferability of credits between institutions. It hopes that other United Kingdom universities will become more flexible than they now are in this respect, which would open the way to arrangements allowing a degree student to spend part of his time on Open University courses and part as a full-time student of a conventional

university. The Open University therefore offers credit exemptions in respect of recognized qualifications in higher education. The basic scale allows one credit for each year of full-time study (or its equivalent in part-time study) in approved courses elsewhere, with a maximum of three credits. A degree of some other university, a Certificate in Education gained through the three-year course of a college of education, a Higher National Certificate or a professional qualification of equivalent standing may thus allow the student to concentrate his energies in a narrower field, and shorten his path to a degree. (Most of the 900 students who graduated after the first two years and more than half of the 3,500 who graduated after the first three years were teachers with maximum exemptions.) Some 31 per cent of applicants claimed exemptions in 1973, the average number claimed being 1.2, and on such various grounds as to require the establishment of an exemptions office which has so far evaluated over 900 outside qualifications.

55. It was the structure of the curriculum as described here that enabled the university to make a start in 1971 with a full cross-section of its potential students, though it was as yet ready to offer only four of its five foundation courses. All of the foundation courses, and the first-year courses for which there is most demand, will be offered every year. It may ultimately prove necessary for some of the more advanced courses to be offered in appropriate rotation. University policy is that each course will be offered four times before it is substantially remade but in practice there has been a tendency to extend the life of courses to conserve resources. University courses, especially in the sciences, must be kept up to date and the prospect of a fresh start at known intervals is a spur to radical innovation.

56. In the current year (1975) there are more than 70 separate courses on offer, amounting to 44 full credits. Next year the university hopes to raise the number of courses by 20 and of full credits by 13.

57. There is no doubt that the university has adopted the right kind of structure for its degree courses. Progress so far has, however, thrown up major problems relating to the number and the balance of courses which have been provisionally resolved only after a long debate within the university. The following factors, and the tensions arising from them, have had to be considered in arriving at an agreed long-term programme.

First, there is the basic need for economic working. The fixed, overhead expenses of course development, irrespective of the number of students to be enrolled, account for a very high proportion of the cost of the operation, including as they do the cost in academic man-hours and the broadcasting cost. Cost-effectiveness diminishes rapidly for an individual course as the initial body of foundation-course students is fragmented into smaller and smaller groups of more advanced students. From this point of view, it is desirable to ensure that the initial intake of each faculty is large enough to feed its more advanced courses. Since there is an overwhelmingly greater number of applicants for arts and the social sciences than for science, technology and mathematics (see section IX below) this involves giving a preference to applicants who choose these latter subjects. It is also economically advantageous to limit the number of more advanced courses and to offer only those which seem likely to attract a considerable following. The university could, on purely economic grounds, keep its second-level courses few and fairly general in character, and confine its third- and fourth-year courses to the minimum number which would allow for a varied range of honours degrees. These considerations are, however, cut across by conflicting pressures.

58. The most important of these pressures is that of consumer demand. There is, within the university, one school of thought which would go so far as to abandon any attempt to keep the faculties more or less level in either number of students or number of courses, and which would let these be regulated by 'market' forces. People of this way of thinking point out that the less-popular subjects, particularly mathematics, have a higher drop-out and failure rate than the more popular subjects, and that if the university favours them unduly it is in danger of producing more and more expensive courses for fewer and fewer students. In their view, a major distortion or manipulation of the market pattern implies a paternalistic attitude towards the public which is justified neither by consideration of national need nor by the preferences of the academic community.

59. The argument that national needs call for an admissions policy heavily biased towards the sciences and for a publicity drive to secure more applicants rests indeed on somewhat dubious grounds. It is notoriously difficult to forecast national manpower needs. In the United Kingdom, a phase of concern about the supply of scientists for industry was followed by an expansion and improvement of facilities for science teaching in schools, and by a great increase in the number of places in universities and polytechnics. They are not now fully taken up, and the prospects of employment for science graduates have diminished sharply. There is now a dearth of teachers of English. Nevertheless, given the decision that the university shall teach science and technology, there is a minimum array of courses below which it cannot claim to be offering a proper and viable university provision.

60. Whatever the admissions policy may become, it seems certain that there will be a strong demand by some students for more specialized courses in the discipline which they have chosen as their first foundation course. In spite of the controversy over the 'two cultures' and the efforts of those who would like to break down the barriers between them, United Kingdom education remains obstinately specialist. Boys and girls in sixth forms (i.e. in their last pre-university two years of high school) normally study only two main subjects. When they leave school very few of them have the desire or the basic intellectual equipment to move into other fields of study. Vocational needs and ambitions reinforce the tendency of the scientist to concentrate on his special branch of science. The need for mathematics is a deterrent to the arts student even if he wishes to broaden his interests. Conventional universities can apply constraints on the choice of courses if they wish to do so, and can thereby encourage interdisciplinary thinking. The Open University can do no more than impose its requirement of two foundation courses, allow students to choose as freely as possible from a range of disciplines and place a number of interdisciplinary courses on offer. The interdisciplinary courses for which there is at present the greatest student demand are those which unite neighbouring disciplines, e.g. mathematics and technology; or less closely related disciplines at the few points where there is obvious common ground. For example, a half-credit course on science and the rise of technology since 1800 had an enrolment in 1974 of 896 students, drawn from both the arts and the science entrants, while a half-credit course on the biological bases of behaviour united 967 science and social science students. But what is desired by some honours students as they progress

to the third and fourth levels is specialism of a narrow kind, incapable of a general appeal: for example, the projected third- and fourth-level courses on systems modelling, on earth science topics and methods, and on thought and reality—a course largely concerned with the philosophy of Wittgenstein.

61. Such student pressure for specialist courses finds a strong reinforcement in the views of many of the academic staff. There is a widely held view that an institution worthy of the name of university ought to concern itself with the whole range of the academic subject spectrum. The extreme proponents of this view would even wish to hold back development in the rapidly expanding fields so as to maintain a balanced provision. In any event they believe that the prestige and standing of each faculty is dependent on work of an advanced level. In their view, the university cannot hope to attract and retain staff of university calibre unless they have the opportunity of such work, the absence of which will offer no adequate intellectual stimulus, and will sharply limit the prospects of professional advancement in other universities. The initiative for more specialist courses therefore arises spontaneously within the faculties. Some proposals are of a traditional nature; some deal with the subjects that are currently arousing intellectual excitement in the university world; some have their origins in the special interests of an individual member of staff. In every instance, they must undergo the scrutiny and secure the approval of the senate. The senate must then submit to the Planning Board a bid for the resources necessary to mount them. The sum total of bids so approved is incorporated in the estimates which are at present submitted triennially to the Department of Education and Science. (It may in future be financed like other universities through the University Grants Committee.) The council must approve the estimates, and must authorize the creation of any new academic post called for by new courses, but in this matter it acts only on the recommendation of the senate, and has no power to question any proposal on academic grounds. The Department of Education meets or refuses the triennial estimates on broad financial grounds only. The department has sanctioned its grant for the 1974–76 triennium on the basis that there will be no more than 65 full undergraduate courses (or the equivalent in part-time courses) by 1976.

62. Broadly stated, the main questions arising from the pattern of course development are these. First, should the university aim at a comprehensive provision, and an effort spread over a very wide field, or should it concentrate on doing those things which it can do best and most economically? This is, of course, a question which can be properly asked of any university in an age of increasing specialization if the best use is to be made of specialist staff and expensive resources. Second, how many separate courses should it seek to provide, bearing in mind both the need for economy and the need to present the student with an adequate but not excessive and bewildering range of choice? Third, can the university afford to devote resources of the same kind and on the same scale to advanced courses with small student enrolments—perhaps no more than 200 or 300—as to its foundation courses?

63. In the event, the senate has settled for the time being on 87 full-credit courses (or the equivalent) as a reasonable and practicable long-term target, and has formulated the basic objectives of the university undergraduate programme in the following terms: (a) to provide students with a range of multi-disciplinary foundation courses; (b) to provide students with courses of a range which allows those who do not want to centre their studies on one particular

area to plan a coherent degree programme; (c) to provide students with an opportunity to 'major' in a number of areas of study. The senate has therefore resolved that 22 of these full-credit courses (or their equivalent) shall be 'general' or 'open' courses with minimal prerequisites—courses broad in subject matter and planned to span over the academic divisions within or between faculties.

64. It is already apparent that the provision of such a large number of courses will call for a careful husbanding of resources. The shortage of full-time staff to direct courses and unmanageable complexities of organization if their number were increased make it imperative to confine them to foundation and other courses which could not be offered at all without them; and the number of such courses will have to be strictly limited. On grounds of expense as well as shortage of transmission time it will clearly be impracticable for all courses to have the support of the broadcasting media, especially television. In these and other respects, there must be a radical reconsideration of teaching methods at the more advanced levels. This question is further dealt with below.

VIII Methods of teaching

65. The courses developed by the Open University represent a unique and highly integrated blend of a wide range of teaching materials, for example: correspondence texts, broadcast and study notes, assignments, self-test questions, etc., television programmes, radio programmes, summer schools, home experimental kits, various audio-visual aids (slides, filmstrips, tape recorders, etc.), computer practice (for certain courses only), set books (purchased by the student), and tuition and counselling (provided by correspondence and in face-to-face situations at local study centres).

66. The unique character of the teaching obviously resides not in the use of any or all of these teaching media, but in the degree of integration achieved and in the organic relationship between the planning of course content and the planning of teaching methods for each course. Since these are ensured by a way of working which is perhaps the most significant educational innovation made by the university, and which is central to both its organization and its philosophy, the idea of the course team will be dealt with before turning to the media themselves.

67. The central principle is that the academic content of courses and the ways in which they will be taught must always be thought of as a single operation by a single group of people. Furthermore, the members of the group must approach their task as a democracy of equals, each with specialist knowledge and functions, but all concerned with every aspect of the course. Each course team is an *ad hoc* group entrusted by the university with the total responsibility for a single full-credit or part-credit course. It starts with senate and Planning Board approval of a proposal from a faculty that a course on some specific topic shall be provided. Its task is to consider the needs of the student body that it envisages, to map out in detail the ground to be covered, and to decide how the various teaching methods at its disposal can best be used to attain its objectives. It has as its chairman a senior member of the academic staff nominated by the dean of the faculty concerned. Its members include those of his staff whose special province is involved, together with experts from outside the university if

required. It also includes representatives of those departments of the university primarily concerned with learning strategies, teaching methods and media production, and the BBC radio and television producers who will be responsible for the broadcast components of the course. They are present not as narrow experts in a particular mode of educational communication, but as full course-team members, and are able to make their contribution to the team's thinking about course objectives and content, just as the academic staff may contribute to thinking about presentation. An editor in each team is responsible for the co-ordination of the work.

68. Courses are organized in terms of weekly units, and once the course team as a whole has decided on the basic form and direction of the whole course, the detailed responsiblity for each unit is placed in the hands of either a smaller group or an individual author. Each component item of the unit is scrutinized by either the whole team or the smaller group. Anyone who writes a correspondence text, from professor to assistant lecturer, must present the first and subsequent drafts of his work to his colleagues. The radio or television producer works out the details of agreed programmes with one or two academic colleagues, usually the correspondence-text author or authors, but before they can be transmitted the programmes too must go to the whole course team for approval.

69. The teaching task of the course team, to quote the report of the Planning Committee, is to set in motion 'teaching operations drawing on different media, but using a systems approach with the learner as the key figure'. To adopt a 'systems approach' to teaching is: to specify educational objectives; to break down the student's task into component elements, or successive stages; to identify the learning processes involved; to consider the appropriateness of the teaching methods available in relation to each stage; to combine the methods so that they make an integrated whole; and finally, to provide for feedback, validation and assessment. Guidance in this field is the special function of the member or members of the team drawn from the IET; they too are full course-team members, and their work too is subject to course-team discussion.

70. No co-operative machinery works entirely without friction. It would nevertheless be fair to say that the course-team approach here described has been far more successful than any other in promoting mutual understanding between academics, educational technologists and media experts, and in producing effective multi-media teaching. The members of a course team do not merely co-operate. They unite their efforts and in so doing learn from each other. The academic staff of the Open University is acquiring an imaginative and practical grasp of the possibilities of audio-visual presentation which is unique in the British university world, and from which other universities may have much to learn. The staff of the BBC Open University Department (which has been specially recruited from men and women with appropriate academic qualifications and experience) has grown accustomed to work not as servants of academics, but as partners in a shared academic purpose; and both groups have learnt how to make systematic use of the art and science of educational communication.

71. It should be emphasized that course-team methods of working have given reality to the concept of partnership with the BBC but that the benefit of this working method would be obtainable if the radio and television producers were directly employed by the university.

Correspondence tuition

72. It was recognized from the first that broadcasting could not possibly carry the main expository burden of even a carefully restricted national operation, for sheer lack of available air time. The only method of instruction capable of being made available everywhere, and capable of indefinite extension as new needs arise, is correspondence tuition. In the United Kingdom it affords a customary and professionally recognized highway to the necessary qualifications in accountancy and other fields. It has proved its value as a help to the external student for a London degree.

73. Correspondence teaching allows, as broadcasting does not, for a two-way traffic of ideas. In a literate culture, the printed word is far more effective than pictures and the spoken word in confronting the student with a problem to be solved, or a task to be carried out, at his own pace and in his own time. Whatever the mode of presentation may be, there must be a regular response from the student, and that response calls for individual attention.

74. The enrolled student of the Open University soon finds that the heart of the course lies in the packaged material prepared by the central academic staff and organized (for a full-credit course) in 32 to 34 weekly work-units, which the student receives by post at three- or four-week intervals. The printed material in each package normally amounts to a substantial, well-printed and well-illustrated treatise, specially written by a member or members of the course team. It also directs the student to a limited number of essential textbooks (some of them specially written) with which he or she must be equipped, and to further books for background reading. But its scope goes beyond the printed word, and extends to slides, gramophone records and apparatus for scientific experiments. Every student of the foundation courses in science and technology is furnished with a substantial 'kit' which allows for the necessary experimental work to be done at home and includes a microscope of novel design. (The student only pays a deposit, and the kit must be returned at the end of the course but its cost substantially increases the expense of science courses to the university.) The course books on which the work of the student pivots are further supplemented by notes on the television and radio broadcasts of the week, instructions for carrying out home experiments, miscellaneous administrative information (e.g. about summer schools), self-assessment question papers, and assignments of work, to be either computer-marked or tutor-marked.

75. Each package presents the student with an assignment of written work of one of these kinds. In science and mathematics in particular, but also in arts and the social sciences, considerable use is made of 'multiple-choice' questions which can be marked by computer, but the main reliance in social sciences and the arts subjects is on a tutorial system which allows for individual postal attention. The marks that the student attains in either kind of test are recorded in the computer files. They are recovered in order to keep the student informed of progress, to draw the tutor's attention to the student's specific weaknesses, and finally to serve as part of the assessment of performance at the end of the year, when the student must also take a three-hour written examination. Wherever it is possible, the precise educational objectives of each work-unit are clearly set out, and the student is able to keep track of progress made and enjoy the stimulus that comes from a growing mastery of the subject through self-assessment tests. Alternatively, if the grades are consistently bad, the

student can decide whether to withdraw. So far as the work that is sent to the tutor is concerned, the student has considerable flexibility in the choice of assignments, and the grade is assessed on a stated number of them; for example, the best six out of ten. Once embarked upon a course, the student must keep pace with its demands; but if a credit is not obtained at the end of the year, it can be taken again.

76. It would be completely impracticable for the students' written work to be marked by the central academic staff. Every student sends his or her written material to the part-time course tutor who is responsible for marking it. These tutors are drawn mainly from the serving and retired staff of other universities and institutes of higher and adult education. They are carefully selected but receive relatively little initial training. A substantial handbook of guidance and advice, *Teaching by Correspondence in the Open University*, has, however, been available to them since 1973. Their work is supervised by the full-time staff tutors, who maintain liaison between them and the central academic staff of the university and organize conferences of the part-time staff. Each part-time tutor undertakes to look after a strictly limited number of students, and at present the university has some 4,500 tutors for its 42,000 students. Many of them make themselves available to answer questions either on the telephone or at the local study centres (see paragraphs 85–91 below), and a considerable number of them conduct tutorial classes for their students there. The teaching operation is entirely dependent on the recruitment of an adequate number of tutors. So far the university has had no difficulty on that score.

77. Thanks to the fruitful working relationship between the academic subject specialists and the staff of the IET, the writing of the correspondence texts and devising of the related assignments presents no basic pedagogical problems. The excellence of their printed format and illustrations undoubtedly contributes largely to student morale and incentive, and to confidence in the institution. It owes a great deal to the establishment by the university of a strong design and graphics department with its studio on the campus and of a strong publications division, the staffs of which work in close partnership with the course teams. Printing is mainly in the hands of outside commercial printers.

78. Such problems as exist are largely practical and logistical, and are dealt with elsewhere in this report. It may be noted here that their solution imposes rigid timings and a strict discipline on the work of the course teams.

Face-to-face teaching

Summer schools and study centres

79. Only one element of face-to-face teaching is obligatory for Open University students. All foundation courses and certain other courses have associated with them a requirement that the student must attend a one-week summer school in order that the course can be completed for credit. Exemption can, however, be granted for a variety of reasons on the recommendation of the student's counsellor.

80. In 1974, summer schools were held during the eight weeks from 14 July to 8 September (i.e. during the university vacation period) in co-operating

universities, for nearly 26,000 students. Teaching was shared, as in previous years, between full-time and part-time members of the Open University staff, members of the host universities, and other qualified tutors. In addition to summer schools related to the foundation courses there were schools, obviously with smaller enrolments, for such diverse courses as the second-level 'Electromagnetics and Electronics', and the third-level 'Problems of Philosophy', and certain discipline-based schools, for example in biology, serving several courses, the total amounting to 25.

81. The enthusiasm and zeal of the students have left no room for doubt about the value of this residential sector of the course work for adults without any previous experience of university life. For science students, the main emphasis is on laboratory practice, and for the arts and social science students on seminars. Both groups benefit from the attention to individual needs. Even more important is the opportunity to meet members of the central academic staff of the university who have previously been no more than names or at most faces on the television screen. This, and the daily intercourse with students from every part of the country, make people feel that they are truly the undergraduates of a great national university, and parts of a common enterprise.

82. For these reasons the academic staff are anxious to extend the compulsory-summer-school principle as far as possible. It is already clear, however, that its limits are in sight. The complexity of the timetabling and organization required appear insuperable obstacles. For advanced courses, the possibilities of weekend courses and of field studies as alternatives are already being explored.

83. There are other considerations which cannot be ignored. Most of the students have limited resources. The summer schools are planned to be self-financing, with a present charge to the student of £40.50 a week. This is covered for most students by a discretionary grant from the local education authority, but by no means for all of them. There may be travelling expenses to be borne. Many students have family responsibilities as mothers, or as fathers with wives and children and only short holidays. Some students, without having any handicap which would justify an application for exemption, do not feel equal to the strain of a summer school.

84. Whatever the reasons may be, there is a heavy drop-out of students at this point, amounting in 1973 to 9 per cent of those still enrolled. Some of these might have ceased to be active students already, and their non-attendance at summer schools merely reveals that fact. It seems likely, however, that many students would satisfactorily complete the credit course but for this obstacle; and it is therefore arguable how far compulsion should be applied, except perhaps for science courses. Without it there would certainly be a very high voluntary level of attendance.

Study centres

85. The university has now established 284 study centres throughout the United Kingdom, and the great majority of students are within reasonable distance of one. Organized in thirteen regions, each headed by a regional director, and served by a staff of full-time counsellors and tutors, with the necessary administrative support, they provide the bases for the personal tutorial services to students, and the framework for their corporate life as under-

graduates. They are normally situated in technical colleges, polytechnics or other existing educational institutions, and many of these allow the use of their own libraries, laboratories and social amenities. They are open each weekday evening from 6.30 to at least 9 p.m., and in some instances at weekend times. Most of them were planned to meet the needs of some 75 students originally, rising to twice that number with the growth of the university. There are considerable variations, however, and enrolments range from 40 to 400 students.

86. Every student is assigned on registration to a locally based part-time counsellor whose job it is to guide and advise the student's studies. Each counsellor is normally responsible for some twenty students and is available at the local study centre on specific evenings of the week; students may ask for a personal interview every fortnight. Arrangements are made for counsellors to visit from time to time students who are unable to attend study centres. The counsellors are the students' first and most immediate contact with the university. They can help with any general academic problem that arises, and if they cannot deal with a problem themselves they know to whom it should be referred.

87. The counsellor arranges and may lead discussion groups. In selected centres, specialist tutorial classes are arranged, either during the evening or at weekends. Since it has proved possible to recruit enough correspondence tutors for the first- and second-year courses on an area basis, the tutors can undertake classes for their own assigned students, and the direct personal contact makes the relationship easier and more valuable.

88. Except for the mathematics student, who should from time to time attend one of the 100 centres with access to computer terminals as an integral part of the foundation course, no student is obliged to frequent a study centre. Provided he or she can work on the correspondence packet and receive the broadcast programmes at home, the university at present insists on no condition which imposes attendance on the invalid or on the natural solitary. Nevertheless, some three-quarters of the registered students make use at one time or another of the opportunities that the centres provide, and the encouragement that comes from formal and informal social contacts with fellow-students and staff. Many of the centres have already developed a strong corporate sense, and a vigorous social life.

89. Since attendance is not obligatory, and since the average number of students attending centres in any one week is less than half, they cannot be reckoned as a *sine qua non* of any venture of the Open University type. Nevertheless they are highly valued by those who do use them, and make a strong contribution to the persistence and success rates of the student body. A study of the comparative examination success of those who do and do not attend them will be revealing; this is under way, but it is not yet completed.

90. One of the original motives for establishing the centres was to ensure that students who lived in areas of poor broadcast reception, who found it difficult to concentrate in the family living-room, or who simply preferred to view or listen with a group of fellow-students, could receive the university programmes there. All centres are therefore equipped for the direct reception of both media. The centres in areas of poor reception hold libraries, either on 8 mm film or on video-tape, of all the television programmes so far transmitted, and other centres may borrow copies from the regional headquarters.

91. In practice, the great majority of students (some 80 per cent) prefer to view and listen at home, and many of the others do so at centres only when classes in their subjects are held there on the same evening. A diminishing number of students have not yet equipped themselves with radio and television sets which will receive the BBC's V.H.F. radio transmissions and second television service; but less than 2 per cent of them live in areas where the signals for these are still unsatisfactory. It nevertheless seems inevitable, in view of the shortage of air time, that there will be a shift of emphasis towards the viewing and hearing of recorded programmes at centres rather than of direct transmissions at home. (See section X below). That may well lead to a wider use of the centres for other purposes.

IX The students of the university

92. The Open University requires no formal qualifications of any kind as a condition of entry. For operational reasons, and in the interest of good public relations, it is desirable that the enrolled students should be spread fairly throughout the United Kingdom. The pattern of demand, reflecting that of conventional universities, is very heavily weighted in the direction of the social sciences and the arts, but university policy and the efficient and economic working of the system as it is now constituted call for the admission of a planned number of students to each of the five foundation courses, 45 per cent of the total number of available places being reserved to date for the mathematics, science and technology courses. It is therefore necessary to apply a system of constraints and quotas, but within the limits so imposed applicants are admitted simply in the order in which they apply, except for the small number belonging to categories for which special arrangements have been made: the physically disabled, prisoners and members of the armed forces serving overseas.

93. Since nobody is refused on formal grounds, it is in the interest of the university that applicants should be able to assess their capacities against the demands of the courses. The fact that the broadcast components of all courses are available for sampling on the public channels contributes to that end. It is furthered by the dispatch of a full and informative *Guide for Applicants* to everybody who responds to the university's advertisements by asking for it. More than 155,000 copies were distributed in 1974. Those still in doubt have a counselling service available to them through the regional offices, which can advise them whether they are already equipped for study at the required level, or whether they would be wise to undertake preparatory studies first. Inevitably, however, many of those who persist with their applications and are admitted find that they cannot keep pace with the work. All of those initially accepted are therefore admitted at first as 'provisionally registered' students. They pay an initial tuition fee for the first three months, which is regarded as a probationary period. This arrangement allows for the voluntary withdrawal of students who decide that they cannot cope with or do not have time for the work. In principle it also provides for early exclusion by the university of those who fail to submit the required written work. In practice the university has never applied this rule. At this stage, there is a drop-out of some 25 per cent of the provisionally registered students. This is allowed for in calculating the planned student

population for the year. It leaves behind a body of serious entrants capable of profiting from courses of university level.

94. The intention of the university is that the total number of finally registered students should be taken as the baseline from which future rates of success and failure should be calculated.

95. In 1974, the university had 42,172 finally registered students, distributed fairly equally between first-, second-, third- and fourth-year students, and between the faculties. Its grant from the Department of Education and Science for the triennium 1974–76 was originally based on the maintenance throughout that period of a student population within the range 36,000 to 42,000. The figure was an arbitrary one, determined by government policy on expenditure, and not by the potential demand. The number of applications for 1974 courses was more than 34,000, a slight increase on the previous year's figure. With drop-out and graduation figures running at their established rates the agreed target figure called for an average admission in each of the relevant three years of 15,000 provisionally registered, i.e. 11,250 finally registered students. There was clearly a large gross surplus of applicants, but since 68 per cent of them applied for either the arts or the social sciences foundation courses, the total number was barely sufficient to fill the smaller quotas of the less popular courses in the academic year 1974.

96. The situation was dramatically transformed by a very sharp rise in the number of applications for 1975 foundation courses, the total rising by the closing date to 52,537. This rise, and the changing occupational character of the applicants, made it abundantly clear that the university was not merely satisfying a limited backlog of demand, and that there was likely to be a steady stream of applicants for many years to come in all subjects. It lent force to the university's argument, already put forward, that total student numbers should be substantially raised, with a consequently increased expenditure, but with a considerably decreased cost per student and per graduation. The admission of an additional 6,000 students in 1975 and for one subsequent year was therefore sanctioned by the government, allowing for an intake in that year of 20,000 students and a rise in the total student population to 49,000 by 1976.

97. A substantial proportion of the finally registered students—17 per cent in 1971—do not attend the required summer schools or present themselves for the examinations. A number of these nevertheless continue as active, fee-paying students. In so far as they have chosen to study for study's sake rather than for credits, they are deriving benefit from the course, though they may be excluding others for whom the university might provide the only hope of a degree. Of those taking the examination, only 8 per cent fail to obtain credits. The success rate of finally registered students judged in terms of credits obtained thus stands at the high figure of 75 per cent, though with marked differences between the faculties. At every stage, the drop-out and failure rate is much higher in mathematics than in any other subject.

98. With the average number of courses taken per year standing at 1.2, it seems likely that the time taken for graduation by most students without exemptions will be five or six years.

99. The social and occupational composition of the student body broadly corresponds to the expectations of the Planning Committee. For many adults, the primary motive for undertaking an arduous course of study is vocational. The men and women most likely to be attracted to and to persevere with studies

of university level are those who have maintained the habit of study in adult life, and in particular those who have already earned qualifications which entitle them to credit exemptions and shorten their path to a degree. Three out of four Open University students have previously been involved in part-time education of some sort, and some 30 per cent of them are able to claim at least one credit exemption.

100. The occupational composition of the student body varies considerably from course to course, but in sum total the largest single occupational group consists of teachers, the great majority of them non-graduates for whom a degree will mean higher scales of pay and better career prospects. The next largest group is drawn from full-time housewives, many of whom intend to take up or resume careers from which they have been temporarily excluded by family responsibilities. Draughtsmen, laboratory assistants and technicians are well represented, and so are qualified scientists and engineers seeking to extend their professional scope or to bring their knowledge up to date. There are substantial numbers of men and women from the fields of administration and management, and from the professions and the arts. The only other statistically important single category is that of clerical and office staff. Small groups of special interest include members of the armed forces overseas, for whom a scheme has been worked out in partnership with the educational branches of the services, disabled students, who require special help, such as braille texts for the blind, and a handful of men serving long prison sentences.

101. Changes in the pattern of enrolment since the university started are of considerable significance. The percentage of teacher applicants has dropped from 37 per cent in 1970 to 23 per cent in 1974, though the number of teacher applicants is still very high. There has been a modest but significant increase in the numbers and percentage of skilled manual workers, and of technicians drawn from the science-based industries, induced in some part by special publicity addressed to industry through firms and trade unions. The ratio of women to men has increased and stands now at 42 per cent. A large majority of applicants have in each year been between the ages of 25 and 45, and the average age has been steadily dropping. It therefore seems likely that there will be a continuing flow of young men and women who discover a personal or vocational need for higher education after a few years of working life. The preference of arts and the social sciences over mathematics, technology and science continues, though there has been a very encouraging rise since 1973 in the demand for the science-based subjects. In all subjects there has been a large drop, as the demands of the courses have become better known, in the number of applicants who wish to take two foundation courses concurrently. In 1974, only 12 per cent of the students admitted attempted initially to do so. It is already clear, however, that some 30 per cent of the students who successfully obtain their first foundation course credit feel able to undertake at least one-and-a-half credit courses in their second year.

102. The university has been criticized for its failure to attract applicants from the lower socio-economic groups, and especially from manual workers. Except in so far as it challenges the original intention to create a university and operate in the early years at degree level only the criticism is misconceived. The social and occupational composition of the student body was determined in its main outline by those decisions.

103. The present student population is necessarily a self-selected group of

men and women who believed and who have proved by experience that they are capable of working at university level. The number of applicants without any formal educational qualifications is, however, increasing. In planning its courses, the university bears in mind the fact that many of them will need more help at the commencement of their university studies than the boy or girl fresh from school. The planners of a degree course must nevertheless assume a capacity for handling ideas, and in the sciences a range of mathematical skills which are likely to be outside the range of those who left school at the age of 14 or 15, and have undertaken no further systematic study. For many years now there has been a wide range of opportunities for both vocational and non-vocational study of many kinds and at many levels in local technical colleges, colleges of further education and adult-education classes. The ablest and most ambitious of the early school leavers have taken advantage of those opportunities, and have moved into better jobs than those they started with. The parents of two-thirds of the students of the Open University belong to those lower socio-economic groups from which the university draws only a small percentage, though a considerable absolute number, of its students. In the past, able children from that social background have been much less likely to go on to a university even if they stayed at school long enough to qualify for entrance to one. Of the 3,500 students who graduated in 1974, 14 per cent left school at age 16 or earlier.

104. It is highly improbable that the number of students from the ranks of the unskilled manual workers could in any way be substantially increased. Any further increase in the number of skilled manual workers (many of whom are in fact engaged in technical studies leading to nationally recognized qualifications) seems likely to depend on the provision of preparatory courses directly geared to the foundation courses of the university. Such courses are already provided, with help and guidance from the university, by some local education authority colleges and BBC further education broadcasting has made an important contribution in this field. The university, more assured of its status than it was in its early days, has begun to contemplate a direct entry into that field, using all its developed techniques and resources. In 1974, official spokesmen of the Labour Party, which sponsored the university, once again in office, began to touch on the possibility of a parallel institution which would adopt the same methods but which would provide courses for the widest possible clientele at a lower academic standard than degree level.

105. It is not surprising that the finally registered student body of the university, constituted as it is, should have proved to consist of excellent and hard-working students. The average time that they spend on their course work greatly exceeds the required ten hours a week. Their ability and enthusiasm as displayed at summer schools has surprised and impressed the participating members of conventional university staffs. A great deal of their success is no doubt due to their strong initial motivation. It is not yet possible to say what the various factors in the teaching situation have contributed to their persistence rate. The didactic skill displayed in the course material is clearly of the first importance. Judging by student comment, the attractive presentation of the course books and the professionalism of the broadcasts also play a significant part. There are clearly temperamental differences between students, shown by the preference of some of them for solitary work, and of others for attendance at the study centres and participation in tutorials and self-help study groups.

Some students watch the television programmes and listen to the radio programmes much more frequently than others. Through its IET, the university will be carrying out research to build up a reliable body of knowledge about the motivation, educational and social background, attainments, conceptual apparatus, vocabulary and learning styles of the various categories of enrolled students. A correlation of success rates with preferred methods of study will be of great value, but it may well emphasize the fact that there is no single approach of equal value to all students.

X Broadcasting

106. When the White Paper of 1966, 'A University of the Air', appeared, the title was already a misnomer. It conveyed a wholly exaggerated idea of the contribution which broadcasting might make to the new enterprise. Direct teaching by radio or television can undoubtedly be achieved in some subjects for reasonably mature students; but reliance on the broadcasting media as the main instruments of instruction calls for a very large allotment of air time. It soon became apparent to the original Advisory Committee from whose work the White Paper emerged that air time in the United Kingdom, especially during those hours when the bulk of the potential student audience was at home, would be sharply limited by the competing claims of programmes, including programmes of adult education, designed for the general public. A further limit would clearly be set by the high cost of television. BBC originations (as distinct from repeats) were then running at a total costing figure of £5,275 an hour including all overhead costs, with a comparable figure for radio of £610. Broadcasting must clearly be reserved for those functions which it was best equipped to carry out.

107. The nature of those functions has been established in many different contexts. The strength of the broadcast components of Open University courses lies not in their novelty, but in the thoroughness with which they have been integrated with the whole pattern of the teaching. They can be used to make the initial presentation of a series of topics with the maximum impact, leaving the task of development and consolidation to the correspondence teaching, operating through the package. They can highlight or illustrate points of special difficulty. They can be used from time to time to clear up difficulties common to a number of students in the light of student feedback. They can bring the students into contact with first-rate minds, offer them basic documentary material in the social sciences or convey aesthetic experience in ways that lie outside the scope of the more utilitarian package. They can help the university to explain its working and functions, and help students to feel that they are members of a corporate body, and in touch with its teaching staff.

108. The aims of the programmes are carefully defined. They are subject to close criticism within the course teams. Selected programmes are tested with sample groups before transmission. They are preceded by the dispatch of notes to the student which direct his attention to their purpose and significance, and where necessary supply him with a vocabulary and an apparatus of concepts which will make the broadcast an effective act of communication.

109. In view of their relatively high cost and the very large demands which they make on the time of the academic as well as the broadcasting staff, it is

important that the university should press ahead through its IET with researches designed to assess the contribution which each of the media can make to motivation and to the learning process in specific subjects and specific contexts. Meanwhile, it must answer as best it can two questions of immediate urgency. It must decide whether the programmes related to each of its courses are to be regarded as compulsory for the student, which in practice means whether written assignments and examination questions are to be based directly on them. It must further decide what level of broadcast support should be made available for its more advanced courses, especially for those with small student enrolments. These questions are complicated by the facts that production resources as well as financial resources are limited; that television costs eight times as much as radio; and that air time is already running short.

110. There is little guidance to be had from existing research findings. As Wilbur Schramm has put it, 'Given a reasonably favourable situation, a pupil will learn from any medium—television, radio, programmed instruction, films, filmstrips, tape or others. In general, the same things that control the amount of learning from a teacher face-to-face also control the amount of learning from educational media.' There is no reason for attributing any special magic to any one of them. Their primary importance is as ways of distributing the best teaching (which even in a face-to-face situation uses a wide range of aural and visual resources) to the largest possible audience. Students value the programmes. Each television programme is viewed on an average by 85 per cent and each radio programme heard by 75 per cent of those enrolled for the course. Their subjective assessments and preferences are not necessarily correlated with objective assessments of what has been learnt. In most courses, viewing and listening are regarded as important, but not as a *sine qua non* for the award of a credit. The science and technology faculties are, however, convinced that the teaching of their subjects at a distance is quite impracticable without the use of television as a substitute for laboratory demonstration. They warn potential students not to enrol unless they can be absolutely sure of following the programmes regularly, and they base both tutor-marked and computer-marked assignments on the observation of experiments shown on the television screen. For that reason, science-based courses receive a preferential quota of television programmes which it will be increasingly hard to sustain except at the expense of urgent requests from other course teams.

111. Some of the problems arising from the use of broadcasts, and of the dilemmas which face the university, are closely bound up with its relationship with the BBC. The BBC is an autonomous body. Its use of the channels allotted to it lies wholly within the discretion of its board of governors, and is not subject to government direction. It controls all of the four radio channels with national coverage, and two of the three television channels, the other being devoted to commercial enterprise. Its agreement to set aside a substantial amount of transmission time for Open University programmes was therefore a necessary condition of the whole undertaking. Furthermore, it has educational obligations under the terms of its charter, a long tradition of educational broadcasting to adults as well as to schools, and a strong group of specialized departments engaged in that work. It was only through their help that there was any prospect of producing programmes of the necessary quantity and quality in the time available before the scheduled start of the university's first teaching year.

112. In those circumstances the BBC was unwilling to act as a mere outside

agency of the university. It was concerned that its educational departments should not be regarded simply as experts in the handling of the broadcasting media, but should be able to make a creative contribution to the achievement of the university's academic aims. Its tradition has been to recruit to the educational side of its work men and women who were primarily subject specialists concerned with the teaching content of the programmes, but whose function it was to acquire such a mastery of the broadcasting skills that they could help contributors to make the most effective use of radio and television. Its strongest conviction is that the drawing of rigid lines between the 'educational' and the 'broadcasting' aspects of programmes, and the assignment of these legalistically to different groups of people leads to friction, bad programmes and bad teaching. It believed that an Open University conceived as an alliance between, on the one hand, academics with no knowledge of the broadcasting media planning the content of programmes and, on the other, a set of radio and television producers deemed to be experts only in their craft would have started with a crippling handicap. It therefore aimed in its negotiations with the Planning Committee at the establishment of a relationship of full educational partnership. Since the university must clearly be the final authority in every aspect of its work, that partnership could be assured only through the establishment by the BBC of an educational department which is solely concerned and closely integrated with the university, while remaining operationally an integral part of the BBC.

113. The agreement between the corporation and the university states that 'the radio and television programmes required by the university and provided by the BBC are to be planned on the basis of an educational partnership between university and BBC staff. In practice this partnership will extend over the whole range from the conception of the course to the final production of the programmes.' The need for the help of an independent broadcasting organization thus played a major part in the emergence of the course-team concept, which has led to a notably harmonious collaboration of academics and professional broadcasting staff, and to a closer integration of broadcasting with other modes of teaching than has previously been achieved in Britain.

114. The relationship hinges on the full participation of BBC staff in the course teams. It is carried further into the realm of academic decision-making by co-opting BBC course-team members and their departmental chiefs to the university senate, and to a wide range of senate committees. It is effectively symbolized by the statutory representation of the BBC on the University Council.

115. From a practical point of view, the BBC has undertaken a commitment to produce 1,450 half-hour television programmes of a highly specialized kind within five years, and a like number of half-hour radio programmes (in practice, the normal length of a television programme is 25 minutes, and of a radio programme 20 minutes). With that end in view, it has retained the lease of premises at Alexandra Palace in north London which it had proposed to give up, and has equipped them as the home of a largely self-contained operation devoted solely to Open University purposes with a steady production output of not less than 300 television programmes and 300 radio programmes a year.

116. This massive operation is sustained by a production staff (i.e. producers, production directors, production assistants and research assistants) of nearly one hundred people. The preponderant weight of effort is on the television side, but the aim is to develop a team whose members are capable of handling the

techniques of both radio and television, and who think of their work as an exercise in the two media directed to a single academic end. The team works under the direction of staff with a long experience of BBC educational broadcasting. Most of its members have, however, been specially recruited as subject specialists capable of playing a full part in the work of the course teams side by side with the university's own staff. There is a constant coming and going between the two groups, its only unsatisfactory feature being the time-consuming distance between the two headquarters.

117. The lease of Alexandra Palace will expire before the end of this decade. The university and the BBC have therefore been considering together the future of their joint operation. It has been decided that a new studio complex should be built on the university campus at Milton Keynes, some fifty miles from London. This will be a university and not a BBC building, financed by the Department of Education and Science at a cost estimated in 1973 at over £3 million. The BBC has nevertheless agreed to continue the present partnership, and to conduct there, by its own staff, a detached BBC operation which will still be able to draw upon its central resources. The studios will be capable of maintaining the present rate of output, and of expansion if necessary. They will have colour capacity, and will allow for the production of colour programmes either electronically or on film.

118. Through its arrangements with the BBC the university has been assured of a smoothly running and highly professional broadcasting operation, with access to the services and resources of a great national organization. It has been able to use programmes filmed at home and abroad and full-scale dramatic productions as well as studio programmes. Its academic staff, whose members (though reinforced by distinguished outside contributors) carry the main burden of the expository broadcasting, have learnt how best to use the media through an intimate and continuous working with their BBC colleagues.

119. The contract between the university and the BBC provides that the broadcasting services shall be charged at their cost price. The estimated cost to the university of making and transmitting the 1,450 programmes was put at more than £7 million in 1970 prices. Since the university intends to use each programme as an integral part of a course which will be on offer four times before it is remade, a large part of this sum can be regarded as an initial rather than a continuing expenditure. Broadcasting nevertheless accounts at present for more than one-sixth of the university's current annual expenditure. It must therefore keep constantly under review the effectiveness of this major use of its academic manpower and financial resources.

120. The main stumbling-block in the relationship with the BBC has from the first been the question of air time. No matter how good educational programmes may be, their effective value in broadcast form depends upon their availability at times when the potential audience can receive them. With only two channels at its disposal, and in a competitive situation, the BBC did not feel able to offer any substantial amount of peak evening time for minority purposes. Moreover, it had to consider the claims of its own adult-education programmes in radio and television, which were competing with those of the university. In the event, it was agreed that a maximum of 30 hours of television time on its second channel, BBC 2, and 30 hours of radio time on a VHF channel should be devoted to Open University programmes during 36 weeks of the university's 40-week academic year. Initially the programmes were to be

placed between the hours of 4.30 p.m. and 7.30 p.m. on weekdays, and between the hours of 9 a.m. and 1.30 p.m. on Saturdays and Sundays; as their number grew, the times would be agreed.

121. At the time of the negotiations, the provisional intention of the Planning Committee was that the university should make at least 40 full-credit courses available within five years, and it hoped that each of them could be supported on an average by one television programme and one radio programme each week for the greater part of the academic year, with a repeat in the same week to allow the student a choice of times or an opportunity for a second viewing or hearing. There has been a consequent allotment of 36 programmes in each medium to foundation courses, and an average of 24 in each medium to other full-credit courses.

122. The rapid growth in the number of courses has made it quite impossible to maintain the broadcast components of courses at this level, and has revealed the fundamentally unsatisfactory character of the position. The 1974 television output, including repeats, uses 24½ hours of transmission time a week for television and 20 hours for radio within the times indicated above, yet serves only a total of courses equivalent to 25 full credits. The full 30 hours available cannot possibly accommodate provision on that scale for the planned number of 87 credits, even without repeats. Even more disturbing is the fact that the additional placings which the BBC is prepared to allot to Open University programmes will all be at times which will exclude at least 25 per cent of the potential audience. Men and women in full-time employment cannot be expected to undertake arduous study after midnight or in the very early morning, and a survey has recently shown that one-third of the present students would find it impracticable to do so. The fact that many of them travel considerable distances to and from work makes times later than 7 a.m. or earlier than 6 p.m. impossible for them. The university has nevertheless been obliged in 1974 to accept the period from 6.50 a.m. to 7.30 a.m. as part of its quota of transmission time. The placing of obligatory programmes at unsatisfactory times inevitably reduces the number of enrolments. The placing of optional programmes then means that they will be unavailable to some students and neglected by those who cannot receive them without gross inconvenience. These facts are forcing upon the university a radical reappraisal of the situation.

123. It would be possible to produce shorter programmes, and accommodate more of them in the available time, but very short programmes are less economical in production, cannot develop a theme fully and are less likely to induce students to set aside the time for them. It would be possible to offer the less popular advanced courses only in alternate years, but this would lessen student choice, lengthen the path of some students to a degree and present the problem of organizing discontinuous employment for the part-time tutorial staff concerned. These expedients have therefore been rejected for the present. It will be necessary progressively to discontinue repeats, except for foundation courses. The Broadcasting Committee, which allots a quota of programmes to course teams in response to their reasoned bids, will have to subject those bids to rigorous scrutiny and allow only reduced quotas for many courses. These steps cannot provide a satisfactory solution.

124. The university has therefore undertaken a thorough survey of the technical possibilities and the cost of distributing its audio-visual course components in recorded form. So far as television-type programmes (i.e.

moving pictures accompanied by speech and sound) are concerned, there are various technically efficient modes of recording, on film or on electronic tape or disc. Allowing for the capital cost of the necessary projector or other playback apparatus, most of them are prohibitively expensive as a means of making the programmes available at all study centres. The inclusive cost of television per programme hour tends to obscure the fact that by far the greater part of the sum is the production cost. Broadcasting is still the cheapest mode of distribution for television-type material, and much the cheapest mode of distribution for radio-type material in any country where the universal possession of television and radio receivers can be assumed as a matter of course. Its closest economic rival in the television field is the tele-type disc, and technical progress may in the next few years change the position.

125. Assuming that there can be one broadcast transmission of each television programme, at however poor a time, it is possible to make recordings with video-tape recorders (VTR machines) at study centres for the use of students who missed the transmission. In 1974 the university, as an experiment, equipped six study centres with VTR machines, and with a supply of tapes to be wiped and used again after an appropriate interval. Since 75 per cent of the students who recently answered a sample questionnaire say that they could attend a study centre at least once a fortnight, this appears to be a hopeful direction of advance. In the long run, unless inexpensive home-based viewing devices become available, it seems certain that there must be either a reduced use of video material per course or a shift from home-based to study-centre-based viewing of either VTR or centrally processed recordings.

126. In spite of a similar shortage of air time, the situation is easier in relation to radio-type programmes. Audio cassettes are reasonably cheap. The provision of playback facilities in all study centres presents no difficulty. The necessary playback apparatus is already in the possession of many students, and could be lent, as scientific kits are, to others. The cassette material can be closely related to an accompanying printed text with illustrations. It can be designed to synchronize with a filmstrip or with slides, and teaching material of this kind has been developed with great success for schools by the BBC under the name of Radiovision. Although further research is needed, it is probable that a great deal of the teaching now done by television could be done as effectively, though perhaps less attractively, by radio or by audio-cassettes linked with still pictures or slides.

127. In view of the probable future significance of recorded material for the university, it has arrived at an understanding with the BBC that the Open University Department will undertake to produce such audio-visual programmes and material as are required, even if most of the distribution for any course is to be in recorded form without any original broadcast.

128. In spite of every palliative, the university is closely enmeshed in the consequences of a contract with the BBC which provides a great volume of material for broadcast without any adequate guarantee of suitable transmission time. In the writer's view, it is doubtful whether any teaching venture of the scale on which it now operates can make a comprehensive and effective use of the broadcasting media without having control of a major part of the time on national channels. A great deal could no doubt be done with radio alone, but in so far as television is necessary for science and other teaching it must be universally available and there is as yet no satisfactory substitute for or

supplement to broadcast distribution. The government has under consideration the allocation of a fourth national television channel, and the university has made a bid for it as an educational channel, to be shared with school broadcasting (which operates at complementary times) and other educational purposes. Since the capital cost of the channel has been estimated at upwards of £30 million, it may be allotted to commerce rather than to public purposes, or may be reserved for a later decision. It is conceivable that the university will succeed at an earlier date with a parallel bid for a V.H.F. radio channel, which would give renewed urgency to a reconsideration of the respective teaching roles of the two media.

XI Staff, premises and equipment

129. The staff of the university is much more diverse than that of a conventional institution. It has had to recruit not only the 400 academic members of its central and regional academic staff, a group of librarians, and the members of its IET, with the usual administrative support. It also has a specialized need for a corps of systems-analysts and computer programmers, for typographers, designers, graphic artists and photographers, and for groups of men and women expert in such various fields as copyright, publishing, the management of correspondence services, and the world-wide marketing of printed and audio-visual material. It depends on the services of a large and efficient secretarial and clerical staff, now nearly 700 strong, and must therefore have access to a pool of labour, especially in this field. In September 1973, there were 1,197 people working on the headquarters campus. The regional directors with all their full-time, regionally based supporting staffs, including organizing tutors and senior counsellors, amounted to another 445 people, and they have, in their turn, been responsible for the enlistment of 5,094 part-time tutors and counsellors who are now busy with the students of the 1975 courses.

130. The choice of a permanent headquarters for the Open University was governed by three factors: the need for a campus of considerable size, the prohibitively high cost of land and buildings in the metropolitan area and the need for the university and the BBC studios at Alexandra Palace to be within easy travelling distance of each other. The seventy-acre site finally chosen is at Milton Keynes, in a rural area scheduled as the centre of a large new city which will be developed during the next decade. With the good-will of the planning authority the main complex of permanent buildings has already been completed, and laboratories which will replace the present temporary accommodation are due to be constructed shortly.

131. The campus at present offers no residential accommodation, but there are plans for residential accommodation to meet the needs of regional staff, of overseas visiting staff and of some postgraduate students. There is no need for the lecture rooms and student laboratories of the conventional university. The laboratories and library serve two purposes, offering to the course teams the facilities necessary for course development, but also meeting the basic research needs of the staff and of a small number of research students working under their direction. A single large lecture theatre is used mainly for gatherings of the staff, including the regional staff. Yet small as its conventional needs are, the university has urgent needs of its own. It must provide accommodation not only for the

academic staff, but also for the very large administrative and clerical groups concerned with the admission and registration of students, with the handling of the students' written work, and with the keeping of records. Centralized control of the educational process is dependent on a complex computer system (now operating over 1,000 separate computer programmes) which calls for the support of a data-processing centre with ample storage space. The computer, to cite only some of its major uses, is used for keeping and making available particulars about each student and his progress, for the marking of the multiple-choice-type of student assignments of work, and for accountancy. The package material depends on the services of a design group with its own studio, which must be sited on the campus to allow for close and constant intercourse between its staff and the members of the course teams. The major printed requirements of the university, including the course books and the prospectus, are printed externally by commercial firms, but the university maintains a photolithographic printing shop to deal with notes on the broadcasts and other supplementary material. There is a photographic unit with darkrooms equipped to process full-colour material. The enormous outward post is handled by packaging and addressing machines of the latest design. Extensive warehousing accommodation is required for the storage of printed material and science kits, and this is provided at an off-campus site.

132. Operationally, the university must be run as an efficient factory, with rigid delivery dates, and a need for close discipline in the whole of its interlocking operation. The housing of all of its basic services (except for printing and warehousing) on the one campus makes far easier the necessary degree of control, and contributes largely to mutual understanding between the various groups of staff involved and a sense of partnership in a shared enterprise. The building of the proposed audio-visual block will take still further the establishment of a large and complex self-contained operation.

XII Finance

133. The balance sheet of the university for the calendar year 1973 (which in the Open University is also its academic year) shows a cumulative capital expenditure to the end of that year of £5,231,283, including payments to the BBC for studio alterations and equipment of £1,104,402.

134. Since regional premises are rented, the great bulk of the expenditure has been on buildings and equipment at the Milton Keynes centre. The major buildings still to be begun are a science block with adequate research laboratories to replace the present temporary accommodation, and a studio centre (at an estimated cost of £2 to £3 million in 1973) to accommodate the BBC operation including the production of non-broadcast, audio-visual material when the lease of the present premises expires.

135. The annual recurrent expenditure for 1973 was £11,865,000; of the corresponding income 83 per cent was derived from government grants and 17 per cent from student fees (including summer-school fees), a ratio well in excess of that prevailing in conventional universities which amounted in 1969/70 to only 6 per cent. (It should be borne in mind that student fees are to a considerable extent subsidized by local education authorities, and thus constitute a charge on public funds; see paragraph 144 below.)

136. The most significant fact to emerge from an analysis of the university's expenditure is the relationship between 'fixed' overhead costs (accounting for 74.5 per cent of the total) and 'direct student' costs varying in exact proportion to the number of students (accounting for 25.5 per cent). The principal headings in the first category are academic-staff salaries (which account for most of the cost of course development) and BBC recurrent charges for the production and transmission of radio and television broadcasts, which, at £2,230,500, amounted to 18.7 per cent of the university's recurrent expenditure in 1973. But these 'fixed' costs also contain charges such as expenditure on administration, on computerized records and on local premises that rise with increases in student numbers, though not in direct proportion. The principal items of 'direct student' costs are the salaries of part-time tutors and counsellors, the cost of printed materials and science kits, and the costs of summer schools.

137. The consequence of this pattern of expenditure, which reverses the pattern of conventional universities, is that the marginal cost of each additional student is much less than the existing average cost, and that cost-effectiveness can be considerably increased by increasing the number of students. This fact was strikingly evidenced by the decision of the government in 1974 that it would respond to the large increase in the number of applicants for Open University places by sanctioning an increase in student numbers. Its previously notified grant-in-aid for recurrent expenditure to cover the triennium 1974–76 amounted to £10.6 million, £11.2 million and £11.8 million, on the assumption that the target for undergraduate numbers during that period would be set in the range of 36,000 to 42,000. The gross cost per finally registered student in 1973 was approximately £314, and since a proportion of the students took more than one course, the cost per full course equivalent was £284. In these circumstances, the university was able to undertake to admit an agreed additional 6,000 students in 1975 and 1976 (lifting the total student population from 42,000 to about 49,000) for an addition to the annual grant of only about £1 million, that is, about £150 per student, and thereby to lower the average cost per student over the whole range.

138. The future cost-effectiveness of the university will therefore depend on the size it is allowed to reach more than on any other single factor. Other considerations than the amount of government grant may, however, have a bearing on the question of size. There must, for example, be a limit, not yet in sight, to the number of suitable part-time staff available. Furthermore, the capacity of the computer and of existing systems is not infinite. It is possible that the optimum size may lie within the range of 60,000 to 70,000 students.

139. Another major factor will be the future rate of drop-out, and encouraging as the present persistence rates are it is too early to extrapolate from them with any confidence. It has been calculated that, if present rates persist, some 6,000 out of every 20,000 students admitted will eventually graduate, and that 50 per cent of them will go on to honours degrees. It cannot yet be stated with any certainty what the average time taken will be, but for a student who starts without credit exemption it seems likely to be five or six years.

140. It should not be assumed that the costs of future third- and fourth-level courses will be of the same order as the costs of the present foundation and second-year courses. The average development cost, including broadcasts, of the five foundation courses so far produced has been about £160,000. The average cost of second-year courses in arts and in the social sciences has been

about £76,000 and that of second-year courses in mathematics and science has ranged from £95,000 to £150,000. (Science courses are much more expensive than arts courses in academic staff time and also tend to have a higher television element. The university has recently estimated academic productivity, making a due allowance for the time spent on research not related to course production, as 2.5 units of the standard 32-unit full-credit course per student-year for arts, 2.3 units for social sciences, but only 1.6 units for educational studies and mathematics and 1.4 units for science and technology. In other words, while an arts course requires the work of a team of six for just over two years, a science course calls for twice that number. Because of the need to issue home-experiment kits and to provide laboratory accommodation at weekend and summer schools, science courses are also much more expensive than arts courses in direct student costs.)

141. In these circumstances, it may prove practicable (and in view of the shortage of television time, it may prove absolutely necessary) to use cheaper methods of teaching, with less reliance on television and more on face-to-face tuition for the more advanced courses with their small student numbers. It is already clear that the life of some courses can be extended beyond the scheduled four years, with large savings resulting.

142. Such assessments as have so far taken place have necessarily been based on figures drawn from a period when the university was still in a state of rapid development, when the student population had not yet reached its agreed size and when the number of courses on offer was limited, though an academic staff adequate to produce and maintain a much larger number was already at work, and a stockpiling operation was in progress. A report prepared by staff of the Higher Education Research Unit of the London School of Economics, basing its findings on courses presented in 1971 and 1972, and taking two years as an Open University student as broadly equivalent to one year as a student in a campus university in terms of hours spent on study and of progress towards graduation, concluded that the cost per full-time equivalent student was very substantially less at the Open University than elsewhere. Its findings did, however, suggest that higher-level courses with fewer students would either have to be produced more cheaply, or justified on the ground that they were an integral part of a system providing wider access to complete degree courses rather than on the ground that they were cheap in themselves.

143. It should be borne in mind in any consideration of the costs of the university that the great majority of its students are in full employment, whereas the value of the work foregone by full-time campus students constitutes a part of the full national cost. Finally, it must also be remembered that the Open University is not in direct competition with the campus universities, but was called into being to serve a wholly different group of students, and to achieve purposes that without it would not have been achieved at all.

144. As for the cost borne by the individual student, the 1975 tuition fee for a full-credit course is £25, with half courses *pro rata.* The fee for a one-week foundation course summer school is £38.50, and for the summer schools of other courses is £40.50. The total cost to a student of an honours degree could thus be estimated as £200 for eight full-credit courses, a further £130 for set books, and a minimum of £77 for the summer schools associated with the two compulsory foundation courses. For a science student the cost of summer schools could amount to very much more. In 1972, however, some 70 per cent of the

students who managed to attend their summer school had at least a part of their summer-school fees paid by local education authorities, and it is the hope of the university that this practice will be further extended.

XIII Conclusions

145. This section aims to list the main characteristics of the Open University that seem relevant to the objectives of the project, and to suggest the points at which the experience gained may be relevant to other countries:

(a) The Open University is a new permanent institution, largely educationally autonomous.

(b) The university is a university among existing universities, conforming in the main to their established requirements, though proposing to offer a range of course choice to the individual greater than existing universities do.

(c) The Open University teaching system was devised to make full use of most (but not all) modern educational media, and to draw heavily upon all the relevant pre-existing educational and communications facilities. These facilities are essential to its system, and it is heavily dependent on the following external agencies:
   - (i) Publishers, for guaranteeing the availability of set books.
   - (ii) Booksellers, for stocking them.
   - (iii) Universities, for providing summer-school facilities.
   - (iv) Local education authorities, for providing study-centre facilities, and financial support to students.
   - (v) Public libraries, for providing background reading facilities.
   - (vi) The Post Office, for providing postal services, and British Road Transport, for providing home-kit delivery services.
   - (vii) The BBC for broadcast production and transmission.
   - (viii) Commercial printers, for printing of course units and handbooks.
   - (ix) The full-time staff of other institutions of higher education, whose members are employed by the Open University on a part-time basis.

(d) The Open University's organizational and teaching system, given nation-wide diffusion and large student numbers, can achieve low costs per student.

(e) The Open University devised, in partnership with the BBC, patterns of working relationships among academics, among academics and educational broadcasters and among academics, broadcasters and educational technologists that were new to the United Kingdom. These relationships draw upon the forty years' experience of educational broadcasting guided by national educational advisory agencies, and upon a national aptitude for collaborative work.

(f) At its outset, the Open University had to contend with certain political and professional attitudes which moulded and may continue to influence its form and practice. When the university showed that its system was succeeding, it came under pressure to contribute to other aspects of higher education than its planners had envisaged.

146. The relevance of the Open University to other countries must be considered in the light of these characteristics. It could be studied:

(a) As an ancillary institution of higher education.

(b) As a system of distance learning applicable to university or other levels of age and attainment.
(c) As a model for study of institutions or systems in countries with different educational or political systems, or at different stages of economic and social development.
(d) As a system expressing principles, ideas and techniques that are capable of different expression at lower levels of cost and complexity in other educational and developmental contexts.

147. The transferability of the Open University system or of its teaching material has yet to be fully explored.

Appendix A — Standardized reference data

Country, state or province	*United Kingdom of Great Britain and Northern Ireland*
Area and climate	94,217 square miles. Maritime temperate.
Population	
Total (latest year)	55,515,000 (1972).
Estimated population aged 18	748,600 (1972).
Estimated percentage under 15	24 (1971).
Current annual growth rate (percentage)	0.4 (1965–72).
Government	
Main organizational structure	Unitary, with delegated administrative responsibilities (e.g. for education, to local education authorities).
Political type	Parliamentary democracy; constitutional monarchy.
Economy	
Political type	Predominantly industrialized; State control of some key industries.
Gross national product	
Total (latest year)	£48,216 million (1971) (U.S.$115,000 million).
Per head	£909 (1971) (U.S.$2,600).
Average annual increase	£2,000 million (till 1969) (U.S.$4,760).
Communications	
Ground/air	Quick and easy countrywide system of roads, motorways, bus, rail and air transport services.
Mail/telephone	Adequate postal services. Growing telephone service: now (1972) 31.4 per 100 people.

Broadcasting	
Main system(s) operating/ Principal authorities responsible	The British Broadcasting Corporation (BBC): a public body responsible for the planning, production and transmission of radio and television services. The Independent Broadcasting Authority (IBA): a statutory public body set up to provide transmission facilities for commercial radio and television companies and to regulate their activities.
Radio	
Transmission coverage of main programme services with percentage of population reached	99.35 per cent reached by all channels on F.M.
Receiving capability for main programme services (percentage)	Approaching 100.
Television	
Transmission coverage as defined for radio	BBC 1: 99.5 per cent. BBC 2: 94 per cent. IBA: 99.5 per cent.
Receiving capability for main programme services	96.5 per cent possess television receivers; 88.6 per cent can receive BBC 2.
Monochrome or colour	All new transmissions in colour; 6.7 million possess colour receivers, numbers rising fast (June 1974).
Education	
Type of system(s)	Predominantly publicly controlled and financed. One in 50 children attends private school.
Main authorities responsible and powers	
At school level	Local education authorities subject to financial and administrative influence of government: Department of Education and Science (DES).
At post-secondary level	Almost entirely publicly financed, universities from DES through University Grants Committee (UGC), polytechnics and other higher education institutions from local education authorities and central funding and fees.
End of full-time school attendance	
Legal	Compulsory and free between 5 and 16.
De facto	Increasing numbers stay voluntarily until 18.
Proportion of 18-year-old age group involved in education	
Full-time	3.88 per cent (1971–72).
Part-time	17.6 per cent (1971–72).
Major developments in provision	
Over last five years	Legal school-leaving age raised to 16 (1972–73).

Over next five years	Robbins Report (1963) recommended raising proportion of 18 to 20 age group entering full-time higher education from 8 per cent (1963) to 17 per cent (1980).

Institution/system under study

Brief for study and reason for inclusion	The Open University is the first university to be established solely to teach adult students at a distance. Included as an example of multi-media distance teaching.
Description of subject studied	The institution and its first-degree system.
Origins	Political decision by Labour Government 1964. Established by royal charter 1969.
Educational authority(ies) and roles	Financed by DES and by students' fees initially, later via UGC.
Communications authority(ies) and roles	Partnership with BBC, which provides air time and programmes to requirements of university, prepared in 'course teams'.
Services provided	Wider opportunities of university education to adults both for vocational and non-vocational purposes, through face-to-face and multi-media methods of tuition. Home-based students remaining in employment.
Eligibility to study	
(a) categories	Adults over 21.
(b) qualifications	No formal qualifications. Applications treated subject by subject and area quotas on first-come, first-served basis.
Terminal qualifications	Graduate degrees (honours and ordinary) and sundry postgraduate.
Instructional means used	Multi-media, i.e. set books, correspondence work, home-experimental kits for science students, radio, television. Voluntary attendance at course centres for advice and tuition. Compulsory summer-school attendance.
Personal input from student	Minimum of 10 hours per week over 40 weeks per course taken; common average 10 to 15 hours weekly.
Normal duration of study	Two courses per year maximum permitted, minimum three years and honours four years (8 units). Usual duration 5 to 6 years. Exemptions possible.
Pedagogic effectiveness	Pass rate per course for finally registered students 73.5 per cent (1973), 8 per cent failed examinations (can retake); 17 per cent (1971) did not attend summer school or take final examinations.

Numbers involved

Students	
Intake (latest year)	20,000 from 52,537 applications (1975).
On roll	42,172 finally registered (1974).
Graduating	10,543 (1974).
Academic staff	
Full-time (latest year)	397 (1973).
Part-time	5,231 (1973).
Other professional staff	
Number	Administration: approximately 500.

Finance

Recurrent expenditure	
By providing authorities (latest available year)	£11,865,000 (1973), of which £2,230,500 to BBC. Derived: 83 per cent government, 17 per cent students (often assisted by local education authority).
Average annual outlay by student	Tuition: £25.00 per course. Books. Summer school: £38.40 per course (1975). May be subsidized or paid by local education authority.
Non-recurrent expenditure	
Gross, over first five years of new institution	£5,231,283 (1969–71) including £1,104,402 to BBC for use of premises, equipment etc.
Special assistance received	
Financial	None beyond public funds.
Non-financial	University dependent upon existing educational and communications infrastructure and co-operation with BBC educational services.

Sources of further information

Educational	Director of Information Services, The Open University, Walton Hall, Milton Keynes (United Kingdom). (Information about the marketing and consultancy services of the university can be obtained from the same source.)
Broadcasting	British Broadcasting Corporation, *Educational Television and Radio in Britain*, BBC, 1966 (handbook).

Appendix B Short bibliography

BRITISH BROADCASTING CORPORATION. *BBC handbook 1975*. London, BBC, 1974.

OPEN UNIVERSITY. *Report of the Planning Committee to the Secretary of State for Education and Science*. London, HMSO, 1969.

——. *Report of the vice-chancellor, January 1969 to December 1970. The early development of the Open University*. Milton Keynes, The Open University Press, 1972.

——. *Report of the vice-chancellor 1971. The first teaching year of the Open University*. Milton Keynes, The Open University, 1973.

——. *Report of the vice-chancellor 1972*. Milton Keynes, The Open University Press, 1973.

——. *Report of the vice-chancellor 1973*. Milton Keynes, The Open University Press, 1975.

——. *Guide for applicants for undergraduate courses 1975*. Milton Keynes, The Open University Press, 1974.

——. *BA degree handbook 1975*. Milton Keynes, The Open University Press, 1974.

——. *Courses handbook 1975*. Milton Keynes, The Open University Press, 1974.

UNITED KINGDOM. *A university of the air*. London, HMSO, 1966. (Cmnd 2922.)

Appendix C Biographical note

John Scupham, M.A. Cantab., was the Educational Consultant for the Research Project on Open Learning Systems in Post-Secondary Education. He was formerly Controller of Educational Broadcasting, BBC, and a member of the Planning Committee of the Open University and its governing council.

Open Learning systems in the **United States of America**

A *The 'learning contract': three systems of personalized study*

The Empire State College, New York
The Minnesota Metropolitan State College
The Community College of Vermont

The three case studies in this part of the report deal with variations of the same type of innovation—the 'learning contract' as an alternative to formal campus-based education. This is a personalized course of supervised study which can lead to a recognized academic award. It is student-oriented and experience-based, in place of the traditional instruction-oriented and discipline-based system upon which higher education has traditionally depended. All three institutions are still experimenting with this system on a small scale and it is premature to attempt any systematic assessment of its effectiveness or its likely impact on the assumptions and methods of higher education. The 'learning contract', however, is a challenging conception and, since it is expressly designed to promote 'openness' in post-secondary education, it has considerable potential, not least because it can be introduced with modest resources, applied to pilot groups of students and assimilated by conventional systems without the heavy overheads and substantial planning effort required by more ambitious schemes. It is, essentially, a style of teaching and learning rather than an institution.

The emergence of these recent attempts to serve students who do not wish to engage in formal teaching programmes must be set in the changing context of post-secondary education in the United States. There is an extensive and diversified pattern of formal education for school leavers.

Over half of the 3 million high-school graduates go on each year to some form of further or higher education. There are approximately 7 million full-time students in universities and colleges, another 6 million enrolled part-time, 4 million engaged in some form of correspondence education and millions more engaged in various forms of in-service or professional and vocational training.

To serve this large student population there are: over 1,700 universities and colleges offering first and second degrees; 1,000 junior and community colleges which provide courses up to sub-degree level; and 1,000 technical and vocational institutions. These universities, colleges and other institutions are both publicly supported (state and municipal funds) and privately endowed, but there is general acceptance and interchangeability of the academic awards they offer. Broadly speaking, students who have graduated from high school anywhere in the country may make their way through the system, carrying appropriate credits from one institution to another.

The concept of accumulating and transferable credits lies at the heart of the American system, permitting students to move, to suspend study temporarily and to re-enter the system at a later date. It governs the construction of syllabuses, provides a way of computing the amount of study required (the method of 'credit-hours')[1] and regulates the pattern of assessment for each level of qualification. By means of a network of accrediting agencies and through regulation by state education agencies, the United States system can thus accommodate a very great variety of degree and sub-degree programmes based upon widely differing syllabuses, modes of instruction and means of assessment and examination.

Despite such flexibility, however, a considerable number of those who go on to some form of post-secondary education do not complete their formal studies. Half of those who enter terminate full-time study after two years; only one-third complete a first-degree programme. With the trend towards more 'open admission' policies, the proportion liable to drop out may well increase. There has been much discussion recently of alternative forms of study for students who do not wish, or are unable, to continue in full-time higher education. This discussion also focuses upon the problems of the large number of school leavers who do not initially attempt to study after finishing high school. It is estimated that over 70 million adult United States citizens have never finished high school or taken any formal course of study beyond the secondary level. This problem is particularly acute among ethnic minorities and other socially disadvantaged groups.

In the last few years, United States universities and colleges have been experimenting with programmes designed to cater for students who do not fit the conventional categories of campus-based education. Such students may have dropped out, or at least have become dissatisfied with the formal four-year degree structure. They may have found it difficult, for physical or financial reasons, to attend a university or college: although these are widely dispersed in small towns as well as in the large cities, there is clearly a significant part of the potential student population which does not have easy access to such institutions. Some may aspire to higher education but find that their preliminary education has been inadequate. Others may be adults, already in the labour force, who wish to study for vocational reasons or for personal enrichment and do not find the formalized offerings that are available appropriate to their needs as they perceive them.

The idea of a 'learning contract' rests on several assumptions. First, that a student should be able to work out a programme which seems relevant to

1. To those unfamiliar with the system, it should be explained that in United States colleges and universities the academic year consists of two periods of study, each of about four months ('semesters'). Progress towards a degree is made by obtaining a specified number of credits, or 'credit-hours', amounting in the case of an associate degree to 60, and for a bachelor degree to 120. A 'credit-hour' was originally a measure of the number of hours of contact between tutor and student needed to cover the course; it might be three per week for an arts course, or, for a science course, five, of which two could be for practical work. There was also an informal relationship between the number of credit hours and the hours of private study—a ratio of two or three hours to each credit-hour. Credit-hours obtained in one institution are, subject to detailed regulation, now usually transferable to another. Credit-hours may also be granted for non-academic activities such as a cultural visit, or a period of attachment in another institution (often referred to as 'internship') which may last over a substantial period. The 'credit-hour' system has thus become a form of academic currency greatly facilitating freedom of movement and choice, though it is also open to abuse.

personal needs and capacities. Second, that a student should be able to combine academic disciplines in a project-based mode of learning, and should be able to draw upon a wide range of resources for help—including community agencies and commercial organizations which may provide the 'experience' context for study. Third, that assessment of the student rests upon the achievement of specified knowledge and skills, not on formal examinations. Fourth, that the sponsoring institution is able to vouch for the student's competence and make an award which enables the student to fit into the credit-based system on equal terms with those who have pursued more conventional studies.

As the three case studies reveal, the advocates of the 'learning contract' believe that this innovation has an educational rationale as well as a social utility. If it succeeds, therefore, it is likely to feed back into formal full-time education and lead to changes both in the curriculum and in methods of teaching and learning. While it is particularly appropriate for off-campus study, its essential principles could be adapted for full-time students who are campus-based.

The Empire State College

This college, based at Saratoga Springs in the centre of New York State, was the seventy-second institution of the ramified State University of New York. Its exclusive purpose is to organize courses of study for degrees on a non-residential basis and without the conventional lectures and classes. It currently enrols just over 2,000 students, and recruits slightly more than 300 entrants each year. It is financed in part by public funds and in part by the Ford, Carnegie and Kellogg Foundations. The average age of its students is 33 years, and a high proportion has previously attended full-time colleges or universities.

The Minnesota Metropolitan State College

Situated in St Paul, and founded in 1972, the college is part of the state system and it offers 'Degree Pact' programmes for students over the age of 25 years. It is exclusively concerned with students whose needs are not served by conventional institutions, and it is publicly financed. Its current enrolment is about 1,000 students.

The Community College of Vermont

This college, situated in the centre of a sparsely populated state, was established in 1971 to serve students living in rural areas and small towns. It offers both vocational and non-vocational education to adults, to the level of an 'associate' degree, which is the equivalent of half a normal four-year degree programme. It currently enrols 1,500 students.

All three institutions are thus supervising and assisting students who are studying and working in their own communities, and all three depend heavily on the use of part-time staff and on collaborators in other educational institutions (and, in some cases, 'mentors' in public and commercial institutions to which students are attached or where they are employed). They thus provide important examples of the ways in which off-campus support can be provided for remote students.

The Empire State College, New York

W. C. Meierhenry

Contents

I Introduction

1. The genesis of Empire State College took place in the early 1960s, far ahead of the development of most such innovative colleges. Dr Pitkin, President of Goddard College, Plainfield, Vermont, pioneered the idea that each student should be given the responsibility of designing his own programme and that a degree should be earned after eight full-time semesters of attendance rather than the traditional American approach of a fixed number of semester hours of college credit. Dr Arthur Chickering, now Vice-President for Academic Affairs at Empire State College, was Dean of Student Affairs at Goddard College during this period.

2. At the same time, Dr Ernest L. Boyer, now Chancellor of the State University of New York, was Dean of Upsala College, East Orange, New Jersey, and became well acquainted with President Pitkin and the Goddard College programme. With the organization of the Union for Experimenting Colleges, a meeting was called of those interested in alternative forms of higher education at Goddard College in 1963, which was attended by Dr Boyer among many others. A number of years passed before Dr Boyer became Chancellor of the State University of New York and was in a position to develop the plans for the innovative college now known as Empire State College (ESC). It was through the efforts of Chancellor Boyer, supported by Governor Nelson Rockefeller of New York, along with sympathetic legislative bodies that ESC was authorized to begin operation.

3. ESC was developed to serve the educational needs of a contemporary society. Basic changes in energy and work, in population and human relations, in generating information and in the exchange of knowledge and experiences have created fundamental changes in human existence and human requirements. The new college was to explore new ways of educating and reaching people and to provide an education for people who could not or do not wish to devote four years of their lives to being physically present in a classroom on a traditional campus.

4. ESC was therefore committed to flexibility and individual learning. The college believed that the quality of education would suffer if students were treated as standardized products on some sort of educational assembly line. ESC's strongest conviction was that students of all ages and situations could be treated as individual human beings, and that the quality of education would rise as ways were found to help such people learn what they wanted to know.

5. ESC is a state-wide institution. It has no campuses and does not duplicate the specialized faculties or libraries common to residential campuses. The college seeks to make available any learning resources necessary for a student's education. Arrangements have been made so that students can move easily from one state university campus to another. A network of educational arrangements providing readily available resources which can be used in the learning centres, sometimes at home or on the job, but always designed to meet each individual's capacities, obligations and interests, has been developed. There is a close working relationship between ESC and other institutions of higher learning, as well as between ESC and community and governmental agencies, industrial and labour bodies and the population at large.

6. The college is not designed for everyone and does not seek to replace traditional campus-oriented education. It welcomes students who want to learn; who think they can function effectively without some of the regular supports of the familiar campus; who want to explore the extent to which they can work independently; who want contact with the faculty on an individual basis; who can and will rise to a challenge.

7. The primary distinction between a traditional programme and the ESC approach is that students pursue most of their college education without residing on a campus or meeting in a classroom. There are opportunities to spend a semester, or more, living and working on a campus or participating in short weekend and summer schools. However, most of the academic programme is pursued at home or in other non-campus situations.

8. A student creates an individual degree programme by harmonizing three principal elements. The first element is the student's goals, capacities and aspirations. Each student *initiates a programme* which responds seriously and concretely to these factors. Since the student takes the major responsibility for learning, this first element is a fundamental and essential part of every effective programme. Second, each student is expected to *demonstrate achievement* in the broad areas of intellectual competence and also to strive for personal development. It is through demonstrating these competencies that the degree requirements are met. Third, each student engages in several *modes of learning* in those areas of study in which the college has approved programmes, experienced faculty (academic staff), appropriate inter-institutional relationships and adequate learning resources. The major modes of learning and areas of study and the frameworks for judgement proposed for each are described later in this report.

II Critical elements in operation

9. As a non-traditional college ESC includes many interesting and unusual elements. Among those demanding special attention are the types of degrees, the time to be spent, the nature of students, mentors (faculty), and learning contracts and the evaluation of experiences to determine whether they have contributed to the students' objective as identified in the learning contract and regional learning centres.

Degrees

10. ESC awards the following degrees: (a) Associate in Arts (A.A.); (b) Associate in Science (A.S.); (c) Bachelor of Arts (B.A.); and (d) Bachelor of Science (B.S.).

Time to be spent

11. The amount of time required to complete a degree varies because ESC operates year-round and allows flexibility for students who have either prior schooling or other previous experience which has been approved for credit or advanced standing. However, there is a minimum time-schedule for completion of degrees. At least three months of full-time or six months of half-time study must be completed for the A.A. or A.S. degree, and six months of full-time or twelve months of half-time for the B.A. or B.S. degree.

12. Any student with 54 or more units of transfer credit will be considered an upper-division student. This includes: (a) a two-year college graduate with an associate degree; (b) a student bringing transfer credit approved by the ESC faculty; (c) a student whose application for advanced standing through presentation of other prior learning experience has been approved by the faculty.

13. Units of credit are described in months of study. Thus, the full-time student should, on average, expect to spend 32 months to complete the work for the B.A. or B.S. degrees, or 16 months for the A.A. or A.S. degrees.

14. On this basis, students are classified as follows: 1 to 16 months, lower division; 17 to 32 months, upper division.

15. These classifications are consistent with traditional arrangements whereby students are enrolled for approximately eight months each calendar year and spend two or four years for the A.A. and A.S. or the B.A. and B.S. degrees. Because ESC operates year-round, however, the student who carries out full-time learning contracts continuously can obtain the A.A. or A.S. degree in one and a half years, and the B.A. or B.S. degree in three. These general time expectations are treated flexibly, depending upon the performance of the individual student. Some students may complete learning contracts in more, or less, time than specified. In such cases the student receives credit for the time specified.

Students

16. The flexible arrangements and varied resources of ESC make it particularly suited for:

(a) A young person who wishes to take major responsibility for planning his own programme and carrying it out.

(b) An older person who wishes for further education which suits his or her particular interests and which recognizes the experience and knowledge he or she already has.

(c) A person on the job who has completed courses offered by an employer or union.

(d) A veteran serviceman or woman who brings studies undertaken during military service.
(e) A retired person pursuing a new interest or new career.
(f) A man or woman of any age who must pursue education while continuing substantial employment in or out of the home.

17. All such individuals are potential ESC students. Their interests, occupations and ages range widely: school teacher; labour union official; government worker; poet; secretary; policeman; photographer; businessman; computer programmer; artist; housewife. Their backgrounds are diverse, but each would consider ESC, for specific reasons.

18. Some would come for the freedom and responsibility inherent in independent study, others to incorporate already gained competencies into academic studies and still others, because of work or family responsibilities, would be attracted by the possibility of study without long residential requirements. For half-time students particularly, individual programming means achieving goals within a reasonable length of time. For such students, the possibility of working at their own time and pace can eliminate the frustrations resulting from incorporating their job, family responsibilities and educational ambitions into a too exhausting timetable.

19. Admission to ESC is made without regard to the race, sex, religion or national origin of the student. There are two principal requirements: (a) possession of a high-school diploma, its equivalent, or the ability to do college work demonstrated by an applicant's presentation of completed work or life responsibilities; (b) the ability of the learning centre to meet the applicant's expressed educational objectives.

20. To qualify for ESC, students must have the equivalent of a high-school education. Students who have not graduated at high school can present the General Education Development Diploma (High School Equivalency). Persons who have not completed high school but have reached the age of 22 and have been involved in activities that relate to their education may also qualify for admission.

Mentor

21. Faculty members at ESC are called mentors. Such a title suggests that the role of the faculty member is to serve at various times as a helper, adviser, counsellor and a teacher. As a mentor the faculty member serves in many more roles than does a typical professor on a college staff.

22. Each mentor in the learning centre is responsible for approximately thirty different students. In addition, he or she contributes to programme planning and developing learning resources for the centre and for the college. The mentor's principal responsibility is to his or her students and for this reason the college employs mentors who take that responsibility seriously.

Learning contract

23. Learning operations at ESC are framed in a particular context. The learning contract, as a pedagogic instrument, has no immediate parallels with

the course descriptions in conventional departmental settings. The mentor is asked to describe the learning operation in more detail than is the professor in a conventional college. At the same time, he or she is often engaged in learning activities which are unique, which resist classification and which often engage the mentor at the edge of his or her competency. Moreover, the individual mentor at ESC is required to design a much larger part of the student's studies than does a single faculty member in a conventional departmental setting.

24. Where mentors are called upon to operate outside their specific area of competence, they turn to other resources. These may range widely but they must have one attribute in common: they must represent intellectually sound learning processes designed by persons into whose specific areas of competence they fall. These learning processes may include: tutorial relationships; courses offered at other institutions; correspondence material; special membership programmes; and programmes developed by ESC and other bodies.

25. Another factor which determines the particular content and role of the learning contract is the nature of the discipline studied. Although the learning contract is central to the operation at ESC and although a generalized format of the contract can be given, the content of the learning contract and the procedures surrounding it will vary greatly, depending upon the nature of the material to be studied and the nature and conditions of the person involved in the learning process. Some learning contracts are difficult to predict. Thus a learning contract in science may very well be quite straightforward. In contrast, one in the creative arts may, of necessity, be quite open, flexible and subject to progressive development.

Evaluation

26. Generally, two phases of the student's degree programme require evaluation procedures. In the first place, most students at ESC will present past experiences which they believe to be equivalent to academic credit. Recognition of such experiences, known as 'advanced standing', is based on prior learning and must meet three requirements: (a) the 'learnings' for which recognition is requested must be articulated; (b) the learnings must be pertinent to the student's goals and consistent with the educational goals of the college; (c) to support the learnings claimed, evidence must be produced, such as transcripts, certificates, licences, examination scores and other documents. It may be necessary to consider tests, demonstrations and other performance alternatives and to consult persons who can render sound judgements about special areas of competence and knowledge.

27. In the second place, when the work of a learning contract has been completed, the student and his or her mentor meet in an evaluation conference. During this conference, the work of the learning contract is reviewed and the evidence of learnings is examined. This evidence may include: notes of conferences or other communications between the student and his or her mentor when work and learning activities were discussed and examined; reactions and evaluative comments from tutors or field supervisors concerning on-the-job performance; papers written, or other items; and grades and teacher comments from courses taken elsewhere.

Regional learning centres

28. ESC operates through a network of area learning centres. These centres are not miniature campuses but rather meeting-places where students can confer with faculty members about their work; they also serve as the location for the 'Orientation Workshop', designed to introduce new students to the educational procedures and resources of the college. Each centre is a major clearing-house in its region for resources useful in the planning of non-traditional approaches to study. Each centre maintains directories of the public and private learning resources in its area.

29. By 1975, eight centres were to have been established, each staffed by a core of faculty mentors and administrators, and serving about 600 full- and part-time students. Once these centres have acquired a full complement of students and mentors, they will establish additional meeting-places on campuses, as well as in storefronts, libraries and museums. The centres already in existence are described below.

Albany Learning Center

30. The Albany Learning Center is located near the Albany campus of the State University of New York and is surrounded by the extensive educational resources of the capital district and the historic Northeast.

Genesee Valley Learning Center

31. The Genesee Valley Learning Center is adjacent to the downtown branch of the State University College at Brockport. Various co-operative arrangements with other institutions were negotiated shortly after its formal opening in January 1972, including provisions to: exchange students and programmes with state university colleges at Brockport and Genesee, and Monroe Community College; secure student-teacher positions in a local school; and use the laboratory facilities of the American Red Cross Blood Bank under the guidance of its professional staff.

New York City Learning Center

32. There are two divisions of the New York City Learning Center, the Labour Division and the Metropolitan Division. The Labour Division provides an opportunity for union members in New York City to go to a college designed for their needs, interests and aspirations. It offers three degrees: Associate in Science in Industrial and Labour Relations, Associate in Arts with an option of concentration in labour studies, and Bachelor of Arts. Labour students are given appropriate help in the skills they may require before they can begin the programme. The Labour Division operates on a quarter system, beginning early in September.

33. The Metropolitan Division offers programmes of study for other students in the New York City area. It is, of course, uniquely situated to take advantage

of the wealth of educational and research opportunities in the metropolitan area. Many co-operative arrangements with the varied institutions of this location are now being pursued.

Long Island Learning Center

34. The Long Island Learning Center is located on the campus of the State University College at Old Westbury. The programme of this centre will be developed in close co-operation with the private and public colleges of the region and have important links in industry and labour.

The College-wide Center for Organized Programmes

35. The College-wide Center, which offers study through organized programmes, is located at Saratoga Springs. Members of the Learning Resources faculty and the administrative staff of the Coordinating Center are available to work directly with the students, and since it is the headquarters of learning-resource development, students at this centre will have an opportunity to visit faculty from other institutions.

36. Students may also elect to participate in organized programmes, based upon independent study of specially prepared learning packages, video-tapes and correspondence courses.

The Coordinating Center

37. The Coordinating Center for the entire network of learning centres is at Saratoga Springs. Here central administrative services such as research, programme development, permanent record-keeping and business affairs are transacted.

III Procedures to be followed by students

38. In order to give a better understanding of how ESC operates (i.e. procedures to be followed, types of learning contracts to be developed, resources to be identified and other aspects of its operation) information is given in the sections which follow.

Application

39. In order to be admitted to ESC a prospective student must first complete the standard application form used by all State University of New York (SUNY) institutions. Second, he must answer the Empire State College prospectus which includes such questions as:

(a) What are your vocational, professional or educational goals?

(b) What kinds of learning resources do you have available to assist you in meeting your educational goals?
(c) What kinds of work experience or other activities might your studies include?
(d) What experiences, other than school or college, seem to be pertinent to your admission to Empire State?
(e) What were the reasons you chose Empire State rather than another college?
(f) What are your long-range educational, vocational or professional plans or aspirations? In what ways would the fulfillment of these plans affect your life style?
(g) What are your current responsibilities and obligations? Which of these would continue as you pursue your programme at Empire State College?

Orientation

40. Each prospective student is then required to attend an Orientation Workshop, where he becomes well acquainted with ESC and should be able to determine whether or not the college meets his needs.

41. A letter of admission indicates the date of the Orientation Workshop to which the student is invited. This may be one or more months after he has been accepted.

42. Student orientation includes: (a) registration; (b) testing; (c) explanation of how the college works together with sample learning programmes; (d) introduction to and preliminary discussion with the faculty; and (e) sharing interests and plans, and becoming acquainted with other students.

Advanced standing

43. Empire State College recognizes that significant learning may be obtained outside formal educational settings—at work, at home, in community activities, through travel, and from individual reading and study. Older students may bring a knowledge and competence developed from life experiences which equal or surpass those of the typical younger college student. ESC will evaluate these learnings and take them into account. Up to 30 months of advanced standing can be granted toward a bachelor degree, and up to 15 months toward an associate degree.

44. Advanced standing within the college is integrally related to Empire State's educational objectives and is more than a simple addition of past 'credits'. Judgements about advanced standing for prior learning have as their terms of reference generally accepted expectations of standards for college-level work. Where a substantial amount of advanced standing is to be granted, it is assumed that the previous experience is consistent with the student's current goals, and that the time remaining is sufficient to satisfy both the student's aims and the college objectives.

45. Initiative and responsibility in applying for advanced standing rest with the student. He or she begins by preparing a 'Portfolio', with the help of the mentor, and may call on other faculty members for advice and assistance in doing so. At this stage, mentors operate as consultants, not as judges. Any student who wishes to apply for advanced standing must notify the associate dean that he or she is in the process of preparing a Portfolio. A student who expects to be granted substantial blocks of time is advised to act rapidly to

prepare the Portfolio and to obtain copies of the necessary supporting documents.

46. A student's Portfolio is composed of (a) an initial summary, (b) a general essay, and (c) an appendix of supporting evidence.

(a) The *initial summary* clearly and concisely states the total amount of advanced standing which the student seeks, as well as giving a breakdown of the months spent on each major activity.

(b) In the *general essay* the student describes his or her long-range plans and specific educational objectives. The student describes the past experiences and the kinds of learnings for which recognition is sought and indicates how these past learnings are related to educational and career goals. When a student is seeking a substantial amount of advanced standing, this general essay should also include a brief description of the Programme of Study and the estimated time required to complete it. Then, by considering the relationship between the Programme of Study and previous learnings, the student should arrive at an estimate of where he or she stands in relation to the degree that is sought.

(c) The *appendix of supporting evidence*, with a table of contents, contains the documents, transcripts, letters, certificates and other materials which the student submits to illustrate and document previous learnings. These materials are integrally related to the student's general essay and should be mentioned in the essay by means of footnotes. Evidence is not limited to written materials. The following list offers examples of evidence and experiences which can be considered:

(i) Accredited work undertaken at another educational institution will be fully accepted.

(ii) Transcripts, certificates of completion, or other evidence from non-accredited, proprietary institutions, or other organizations, may be submitted.

(iii) Written examinations, standardized or local, may be used as evidence of learning.

(iv) Licences may be taken as evidence of competence if it is known that a student had to pass a very stiff examination or meet certain performance standards.

(v) Membership in a professional or trade association may be accepted for credit, provided that enough is known about the student's requirements for membership or a given class of membership.

(vi) Products may be submitted or created: works, books published, pictures painted, music written, patents obtained, machines designed, scientific exhibits, intellectual autobiographies.

(vii) Performance may be observed. If the student can, say, speak fluent German, play the piano, draw a portrait, or operate a machine, this accomplishment can be demonstrated to skilled judges. The standing granted varies with the level of skill demonstrated or with the relevance of the performance to the student's objectives.

(viii) 'Eyewitness reports' from colleagues or supervisors can be solicited to support a competence which cannot be demonstrated or an experience which cannot otherwise be verified.

(ix) Interviews or oral examinations may be used to establish the student's level of knowledge or understanding in a field in which experience has been the source of competence. Such examinations are generally less reliable than written ones. Considerable reliance may have to be placed on the skills of the interviewer.

47. The evaluation committee examines the Portfolio, meets the student and his or her mentor and then decides how much advanced standing can be granted. Its members then prepare a transcript statement for the student's record, indicating the nature of their action and summarizing the bases on which their judgements rest.

Learning contracts

48. The learning contract can be an instrument for helping the student to conceptualize and give focus to the work to be done. It is a single unit which includes both the initial planning statement and the final digest and evaluation. Individual learning contracts differ in as many ways as there are differences in student goals, learning resources and approaches among mentors, but to the extent that the concept is valid, all good learning contracts probably have some qualities in common. At the most general level, they reflect careful planning and full consideration of the evaluation requirements of the learning experiences that they represent. More specifically, contracts show that attention has been given to the aspects described in the categories below. These dimensions of the learning experience may sometimes be identified in the initial learning contract, and sometimes in the digest and evaluation.

49. Learning contracts can cope with a certain degree of unpredictability by including the following elements: (a) an initial description of the precise problems on which the student will be working; (b) the time stipulated for that work; (c) after the work is completed, a description of the completed work and the evaluation of the learning activity.

Student purposes and background

50. A learning contract that makes explicit a student's long-range goals and specific purposes provides a context within which learning activities and materials can be viewed and understood. The stated goals and purposes serve as guides and reminders to both student and mentor as the contract proceeds, and they assist others who wish to understand the undertaking.

51. A knowledge of the student's background is sometimes important to the understanding of the initial contract. This background need not be written for each new contract, but from time to time student or mentor may wish to make modifications and it should always be readily available.

Diversity and variety, unity and intensiveness, compatibility with the discipline

52. Contracts that help the student move toward his goals by experiencing a variety of media and learning activities give him the opportunity to develop and exploit his abilities and his special style of learning. Human interaction,

work and field experiences, film, radio and television, in addition to printed materials, all are valuable in learning and may contribute richness through diversity and variety in a contract. Each particular area of study determines the scope of each contract but it is important that a student pursues a subject to a degree of complexity and to a level of intensity warranted by the subject itself. Field and work experience, for example, take on added value when supported by immersion in theory and research findings.

Time requirements

53. Special attention needs to be paid to the time demands of learning activities. This is a complex issue requiring continuing study. Meanwhile it can be said that those making decisions about the duration of a learning contract, and whether it needs to be full- or part-time, should take into consideration the nature of the included learning activities, the level of required skills possessed by the student and the time available to him. The best and most realistic balance possible should be sought in relation to the goals of the contract. Certain kinds of learning activities cannot be spread thinly, just as others cannot be compressed.

Bibliography and other learning materials and resources

54. Bibliographic references selected for inclusion in the learning contract more clearly contribute to the goals and purposes of that plan of study when they are appropriate to the student's background and level of comprehension. Mentors may want to consider the appropriateness of primary as against secondary sources, historical as against contemporary perspectives and other alternative frames of reference. They may want to suggest bridges between theory and practice and bridges between several disciplines. An initial bibliography may serve as a point of departure for the student and mentor to develop a more adequate bibliography as learning progresses.

Mentor role

55. ESC expects that there will be an increased use of consultants and tutors to supplement the mentor's capabilities and competencies. Delineation of the role and responsibilities of the mentor shapes the student expectations. Times and purposes of meetings and conferences between mentor and student should be specified in order to help structure the learning activity. A mentor in the learning arrangement needs to consider himself not necessarily as the teacher but rather as the co-ordinator of the student's education, making available to him as many routes as possible.

Degree expectations

56. As indicated earlier, at present ESC offers its students degree programmes leading to the B.A., B.S., A.A. and A.S. Each degree programme requires a

concentration of learning with a clearly defined rationale and general learning that supports the concentration and provides for breadth of education. The extent of concentration is determined by the goals of the student, the modes of learning pursued and the area or areas of study that are tackled.

57. The B.A. is awarded to students whose degree programme contains no more than 8 contract-months of work outside the liberal arts. The B.S. is awarded to students whose degree programme contains more than 8 and less than 17 contract-months of work outside the liberal arts. Similarly, the student is awarded an A.A. or A.S. with 4 contract-months or 5 to 8 contract-months respectively of work outside the liberal arts. Students whose programmes of study fall within certain frameworks may find that, in contrast to other students, external requirements may limit or determine certain aspects of their studies. Student degree programmes should be described in terms which most effectively communicate their prospective studies as well as in terms of modes of learning and areas of study. When a student's concentration is recognized to have been largely completed prior to enrolment in ESC, the degree programme emphasizes the need to broaden general learning through liberal studies.

58. Associate-degree programmes emphasize general learning to establish a base for future concentration, while bachelor-degree programmes emphasize depth of concentration as well as broad general learning. With this in mind, associate-degree programmes are constructed within the same modes and areas of study as those for bachelor degrees. Associate-degree programmes are expected to employ the same intellectual competencies as bachelor-degree programmes.

59. The interests, needs and goals a student brings to the college are met through individually developed programmes which combine, or fall within, one or more major modes and areas of study.

60. The following are the major modes available to students:

Disciplinary. In pursuing studies in a particular discipline, the students will be guided by its existing framework. Within its boundaries, the student develops a programme that will lead to an understanding of its structure, methods and content.

Interdisciplinary. Students who wish to investigate two or more disciplines may organize a programme of study in the interdisciplinary mode. The student, in developing a degree programme, must identify the disciplines to be combined and the supporting knowledge required to provide background or focus to the programme.

Problem-oriented. A student may approach a programme by concentrating on a particular problem or set of problems. The student attempts to master the knowledge and skills necessary for an analysis of the attack on the problem. The fundamental aspect of this mode is that the student formulates a well-defined problem and explores and evaluates various possible solutions to it.

Thematic. In the thematic mode, the student studies a particular theme or set of ideas that interconnects a body of learning within an area or combination of areas of study. This is different from the problem-oriented mode; in the thematic mode, the student does not seek a solution but rather attempts to understand the way in which a particular theme repeatedly appears within human experience.

Professional/vocational. This mode is a preparation for a particular vocation or profession. The main focus of study is on specific job-related knowledge and skills; such a programme involves consideration of the conceptual foundations of a field, the professional role of the student and relationships to society at large. In cases where training is technical or specialized, the specific training may occur on the job or at other higher-education institutions.

61. The areas of study currently available to students are the following:

The arts. Art studies at ESC include work in the visual and performing arts, creative writing and historical and critical studies in art. Students may devise programmes which are combinations of both the theoretical and the practical, the critical and the creative.

Business and economics. Studies in business and economics in the college prepare a student to understand the business environment and its technology. They include operational business skills, economic theory and method, and the social, political and legal context of business.

Community and social services. This area includes both theoretical and applied studies in the broad range of human services. Students may concentrate on the analysis of the structure and performance of human services and on the various technical skills involved in the performance of these services.

Social theory, social structure and change

62. This general area consists of what are usually thought of as the social sciences, with interests in social structures and social change. It is not an end in itself but a tool for understanding social, political and economic structures and processes which shape and constrain human experiences and potentials. It is concerned with structures, processes, issues and policies.

63. The degree requirements of ESC include explicit attention to general college objectives in each degree programme. Students must demonstrate their ability to carry out activities or accomplish ends that attest to their intellectual development within the following categories:

Basic skills. To read, speak and write clearly, correctly and effectively; to demonstrate the necessary quantitative skills; or to perform technical and physical skills essential to a programme.

Knowledge. Knowledge is the recall of different levels of abstraction, from facts, to theories, to methods of inquiry. It involves the identification and gathering of relevant data such as the classification systems of a body of knowledge, the range of activities in a given society or the products of a particular artist.

Comprehension. Comprehension emphasizes demonstration of levels of understanding in known terms. The practical result may be a paper, a painting, an experiment or a field trip. Not only must ideas be comprehended, but also relationships must be explored and implications developed. Comprehension includes translation, interpretation and extrapolation.

Application. Application is the ability to apply learning to a new situation and to transfer abstractions to concrete situations. Applications may be verbal, i.e. a paper in which theoretical ideas are applied to a given situation, or may be demonstrated by the use of known information for solving a problem.

Analysis. At the analysis level, there is emphasis on the breakdown of ideas or materials into parts in order to explain relationships and clarify the organization of these parts. Analysis is the competence underlying the study of a text, genre, movement or problem. Providing explanations, distinguishing facts from hypotheses and perceiving patterns and parallels are activities related to analysis.

Evaluation. Evaluation is the articulation of conscious value judgements based on criteria. The development of new criteria may often be required. The ability to judge the work of others, to perceive values and to distinguish opinions from judgements supported by specific standards are illustrative of this level of intellectual competence.

Synthesis. At the synthesis level, elements are combined and arranged in order to create a whole which was clearly not there before. The ability to synthesize demonstrates the intellectual competence to form a new hypothesis, organize a new experiment, present a new artistic product, propose a new solution to a given problem or generate a new theory or principle.

64. The college aims to help students develop intellectually in these major areas, while recognizing that some or most of these developments may be demonstrated through assessment of what was learned before they enrolled, while others will be met through learning contracts.

Evaluation of learning-contract experiences

65. Evaluation of learning has several components. First, there is a continuing evaluation which takes place throughout the student-mentor relationship. Second, there is the evaluation of the products resulting from the learning-contract activities. Third, the criteria for evaluation itself are constantly evolving.

66. Fulfilment of a contract means that a student and mentor agree that the purposes of the contract have been accomplished. This agreement is facilitated when the learning contract specifies at the outset what will represent an accomplishment and how it will be observed, though this is not always necessary.

67. Evaluation can include written or oral elements or performances, which are objective or subjective; but in all cases these elements should relate to learning-contract goals and provide public evidence of the student's accomplishment, particularly in the case of the oral examination by the mentor directly. The mentor should make clear the distinction between such a formal examination and an informal discussion. A specific report on such examinations and what they cover should be provided by the mentor or the tutor operating within their competence. Open-ended, process-oriented arrangements, sometimes even with no detailed written evaluation, are educationally defensible and even desirable. Where the responsible teacher is in clear command of the subject, the oral exchange between the student and the teacher during the process of work and the presentation of completed artefacts approved by the teacher can constitute sufficient evaluation.

Resources

68. ESC students have a relatively wide range of aids to learning under the overall planning and review of a mentor or a unit co-ordinator. Programme development is facilitated by the ability of the student to utilize the resources of the college and its faculty, as well as human and material resources outside of

the college. The availability of this method of operation enables the college to accommodate a broader range of students than would be possible if the college faculty and facilities were the students' only resources. These resources include:

Organized programmes. For broad curricular areas, the faculty has developed full programme study materials. These are known as organized programmes and may be pursued directly with a mentor or by letter and cassette through the Saratoga Center.

Every time a mentor prepares a contract with a student, he or she is at once professor and programme developer. At times, a student's interests, abilities and goals are so clearly delineated that the mentor can write not only a first learning contract but also project a long-range programme of study. Sometimes, he or she realizes almost at once that one learning contract at a time, each offering new elements, would be in the student's best interest until his or her intellectual interests begin to take shape. For the most part, though, ESC students, while seeking alternatives to 'required courses' and 'credit-hours', also want an estimated time needed for a degree and suggested methods of progression, before they invest their time and money. With these ideas in mind, curriculum planning at ESC includes a series of unique study programmes:

(a) They deliberately avoid locked-in curricula or rigid sequential programmes; thus a student may adapt any part of an organized programme of study to his or her needs.

(b) They take into account differing points of entry for individual students; each organized programme begins at a basic level and proceeds through increasing levels of complexity.

(c) Each organized programme is made up of separable units which have their own integrity as units of disciplined work, but also have functional relationships to each other.

(d) Each organized programme begins with brief exploratory exercises to allow both student and mentor to judge relevance and level of entry.

Formal courses. As a part of the contract, an ESC student may take a scheduled credit course at any accredited institution of higher learning. If this course is undertaken at a state-university-operated campus, ESC covers the entire cost of tuition. If the student attends a course at a private university or locally sponsored community college, ESC waives that proportion of the tuition fee on a per credit-hour basis that he would have paid by attending a state-supported campus.

Independent study and media courses. The State University of New York now has more than 87 undergraduate independent study courses in 30 areas of study. Many of these courses are supplemented by films, video-tapes, audio cassettes, slides and laboratory kits. The university also has more than 75 television courses in the arts and humanities, mathematics and physical sciences and the social and behavioural sciences. All are available to ESC students. In addition, programme developers in the Saratoga Coordinating Center are cataloguing available courses, films, and tapes produced by universities and other educational agencies throughout the country.

For the student who wants a particular course, or for part-time students whose family or job responsibilities prevent them from fitting more than an occasional course into their free time, the ability to integrate these studies into a total programme is a distinct advantage.

With the approval of his or her mentor, a student may attend certain non-credit courses run by industry, government and social agencies, and institutions of higher learning, as part of his or her programme.

Independent study areas available through correspondence courses. The following study areas are available: anthropology, business, civil and construction technology, criminology, data processing, economics, education, electrical technology, engineering drawing, engineering mechanics, engineering science, English, fire science, geography, history, home economics, languages, law enforcement, marine technology, mathematics, philosophy, physics, political science, psychology, recreation, sociology, speech.

Community resources. ESC is a college in the community in the truest sense. The community is the campus. Its learning centres were not designed as a new type of campus attempting to duplicate libraries, cultural programmes and other available resources. The college does not intend to substitute an imposed and artificial community for the real community all around us; rather it considers the value of the resources of the community and makes them available to all its students.

Empire State students are now interns in government and social agencies; they are working and studying with theatre and dance groups, museums, television and radio stations, local libraries, laboratories and language centres.

Co-operative study. Some students, particularly those who live at some distance from a learning centre, develop their own interacting community. Instead of looking to the college to develop this creative interaction, the students form their own groups. This is a desirable objective for any student; at ESC, it is almost essential. Other students have organized seminars in literature, film and community action. Meetings are held in the learning centres or in the homes of students or mentors.

ESC accepts the idea of co-operative study. This means that a group of students may write a collective learning contract with a group of mentors. For example, the Adirondacks provide a rich field for study and research, and where a number of students are interested in such a particular geographical area, a co-operative study could result. Thus, the history of the French and Indian Wars, Indian anthropology, the art of the Hudson River school, rural studies, changing land values, the literature of the region—all could be incorporated into a single learning contract, involving various students interested in separate aspects, but all contributing to the whole. Thus, each student would be pursuing an individual programme, but its breadth and depth would be enhanced by its being apart of a larger study in which others were participating.

Short-term residencies. As part of its organized programmes of study, the college offers a series of short residential terms. These intensive study periods allow students otherwise unable to attend a campus for a semester or year to experience learning with a group of fellow-students. Although attendance at a residency is not required for a degree at ESC, all students are encouraged to give serious consideration to its educational value in their total programme of study. Residencies are scheduled on SUNY campuses located around the state.

Students engaged in co-operative study may also wish to plan short-term residential experiences. Potential teachers assisting in schools, students pursuing diverse kinds of urban or ecological studies, students of foreign language, philosophy, literature, history, economics, human development, social problems, the plastic or performing arts—these and many other interest groups can put occasional long investigations together to excellent use, sharing experiences, products and insights, sharpening skills and concepts, increasing the store of working knowledge. There are also opportunities to participate in workshops and colloquia with visiting and resident scholars.

Where such meetings take place is unimportant. A temporarily vacated college dormitory will do; an old house in the country is ideal; an offseason motel or hotel, if sufficiently inexpensive, can serve. The significant thing for such short-term intensive sessions is not what the environment has to offer, but what the persons bring to the environment and create for themselves while they are there.

International studies. Travel has long been one of the broadening elements of education. For this reason, ESC has organized international programmes of study and has resident mentors overseas to work with students. Several students are now in Europe completing their academic assignments at designated places and reporting back to a mentor in their own learning centre or to the overseas mentors by means of reports, letters and audio-tapes.

The college now has an overseas learning centre in London. As part of their learning contracts, students may make use of the richness of formal offerings in European institutions, as well as of courses associated with the international programmes of other SUNY units. Students may also elect to work with organized and multidisciplinary programmes developed by ESC, such as 'The Culture of Cities', 'Contemporary British Theatre', or 'Comparative Education'.

Programmes and activities may include: living with a family; visiting historical sites and cultural events and exhibits; working on farms, in factories, or offices; studying in universities and art, drama and music schools; studying independently; studying trade unions; or participating in archaeological digs.

Other specialized programmes. As ESC continues to grow, educational opportunities in other areas of particular interest will increase. The Martin Luther King Center, Metropolitan Museum of Modern Art, Fashion Institute of Technology and Lincoln Center would provide opportunities in New York City, as would the Mental Health Center and State Education Museum and Library in Albany and the Head Start Programme in Lewis County.

'*Modules*'. A unique approach at ESC is the writing of 'modules' by a special staff at the college headquarters at Saratoga Springs. Over 200 have been produced on a wide range of subjects and topics such as 'The World of Work', 'Aristotle', 'Renaissance 1', and 'The Nature of Mathematics'. These 'modules' are not a printed lecture nor are they programmed material. They represent a statement by a specialist on the topic to motivate and provide information for the student. Each mentor has a complete list of such 'modules' and may select one or more to help the student with an objective in the learning contract.

Programme approval

69. The student submits his programme for approval when six to nine

months of full-time study, or the equivalent period of half-time study, remain to complete the A.A. degree programme, or when twelve to eighteen months of full-time study or its equivalent remain for the B.A. degree, and when the major elements of the work still to be done can be described with reasonable clarity and conviction.

70. A student seeks programme approval by submitting an application which describes: (a) his past educational and occupational experiences and activities, undertaken while enrolled at ESC or prior to enrolment, or both; (b) the major interests, plans, or aspirations he wants to pursue; and (c) the major areas and activities to be undertaken, the mentor or mentors with whom he or she works, any major outside resources to be used, and the time required to complete the projects. This application need not spell out in detail particular learning contracts or specific learning activities but it should provide a clear framework within which the pertinence of those particulars will be apparent. Students call on mentors for whatever assistance they require in developing well-balanced programmes and in preparing their applications.

Transcript

71. The transcript will include the following items in addition to basic information about the student: (a) a brief statement of the programme of study and faculty approval; (b) when appropriate, a brief description of the amount of advanced standing granted and the major learnings on which it rests; (c) a digest and evaluation from each successfully completed contract. When transcripts are sent from the college to potential employers or to other educational institutions, they will be accompanied by a description of the college programme, its record system and the procedures for judging student progress and awarding degrees. If an employer or other educational institution asks for clarification of a transcript, or translation into its own terms, the college will respond as fully and as accurately as possible.

Faculty

72. ESC mentors average 40.6 years with a range of 24 to 69 years. Ten are in their twenties, twenty-six are in their thirties, ten in their forties, fifteen in their fifties, and one in his sixties. Forty-three (69 per cent) mentors and deans are men and nineteen (31 per cent) are women, a ratio that is fairly consistent throughout the centres. Though most mentors were born in the north-eastern United States, many have travelled extensively in their country and Europe. Also, a few have travelled to and lived in South America, Africa and Asia. Thirty-five mentors (57 per cent) and centre deans hold terminal degrees (doctorates, etc.), many from institutions of high repute. Seventeen (27 per cent) more are candidates for terminal degrees, nine at Long Island.

73. The mentors as a group are experienced faculty members. Thirty-one (55 per cent) have at least five years' experience of college teaching. Since they are required to perform a variety of untraditional faculty tasks, it might be expected that they would be non-specialists, but other evidence exists. The group has published twenty-two books, three monographs, over 120 articles,

eighty-five papers, fifty-five reviews, six essays and it has even produced a few films. In all, fifty mentors and centre deans (81 per cent) have had writings published. Another aspect of the mentors' particular skills is indicated in a partial list of past non-academic jobs held: president of a local labour union, computer designer, real estate manager, co-ordinator of a model cities programme, marketing executive, medical research librarian, editor.

74. In general, mentors are much like their faculty colleagues at other institutions. ESC mentors are both young and old, published and unpublished, with full credentials. Perhaps they are a little more oriented to private and independent educational practices and a little more varied in background experiences, but the importance of these factors cannot be determined at this time.

IV Profiles (students and graduates)

75. In May 1973, the folders of 500 active students, approximately one-third of the students at each regional centre, were examined. The average age of the students in the sample was found to be 33.5, ranging from 16 to 66 years. Forty-five per cent of the students were female. More than half of the students in the sample were married and two-thirds had been.

76. ESC seems to have attracted many people who maintain full-time jobs while studying (54 per cent). The number of people estimating their educational level at two years of college or more on the ESC admissions prospectus is also high (66 per cent). Assuming that the admissions question is fairly accurate in determining the extent to which students with formal credit enrol at the college, the high percentage of 'two-year-plus estimaters' from Long Island (76 per cent) is no surprise. Traditionally, a high percentage of secondary-school graduates in that region go directly to college. It appears that many who never managed to finish their higher learning are now enrolling at ESC.

77. By 1 July 1973, ESC had 95 graduates. Seventy-one (75 per cent) received B.A. degrees, 16 (17 per cent) B.S. degrees, 4 (4 per cent) A.A. degrees, and 4 (4 per cent) A.S. degrees. Fifty-one (54 per cent) of the graduates are female and 44 (46 per cent) male. Seventy-two (75 per cent) are married, 21 (22 per cent) are single, and 2 (2 per cent) divorced.

78. Sixty-eight (72 per cent) graduates had two or more years of college before coming to ESC and 80 per cent received 30 months' advance standing, which accounts for the short time needed by these students to complete degrees. This also helps explain why only 10 out of the 95 graduates engaged in four or more contracts.

79. The youngest graduate is a 19-year-old man, a mental-health worker who studied education for the emotionally disturbed, to receive a B.A. The oldest graduate is a 72-year-old actress who received her B.A. by studying the theatre and its relationship to education. The average age of all graduates is 37.6 years, with a distribution approximating a bell-shaped curve.

80. Seventy-three (77 per cent) graduates are employed in a wide range of occupations with the heaviest concentration among professionals, supervisors and public officials. Some specific jobs held by graduates include automobile worker, music teacher, co-ordinator of health occupation centre, senior training engineer, addiction specialist, police lieutenant, supervisor of instructional media centre, and social service investigator.

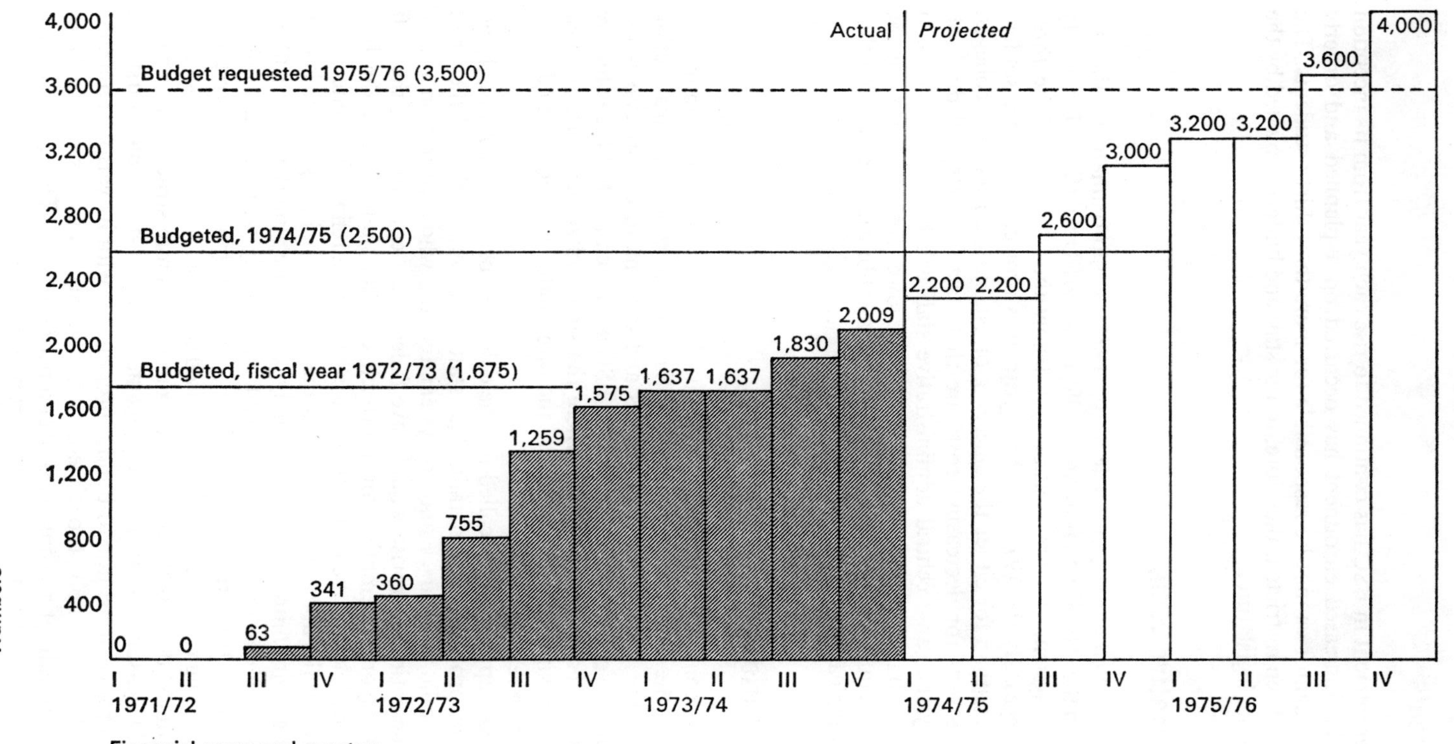

FIG. 1. Empire State College: nine-month comparable full-time equivalent (FTE) growth in numbers, actual and projected (by quarters (I–IV) from financial year 1971/72 to financial year 1975/76). (Actual figures represent nine-month comparable FTE on last day of appropriate quarter.)

V Enrolments

81. The enrolment in ESC has continued to rise each year from its inception (see Figure 1). Increased enrolment has occurred on a planned and orderly basis, since a mentor cannot be responsible for more than thirty students. The enrolment has been restricted, therefore, to the staff and budget provided by the New York State legislature.

VI Comparative costs

82. The projected costs per student for 1974/75 approximate to the per student costs in the established four-year colleges in the SUNY (State University of New York) system and are considerably below those of two of the three emerging colleges. By the 1975/76 school year, it is projected that per student costs will be less than for either the emerging or established four-year colleges. Among the reasons for decreasing costs are that start-up costs will diminish and essentially the same central administrative staff will be able to handle a much larger enrolment. Among the reasons for the lower cost per student is the fact that ESC requires no buildings, capital outlay, libraries, health or other such services typical of traditional colleges.

VII Observations

83. There is considerable excitement about the ESC programme among the central staff in the Coordinating Center at Saratoga Springs. The real action takes place at the various learning centres and even more enthusiasm is expressed by those working at that level. The ESC approach implies the extensive use of decentralized learning centres where the staff and students are in close geographical proximity to each other and are quite well acquainted with possible learning resources.

84. The ESC approach has called for the college to become operational and then work out problems and details. The staff is convinced that if they had attempted to validate courses and to systematize the whole operation before beginning, the entire enterprise would have failed. As a consequence, the staff believes that anyone attempting an approach to ESC should make the best initial plans possible but then begin operation and make refinements later.

85. Related to the above is the fact that the instructional programme is now beginning to acquire more structure. Initially, there were almost no curriculum guidelines and the contract for each student was entirely an individual matter with each mentor. With the passing of time, there is much more interest in developing learning resources which can be used by many students. The development of 'modules' described earlier is an example of more structured learning resources. The reasons for such developments are at least twofold. First, the time required for each mentor to build a programme with its various contracts for each student is simply too time-consuming. Such an extreme form of individualization cannot be supported over a period of time. The second reason for more structured learning experiences grows out of the fact that even though each student has individual and personal learning needs, there are also many

common interests and needs. Therefore, it is possible to develop 'modules' and other learning resources in advance for many students to make use of.

86. In addition to developing more structure, the staff is attempting to locate and/or develop many more materials at the beginning levels in different subject-matter areas. Although there is not a surplus of learning resources at any level, the staff reports a great paucity of such resources for students just beginning their study of a field of knowledge.

87. The orientation and enrolment procedures demand highly literate persons with a good deal of self-discipline. Therefore, the individuals who persist through the orientation period are those who are more likely to be successful in the ESC approach, which requires so much individual initiative. As indicated in section I, ESC is not for everyone and the orientation procedures are designed to eliminate at least some persons who will not be able to profit from such a programme.

88. It is interesting to observe that a small number of credits is given for prior experiences, including work experiences. One might expect that those doing the evaluating of such previous experience would be rather generous in giving such credits, but the evidence suggests otherwise.

89. A related point is the continuing problem of defining what is 'academic' and what is 'occupational', 'work' and/or 'vocational'. The question of determining and specifying what part of a student's work experience constitutes a learning for which college credit should be given continues to be a perplexing one because, as indicated by two evaluation specialists at ESC,

> Empire State College is not in the business of estimating the worth of one's life, nor can the student simply 'cash in' a miscellaneous rack of prior learning, including formally gained college credits toward a degree or even a better part of one. He must present a cogent case that his college-level learnings, whatever the source, have contributed to his development into the kind of educated person he aims to be.

VIII Recommendations

90. The following recommendations have come out of this study:

(a) A prerequisite for a programme similar to ESC to be successful is to have available at a local level extensive human and physical resources. Since much of a student's programme is built upon non-formal course requirements, it is necessary to have a wide range of resources available to the student.

(b) Some type of prior work experience before enrolment is desirable for students. Since much of the programme developed for a student takes into account past, present or future experiences, such prior job experiences are highly desirable.

(c) A potential student body with a high degree of motivation and desire for formal education is necessary for an approach such as that of ESC to be successful. Only students who have a good deal of initiative and self-discipline will be successful in such an individualized programme.

(d) A programme of the type usually developed for ESC students is highly academic and requires a high degree of literacy on the part of students. Therefore, again, a potential student body must exist with such characteristics.

(e) Suitable faculty (staff) must be available to fill the posts of mentor, whose role is quite different from that of professors in conventional institutions.
(f) The belief that it is possible to express through written documents ('contracts') what is necessary to justify the award of a bachelor degree must be firmly held.
(g) The possibility of translating life experiences into measurable units of college credit must be considered feasible and possible.

Appendix A Standardized reference data

Country, state or province	*United States of America: New York State*
Area and climate	49,576 square miles. Temperate.
Population	
Total (latest year)	18,237,000 (1971).
Estimated population aged 18	909,000 (18 to 20 years).
Estimated percentage under 15	24 (under 14 years).
Current annual growth rate (percentage)	0.3 (1970–72).
Government	
Main organizational structure	Partially autonomous state under federal control of United States of America. Elected state legislature.
Political type	Democratic state organization.
Economy	
Political type	Predominantly industrial, particularly business. No state or federal control.
Gross national product	
Total (latest year)	$1,151,400 million (1972) (United States).
Per head	$5,515 (1972).
Average annual increase (percentage)	2.
Communications	
Ground/air	Very good system of roads, motorways, bus and air transport services. Rail poor: freight only.
Mail/telephone	Good postal services; 95 per cent of households with telephones (1972).

Broadcasting

Main system(s) operating	A.M., F.M.; television.
Principal authorities responsible	Only private commercial bodies under aegis of United States Federal Communications Commission. Four major broadcasting networks with, nationally, 650 television stations and 6,033 radio stations.
Radio	
Transmission coverage of main programme services with percentage of population reached	100.
Receiving capability for main programme services (percentage)	100.
Television	
Transmission coverage as defined for radio	100.
Receiving capability for main programme services (percentage)	100.
Monochrome or colour	Both monochrome and colour.

Education

Type of systems(s)	Under state control at advisory innovative level.
Main authorities responsible and powers	
At school level	Local school districts' main responsibility, providing 57 per cent of budget; the state provides 40 per cent and Congress only 3 per cent. Private, autonomous schools are 80 per cent Roman Catholic, 10 per cent Protestant and 10 per cent non-sectarian.
At post-secondary level	More than two-thirds of the 1,800 post-secondary institutions are private and receive no direct support from government sources.
End of full-time school attendance	
Legal	16 years.
De facto	16 years; many stay on until graduation (17).
Proportion of 18-year-old age group involved in education	
Full-time	182,072 (18- and 19-year-olds).
Part-time	98,794.
Major development in provision	
Over the next five years	Projected growth in numbers (full-time equivalents): financial year 1974/75, 2,200 to 3,000; financial year 1975/76, 3,200 to 4,000.

Institution/system under study — Empire State College

Brief for study and reason for inclusion

Empire State College (ESC) represents a major effort by the State University of New York System (SUNY) to discover whether alternative approaches to higher education can serve more flexibly the needs of individual students, while maintaining quality and educational effectiveness comparable to that available on traditional campuses.

Main features of subject studied

Availability of flexible learning resources through ESC.

Origins
Established in 1971 by SUNY Board of Trustees with strong urging of Chancellor Boyer and Governor Rockefeller to the legislature.

Educational authority and roles
State University of New York (of which ESC is one of thirty-four state-supported campuses) is controlled by a fifteen-member Board of Trustees.

Communications authority(ies) and roles
No direct relationship to mass media except as student may use to fulfil contract.

Services provided
ESC serves the educational needs of a contemporary society. This new college has a mandate to explore new ways of educating people, new ways of reaching them. ESC was created to provide an education for people who cannot or did not wish to devote four years of their lives to sitting in a classroom on a traditional campus.

Eligibility to study

(a) categories
Anyone 16 years or older but generally much older (average age 33.5 years). Very varied backgrounds.

(b) qualifications
High-school graduation or equivalent together with ability of ESC to meet applicant's educational needs.

Terminal qualifications
Associate in Arts (A.A.) and Science (A.S.) degrees (two years); Bachelor of Arts (B.A.) and Science (B.S.) degrees (four years).

Instructional means used
Predominantly student-organized programmes with mentors, formal courses, independent study and media, community resources co-operative study, short-term residencies. International studies in area learning centres.

Personal input from student
Flexible: minimum three months full-time A.A./A.S.; minimum six months full-time B.A./B.S. Eighteen months usual, average thirty-two months full-time.

Normal duration of study	Of the first ninety-five graduates, seventy-eight (72 per cent) had college work before coming to ESC and 80 per cent received thirty months advanced standing. Thus, it seems that the average student completes his work in approximately one year but in no instance less than six months.
Pedagogic effectiveness	In a recent 'mini'-study of 27 graduates, of those queried 13 had applied to graduate schools and 7 were accepted, 1 was rejected, and 5 were still waiting to hear as to whether they were admitted. Also, attrition data suggest that about 10 per cent of students who actually enrol withdraw.
Numbers involved	
Students	
Intake (latest year)	373 (1973/74).
On roll	Increased from 1,637 full-time equivalent (autumn 1973) to 2,166 (30 April 1974).
Graduating	Ninety-five graduates (July 1973).
Academic staff	
Full-time	Sixty-two (total for all four learning centres located at Genesee Valley, Long Island, Metropolitan and Northeast).
Part-time	No part-time or adjunct faculty.
Other professional staff	
Number	Twenty-seven persons are on administrative staff at Saratoga Springs, New York, plus twenty development and visiting faculty, the latter being professional staff involved in curriculum and course development.
Finance	
Recurrent expenditure	
By providing authorities (latest available year)	State funds: 1972/73, $2,373,000; 1973/74, $3,738,000; 1974/75, $4,760,000.
Average annual outlay by student	For 1973/74, cost per full-time equivalent was $2,073.
Non-recurrent expenditure	
Gross, over first five years of new institution	No new facilities constructed. Old Skidmore College Campus purchased for central administration at Saratoga Springs and four learning centres rent facilities.
Special assistance received	
Financial	In 1973/74, $577,000 from Ford and Carnegie Foundations; in 1974/75, $725,000 from Kellogg Foundation.
Non-financial	None.

Sources of further information

Educational	Empire State College, 2 Union Avenue, Saratoga Springs, New York 12866.
Broadcasting	No direct affiliation with either radio or television.

Appendix B **Short bibliography**

CARNEGIE COMMISSION ON HIGHER EDUCATION. *Less time, more options: education beyond the high school.* New York, N.Y., McGraw-Hill, 1971.

——. *Toward a learning society: alternative channels to life, work and service.* New York, N.Y., McGraw-Hill, 1973.

CROSS, P.; VALLEY, J. *et al. Planning non-traditional programs: an analysis of the issues of postsecondary education.* San Francisco, Calif., Jossey-Bass, 1974.

FURNISS, W. TODD. (ed.). *Higher education for everybody.* Washington, D.C., American Council on Education, 1971.

GOULD, S. *Diversity by design.* San Francisco, Calif., Jossey-Bass, 1973.

HESBURG, T.; MILLER, P. A.; WHARTON, C. *Patterns for lifelong learning.* San Francisco, Calif., Jossey-Bass, 1973.

HOULE, C. *The external degree.* San Francisco, Calif., Jossey-Bass, 1973.

ILLICH, I. *De-schooling society.* New York, N.Y., Harper & Row, 1971.

Appendix C **Biographical note**

Dr Wesley C. Meierhenry is currently Chairman and Professor of the Department of Adult and Continuing Education, and Professor of Educational Administration and History and Philosophy of Education, at the University of Nebraska, Lincoln, Nebraska (United States of America).

The Minnesota Metropolitan State College, Minneapolis/St Paul

W. C. Meierhenry

Contents

I Introduction

1. Minnesota Metropolitan State College (MMSC) is an upper division (last two years of college) which opened in February 1972. The first proposal made in 1969 by Chancellor Mitau of the state college system to the state legislature was to establish a four-year state college in the Metropolitan Minneapolis/St Paul area. The proposal did not receive sufficient legislative support at the time so subsequently a report was prepared by a Citizens League Committee on Higher Education which had much to do with the approval of the new college by the legislature in 1971.

2. The Citizens Committee, which studied the need for a new and different type of higher education institution, examined such data as the increase in the number of students who would be seeking higher education in the Twin Cities (Minneapolis/St Paul) area. It also considered whether such expanded opportunities should follow traditional patterns or require new approaches and analysed the capacity of the current institutions to meet the additional enrolment and new approaches. As part of its deliberations, the committee examined many reports dealing with higher education in Minnesota and also considered such national reports as the Carnegie Commission on Higher Education's *Less Time, More Options: Education Beyond the High School*, and *Report on Higher Education*, by Frank Newman.

3. The committee then made their recommendations to the legislature; their report had a substantial impact on legislators and led to the funding of the college and its initial operation.

4. One of its recommendations was that a new Urban College of Minnesota, identified by its educational mission and programme, should be established by the 1971 legislature to make close-to-home college education and training available to additional thousands of primarily Twin Cities area residents. The legislature was asked to require the Urban College:

(a) To offer courses and study space at locations throughout the Twin Cities area, making use of a variety of under-used existing buildings, such as space in private colleges. The new kind of college proposed would not have the traditional type of college campus. If any new buildings were to be requested of the legislature in the future, the legislature was to insist that there be a clear demonstration that all possibilities for use of existing facilities had been exhausted.

(b) To serve primarily (i) persons who have been employed for several years and who may desire to continue their employment while obtaining additional education, and (ii) persons who attended other post-high-school institutions, such as junior colleges or vocational schools, and desire to continue their education. No qualified student should be denied the right to attend for lack of financial resources.

(c) To emphasize teaching, not research, and for its curriculum to be 'career-oriented', that is, closely co-ordinated with the employment students will undertake upon completion of their education.

(d) To offer courses at all convenient hours during the week and at weekends, as well as during the traditional Monday to Friday regular daylight class hours.

(e) To seek to bring the teachers to the areas where the students live and work, rather than have the students go to a central campus where the teachers traditionally are.

(f) To have its official 'headquarters', in addition to the numerous satellite locations at which the Urban College will have facilities, located (i) centrally to serve the maximum number of students, (ii) near public transport, (iii) near employment centres, and (iv) where persons living in lower-income areas can easily be served. Two headquarters, in or near each of the downtowns of St Paul and Minneapolis, would most likely satisfy these criteria.

5. As a result of the legislative mandates, five basic tenets were developed for MMSC and continue to guide its operation up to the present time. They are as follows:

(a) The college vests in each individual student responsibility for, and authority over, his or her education. The college vests in its officers and faculty responsibility for teaching and for determining whether or not a student has given adequate evidence that he has achieved his or her educational objectives.

(b) The college records a student's educational progress in terms of the competencies the student achieves and not in terms of the number of courses or other units of experience in which the student undertakes to achieve competencies.

(c) The college believes that, whenever appropriate, students should be encouraged to achieve their educational goals by making use of community resources, including human resources and events controlled by agencies and organizations external to the college.

(d) The college recommends that each student receiving a degree demonstrate a high level of competence in each of these areas of life: (i) communications and basic learning; (ii) the responsibilities of a self-governing member of a self-governing community; (iii) work; (iv) recreation; and (v) personal development and social awareness. To achieve competence in these areas means that students must know and employ many of the arts, sciences, humanities and applied disciplines. It also frequently means that students must have types of knowledge and understanding which vary significantly from those usually associated with higher education, especially in the field of experience-based and practical knowledge. The college respects this broadening of the concept of knowledge.

(e) The college expects that those upon whom it confers degrees will be lifelong, self-directed learners committed to achieving excellence in their learning.

II Critical elements in operation

6. There are many distinguishing characteristics of MMSC growing out of these five tenets, but the type of student, the use of pacts and the emphasis on competencies, with the accompanying procedures as to how these competencies are to be identified and assessed, are the most significant factors.

Student eligibility

7. Candidature implies that a student has been accepted for a degree programme. Before being accepted as a candidate for a bachelor of arts degree, an individual must meet one of the following requirements:

(a) Possess an associate degree (two years of college).

(b) Have completed a minimum of 90 quarter or 60 semester credit-hours (considered to be two years of college) in a lower division undergraduate programme at a college or university in which he achieved an average grade of two or above on a four-point scale.

(c) Have satisfactorily completed the equivalent of a minimum of 90 quarter credit-hours (considered to be two years of college) in formal, post-secondary programmes in an institution authorized to offer such programmes, e.g. a vocational-technical institute or school, a community college, a school of nursing, or an armed forces school or institute.

(d) Have satisfactorily completed the course in individualized educational planning (IEPC).

8. MMSC is, therefore, only for those individuals who have the equivalent of the first two years of college. It is also expected that students will be a minimum of 25 years of age and either have engaged, or currently be engaged, in some type of work experience.

Facts

9. A fundamental aspect of MMSC is the pact (or contract) which the student develops in proposing to meet the academic requirements needed to complete a bachelor's degree. A draft of a degree pact consists of the following elements:

(a) A statement of a maximum of eighteen specific competencies which are required to fulfil the student's educational goals and qualify him or her for a bachelor's degree. Each competency must conform to the technical definition of a competency (see paragraph 10 below). At least one competency must be included in each of the competency areas referred to above in paragraph 5(d). The number of competencies listed may be reduced at the rate of one competency per five quarter-hours above the 90 accepted for admission purposes, except that the draft degree pact must list a minimum of 9 competencies, since a minimum of the equivalent of one year must be completed at MMSC in order to obtain a degree.

(b) A statement of the learning strategies the student would undertake to achieve any of the competencies he or she does not already possess.

(c) A statement of the types of evidence the student would offer (including tests and other measuring techniques) to prove, demonstrate, or verify that he possesses the claimed competency. Such evidence must conform to college standards.

(d) A brief statement by the student indicating the relationship of the eighteen specific competencies to one or more life goals, which life goal or goals shall also be set forth in writing and attached to the draft degree pact.

(e) The student is responsible for development of the pact, the identification and description of competencies to be achieved and the means by which the competency will be verified. The faculty is available for advice and consultation but not for preparing any of these items.

Competency

10. Since competencies make up the pact and form the basis of the academic programme it is necessary to understand its definition as used by MMSC. In the technical sense, the term 'competency' means the ability to exhibit the level of performance required in the successful attainment of a particular goal. A student proves, demonstrates or verifies that he has this ability by referring to an assessment of his behaviour (including both written and spoken evidence). The behaviour itself is not the competency but it should be an indication, to qualified observers, that the specific competency exists and would continue to do so.

There are three levels of competency and in order of complexity:

(a) *Knowing*. To know means to have learned and retained, and to be able to recall, the theory and method or the history and literature, the applicability and the context of a discipline in relation to a particular competency.

(b) *Applying*. To apply means to be able and willing to use the theory and method or the history and literature and the context of a discipline in new situations as well as routine ones, and to be able and willing to analyse relationships, including similarities and differences, in relation to a particular competency.

(c) *Evaluating*. To evaluate means to be able to judge the value of a particular competency, that is, the value of the theory and method or the history and literature, the applicability and the context of a discipline in relation to a goal or stated criteria. This evaluation process implies an informed judgement, one that is grounded in knowing and applying levels of performance, with the additional ability to support that judgement by rational argument and the discriminating use of evidence.

In addition to relating the competency to one of the five competency areas referred to above (see paragraph 5(d)), the level at which that competency will be reached (knowing, applying or evaluating) must also be identified.

Assessment

11. A most critical issue, in so far as the MMSC programme and its consequent academic credibility are concerned, is the validity of the assessment procedures which verify the existence of the competency identified in the pact. The student may prove that he or she possesses the competency by many kinds of evidence. Guidelines for judging adequacy of evidence and suggested assess-

ment techniques of MMSC are considered in detail in the section which follows.

III Procedures to be followed by students

12. In order to give a better understanding of how MMSC operates, the procedures and types of contracts which the student usually forms with the college are found in the paragraphs which follow. These steps or procedures are not necessarily linear in nature since several of them may take place at the same time.

Orientation

13. The orientation process is a very significant aspect of MMSC. It is a structured, intensive, six-week Individualized Educational Planning Course (IEPC) at the end of which the student must know, and be able to apply and evaluate, the educational concepts and procedures of the college, and develop and submit a satisfactory draft degree pact. On the basis of the student's performance in the IEPC and the quality of the draft degree pact, the college decides whether to admit the student to candidature for the bachelor of arts degree. The orientation had by spring 1974 become more formalized, for several reasons. First, there is the need to accomplish some activities on a group basis and thereby help to eliminate as much individual activity as possible for the faculty, including pact development. A second objective is to clarify very early in the student's relationship with the college the philosophy, approach and operation of the college, especially in regard to student responsibility for completion of every aspect of the programme. The result is that self-selection of those individuals who either do or do not fit the MMSC purposes and operations takes place early.

Faculty

14. As part of the orientation procedure, the student becomes familiar with the two types of faculty members at MMSC. First is a small number of full-time faculty members, one of whom may serve as an adviser to the student in such matters as the development and approval of the pact, the strategies to meet the pact, the assessment procedures to verify the competencies and the development of the transcript.

15. Most likely, however, the student becomes associated with a 'community faculty' member. Such people are usually full-time employees in the community and have background, experience and competency in some area of interest to the student. They assist the student to meet the various requirements of the college in the same way that full-time faculty members are expected to do (see paragraph 55 below).

Competency levels

16. The pact must identify to which of the five areas of life listed in paragraph

5(d) above the competencies will be related. The college issues general statements followed by suggested checklists to help in examining students for admission, to help students who have been admitted with their own personal assessment, and to help decide if the student is ready to be recommended for graduation. A summary of the general statements, each followed by its checklist, is given below.

Communications and basic learning competence

17. MMSC stresses the need for educated individuals to be both effective receivers and skilful disseminators of knowledge and hopes that the student will want to be a fully functioning self-directed learner. There are a number of areas in which he or she can set himself or herself goals as an aid to achieving competency as a communicator.

18. Messages may be written, oral, pictorial or non-verbal and the student may need to demonstrate competency in more than one or in all of these ways.

19. There are also symbol systems or languages, which the student can learn: standard English, colloquial English, technical English, musical notation, colour and forms, textured materials, body language and movements, mathematics, statistics, accounting, computer languages (such as Fortran and Cobol) and foreign languages (e.g. Spanish, Japanese and Russian).

20. In short, learning to communicate effectively will be a part of almost everything else the student does. Every learning activity engaged in will require the student to be either an effective creator or an effective interpreter of communications.

Personal development and social awareness

21. This is the ability to look at oneself, to identify one's strengths and limitations, to be able to set goals as a result of assessing oneself, and to plan and carry out strategies which make possible the realization of those goals.

22. Knowledge of the social patterns, modes and customs of the student's own background and the background of others can be an integral part of the social awareness component of this competency.

23. The knowledge possessed by the student of groups and individuals and how they function will help to clarify the student's own values. Conversely, clarification of the student's own values helps his or her understanding and evaluation of others. There are numerous ways by which such understanding can be achieved.

Civic competence

24. This is the ability to form ideas and be an active participant in community affairs. The decisions made by communities are neither entirely 'political' nor are they decisions relating solely to government.

25. A wide array of activities of secular and non-secular voluntary groups enables the student as a citizen to contribute to the civic process.

26. Knowlege and analysis of economic, cultural, religious and social decisions make possible informed participation in the civic process. Understanding can be gained either while participating, or as a preparation for involvement, in civic activities.

27. MMSC aims to assist its students to become self-governing members of their communities; to become citizens in the classic sense of the term.

Recreational competence

28. This is the ability to explore new interests and activities and enlarge on old ones, so that one can constantly draw on these resources for continued growth and enrichment of one's quality of life.

29. For most people the need for recreation and renewal is intermingled with vocational obligations. As our society moves towards the thirty-five hour or four-day working week, and is forced to re-examine the role and meaning of work, the student must prepare for the changes in life style which such developments imply.

Vocational competence

30. Although MMSC is an undergraduate liberal arts college, it holds that no one should be granted a bachelor's degree who does not have competence in some vocation—a profession, trade or occupation. It is essential that the student shows the knowledge and skills necessary to be a useful and productive person, not only for economic independence but also for reasons of self-esteem and satisfaction.

31. The student should be able to move occupationally within an increasingly unstable job market. The choice of vocation pursued is entirely his or her own, as is the responsibility for securing a particular position.

32. Even if the student enters the college already qualified in a particular vocation, there may be a desire for a secondary vocational competency. If the student's vocational competencies are too specialized, he or she may need to broaden this understanding of them and their relation to contemporary society.

IV Assessment of competence

33. As indicated earlier, a most crucial aspect of MMSC pertains to the assessment of competency. A most important principle is that the same standards for adequate evidence, criteria for judging the adequacy of the evidence and assessment techniques must be applied whether the student is seeking approval for prior experiences to meet a competency or competencies or for a new competency or competencies called for in the pact. The procedures and criteria are presented in some detail below because they are vital to the validity of the MMSC approach.

Standards for adequate evidence

34. Evidence as used at MMSC is defined as information provided by the student to the college in support of a claim to the possession of a specific competency. Assessment, as defined at MMSC, refers to the combined process of measurement and evaluation. Measurement is the process of acquiring information about how much competency a person possesses. Evaluation is a judgement about the value of the degree of competency in relation to a set criterion or an individual educational objective, or in comparison with the performance of others. Below are presented the college guidelines for judging the adequacy of evidence, and suggested techniques for use by students and faculty in gathering and presenting evidence of competency.

Guidelines for judging adequacy of evidence

35. The evidence should be based on an assessment technique that is reasonably accurate and complete in measuring and evaluating the competency as stated in the degree pact. Following the application of an acceptable assessment technique, a concise assessment statement or form should be submitted to the college by the person or persons conducting the assessment.

The college retains the right to determine what evidence is adequate and to ask for additional or substitute evidence. It is the student's responsibility to bear any unusual costs of assessment.

The guidelines are as follows:

(a) In providing an assessment statement to the college, the persons conducting the assessment should comment only on that behaviour or product which they have directly observed or measured. Although statements of both fact and opinion may be made, the evaluator should distinguish between the two.

(b) The assessment statement should rest on assessments made by persons recognized as 'experts' by the Dean of Learning Development. In making his decision as to who is an expert, the dean is guided by the following definition. An expert is one who is recognized, by persons active in the same field, as competently trained and who knows the techniques of assessment pertaining to that field. It is the student's responsibility to inform the college of the qualifications of the person or persons conducting the assessment.

(c) An assessment statement may comment on more than one competency, provided it has been established that the evaluator is qualified to make judgements on all the competencies. Each competency must be commented upon directly and separately in the assessment statement.

(d) The evidence should be based on an assessment technique which, if repeated, would yield nearly the same results.

(e) If the evidence is based on activity or an assessment made several years or more in the past, the college reserves the right to ask for a more current assessment.

(f) The evidence should be based on an assessment technique that is practical for the student in terms of cost, complexity and time requirements.

(g) The evidence should be sufficient in quantity to persuade an impartial reviewer that it verifies the claim to competence. Excessive evidence should be avoided.

(h) The language of an assessment statement should be clear and specific and show internal consistency.
(i) Assessment statements should conform to the evaluation terms (knowing, applying and evaluating) as contained in the college's definition of competency.

Suggested assessment techniques

36. The following techniques are not proposed as an all-inclusive list of ways to measure and evaluate. The college hopes that new techniques will be developed by creative students and faculty members. Staff members of the Office of Learning Development can be consulted on selection or design of assessment techniques. The techniques are broken down into six categories, as follows:

Oral examinations may be conducted by one or more examiners or interviewers, and involve one or more examinees. Questions or problems may be stated in oral or written form, but the responses by the student are oral. In a group interview, several students are expected to respond not only directly to the stated question or problem, but also to each other.

Objective tests are usually 'pencil and paper tests' composed of questions or items for which there is only one correct answer. The form of an objective test may be: (a) true–false; (b) multiple choice; (c) completion; and (d) matching.

Essay tests are characterized by the presentation of a question or task to which the student responds by organizing and writing an answer.

Situation tests involve planned observation of the student in a natural setting. Generally, a rating scale is used to facilitate the recording of items measured through observation. Frequently, specific performance measures can be employed, e.g. typing and shorthand tests, listening tests in music and foreign languages, etc.

Simulation games require that the student's responding behaviour should take place in a situation constructed to be as much like a natural situation as possible. Observations and judgements are then made by examiners of individuals and/or group behaviour.

Product assessment is employed when not the processes by which the student arrived at the product are to be measured or evaluated, but the product itself, e.g. art, music, creative writing, play production.

It is also possible to use standardized tests, such as the College Level Examination Programme (CLEP) to test competencies. Normally an individual would choose this method when his or her experiences more nearly coincided with the regular college courses. MMSC allows up to nine competencies to be met by CLEP examinations.

V Learning strategies for developing competencies

37. The college encourages and accepts a wide range of experiences to meet the competencies. Some of the more common means followed by students are identified and discussed briefly below.

MMSC group-learning activity

38. The full-time faculty members (in contrast to 'community faculty') will frequently organize group-learning experiences for students. Student attendance and participation are voluntary, but successful completion of a group-learning opportunity will generally meet the requirements for one competency. The learning-experience group never meets where the administrative staff and faculty are housed but rather somewhere in the community, for example, in churches, libraries, business establishments, art galleries or homes. Thus the faculty holds to the philosophy that there is not a college campus in the traditional use of the term. Sometimes the community faculty also organize group-learning experiences. They follow the same general approaches and procedures as do the full-time faculty.

Group learning outside the MMSC

39. A second type of group-learning experience is that provided through some other community organization or institution. Students are informed of the existence of such possible learning experiences through a weekly publication of MMSC entitled *Catalyst*. This publication lists learning opportunities of possible interest to students but does not evaluate them, leaving this function to the student who wishes to make use of them to fulfil part or all of the requirements for a competency.

40. Students may also participate in the regular college classes offered by one of the many colleges or universities in the Twin City area. Attendance at, and a grade for, such a course does not of itself meet the competency; the student must go through the same steps of describing it in a pact. If the tuition fee for such a course is greater than the college's standard charge, then the student must pay the balance (see paragraph 50(a) below).

Internships

41. Learning achieved through critical observation, orientation or participation at a variety of agencies and institutions in the Twin Cities, or learning opportunities that involve a newly designated project at one's place of employment, are utilized by students for one or more competencies. The college makes special efforts to identify internship opportunities, since part of its philosophy is their commitment to work experience related to the student's job. In addition to internships, the college encourages the use of projects and activities at the place of work which differ from the student's regular job assignment but may be considered as a possible way of developing one or more competencies.

Supervised study

42. In order to develop a competency a student may arrange a tutorial with a regular faculty member, a community faculty member, or someone in the community who does not have a direct relationship to the college but who has a

particular background which makes that person an appropriate individual to provide the tutoring.

43. A student may wish to develop a competency through in-service training which involves a supervisor working with a student, or by the development of a research project requiring consultation and direction.

Self-directed study

44. The student may only utilize an instructor to evaluate a project which the student has carried out on his or her own. Under this arrangement, the instructor often meets the student only twice, the first meeting being to set up the project and the second to provide the final assessment.

45. Under this arrangement, the student may work with a local community service agency, follow a television course broadcast by a local television station, undertake travel, study programmed tests or make use of any other specific project that is of interest.

VI Preparation of transcript

46. The transcript of a graduate of MMSC appears very different from the traditional transcript which, in a United States university, generally consists of grades based on semester or quarter hours. As the student approaches graduation, considerable time and energy is devoted to helping to develop the transcript.

47. The official transcript for a student, which is obviously closely related to the pact, consists of the following elements:

(a) A statement of the credits accepted for transfer from other post-secondary institutions, including the name of each institution and the date the credit was awarded.

(b) A list of all formal courses and other formal learning activities in which the student took part (in accordance with his or her degree pact) after admission to the college, including courses and other formal learning activities sponsored by the college and those sponsored by other individuals, organizations, institutions, agencies or companies. This list also includes the following information: the name of the sponsoring institution, etc.; the dates during which the student participated; the name of the instructors or other responsible individual(s); a title; and whenever possible, a brief description of the material covered and the methods of instruction.

(c) A list of competencies which the student has demonstrated or verified he or she possesses. This list includes the following information about each competency: a title and brief description of the competency; a description of the evidence which proves that the student possesses the competency; the name of the individual (or individuals) who evaluates the evidence and determines that it is adequate; the date the evidence was officially evaluated and the competency recorded.

VII Tuition, 'Learning Activity Agreement' and resource

Charge

48. As indicated earlier a student must enrol for a minimum of a one-year programme or a maximum of the equivalent of two years' study. A student must complete a minimum of 18 competencies in two years or 9 competencies in one year. The college makes available financial resource credit (much like bank credit), which may be used by the student to purchase various types of learning activities or strategies to develop the competency identified in the pact.

49. The form 'Learning Activity Agreement' is employed to serve the following three purposes:

Registration constitutes notification to MMSC that he or she intends to engage in a particular learning activity at a specific cost that relates to his or her pact and competency goals.

Negotiation provides reference to the pact as to which competency or competencies are to be attained, specific strategies as to how, and criteria for assessment/evaluation of the level of competency to be attained.

Assessment/evaluation is the instructor's indication of actual accomplishment in reference to original goals and intent.

Procedures and responsibility for the Learning Activity Agreement are as given below.

Registration

50. It is the student's responsibility to register all his learning activities with the Division of Academic Affairs, by telephone, mail or in person:

(a) The student must provide, at the time of registration, all the information indicated in the registration section of the agreement. Additionally, the student must indicate the cost of the learning activity if the amount is above the established rates of the college (for example, if the registration relates to enrolment at an educational institution where a tuition fee of $50 is charged, this would be the amount charged to the student and paid directly to that institution by MMSC).

(b) The Records Clerk will enter the registration information, record the item to the student's resource account, and issue the agreement to the student (a copy of the registration section will be forwarded to the adviser for information purposes). In the case of registration for an MMSC-sponsored course, the agreement will be made available to the instructor for use with the student at the first class-session.

Negotiation-assessment/evaluation

51. When the agreement is issued to the student, it is his responsibility to negotiate specific terms with the instructor. They must relate to and be in accordance with the pact.

It is the student's responsibility to gain his or her adviser's approval of the negotiated items, of the wording of the narrative transcript and of the agreed outcome. This may be done by mail, telephone or in person—with the adviser's signature or oral approval for signature at a later date.

After negotiation, it is the instructor's responsibility to retain the agreement until the student has completed the learning activity and the instructor has written the assessment/evaluation (two weeks is the normal period for this to be written). The student must approve and sign this section.

52. This form and procedure formalize into a contract the competency to be attained, the strategy to be followed and the assessment techniques and criteria to be used, along with commitment of resources required for the student's resource credit. When the competency has been successfully completed, this procedure also results in the payment of fees to the adviser with whom the Learning Activity Agreement was made, except that no payment is ever made directly to a regular faculty member receiving a fixed salary.

VIII Faculty

53. MMSC faculty had very little turnover during the year 1973/74. At the time of writing, a total of twenty-five persons held faculty rank, thirteen of whom performed faculty activities on a full-time basis and twelve of whom carried joint administrative/faculty appointments. Eleven MMSC faculty members held an earned doctorate, eleven held master's degrees and three held bachelor degrees. In terms of faculty rank, MMSC had four full professors, six associate professors, twelve assistant professors and three instructors.

54. One significant difference in the activities of MMSC full-time faculty members is that their time has been divided into functional areas with approximately half being assigned to the learning development area, to concentrate on such activities as advising, assessment, IEPC and pact review, the other half of their time being assigned to learning resources, to carry out such responsibilities as course and programme development and recruitment, selection and evaluation of community faculty.

55. There are several hundred community faculty members, that is, persons not employed full-time by MMSC but who have expertise they are able to share with MMSC students, who are the primary instructional staff of the college. Students sometimes suggest citizens of the community with high skills in a specific area to serve as community faculty members even though they have no official status.

IX Governance structure

56. A major step towards developing an effective governing structure was taken in the spring of 1973 when the college moved from a College Assembly (town-hall meeting) to an elected representative system headed by the College Governance Council. The council consists of twenty representatives from all college components, including seven students, seven faculty (four full-time faculty and three community faculty), three administrators, two professional support personnel and two members of the College Association (the College Association is an open-membership citizens' and alumni organization). The Governance Council meets at least once a month and may make recommenda-

tions to the president on any matter which in its judgement affects the welfare of the college. The Governance Council must review and approve all college regulations before they become effective.

57. The council has established two standing committees, the Academic Affairs Committee and the Administrative Affairs Committee. A third group, the Human Rights Compliance Commission, reports formally to the Human Rights Compliance Commission of the Minnesota State College System and the president of the MMSC and informally to the Governance Council. The Academic Affairs and the Administrative Affairs standing committees are made up of representatives of each of the components of the college and serve in advisory capacities to the Governance Council, the president and the college.

X Satellites

58. The college is in the process of organizing two satellites or resource centres. It is expected that many additional satellites will be developed over a period of years to decentralize the full-time faculty and place the new satellites closer to the homes of the students.

59. The several regular faculty members who will be moved to each of the two satellites now being planned will be involved in pact development, assessment and learning strategies at the satellite level. Administrative functions only will be performed by a small staff centrally located but not constituting a formal campus.

XI Profiles

Student profile

60. Enrolment at MMSC increased from 502 to over 700 (head count) during 1973/74. It was deliberately stabilized between November 1973 and April 1974 to permit the college to review its educational policies and procedures and to incorporate necessary changes. The college did not implement a comprehensive recruitment programme, inasmuch as enrolment was stabilized throughout most of the year and only replacements for graduates and drop-outs were admitted. However, the college plans to increase enrolment significantly and establish a consistent growth rate. Enrolment projections for the next few years are:

Financial year	*Head count*	*Full-time equivalent (average)*
1975	1,200	900
1976	1,500	1,200
1977	2,667	2,000

61. The demographic and educational characteristics of the MMSC student body indicate that the median age of the students is 33 years with only 5 per cent being of conventional college age, that is, 18 to 22 years. Approximately 68 per cent of MMSC students are employed on a full-time basis while 70 per cent are married. The racial composition of the students closely parallels that of the catchment area of the college, where over 98 per cent of the students reside. Males comprise 61 per cent of the student body.

1. Student data as of 20 May 1974

Students	*Number*	*Percentage*	*Median age*	*Age range*
Female	235	39	36.0	20 to 72
Male	364	61	30.6	
Total	599	100	32.1	

Age distribution	*Percentage*	*Admission basis*	*Percentage*
21 or younger	1	Transfer of college credit	88
22 to 29	38	Equivalence through experience	12
30 to 39	32		
40 to 49	21		
50 to 59	7		
60 and older	1	*Date of last college attendance*	*Percentage*
Number of college credits		1970–73	58
at admission	*Percentage*	1966–69	17
None	5	1961–65	10
89 hours or less	15	1950–60	6
90 to 134 hours	56	Before 1950	4
135 hours or more	24	None	4

62. In addition to students enrolled for the bachelor of arts degree, non-degree students enrol at MMSC for specific cluster competencies to gain particular qualifications and, also, for continuing education purposes.

63. By 15 May 1974, 104 students had graduated from MMSC. Profiles of MMSC graduates, as of 15 May 1974, are shown in table 2.

XII Observations

64. The observation of the writer is that there is a high degree of motivation and excitement among both faculty and students at MMSC. The impression he got when visiting staff and students is that all feel involved in a significant new approach to higher education.

65. The MMSC programme has been changed and modified frequently since the opening of the college in 1972. There are movements towards more structure and more group activities. Nevertheless, a good deal of ambiguity and flexibility continues to characterize the programmes, some of which is desirable and some undesirable. One of the great temptations in developing a non-traditional programme is to institutionalize it, so that before long it has as much or even more rigidity than traditional programmes; the danger is the introduction of too much structure with consequent rigidity. The opposite problem is that, when too little structure exists and too few policies and procedures are outlined, the programme becomes chaotic because no one knows and understands what is or should be taking place.

66. The overall impression of the writer is that MMSC has survived its earlier days when procedures and policies were less well developed than they are now. The college was then flooded with applications from individuals who

2. Graduate profile as of 15 May 1974

Students	*Number*	*Percentage*	*Median age*[1]	*Age range*
Female	53	51	44.4	23 to 65
Male	51	49	41.0	
Total	104	100	43.0	

Age distribution	*Percentage*
21 or younger	0
22 to 29	22
30 to 39	20
40 to 49	30
50 to 59	25
60 or older	3

Number of college credits at admission	*Percentage*
None	6
89 hours or less	14
90 to 134 hours	47
135 or more hours	33

Admission basis	*Number*	*Percentage*
Transfer of college credit	92	88
Equivalence through experience	12	12

1. At time of graduation.

expected to obtain a bachelor degree solely on the basis of work experience and/or miscellaneous and undocumented activities. When it became known that the programme called for learning experiences classified as cognitive or affective or as skills which would be assessed and evaluated (although any strategy could be pursued in achieving them), then those for whom this approach to education appealed enrolled with the college. The writer is convinced that those who do complete the programme probably enjoy an education with greater breadth and depth and more design than does a student who completes a typical four-year course in a United States college or university.

XIII Recommendations

67. An initial requirement for a programme similar to MMSC is the availability of human and physical resources that can be employed for educational purposes. If a programme similar to MMSC were to be undertaken in a developing country, there would have to be a supply of competent individuals to serve as community faculty staff. There would need to be all types of institutions and of business and industrial groups from which students could obtain educational experiences and/or internships.

68. A second major requirement is that prospective students must possess a high degree of interest and motivation to secure an education. Further, they need to be highly literate, well organized and individually motivated because many of the methods used at MMSC are verbal and the students are mainly responsible for designing and implementing their own educational pacts.

69. The costs are greater at least during the start-up period than they are for traditional educational programmes. At MMSC the current costs for students are approximately $1,800 per year (hoped to be $1,500 in 1975), while the costs

in regular state colleges in Minnesota are approximately $1,200. Although there are practically no costs for buildings, equipment and materials, the high degree of individualization is one of the factors that makes the programme more costly, at least during the initial stages of development. Moreover, the development of individualized instruction materials and approaches is expensive.

70. Any developing country considering the MMSC model should be committed to the basic philosophy that work experience is desirable and necessary and may have academic value. In many cultures there is a dichotomy between work and education, a feeling that physical labour is to be avoided and that education is an escape route. The MMSC model places high value on employment as an essential and necessary base from which education should proceed.

71. The increasing use of the internship as an educational experience may have much to recommend it in a developing country. The MMSC model might be more applicable to secondary education and lower-collegiate work if work experience and internships were built-in for persons engaged in agriculture or employed in simple industries.

Appendix A Standardized reference data

Country, state or province	*United States of America: State of Minnesota*
Area and climate	84,068 square miles. Temperate.
Population	
Total (latest year)	3,805,000 (1971).
Estimated population aged 18	223,000 (18 to 20 years).
Estimated percentage under 15	27 (under 14 years).
Current annual growth rate	1.1 (1970–72).
Government	
Main organizational structure	Partially autonomous state under federal control of United States of America. Elected state legislature.
Political type	Democratic state organization.
Economy	
Political type	Mixed: arable farming and industry. No state or federal controls.
Gross national product	
Total (latest year)	$1,151,400 million (1972) (United States).
Per head	$5,515 (1972).
Average annual increase (percentage)	2.
Communications	
Ground/air	Very good air and road transport, rail poor except some freight.
Mail/telephone	Good postal service; 62.8 per 100 people with telephone (1972).
Broadcasting	
Main system(s) operating	A.M., F.M.; television.

Principal authorities responsible	Only private commercial companies under aegis of United States Federal Communications Commission. Four major broadcasting networks with, nationally, 650 television stations and 6,033 radio stations.
Radio	
Transmission coverage of main programme services with percentage of population reached	100.
Receiving capability for main programme services (percentage)	100.
Television	
Transmission coverage as defined for radio	100.
Receiving capability for main programme services (percentage)	100.
Monochrome or colour	Both monochrome and colour.

Education

Type of system(s)	Public and private.
Main authorities responsible and powers	
At school level	Local, state and federal government.
At post-secondary level	State and federal government.
End of full-time school attendance	
Legal	16 years.
De facto	16 years.
Proportion of 18-year-old age group involved in education	
Full-time	41,951.
Part-time	11,575.
Major developments in provision	
Over next five years	Projected enrolments (head count) by financial year (in parentheses: full-time equivalent, average): 1975, 1,200 (900); 1976, 1,500 (1,200); 1977, 2,667 (2,000).

Institution/system under study — *Minnesota Metropolitan State College, Minneapolis/St Paul*

Brief for study and reason for inclusion	A newly chartered institution of higher education devoted entirely to meeting the needs of clientele not now served by traditional higher-education institutions. One of few institutions in the United States in which every aspect of programme and facilities has been developed to serve needs of non-traditional student.

Main features of subject studied

Origins	Political decision by legislature in 1971.

Educational authority(ies) and roles	In response to *Citizens League Report* April 1971.
Communications authority(ies) and roles	Not directly related to mass-media systems.
Services provided	To make close-to-home college education and training available to thousands of primarily Twin Cities residents. Should serve primarily (a) persons who have been employed several years and who may desire to continue their employment while obtaining additional education, (b) persons who have already attended other post-secondary institutions such as junior colleges or vocational schools and desire to continue their education.
Eligibility to study	
(a) categories	See 'Services Provided' above.
(b) qualifications	Two years of college or its equivalent. Those who apply under the equivalency procedures are to be a minimum of 25 years of age.
Terminal qualifications	Bachelor of arts degree.
Instructional means used	Group learning under resident and community faculty; community organizations or institutions; internships; supervised study and self-directed study.
Personal input from student	When competencies are met, nine in one year, no set time schedule.
Normal duration of study	No limit.
Pedagogic effectiveness	From February 1972, when college opened, to May 1974, drop-out rate about 27 per cent; now approximately 15 per cent.

Numbers involved

Students	
Intake (latest year)	200 between 1973 and 1974.
On roll	700 (head count) as of April 1974.
Graduating	Total of graduates up to May 1971: 104.
Academic staff	
Full-time	Twenty-five (thirteen full-time faculty staff and twelve who carry joint administrative faculty appointments).
Part-time	Approximately 200 community faculty staff.
Other professional staff	
Number	Twelve community faculty members provide advisory services to students while college seeks full-time staff.

Finance

Recurrent expenditure	
By providing authorities, latest available year	1974–75 biennium Minnesota legislature appropriation: $1.75 million.
Average annual outlay by student	$1,450 for twelve-month period.

Non-recurrent expenditure	
Gross, over first five years of new institution	None for buildings or resources such as library or laboratories. Only outlay for space has been rental of modest office space to house administration and faculty.
Special assistance received	
Financial	Outside funds are as follows: Fund for Post-Secondary Education (three years), $455,630; Hill Family Foundation, $71,000; Rehabilitation Services, $61,672; Veterans Administration, $4,000; Law Enforcement Education Programme, $10,000; Ford Foundation Venture Fund, $120,000; total $722,302.
Non-financial	All space for classes in community such as libraries, churches, non-profit agencies, etc. contributed free of charge.

Sources of further information

Educational	Write to: Minnesota Metropolitan State College, Metro Square, Seventh and Robert, St Paul, Minnesota, 55101.
Broadcasting	No broadcasting involved unless by student to use the medium to develop a competency.

Appendix B **Short bibliography**

CARNEGIE COMMISSION ON HIGHER EDUCATION. *Less time, more options: education beyond the high school.* New York, N.Y., McGraw-Hill, 1971.

——. *Toward a learning society: alternative channels to life, work and service.* New York, N.Y., McGraw-Hill, 1973.

CROSS, P.; VALLEY, J. *et al. Planning non-traditional programs: an analysis of the issues of postsecondary education.* San Francisco, Calif., Jossey-Bass, 1974.

FURNISS, W. TODD. (ed.). *Higher education for everybody.* Washington, D.C., American Council on Education, 1971.

GOULD, S. *Diversity by design.* San Francisco, Calif., Jossey-Bass, 1973.

HESBURG, T.; MILLER, P. A.; WHARTON, C. *Patterns for lifelong learning.* San Francisco, Calif., Jossey-Bass, 1973.

HOULE, C. *The external degree.* San Francisco, Calif., Jossey-Bass, 1973.

ILLICH, I. *De-schooling society.* New York, N.Y., Harper & Row, 1971.

Appendix C **Biographical note**

Dr Wesley C. Meierhenry is currently Chairman and Professor of the Department of Adult and Continuing Education, and Professor of Educational Administration and History and Philosophy of Education, at the University of Nebraska, Lincoln, Nebraska (United States of America).

The Community College of Vermont

David C. Kinsey

Contents

I Introduction

1. The Community College of Vermont (CCV) was founded in 1970 to enable state residents to continue their education directly in their own communities. A member of the Vermont State College System, it is an outgrowth of the United States community-college tradition in which courses and other educational services are provided for those who wish to complete the equivalent of the first two years of a college education with an associate degree, to obtain vocational training or to promote personal development. Within this context, it has a number of characteristics and adaptations that make it noteworthy as an educational innovation in Open Learning.

2. The CCV is an open-access programme designed to serve Vermonters who are unable to take advantage of other educational opportunities in the state. Anyone may enrol regardless of age, financial means, geographical location or previous educational experience. The college has no campus and uses existing community buildings for classroom and office space. Classes are taught by part-time teachers from the community, people who usually have regular jobs practising the skills they teach and who are given professional support by the college. Courses and individual learning programmes are designed around student interests and needs. For those seeking academic qualifications, degree programmes are competency-based; the student, with the help of a CCV counsellor, draws up a learning contract that describes the selected competencies to be acquired and the means to obtain them. The degree is awarded when the student demonstrates he has achieved the designated competencies, regardless of the time taken or whether they have been acquired through courses or other means. The organizational system of CCV balances central control and support with a responsiveness to local needs and individual initiative; in both managerial and instructional activities the principle of accountability to agreed objectives is employed. In its overall operation, the programme involves low costs to the college and students.

3. The significance of CCV for those who plan Open Learning systems lies in the way it has attempted to meet many of the basic needs faced by such programmes. It provides an example of an approach to dealing with the following common problems:

Reaching a population unserved by formal or existing educational facilities.

Designing a programme that takes into account the abilities and limitations of students, what the student wants and needs, and what the society needs.

Determining what to learn, and if it is learned, while providing for individual differences as well as for system uniformity and quality control.

Assuring effective adaptation and delivery of services to diverse and remote settings.

Making optimal use of physical and human resources in the region while implementing the programme.

Keeping start-up and operating costs low.

4. This survey of CCV is presented according to the categories established for other case studies on Open Learning systems. While the emphasis here will be on the CCV programme of direct educational services to students, it should be noted that CCV has the additional functions of giving training under contract for specialized agencies and serving as a catalyst for the co-ordination and improvement of the educational services of various bodies in the state.

5. The introduction and conclusion may be read for a general view of the case and its usefulness. The body of the study describes some of the particular aspects and problems of this approach.

II State context

6. Vermont is a small, rural and mountainous state, with most of its population of 450,000 living in numerous rural towns and eight small cities. Having some characteristics of a developing area, the economy depends upon specialized agriculture, owing to poor soil, quarries, small industries and tourism. The traditional Vermonters are relatively poor, with 12 per cent of the population living below the official poverty level; they are also, however, noted for their independent, industrious and resourceful qualities. In recent years there has been a significant new element of young adults and older professionals who have moved from urbanized states to take up residence in Vermont, often in rural areas. The population as a whole has an unusual mixture of both strongly conservative and markedly progressive attitudes. There is a representative state government and good communications by road, post and telephone, although some small areas have poor radio and television reception because of the terrain.

7. In 1973 Vermont ranked thirty-third out of fifty states in *per capita* income, but it was third in its per pupil expenditures on public education. Of the total of $171 million spent on public education in that year, $52 million came from the state, which devoted 38 per cent of its budget to formal public schools. The expenditures on the six public colleges or universities represented 31 per cent of the total costs of public education. About one-quarter of the cost of public higher education was covered by the state budget; the rest came from tuition, grants from the federal government, private foundations and other sources.

8. Almost all of the enrolments in eight-year elementary and four-year secondary (high school) education are in public schools. These are under the direct control of local school boards and the overall supervision of the state Department of Education. Recent expansion on these levels has meant that, despite a 30 per cent drop-out rate before the completion of the full primary–secondary sequence, the median number of years of schooling obtained by the Vermont population rose from 10.9 years in 1960 to 12.2 years in 1970. The secondary school enrolments are about normal for the United States, but the

number of Vermonters who go on to college is approximately 20 per cent below the national average. Only 38 per cent of the high-school graduates of 1972 subsequently entered college, and another 5 per cent undertook some form of specialized vocational training.

9. The options for higher education in Vermont for secondary school graduates are six public and eighteen private institutions. Although half of the enrolments in higher education are in private colleges, the vast majority of their students are from outside the state. The most esteemed higher institution that appeals to local residents is the University of Vermont (UVM), established in 1791. A public institution with partial state funding, UVM has its own board of trustees and considerable autonomy. In the past two decades, four other public colleges have been organized under the Vermont State College (VSC) system, which also has its own board of trustees and receives state financial support. CCV was added to the VSC system as a fifth member. The normal undergraduate programme is for four years, leading to a bachelor's degree. Two-year programmes for an associate degree are provided at UVM and in two of the VSC institutions; and one VSC member is a two-year technical college with its own degree.

10. Colleges in Vermont have had an increasing problem with funding in recent years, and there has been a lack of co-ordinated planning for higher education. While there is mounting pressure to accommodate more students, costs have also risen and the proportion of the state budget devoted to education has declined. Consequently, higher tuition fees have been charged and more attention has been given to part-time study and external education as a means of allowing students to hold a job while studying. Grants from the federal government have been an important source of income for higher education, although these are now more difficult to obtain. A state-wide commission has been established to screen and co-ordinate requests for federal support, and in time federal funds may be processed directly through this body. Vermont is one of three states without a public planning organization for higher education, though the UVM and VSC governing bodies, the Higher Education Council and the state budgetary process serve some of the functions related to planning.

11. There are various, but limited, opportunities to continue their education for those with an incomplete or complete high-school education who cannot be full-time college students. Approximately one-quarter of the total Vermont population is composed of people over 16 years of age who have less than a complete high-school education. The small and federally supported Adult Basic Education programme offers free literacy activities for this group and prepares candidates to take the High-School Equivalency examination. A very small number of this group, or of the high-school graduates who do not go to college, have access to a few manpower or new career training programmes. External programmes at UVM and at one of the state colleges also provide an opportunity for continuing education, but these are for high-school graduates, who generally require some financial aid, and often are on a higher college or even post-college level. Before the establishment of CCV, there was clearly a large segment of the population not being served by existing programmes, e.g. those people with a complete or nearly complete high-school education, limited financial means or poor geographical access to institutions, who wanted to have a chance to study for a college degree or develop occupational skills for middle-level jobs.

III Origin and development

12. The idea of creating a community college to meet unfilled needs in Vermont for post-secondary education was first presented by a commission appointed in 1968 to examine the feasibility of establishing an additional state technical college. Under the direction of the state Commissioner of Education, Harvey Scribner, this study concluded that such an institution would be highly expensive and would not meet state-wide needs. Instead, it recommended the development of a regional community college system for Vermont. However, no action was taken until Scribner revived the idea at the annual New Careers Conference in 1970.

13. The fact that effective steps were then taken to implement this recommendation was due to a convergence of personal influence and immediately available outside funds. At the conference was Tom Davis, state director of the federal Office of Economic Opportunity (OEO) programme and son of the Governor of Vermont. Davis knew that OEO had some uncommitted funds at the end of the fiscal year, and with others drew up a letter of interest and submitted it to Washington. When an OEO grant of $59,000 was awarded, the governor was prompted to appoint a Vermont Regional Community College Commission (VRCCC) to oversee the pre-planning phase of the grant to establish a community-college demonstration model. The new head of one of the state colleges, William Craig, was appointed president of the commission, which included representatives of the state government, agencies and educational institutions. Peter Smith, a young man from an old and influential Vermont family who had been working under Scribner, was named Project Director.

14. The mandate of the commission was to establish a demonstration model that would: (a) research and demonstrate the feasibility of a non-campus and community-oriented programme for academic and professional training; and (b) train state-level personnel in the effective co-ordination of educational and career programmes for the disadvantaged population. It hypothesized that education can be taken to the consumers to meet their expressed needs, and that many of these educational needs can be met through the utilization and co-ordination of existing resources.

15. In carrying out the mandate in 1970/71, Smith had a small staff of young people, some of whom had done graduate study in education, who were dedicated to this idea and willing to work on demanding tasks for modest salaries. Rather than spend an extended period in preparatory design and surveys, they elected to carry out trial operations in the field early in the planning phase of the grant. They established and staffed three regional sites in north-east, central and south-east Vermont, where free courses based on student demand and taught by volunteer community teachers were offered. There was also a special projects team that worked in other regions to co-ordinate and run training programmes in co-operation with state and federal agencies.

16. The conceptual value of this planning-around-action approach was that it both tested and demonstrated the potential demand for services, and gave direct experience with real operational problems that should be considered in subsequent planning and design. It also served a political need. To gain acceptance of such an innovative idea and to acquire further funds some visible short-term results were needed. The governor gave permission for VRCCC to

be incorporated as a private non-profit organization, which gave flexibility in fund-raising. The fact that potential sources of opposition in the state educational establishment were quiet was perhaps due to the non-competitive nature of the college's outside funding and a belief that over a period of time it would not succeed. But the field demonstration of the programme's feasibility and its potential for low-cost education did provide a realistic basis for the development, evaluation and revision of operations, and for the training of staff. It also helped to attract additional outside funds.

17. From the beginning it was apparent that some important decisions would have to be made about the future form and organizational links of the college. Would it be a community programme that primarily helped low-income people to develop vocational skills, or would it also provide a means for the disadvantaged to get a formal academic degree in the public higher-education system? Some representatives of agencies concerned with low-income families argued for the former; most of the staff who had personally experienced the formal system wanted to get out of it, and were initially interested in this programme because it was 'going to the people' with an educational alternative to the formal system. But the field testing indicated that many of the disadvantaged clientele wanted to get *into* the system, to have a chance to obtain a recognized degree. While this difference in orientation has persistently posed problems, from the early days it was clear to Smith and others that the mixture of services should include programme options for a recognized degree. Despite the advice of some members of the commission to organize degree programmes quickly, this was done gradually in stages on the basis of field assessment and consultation. This permitted programme relevance and originality, as well as a timing that allowed the degree programmes to be integrated with the answer to a second basic question.

18. Would the college remain as a separate entity, have its own board, grant its own degree and depend on outside funds? Or would it become a unit in the state college system? Again, some favoured the first on grounds of greater flexibility, but it was apparent to Smith that this would be unstable and merger was the only politically and financially feasible course to take. A number of factors favoured joining the VSC system rather than the University of Vermont: VSC had the statutory power to create new entities without special legislation and was administratively more sympathetic. With the help of the provost of VSC, official evaluations of the college were carried out in the spring of 1972 and reports were favourable on merger. The VSC board agreed in principle, but disagreed as to when. Smith argued successfully that immediate approval was necessary to aid fund-raising for the following year. In September the college, renamed Community College of Vermont, became the fifth member of VSC, was placed under its board, and the initial degree programme in Human Services was approved.

19. This agreement was reached on the condition that the VCC budget would be entered as a separate item in the next year's request for state funds, and hence would have to be approved by the state legislature without cutting into the regular VSC allotment. While this appropriation of $50,000 represented the first formal state expenditure on VCC, the arrangement was still unstable and it was indicated in the executive budget of the state that in future the allocations to VCC would continue to be relatively small. With the aid of further foundation and federal grants, and the decision to charge a small tuition fee, VCC continued

to improve its external relations and internal development in 1973. It held its first graduation, had two additional degree programmes in Administrative Services and General Studies approved by VSC, and became a member of the Vermont Higher Education Council. Its second request for state funds was approved, with a cut from what was asked, but in 1974 it was agreed that its requests should be incorporated into the overall VSC budget. Henceforth the proportionate amount of state funds available to CCV will be worked out internally within VSC. The prospects for a sympathetic hearing within the constraints faced by that body were further improved when William Craig, the past head of the VRCCC, was named chancellor of the VSC system; he brought with him, as an assistant, the planner who had played a central role in the development of CCV.

20. The timing and manner of CCV's emergence appear to have been propitious. The fact that it started at a time when there was no state mechanism for the planning and control of all post-secondary education was probably an advantage. The influence of bureaucracy and vested interests in such a body might well have blocked the political or economic channels that CCV needed in order to survive. With an established position in the state college system, President Peter Smith and CCV have been assured that they will play the central role in activities concerning two-year college education throughout Vermont.

21. By the end of 1974 CCV had a well-developed administrative and delivery system, and was operating a year-round educational programme that enrolled about 1,500 students in regional sites in the eastern half of the state. In addition, it had worked out a number of co-operative links with other agencies for the joint improvement of educational services.

IV Organization and management

22. The Community College has two basic organizational tasks: to deliver educational services to its students through the staff and existing community resources, and to create collaborative relationships with other agencies in order to provide improved and co-ordinated services. The first task absorbed most attention in the early years and is our primary concern here. In organizing this system, the intent was to combine decentralized authority in field offices that could be responsive to particular local needs and initiate activity with a centralized body that had overall responsibility and co-ordinating authority as well as an ability to provide supporting services to the sites. On both levels management is guided by agreed annual objectives.

23. As with other state colleges, CCV is under the board of trustees and the chancellor of VSC, and in major academic programmes and budgetary matters it follows their guidelines and must receive their approval. It has its own advisory board which is consulted on the initiative of the president. The president's team includes four officers who, on a college-wide administrative level, are responsible for guiding the planning and evaluation in terms of yearly goals, development of new programmes and public information. Beyond this the administration is divided into supporting services of the central office that maintain the delivery of educational services of the college, and delivery services in the regional sites that are concerned with direct provision of educational services to students.

24. Institutional support from the central office is handled by two teams, one for Learning Services and the other for Administrative Services. The director and four members of Learning Services are responsible for assisting with curriculum development, media and materials, staff training, teacher and student support, and registrar services. The director and two members of Administrative Services deal with financial and personnel services as well as student financial aid. In each regional site there is a director and usually two 'teacher supporters', four 'student supporters' or counsellors and two office managers. These field-site teams are responsible for the mobilization of human and physical resources in the communities into courses and programmes to meet the needs of students.

25. In performing their various delivery functions, personnel in the regional sites receive assistance from specified units of the central office. The regional site director, who handles the administrative support for the site staff and the liaison between them and community groups, obtains help from the president, his team, and Administrative Services. The teacher supporters are responsible for developing courses and recruiting, training and evaluating the part-time teachers from the community as well as assuring the delivery of materials to teachers. They are aided by Learning and Administrative Services. The counsellors, who along with the teachers have direct contact with students, may turn to the same two services. Special community groups on the site level, such as the local review committees which personally guide and evaluate degree students (see section VII below), are also given aid and guidance by Learning Services.

26. Planning, under the guidance of the planning officer of the president's team, is a recurring process that involves staff on the site and central office levels. In the first period of trial-site programmes and learning from experience much of the officer's time was spent advising and training site personnel in a rational process of planning for local programmes. On the basis of this field experience, guidelines were established for preparing annual site plans. In addition, an overall information system was created to give measures of progress in the framework of the plans and to provide feedback to the sites for evaluation and further planning. This information is supplemented by the use of student and teacher evaluation questionnaires after each course. As CCV became more organized, the planning officer was responsible for guiding an all-college goal-setting process involving broad participation, and for the supervision of studies or surveys of organizational and student progress. Recently an additional procedure has been adopted whereby, after the college goals for the following year are established, each site proposes and designs special projects to determine how the goals can be met in its region. Projects are carried out by site personnel with the help of central staff, and results are considered in preparing the next site plan. The college has instituted a programme budgeting system that presents the budget in functional categories so that the financial implications of programmes can be considered more readily in planning.

27. In respect to decision-making, issues of college-wide importance are acted upon in monthly meetings of the president and field-site directors. The College Council, also meeting each month, can recommend action and give advice or reactions to decisions before the president and directors. The council represents the views of the staff and is made up of five members elected by the

staff each year. The institutional support teams of the central office oversee the implementation of decisions, and the field-site teams can express ideas or concerns through the council or directly. Implementation of a decision is delayed for thirty days, during which time college members can make an appeal for reconsideration. For the most part, matters not of college-wide importance are left to the discretion of the sites.

28. Decisions on co-operative activities with and through other agencies start with a proposal to the president and site directors, who refer it to one of the support teams to develop. If the president and directors approve the elaborated proposal, they have the team draw up a contract and, if acceptable, it is issued. Examples of this type of activity include a 'Credit Banking' system with another of the state colleges where Vermonters may keep on file documentation of their credit-worthy experience, or co-operation in providing educational services with a vocational centre.

29. The college began with a demanding array of enthusiastic staff activities. In developing this organizational system there was an attempt to maintain room for initiative and the flow of energy while establishing an order that would provide the rest needed to sustain activity during the period. Owing to the geographical dispersion and decentralization required to keep the programme close to communities and students, there are tensions between units that come and go despite remedial efforts. The management, however, feels this is an inevitable feature of such a scheme, and even desirable in assuring the vitality and responsiveness of the system.

V Staff

30. The staff arrangements of the community college are characterized by a small body of regular, continuous administrators and professionals, and a heavy dependence on part-time or temporary personnel from the communities. A major function of the regular staff is to give support to part-time local teachers who conduct courses and to students who design and carry out their own particular learning programmes.

31. At the end of 1974 there were forty members of the regular staff, eighteen of whom were in the central office and twenty-two in the regional sites. The most important element on the temporary staff are the 150-odd community teachers who are contracted to give specific courses. In addition, temporary contracts are given to consultants and personnel in co-operating agencies for programme development, and to a person to develop work-study programmes for students. Occasionally students are given temporary employment in the offices and members of the community serve voluntarily on specific committees.

32. For the most part the regular staff are young adults who have college degrees and some training or experience in their respective areas. Candidates are located through public announcement and a search committee, and after selection are given a job orientation and a renewable contract of at least one year's duration. Despite this and relatively low salaries, it has been possible to obtain an able and dedicated staff, attracted by the novelty and spirit of the college, the opportunities for a constructive contribution to its evolution, and the cause of helping a disadvantaged population. Several have additional or personal sources of financial support outside the college. Because of the

particular demands of this type of programme and gaps in staff preparation, in-service training by central staff or special outside consultants has played an important part in personnel development.

33. The teachers are usually local people who are employed full-time practising the skills they teach. Thus a craftsman may give an evening course on his speciality, a secretary on office skills, a day-care centre specialist on child development or a town official on local government. A teacher is recruited by the teacher supporter on the regular staff of the regional site; he judges the teacher's competence and prepares a contract for the course. The teacher is paid $225 for a fifteen-week course, meeting three hours a week, if there are five or more students; if there are fewer students, he is paid $50 per student per term. The contract is only for leading the course and evaluating students. The fact that there are no administrative, counselling or research responsibilities is attractive to someone with competence and interest but limited time. For a number of teachers the interest has been sufficient for them to make further contracts for subsequent courses. The teacher supporter is responsible for helping the teacher with pre-service orientation and planning, for assisting with materials and information during the course, and for aiding with evaluation at the end.

34. Since it was assumed at the outset that few course teachers would have had previous teaching experience, it was expected that the teacher supporter would have to play an important guidance role in regard to pedagogical methods. Unexpectedly it has turned out that about three-quarters of the course instructors have had previous teaching experience of some kind. The implications of this will be discussed in section VIII below.

VI Students

35. The Community College follows the principle of open access, in which there are no formal entry requirements of any kind. However the target group for the programme consists of those who are denied access to further education because of their geographical location, level of prior educational attainment, or poverty. To serve such a population obviously requires special measures of psychological, pedagogical or financial support beyond those offered by an ordinary college.

36. By spring 1974, the college enrolment had grown to over 1,400 students. About 85 per cent of these were considered to be in the target population, a composite index of those who reported that they had no alternative access to education (78 per cent), had less than a complete high-school education (8 per cent), and had a low income at the welfare level (43 per cent). The programme as a whole appealed mainly to adults between 20 and 45 years old, the average age being 28 years. Approximately two-thirds of the student body were employed full- or part-time, and had less than two years of college education. Whether due to a greater availability of time or other factors, females predominated over males in a ratio of 2 to 1.

37. It is evident that most students who make use of CCV services do so for the practical purposes of developing skills to improve their career prospects. In 1973, student questionnaires indicated that 51 per cent wanted directly to improve their employment-related skills, 37 per cent wished to work for a

recognized degree and the remainder were interested on grounds of general personal development or recreation.

38. The disadvantaged target population has numerous barriers to continuing their education, derived from isolation, previous educational failure or poverty. A certain number of potential students learn of CCV through friends, the media and direct contact with staff, but the regional sites have had to experiment with special outreach efforts to contact a dispersed population. Taking into account the limited staff time available, such measures have included mailings, public speakers and the improvement of agency referrals. Once a potential student has expressed interest, educational counsellors help individuals or groups to identify personal goals and match the student's needs with what CCV can offer. As an enrolled student, the individual may receive help from counsellors on personal needs, vocational information and the design of a degree programme. In cases where problems such as transport or need for baby-sitting hinder study, the counsellor may be able to facilitate support through student financial aid provisions.

39. Of the students enrolled in a given term, about one-third are continuing students. Since this is about the proportion working for a degree, it indicates that the majority of the student body tends to be in flux with students moving in and out to take courses that meet their needs. A student takes courses at his own pace as he is able to find the time.

40. In the short history of CCV, 57 students had graduated with an associate degree by the summer of 1974. A follow-up of these graduates showed that: 63 per cent found employment in social and administrative service jobs on a paraprofessional level; 11 per cent were unemployed (but over half by choice); and 26 per cent were continuing their college education at four-year institutions. Consequently, the early evidence indicates that the CCV degree programme can provide a successful second chance and gateway to occupational advancement or a complete college education.

VII Courses and curriculum

41. The two basic principles that guide the CCV educational system are: (a) that the college should respond to the learning needs of students, whether these are for a formal academic degree, vocational training or personal development, and (b) that for academic certification, the college should evaluate learning according to demonstrated competency regardless of when, where or how it was learned. In applying these principles, CCV makes an important distinction between courses and degree programmes. Courses, which are created to meet a variety of expressed needs, are single units without any sequence. They may vary from region to region, and from term to term, depending upon the demand and the availability of teachers to lead them. On the other hand, a degree programme in a given field is defined in terms of the central skills to be attained if one is to have adequate competency in that field and receive a degree. A student who contracts for a degree programme may elect to develop certain competencies in his programme by taking CCV courses; but he may also do this through other means. Theoretically a student might be able to demonstrate the necessary competencies and receive a degree without taking any CCV courses.

42. A course may originate from the request of a potential student or a proposal from a potential teacher. In either case, the regional office tries to make a preliminary assessment of the broader demand for such a course, as well as of the teacher's interest, before approving it. Alternatively, the staff may initiate the idea for a course on the basis of an apparent need, find a teacher and verify the demand by the extent of student enrolment.

43. The initial course planning is done by the teacher and a teacher supporter, who prepare a brief statement of the list of courses for the coming term and a more detailed proposal. The proposal is then negotiated and revised with the students at the beginning of the course; and shortly thereafter the teacher, teacher supporter and students agree upon a final course description that identifies objectives, means and completion requirements in a single page. At the end of the course an evaluation sheet is filled in, with assessments and recommendations by the student and the teacher's evaluation of the student. These two pages become the student's 'transcript' if he had earlier elected to take the course for credit and later needs a transcript for use outside CCV.

44. Each regional site publishes and distributes a separate annotated list of courses before each of the three terms. A course meets for three hours a week during the fifteen-week terms in the autumn and spring, and with additional hours during the eight-week summer term. Course topics may range from automobile maintenance, typing and how to start a small business, to child development, English composition and literature. There is an effort on the part of the staff to balance practical courses with some offerings in academic areas, such as the social sciences and humanities. This is done not only to serve degree students but also to avoid becoming categorized as a lower-class vocational college in the eyes of the public. In addition to formal courses, each region also arranges 'special features', such as counselling groups, arrangements for on-the-job learning experiences and educational trips.

45. The degree programmes lead to an Associate degree which, in the state colleges and elsewhere, is awarded after a two-year college programme. But, unlike the general practice of requiring 60 credit hours, at CCV it is based on demonstrated competencies without reference to credits or time spent. Typically the programmes qualify the student for paraprofessional roles in different occupations, or for transfer into the third year of a regular four-year college. At present there are degree programmes in three areas. The first, in Human Services, has study-area specialities for education, child development and counselling; and the second, for Administratives Services, has specialities in office occupations, marketing and business management. The third programme, in General Studies, permits the student to choose what his own content and purposes are to be. Here the programme deals with the process of how to learn and identifies intellectual, social and physical competencies pertinent to successful achievement in any speciality.

46. Guidelines for each programme area were developed by a special State Advisory Committee of Vermonters appointed by the CCV president. A committee is composed of three practitioners in the area, three active teachers in the area, three potential students and the president or his representative. The Committee for Human Services, for instance, assessed the projected demands for manpower in this area and determined the central skills needed to perform effectively in Human Services. The resulting guideline presents the 'core goals' for the whole programme in Human Services in terms of nine general com-

petencies, with explanations and examples of each. For each speciality selected as having promise on the job market, six 'study-area goals' or specific competencies are given, again with explanations and examples. Finally there is a section that describes and gives skill requirements for sample jobs in human services, and lists resources that the student may consult for further employment information. The programme guidelines for Human Services and Administrative Services, which follow a similar format, have a clear orientation for certain vocational roles. However, a significant number of students want to pursue vocational studies outside these areas, to obtain advanced entry into other educational institutions, or to study areas of special personal interest. Guidelines for the General Studies programme were formulated to serve these needs.

47. To obtain an associate degree the student has to demonstrate competencies in fifteen of the core and study-area goals of the programme. A certificate may be issued if eight competencies are demonstrated. In his learning contract (see section VIII below) the student identifies the competency goals to be achieved in the context of the programme's guidelines and indicates the means by which they will be attained. For any given competency, students may receive credit if they can demonstrate that they have already achieved it through experience, independent study or other means. One method of demonstrating this is the College Level Examination Program, a nation-wide test which CCV is authorized to give, that determines if a student has skills and knowledge on a second-year college level in various fields.

48. Formally the CCV Review Board at the central office is the final authority that approves the successful completion of a learning contract before the degree is awarded. In practice the basic evaluation and recommendation for a degree are made in the regional sites by a local review committee. This innovative body meets with the student, guides him in the development of the contract and decides if it has been successfully completed. Its members, under the chairmanship of the site director, include a member of the CCV Review Board (if the director is not also on that board), a local student, a teacher and a practising expert or professional, all of whom are in fields related to that of the candidate. Operational guidelines are provided for the local review board, and an effort is made to select members with high standards who can make wise judgements as to whether sufficient competency has been attained. When it decides that the contract has been completed, the contract and evidence are sent to the central CCV Review Board, which mainly serves to assure college-wide consistency in meeting degree requirements.

49. The Vermont State College system recognizes the CCV associate degree and graduates may transfer directly into third-year college courses. Students have also been able to obtain credit for individual CCV courses when entering other institutions.

50. Notwithstanding its difficulties, students have responded favourably to the stimulation, flexibility and relevance of the contract-competency system. The main problems seem to be those of definition and standards. Some of the persistent questions are: What precisely is a competency within the broader statements in the programme guidelines? What constitutes a sufficient demonstration of attainment? And, how much competency is enough for a degree? As experience with contracting accumulates, CCV is continually trying to improve the local review committees and the guidelines for contracting so that there may be more precision in these difficult issues.

VIII Teaching methods and materials

51. The college has a student-oriented approach which tries to adapt the institution to the student rather than assume the student should adapt to the institution. In this there is an inevitable tension between the need for some outer direction and institutional control on the one hand, and the objective of maintaining a responsiveness to student desires and initiative on the other. Accepting the necessity and desirability of this tension, the design and methods of the CCV programme represent an effort to assure that the latter objective will not be submerged by the usual forces of institutionalization.

52. In principle, CCV assumes that the relevance and motivation for study will be greater if the student can play a significant role in determining the design and objectives of his course work or degree programme. It is also believed that learning will be more effective and continuous if, in the process, a student can learn how to learn and be his own educational programmer. However, the manner in which such concepts are applied differs between courses and degree programmes. Thus it is best to consider separately for each of these two dimensions the methods employed and the aspects of the learning-support system that facilitate their use.

53. The teaching methods used in courses vary according to the nature of the subject, teacher and students. While occasionally there are lectures and guest speakers, more typically there are demonstrations, discussions, problem-solving, simulation exercises, and individual or small group projects. Sometimes courses are organized around a special Educational Television (ETV) or other audio-visual series, with readings and discussion. Recently there has been an increased use of audio-visual materials and kits as supplementary aids for a course.

54. In addition to providing administrative, planning and evaluation support for teachers, the regional teacher supporters are also supposed to assist with teaching methods and in-service training. For various reasons, there has been more success with the former than with the latter. Teacher supporters have been weighed down with administrative tasks, which are particularly demanding in this system, and in practice they have little time to help in training or methods. Furthermore, most of the teachers have had previous teaching experience and tend to want to do things their own way. This has often meant that there is some resistance to the idea of designing a course around behavioural objectives of what a student will be able to do at the end; and there is even a reluctance about in-service training. Since there is a limited supply of community teachers willing to work for nominal pay, and the freedom from administrative and other demands on their time is part of the attraction, there can only be gentle persuasion on the part of CCV in matters of methods and training. One alternative being planned is to encourage teachers to meet together periodically to stimulate and encourage themselves.

55. Arrangements for course use of ETV programmes and the supply of audio-visual and other materials are facilitated by the central office. However, the geographical dispersion of courses presents delivery problems. Current efforts to remedy this difficulty include the establishment of resource centres for media and materials in the sites and co-operative arrangements with local public libraries to serve course needs.

56. The essential educational method and instrument for completing a

degree programme is the student contract. At CCV the contract procedure places the burden of initiative and responsibility on the student. It involves a process that helps students to learn how to become their own teachers. Along the way they are given counselling and guidance, but they are themselves accountable for the design and evidence that their competency goals have been achieved. The ultimate criterion is what has been learned, and this means that courses, qualifications of teachers and activities are significant only in so far as they have resulted in actual competencies.

57. Initially the candidate consults the degree programme guidelines, selects the twelve to fifteen programme goals that are most in line with his or her personal needs and determines his or her objectives. Then, with the advice of a counsellor, he or she writes a preliminary learning plan that answers the following questions: 'In respect to my objectives: (a) What do I already know? (b) What do I want to learn? (c) How do I want to learn it? (d) How will I know when I have learned it?' Next he or she meets a local review committee, perhaps accompanied by his or her counsellor, for initial approval of the plan and guidance. After this the student carries out his or her planned contract. If the candidate has already acquired necessary competencies through prior learning, he or she may gather documentation or evidence to prove this, or take the College Level Examination Program test. Means for acquiring new competencies may include taking courses, independent study, on-the-job training, the use of kits or correspondence courses. When the contract has been completed, the student prepares a short statement that describes his or her learning experiences and provides documentation to confirm the resulting competencies for each of the personal objectives related to programme goals. With this completed contract the candidate again meets the local review committee to evaluate and confirm successful completion. In rare cases where there has been a large amount of unrecognized prior learning, the process may be completed in a matter of weeks or months; but most typically it takes about two years.

58. Considering the non-traditional nature of the students and the conceptual demands of this approach, it is apparent that counselling plays a key role throughout the contracting procedure. While much progress has been made in developing the capacity of counsellors through in-service training, there have been some persistent problems. Many students have difficulty with the unfamiliar tasks of specifying their learning objectives in behavioural terms and in documenting competencies. As student enrolments grow it is increasingly difficult for counsellors to have adequate time for one-to-one counselling. This has resulted in experimentation with a variety of alternative counselling techniques. For instance, in 'contracting groups' a counsellor meets a number of students at the same time, helping them either with the preliminary tasks of clarifying personal values and goals or with the specification of detailed learning plans. Or a CCV teacher with counselling experience is contracted to run a counselling group, and is occasionally assisted by graduates of the programme who have been through the process and can provide insights or encouragement. Peer counselling has been started, in which a student working for a degree programme in counselling is given training and financial aid to counsel other students. Besides providing a needed service, the counselling student is also able to develop competencies for his or her own degree programme.

IX Finances

59. The financial mission of CCV has two fundamental purposes. The first is to provide post-secondary education at a cost that is significantly lower than that of the usual colleges and universities. This is done by the utilization of existing physical and human resources in communities and by co-operation with other agencies and institutions in the delivery of educational services. The second objective is to reduce or remove financial constraints as a barrier for potential students who could not otherwise continue their education. The means for doing this include a minimal and flexible tuition fee-paying policy as well as a liberal financial-aid programme for students.

60. The expense of starting a non-campus college of the CCV model is far below that of a conventional college, and students are served much sooner. In its first complete fiscal year (1971/72), CCV spent $207,000 and enrolled 750 students; in the second year (1972/73) the figures were $420,000 and 1,200 students. By contrast, in 1971 a state committee estimated that by 1980 it would cost $14 million to construct the physical plant, exclusive of dormitories, for one new state college of about 1,000 students. With the virtual elimination of capital costs, the CCV budget is essentially an operating budget. These recurrent expenses of CCV are considerably less than those of a conventional college since there are no salaries and benefits for a full-time faculty roll, insignificant costs for items such as plant maintenance and research and lower allocations for an administrative staff. An important implication of this model is that a greater proportion of available funds is devoted to activities directly related to instruction: these represent two-thirds of the CCV budget, but only one-half of the regular state college budgets.

61. In the interests of facilitating enrolment of poor students, there is a tuition fee of only $30 per course. This is less than one-third the amount charged per course in other state institutions. In 1973/74 a radical 'bank-by-mail' experiment was started for tuition payments. In this system students mail their tuition fees directly to a CCV bank account. This procedure depends on the students' sense of responsibility and there is no formal control on who actually pays and whether the full amount is deposited. This saves the college the salary and expenses involved in a formal collecting procedure, and it was hypothesized that this saving would be greater than the loss in unpaid tuition fees. This has proved to be the case. In the first year students paid 72 per cent of what the traditional system would have guaranteed, which is well above the break-even point for success of the new system.

62. Financial aid for needy students is available in the form of individual grants, educational loans or help with work-study arrangements. The various forms of aid, which are mostly from federal or private foundation sources, have different stipulations or eligibility requirements. Except for scholarships awarded on the basis of scholastic achievement, aid is given on grounds of need and may be used for tuition fees, materials, transport or other reasonable necessities. Students from families whose incomes are below certain minimal levels are eligible to have all college-related costs met, including basic living costs.

63. The CCV programme began with a dependence on federal funds from Washington and was supplemented with a private foundation grant. In its brief history, progress has been made in developing local funds. These include

allocations from the state budget, tuition fee receipts and special service contracts with other agencies. In addition, various in-kind services have been provided by communities and the state in the form of class or office space, technical advice and co-operative assistance. Despite such progress, in 1974/75 only one-third of the CCV budget was covered by state allocations and tuition fees (23 per cent and 9 per cent respectively), whereas two-thirds of the budgets of other state colleges come from these sources. Thus CCV still must raise two-thirds of its funds from federal and private bodies.

64. The continuation of this dependence on outside funds poses a major problem for the future. In the first years, when CCV attracted attention as a promising innovation, such resources were more available than they are now, in a period of rising inflation. On the other hand, since the programme is largely aimed at a poor target population, CCV has fewer possibilities than the other state colleges to make up some of the difference through increased tuition fees. And while its share of the overall state allocations for the state colleges has steadily progressed, further increases will be difficult in view of their competition with established institutions. CCV will argue for a higher share on the grounds that its model, and the co-ordinated use of available resources, are the financially necessary path of the future. Much depends on the success of this argument with potential funding sources in and outside the state.

X Conclusion

65. The CCV model builds upon the American tradition of community colleges and the more recent educational innovations of contract learning and competency-based credits. But the way it has applied these concepts to the common needs that face an open learning system and the particular conditions of Vermont represents a significant innovation in its own right. The result is a post-secondary educational programme with lower costs and a greater degree of social justice for a dispersed, underprivileged population not served by conventional education than is the case in most other efforts. While there is an emphasis on meeting individual needs for self-improvement, a number of development requirements of the society as a whole are also served. CCV relieves the pressure for initial entry into regular post-secondary institutions, provides needed skills on the paraprofessional level and facilitates the co-ordination or mobilization of existing resources.

66. As an organization, CCV is a regional system that supports and co-ordinates decentralized programmes on the local level. Thus it is not a traditional institution with a physical plant or single community base; nor is it basically a central programme that reaches out to students who follow a prescribed course of study. Educational services through CCV and community personnel are directly given in local settings and are adapted to specific needs without up-rooting students from homes or jobs. As a pedagogic system, the focus is on students' authority and responsibility in designing their own education. This is done within a framework of assistance and guidelines with respect to preparing a learning contract and achieving designated competencies. The competencies, however, may be of an academic or non-academic nature, and the means to attain them may be those of a formal or non-formal education.

67. The CCV approach involves several assumptions which, in the case of

Vermont, have had varying degrees of confirmation. With regard to the nature of existing resources, the assumptions have been borne out that in the communities there are adequate locations that can be donated for classes and teachers who will give courses for a nominal fee. However, the belief that there are other agencies already providing complementary services, such as employment and career counselling, which CCV would not have to offer has proved to be more problematic. The educational assumptions that underprivileged students can learn along the lines of this pedagogic system and that community teachers can teach in an innovative manner appear to have had partial but not complete affirmation. This, and the premise that the basic competencies identified in different programmes are universally applicable for those areas, still need evaluation. To date the system as a whole has been evaluated essentially on grounds of its growth, which has been impressive. Nevertheless, specific outcome assessments are desirable, both for CCV itself and for those considering the use of its model or techniques.

68. Of its dual roles, namely, providing direct services and facilitating co-ordination with other agencies or programmes, CCV so far has been most productive with the former. While further refinement and evaluation are necessary, the major work of the future in the delivery of direct services relates to its financing and its geographical expansion to other regions of the state. The frontier of new innovative activity in the future appears to be in the field of co-operation and co-ordination. One of these activities will be the co-operative development of a regional 'credit-banking' system for recording educational experience of individuals that is worthy of academic credit. Another will be learning how to develop links, monitoring and quality control with other agencies in the delivery of educational services to those who are not in the conventional colleges.

69. The development of the CCV programme of direct services was made possible by a number of conditions. The extent to which some of these are necessary preconditions for a programme of this type needs further assessment. They are, however, important for this case and should be kept in mind if a similar approach is contemplated elsewhere. These enabling conditions have included:

(a) A core group of qualified, energetic personnel who were committed to the concept of student authority in educational programming, who viewed themselves as facilitators, and who were able to analyse and use the conditions in which they found themselves.

(b) A political and social context in which there was some readiness to consider innovations in educational practice and a democratic belief in the rights of all to have some post-secondary education.

(c) An expansion of formal secondary education to the extent that there was a large reservoir of potential students with some secondary education as a starting point.

(d) A tradition of popular and comprehensive higher education where it is relatively easy for a qualified student to transfer into a formal college, an opportunity which encourages those with academic motivation to participate in this non-traditional programme as a doorway to a conventional college and a higher degree.

(e) A perception on the part of potential students that there are actual opportunities for advancement in old or new jobs if vocational skills are increased.

(f) A substantial infrastructure of physical and human resources in communities, such as libraries, technological aids and educated local people.
(g) The possibility of federal and private financial aid for an innovative programme in a relatively poor state where the educational budget was already strained.

70. This case study of CCV can be useful as a source of ideas for those who design and plan innovative educational programmes in other places. Rather than attempt an integral and automatic transfer of the model to another location, it would be necessary to adapt and experiment with such ideas in the light of the particular needs, constraints and resources of the new setting. The form and techniques of the CCV programme are the result of a development process. This included: a determination of which needs were not, or could not be, met by the existing system in Vermont; an assessment of the approach, focus and sequence of an alternative activity that would build on available capacities and have the best prospect of serving unmet needs, and a consideration of how this could be most effectively related to other existing programmes. A similar process should precede the adaptation of ideas from this case to an area with other conditions.

71. Theoretically the example of CCV could be viewed as a possible scheme for a national or regional programme, as a programme for specific communities with requisite conditions, or as an extension activity of an existing educational institution. In practice, however, the overall model presumes the existence of a relatively sophisticated infrastructure and conditions that are present in only a few countries or areas. And even here a recasting would be necessary. Some of the individual features of the CCV case are more likely to be of use: its method of utilizing local resources, the application of pedagogic methods such as contract learning and competency-based programming or the administrative and support system for local educators and students. Such specific principles, ideas or techniques could be studied and tried in some form as components of other formal or non-formal educational programmes.

Appendix A Standardized reference data

Country, state or province	*United States of America: State of Vermont*
Area and climate	9,609 square miles. Temperate.
Population	
Total (latest year)	444,330 (1970).
Current annual growth rate (percentage)	14.2 (1960–70).
Government	
Main organizational structure	Partially autonomous state under federal control of United States of America.
Political type	Democratic state organization.
Economy	
Political type	Predominantly livestock agricultural, no state or federal controls.
Gross national product	
Total (latest year)	$1,151,400 million (1972) (United States).
Per head	$3,865 (1972).
Average annual increase (percentage)	2.
Communications	
Ground/air	Very good road services. Poor rail and air systems.
Mail/telephone	Adequate postal services; good telephone service to 99 per cent of all households.
Broadcasting	
Main system(s) operating/ Principal authorities responsible	Mainly commercial companies under aegis of United States Federal Communications Commission. Vermont Educational Television station.

Radio	
Transmission coverage of main programme services with percentage of population reached	Good. Approaching 100 per cent.
Receiving capability for main programme services (percentage)	100.
Television	
Transmission coverage as defined for radio	Scattered reception.
Receiving capability for main programme services	164,000 households have television; four television receivers per school.
Monochrome or colour	Colour.
Education	
Type of system(s)	Under state control at advisory and innovative levels.
Main authorities responsible and powers	
At school level	Local school districts have main responsibility providing 57 per cent of budget; state provides 40 per cent, Congress 3 per cent. Private schools autonomous. Public 437, private 50.
At post-secondary level	Six public, 18 private.
End of full-time school attendance	
Legal	Compulsory and free between 5 and 18 years.
De facto	30 per cent drop out before completing secondary school.
Proportion of 18-year-old age group involved in education	
Full-time	64 per cent (1970).
Major developments in provision	
Over last five years	Increase of 5.1 per cent per annum of full-time students in public higher education.
Over next five years	Projected annual increase until 1980: University of Vermont, 1.8 per cent of budget; Vermont State colleges, 5 per cent of budget.

Institution/system under study — *Community College of Vermont*

Brief for study and reason for inclusion	College serves a rural community with characteristics of a developing country and offers opportunities for gaining qualifications based on 'competencies'.

Main features of subject studied	
Origins	Commission (1968) under Commissioner for Education set up to research possibility of another state technical college. Commission (1970) recommended a regional community college. College founded 1971.
Education authority	Vermont Higher Education Council.
Services provided	Wider opportunities of post-secondary education to adults, both for vocational and non-vocational purposes.
Eligibility to study	
(a) categories	All adults over 18.
(b) qualifications	No formal qualifications.
Terminal qualifications	Associate degree, or certificate on completion of half degree requirements.
Personal input from students	Three hours per week over 38 weeks; additional hours in summer term; also educational trips; counselling groups.
Numbers involved	
Students	
Intake (latest year)	1,500 (1974).
Academic staff	
Full-time	40.
Part-time	150.
Finance	
Recurrent expenditure	
By providing authorities (latest year)	$685,205 (1974).
Average annual outlay by student	$30 per course, including books, travel.
Non-recurrent expenditure	
Gross, over first five years of new institution	No capital expenditure since CCV is non-campus and facilities are rented.
Special assistance received	
Non-financial	Dependent upon existing state services, e.g. technical advice assistance.

Source of further information	The Principal, The Community College of Vermont, P.O. Box 81, Montpelier, Vermont 05602.

Appendix B Short bibliography

HOCHSCHILD, S. F.; JOHNSTON, J. G. *Postsecondary education access study*. Montpelier, Vt, State of Vermont Commission on Higher Education Facilities, 1974. (Interim reports.)

SMALLWOOD, F. *Higher education in Vermont: past, present and future*. Burlington, Vt, Joint Committee on Higher Education Planning, 1971.

VERMONT EDUCATIONAL TELEVISION NETWORK. *Vermont Educational Television handbook*.

Vermont year book: 1974. Chester, Vt, The National Survey, 1974.

Appendix C Biographical note

David Kinsey, M.A., Ph.D., has been a director of work-camp programmes in Algeria, France, Israel and the Middle East during 1951–56 and in Tunisia in 1965–66. His teaching experience ranges from that of teacher at the Social Studies Department, Connecticut (North Haven) to assistant professor, Graduate School of Education, Harvard University (1966–73). He was a research associate at Harvard from 1964 to 1973 and has acted as a consultant for Harvard University in Tunisia and Jordan, as well as for the United Nations Development Programme on a UNDP/Unesco mission in the Ivory Coast (1970), the American Friends Service Commission (1972) and the Education Development Centre, Newton, Massachusetts (1974 to date). He has also been adviser/consultant on education for the Ford Foundation since 1973.

B *Open university*

UMA/SUN: the Nebraska approach to a regional University of Mid-America

Charles A. Wedemeyer

Contents

I Introduction

1. The State University of Nebraska (SUN) and the regional University of Mid-America (UMA), which is its conceptual child, constitute a new phenomenon in United States post-secondary education. These institutions, now linked in parallel development, are not novel because they are 'open'. Open education is no longer new, although the immediate precedents of this movement go back only ten years. What is new in SUN and UMA is: the scale of development; its regionalization; the mechanisms used to create a regional institution that is credible and legitimate; the emphasis on research and evaluation; and the role of the United States Federal Government in funding and guiding development.

2. There are few technological or educational innovations in the UMA/SUN model which were not pioneered elsewhere. The philosophical, social, economic, political and educational issues out of which the Open Learning concept emerged have already been documented, and are not uniquely indigenous to Nebraska or Mid-America.

3. Nevertheless, for the United States and possibly for some other countries the development of UMA/SUN may have significance as a case study in the orderly yet creative reform of state post-secondary systems to serve larger regional and educational needs. Because change has been conducted within the customary development channels, destructive division has been avoided.

4. The analysis which follows is based upon November 1974 documentation. It should be remembered, however, that UMA/SUN is at the threshold of its development, and that this American regional open university enterprise may change before it is fully established in 1980.

II The State of Nebraska

5. Eighteenth-century French fur traders, bartering with the Pawnee, Sioux, Omaha and other Indian tribes, were the earliest white visitors to the Nebraska area. The name is from the Omaha, meaning wide river, a reference to the Missouri River which forms Nebraska's eastern and part of its northern border. The state now has a population of about 1.5 million.

6. The Nebraska state motto is 'Equality before the law'. Its nickname is the Cornhusker State, a reference to the large plantings of Indian corn (maize) in

this area. The state has a severe climate with cold winters and heavy snows, and hot, humid summers. About 20 per cent of the employed Nebraskans work in agriculture, the remainder in trade, government and manufacturing. The public elementary/secondary schools enrol nearly 500,000 children. The Nebraska State Department of Public Instruction, headed by a superintendent, administers the schools. The capital is Lincoln, which is also the seat of the University of Nebraska, a land-grant institution with an enrolment of 36,114 and three campuses headed by a president. There are also four state colleges, not part of the university system, and eleven locally controlled community colleges.

7. The University of Nebraska includes an Extension Division and an Agricultural Extension Service. The Extension Division is widely known for the excellence of its correspondence courses on the high-school and college levels. Its high-school courses have been important in enriching the curricula and learning opportunities of students in the many small high schools in the state. The Great Plains National Instructional Television Library is also located at the University of Nebraska.

8. The University of Nebraska has a tradition of serving state needs through extension services and modern technology.

III The origin and history of UMA/SUN

9. The idea of an open university for the state of Nebraska had its origins in the late 1960s. Dissent and protest over the Viet-Nam war, the drive for racial equality and civil rights, the rise of the women's liberation movement, and a deepening concern for the reform of education—these and other issues sparked off nearly a decade of innovation and experimentation, especially in higher and adult education.

10. The youth culture, the drug scene, the hippie-yippie groups, the challenge to established institutional patterns and moralities, the radicalization of student organizations, all these had initial and direct impact on higher education. But in addition, for perhaps the first time, the mass media were used for the direct communication of the real or fancied grievances that animated a very vocal segment of United States colleges and universities. This use of mass media for the exploration and presentation of public grievances was both a reflection of the mood of the country respecting great and divisive issues, and an element contributing to the mood. An intellectual, political and educational climate evolved which encouraged the search for alternatives to the institutional *status quo*.

11. The earliest experiment in open, mediated higher education made its appearance in 1964 and continued under a grant from the Carnegie Corporation for four years. This was the Articulated Instructional Media (AIM) experiment in Wisconsin. It had an impact on the development of the Open University in the United Kingdom, and stimulated a number of investigations into the development of open universities in the United States, Canada and elsewhere. In New York State, the New York Proficiency Examination Programme explored new means of evaluating the achievements of learners who had followed non-traditional (generally not credit-earning) paths to learning.

12. New York was also studying the formation of a system (Empire State College) which would serve persons who could not go to a campus for full-time

learning, and the seeds for the University Without Walls programme were stirring in Antioch, Ohio, leading eventually to a consortium of co-operating colleges and universities experimenting with new approaches.

13. In 1967, note was made of the societal changes that were bringing about the obsolescence of higher-education patterns that had their origin in earlier times and contexts, and new guidelines for institutional development were suggested which pointed towards more Open Learning through the employment of mediated instructional systems. Educational journals as well as the public press gave space and attention to issues of institutional change.

14. The self-actualizing independent learner, capable of getting his education from many sources at a distance, re-emerged in a new context. Long an ideal, the 'self-made person' had been the frontier's answer to the deprivations associated with pioneering.

15. When the spread of schooling made an anachronism of the example of Abraham Lincoln studying law by the light of a prairie-cabin fireplace, the independent-learner image waned, although the practice continued through the growth of correspondence study. Correspondence study laid a basis for learning by the electronic media.

16. In 1969, in the United Kingdom, the Open University was chartered and the development of the university began to take place at Milton Keynes. A steady drumbeat of articles, descriptive of new experiments in mediated and more open forms of instruction, laid a theoretical and pragmatic basis for various commissions in the United States charged with evaluating the need for institutional change, more open forms of learning, and mediated instructional patterns and options.

17. The Commission on Non-Traditional Study reviewed the status of innovative experiments on a national basis, and various states studied their needs to recommend new institutional development.

18. Two national reports on higher education—the Carnegie Commission Report and the Newman Report—emphasized that, despite the vast number of institutions offering some form of post-secondary education, there still remained a significant national population which could not take advantage of the opportunities offered by on-campus programmes.

The origins of SUN

19. The ferment in higher education and concern over adults' lack of access to higher education posed a question in Nebraska: if the citizens of Nebraska were not able to take advantage of the many existing opportunities for higher education, could not the well-established Nebraska Educational Television network be given an important role in alleviating the situation?

20. In April 1971, a university-wide committee was named to study this question.

21. In June 1971, the committee presented its report to President Varner and the board of regents of the University of Nebraska. The report recommended the establishment of the State University of Nebraska project, thereafter known as the SUN project.

22. The preamble of the report noted that 'The present system of higher education is faced with challenges from many segments of society', and that:

A burgeoning educational system has not yet been able to absorb pressures created by an expanding population, a tremendous growth in knowledge and technology, and in increasingly broad-based appreciation of the personal values to be gained from higher education . . . it has not been able to reach all the potential students desiring and deserving educational opportunities. . . . The resources available on established campuses are insufficient to meet the increasing need. . . . Developments of new methods of packaging and delivery of quality educational programmes may provide some answers to today's challenges to the university system.

23. The rationale behind the recommendation to create SUN, and the SUN institutional concept itself, were a restatement of similar proposals which had erupted earlier in several other states, and which would continue to surface through the early 1970s wherever university reform and development were under study. The consistency of such reports was indicative of the prevailing mood of reform in United States higher education. While there were specific differences occasioned by the time, place, local situations and traditions, there were common themes: higher education should be made more 'open'; new learner groups must be accommodated; technology could be a means for improving access to education and improving instruction; United States higher education could reform and extend itself either through evolving new and separate institutions (as in the case of SUN, Minnesota Metropolitan State College, Empire State College) or through the adaptation of present institutions. The sparks struck by the early AIM programme and the success of the Open University in the United Kingdom had lighted a series of academic brush fires.

24. The basic premises of the Nebraska SUN proposal were spelled out in the 1971 report:

1. A non-residential curriculum can be developed which will maintain the high quality of expectations and performance typical of existing residential university systems.
2. Such a programme would be appropriate to two facets of the mission of a university; transmitting knowledge and skills to desirous students, and serving the educational needs of the citizens to whom the school is responsible.
3. Any new approach to higher education should amalgamate the educational resources existing in Nebraska and develop new assets so that a continuing programme of higher education may become a part of the fabric of life for the state's citizens. Some single educational unit, reasonably the University of Nebraska, could provide leadership.
4. Many potential students, in all walks of life and adult age groups, are seeking opportunities to extend their education.
5. College instruction should provide much more opportunity for 'drop-in' and 'drop-out' types of students, as well as those who may wish to qualify for certificates, an associate degree, or the more traditional degrees. Provisions must be made for alternate forms of recognition for college work.
6. A broad range of educators would be involved in any new approach, a considerable dividend in unifying the total higher educational system.
7. An independent SUN faculty and staff is essential to the development of the curriculum and of the delivery system. Variable periods of in-residence in an academic setting will be important to student–faculty cohesion, to nurturing the innate motivation of students, and to monitoring and evaluating student progress.

25. The SUN instructional design was to be developed by a team of individuals, each with a particular expertise, working on a full-time basis. The team members were to include: an educational psychologist, a test designer,

an instructional designer, content specialists, media producers, writers and directors, a cinematographer and a graphic artist. The development was to include, in addition to television, all other educational media that would promote learning activities.

26. The report pointed out that:

If the courses at the State University of Nebraska are to be equal or superior to those at established residential campuses, it is evident that a new type of instructional team must be established. This team should be responsible for translating general objectives into specific learning units; for developing integrated learning kits, media, and face-to-face instruction and for constructing appropriate evaluation instruments. Designing the new courses will require more extensive and different kinds of preparation than the individual professor puts into his own class planning.

The course-development concept indicates how widespread was the influence of AIM and the Open University, and also how different investigators, working independently in various places, tended rather consistently to reach and confirm similar conclusions about the process of course development.

27. The SUN design further outlined a delivery system in which learning centres would be a focal point. Supplied with technological equipment appropriate to the educational media used, and resource materials and video cassettes of all television programmes associated with each course, learning centres were to be located on college campuses, in public schools and libraries, and educational service units. The Wide Area Telephone Service (WATS), enabling callers to telephone free, would be used for direct communication between students and faculty.

28. The 1971 SUN report noted that 'identification of groups who might be served by the State University of Nebraska is basic to the plan'. Preliminary studies indicated two primary categories:

College-bound groups. Persons who may at a later time matriculate at a residential campus: (a) traditional freshman group; (b) accelerated group (complete freshman year while still in high school).

Non-college-bound group. Persons unlikely ever to matriculate on residential campus: (a) vocational group; (b) professional group; (c) personal enrichment group.

29. The SUN design called for a special faculty to teach the courses offered, normally those in the first two years of college.

Grant proposals and development

30. With the acceptance of the report by President Varner and the regents, a request for a planning grant was forwarded to the National Center for Educational Technology of the United States Office of Education.

31. Initial funding of $25,000 was received for the following proposals: (a) to examine some key issues related to credit-by-examination and to provide the skeletal framework for establishing a Nebraska College equivalency programme; (b) to conduct a major clientele study.

32. The results of the clientele study indicated that 1.7 per cent of the adult population of Nebraska were potential enrollees of the programme. (This approximates 20,000 to 24,000 individuals.)

33. At this point, the officials of the United States Office of Education began to see in SUN the potential for a regional model for the states surrounding Nebraska, and possibly for the nation.

34. Another grant of $50,000 was awarded to SUN for the study of problems concerning regional institutional relationships, public broadcast television and delivery.

35. A third grant in 1972 funded a research and development phase.

36. A fourth grant in 1973 extended the research and development phase (the production of thirty television segments) to field testing.

Five-year developmental period

37. By December 1973, SUN had completed the tasks associated with each of the four grants and was ready to enter into a five-year developmental period.

38. In January 1974, the National Institute of Education (NIE) awarded a continuation grant of $934,581 for the calendar year to accomplish work assignments essential to the orderly development of a post-secondary Open Learning model in Mid-America.

39. A $92,000 planning grant from the National Endowment of the Humanities was received to design 'The Great Plains: Cultural History', and to develop three lessons within the course.

40. The total of grants from the United States Office of Education and the National Institute of Education was now $1,798,940. With a grant of $200,000 from the Edna McConnell Clark Foundation, and the $92,000 from the National Endowment of the Humanities, the total SUN grant support as of 1 March 1974 totalled $2,090,940.

41. In June 1974, the NIE (under whose largesse the primary development of SUN would continue) initiated an intensive review of SUN's accomplishments, and SUN appointed an advisory committee of national authorities in non-traditional education to assess its progress and advise SUN in the preparation of its NIE proposal for the development of the University of Mid-America (UMA), a model regional Open Learning system. In effect, the proposal then changed from a proposal to establish SUN to a proposal to establish UMA/SUN.

IV Staffing for planning and development

42. While there was general intellectual and political readiness for open forms of post-secondary and higher education in the United States, there was no equivalent readiness in the academic area. Institutional reform was not lacking in strong and innovative leadership, but the bulk of United States academics had attitudes from scepticism to outright hostility. Most of the leaders in open education were virtually without academic followers, a situation not unlike that in the United Kingdom when the Open University concept and structure were being developed, or the situation in Wisconsin (1964–69) during the AIM experiment.

43. The process of adoption of change involves the following steps: (a) innovators propose change which is regarded as heresy; (b) leaders (opinion-makers) adopt change for limited application to test out results; (c) enlightened

followers accept proven changes and spread adoption; (d) followers change as new practices are demonstrably superior, and as failure to change is clearly a disadvantage; (e) everyone wants to 'get on the bandwagon'; (f) the heresy proposed by the innovators becomes the new norm.

This process indicates the complexity of institutional reform, and underlines the importance of people and roles in it.

44. The group which studied and proposed the open-education project for Nebraska, with the tantalizing prospect of regional adoption, was a special committee which reported to the president and regents of the University of Nebraska. Even the regents do not have authority over all higher education in Nebraska, but only over those state-supported institutions in the University of Nebraska system. Certainly they had no authority over any higher education in their sister sovereign states. Furthermore, the regents have policy control over only those funds that are appropriated by the Nebraska unicameral legislature, or that come under their control through gifts, grants and contracts. The regents cannot directly raise taxes for higher education. They must submit requests to the legislature for all support received.

45. Accreditation, the acceptance of a university's credits and degrees beyond its boundaries, is vested in regional bodies (i.e. the North Central Association of Secondary Schools and Colleges) which act as quasi-public offices in the maintenance of academic standards and their recognition.

46. Hence the proposal of a regional open university in the United States poses policy, strategic, tactical and logistic problems that are nearly without precedent. What precedents exist are largely non-educational (crime prevention, power transmission, etc.). Consequently, most of the problems relating to the conceptualizing and planning for the University of Mid-America had to be approached almost *de novo*. It is in this context that the planning and development staff takes on extraordinary importance in conceptualizing innovation. Yet they must also be recognized and accepted by their academic peers in order to win that degree of trust (something like the 'willing suspension of disbelief' of the theatre) necessary for the unhampered development of seminal ideas.

47. Since academic acceptance is largely based upon a person's competence respecting what is known about the past and present in a discipline, and the job of innovation is largely a matter of thinking about the restructuring of education in the future, these requirements would seem often to be in conflict. Hence the innovator must be a person of some patience who can sense when it is prudent to go slowly while trust is developing, yet persisting in the face of the often negative feedback from academics. Willingness to do things over and over for the sceptical lookers-on or participants is necessary. The innovator needs both an emotional commitment to the ultimate achievement desired (intrinsic goal orientation) and a professional detachment or objectivity regarding the processes of reaching the goals and confronting the oppositions that will be met along the way. Very few people have all the characteristics mentioned, which is one of the reasons why a team approach, with an astute manager or executive who understands the employment of the diversified talent that makes up the team, is desirable.

48. It is also important that initially the planning and development function and staff be located in the institutional structure where it will be the least vulnerable to attack from within, for that is where the opposition will occur

first. Hence it is often the policy in United States universities to attach planning and development to the president's office. This is also prudent from the point of view of the president, who, of all the institution's officers, must bear the greatest responsibilities for development. The president is the only officer who can shape development congruent with policy. A president can oversee the development process, affect it by counsel and direction, and nourish it because of the extraordinary power he wields with the regents and top state officers. But also, he needs to be close to development so that he can gauge the points at which opposition is likely to erupt, and through careful deployment of staff, minimize internal disruption. At some point when the innovation becomes operational, a different structure will be needed, and through close association with its development, the president may be able to effect the appropriate structure required when the project must meet opposition primarily from the outside.

49. Opposition is not necessarily inimical to orderly and imaginative development. Indeed, the quality of opposition which any innovation receives is perhaps as important as the creativity of its advocates. The process of encountering opposition, whether from within or without, is the process of defining, clarifying, illustrating, convincing with solid theory and hard evidence, moving from concept to clear objectives, and removing or meliorating the threats implicit in new proposals.

50. Staffing for UMA/SUN planning and development began at the systems level under the vice-president of the University of Nebraska system, and with the executive director of SUN (also general manager of the Nebraska Educational Television network) as 'Special Assistant to the President', indicating the direct relationship of SUN to the president of the university system. A former dean of the College of Arts and Sciences of the Lincoln campus of the University of Nebraska was named provost of UMA/SUN.

51. In general, UMA itself is a central course-development and evaluation agency that makes courses available to individual state institutions for delivery as those states determine. UMA co-ordinates state delivery systems, the link between the learners and the UMA course-development and evaluation activity. SUN, on the other hand, continues as a model state-wide delivery system, useful for the development of systems in other states.

52. The post-secondary Open Learning model which UMA/SUN proposed has the following characteristics:

(a) A policy of unrestricted admission for adults.
(b) Learning opportunities based on an understanding of the needs and educational objectives of the learners.
(c) Meeting the learner where he or she is educationally, by recognizing individual differences in entry levels.
(d) Enabling the learner to learn at times and at places convenient to him, without prohibitive interference with job, family or other obligations.
(e) Reducing constraints on how people learn by employing a variety of media and materials.
(f) Allowing the student flexibility in constructing his own learning sequence. UMA/SUN 'courses' do not have single entry and exit points, nor single achievement requirements.
(g) Encouraging the offering of interdisciplinary courses.
(h) Using local and regional resources to exploit the opportunities available to the learner in his own environment.

(i) Offering programmes without economic penalty to learners, and at reasonable cost to society.
(j) Emphasizing learning rather than the meeting of arbitrary standards of time, course or curriculum requirements; but with academic quality equal to that of a traditional university, so that work accomplished is fully accepted by other institutions.
(k) Openness in self-examination, research and evaluation.

53. In the five-year period, UMA/SUN will explore a variety of *issues* which underlie the philosophical and procedural policies of the organization (e.g. whether UMA/SUN should offer credit for work experience); produce certain kinds of *products* (e.g. courses capable of being delivered to adults in their homes); and provide certain *services* (e.g. student counselling, and consulting services to individual states wishing to establish Open Learning delivery systems).

V Organization and administration: consortium planning and development

54. The process by which SUN reached decisions respecting the creation of UMA is instructive.

55. A regional approach to Open Learning, it was assumed, would help insure both to SUN and interested funding agencies that Open Learning courses developed at high cost in Nebraska would prove acceptable for use with populations beyond the state boundaries. Since the major expenses of an Open Learning system are in course development, regional delivery would clearly be economically advantageous, providing a greater financial return per dollar invested in course development. Economically, there is an advantage in an organization which both expands the learner market and attracts fiscal commitments under a long-term programme. Further, a regional system provides SUN with the advice necessary to ensure that courses are relevant, accepted on a wider geographical basis, and benefit from regional input into development and co-ordination of delivery.

56. Discussions with the presidents of the universities in the Mid-America State Universities Association (MASUA) evolved a plan for the development of a regional Open Learning consortium (UMA), the instrument for the development and production of Open Learning 'courseware' and the regional delivery systems.

57. The plan adopted represents a middle-ground position respecting course production and delivery. Although it was recognized that delivery of courses is legally each state's prerogative and one most logically left to states for political and economic reasons, the regional planners wanted to retain a relationship between courseware and delivery.

58. It was agreed that course development and distribution processes must be centralized to avoid duplication. The major source of expense in any such system is course development. These costs are relatively fixed; they do not increase in proportion to enrolment. Therefore, the broader the economic base of the consortium, and the larger the potential audience, the greater the prospects for economic viability. It seemed essential that development costs be kept relatively constant through the control of the regional entity. Hence, institutions of the participating states are responsible for delivery, but UMA co-ordinates

delivery. Responsibilities for course development, research, creation of public understanding and awareness, and faculty training were given to the regional entity (as eventually, perhaps, degree-granting responsibilities will be). This plan, it was hoped, would avoid practical political difficulties.

59. UMA is a non-profit corporation, governed by a board of trustees, with the advice of an academic council and other consultant groups. The University of Nebraska offered to relinquish leadership to a regional staff as of January 1975. The planners, however, favoured an evolutionary transition. Consequently, UMA is managed, under a sub-contract, by the University of Nebraska, and the SUN staff continues its UMA staff role in carrying out major regional responsibilities. The separation of the staffs of SUN and UMA will occur gradually. In the interim, SUN delivery in Nebraska will be the test-bed for regional delivery.

60. An issue affecting the organization and administration of UMA concerned the composition of UMA itself. Not all MASUA institutions will participate initially in UMA. At present, five universities in four states participate (Kansas State University, Iowa State University and the Universities of Kansas, Nebraska and Missouri). Furthermore, some institutions outside MASUA have indicated interest in joining UMA. The need for the system to be operational by January 1975, and the lack of an immediately available mechanism for co-operation with non-MASUA institutions, dictated the policy that MASUA institutions be the founding participants, with the possibilities for further expansion to be considered later. This policy preserved for UMA the practical advantage of starting out with a smaller number of states and institutions while working out the complex problems of a regional university. As UMA gains experience, it can turn to other states and institutions to expand the participation base.

61. The four states initially participating are committed to developing and funding state-wide Open Learning delivery systems aimed at new populations of adult learners. Each state is pledged to provide the participation and co-operation of all its institutions of post-secondary education and, during the calendar year 1975, to assume 50 per cent of the costs of delivery-system planning and development.

62. The complex arrangements necessary for the creation of a regional university including different states, each of which has sovereign control of education, is a formidable task.

63. Agreements across state lines must have the approval of governors of the states, legislatures, boards of regents (or trustees) of participating universities, presidents, chancellors, deans and faculties. Narrowness of vision, a competitive or adversary position, protectionism, distrust of others for whatever reason—any of these could imperil the creation of a regional institution. Approval, significant as it is, is only the beginning, and other problems remain. Public subsidy requires legislative appropriation in each participating state. The flow of money across state boundaries requires authorization. Employment of academic staff at participating institutions in other states involves approvals all along the line.

64. If funding is also received from the federal government, additional approvals are required. The existence of UMA is proof that a public, regional, educational institution in Mid-America is not impossible. It remains to be seen whether the organization can do what its framers intend.

65. It is noteworthy that the authority for the planning, development and operation of UMA is an association of state universities—MASUA. Without such an association, the enterprise would have been more difficult. The existence of MASUA (a multi-state multi-institutional entity) offered the surest approach to the development of a regional institution.

66. The structure, organization and administration of UMA/SUN will undoubtedly undergo modification as programme issues, tasks and operations teach the regional body how to cope. A simplified expression of the organization of UMA/SUN is given in Figure 1.

VI The target studies

67. A new concept—a new institution—does not have a ready-made clientele. It must find its intended clientele and serve it. For a viable educational institution, the selection of the target populations is the starting-point.

68. In educational institutions built upon predetermined goals, the curriculum is an important determinant of clientele. UMA/SUN determined to offer a curriculum broader than traditional degree programmes, including new kinds of credit and non-credit offerings, in the hope that a broad spectrum of student needs would be met. In an information leaflet, SUN declares its hope of making higher education more accessible to all persons: 'Are there people not now pursuing a college education who might take courses if an Open Learning programme becomes available? If enough people are interested, what are their unique interests, needs and abilities?'

69. Three client groups for external degree programmes have been identified and numbers in each group estimated for 1971, and projected to 1990 (for the United States as a whole):

Client groups (25 years of age or over)	*Number 1971 (in millions)*	*Number projected to 1990 (in millions)*
High-school drop-outs	18	20
High-school diploma, no college	38	58
Some college	11	22

70. SUN found that in 1970 Nebraska had 125,941 males and 129,976 females in the 21-to-34-year age group, the period during which there is the highest participation rate in adult-education programmes. In the 31-to-52 age category, Nebraska had 156,074 males and 159,970 females. Annual eleventh- and twelfth-grade populations are close to 50,000.

71. The educational characteristics of Nebraska and UMA region citizens were revealed through census data, a state interest survey and two regional market surveys.

72. On the basis of data yielded by these studies, UMA/SUN is committed to at least two target groups: (a) the bright high-school student who would like to accelerate his or her educational programme, and (b) the adult who, for various reasons, cannot take college courses in a campus setting.

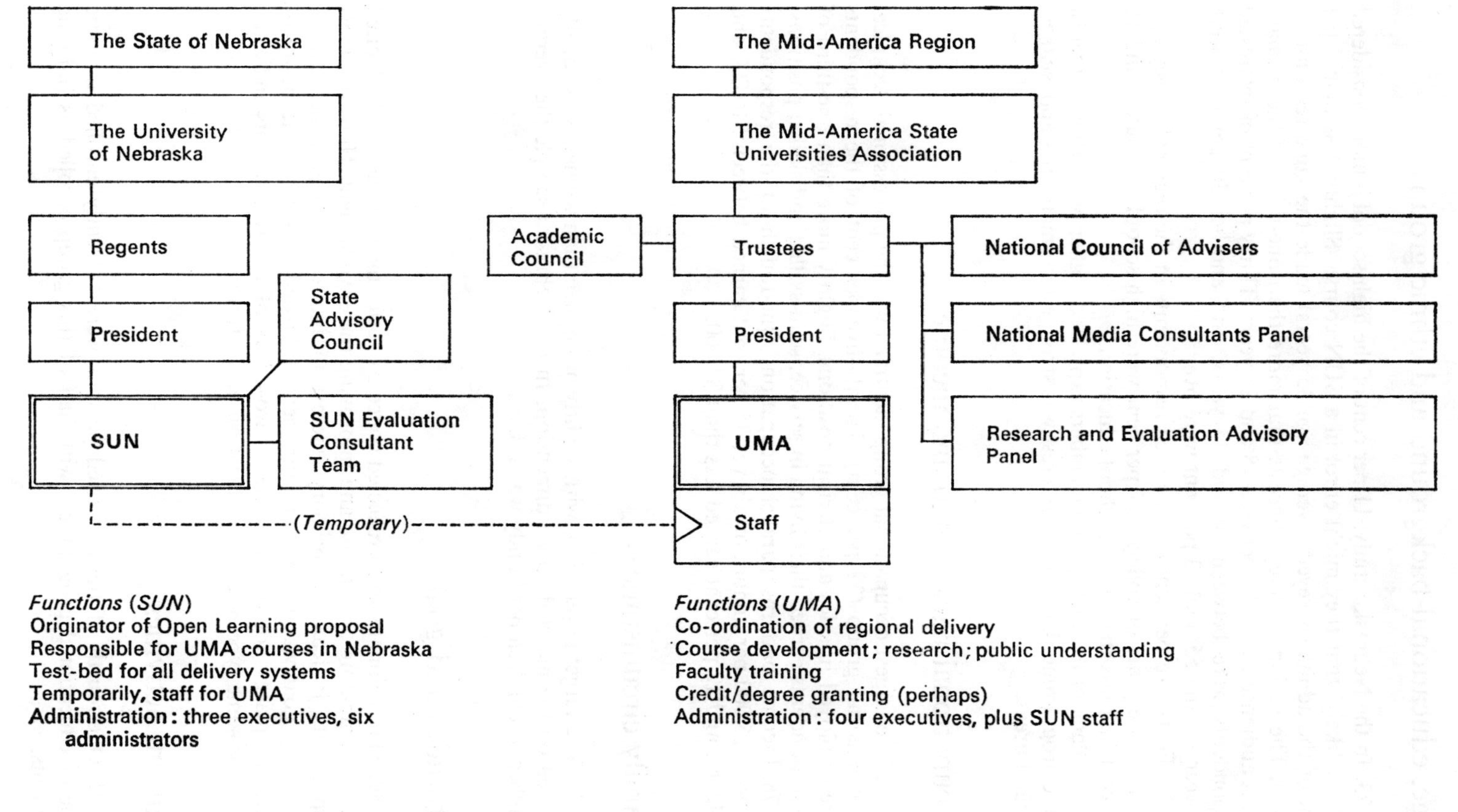
The State of Nebraska
The University of Nebraska
Regents
President
SUN
State Advisory Council
SUN Evaluation Consultant Team
(Temporary)
Academic Council
The Mid-America Region
The Mid-America State Universities Association
Trustees
President
UMA
Staff
National Council of Advisers
National Media Consultants Panel
Research and Evaluation Advisory Panel
Functions (SUN)
Originator of Open Learning proposal
Responsible for UMA courses in Nebraska
Test-bed for all delivery systems
Temporarily, staff for UMA
Administration: three executives, six administrators
Functions (UMA)
Co-ordination of regional delivery
Course development; research; public understanding
Faculty training
Credit/degree granting (perhaps)
Administration: four executives, plus SUN staff

FIG. 1. UMA/SUN structure and organization

Age, educational background and ethnic group

73. In the Nebraska study, 11 per cent of the high-school juniors considered it 'very likely' that they might enrol in a SUN course. Slightly less than 7 per cent of the adults surveyed (average age 35 years) made the same response.

74. The regional survey suggests that more than one-third of the primary target audience would be between 18 and 25 years. Thirty per cent of interested respondents were between 26 and 39 years, and another 30 per cent were between 40 and 55. Only 3 per cent were over 55.

75. Forty-five per cent of interested respondents in the regional survey had one or more years of college; 27 per cent were high-school graduates; and 16 per cent had less than a high-school education.

76. Black or minority group members expressed higher proportional interest in the programme than others. Interest was strongest in small cities and weakest in rural areas.

Occupational background and income

77. The largest occupational group identified was the professional, technical or managerial group (32 per cent). Twenty-five per cent of the respondents were employed in sales and clerical positions. Slightly more than one-third of the respondents earned their living in service, semi-skilled and skilled positions.

78. Income patterns parallel occupation. One-fourth of the respondents earned $15,000 per annum or above; 35 per cent earned between $10,000 and $14,999; and 12 per cent earned less than $4,000.

Family circumstances

79. The target population, with slightly more men than women, was equally divided on the married–single dimension. In the Nebraska sample the average number of children per family was 1.8.

Attitudes and goals

80. The regional survey reflected concerns about major issues in the United States: combating drug abuse and improving the environment. However, most respondents indicated a primary interest in improving their education. A secondary goal was saving for retirement, followed closely by the desire to travel to places not before visited. Two-thirds of the respondents indicated plans for some type of college education in the future.

Current activities

81. One-fourth of the interested persons were currently enrolled in some type of educational programme, with half of this group enrolled as full-time students.

Interests expressed

82. The potential audience rated convenience as the major advantage of a programme like SUN. Being able to work at one's own pace was seen as a prominent advantage, plus the fact that the programme is open to everyone. The major negative response expressed concern that the new programme might not provide adequate personal relationships with instructors.

83. The most frequently requested courses were psychology, sociology, mathematics and accounting.

84. Prominent reasons for taking courses included 'improving my mind' and 'gaining an understanding of this world' (two-thirds). One-third hoped college courses would qualify them for a better job, and one-fourth of the target group intended to obtain a degree. Almost half indicated they would be interested in taking and paying for a non-credit SUN course.

The potential target population

85. Data yielded by the surveys indicate that 20 per cent of the population of the UMA/SUN area are interested in the benefits continuing education can provide. In an eight-state area surveyed there appear to be 202,000 people interested in taking SUN courses. General interest surveys, however, yield quite gross responses which gave validity only as indicators. If the institution could be created as the respondents perceive it, the indicators might be confirmed by enrolments. However, if the institution does not fit the expectations of respondents, a different enrolment pattern results.

First SUN enrolments

86. The first (October 1974) courses offered by SUN (accounting and psychology) enrolled nearly 600 students. This test population ranged in age from 13 to 69 years, with a median age of 41. Most enrolments came from the 25-to-54-year age group. Females outnumbered males; credit enrolments outnumbered non-credit; and half of the enrolled students had previous college experience.

87. The initial enrolment is too small, and the courses offered too limited, to yield definitive information about UMA/SUN's eventual student body.

VII Curriculum and learning goals

88. Concepts of curriculum imply institutional goals and define target learner groups.

89. The decisions regarding the UMA/SUN curriculum (and those still to be made) while not unlike curricula decisions elsewhere, are more than ordinarily significant simply because UMA/SUN is in many respects a *de novo* enterprise in the United States higher-education scene. The UMA planners have stated that, by 1980, UMA will have planned and developed a curriculum that both recognizes and honours the characteristics of an Open Learning system. The

curriculum will affirm that one of the major purposes of post-secondary education is to contribute to the self-development of individuals and to foster a society of people who are able to lead rich, full lives.

90. The planners point out that the curriculum scenario for 1980 (the end of the five-year development period) requires a curriculum sensitive to 'the differing needs and hopes' of a range of learners.

91. This attention to individuals will not simply be rhetoric. Learners will participate in curriculum development and decision-making by providing continual feedback to course-development teams. The curriculum will contain experiences designed to increase the capacity of individuals to function as citizens in a democratic society. The UMA curriculum will strike a balance between specific career training and a liberal arts education.

92. Any curriculum is an indirect expression of the philosophy, or 'learning goals', that the institution either has determined for its learners, or that the learners have determined (by their free choices and feedback) for the institution.

93. The UMA learning goals do not, of course, constitute a curriculum. But under these goals, UMA hopes to have fifty-five courses developed by 1980 (eleven new courses each year during the five-year development period) meeting a blend of academic and continuing educational needs.

94. Of the fifty-five new courses, most will be credit offerings applicable to the bachelor-degree curriculum. The remaining courses will be 'modularized'; portions may be taken for credit or no credit according to student needs. Experience may dictate a change in the ratio of courses in the two broad UMA curricula.

95. Whether UMA's learning goals will be congruent with learners' goals and needs will not be known until a sufficient number of learners make this known through the exercise of free and open choice, and feedback to UMA. The learning goals developed by the Academic Council indicate an eagerness to involve learners and a willingness to listen.

VIII Course development and production

96. The UMA five-year course-development plan starts from the working base established in 1974. That base includes the development and production of two pilot or prototype courses offered to limited enrolments in September 1974. It is therefore important to examine the processes used in prototype development and production, for these will be carried forward into the five-year period, during which an additional fifty-five courses will be prepared.

97. The prototype courses were selected on the basis of market surveys. The introductory accounting course, it was decided, would be wholly designed, developed and produced by SUN, whereas the course in general psychology would be developed from existing materials. Thus the prototype phase will yield experience in two courseware development processes.

Five SUN production formats

98. With an eye on production costs, estimated enrolments and learner needs, SUN set up five formats for UMA course production:

Approach A is a procedure by which a course is designed, produced and tested within a minimum period of twelve months. This is the most expensive approach, with extensive use of television.

Approach B is a format making less use of television, in which a course is designed, produced, and tested with an eleven-month limit.

Approach C does not require television, but will make extensive use of print and audio components in a nine-month production format.

Approach D involves the acquisition of a course by UMA and its use with minimal print adaptation in three months.

Approach E is the acquisition of a course which must be adapted within nine months.

99. UMA must make a large number of courses available to students, yet budget constraints do not permit many courses to be developed by the costlier A or B approaches. Therefore it is necessary that a large number of courses be acquired and/or adapted. Using a mix of development formats, UMA will offer a variety of high-quality courses to learners at a low cost, while retaining the ability to experiment with different media, course formats and sequences. (The great variety of educational objectives mentioned in paragraph 24 above should be recalled at this point.)

The SUN-produced introductory accounting course

100. The accounting course team is led by an executive producer and two professors as resident content consultants. The team includes an instructional designer, a professional writer, a research associate and media production specialists. A senior content advisory panel works with the course team in defining course objectives and content.

101. The three-credit-hour accounting course has five components: television, audio cassettes, newspapers, text and study guide.

102. In the fifteen colour-television components, professional actors convey the content material.

103. The course team specified fifteen audio cassettes to guide the learners, reinforce learning and test achievement. The audio component functions with a study guide/workbook.

104. A print component, to appear each week prior to the television lesson, will be included in Nebraska's largest newspaper. Formative evaluation is employed as the various course segments are developed and produced.

105. On the basis of experience with the accounting course, SUN has already decided that the course team can be strengthened by assigning more responsibility to the resident content consultant and the instructional designer. A National Media Consultant Panel has been set up to advise on media and production problems.

Acquisition and adaptation of the 'Psychology Today' course

106. Course acquisition is not easily accomplished and experience during 1974 has identified a variety of constraints, conditions of use and terms of sale respecting acquisition.

107. These variables present problems in budgeting. It is difficult to determine the fixed expenditure per course to be acquired, particularly when per-student costs must be anticipated on the basis of future enrolment estimates.

108. As with acquisition, adaptation procedures vary according to the specific course and its components. Courses considered range from existing television courses to Open University foundation courses and correspondence courses. However, a generalized model for the adaptation process will include one, some, or all of the following possibilities: revision of, and/or additions to, television segments, study guide, audio component, text; additional components such as newspaper modules; and restructuring of the course content itself.

109. SUN obtained a complete inventory of the 'Psychology Today' course materials: video-tapes, textbooks, study guides, and self-check quizzes. The course team included two content consultants, an executive producer, instructional designer and production personnel.

110. The course team decided that the SUN adaptation would be an introductory psychology course of 15 units, and an identical number of television presentations, with basic text, study guide and television segments providing the core of the SUN course. The television programmes and study guides were interrelated, so that the learner would have in these two elements the essential content of the course.

111. The SUN research and evaluation staff developed quiz and examination items. Each unit of instruction has a self-administered quiz in the study guide based on the television segment and the required reading. Examinations, for purposes of establishing grades, awarding credit and certifying course completion are provided for each cluster of instructional units.

112. While a primary responsibility during the five-year developmental period will be to make available a variety of 'courses', related questions emerge, such as the following: How can courses be designed to provide maximum flexibility? What are the potentials and limitations of the various media components? How effective is the course development process?

113. As courses are used and UMA becomes aware of learners' reactions, two other problems emerge: first, the need to revise courses, not only to avoid their obsolescence, but also to increase their appeal, effectiveness and flexibility; and second, to increase their effectiveness in relation to the costs of their development. By 1980, UMA hopes to have completed the cataloguing and evaluating of relevant Open Learning courseware in existence throughout the world.

IX Delivery and access systems

114. Learning occurs where the learners are. Unless the courses, materials, seminars and other educational opportunities are brought to the learners, there is no SUN, and no reason for UMA. The delivery system acquaints SUN with the needs and objectives of learners, channels instruction and counselling to the learner, and employs local and regional resources to enrich the learner's environment.

115. The SUN model delivery system is a test-bed for UMA courseware; it is the setting in which all delivery mechanisms will be evaluated and modified by experience; it is a model for the UMA system and other regions.

The learning centre

116. A learning centre is a means by which delivered courses are made accessible and a place where learners can: receive advice and counsel; register for courses; learn at an individually determined pace; meet other learners and faculty members; and use educational resources.

177. Learning centres are located on local college campuses, in shopping centres, libraries, or mobile vans. The centre houses the staff, contains complete sets of courses and materials, and provides places for learners to work independently or in groups.

118. SUN has four experimental learning centres—in Lincoln, Omaha, Scottsbluff and Kearney. These are pilot operations. The five-year operational plan calls for fifteen strategically located centres throughout Nebraska.

119. Using the centre is optional for the student. There the student works out his own path to a learning goal by selecting options to meet his particular needs. Tests will be administered at centres, and copies of student records will be kept, as well as at SUN central. A toll-free, inward WATS line is available to students who wish to call faculty members with specific course questions, or to call SUN staff about registration, records, fees or other matters.

120. The prototype learning centre located in Lincoln is the test site for all learning centres. Every function of the centre will be evaluated to determine the extent to which it contributes to student learning experience.

121. The Omaha learning centre, established in conjunction with the University of Nebraska, Omaha, is located on the ground floor of an office building in the heart of the city. The Kearney centre was strategically placed in two rooms of the library of Kearney State College. The Scottsbluff facility was developed in co-operation with the Nebraska Western Community College, and occupies space in the Panhandle Agricultural Experiment Station.

122. The effectiveness of the centres will be assessed by studying the progress of student users and non-users.

123. The learning centre is the student's major communications link with SUN. All of SUN's activities concerning the student and instruction are focused there.

Admissions

124. A policy of open admissions ensures that programmes are open to all students. Students who are unable or unqualified to complete a course may drop out without penalty at any time during the first four weeks after enrolment.

Registration

125. A student may register in person at a learning centre, or by mail through the central SUN office. If the latter, he will be referred to the learning centre nearest his home, where he will receive a package of materials including the study guide, text, audio cassettes, audio player (if requested) and the instructional kit for the course in which he is registered.

Accreditation

126. Accreditation is obtained through the academic departments of the University of Nebraska, Lincoln (UNL), and the University of Nebraska at Omaha (UNO). Accreditation ensures the transferability of SUN credits to other colleges and universities. The possibility that UMA itself (or its associated delivery systems) may in future grant credit and degrees will be studied as a part of the five-year plan. As a first step towards this goal, the North Central Association of Colleges and Secondary Schools has ruled that all SUN courses approved by the university's board of regents are eligible for accreditation.

Information dissemination

127. SUN's clientele will not be the conventional on-campus student. The adult learner needs to be made aware of SUN. A programme of information dissemination to attract potential learners to SUN is necessary, using news media, public relations, brochures and posters, as well as the information systems of regional post-secondary institutions.

Broadcasting

128. The Nebraska Educational Television network, which covers the entire state and overlaps into areas of South Dakota, Wyoming, Colorado, Kansas, Missouri and Iowa, will telecast each of the television modules twice per week. Video cassettes will be made available at the learning centres for students whose schedules do not permit them to watch the telecasts, or for those who begin courses at times that do not correspond to the telecast schedule.

129. By 1980, the model state-wide delivery system will be fully operational, and versions appropriate to the three other participating states will have been worked out.

X Research and evaluation

130. Most innovative ventures are not permitted the time, funds, staff and facilities for research-evaluation that have been a substantial portion of the SUN and projected UMA/SUN budgets. For example, in the yearly budgets anticipated for 1975–79, research and evaluation accounts for about 23 per cent of the costs associated with administration (about $300,000 each year out of about $1.4 million). However, the proportion of research-evaluation costs to the total cost of the UMA/SUN operation is less than 5 per cent.

131. There is always tension in new institutional developments between two opposite forces: (a) the drive to become operational quickly, before support fades and so that 'success' can be demonstrated; and (b) the need to find out how to proceed with the best probability for success. The need to know what, why and how to do things is usually in conflict with the strong desire in any new venture to do something quickly.

132. The development of UMA/SUN has been more complex than may be apparent. While the federal government cannot control education, it can and

does provide funds for education, and can effect a measure of 'control' through setting up standards, requirements and criteria which must be met whenever federal funds are used.

133. SUN and UMA are heavily (though not exclusively) financed by federal funds, chiefly from the National Institute of Education (NIE). The NIE official under whose charge the UMA/SUN project falls is Dr Jerome E. Lord, Project Officer in the Division of Productivity and Technology of the NIE.

134. The separate entities in the project (the University of Nebraska, SUN, UMA, the states and universities collaborating, the communities involved and NIE) each have responsibilities leading back to different authorization, funding and control bodies. Indeed, it would be unlikely that, in an organizational mix of such complexity, there would be absolute identity and agreement about issues. Furthermore, innovative leaders who are drawn to projects such as UMA/SUN are themselves generally strong and confident people with a sense of mission. Healthy debate on issues is required.

135. What is significant is that the debate is not confined to UMA/SUN, but includes NIE. NIE has exercised an active rather than passive role regarding this project, nowhere more evident than in encouraging SUN to become regional and to employ research and evaluation as a guide to development. This emphasis has slowed the operational phases of UMA/SUN development, but it has provided the project with a far more secure base of knowledge for decision-making and operational practices than would otherwise have been possible. In view of the rapid rate at which even new institutions become rigid, this influence may help to keep UMA/SUN more open and innovative during the next five critical years.

136. The UMA/SUN Office of Research and Evaluation provides services to course designers, producers, content specialists and others associated directly with the design and implementation of SUN courses. Evaluation plays an important role in course design and development.

137. Evaluation requires information-gathering concerning developmental and operational decisions. As such, evaluation is a here-and-now phenomenon. Research, on the other hand, is concerned with the derivation of general principles and guidelines for long-range planning. Evaluation is decision-oriented, while research is conclusion-oriented.

138. The UMA/SUN Office of Research and Evaluation work proposal for 1975/76 identifies eighteen tasks leading to decision-making. The success of each of these tasks is dependent upon a research or evaluative effort (or both) prior to decision-making. A less sophisticated, or less funded and guided project, would attempt decision without preliminary study. From the point of view of NIE, a too rapid development of the operational system would foreclose the careful consideration of alternative strategies as each issue is faced.

XI Finance and cost-effectiveness measures

139. Financing a project such as SUN is simple compared to financing UMA.

140. The cash-flow models for SUN and UMA for the five-year period 1975–79 give the essential financial picture and will be used here to provide an overall picture of funding: where the money comes from and where it goes.

141. The figures presented below are estimates worked up for submission

to NIE as the basis for continued funding. There is no certainty that UMA/SUN will be funded at the levels given here. It would be prudent to assume that the actual funding for the periods indicated will be different. However, the cash-flow models show with reasonable accuracy how the financing of UMA/SUN will be carried out.

UMA cash-flow model assumptions

142. A number of assumptions underlie the five-year cash budget for UMA and SUN.

Cost centres

143. There are two cost centres for UMA: administration and course development. There are three cost centres for SUN: general administration, academic services and student services.

Tuition income

144. Dependent upon factors such as type of course and ability of the student to pay, several tuition rates will be employed. Tuition income was calculated at an average of $18 per credit hour for the first six months of 1975, and an average of $20 per credit hour thereafter. It was also assumed that non-credit course income will average $25 per course. It was assumed that 60 per cent of the adult learners will enrol for credit, and 40 per cent will audit on a not-for-credit basis.

Materials fees

145. Course materials will be charged to students at cost. Total costs of course materials will be balanced by the income from student fees.

State appropriation

146. The present assumption is that SUN will receive $1.25 of state appropriation for each dollar of tuition fee from students. Other UMA states will be similarly subsidized by their respective state appropriations.

Learning centres

147. The SUN plan calls for fifteen learning centres strategically located throughout Nebraska. Each learning centre will have a co-ordinator and an assistant, and will operate in co-operation with other post-secondary institutions, thus affording some cost sharing. Each learning centre will have a full set of course materials, including audio and video cassettes where required.

Faculty and graduate assistants

148. Each course required a three-quarter full-time equivalent (FTE) faculty member and a graduate assistant at half FTE.

Telephone

149. Use of WATS lines will link faculty and students in Nebraska.

Lease income

150. Courses will be leased throughout the country at an average $3,000 per lease.

Course development

151. The full production cost of each course is included in the year that production is scheduled to start.

Membership contribution (UMA)

152. Each state will make a contribution of $25,000, increasing by $25,000 each year, and levelling off at $150,000 per state in 1980. Members of UMA will be exempt from lease expense.

153. In 1975, income and expenditures anticipated by SUN are $781,900. This sum is to be realized from the following sources: tuition, $253,800; materials, $121,800; state appropriation, $158,600; private grants, $60,000; NIE grant, $187,700.

154. In 1975, UMA income and expenditures are expected to total $4,375,600 from the following sources: federal grants, NIE $3,332,200, other $578,400; private grants $300,000; lease income $60,000; membership contributions $105,000.

155. The UMA/SUN total (income and expenditures) is $5,157,500.

156. In the five years 1975–79, total SUN income and expenditure is projected at $6,765,700. In the same period, the UMA total is projected at $22,348,900. For the five years, the two systems together will take in and spend an estimated $29,114,600.

157. Expenditures for UMA in 1975, in the cost centres of administration and course development, are projected as follows: *Administration:* general administration, $427,200; academic administration, $350,100; public affairs and information services, $81,000; course acquisition, $50,300; production services, $180,400; research and evaluation, $299,600; instructional design, $92,300. *Course development:* course development costs, $2,781,000; course revision costs, $113,700. *Total:* $4,375,600.

158. Expenditures (delivery costs) for SUN in 1975 are estimated to be: general administration, $94,100; academic services, $636,700; student services, $51,100; total, $781,900.

159. UMA/SUN have also begun the development of an economic model which goes beyond the analysis of balanced cash flow, to assess costs and benefits. The economic model makes use of the data base developed for the cash-flow model, but extends the analysis to include studies of alternative assumptions to determine the overall characteristics of a system's economic viability, as well as making comparisons with costs of other institutions.

160. The analysis of costs must be made in a 'steady-state' environment, recognizing that the establishment and development of a totally new enterprise entails large costs that do not continue throughout the life of the organization.

161. The cash-flow model includes incomes for SUN and UMA which are subsidies from several sources, chiefly NIE.

162. By 1980, UMA and its associated delivery systems must become 'self-supporting' in the sense that continued funding from NIE is no longer required.

163. Long-range economic modelling for UMA/SUN thus includes the all-important consideration of eventual self-sufficiency, which means, in the United States context, survival without continuing federal subsidy. To accomplish this, the UMA/SUN systems must find ways to serve learners at a cost-effectiveness level that will be no higher, and hopefully lower, than conventional institutions in order to justify state and regional support.

Postscript (June 1975)

An element of now increasing importance is the income from sale or hire of UMA/SUN courses to other users ('leasage'): schools, colleges, trade unions and other non-educational institutions. It is hoped that by 1980 this source of income may rise to one-third of the total budget expenditure.

XII Facilities and resources

164. The University of Nebraska became the fulcrum for leverage in the effort to create a regional open university for a variety of reasons:

President Varner, who took the SUN project into his office for initial development, is a leader of state and regional credibility.

Nebraska already operates a public television network which provides good-quality reception to 90 per cent of the residents of the state, and overlaps contiguous states.

The Nebraska Educational Telecommunications Center represents a significant base for UMA/SUN.

Inter-institutional and inter-state co-operation on a regional basis has strong support.

Innovative higher education has strong political support.

SUN and UMA are not 'locked into' present-day technology.

There is willingness to permit innovators to take planning roles.

Production facilities and resources have good links with academic resources for instructional improvement and innovation.

The Great Plains Instructional Television Library is located in Lincoln.

Resources include highly qualified academic and professional media personnel, and national authorities in advisory and consultative roles.

The Mid-American State Universities Association is an existing consortium committed to the regional concept of UMA/SUN.

The MASUA consortium provides access to the academic, professional and technical resources and facilities of the UMA region.

A sufficient regional population base exists so that, even at a 2 per cent enrolment ratio, there will be an adequate level of aggregation for UMA/SUN to achieve economic viability.

XIII Conclusion

165. SUN and UMA are developing according to a clearly stated philosophy, rationale and objectives. The SUN staff, which is also for the time being the staff of UMA, is motivated and capable. Institutional support in Nebraska, Iowa, Kansas and Missouri—expressed through the MASUA consortium—appears to be solid. Financially, according to present indications, there is unprecedented federal funding until 1980.

166. Leadership in Nebraska and the UMA region is skilful, committed and politically credible. Target learners seem to be responsive. Institutionally, there is a healthy concern with knowing why as well as how before undertaking specific action, and of trying to preserve flexibility and openness so that learner feedback can modify programmes, structure and organization. The facilities and resources of the region are a cornucopia of riches that can be poured into the enterprise.

167. The UMA/SUN Open Learning emphasis is consistent with the region's historical acceptance of university extension, independent study, distant learners and mediated instruction. The dialectical relationship of UMA/SUN to the National Institute of Education opens new potentials for state–region–federal collaboration respecting large educational needs and issues.

168. Whether UMA/SUN will succeed is of course not now known. Seldom, however, have large undertakings towards great educational and social ends been so carefully planned, so painstakingly researched, as UMA/SUN's. Even so, some dissonances strike the observer and suggest areas in which study and action may be needed to improve the probability of achievement of goals.

Institutionalizing creativity. It is difficult to institutionalize so fragile a thing as creativity. Innovation depends on creative people in open situations. Will the structures for accountability to traditional institutional and academic authority thwart creativity and innovation? Will UMA/SUN, once in operation, choose itself to make processes rigid, limit goals and routinize operations to that which is 'successful' in a more conventional sense? Pioneering institutions tend to assume that the initial creative thrust will continue because that's the way it all started; but the history of institution-building confirms that, relatively quickly, all institutions tend towards establishment, *status quo* and conserving behaviours. How will UMA/SUN, with its inherent dependencies on conservative authorities, counteract this tendency?

Developing non-traditional courseware. Courseware development is likely to be UMA/SUN's most important continuing activity in bringing resources of knowledge to learners. Will UMA/SUN be squeezed into an inarticulate, ineffective status between the immovable object (the need for subject matter from academic sources) and the irresistible force (the avowed intention of responsibly involving learners in an open format)? The course-team method adopted is the best mechanism for developing courseware, but it too can be eroded by the conserving and conforming pressures on the certification-accreditation processes. How will UMA/SUN avoid the trap of developing traditional courseware for use in a non-traditional system?

University extension. The only important area seemingly not represented on the SUN staff is university extension. No personnel, it would seem, would have more acquaintance with the practical problems of concept implementation, or be more favourable to the open learning concept than those in extension.

No group would have more expertise in 'distant' learning, and direct knowledge of the client groups that SUN is attempting to reach. Are there ways in which the expertise and support of extension can be employed in strengthening the programme?

Learner-initiated communications. The communications loop from institution to learner is clearly defined; the loop from learner to institution is less clear. In a learner-centred programme, the learner-initiated communications must be carefully arranged for, and the channels made clear and open.

The independent/distant learner. UMA/SUN convey the intention of being learner-centred. Perhaps, however, they are primarily instruction-centred. To become more learner- and learning-centred it would seem that courseware and delivery problems would have to be consistently approached from the theory and point of view of the independent/distant learner, an approach not generally within the experience or expertise of regular campus-based academics or media personnel. It may be desirable to provide an orientation to courseware and delivery personnel in independent learning.

169. The UMA/SUN model may become the model for other United States regional, open post-secondary institutions. It may even be looked at as a potential model for other countries. Transfer or borrowing is, however, fraught with difficulties.

170. Educational institutions express, in very concrete ways, the political, social, cultural and economic conditions and values of the country in which they emerge. Each institution acquires its character from the total context in which it exists, and that context, more than anything else, is what is indigenous. While the borrower can adopt the concept, technology and even the substance of an innovation, he cannot easily borrow the context which, in the other country, made the programme viable.

171. Borrowings which are dependent upon a suitable context for viability will generally fail in another country; but if the borrower's context is as good or better than that in which the innovation originated, the borrowing may be successful. It remains to be seen whether the complex contextual mix, out of which SUN and UMA emerged, exists or can be replicated elsewhere.

Appendix A — Standardized reference data

Country, state or province	*United States of America: States of Iowa, Kansas, Missouri, Nebraska*
Area and climate	Iowa: 56,290 square miles. Kansas: 82,264 square miles. Missouri: 69,686 square miles. Nebraska: 77,227 square miles. Total: 285,467 square miles. Nebraska: harsh, cold winters with heavy snows; hot humid summers.
Population	
Total (latest year)	11,189,861 (1970).
Estimated population aged 18	3,714,000 (1970).
Estimated percentage under 15	28.
Current annual growth rate (percentage)	Iowa: 0.9 per cent; Kansas: 0.2 per cent; Missouri: 0.7 per cent; Nebraska: 1.2 per cent.
Government	
Main organizational structure	Partially autonomous states within federation of United States. Elected state legislature.
Political type	Democratic state organization within parliamentary democratic republic.
Economy	Primarily agricultural states specializing in arable farming. No state or federal control.
Gross National Product	
Total (latest year)	$1,151,400 million (1971) (United States).
Per head	$5,073.
Average annual increase (percentage)	2.

Communications

Ground/air	Very good system of roads, motorways, bus and air transport services. Rail poor: freight only.
Mail/telephone	Good postal services; very good telephone services, 62.8 per 100 inhabitants.

Broadcasting

Main system(s) operating	A.M., F.M.; television.
Principal authority(ies) responsible	Only private commercial companies under aegis of United States Federal Communications Commission. Four major broadcasting networks with, nationally, 650 television stations and 6,033 radio stations.

Radio

Transmission coverage of main programme services with percentage of population reached	98.
Receving capability for main programme services (percentage)	98.

Television

Transmission coverage as defined for radio	97 to 98.
Receving capability for main programme services (percentage)	Virtually 100.
Monochrome or colour	96 per cent colour.

Education

Type of system(s)	Under state control at advisory innovative level.

Main authorities responsible and powers

At school level/At post-secondary level	Local school districts' main responsibility, providing 57 per cent of budget; state provides 40 per cent and Congress only 3 per cent. Private, autonomous schools are 80 per cent Roman Catholic, 10 per cent Protestant, 10 per cent non-sectarian. More than two-thirds of the 1,800 post-secondary institutions are private and receive no direct support from government sources.

End of full-time school attendance

Legal	Compulsory and free between 6/7 and 16.
De facto	Many stay on until graduation (17).

Proportion of 18-year-old age group involved in education

Full-time	70 per cent.
Part-time	20 per cent.

Major developments in provision

Over last five years/Over next five years	Plans for increasing possibilities for combining work and learning.

Institution/system under study	*UMA/SUN (not fully operational until 1980)*
Brief for study and reason for inclusion	Probable model for other regional groupings as a major television-based university-level system for external courses over a large region, based in Nebraska.
Main features of subject studied	
Origins	Study Committee, University of Nebraska, 1971; series of grants for development leading to 1974 proposal for five-year full development by 1980.
Educational authority(ies) and roles	Combined effort of University of Nebraska and UMA-MASUA: four states and five institutions.
Services provided	Educational openings for adult learners who are home- and work-based.
Eligibility to study	
(a) categories	Post high school: provisionally a programme for advanced high-school students.
(b) qualifications	Open entry.
Terminal qualifications	Associate (external) degree. Full qualification planned.
Instructional means used	Multi-media, i.e. television, audio cassettes, correspondence work, newspaper units, learning centres.

Sources of further information

Educational	State University of Nebraska, P.O. Box 82446, Lincoln, Nebraska, 68501.
Broadcasting	State University of Nebraska, P.O. Box 82446, Lincoln, Nebraska, 68501.

Appendix B **Short bibliography**

ADVISORY COMMITTEE ON ISSUES IN EDUCATIONAL TECHNOLOGY. *Issues and public policies in educational technology*. New York, N.Y., Commission on Education, National Academy of Engineering, C. D. Heath, 1974.

BEREDAY, G. Z. *Universities for all*. San Francisco, Calif., Jossey-Bass, 1973.

CARNEGIE COMMISSION ON HIGHER EDUCATION. *Toward a learning society: alternative channels to life, work and service*. New York, N.Y., McGraw-Hill, 1973.

GOULD, S.; CROSS, P. (eds.). *Explorations in non-traditional study*. San Francisco, Calif., Jossey-Bass, 1972.

MILTON, O. *Alternatives to the traditional.* San Francisco, Calif., Jossey-Bass, 1973.
NEWMAN, F. (Task Force chairman). *Report on higher education.* Washington, D.C., Department of Health, Education and Welfare, United States Office of Education, 1971.
PERRY, W. *The early development of the Open University.* Milton Keynes, The Open University Press, 1972.
WEDEMEYER, C. A. The open school: education's Runnymede? *Educational technology*, vol. 12, 1972. (Also available on audio-cassette.)
WEDEMEYER, C. A.; NAJEM, R. *AIM—from concept to reality. The Articulated Instructional Media Program at Wisconsin.* Syracruse, N.Y., Syracuse University, 1969. (Publications in continuing education.)
WEDEMEYER, C. A.; NEWSOM, C.; MCNEIL, D.; WITHERSPOON, J. *Open learning systems. A report.* Washington, D.C., National Association of Educational Broadcasters, 1974.

Appendix C Biographical note

Charles A. Wedemeyer is the Lighty Professor of Education at the University of Wisconsin. He was the initiator of the Wisconsin AIM experiment (the first model of an open, mediated, higher-education system for distant adults), a consultant to the United Kingdom Open University and to UMA/SUN and has written widely on independent learning.

The use of **satellites** in Open Learning systems[1]

Norman C. Dahl

Contents

1. This study was commissioned on account of the widespread interest in the possibility of using distribution satellites to accelerate the extension of educational facilities to populations not now, or not adequately, served. It was felt that, though the study does not conform to the criteria which have been used to guide the choice of other subjects, and though there is no direct connexion between Open Learning for adults and the use of satellite transmissions, a publication in 1975 which ignored this facility would be open to criticism.

The study was completed late in 1974 so that certain developments announced as due to take place may since have actually occurred.

I Introduction

1. The purpose of this case study is to identify and discuss the issues which will be involved in planning for and using a communications satellite in an Open Learning system. Many Open Learning systems will make use of radio and/or television for some parts of the learning process. In some cases the conditions will make it natural to consider whether it would be better to deliver the radio and television programmes via a communications-satellite system rather than via the conventional means of a terrestrial broadcasting system. In dealing with this question, the level and detail of discussion will aim to give senior officials with educational planning responsibilities a useful overall view from which to start a detailed examination of possible satellite use for a specific educational purpose.

2. The case study begins with a brief non-technical review of the currently operating communications satellites and of design trends for future satellites. This is followed by a discussion of the issues, technical and other, involved in choosing between a satellite or a terrestrial system. Next, there is an identification and discussion of the factors involved in the use of a satellite for educational purposes.[1] This, in turn, is followed by a review of present and projected experiments in the educational use of satellites with an emphasis upon how these factors have influenced the planning and operation of the experiments. Finally, the report considers what the foregoing implies for the use of satellites in Open Learning systems at the post-secondary level.

3. It will become evident on reading the case study that decisions with respect to satellite use are hard to make, because the issues are complex and there has been very little experience with educational use. As frequently happens in situations where both clarity and experience are lacking, discussion has tended to polarize into full support for, or total opposition to, the use of satellites for education. In the short run neither extreme can be justified by either analysis or experience and in the long run it is likely that, as usual, truth will reside in an intermediate ground. This report looks for the current location of that intermediate ground.

1. See: Kenneth A. Polcyn, *An Educator's Guide to Communication Satellite Technology*, p. 3–8, Washington, D.C., Academy for Educational Development, 1973.

II Present and projected communications satellites

4. A telecommunications satellite is a device which receives electromagnetic (radio) waves transmitted from one point on earth and retransmits them to one or more other receiving points on earth. The originating earth station encodes the electronic symbols representing the voice, music, television, computer data or other message on to electromagnetic waves and equipment at the receiving point decodes the message and transforms it into an electronic form which will drive a presentation device appropriate for the message, such as a radio or a television set. Specifications of the details of a television image (detailed geometry, brightness and colour) require about a thousand times more information than is required to specify the details of a voice message (frequencies and volume). Consequently, a satellite designed to transmit a television message will require much more capacity than one designed only for radio traffic; alternatively, a satellite with television capability will also have the capacity to transmit several hundred voice messages simultaneously.

5. There are two major communications-satellite systems now in operation: the International Telecommunications Satellite consortium (Intelsat) system in which most of the non-Communist countries participate and the Intersputnik system maintained by the Communist nations. The Intelsat system uses a series of satellites in synchronous orbit at various longitudinal locations 35,680 kilometres above the earth in the equatorial plane; in such orbit the satellite moves through space so as to remain stationary with respect to the earth. The Intersputnik system is much less extensive and uses satellites which are in highly elliptical orbits (ranging from 500 kilometres to 40,000 kilometres from the earth in one orbit) in planes inclined to the equatorial plane. These differences in orbits result from both technical and geographic location considerations. In addition to these systems, Canada has two synchronous satellites (Anik I and Anik II) which it uses for communications within Canada. In the United States the Western Union company offers domestic communications services via two synchronous orbit satellites (Westar I and II) and other private communications companies are also planning to launch satellites. Other countries are in various stages of planning and development or procurement of domestic communications satellites.[1] It is reasonable to assume that both the Soviet Union and the United States have military communications-satellite systems which exceed the Intersputnik and Intelsat systems in both capacity and technical sophistication.

Depending on the capabilities of the satellite and the ground sending and receiving stations it is possible to identify three functionally different communications-satellite systems: point-to-point; distribution; and direct broadcast.

6. The *point-to-point system* uses a satellite having a relatively low-powered transmitter which broadcasts signals over a vast area. Because of the low power and large area the signals reaching the ground are very weak, necessitating antennas about 85 feet in diameter and elaborate ground receivers for signal detection and amplification. Within a country the signals are routed into appropriate terrestrial systems (telephone, microwave, broadcasting, etc.) for distribution. The early Intelsat satellites were of this type and the costs of

1. Polcyn, op. cit., p. 23–25.

ground stations varied from about U.S.$2.5 million to $4 million depending on the density of traffic to be carried.

7. In a *distribution system* the satellite has both more transmission power and antennas which can focus the radiated energy on a limited geographical area. The resulting stronger signals allow the use of antennas of only about 40 feet in diameter and less elaborate electronics in the earth stations, reducing the cost to between $100,000 and $200,000 for receive-only stations and $300,000 and $500,000 for receive-transmit stations. The lower cost of the ground stations makes it possible for more locations to be supplied, thus allowing them to feed the signals into local broadcasting systems and to eliminate the need for the complex interconnective microwave and/or cable system required for signal distribution with the point-to-point satellite. The Intelsat IV satellite, which has a capacity of more than 3,000 telephone circuits or 12 television channels, has capabilities for operating as a distribution satellite although it is used mainly as part of a point-to-point system. Canada uses the Anik satellites, which have similar capacity, in a distribution system involving some seventy earth stations. The U.S.S.R. also has a distribution system and various other countries, including Brazil, France, India, Iran, Japan, the United States and the Federal Republic of Germany, are reported to be seriously considering such a system.[1]

8. A *broadcast system* uses a satellite with very large transmitting power to produce a signal strength which can be picked up by a very small and relatively inexpensive earth terminal attached to an individual television set. In May 1974, as part of its Applications Technology Satellite (ATS) programme, the United States National Aeronautics and Space Administration (NASA) launched and put into synchronous orbit the ATS-F satellite, which was renamed ATS-6 when it reached orbit. In addition to about twenty scientific and technological experiments, the ATS-6 will carry out experiments to determine the feasibility of broadcast satellite transmission. Through a combination of higher transmitting intensity, use of a larger and more efficient antenna and more accurate pointing of the antenna at a specified spot on the earth, it is expected that the ATS-6 will produce a signal strength on the earth about fifty times as strong as that from Intelsat IV. The earth station capable of receiving this signal and amplifying it to drive a single television set will require an antenna of only about 10 feet in diameter and is expected to cost about $3,000. During the first year the experiments will involve television to the United States while the ATS-6 is in synchronous orbit at a point roughly above the Galapagos Islands, and in June 1975 the satellite will be moved into orbit above Kenya where it will remain for another year in an experiment involving television transmission to India. The nature of these two experimental broadcast programmes will be described and discussed in some detail in section V below.

9. The general trend in communications-satellite design, spurred by advances in solid-state electronic technology and growing experience in space technology, is to make the satellites more and more sophisticated, so as to permit the use of simpler and less expensive ground stations, both transmitting and receiving. Along with this there is emphasis on increasing satellite capability to broadcast several programmes simultaneously, each to a different region of a country, by means of antennas which focus the signal for each programme on a specific geographical area. It is not yet clear how fast or how extensive the growth of

1. Polcyn, op. cit., p. 9.

broadcast satellites will be. The ATS-6 is to be the last satellite in NASA's ATS series and the only further scheduled experimental work in satellite communications by NASA is a joint venture with Canada involving the launching in 1975 of a Communications Technology Satellite (CTS) which will be used in experiments to advance the state of the art in spacecraft and related ground technologies for future educational broadcasting and remote-area communications.[1] The future developments in broadcast satellites will depend to a large degree upon the success of commercial satellite and communications companies in selling their systems, and this success will be constrained by economic, cultural and political factors relating to how much, and what kinds of, communications a country feels it needs, wants or can pay for.

III Making the choice between a satellite and a terrestrial communications system

10. The decision as to whether a country will opt for a satellite or for an expanded terrestrial communications system always is, ultimately, a political decision. This is so because the performance and the deployment techniques of the two systems are fundamentally different[2] and because the benefits accruing from different uses are frequently incommensurable. For example, the relative priority between the need to expand the telephone service linking the major industrial areas and the need to reach remote areas with social-service information cannot be decided on the basis of quantitative analysis alone and must include some arbitrary assignment of value. This defines a political process. Even when the decision relates to competing commercial communications systems the political process will be felt in relation to such matters as the setting of rate structures and specification of the kinds of services which can be offered on the two kinds of systems.

11. Although the final decision is political, it is important that this decision be based on as much analysis as can be assembled about the costs and benefits likely to be associated with different uses of the systems. Such analysis will not make incommensurable benefits comparable but it will impose a discipline on the proponents of any specific use to make more explicit their assumptions and experience, and will thereby reveal where they are on solid ground and where they may be indulging in wishful thinking.

12. In some areas of use (e.g. telephone, telegraph, computer data), it is possible to make quantitative comparisons of the costs and benefits of a satellite system as opposed to a terrestrial one. This is possible because most aspects of their use can be quantified and considerable experience has been gained with such systems. Although experience demonstrates that growth patterns cannot be predicted with accuracy, it is possible to construct a range of estimates of the patterns of future traffic, numerically and geographically, on the basis of current traffic and projected national development plans.[3] Using this range of

1. Polcyn, op. cit., p. 27.
2. Robert Butman, George Rathjens and Colin J. Warren, *Technical-Economic Considerations in Public Service Broadcast Communications for Developing Countries*, Cambridge, Mass., Massachusetts Institute of Technology, 1973.
3. See, for example: R. C. Butman, *Telecommunications Development in Indonesia*, Cambridge, Mass., Massachusetts Institute of Technology, 1974.

estimates, together with the geographic features of the country (total area, compactness, hilliness, etc.), calculations can be made of the capital and operating costs required to handle the traffic with a satellite system, a terrestrial system or some hybrid combination. However, these costs will vary depending upon the estimates of future traffic and it is possible that no system will have a clear advantage over the entire range. Thus, in order to select the most economical system it will be necessary to make a judgement as to the most likely pattern of traffic growth. Since, generally speaking, the advantage of satellite communications increases with the size of the area to be served and the traffic to be carried,[1] a dedicated proponent of satellites might, at this point, be inclined to opt for a high traffic estimate and an equally dedicated proponent of microwave systems might be inclined towards a low estimate. Thus, even for these uses, the outcome of a quantitative comparison will have to be decided in some cases by a non-quantitative process.

13. In other areas of use (and education is one of these) it is even more difficult to develop a solid basis on which to choose between a satellite or a terrestrial communications system. Indeed, wrestling with this choice in connexion with educational objectives implies the prior decision to make extensive use of television and/or radio and perhaps the making of this prior decision is an even more crucial choice. Past experience leaves no doubt that radio and television can contribute effectively to education. However, not all applications have been successful and success or failure has been found to be due to complex interactions among many factors, only some of which are educational. Thus, when considering any specific application, there is room for differing opinions as to whether the use will be appropriate or cost-effective. This is particularly true with respect to applications in developing countries where both financial and human resources are in short supply and the costs of misallocation are thus more significant than in the developed countries. There is a large number of reports and studies which deal with many questions surrounding the educational and cost effectiveness of radio and television[2] but this discussion will not be summarized here. Rather, it will be assumed that those responsible for an educational project will study this past experience in detail, and the focus of what follows will be kept on the additional considerations brought in by use of a satellite.

14. As yet there is no satellite dedicated wholly or primarily to educational uses, nor, for that matter, is there any major terrestrial educational communications system so designated. From this it is reasonable to infer that educational needs have not been a major determinant in shaping communications systems. It is a moot question when, or whether, the accumulating experience with

1. Polcyn, op. cit., p. 14.
2. See, for example: James W. Armsey and Norman C. Dahl, *An Inquiry into the Uses of Instructional Technology*, New York, N.Y., The Ford Foundation, 1973; Dean Jamison and Steven Klees, *The Cost of Instructional Radio and Television for Developing Countries*, Education Resources Information Centre, 1973 (ERIC doc. EDO77213); Dean Jamison, Patrick Suppes and Stuart Wells, 'The Effectiveness of Alternative Instructional Media: A Survey', *Review of Educational Research*, Vol. 44, 1974 (ERIC doc. EDO76058); Emile G. McAnany, *Radio's Role in Development: Five Strategies of Use*, Washington, D.C., Academy for Educational Development, 1973; Carroll V. Newsom, 'Communications Satellites: A New Hazard for World Cultures', *Educational Broadcasting Review*, April 1973; Wilbur Schramm, *Big Media, Little Media*, Palo Alto, Calif., Institute for Communications Research, Stanford University, 1973 (ERIC doc. EDO77186).

educational use of television and radio will cause a change in this situation and educational uses will come to have major influences on the design of communications systems. In any event it seems likely that in the short run, say for the next decade, educators in most countries will have available, at most, only partial use of satellites, whose major function is non-educational. Under these conditions the economic basis of choice between the use of a satellite or a terrestrial system would be the add-on costs of the educational use. But it is also possible that the choice may be made on some other grounds. Indeed, one of the major arguments advanced for the use of a satellite is that it can provide widespread educational services to rural areas much more quickly than could be done by expanding a terrestrial microwave system.

IV Factors involved in the use of satellites for education

15. The radio listeners or the television viewers receiving educational programmes cannot detect whether the signals are delivered by a satellite or by a terrestrial broadcasting system. But those with overall responsibility for the educational content carried by the signals perceive great differences, depending on which system is used.

16. Most of these differences stem from the inherent capacity of the satellite to operate on a very large scale. Moreover, the capacity to deliver programmes on all the radio and television receivers in a large area exists from the moment the satellite is in orbit, provided the receivers have been equipped to receive the satellite signals. In contrast, the signals from ground-based transmitters are limited in their geographical coverage by interactions with the earth's surface and the ionized layers in the atmosphere. Thus, a signal coverage of a large area can be accomplished only by locating sufficient transmitters in the area so that all locations receive a signal from at least one transmitter and then connecting all the transmitters into a system by some means such as microwave links. The usual experience is that such terrestrial systems come into existence only over a period of years. The pace of expansion throughout the area is constrained by such matters as the physical difficulties of construction in remote and rugged terrain and the essentially linear, or incremental, nature of the expansion process. In comparing the two systems, the satellite system might be characterized as a 'lumpy' technology which must be absorbed in more or less full-scale size and the terrestrial system as an 'incremental' technology which can be absorbed gradually as the system grows over time.

17. The scale aspect of the satellite system brings some complications along with its obvious benefits. A complication which springs immediately to mind is that the capacity of a satellite may be much larger than is needed by a country. There does not seem to be any easy way out of this situation. One suggestion has been the use of regional satellites whose cost and capacity could be shared by several adjoining countries. However, to realize savings it may be necessary to share common curricula across national, cultural and linguistic boundaries and, thus far, such requirements have been obstacles to agreements to invest in regional educational satellites.[1]

1. Bert Cowlan, 'Educational Satellites over Africa: An Unlikely Scenario', *Educational Broadcasting International*, Vol. 7, No. 3, September 1974.

18. Within a country large enough to use an educational satellite for its own purposes, the scale of the satellite's capabilities imposes the need for a large organization to deal with both the geographical and functional aspects of that satellite. The operational responsibility for the satellite is likely to rest with a ministry of communications or a ministry of information and broadcasting. Thus the ministries responsible for the substantive aspects of the educational programmes, such as education, health, agriculture, etc., will have to co-ordinate at the national level not only among themselves but with the ministry responsible for the operation of the satellite. Detailed organization and co-ordination at the local level is vital, not only with the educational authorities and teachers but with other elements of government that have administrative responsibility and control. For example, the simple physical matter of providing electricity to power a television set located in a particular schoolroom may prove to be a far from simple administrative matter. Further, since there are various levels of governmental authority between the local and national levels it will be necessary to have organizational relations with this intermediate governmental machinery. In using a satellite to take advantage of its capability to reach widely dispersed sites, therefore, the managers of the educational programmes must assume the responsibility of developing an organizational structure which itself is widely dispersed, both hierarchically and geographically. To develop an effective structure of this kind is no simple matter at any time in any country.

19. When a country goes through its first exercise in planning for use of a satellite for educational purposes, a probable major problem will be the availability of trained manpower that can contribute to a realistic planning analysis. While it may be both possible and necessary to get assistance from other countries, care should be taken that knowledgeable nationals are in effective control of the planning. If such people are not available within the country because there has been little educational use of radio or television, then the prudent course would be to delay the project planning until capable people can be sent abroad to get the required experience or training.

20. The implementation phase will bring another set of requirements for staff with new skills. The educational use of radio or television involves a wide variety of problems which are not part of the usual educational training or experience and hence in most countries the personnel needed for implementation do not exist. Thus, high priority should be given to the specification of the skills needed and the setting up of various kinds of programmes to train the necessary staff. Delaying such training will result in either the project falling behind schedule because of lack of staff with particular qualifications, or in poor performance because the project has gone ahead with unqualified staff.

21. It is obvious that the most critical factor in implementation is the effectiveness of the set of materials and activities—the software—designed to produce the desired learning in the users. It is not obvious how effective software is to be produced for any particular situation. There are, however, general guidelines which can be drawn from the experience of the past two decades. It has been found that in order to design effective software it is necessary to conceptualize the educational problem and state the objectives in such a way that the software designers and producers have specific goals to guide them. The extent to which learners reach these stated objectives will give a measure of the effectiveness of the software and provide a basis for redesign and improve-

ment. In using various media it has become evident that most effective learning is accomplished through a combination of media, and that variation in learning is more dependent on how a medium is used rather than which one is used.[1] It has also been found that when using radio or television the effectiveness of the broadcast material is critically dependent on what goes on at the receiving end, on what interaction the learner has with it. Passive listening or viewing does not lead to learning.

22. Another important lesson from experience with the development of multi-media software for wide distribution has been the discovery that the only reliable way to create effective learning materials is through a design and development process which involves reiterative testing and revision of the materials until it is proved that students learn well when using the materials in actual school environments. It has also been found that this process requires a team approach in which there is collaboration among subject-matter specialists, educational technologists and media-production specialists.[2] Teachers are the key to the effective use of the finished materials. Not only must there be close collaboration with a limited number of classroom teachers during the testing and revising cycles, but teacher-training programmes must be included in the implementation process from the outset.

23. The use of a satellite does not eliminate the need for good ground communication with the receiving sites. Ground communication will be needed to supply printed materials and mail, to allow supervisory and evaluative personnel to visit the sites and to ensure that the equipment can be maintained and serviced. It is not possible to overemphasize the importance of planning to ensure the maintenance of the equipment. This is particularly applicable to developing countries where in most rural areas there is little experience with any kind of equipment and no tradition of maintenance. By way of example, in visits to 44 Mexican primary schools which supposedly were using 90 minutes of radio broadcasting a day, it was found that only 18 schools had a functioning radio on the day of the visit.[3] Good maintenance will require not only good technical competence but good administrative supervision.

24. Although the costs of an educational programme using a satellite may be large in absolute terms, the per-student cost can be small provided the number of users is large enough. The major costs are hardware costs, software costs and system-operating costs. The hardware costs for a specific system can be determined in advance with a reasonable degree of precision although it is difficult to speak of typical system-cost figures because '. . . the cost of direct broadcast-satellite systems depends on many variables such as type of service, receivers, frequencies, satellite power, satellite coverage area and software'.[4] Software costs can vary over a wide range depending upon local circumstances. As a general guideline for planning, it must be recognized that effective radio or television educational programmes will require high standards of design and production and this will determine the production costs in terms of human talent

1. Schramm, op. cit.
2. David Hawkridge, 'The Open University and Educational Technology', *The Times Educational Supplement*, April 1971.
3. Peter L. Spain, 'A Report on the System of Radioprimaria in the State of San Luis Potosi', in: *Instructional Technology Report*, Washington, D.C., Information Center on Instructional Technology, Academy for Educational Development, 1974.
4. Polcyn, op. cit., p. 21.

and staging. The money costs will depend upon the local rates for the necessary talent and staging. In addition there will be software costs for programme testing and revision and for development and production of the printed and other materials sent to the users at each site.

25. The system-operating costs will include such costs as personnel, ground communications with receiving sites, fixed facilities at receiving sites and maintenance of hardware. A critical segment of the personnel will be the teachers or other staff who work with the users at each site. The entire effort will fail if such staff do not have the capability to stimulate the users to interact and work with the content of the broadcast programme.

26. A recent study on the costs of instructional radio and television via terrestrial systems in developing countries[1] reported television costs ranging from U.S.$0.062 to $1.10 per student hour and radio costs ranging from U.S.$0.014 to $0.058. The projects from which these figures came were all different in character and involved quite widely varying numbers of students so the range in costs is not surprising. The much lower figures for radio are borne out by other studies.[2] These result from both lower capital costs for hardware and lower software production costs.

27. It is likely that the actual student-hour costs during operation will be higher than those predicted during the planning stage. Proponents of projects tend to be optimistic and thus to overestimate acceptance and underestimate difficulties. Similarly, both hardware and software costs seem to have an almost natural tendency to grow during implementation as those responsible try to do a 'better' job and sometimes add marginal improvements at considerable costs. Student-hour costs could also increase as a result of funding cuts which eliminate some planned uses and leave the capital costs to be distributed over a smaller number of users. Thus, while the student-per-hour-use cost is an important criterion for helping to decide whether or not to go ahead with a project, the 'lumpiness' of the technology makes this cost figure subject to substantial change owing to budget decisions which might be taken after the hardware has been committed.

V Current and projected experiments in the educational use of satellites

28. In this section brief descriptions are presented of current and projected experiments in educational use of satellites. All of those described make use of one of NASA's Applications Technology Satellites or Canada's soon to be launched Communications Technology Satellite. While it is possible that the U.S.S.R. is conducting experiments, there has been no published account of such work.

State of Hawaii experiment with ATS-1

29. In 1971, the University of Hawaii began experiments which used the ATS-1 to relay voice and facsimile messages between its campuses on the

1. Jamison and Klees, op. cit.
2. Schramm, op. cit.

islands of Oahu and Hawaii, which are some 400 kilometres apart. In 1972 the experiment began to include other islands in the Pacific and today there are about ten other users stretching as far as New Zealand. Some stations have only voice communication while others also have capabilities for receiving and transmitting slow-scan television and teletype signals. Relatively inexpensive ground terminals for these two types of service have been developed by the University of Hawaii costing, respectively, about $1,500 and $7,000.

30. Various uses have been made of the system, including library exchanges, medical conferencing, student debates, teacher training and collaborative marine research. The type and quantity of exchanges are determined by the users, up to the total of 12.5 hours per week for which the ATS-1 is available for this service.

31. This experiment, in which institutions at widely separated distances share scarce resources, is an excellent demonstration of satellite capability. Financing for the ground stations and general administration has been relatively low, less than $100,000. Each institution is responsible for its own personnel and programme exchange costs.

Stanford University/Brazil experiment with ATS-3

32. Beginning in the late 1960s, the Brazilian Institute of Space Research (INPE) began to investigate the possible uses of satellites by Brazil. INPE concluded that the size and development problems of Brazil were such that a satellite information-distribution system could make major contributions in education and communication, and developed a phased plan for proceeding towards such a system. Phase one, which is aimed at gaining experience with both the technical and educational aspects of satellite transmission, began in 1972 in collaboration with Stanford University. This programme uses the ATS-3 for the transmission of voice and slow-scan television broadcasts from Stanford and cultural programmes from Brazil. The voice element provides two-way communication, which allows for interaction during lectures and seminars. Phase two planned for the use of the ATS-6 in educational experiments involving both terrestrial and satellite communication but at the time of writing there has been no announcement that time on ATS-6 will be made available. Phase three planned for Brazil to establish its own domestic satellite system for educational and communications uses. As yet Brazil has not announced any specific decision to move ahead on phase three.

State of Alaska experiments with ATS-1 and ATS-6

33. Alaska has a small and dispersed population and geographic and atmospheric conditions which make radio communication difficult and uncertain. In 1969, Alaska proposed to NASA an experimental programme which would use ATS-1 to deliver television and radio signals to remote communities in Alaska. However, it was found that earth stations capable of receiving television would cost far too much, about $200,000, and the programme therefore went ahead using only radio, with the television experimentation being deferred until the more powerful ATS-6 would be available. In 1971 VHF receiver-

transmitter earth stations were established in twenty-six villages. These earth stations consisted of an antenna and a two-way radio, the latter costing about $40. Through ATS-1 the villages could communicate with each other and with larger earth stations at Fairbanks and Anchorage.

34. Three experimental projects were initiated in 1971: delivery of medical services to the twenty-six villages, receipt of national public radio programmes from the United States south of Canada and delivery of subject-matter programmes to schools in the villages. In addition, the villages were encouraged to use the system for communication with each other. The medical programme has consisted of using the satellite to provide voice communication between village health aides and physicians in Fairbanks. The health aide, who has had up to sixteen weeks of training and is equipped with a medical first-aid manual and a basic drug kit, confers with the physician about diagnosis of difficult cases. When the diagnosis indicates a medical problem which the aide cannot treat the patient is evacuated. Means for such consultation existed previously via shortwave radio but terrain and atmospheric conditions often made the quality of communication poor and frequently delayed the contact, sometimes for as long as a week. The reliable communication available via the satellite has improved the quality of health care and increased the confidence of the villagers in the health-aide system.

35. The experience with the educational and inter-village communications programmes has been less successful: '. . . in many instances the populace was inadequately prepared to participate. For example, failure to involve local groups during the planning phases or to explain the purpose of the equipment has plagued the experiment, resulting in few objectives being achieved'.[1] This and other lessons have influenced Alaska's planning for use of the ATS-6 which became available in May 1974 for a one-year period during which separate experimental programmes will be carried out in Alaska, the Rocky Mountain region and the Appalachian region.

36. For these experiments the ATS-6 will be able to relay two separate colour-television signals in the 2,500 megahertz range, each with four voice channels. Ground stations capable of receiving the television signal and feeding a single television set will require an antenna about 10 feet in diameter and cost roughly $4,000, including $1,000 for installation. There will also be more expensive stations with the additional capacity of sending a television signal to the ATS-6.

37. The Alaska ATS-6 programme will continue to focus on the areas of medicine, education and public broadcasting. Ground stations will be set up in eighteen communities, five of them as receive-transmit stations. Each community will also have two-way voice communication via the ATS-1.

38. Two of the communities with the receiver-transmitter stations will use these to add two-way television communication to the health aide/physician diagnostic conferences. This experiment is aimed at testing the expectation that the addition of television will substantially improve diagnosis and reduce the frequency of specialists' visits to remote villages.

39. Experiments will also be carried out to explore the possibilities of providing instruction to medical students located in an area in which there is no medical school. Faculty members at the University of Washington Medical

1. Polcyn, op. cit., p. 55.

School in Seattle will give classes in basic sciences to first-year medical students in Fairbanks. The students will have two-way voice and video interactions with the faculty staff in the form of lectures and discussions and they will study some of their courses in computer-aided format supplied via the ATS-6.

40. The education programming will have four components: English-language skills for pre-school and primary children, early childhood education, health education and in-service teacher training. The television teachers will have two-way voice communication with the classrooms and the classroom teachers will receive manuals containing programme goals and objectives, descriptions of programme content, lesson guides and suggestions for teaching activities.

41. The major element in the public broadcasting activity will be a programme series called the 'Alaska Native Magazine' with the audio part presented in English and up to three native languages simultaneously. Matters of interest and concern to the communities will be featured. The programme will include intervals during which the viewers can use the two-way voice circuit to discuss issues in the current programme and express preferences for future programme materials.

42. The ATS-6 will be available to Alaska for only about ten hours a week. Probably for this reason as well as the limited number of potential viewers the emphasis on evaluation appears to be on process rather than on product.[1] Given these conditions the conclusions which can be drawn are not likely to be compelling.

43. It is difficult to estimate the true cost of these experiments since the largest cost, that of the ATS-6, must be allocated over about twenty different experiments. NASA states that the cost of the ATS-6 mission, including development and running all the experiments, is about $200 million, including about $25 million for launching the mission. As of 1973 the anticipated budget for the ground components of the Alaska experiments was approximately $3 million.[2]

Rocky Mountain region experiment with ATS-6

44. Six states lying along the Rocky Mountain range in the western United States joined together in 1966 to form the Federation of Rocky Mountain States, for the purpose of promoting joint economic, educational and other social interests of the region. Beginning in 1969 the federation began to explore the possibilities of using an ATS satellite in experiments to improve the quality of education in small, isolated schools in the region. Early in 1971, the federation obtained a small grant from the United States Department of Health, Education and Welfare (HEW) to prepare a detailed plan for an educational experiment with the ATS-6, then scheduled for launching in 1973. Later, in 1971, the federation submitted a $26 million proposal for a three-year project for experi-

1. Bert Cowlan, 'An Educational Television Satellite Experiment: Federation of Rocky Mountain States', in: *Broadcast Satellites for Educational Development: The Experiments in Brazil, India and the United States*, p. 66, Washington, D.C., Academy for Educational Development, 1973.
2. Cowlan, 'An Educational Television Satellite Experiment . . . ', op. cit., p. 65–68.

mental programmes in early childhood education, career development and higher education to be delivered to some 500 communities equipped with ground stations, hopefully capable of transmitting as well as receiving television signals.

45. In the autumn of 1974, under HEW funding arrangements which will bring the total expenditures on the project from inception to completion to a total of about $10.5 million, the federation began a year's operation with ATS-6 in which programmes in career education will be delivered to sixty-eight communities equipped with low-cost receive-only ground stations. The process by which the project changed from the proposal of 1971 to the actual operations of 1974 was complicated and sometimes stormy. A 1973 review of the project makes the following observations about the several levels of government (federal, regional, state and local) and the many non-governmental groups involved in the planning process:

> A wide variety of organizations were involved in planning, besides those mentioned. The specifics of what had been planned and of how the project reached its current level of funding are not as important as understanding the process involved. It was a complex one of needs assessment, changing focus, fiscal realities, legislative complications, managerial and staffing problems, and altering priorities. The preferences of the individual states and of the Federal policy planners entered into this process. So, too, did technological problems and limitations.[1]

The review also makes the point that these kinds of problems are going to be part of any major educational-satellite programme:

> It does appear important, though, to state that goals and objectives for projects using new technologies are not easily formulated. Nor is the management of large, complex, and untried systems easy to analyze. The planning, management and maintenance of a project of the scope of the Rocky Mountain experiment require not only money but also manpower. Furthermore, the manpower must be highly skilled, and the team must be able to learn and appreciate vocabularies of different disciplines, so that it can deal with the forces that can result from education, communication and technology.[2]

46. The ground stations are the same as those used in the Alaska experiment. Fifty-six of these stations are located in rural, isolated communities and about half of these also have two-way voice communication via the ATS-3. The other 12 are located in cities or towns which have public broadcasting service stations; these stations rebroadcast the programmes to near-by schools.

47. The career education is for junior high-school students and the programming emphasizes three areas: dissemination of career information, techniques of self-assessment and instruction in making decisions about career options. The teachers received in-service training programmes at the start of the school year and there will be further broadcasts during the year. Teacher's guides, student workbooks and other supplementary materials will be delivered to the schools. The television programmes and supplementary materials are being prepared by an organization patterned on the 'course team' concept of the United Kingdom's Open University.

1. Cowlan, 'An Educational Television Satellite Experiment . . .', op. cit., p. 8.
2. Cowlan, 'An Educational Television Satellite Experiment . . .', op. cit., p. 2.

48. Another aspect of satellite use being explored is the delivery of audio-visual materials to remote schools. Each school will be given a catalogue listing some 500 titles on various subjects. The request of a teacher for a particular title will be sent to the television transmitter station in Denver where the audio-visual materials are located. The Denver station will send the material to the ATS-6 which will retransmit and the requesting school will record it on a video-tape recorder for later use at a convenient time.

49. The total system use will be about twelve to thirteen hours a week, including use every three weeks to deliver an evening programme designed to interest adults in the rural communities. The aim here is to see whether it is possible to use expressed viewer preferences to develop community-oriented programmes which have wide appeal.

50. The project has had a research and evaluation component almost from the beginning and detailed evaluation will be carried out during the year of ATS-6 operations and in a follow-up period after this. Very few major projects have had this degree of evaluation and thus the reports are likely to be of value to others contemplating large systems. Since the complexity approaches that which would be encountered in establishing a national system of moderate size, the results should be particularly interesting to many developing countries.

Appalachian region experiment with ATS-6

51. The Appalachian region lies in the eastern United States stretching over thirteen states from northern Mississippi to southern New York, a distance of about 1,500 kilometres. Although the terrain is not as rugged as the Rocky Mountain region it is a mountainous area in which there are many rural, isolated communities and relatively poor communications and transport. The development of the region has been retarded and in 1965 the Appalachian Regional Commission, a federal-state agency, was created to stimulate and co-ordinate economic and social development.

52. Since the ATS-6 was available in 1974–75, the commission is experimenting with in-service teacher training under a $1.2 million budget from HEW. Fifteen sites are equipped with receive-only ground stations. The sites are grouped in clusters of three, one site having two-way voice communication with the television-originating centre via the ATS-3 and the other two sites being connected to it by land lines.

53. During the summer of 1974 separate courses in early reading and career education were offered to about 300 elementary teachers from schools surrounding the sites. Each course had three elements in addition to textbooks and supplementary printed materials: twelve 30-minute pre-taped television programmes, twelve 15-minute programmes of audio-based programmed instruction, and four 45-minute live television seminars with provision for audio interaction. The teachers received college credit for the courses. During the coming school year, in-service courses in career education will be offered to both senior- and junior-high-school teachers. A major element in each course will be a series of live television seminars with audio interaction. Teachers who have taken one of the courses will be able to use the system to get specialized information to help them in dealing with problems which may come up in their teaching.

54. During the year, a parallel programme of in-service continuing medical education will be provided to doctors in ten hospitals which have been equipped with ground stations. The educational and medical uses together will total about five hours a week.

Canadian experiments with CTS

55. Canada and the United States are engaged in a joint venture involving the launching of the Communications Technology Satellite (CTS) late in 1975. Some forty experiments are scheduled to be carried out during the expected two-year minimum lifetime of the CTS and several of these will explore issues in education. The CTS has more radiating power than the ATS-6 but its signal strength on the ground is about the same, owing to different antenna configuration. Television ground stations of both 8 and 10 feet antenna-diameter will be used as well as radio ground stations giving receive-transmit capability with antennas only 3 feet in diameter.

56. One experiment will try out different kinds of communications and educational services for Indian communities in northern Ontario which are widely dispersed and frequently have no road connexions. The programme is being planned jointly by the tribal council representing the Indians in the area and the Ontario Educational Communications Authority. It is hoped that the experiment will yield results which can provide the basis for design of a full-scale, more permanent communications system for this region.[1]

57. In another experiment aimed at northern Ontario, Lakeland University will use the CTS for in-service training of teachers in remote schools. Frequently these teachers have had little more formal education than the students they teach and the aim is to see what can be done to increase this gap through remote, interactive teaching programmes.

58. Yet another remote area use will couple the University of Western Ontario with the community of Yellowknife, located on Great Slave Lake in the far north of Canada. Experiments will be conducted in computer-aided instruction for which the university has converted the instruction into the local language used in Yellowknife.

59. One experiment will link the cable system in a community in the province of Saskatchewan with a cable system in a community in the province of Quebec some 1,500 kilometres away. Most inhabitants of the Saskatchewan community are French-speaking and this connexion will give them access to the French culture of Quebec.

60. Canada and the United States will carry out one collaborative educational experiment with the CTS. Carleton University in Ottawa and Stanford University in California will explore the possibilities for sharing faculty resources via satellite. By means of one-way television and two-way voice circuits, selected graduate courses from Carleton will be available to students at Stanford, and vice versa. If successful this might have interesting implications for higher education.

1. *Educational and Social Implications of the Use of the Communications Technology Satellite*, p. 7, Toronto, The Ontario Educational Communications Authority, 19 February 1974.

Indian experiment with ATS-6

61. India began to use television in 1959 with a station in Delhi which broadcast educational, social and cultural programmes to schools and community-viewing centres in Delhi and the near-by area. In 1965 daily general programming was added and in 1971 the range of the station was increased to sixty kilometres. The Ministry of Information and Broadcasting, which has the prime responsibility for national television and radio broadcasting through All India Radio (AIR), developed a plan for expansion of television which was based on building stations in other metropolitan areas and subsequently extending to rural areas. In 1972, a second station was started in Bombay and four or five others have followed since.

62. In the mid-1960s the director of the Indian Space Research Organization (ISRO), an internationally respected scientist with wide connexions both in India and abroad, became convinced that the AIR scheme of television expansion needed to be augmented by a satellite system so that the rural areas could be better served with education and communications needed to bring them into the main stream of India's development. Shortly thereafter he became Secretary (head) of the Department of Atomic Energy (DAE), which was the supervising agency for ISRO, and in this position he continued to advocate such a satellite. While the satellite concept was not embraced by AIR or the Department of Communications, the Secretary was successful in getting Government of India approval in 1969 for the DAE to enter into a memorandum of agreement with the United States National Aeronautics and Space Administration (NASA) to conduct jointly in 1972–73 an instructional television experiment in India using NASA's ATS-F satellite (subsequently to be named ATS-6 when it reached synchronous equatorial orbit). Named the Satellite Instructional Television Experiment (SITE), this experiment was to consist of direct broadcast of television and two audio channels to some 5,000 widely dispersed villages equipped with television sets, fed by relatively simple ground terminals and, also, to other villages through rediffusion from standard television transmitters. The agreement listed general objectives of demonstrating how satellite technology could contribute to education, mass communications and national development and cited as specific objectives the contributions which could be made towards health and family planning, improved agricultural practices, national integration and primary education. NASA was to be responsible for positioning and maintaining the satellite, the DAE for providing and maintaining all ground hardware and for all programming. At the time the agreement was signed, DAE announced that SITE was the first step towards the development of an Indian domestic communications satellite (INSAT).

63. While needed hardware (ground terminals and rugged solid-state television sets suitable for use in villages) had not been made in India the potential existed for designing and producing it. The Secretary of DAE apparently felt that the same could not be said of the potential for producing the software because he proposed organizational arrangements in which AIR would share software production with other independent producing units. The discussions on software responsibility dragged on and the issue was only resolved after the sudden death of the Secretary in late 1971, when the responsibility was given to AIR. ISRO retained responsibility for all other operational aspects of SITE.

64. SITE was to begin operations in the summer of 1975 when the ATS-6 was moved to an orbital position above Kenya after completion of the educational experiments in the United States. The main features of the plan made in 1973 are as follows. In the SITE experiment the ATS-6 will be broadcasting in the 860 megahertz range with one video signal and two audio channels, with the programmes being sent to it from large ground stations at Ahmedabad or Delhi. About 2,400 villages will be equipped to view the programmes on television sets fed by low-cost ground stations which have a 10-foot diameter antenna. These villages are located in clusters of about 400 in each of six states, most of which have differing languages. The states (and their languages) are: Andhra Pradesh (Telugu), Mysore (Kannada), Madhya Pradesh (Hindi), Orissa (Oriya), Bihar (Hindi) and Rajasthan (Hindi). Where regular television transmitters exist in these states some villages near the transmitter will be equipped with television sets to receive the programmes via retransmission of the satellite signal. Because of a number of constraints (time, language, agricultural problems etc.) most of the programming will be time-phased in about half-hour segments, with the programme in each segment carrying a picture and two languages appropriate to two clusters. The groupings of the clusters will be: Andhra Pradesh and Mysore; Madhya Pradesh and Orissa; and Bihar and Rajasthan, which will require only one voice channel, Hindi.

65. There will be a total of about four hours of broadcasting per day, one and a half hours in the morning to children in primary schools and two and a half hours in the evening to adults who come to the schools for community viewing. Although the entire four hours can be received by all clusters the daily programming beamed at any one cluster will be only one half hour for the children and about one hour for the adults (one half hour of the evening broadcast will be audio-only general entertainment in Hindi, the national language).

66. Most of the schools will be one-room, one-teacher schools so the programmes will be viewed by a group of children between the ages of 5 and 12 years. Under these conditions it was decided that curricula-related programmes would not work. The general plan is to have the content supplemental in such subject areas as health and natural science but supportive where possible in such areas as numerical concepts. A magazine format will be employed with several short segments in one programme, some aimed at the 5-to-8 age group and others at the 9-to-12 group.

67. The adult programmes also will have a magazine format. An entertainment segment will be included in each programme. Most will also include something specifically related to agriculture in the region of the cluster; it is anticipated that this will entail difficulties because two clusters must share the same visuals. Health and nutrition, indirect motivations towards family planning, exploration of the cultural diversity of India and matters related to development form the basis of other segments.

68. AIR estimates that in order to meet all the broadcast requirements, and allowing for the use of already existing film materials, it will be necessary to produce somewhat more than 1,100 hours of programming. As of the summer of 1974, it appeared that AIR had about 50 hours of this new programming in hand. If this figure is approximately correct it will be necessary over the next two years to produce programmes at the rate of about 500 hours per year in order to meet the broadcast schedule. Producing good programmes at this rate

will be a formidable task, even though there will be a number of them for which visuals and the basic scripts will be the same. However, AIR has completed two new production studios this summer, to give a total of three, and has located film field units in each of the six cluster regions, so that it has a considerably increased production capacity. Further, it has put together a capable management and production team. However, AIR must depend upon the ministries that use the programmes (education, agriculture, health and family planning) for setting programme objectives and providing substantive programme content; thus the rate of production is not entirely under AIR's control. There is in evidence no superior authority which can compel the user ministries to work together with AIR as a team against a fixed production schedule and this may result in the schedule not being met.

69. In looking at other activities in SITE at this time there are a number of areas where the lack of a central co-ordinating authority may be seen. All the necessary activities appear to be going on—hardware procurement, site selection and preparation, maintenance planning, teacher training, evaluation, central, state and local co-ordination, etc.—but not always marching to the same drum. As is evident from the Rocky Mountain experience, planning and executing a satellite project is a complicated and exacting management job, and perhaps SITE has had an even more difficult management task because of the untimely death of its founder. None the less, the outcome of the project, two years hence, will be of great interest and value to India as well as to others who want to know what role the satellite can play in development, in a real situation.

VI Satellites and Open Learning systems

70. From the foregoing discussion of satellites and the review of current experimental uses in education it is possible to conclude that the evidence for or against the use of satellites is not yet compelling. Further, it seems that satellite education systems have planning and management complexities which make it unlikely that the current experiments will yield a clear picture of the best that might be attainable in either educational effectiveness or cost levels.

71. Given this situation it would appear that for some years the arguments for satellite use will have to be based either on the need for more experimental evidence or on the need for a particular social action. Both of these are legitimate arguments whose priority can be evaluated by the political process.

72. The issue of possible use of a satellite to provide service to an Open Learning system brings in additional considerations. In most Open Learning systems the students or users are spread geographically and tend to operate as individuals. A satellite has the advantage that it can reach anywhere, but ground hardware costs would be large if only one or a few used each ground terminal. Additionally, per-user costs for the space hardware would be high unless there were a large number of users. Another feature of some Open Learning systems is the variety of study programmes pursued by the users. Here the satellite system would be at a disadvantage because one of its primary characteristics is its ability to deliver the same programme to every point in a wide area, although the situation would be better if radio were used instead of television, since the television bandwidth could be used to transmit a large number of different voice channels.

73. Summing up, given that the case for satellite use in formal education is still an open question, it would seem sensible to conclude that it is better to wait for the resolution of that question before introducing the added complications which come with the subject matter and geographic diversities of Open Learning systems.

Appendix Biographical note

Dr Norman C. Dahl is an educational consultant who has been Professor of Mechanical Engineering at Massachusetts Institute of Technology and Deputy Representative of the Ford Foundation in India. He has studied education and advised on educational matters in many countries.

General bibliography

This short bibliography is intended for those who wish to read further about the general issues dealt with in this book. It does not attempt to deal with the subjects covered in the case studies, each of which contains a bibliography and names and addresses of people and offices from which further information can be obtained. Nor does it cover all the official regular publications of government departments, or specialized journals and magazines.

COMMISSION ON NON-TRADITIONAL STUDY, THE. *Diversity by design*. San Francisco, Calif., Washington, D.C., London, Jossey-Bass, 1973. Final report of the commission (formed in 1971).

COUNCIL FOR CULTURAL COOPERATION, THE. *The combined use of radio and television and correspondence courses in higher education*. Strasbourg, Council of Europe, 1974.

EDSTRÖM, LARS-OLOF; ERDOS, RENÉE; PROSSER, ROY (eds.). *Mass education: studies in adult education and teaching by correspondence in some developing countries*. Uppsala, The Dag Hammarskjöld Foundation, 1970.

GOULD, S. B.; GROSS, K. P. (eds.). *Explorations in non-traditional study*. San Francisco, Calif., Jossey-Bass, 1972.

HOULE, C. O. *The external degree*. San Francisco, Calif., Jossey-Bass, 1973.

INTERNATIONAL COMMISSION ON THE DEVELOPMENT OF EDUCATION, THE. *Learning to be*. Paris, Unesco, 1972. Report to Unesco by the commission (chairman Edgar Faure; established 1971).

ORGANIZATION FOR ECONOMIC CO-OPERATION AND DEVELOPMENT. *Recurrent education: a strategy for lifelong education*. Paris, OECD.

POLCYN, K. A. *An educator's guide to communication satellite technology*. Washington, D.C., Academy for Educational Development, 1973.

SCHRAMM, W. (ed.). *New educational media in action: case studies for planners*, vols. 1–3. Paris, Unesco/IIEP, 1967.

SCHRAMM, W.; COOMBS, P. H.; KAHNERT, F.; LYLE, J. *The new media: memo to educational planners*. Paris, Unesco/IIEP, 1967.

Short list of reference works

Educational media year book, James Brown, San José University
Obtainable from R. B. Bowker & Co., 1180 Avenue of the Americas, New York, N.Y. 10036 (United States of America).

International foundation directory, 1974
Obtainable from Europa Publications, 18 Bedford Square, London, WC1 BEJN (United Kingdom).

Sources of information on international and Commonwealth organisations, 1975, London, HMSO
Obtainable from Information Division, Department of Education and Science, Elizabeth House, York Road, London SE1 (United Kingdom).

World of learning, 1974–6
Obtainable from Europa Publications, 18 Bedford Square, London WC1 BEJN (United Kingdom).

Yearbook of international organisations, 1975
Obtainable from the Union of International Associations, 1 Rue aux Laines, 1000 Brussels (Belgium).

[A]ED. 75/D-85/A